Oh My Goddess!

ああっ女神さまっ **The Phantom Racer**

Oh My Goddess!

ああっ女神さまっ **The Phantom Racer**

v.18

STORY AND ART BY

Kosuke Fujishima

TRANSLATION BY

Dana Lewis & Toren Smith

LETTERING AND TOUCH-UP BY

Susie Lee with Betty Dong & Jon Babcock,
with Tom2K

DARK HORSE MANGA™

PUBLISHER
Mike Richardson

SERIES EDITOR
Tim Ervin-Gore

COLLECTION EDITOR
Chris Warner

COLLECTION DESIGNERS
Amy Arendts and Lani Schreibstein

ART DIRECTOR
Lia Ribacchi

English-language version produced by Studio Proteus
for Dark Horse Comics, Inc.

OH MY GODDESS Vol. XVIII: The Phantom Racer

This volume collects issues ninety-six through one-hundred-four of the Dark Horse comic book series *Oh My Goddess!*

Published by
Dark Horse Manga
A division of Dark Horse Comics, Inc.
10956 SE Main Street
Milwaukie, OR 97222

www.darkhorse.com

To find a comics shop in your area, call the Comic Shop
Locator Service toll-free at 1-888-266-4226

First edition: May 2004
ISBN: 1-59307-217-1

1 3 5 7 9 10 8 6 4 2
Printed in Canada

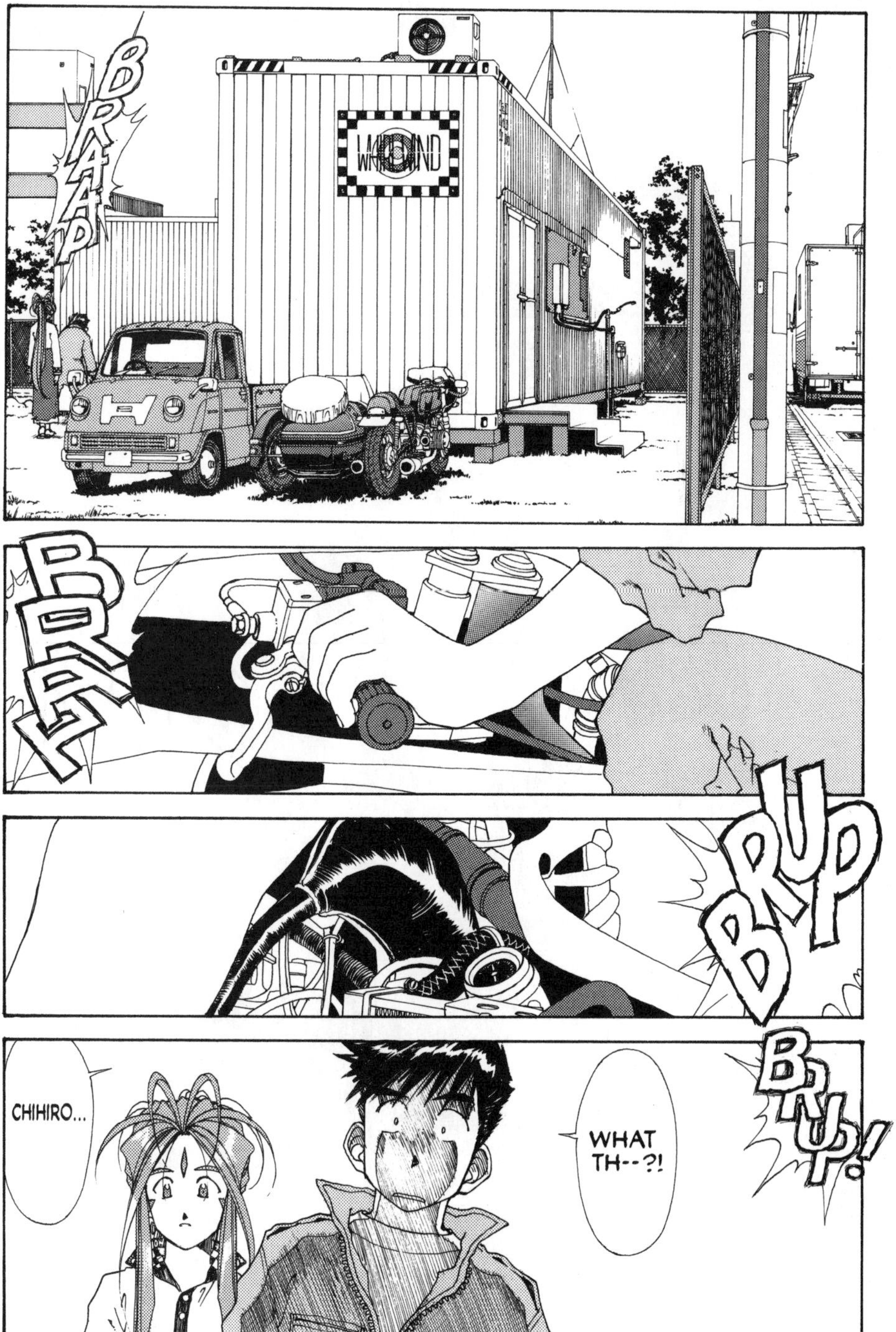
BRAAP
WHIRLWIND
BRAAP
BRUP
CHIHIRO...
WHAT TH--?!
BRUP!

THE GHOST OF THE PASS

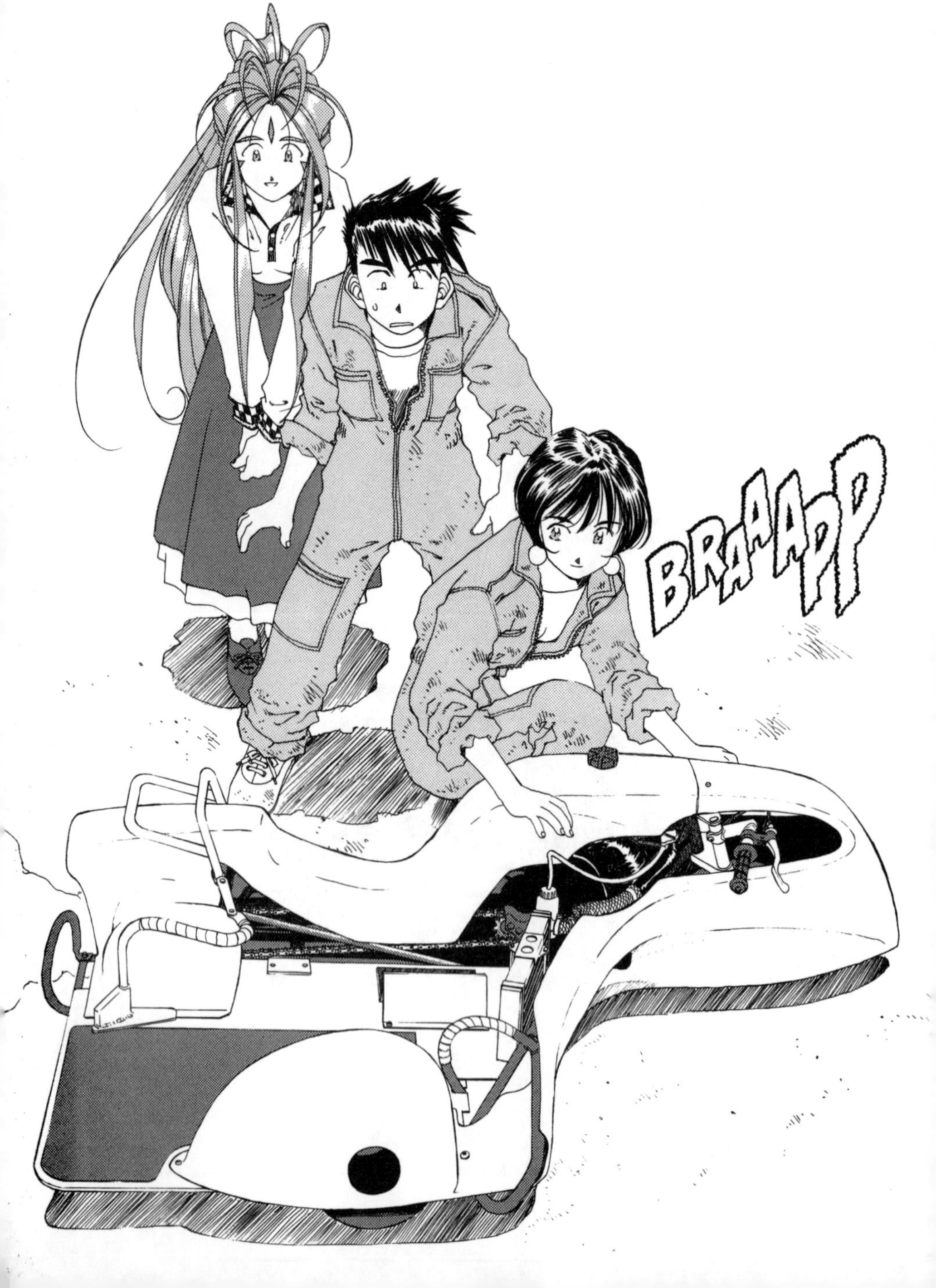
BRAAAPP

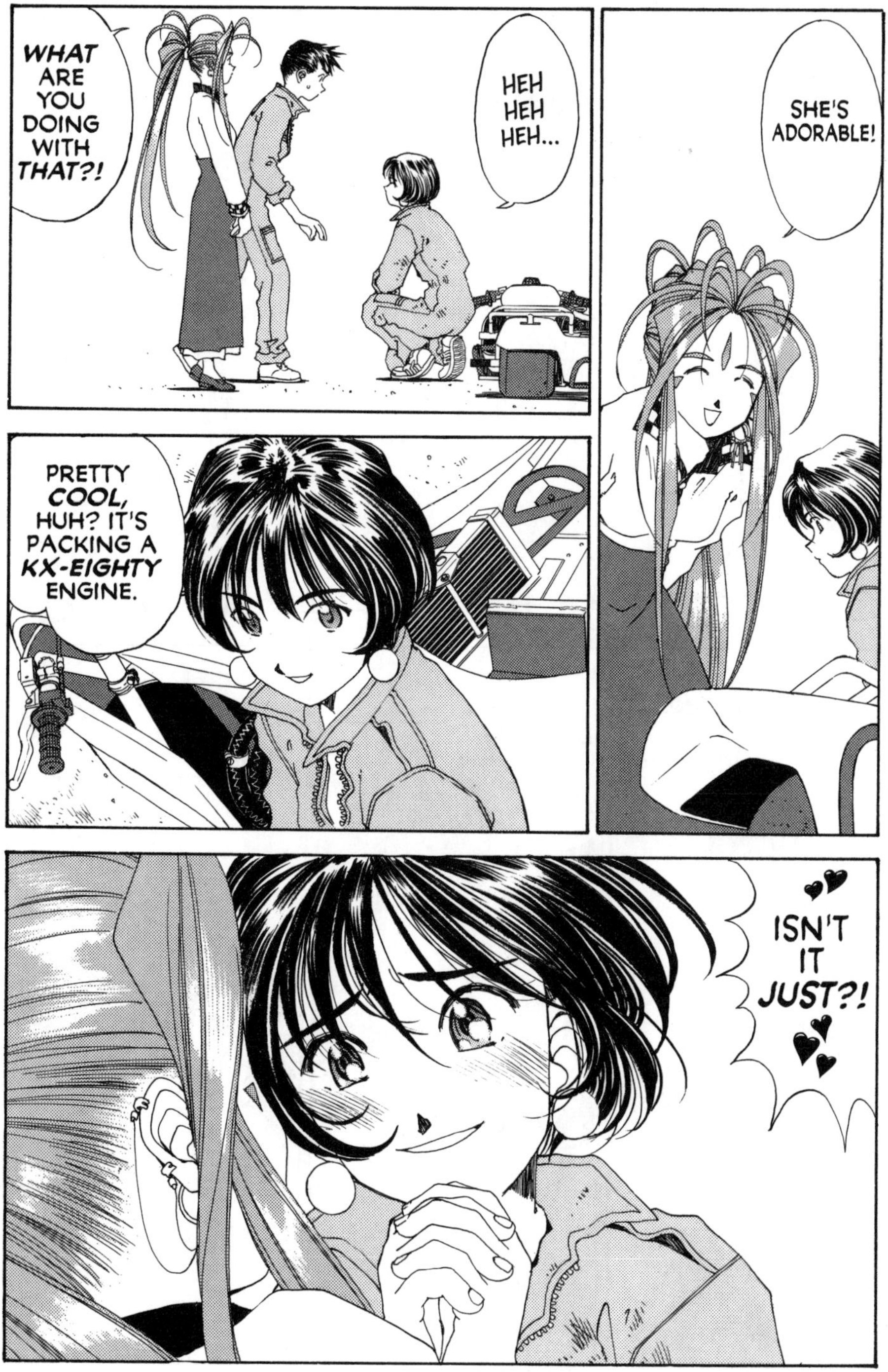
WHAT ARE YOU DOING WITH THAT?!
HEH HEH HEH...
SHE'S ADORABLE!
PRETTY COOL, HUH? IT'S PACKING A KX-EIGHTY ENGINE.
ISN'T IT JUST?!

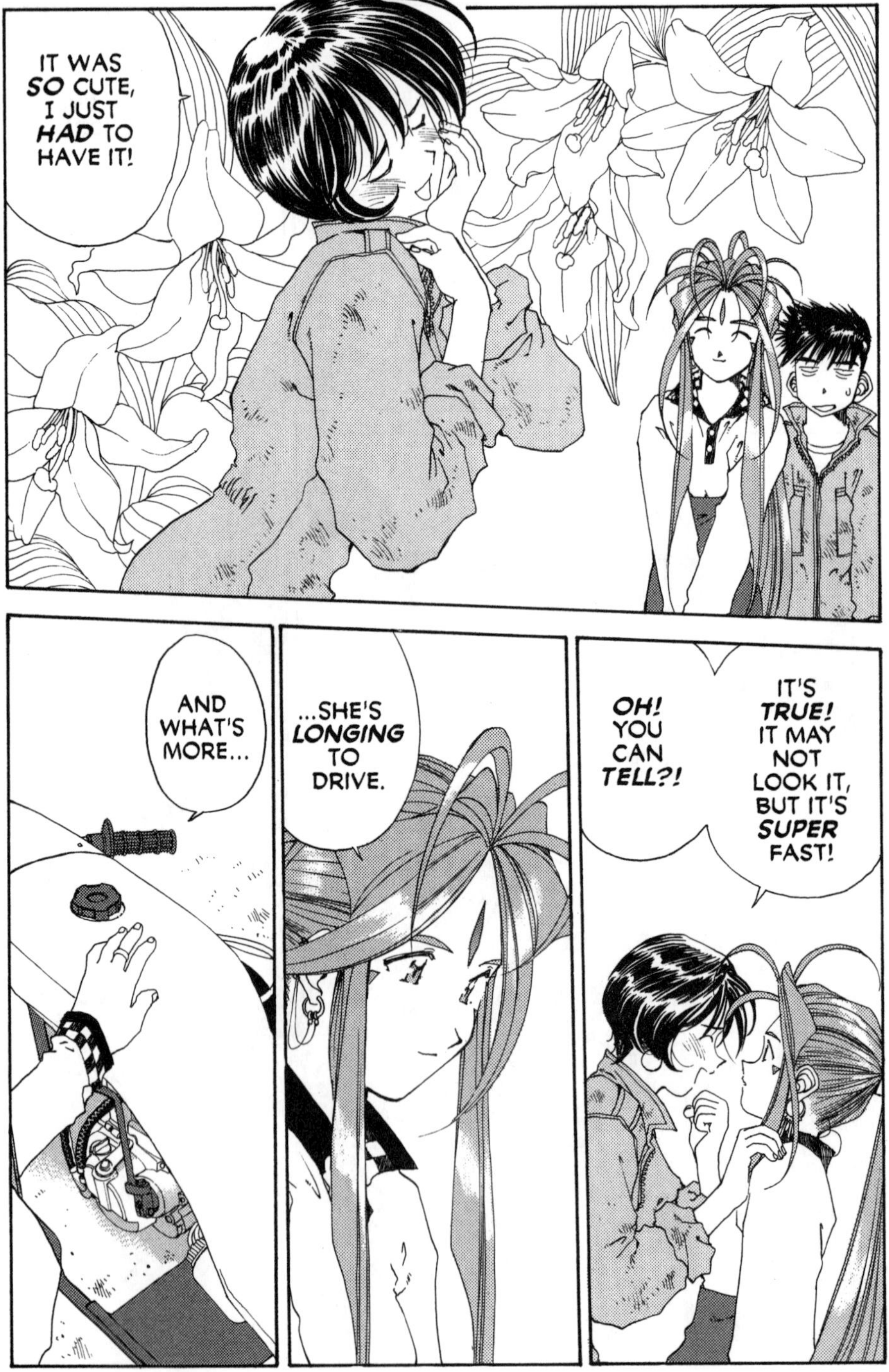
IT WAS SO CUTE, I JUST HAD TO HAVE IT!
AND WHAT'S MORE...
...SHE'S LONGING TO DRIVE.
OH! YOU CAN TELL?!
IT'S TRUE! IT MAY NOT LOOK IT, BUT IT'S SUPER FAST!

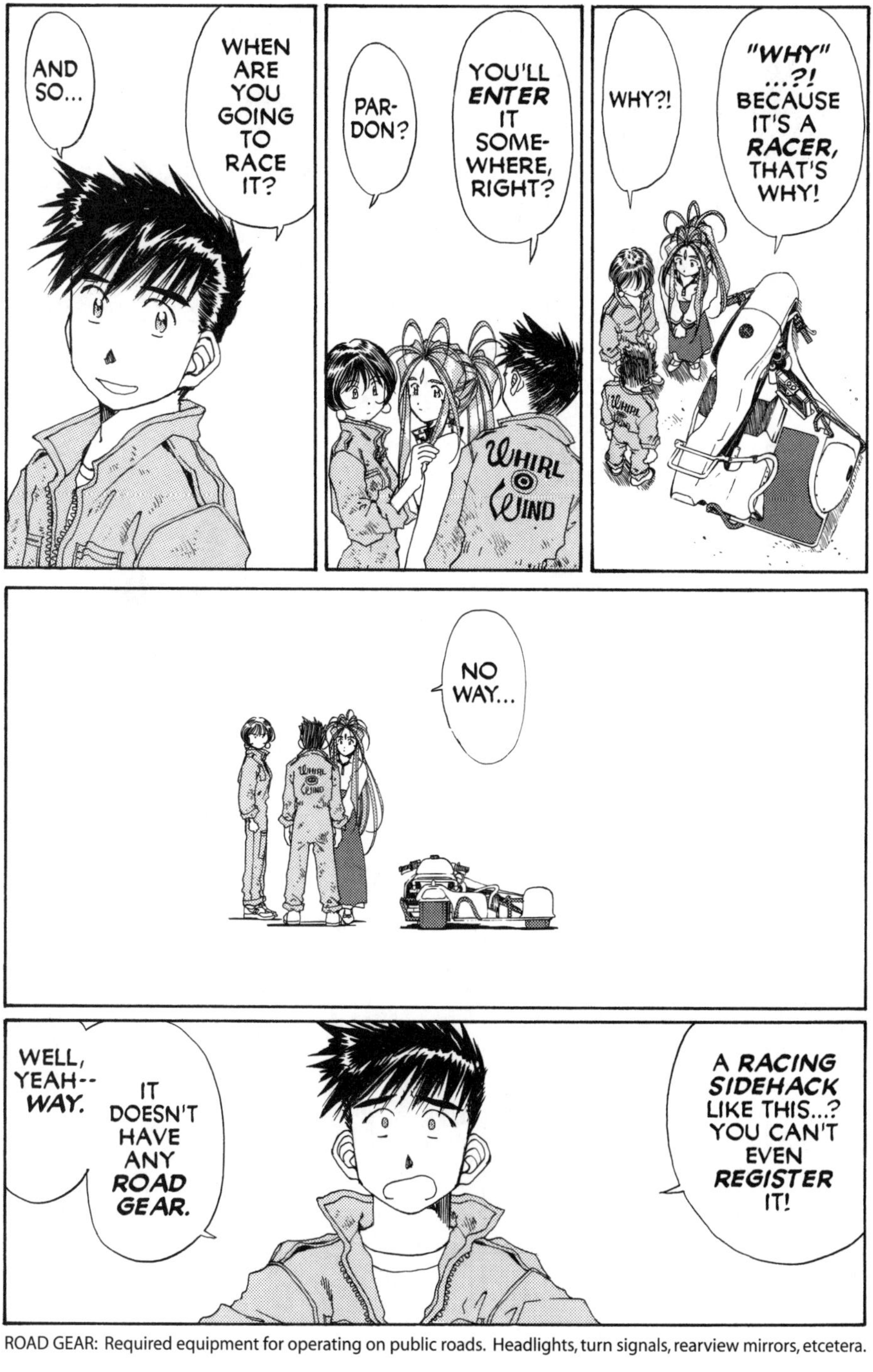
AND SO...
WHEN ARE YOU GOING TO RACE IT?
PAR-DON?
YOU'LL ENTER IT SOME-WHERE, RIGHT?
WHY?!
"WHY" ...?! BECAUSE IT'S A RACER, THAT'S WHY!
NO WAY...
WELL, YEAH-- WAY.
IT DOESN'T HAVE ANY ROAD GEAR.
A RACING SIDEHACK LIKE THIS...? YOU CAN'T EVEN REGISTER IT!

ROAD GEAR: Required equipment for operating on public roads. Headlights, turn signals, rearview mirrors, etcetera.

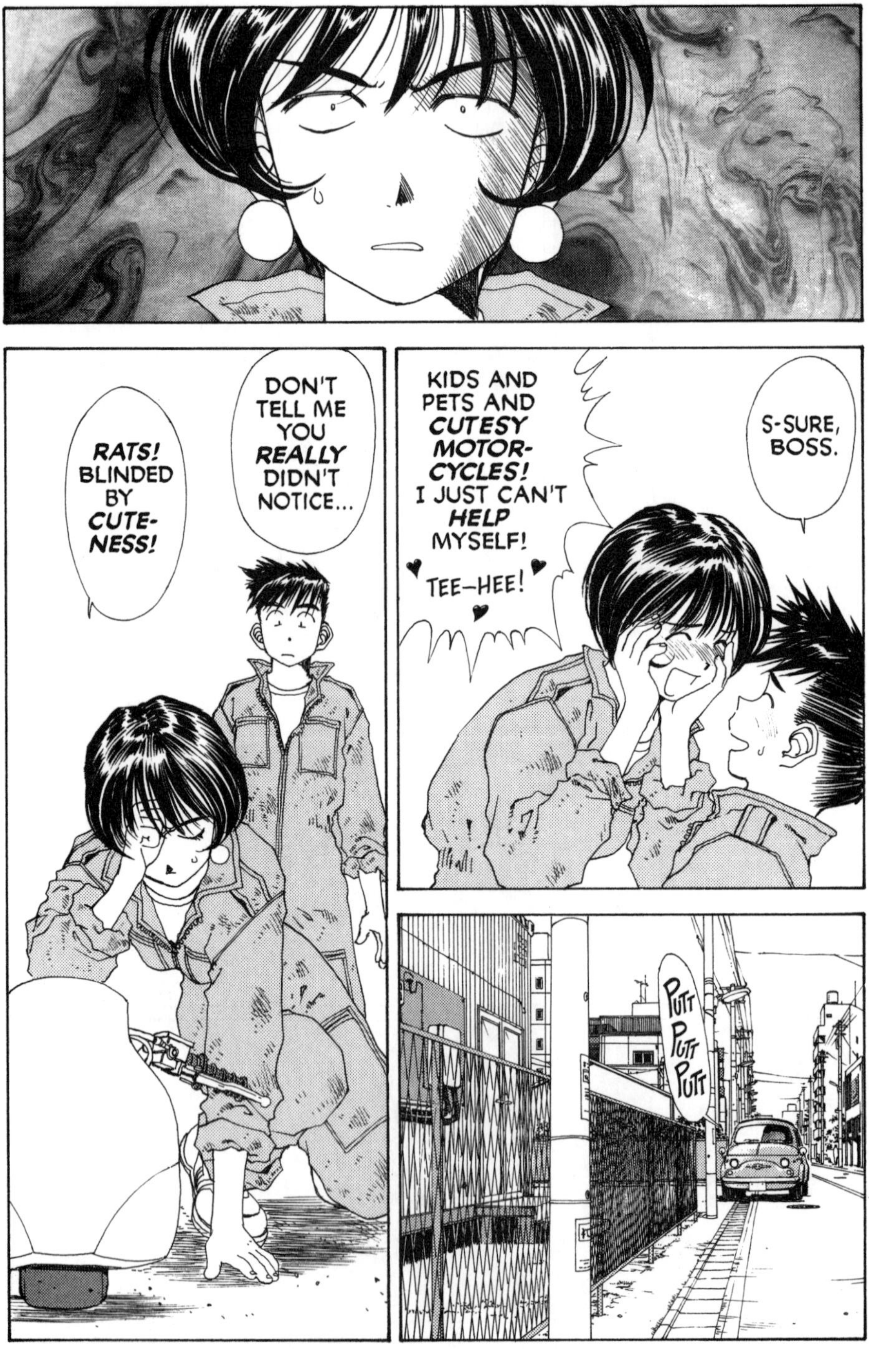
RATS! BLINDED BY CUTE-NESS!
DON'T TELL ME YOU REALLY DIDN'T NOTICE...
KIDS AND PETS AND CUTESY MOTOR-CYCLES! I JUST CAN'T HELP MYSELF!
TEE-HEE!
S-SURE, BOSS.
PUTT PUTT PUTT

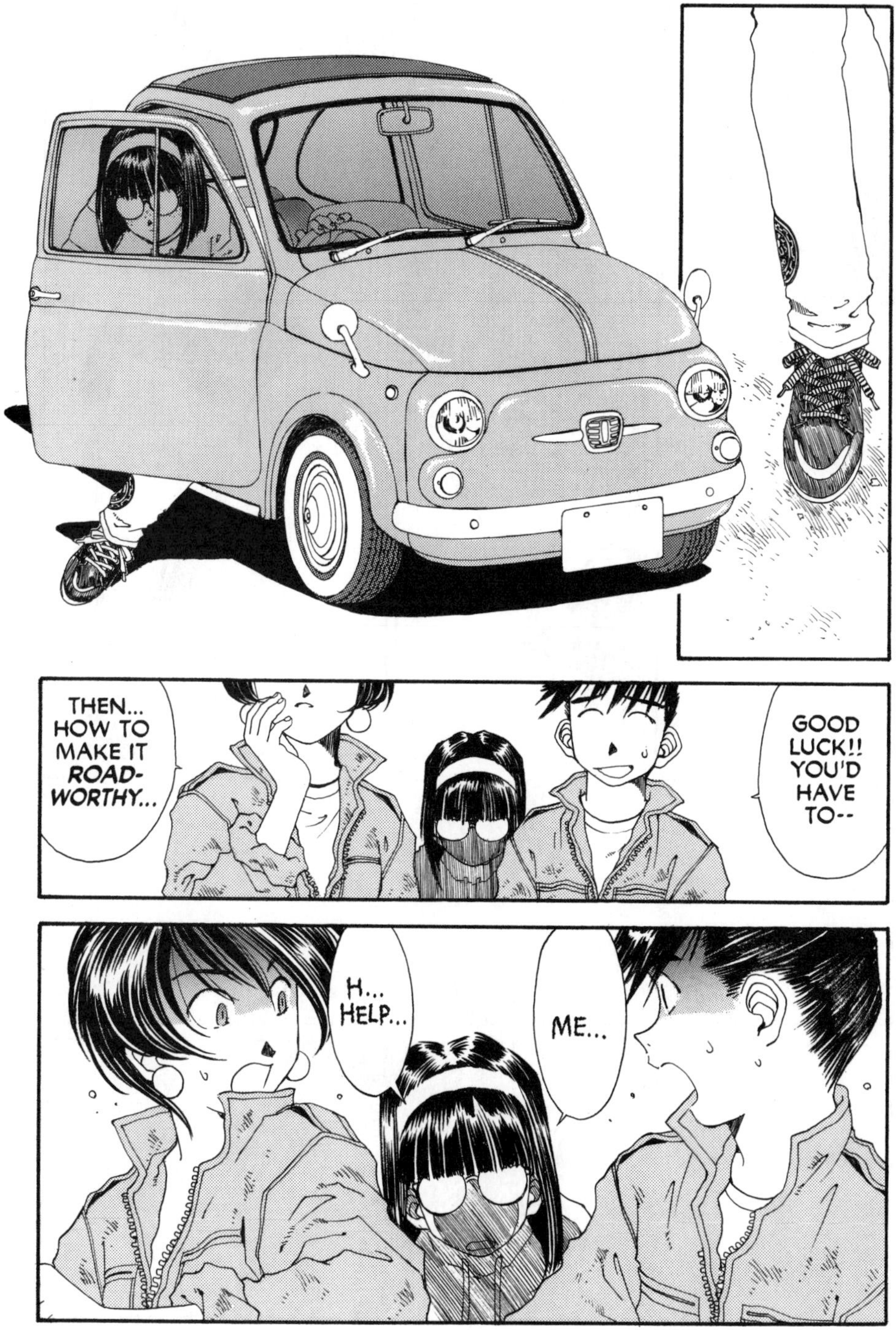
THEN... HOW TO MAKE IT *ROAD-WORTHY*...
GOOD LUCK!! YOU'D HAVE TO--
H... HELP...
ME...

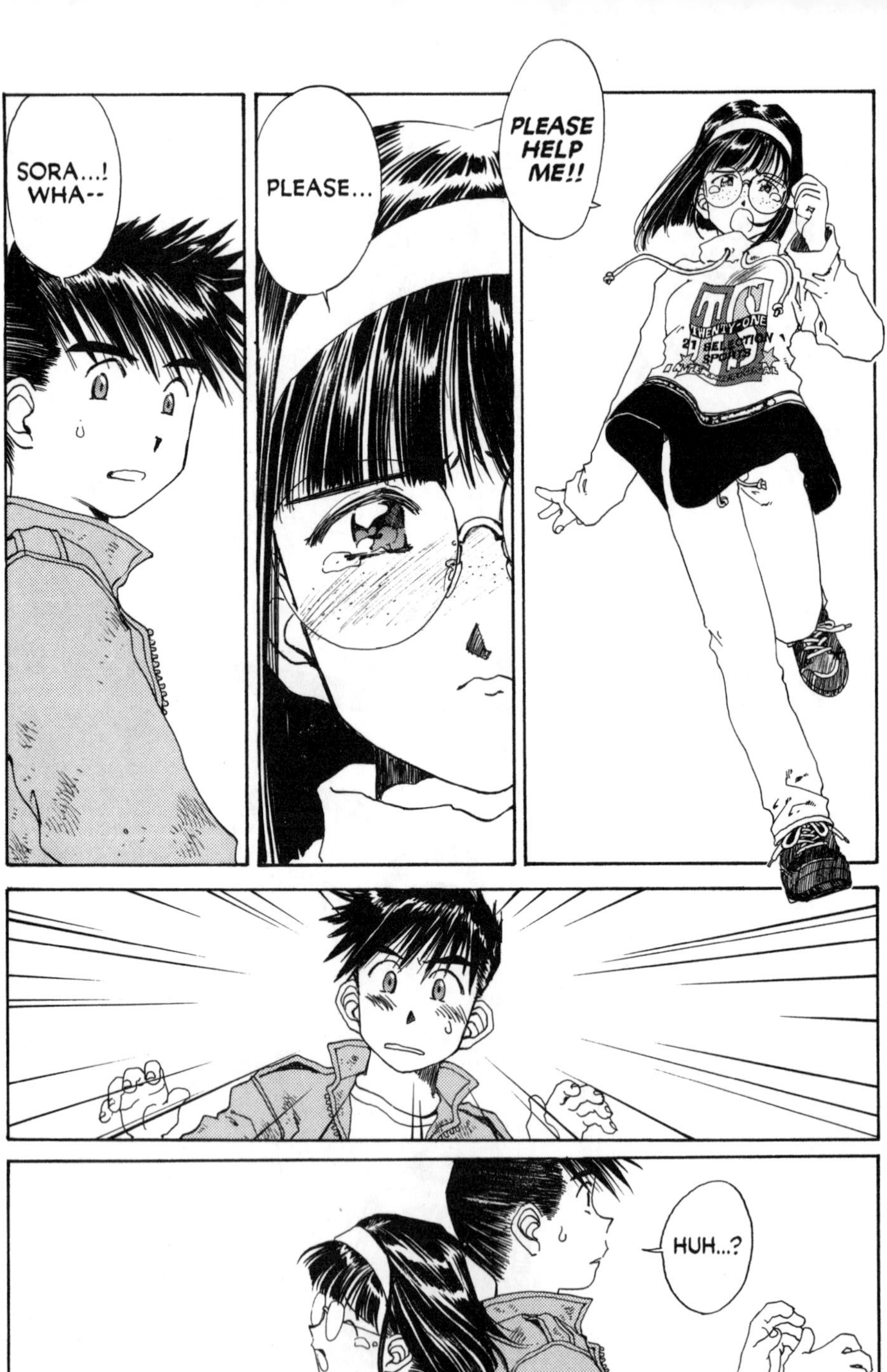
SORA...! WHA--
PLEASE...
PLEASE HELP ME!!
TWENTY-ONE
21 SELECTION SPORTS
HUH...?

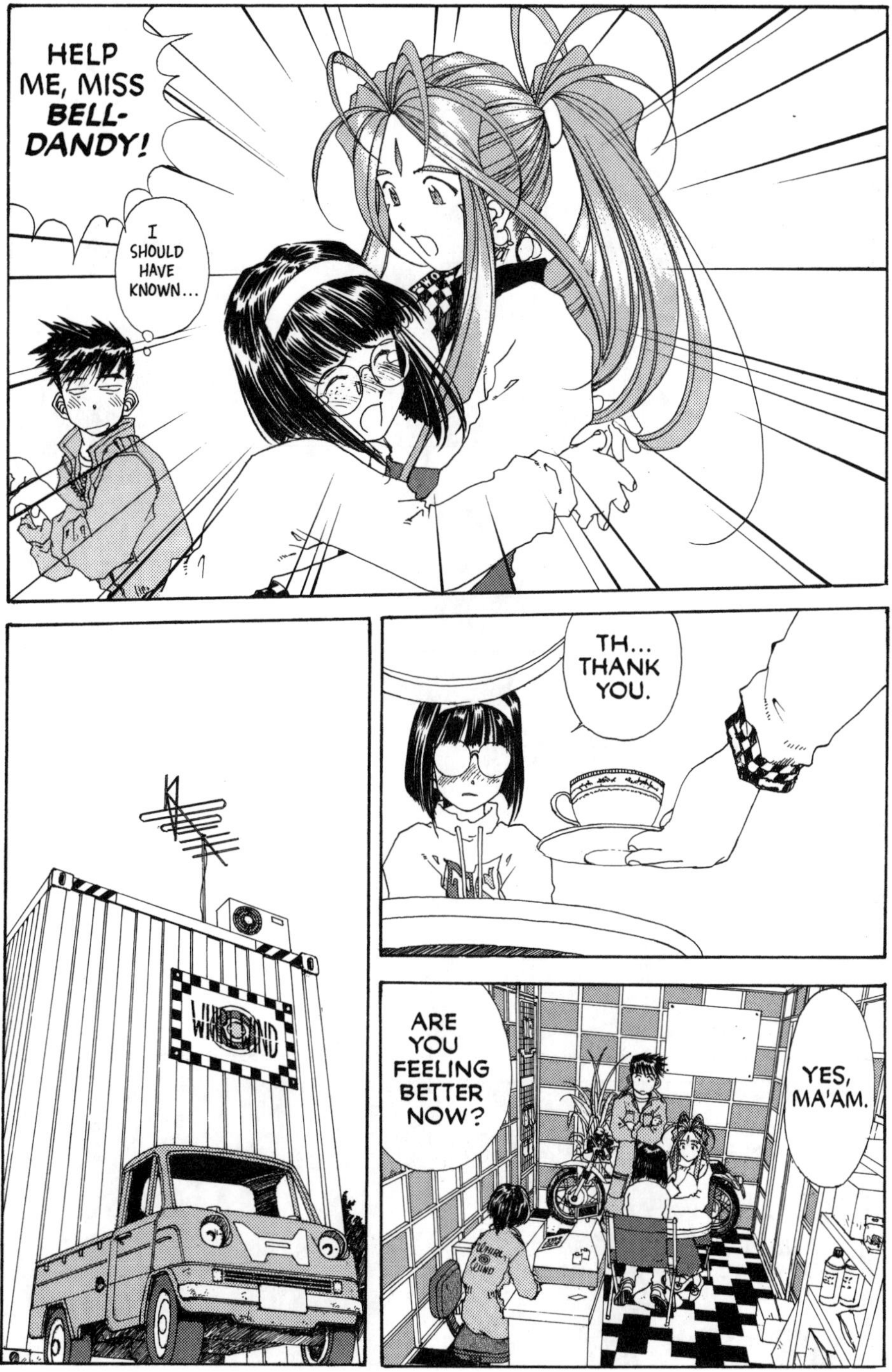

HELP ME, MISS BELL-DANDY!
I SHOULD HAVE KNOWN...
TH... THANK YOU.
ARE YOU FEELING BETTER NOW?
YES, MA'AM.

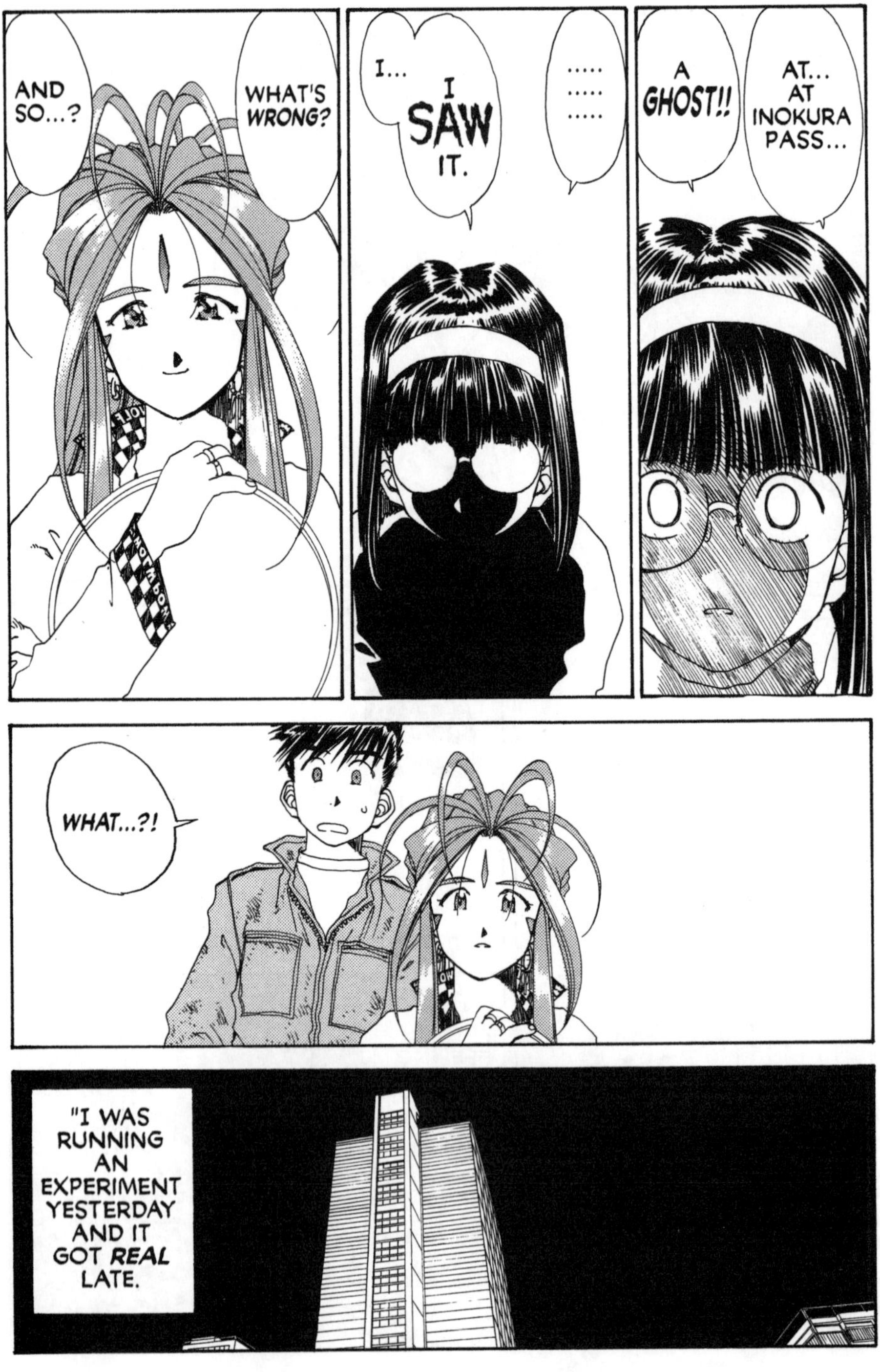
AND SO...?
WHAT'S *WRONG?*
I...
I SAW IT.
.....
.....
.....
A *GHOST!!*
AT... AT INOKURA PASS...
WHAT...?!
"I WAS RUNNING AN EXPERIMENT YESTERDAY AND IT GOT *REAL* LATE.

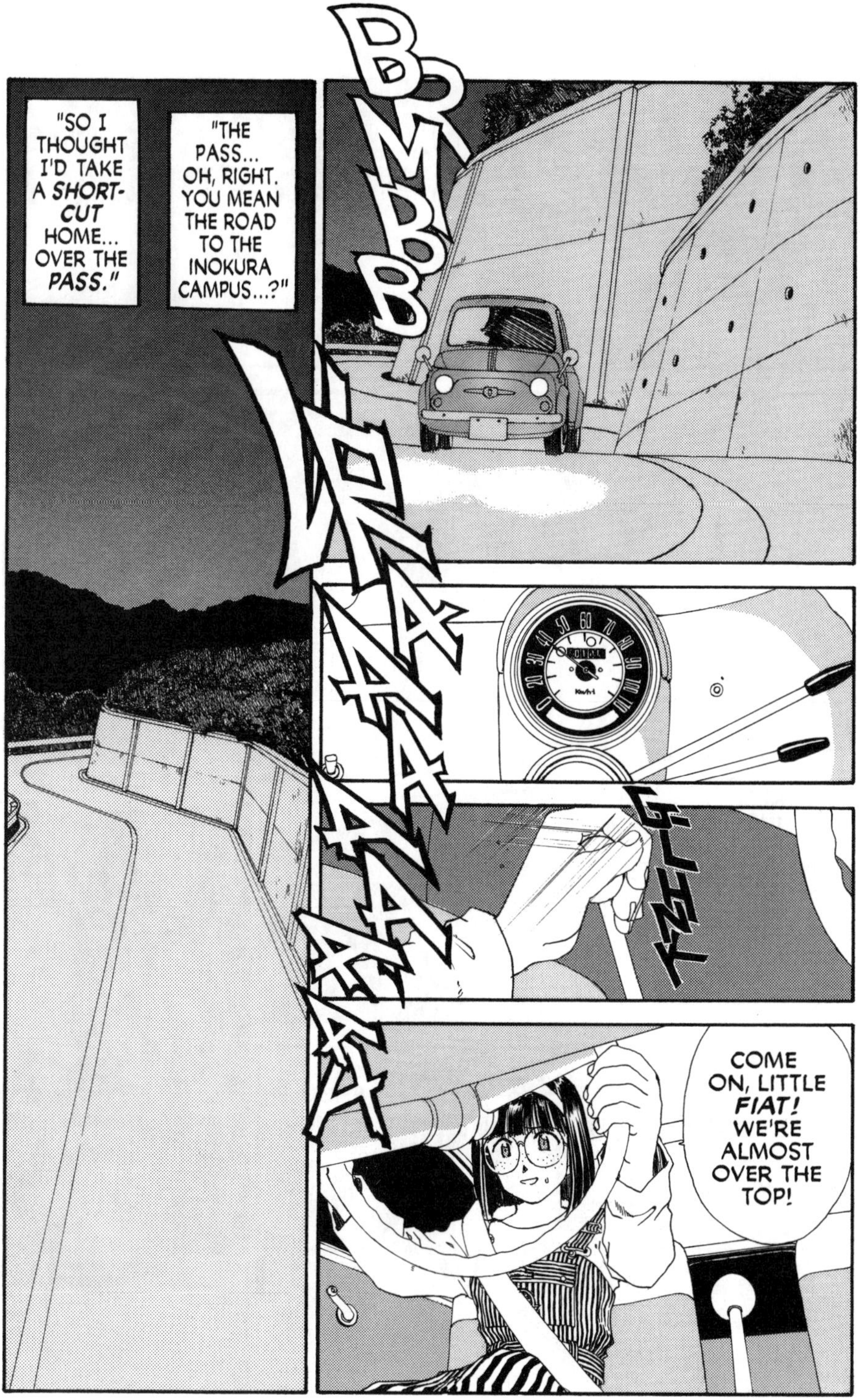
"SO I THOUGHT I'D TAKE A ***SHORT-CUT*** HOME... OVER THE ***PASS.***"
"THE PASS... OH, RIGHT. YOU MEAN THE ROAD TO THE INOKURA CAMPUS...?"
BRMBBB
VRAAAAAAA
GLUNK
COME ON, LITTLE ***FIAT!*** WE'RE ALMOST OVER THE TOP!

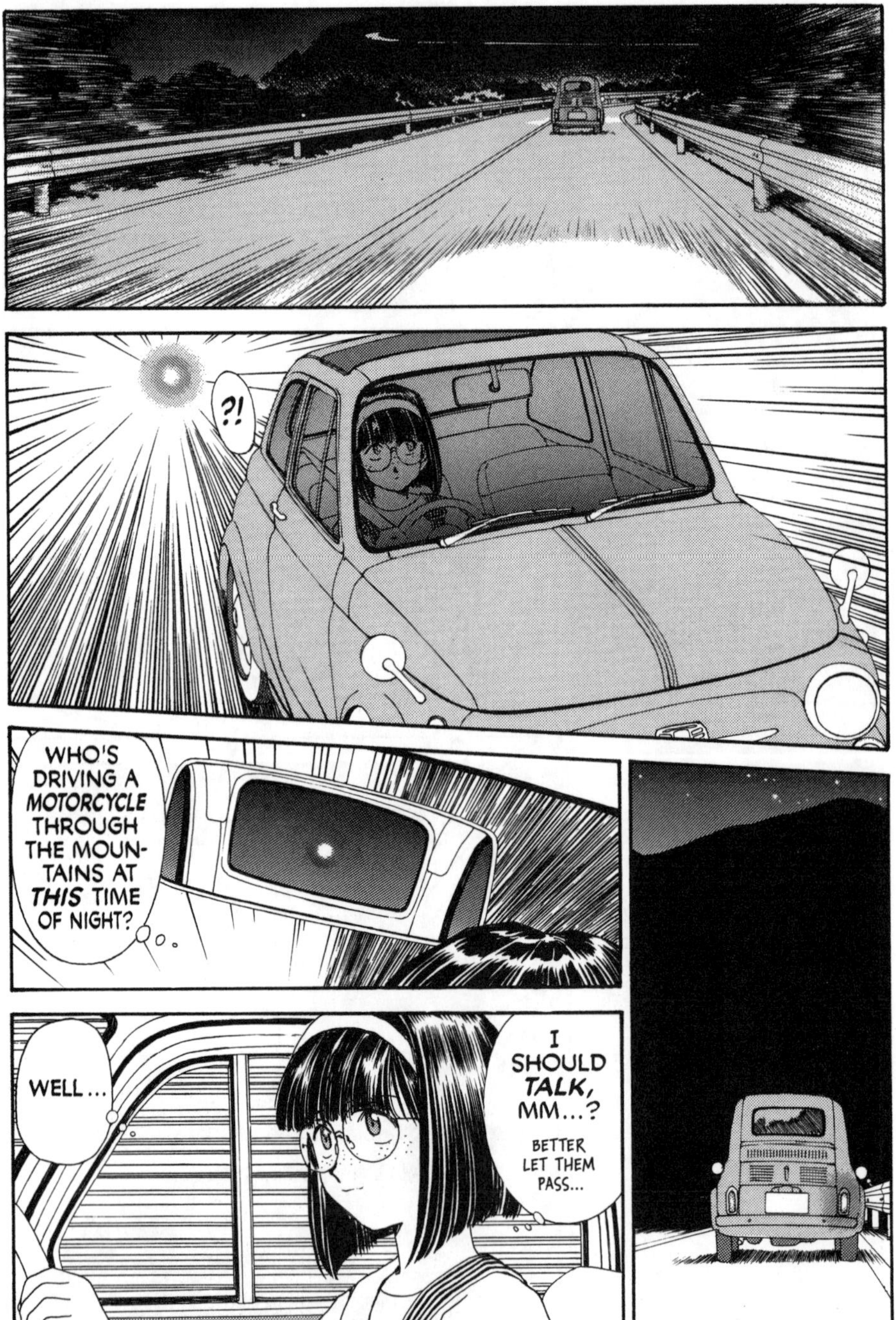
?!
WHO'S DRIVING A *MOTORCYCLE* THROUGH THE MOUN-TAINS AT *THIS* TIME OF NIGHT?
WELL...
I SHOULD *TALK,* MM...?
BETTER LET THEM PASS...

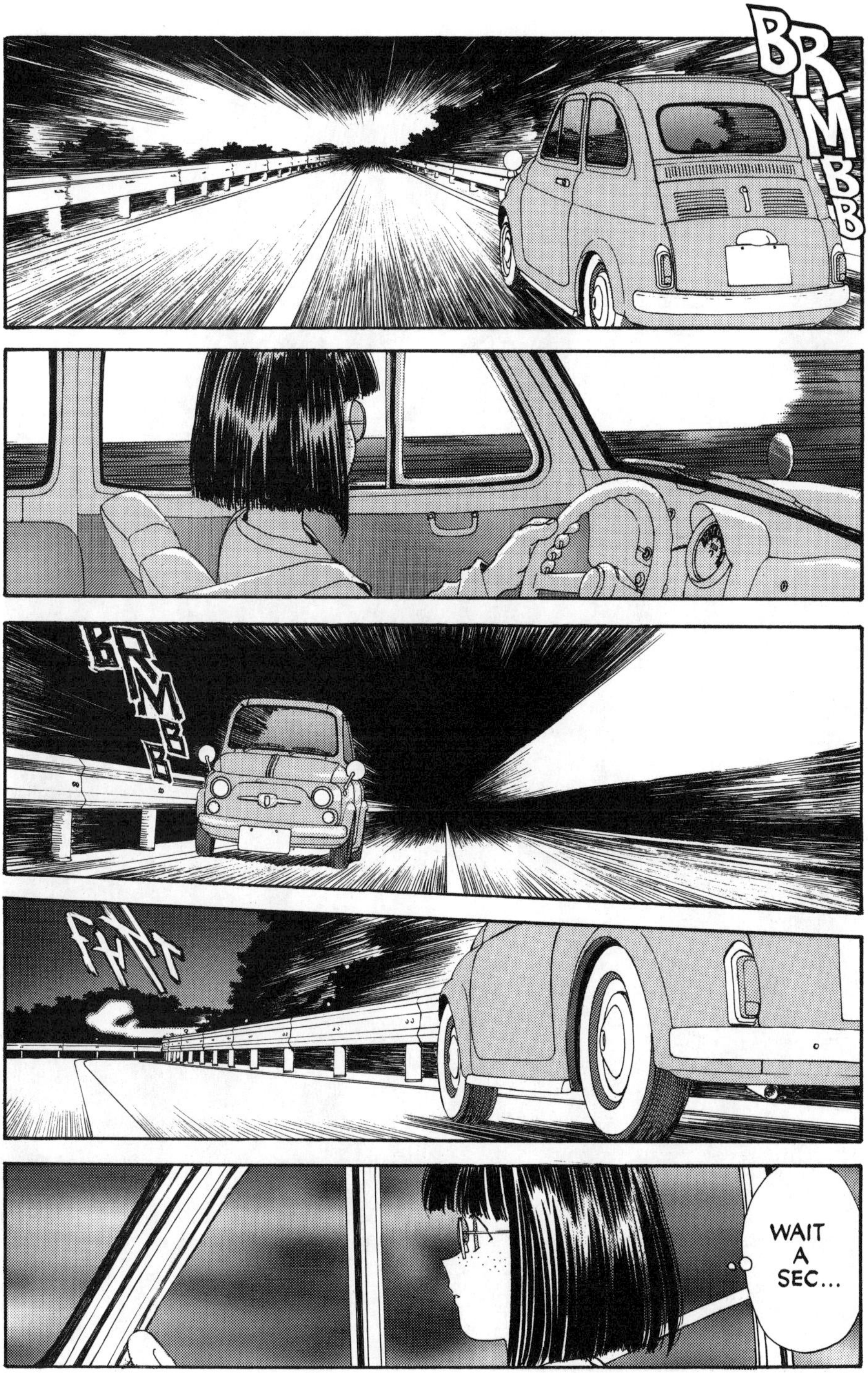
BRMBB
BRMBB
WAIT A SEC...

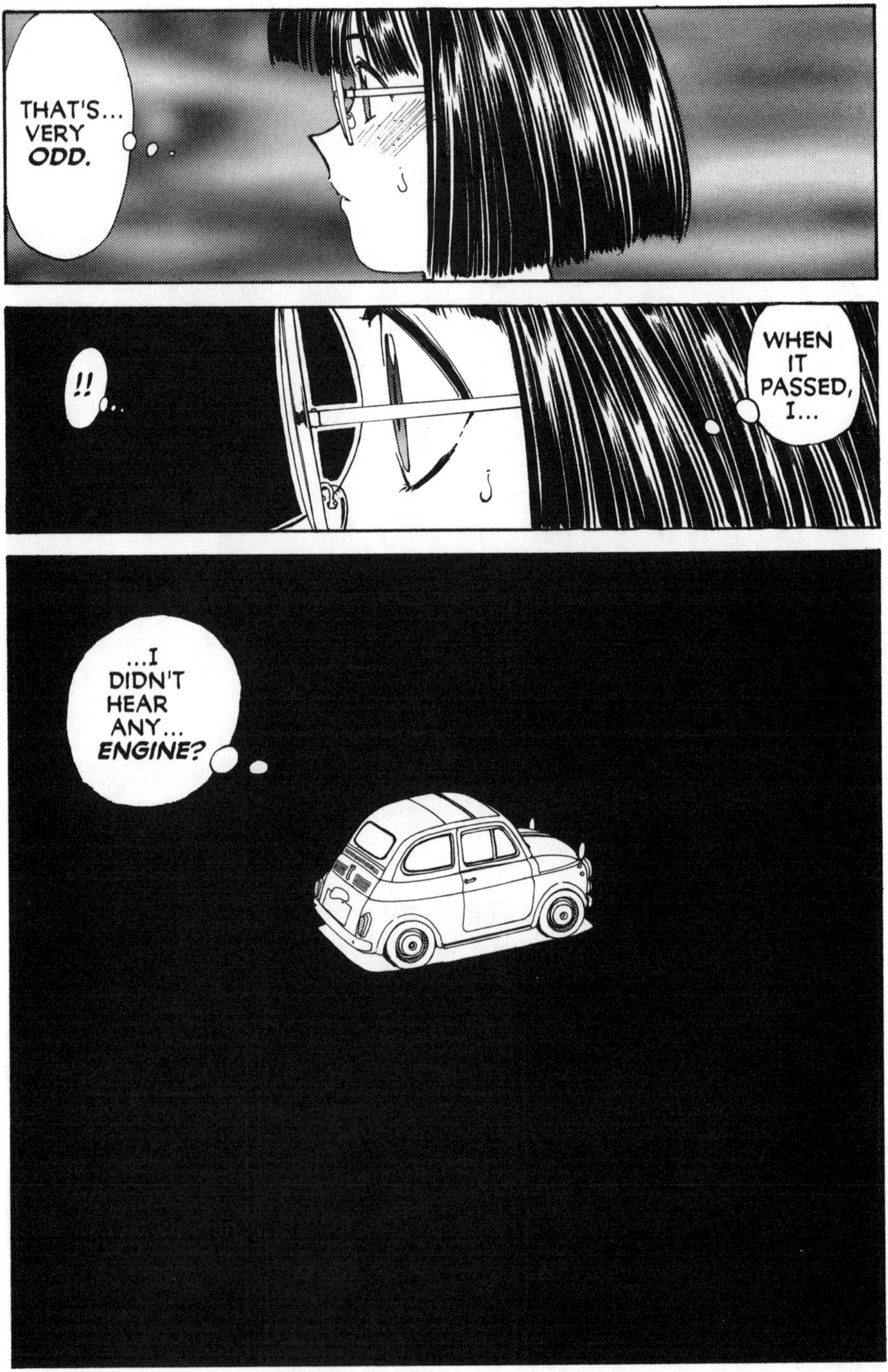
THAT'S... VERY ODD.
!!
WHEN IT PASSED, I...
...I DIDN'T HEAR ANY... ENGINE?

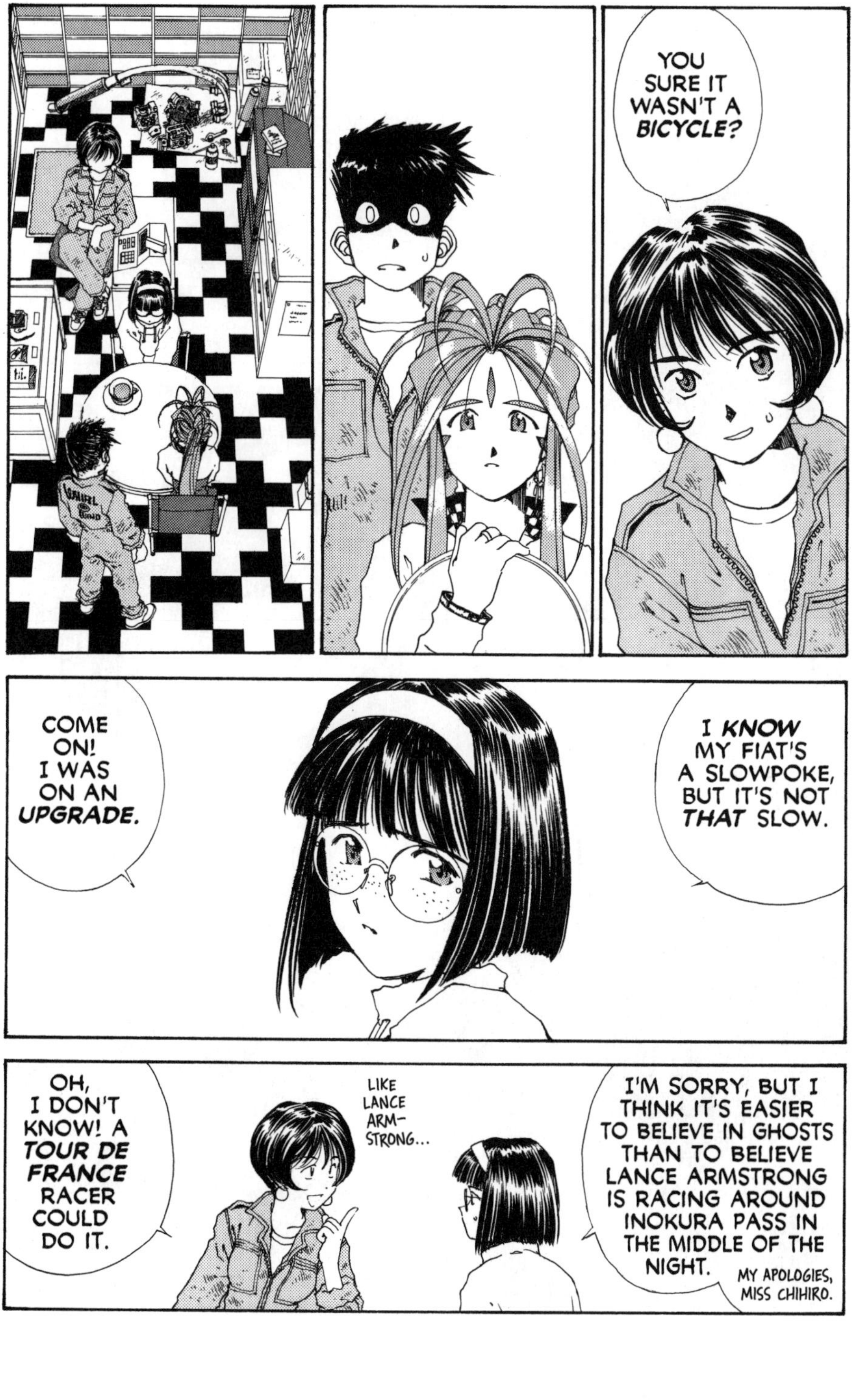
YOU SURE IT WASN'T A *BICYCLE?*
COME ON! I WAS ON AN *UPGRADE.*
I *KNOW* MY FIAT'S A SLOWPOKE, BUT IT'S NOT *THAT* SLOW.
OH, I DON'T KNOW! A *TOUR DE FRANCE* RACER COULD DO IT.
LIKE LANCE ARM-STRONG...
I'M SORRY, BUT I THINK IT'S EASIER TO BELIEVE IN GHOSTS THAN TO BELIEVE LANCE ARMSTRONG IS RACING AROUND INOKURA PASS IN THE MIDDLE OF THE NIGHT.
MY APOLOGIES, MISS CHIHIRO.

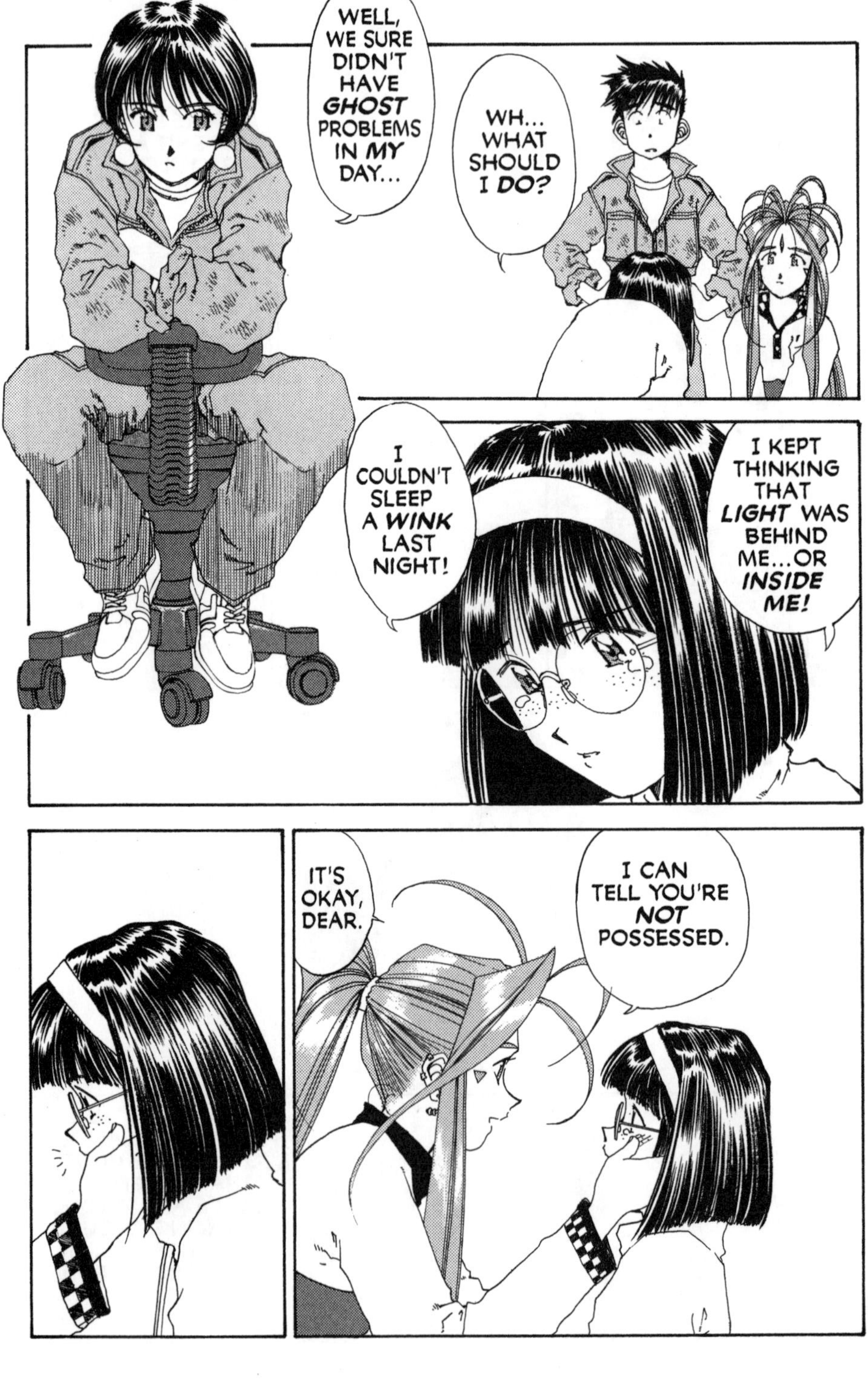
WELL, WE SURE DIDN'T HAVE GHOST PROBLEMS IN MY DAY...
WH... WHAT SHOULD I DO?
I COULDN'T SLEEP A WINK LAST NIGHT!
I KEPT THINKING THAT LIGHT WAS BEHIND ME...OR INSIDE ME!
IT'S OKAY, DEAR.
I CAN TELL YOU'RE NOT POSSESSED.

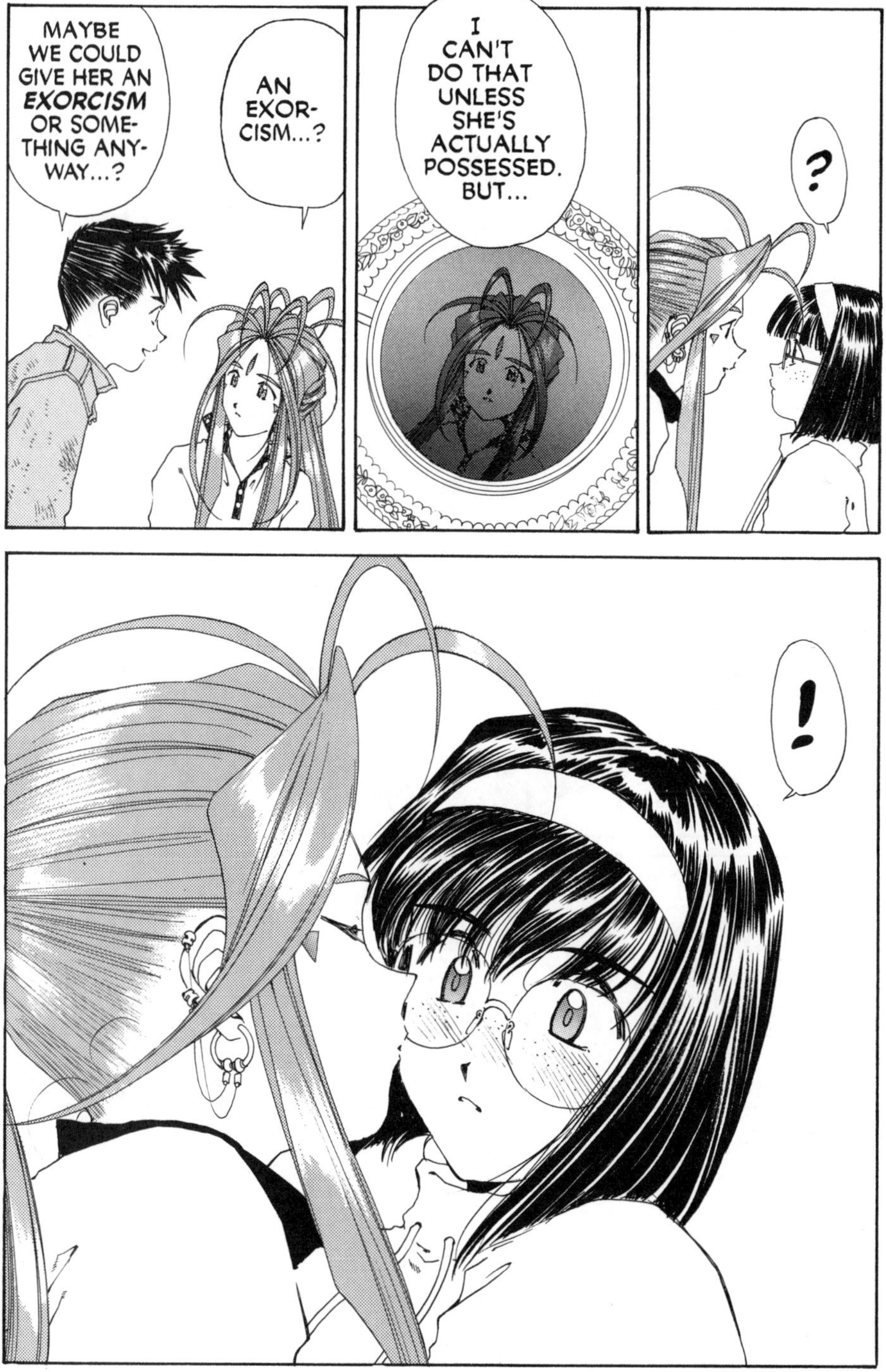
MAYBE WE COULD GIVE HER AN *EXORCISM* OR SOME-THING ANY-WAY...?
AN EXOR-CISM...?
I CAN'T DO THAT UNLESS SHE'S ACTUALLY POSSESSED. BUT...
?
!

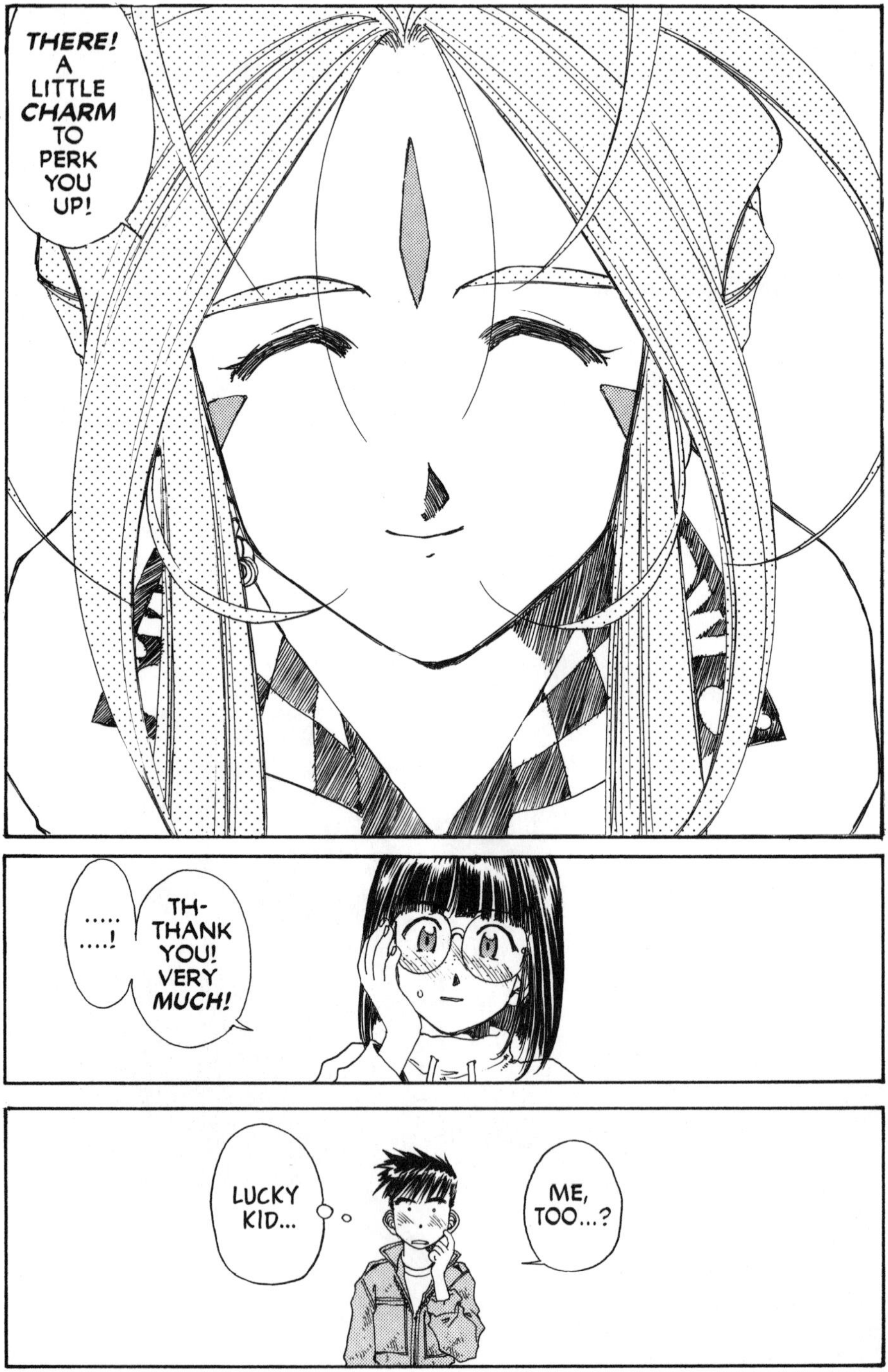
THERE! A LITTLE CHARM TO PERK YOU UP!
....!
TH-THANK YOU! VERY MUCH!
LUCKY KID...
ME, TOO...?

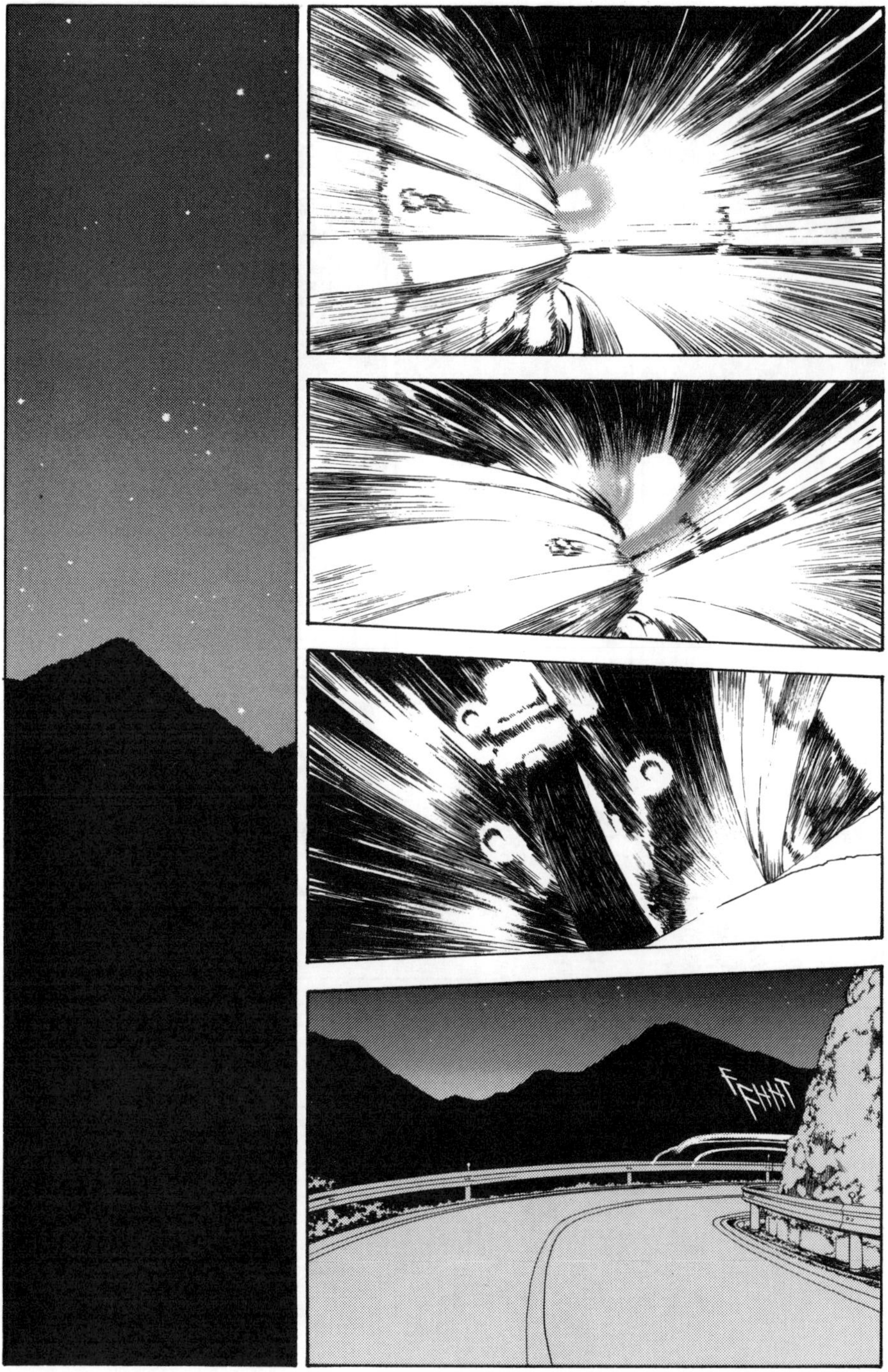
FFHHT

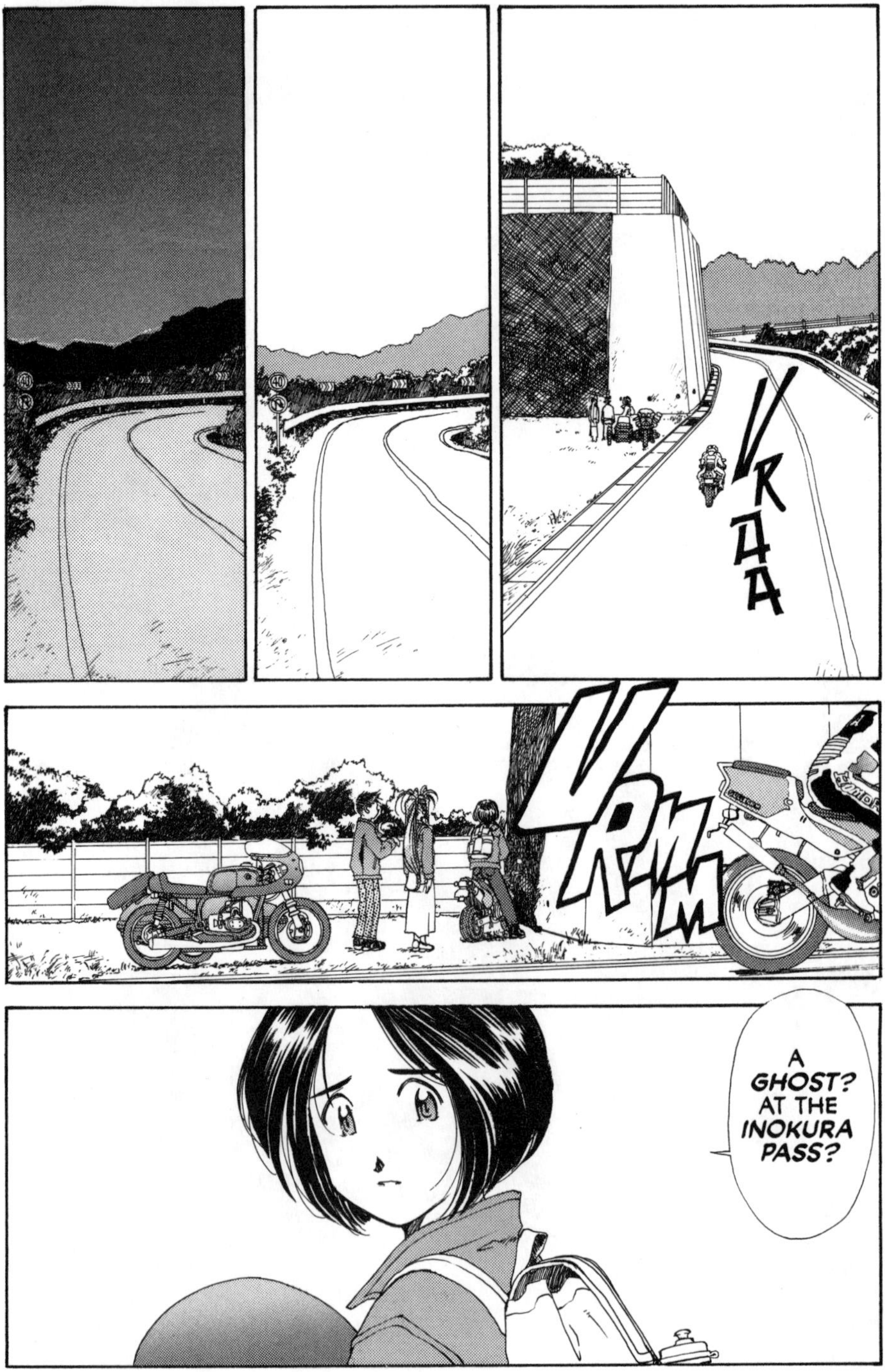
VRAA
VRMM
A GHOST? AT THE INOKURA PASS?

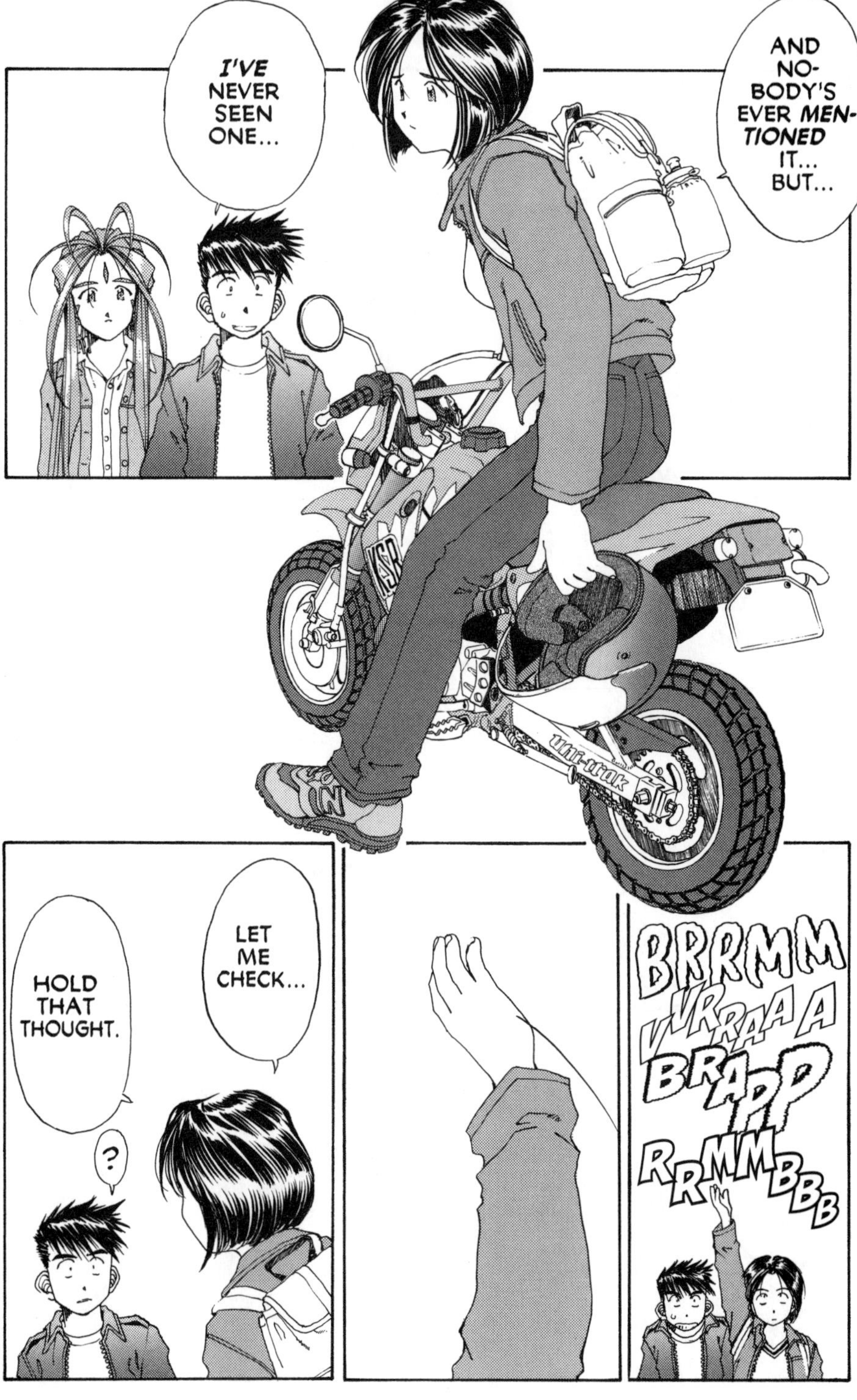
I'VE NEVER SEEN ONE...
AND NO-BODY'S EVER MEN-TIONED IT... BUT...
HOLD THAT THOUGHT.
LET ME CHECK...
?
BRRMM
VRRAAA
BRAPP
RRMMBBB

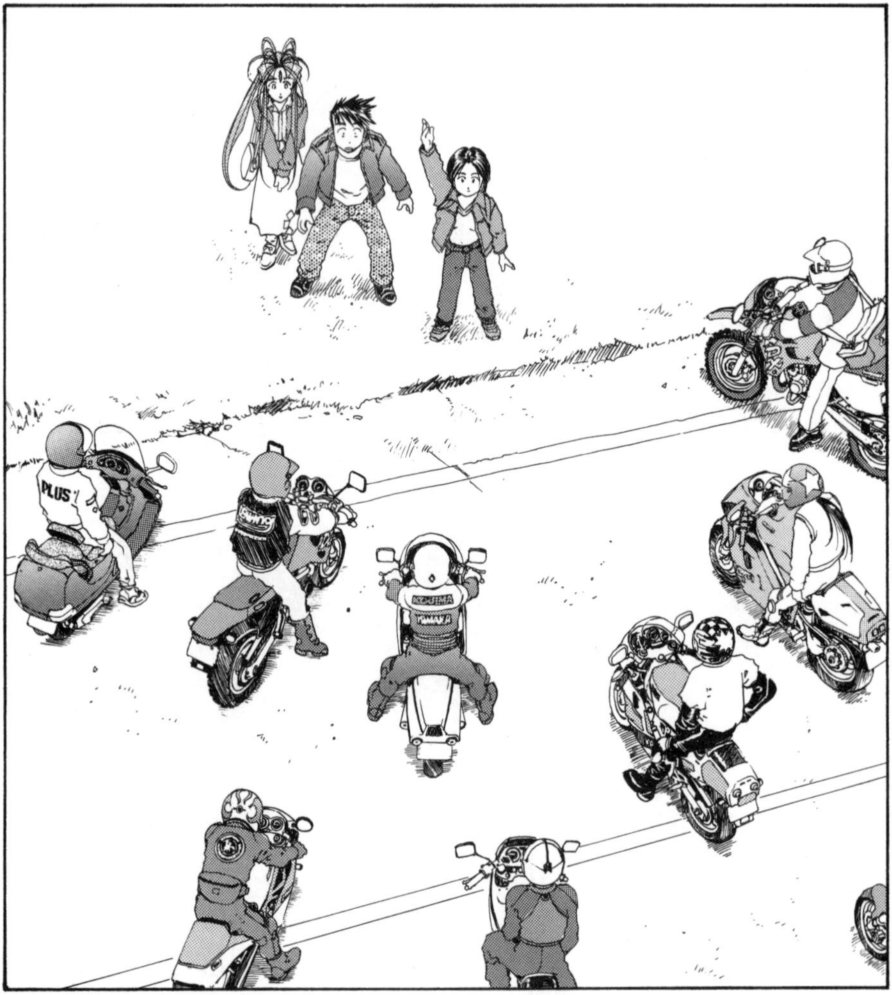

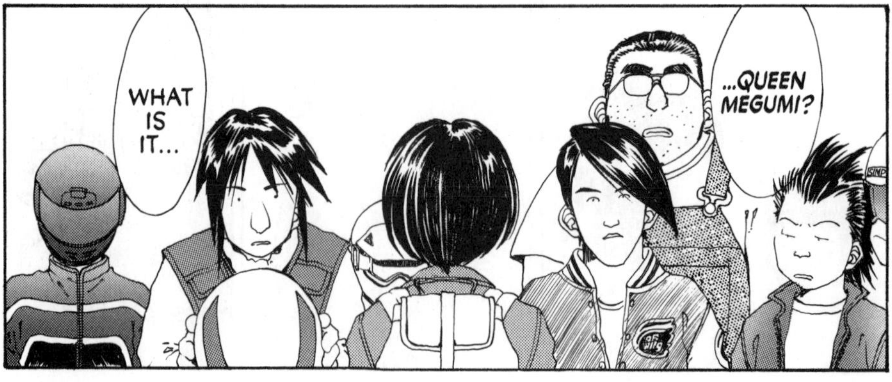
WHAT IS IT...
...QUEEN MEGUMI?

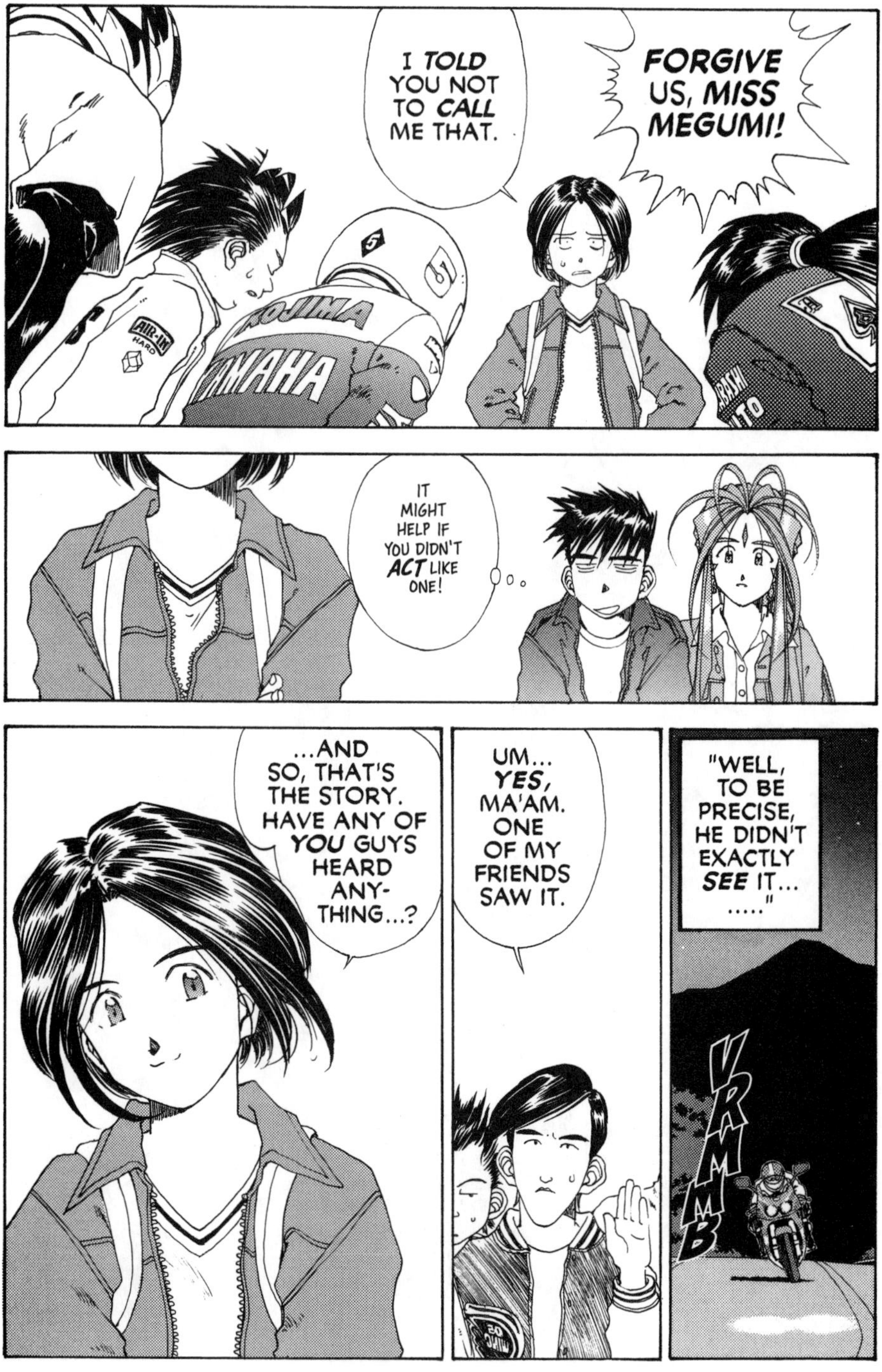
I TOLD YOU NOT TO CALL ME THAT.
FORGIVE US, MISS MEGUMI!
IT MIGHT HELP IF YOU DIDN'T ACT LIKE ONE!
...AND SO, THAT'S THE STORY. HAVE ANY OF YOU GUYS HEARD ANY-THING...?
UM... YES, MA'AM. ONE OF MY FRIENDS SAW IT.
"WELL, TO BE PRECISE, HE DIDN'T EXACTLY SEE IT... ....."
VRMMMB

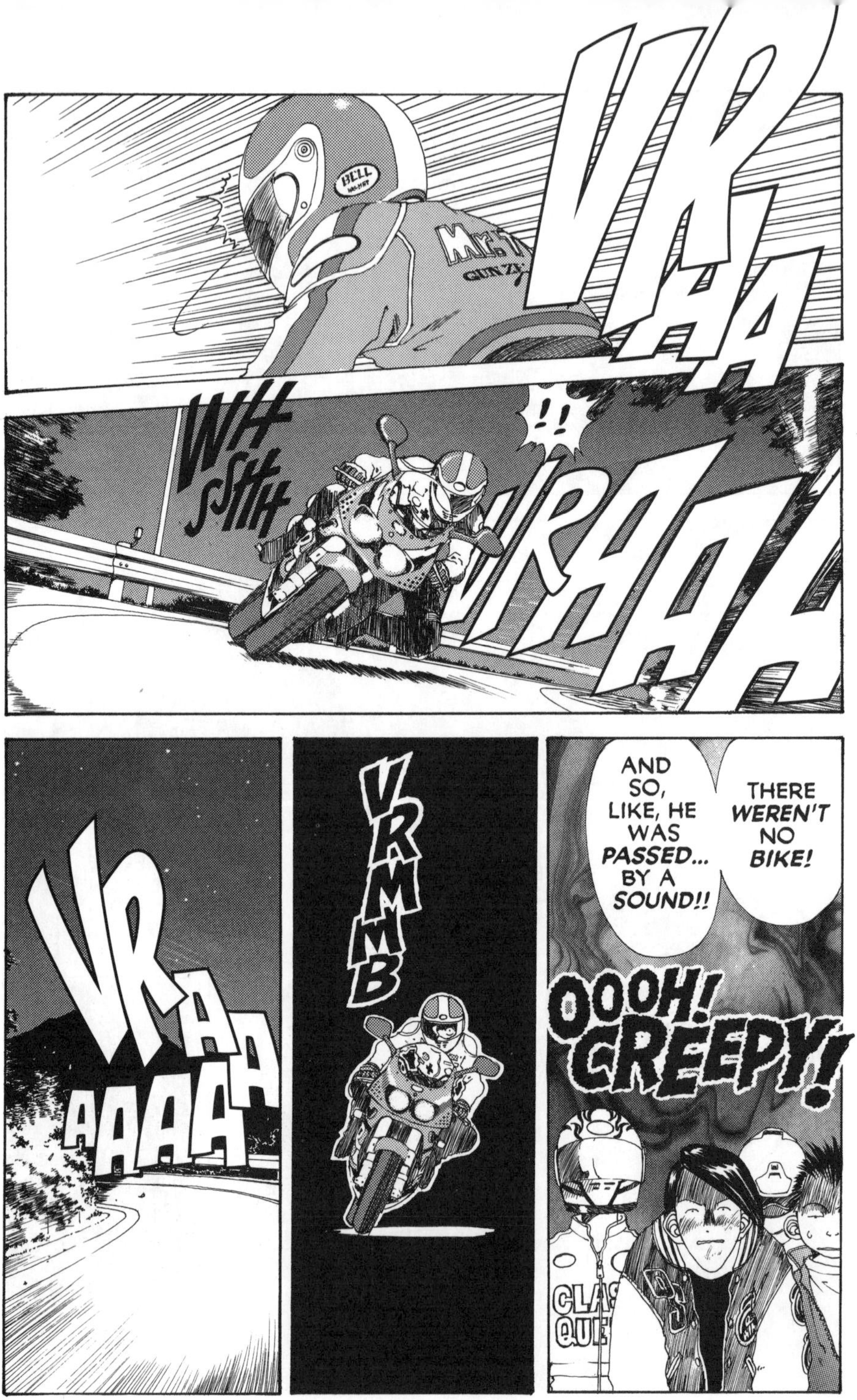
!!
VRMMMB
AND SO, LIKE, HE WAS PASSED... BY A SOUND!!
THERE WEREN'T NO BIKE!
OOOH! CREEPY!

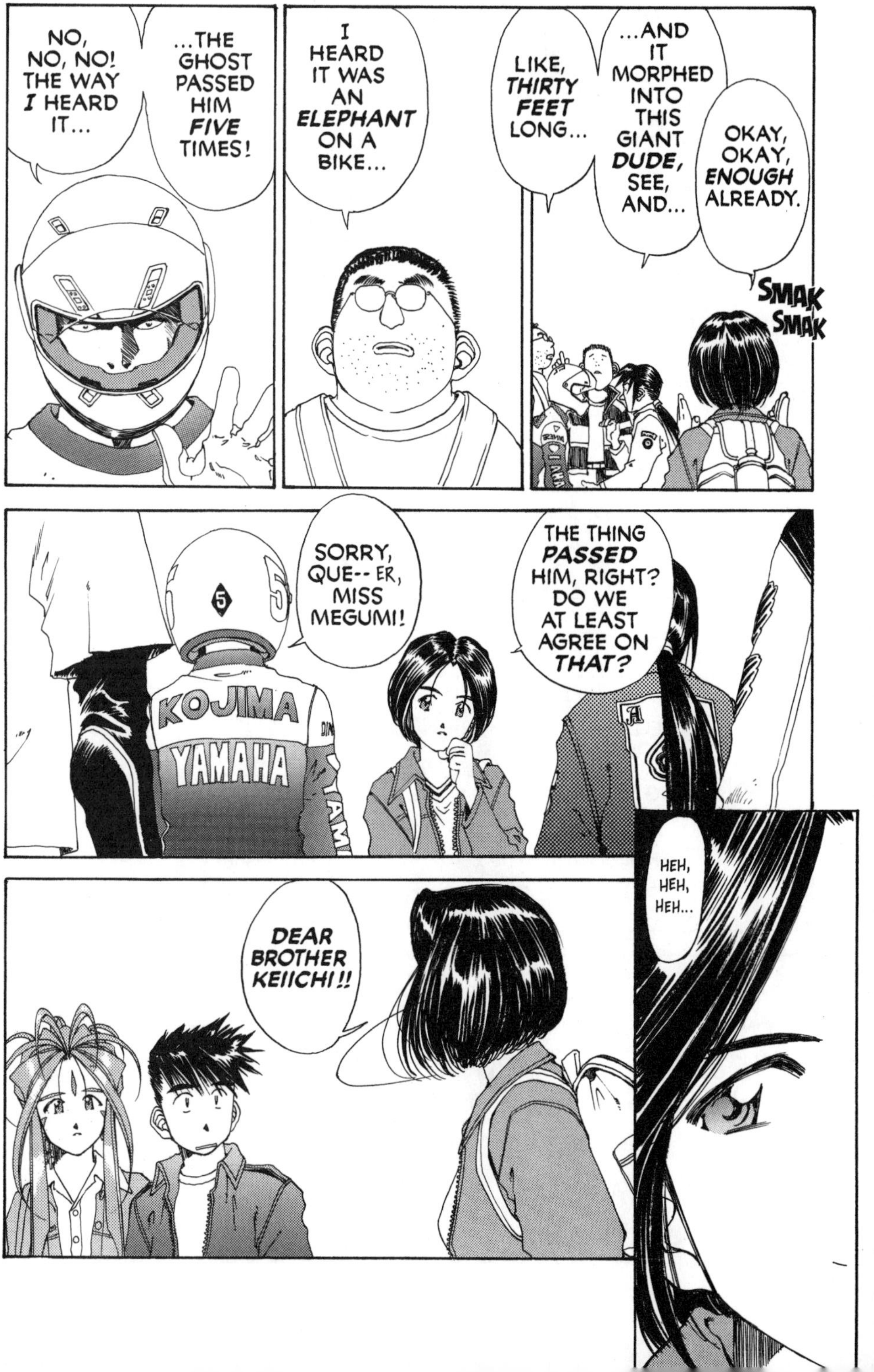
NO, NO, NO! THE WAY I HEARD IT...
...THE GHOST PASSED HIM FIVE TIMES!
I HEARD IT WAS AN ELEPHANT ON A BIKE...
LIKE, THIRTY FEET LONG...
...AND IT MORPHED INTO THIS GIANT DUDE, SEE, AND...
OKAY, OKAY, ENOUGH ALREADY.
SMAK SMAK
SORRY, QUE-- ER, MISS MEGUMI!
KOJIMA
YAMAHA
THE THING PASSED HIM, RIGHT? DO WE AT LEAST AGREE ON THAT?
HEH, HEH, HEH...
DEAR BROTHER KEIICHI!!

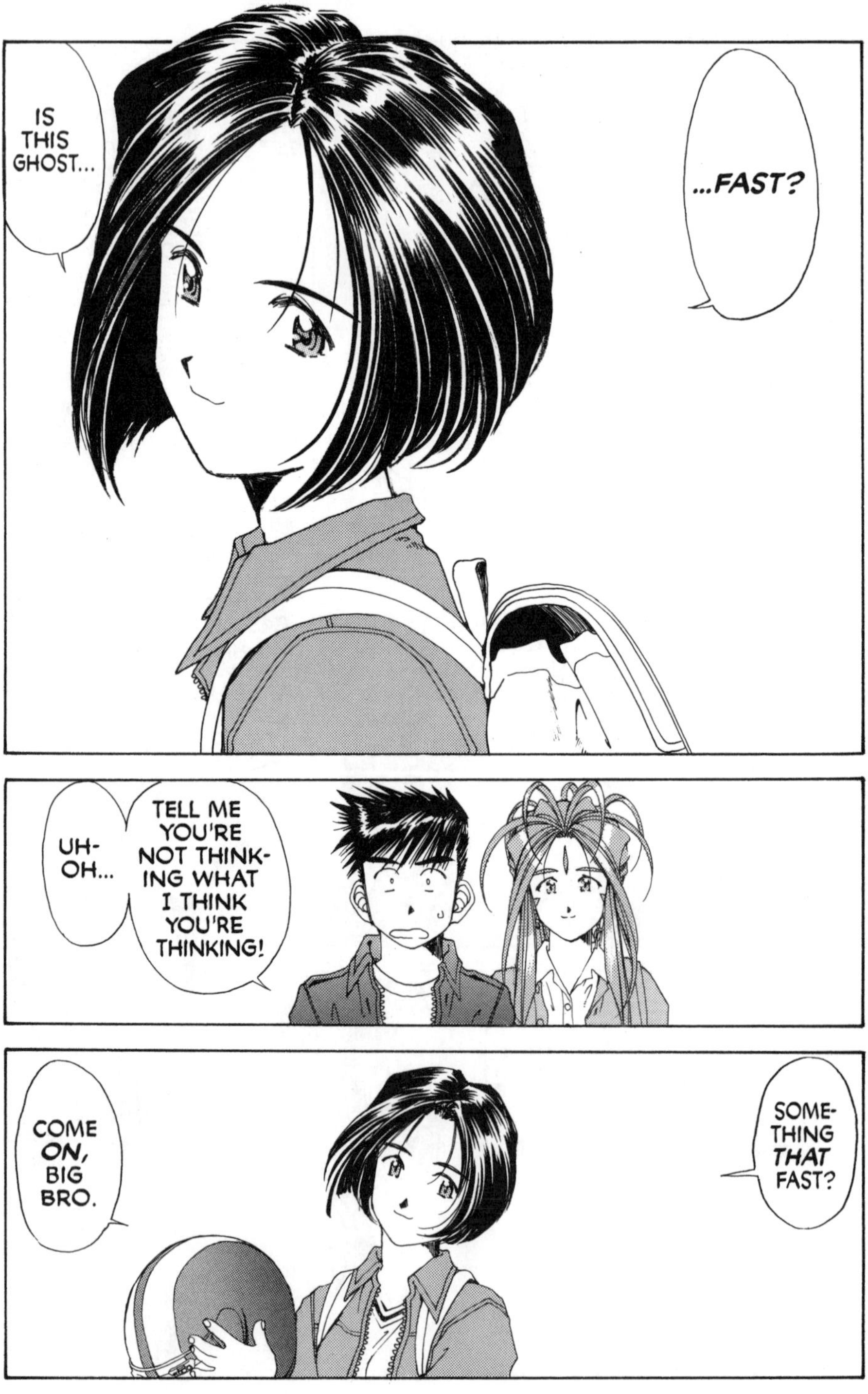
IS THIS GHOST...
...FAST?
UH-OH...
TELL ME YOU'RE NOT THINKING WHAT I THINK YOU'RE THINKING!
COME ON, BIG BRO.
SOMETHING THAT FAST?

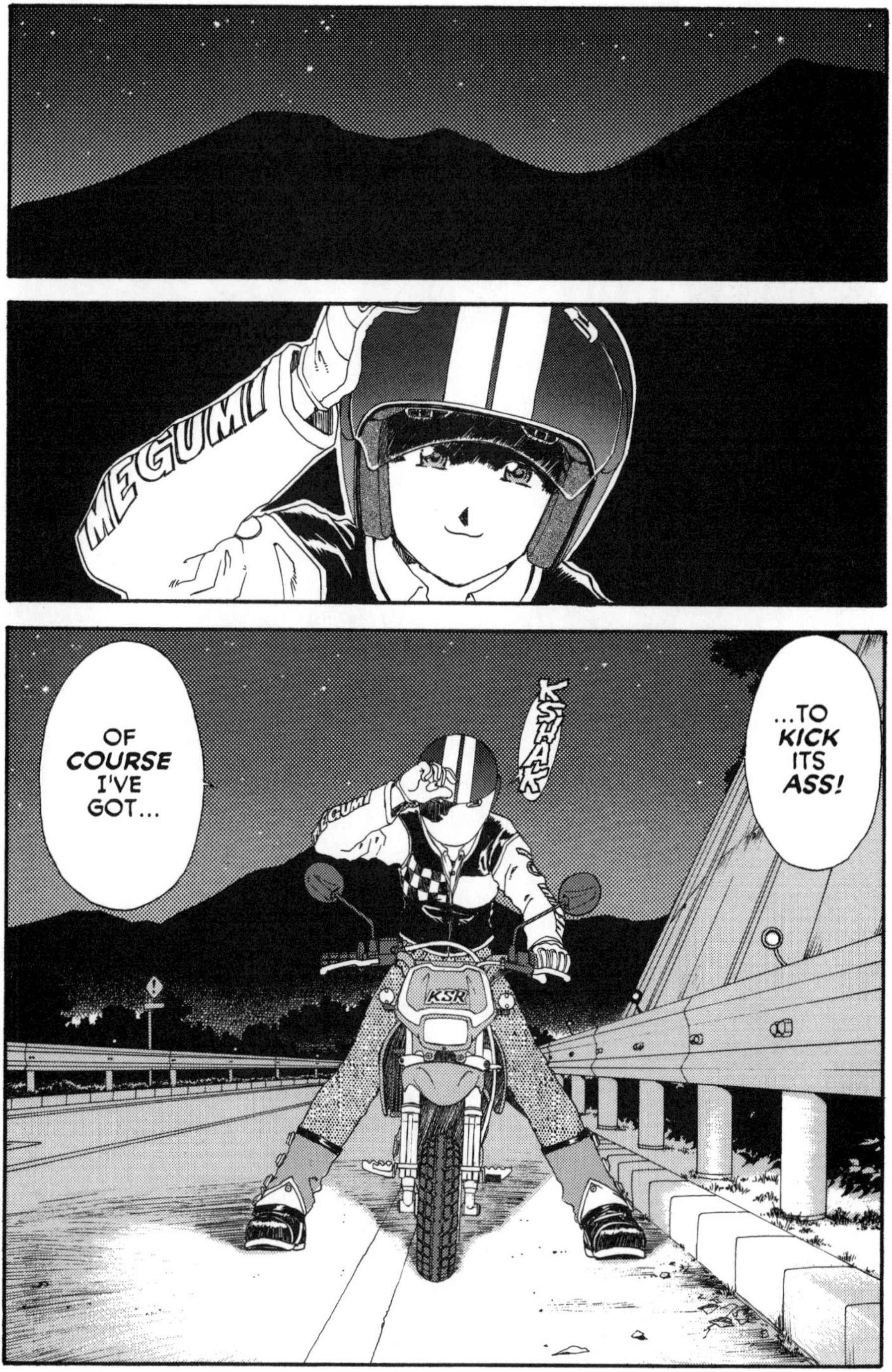
MEGUMI
OF COURSE I'VE GOT...
KSHAK
KSR
...TO KICK ITS ASS!

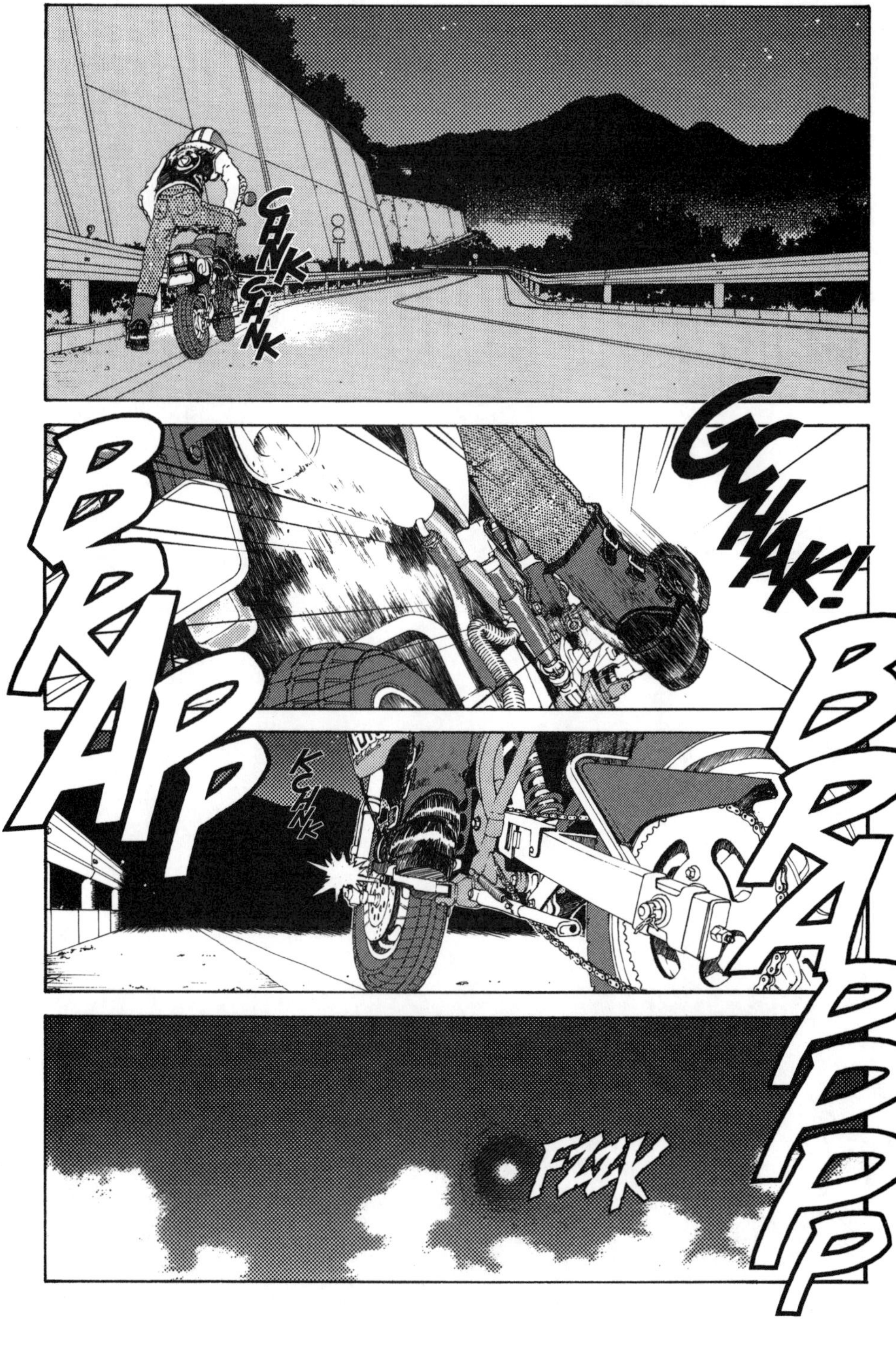
CHNK CHNK CHNK
BRRAP
GCHAK!
KCHNK
BRRAPPPP
FZZK

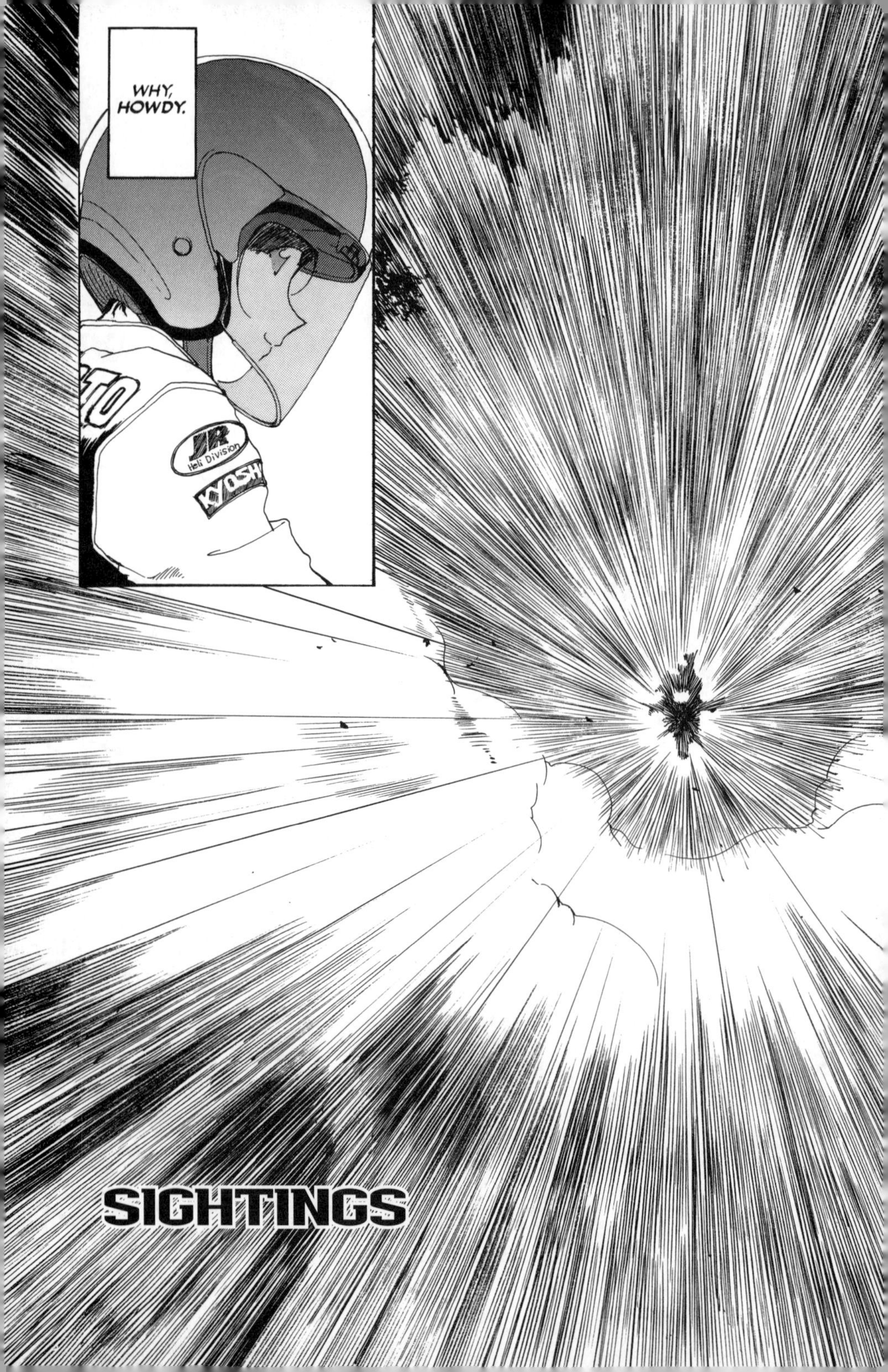
WHY, HOWDY.
JR
Heli Division

SIGHTINGS

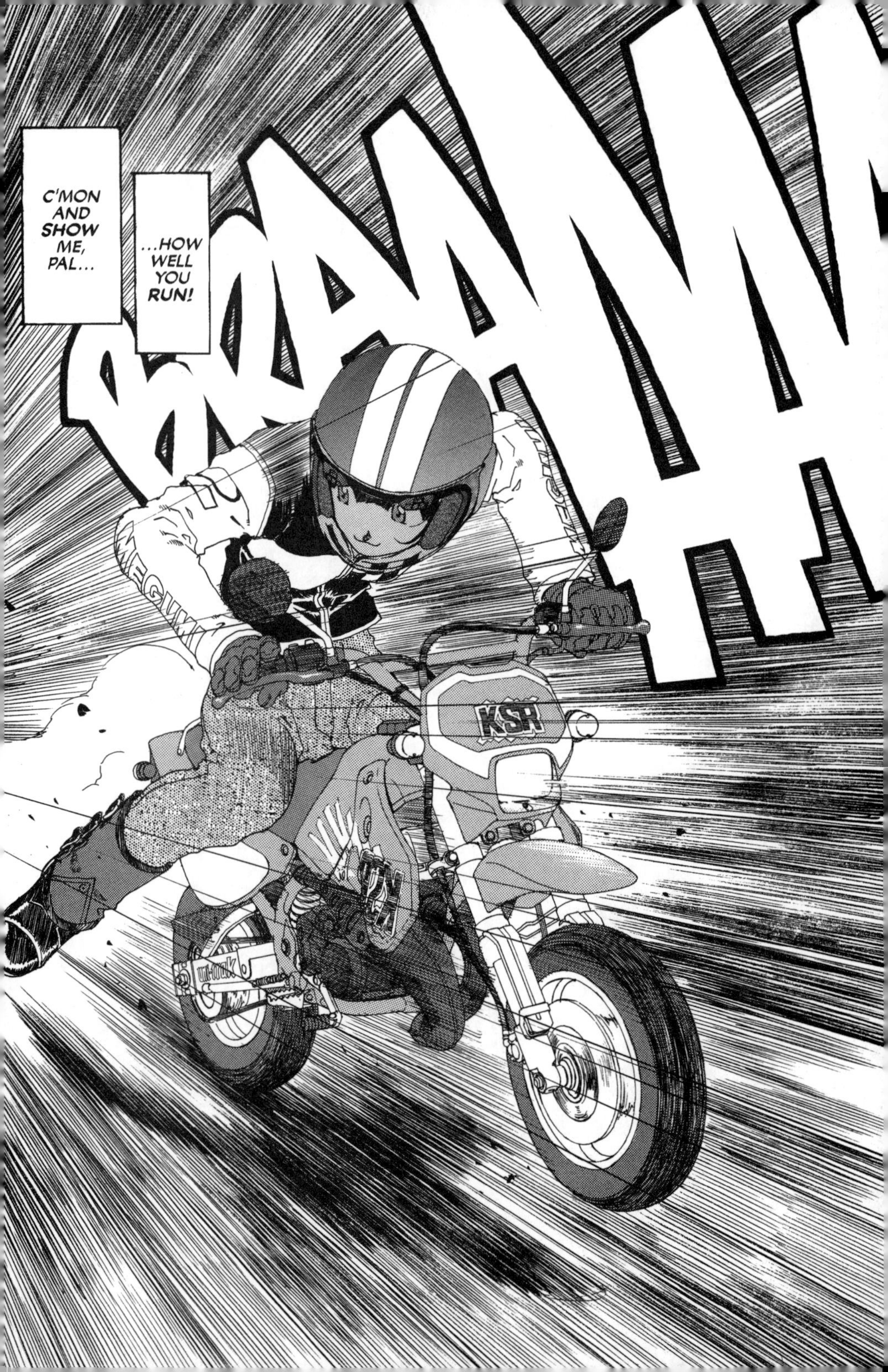
C'MON AND SHOW ME, PAL...
...HOW WELL YOU RUN!

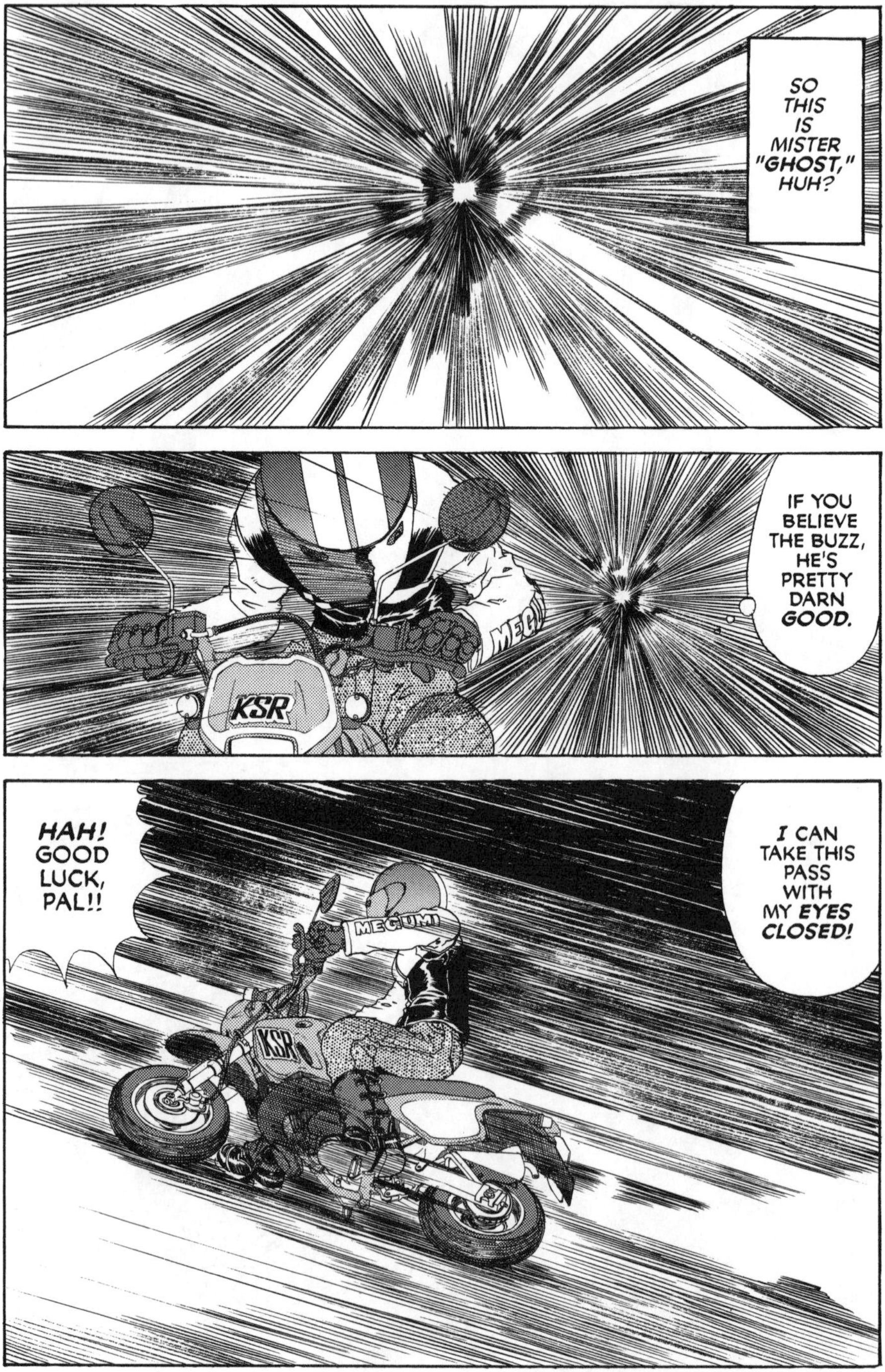
SO THIS IS MISTER "GHOST," HUH?
IF YOU BELIEVE THE BUZZ, HE'S PRETTY DARN GOOD.
KSR
HAH! GOOD LUCK, PAL!!
MEGUMI
KSR
I CAN TAKE THIS PASS WITH MY EYES CLOSED!

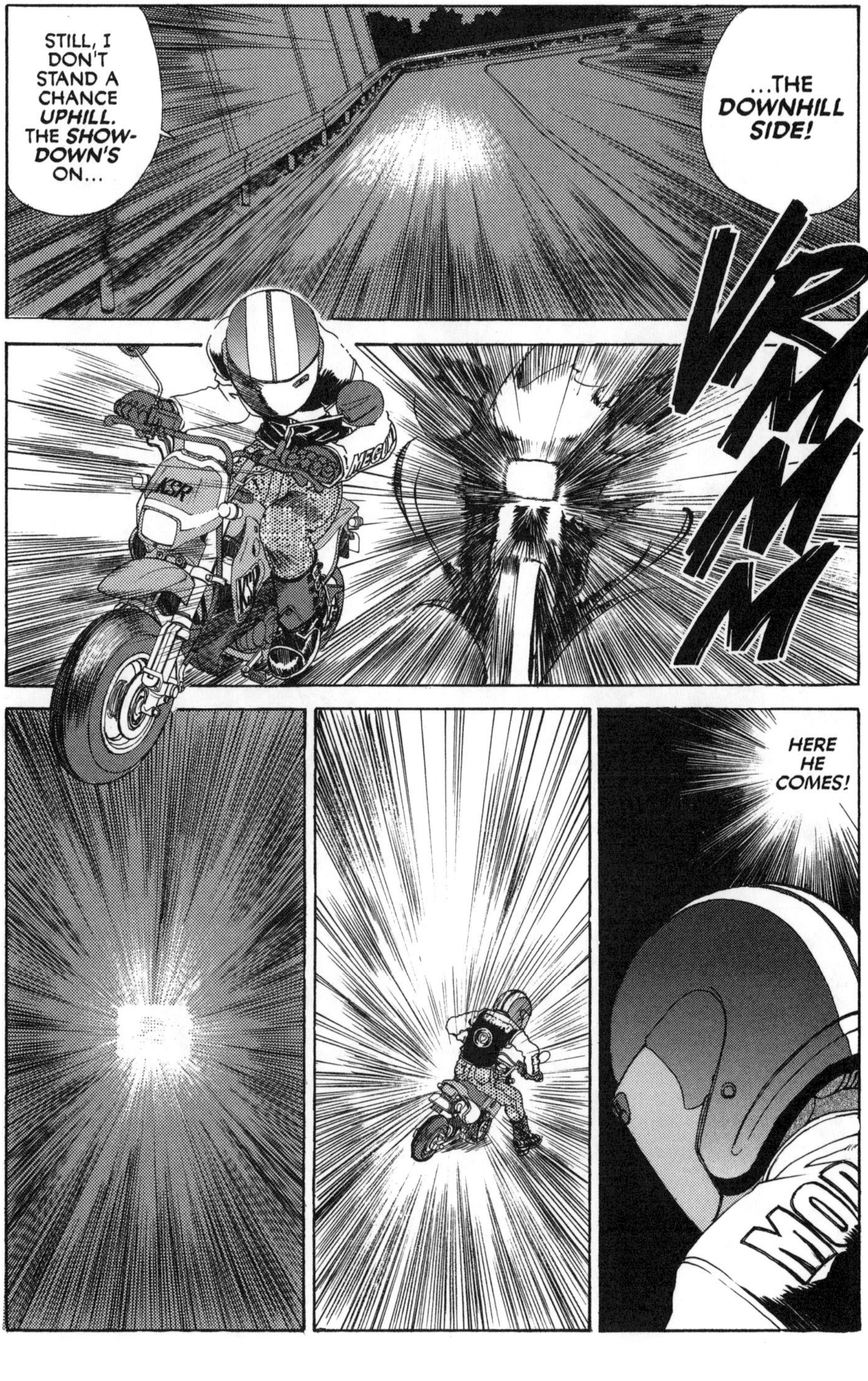
STILL, I DON'T STAND A CHANCE *UPHILL.* THE *SHOW-DOWN'S* ON...
...THE *DOWNHILL SIDE!*
VRMMMM
KSR
HERE HE COMES!

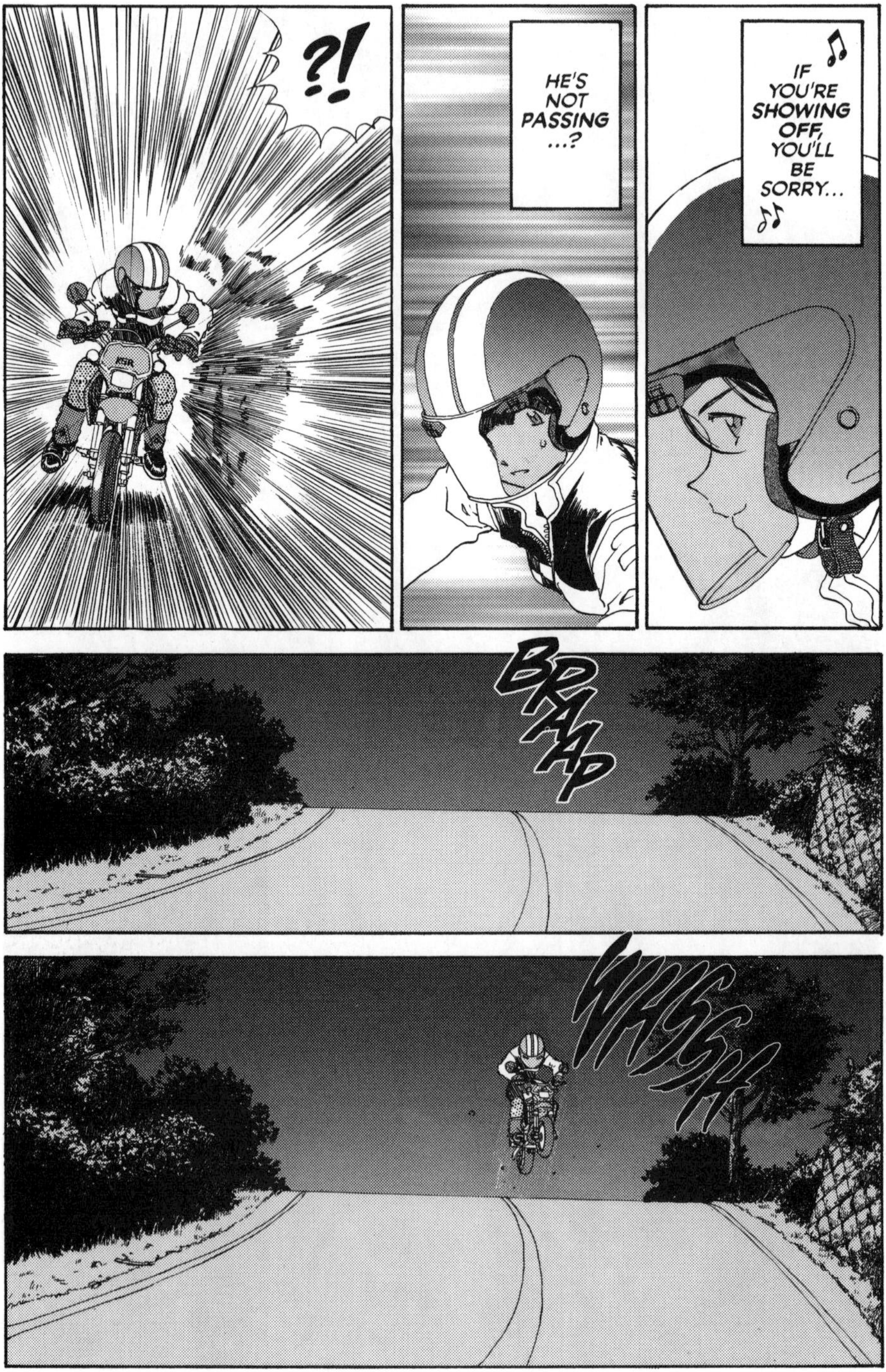
?!
HE'S NOT PASSING ...?
♪ IF YOU'RE SHOWING OFF, YOU'LL BE SORRY... ♪♪
BRAAAP
WHSSH

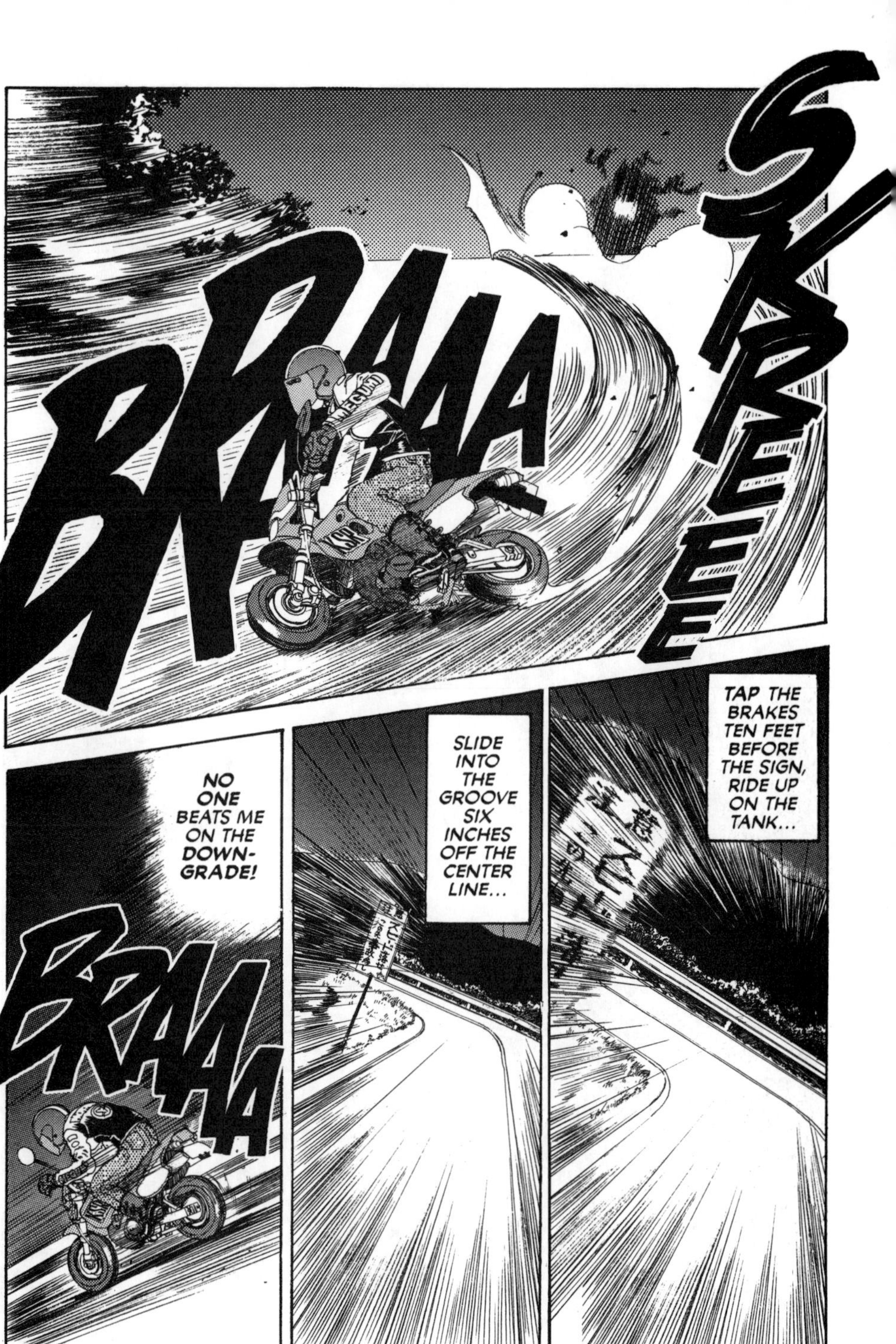
NO ONE BEATS ME ON THE DOWN-GRADE!
SLIDE INTO THE GROOVE SIX INCHES OFF THE CENTER LINE...
TAP THE BRAKES TEN FEET BEFORE THE SIGN, RIDE UP ON THE TANK...

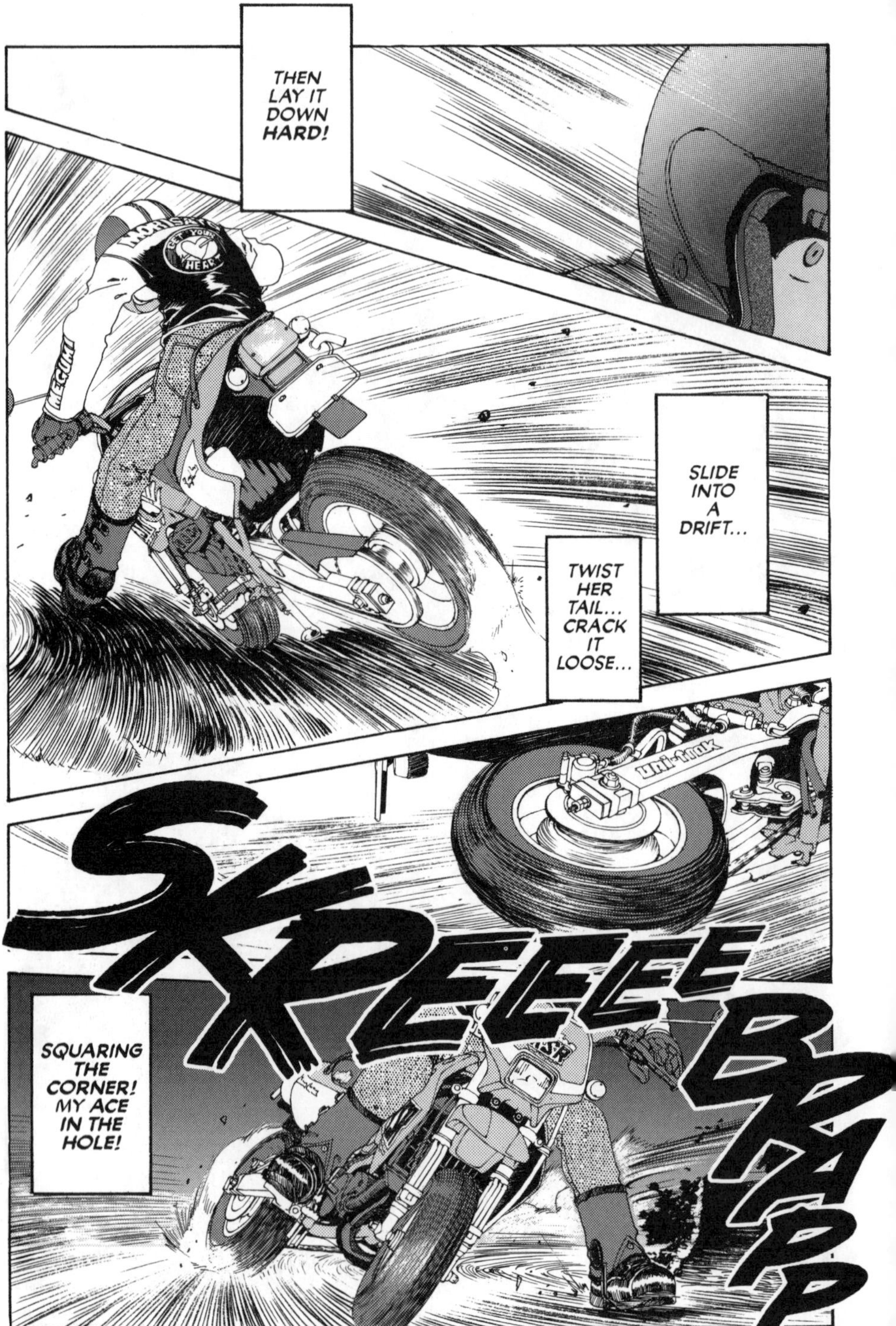
THEN LAY IT DOWN HARD!
MEGUMI
SLIDE INTO A DRIFT...
TWIST HER TAIL... CRACK IT LOOSE...
uni-trak
SKREEEE
SQUARING THE CORNER! MY ACE IN THE HOLE!
BRAAPP

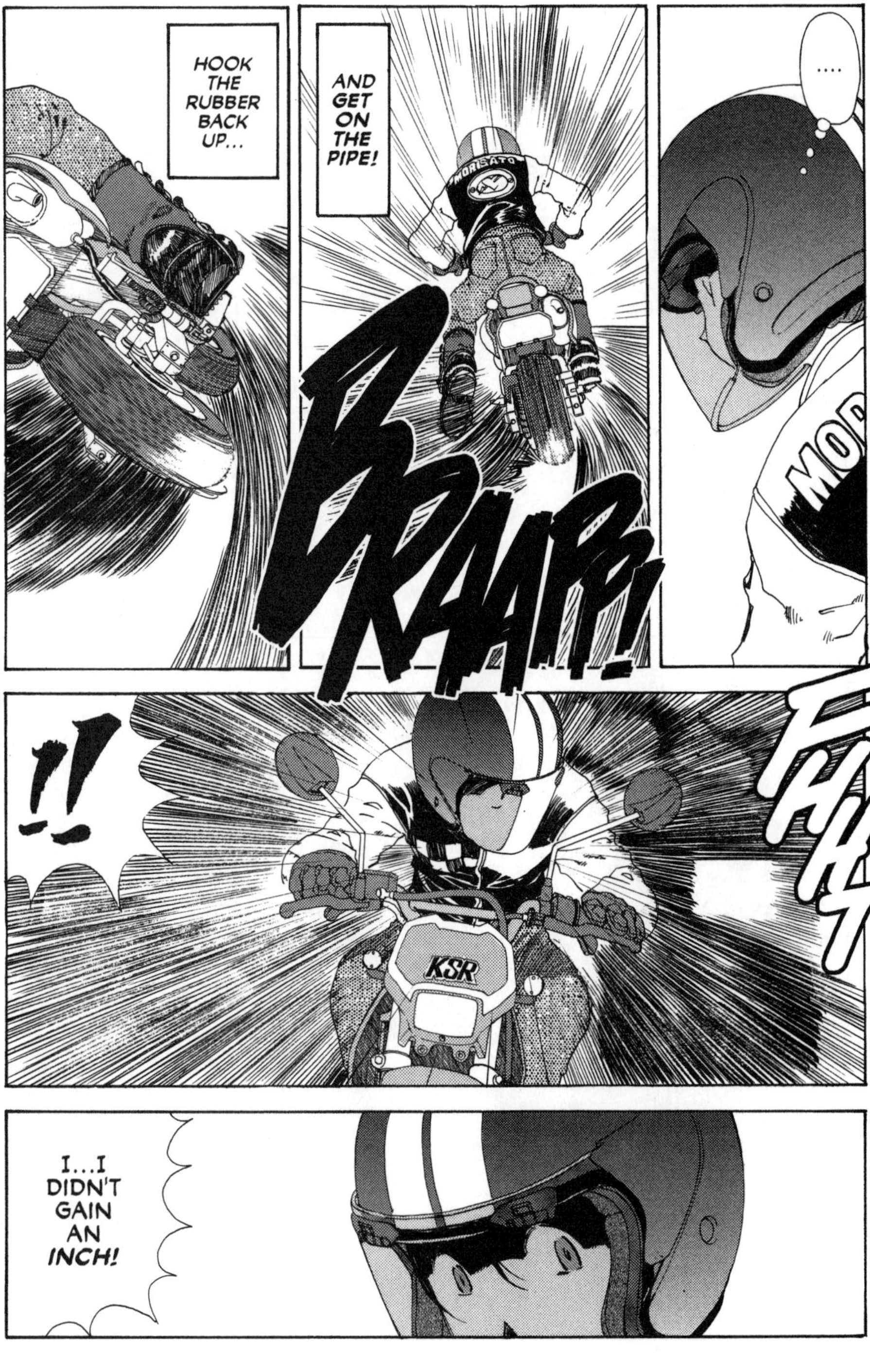
HOOK THE RUBBER BACK UP...
AND GET ON THE PIPE!
....
BRAAAPP!
MORISATO
MOR
!!
FAHH
KSR
I...I DIDN'T GAIN AN *INCH!*

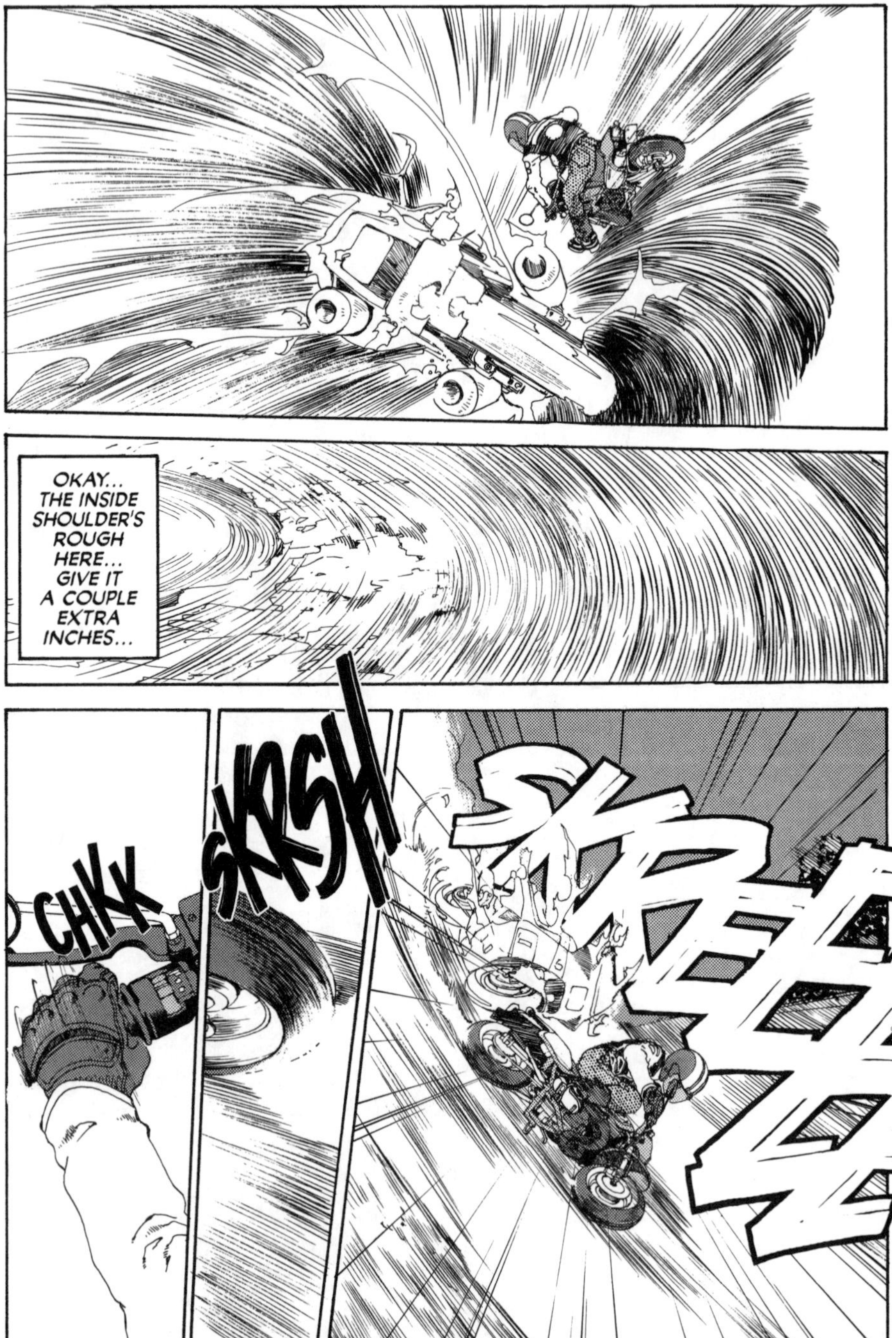
OKAY... THE INSIDE SHOULDER'S ROUGH HERE... GIVE IT A COUPLE EXTRA INCHES...
CHKK
SKRSH
SKREEE

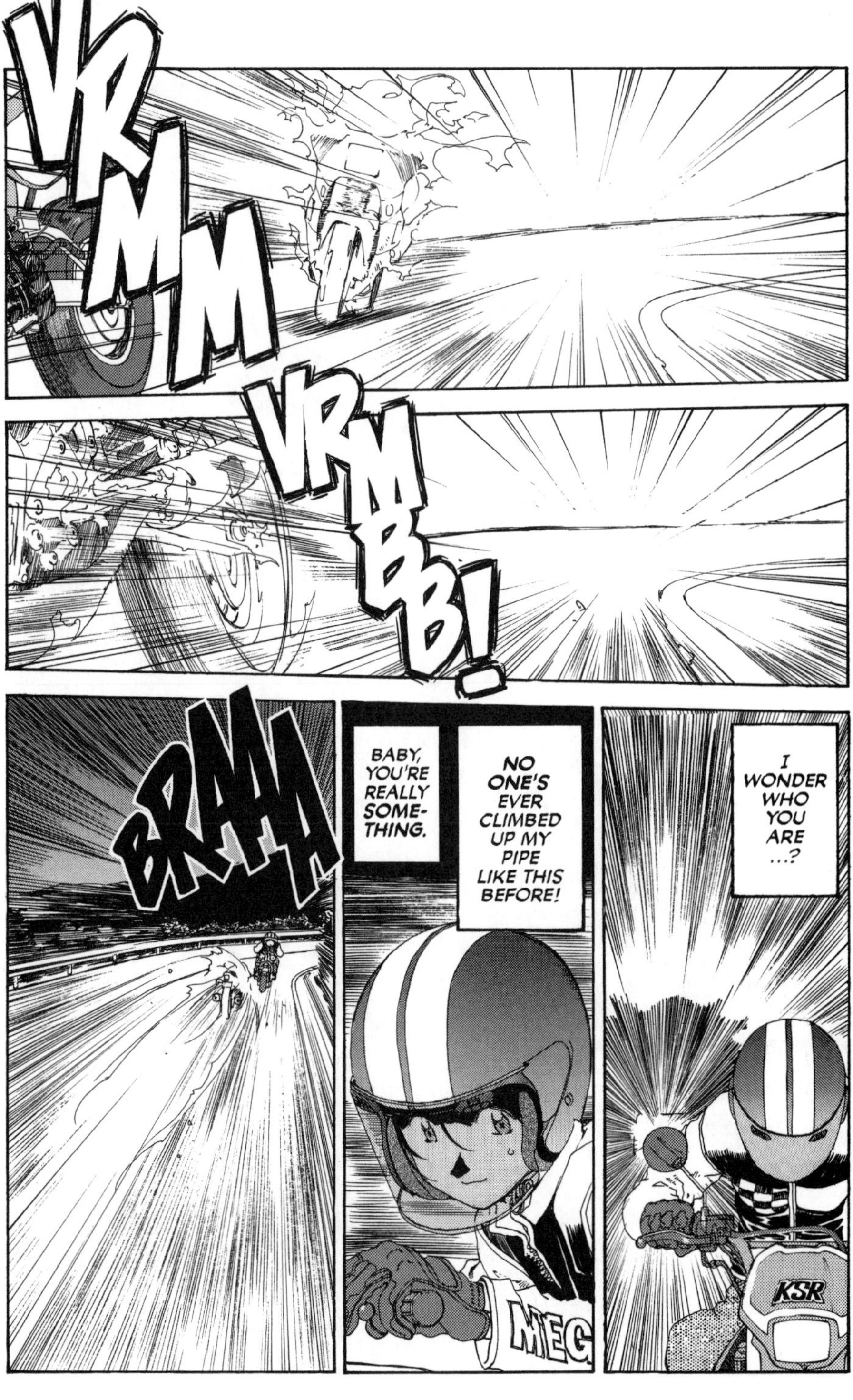
VRMMM
VRMBB!
BRAAA
BABY, YOU'RE REALLY SOME-THING.
NO ONE'S EVER CLIMBED UP MY PIPE LIKE THIS BEFORE!
MEG
I WONDER WHO YOU ARE ...?
KSR

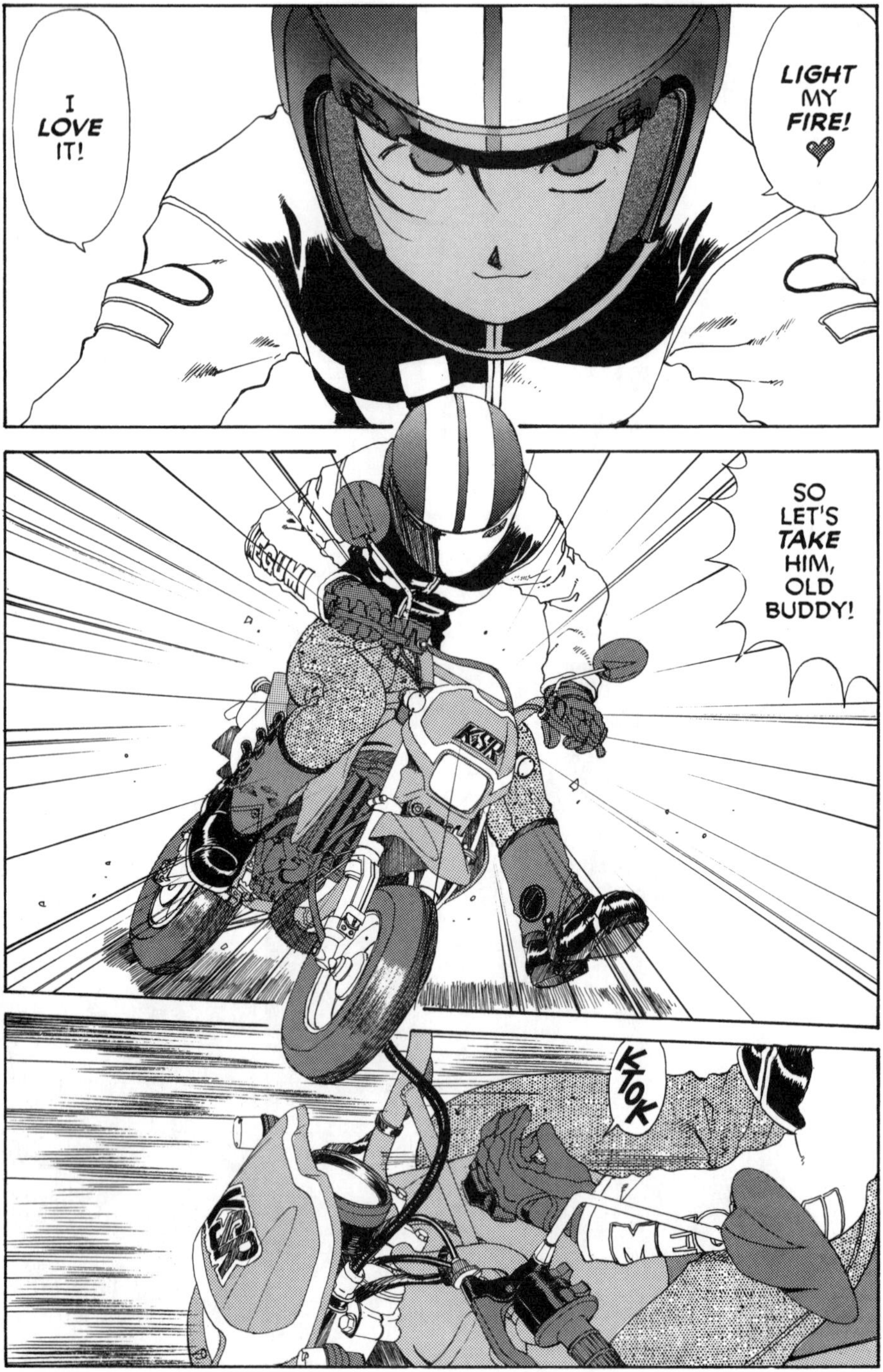
I LOVE IT!
LIGHT MY FIRE! ♥
MEGUMI
KSR
SO LET'S TAKE HIM, OLD BUDDY!
KTOK
KSR
MEG

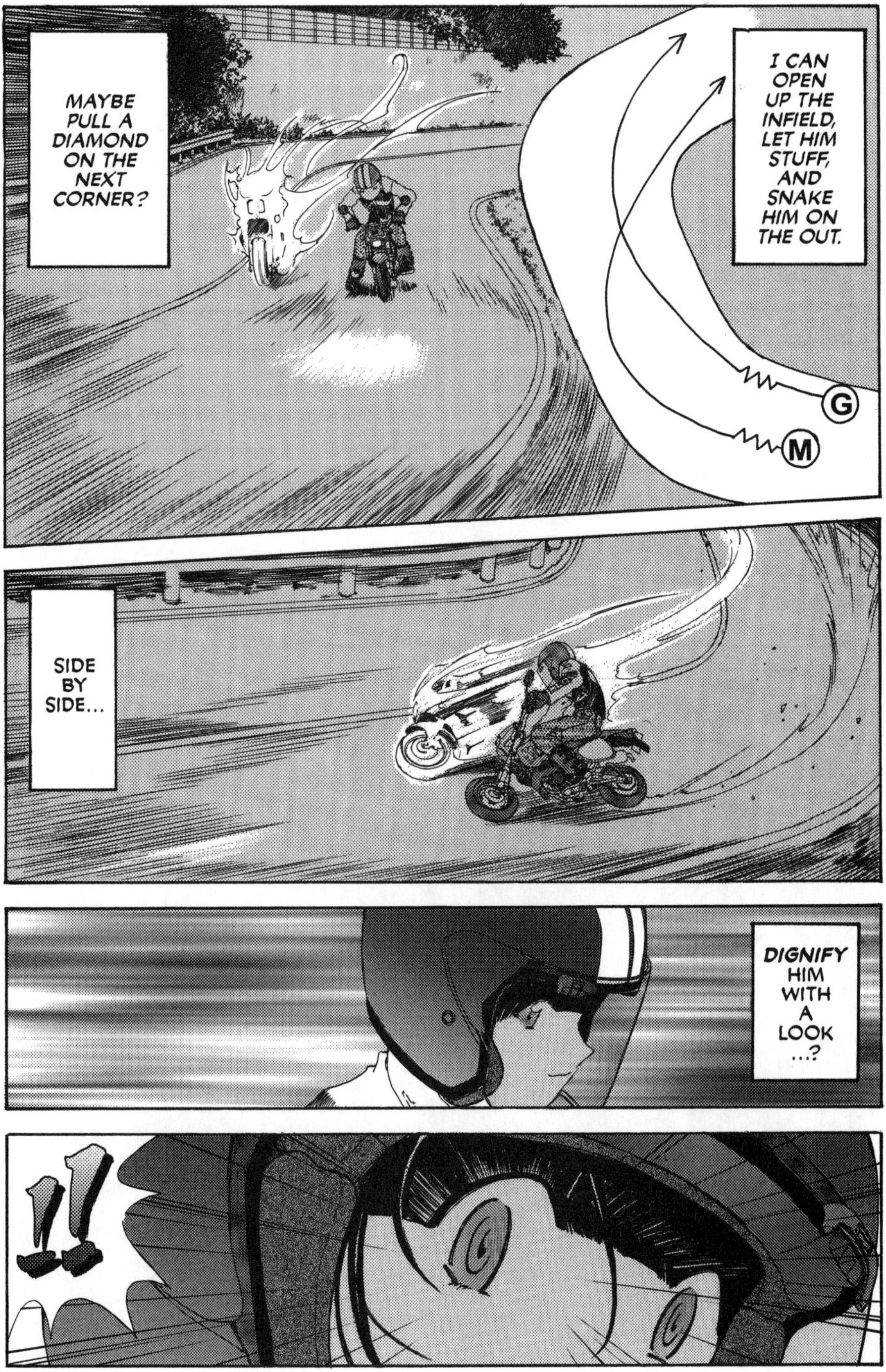
MAYBE PULL A DIAMOND ON THE NEXT CORNER?
I CAN OPEN UP THE INFIELD, LET HIM STUFF, AND SNAKE HIM ON THE OUT.
G
M
SIDE BY SIDE...
DIGNIFY HIM WITH A LOOK ...?
!!

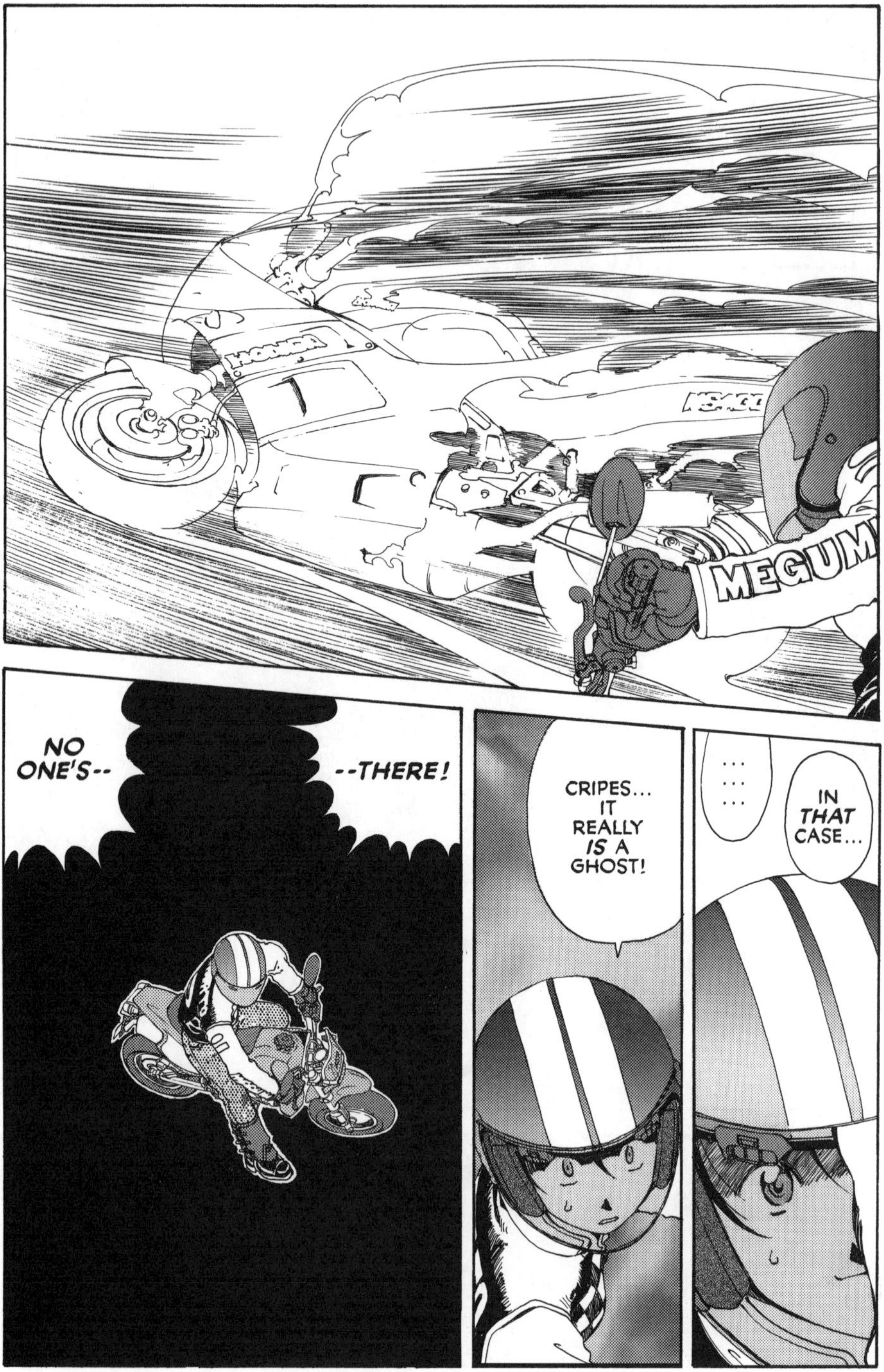
NO ONE'S--
--THERE!
CRIPES... IT REALLY *IS* A GHOST!
......
IN *THAT* CASE...

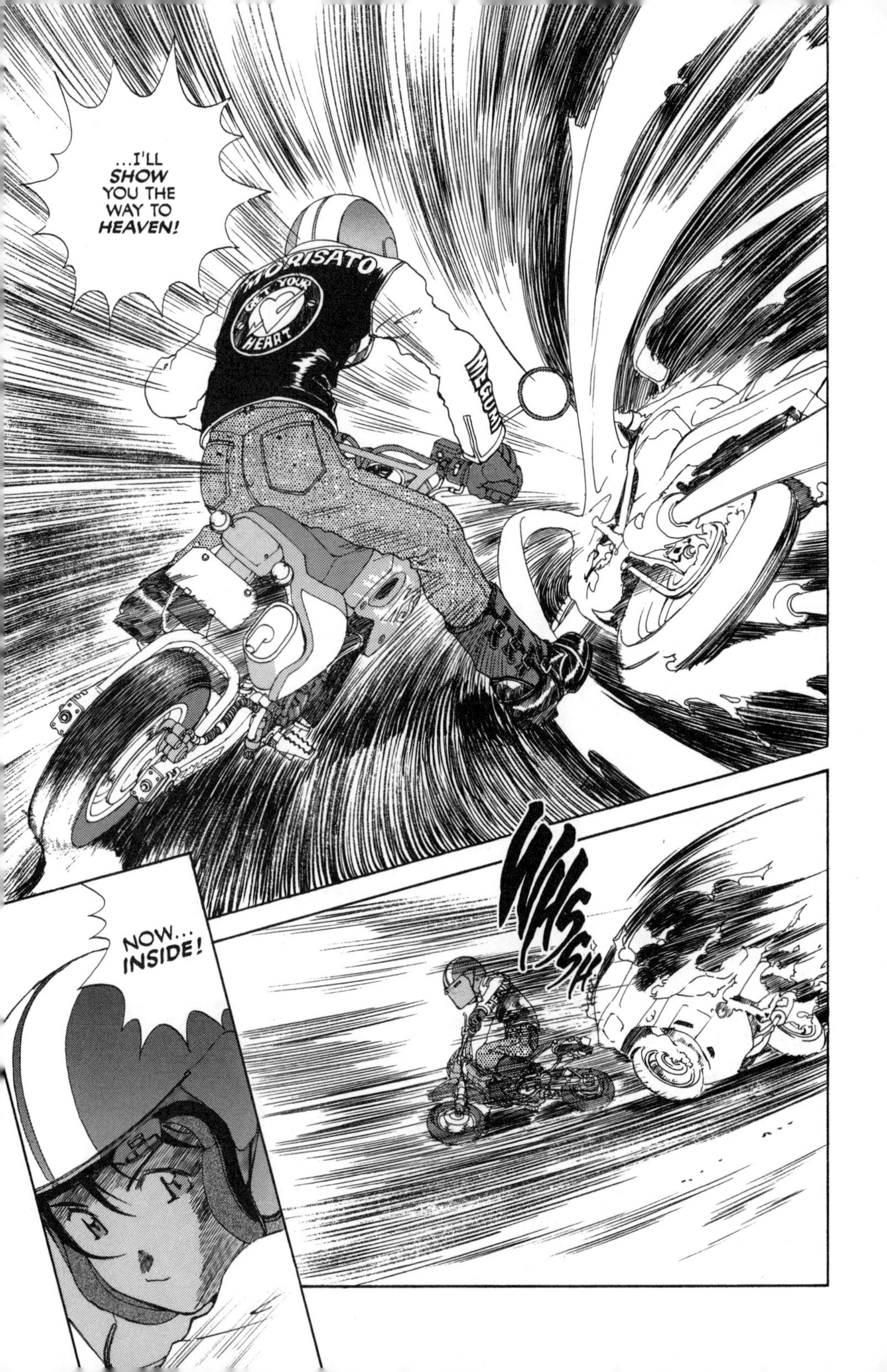
...I'LL SHOW YOU THE WAY TO HEAVEN!
MORISATO
GET YOUR HEART
MEGUMI
NOW... INSIDE!
WHSSH!

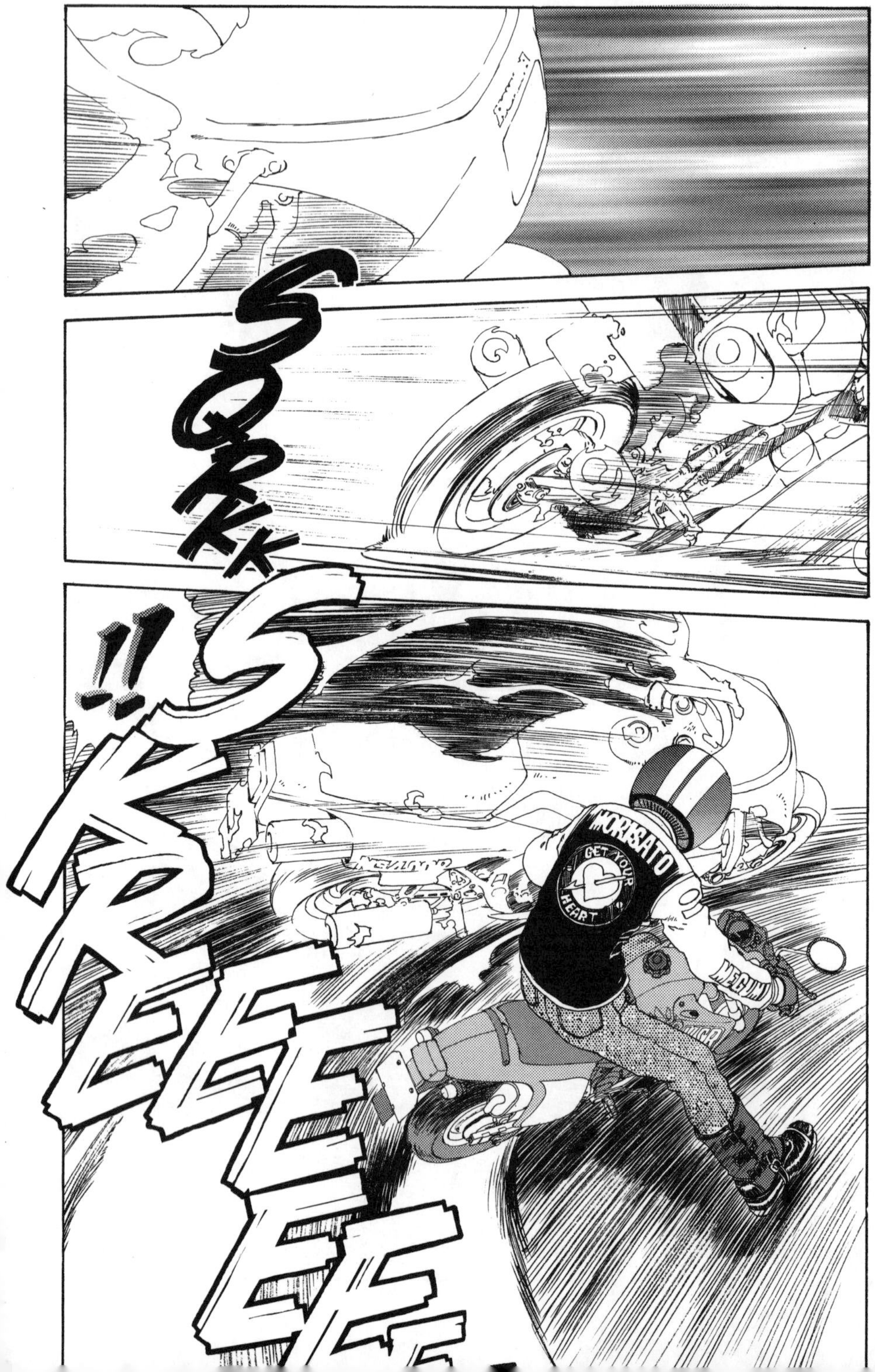
SQRKK
SKREEEEEE!!
MORISATO
GET YOUR HEART
MEGUMI

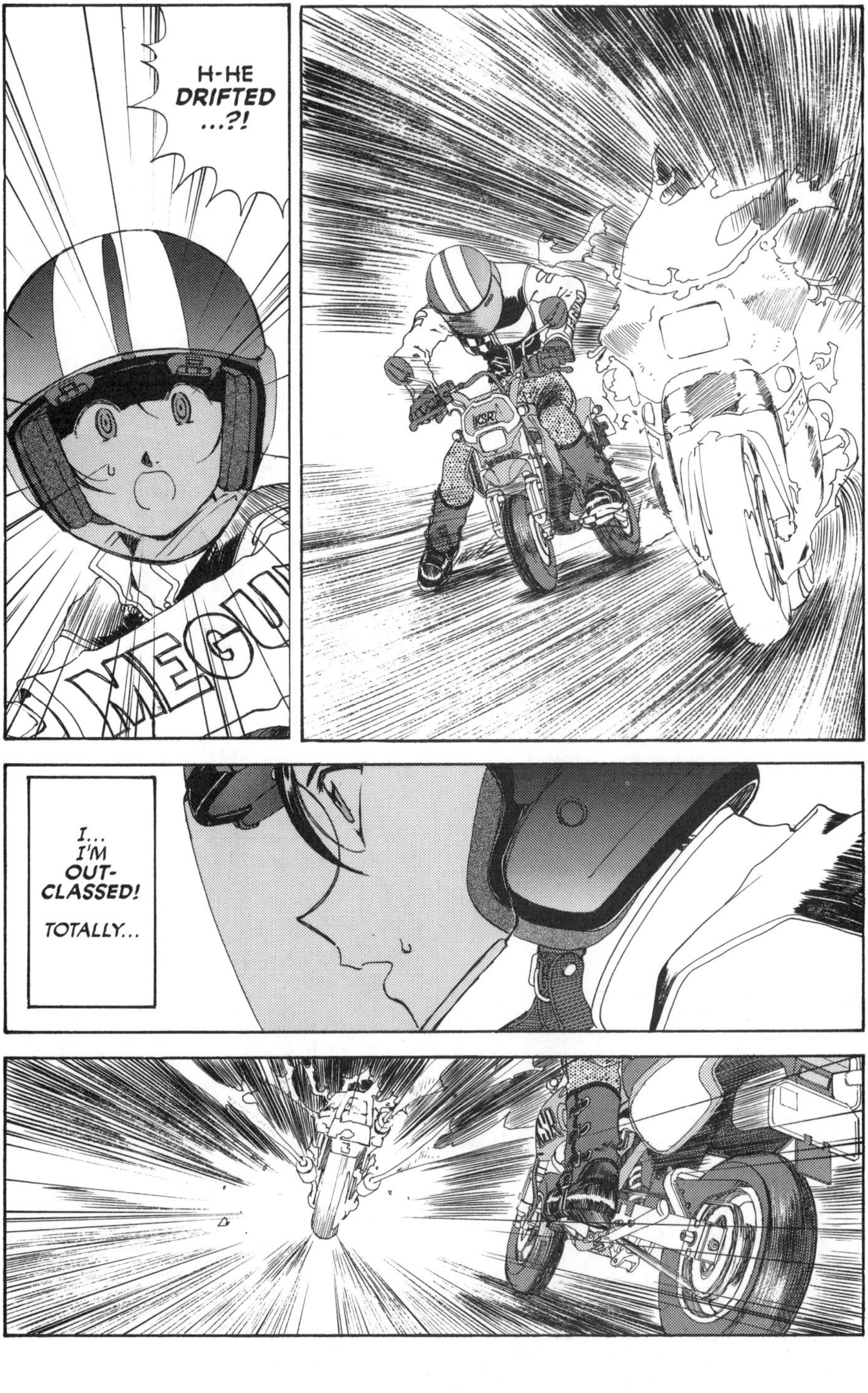
H-HE DRIFTED ...?!
I... I'M OUT-CLASSED!
TOTALLY...

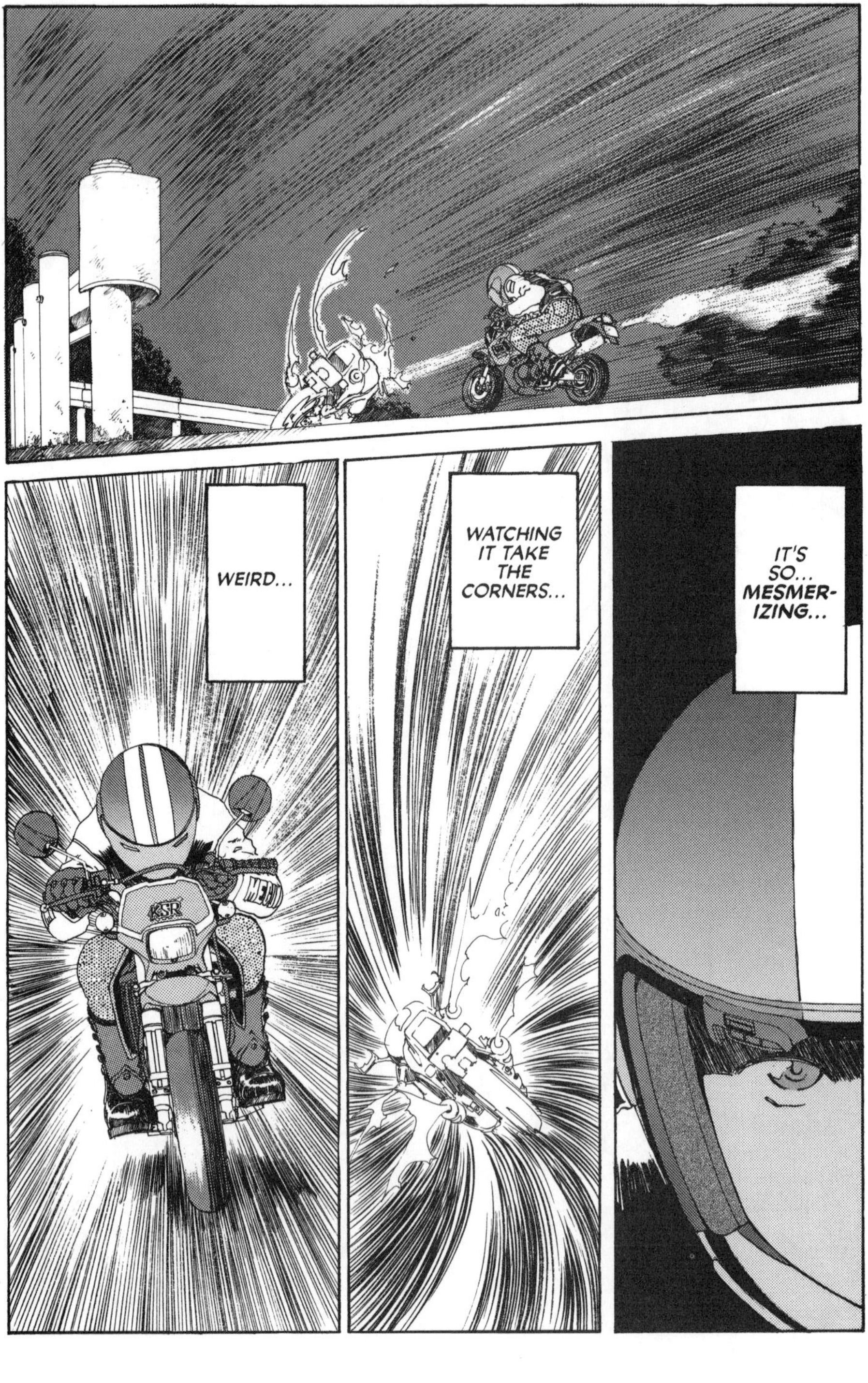
WEIRD...
WATCHING IT TAKE THE CORNERS...
IT'S SO... MESMER-IZING...

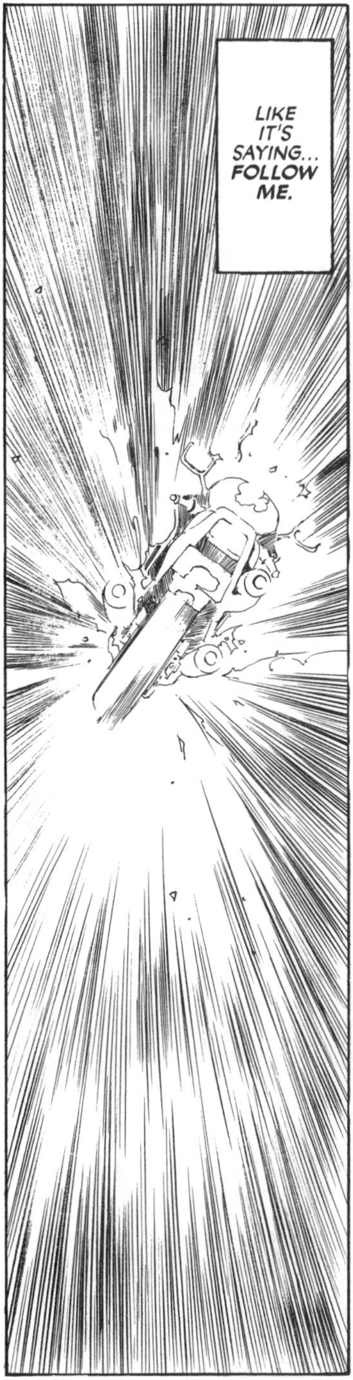
LIKE IT'S SAYING... FOLLOW ME.

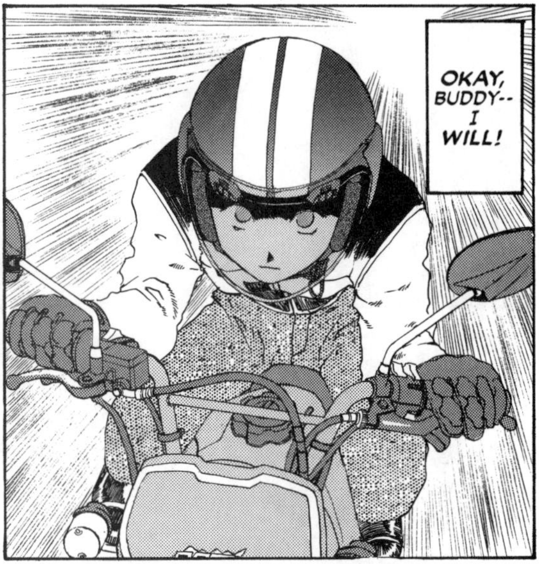
OKAY, BUDDY-- I WILL!

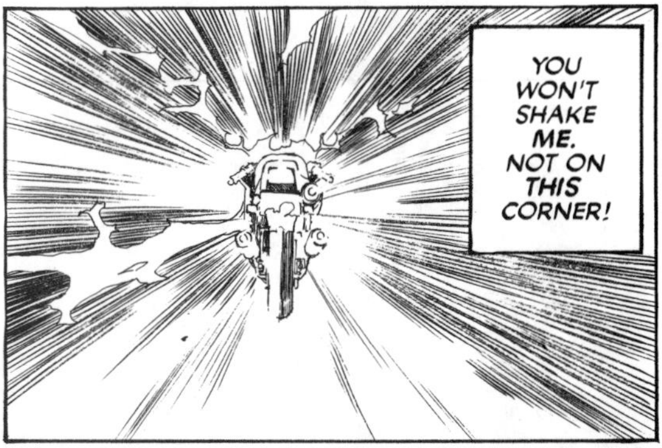
YOU WON'T SHAKE ME. NOT ON THIS CORNER!

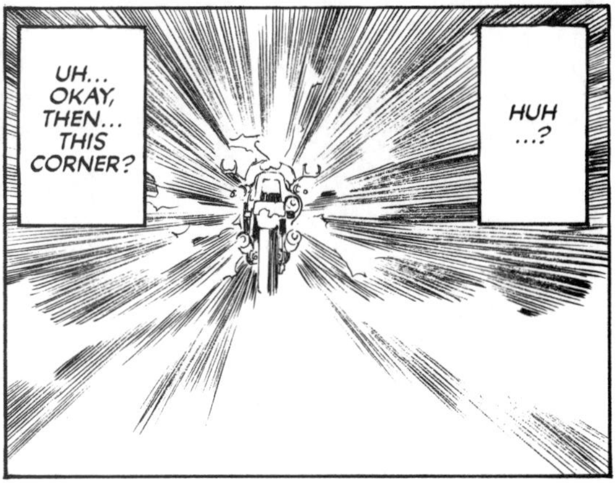
UH... OKAY, THEN... THIS CORNER?
HUH ...?

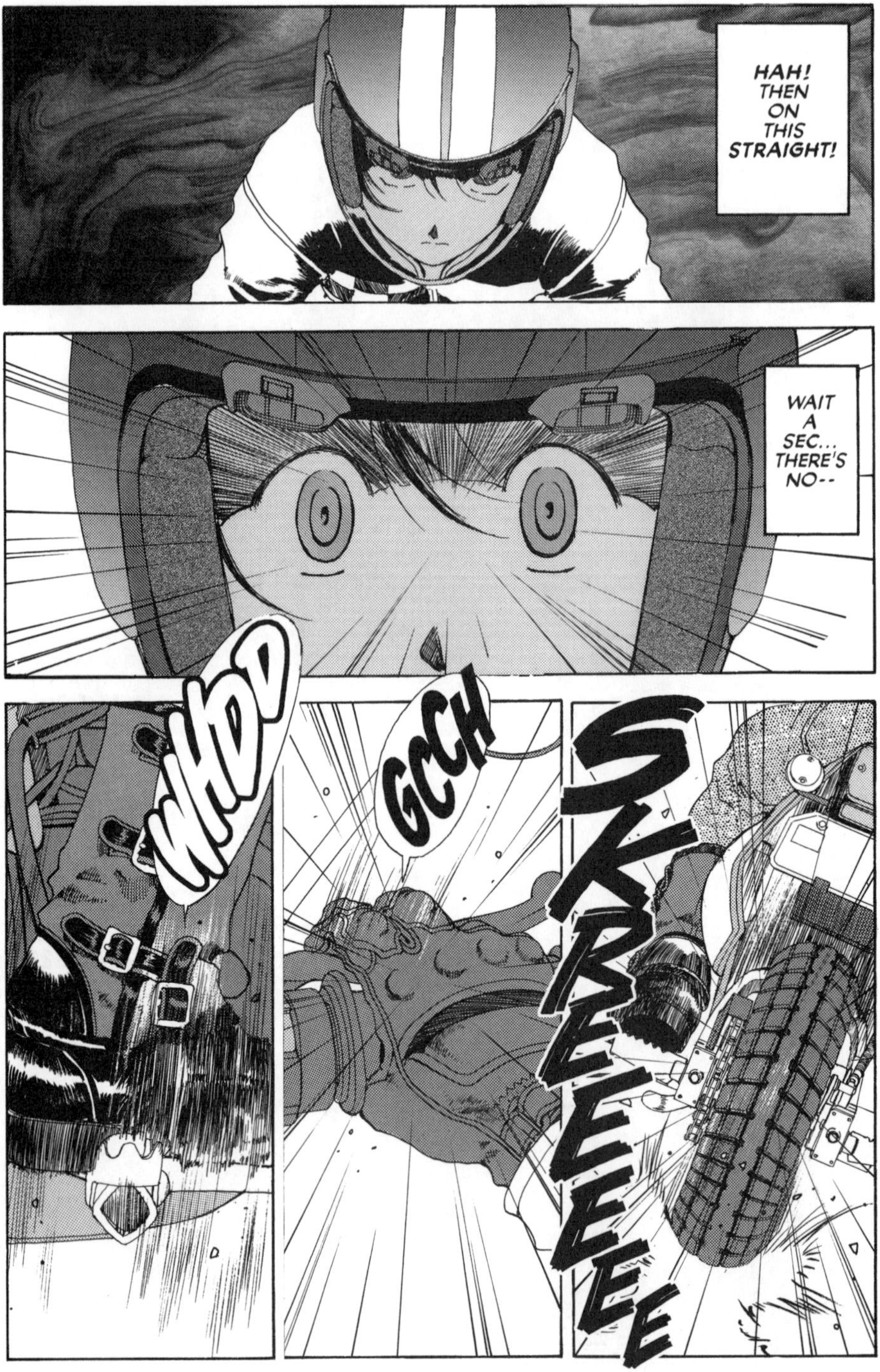
HAH! THEN ON THIS STRAIGHT!
WAIT A SEC... THERE'S NO--
WHOD
GCCH
SKREEEEEEE

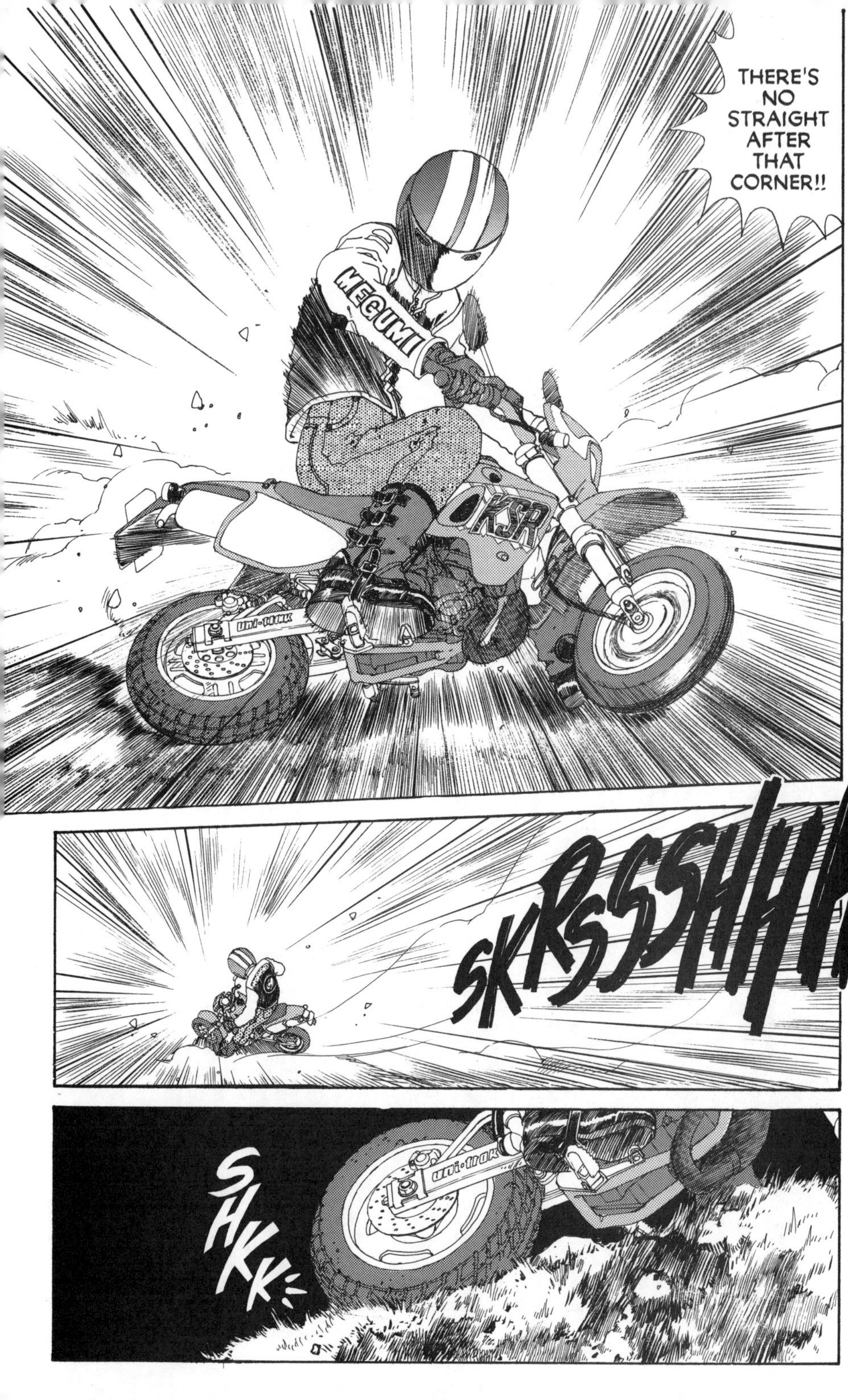
THERE'S NO STRAIGHT AFTER THAT CORNER!!
MEGUMI
KSR
SKRSSSHHH
SHKK

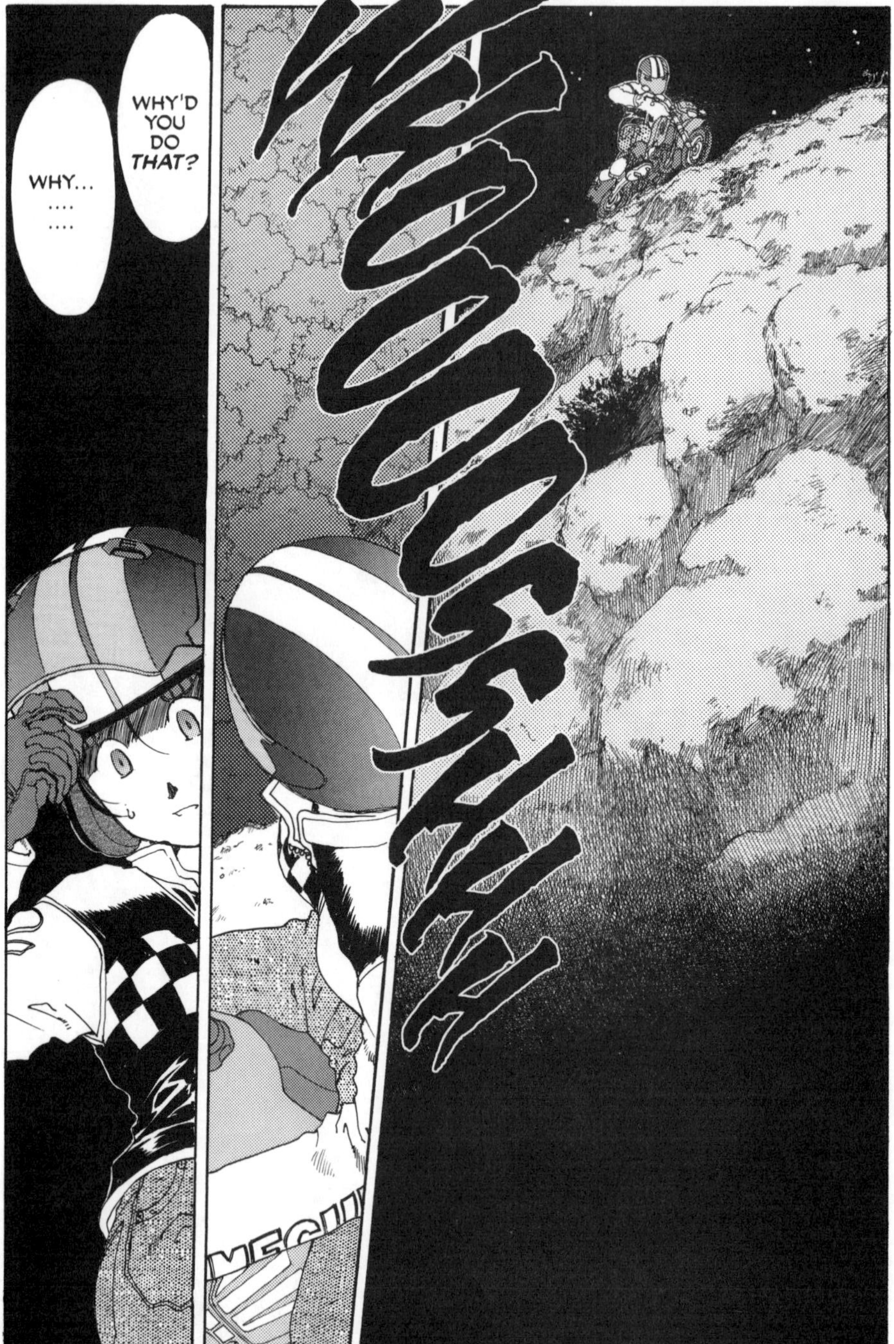
WHY... ....
WHY'D YOU DO *THAT?*

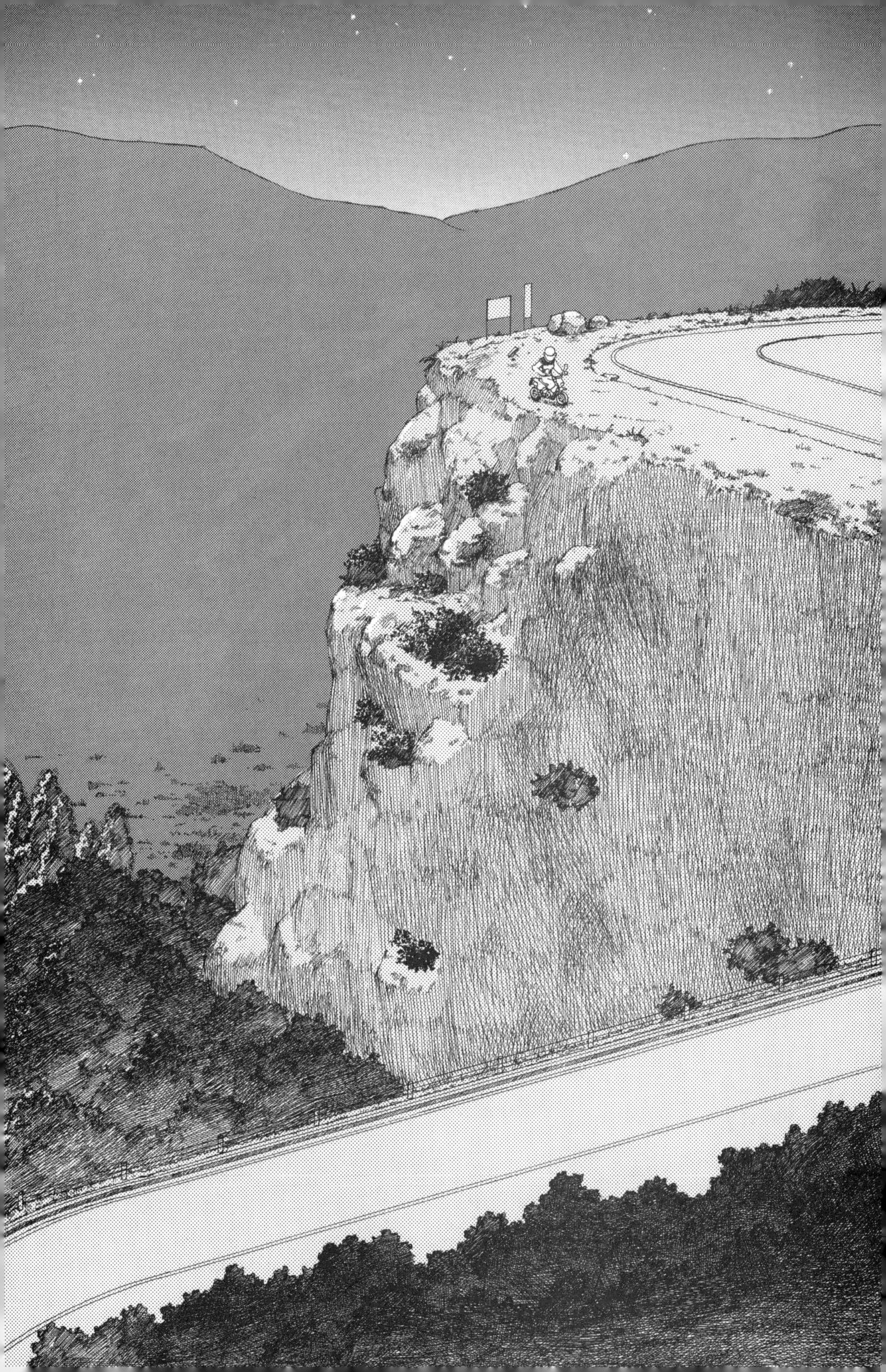

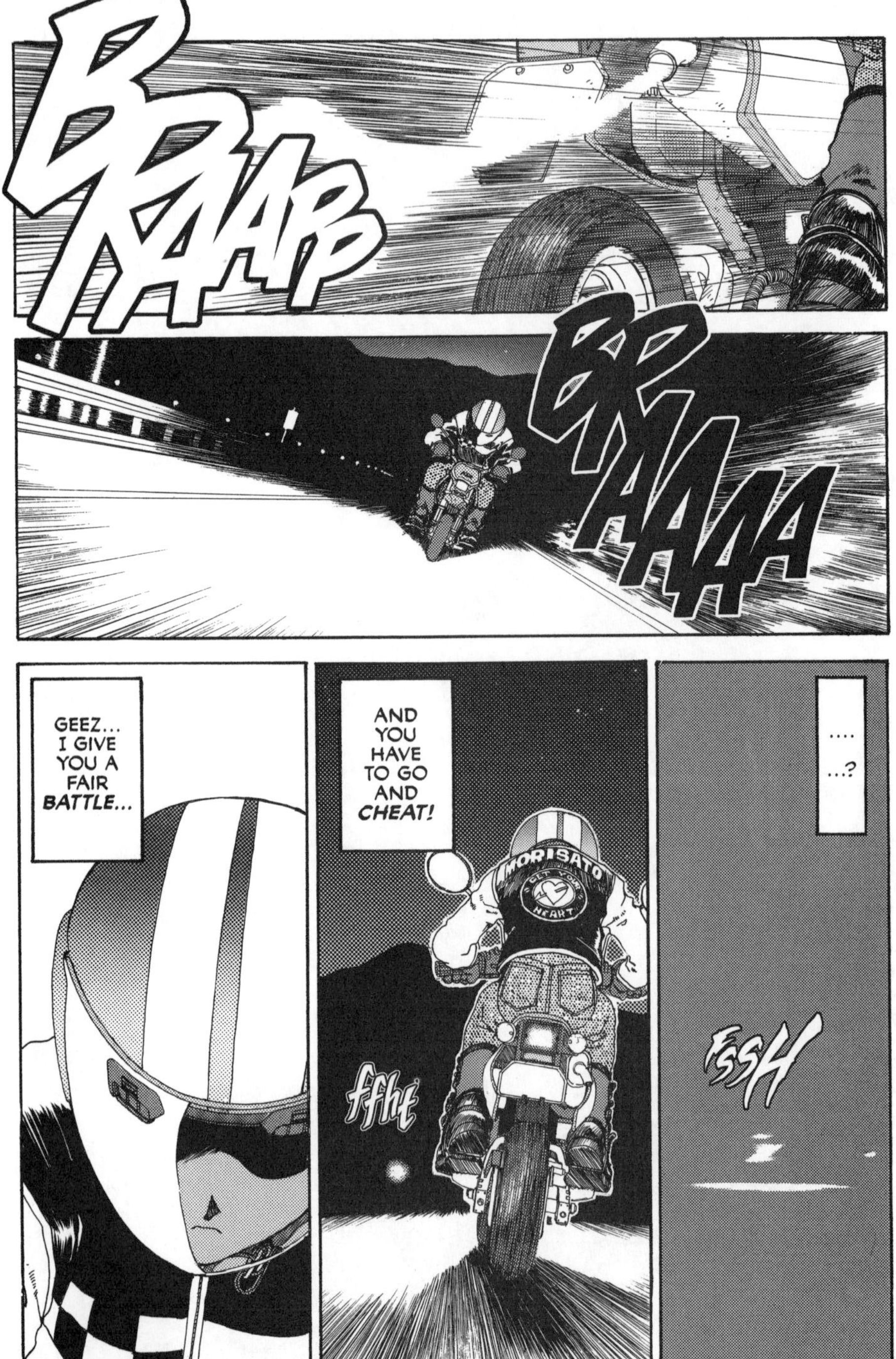
BRRAAPP
BRRAAAAA
GEEZ... I GIVE YOU A FAIR BATTLE...
AND YOU HAVE TO GO AND CHEAT!
MORISATO
....
...?
FFHT
FSSH

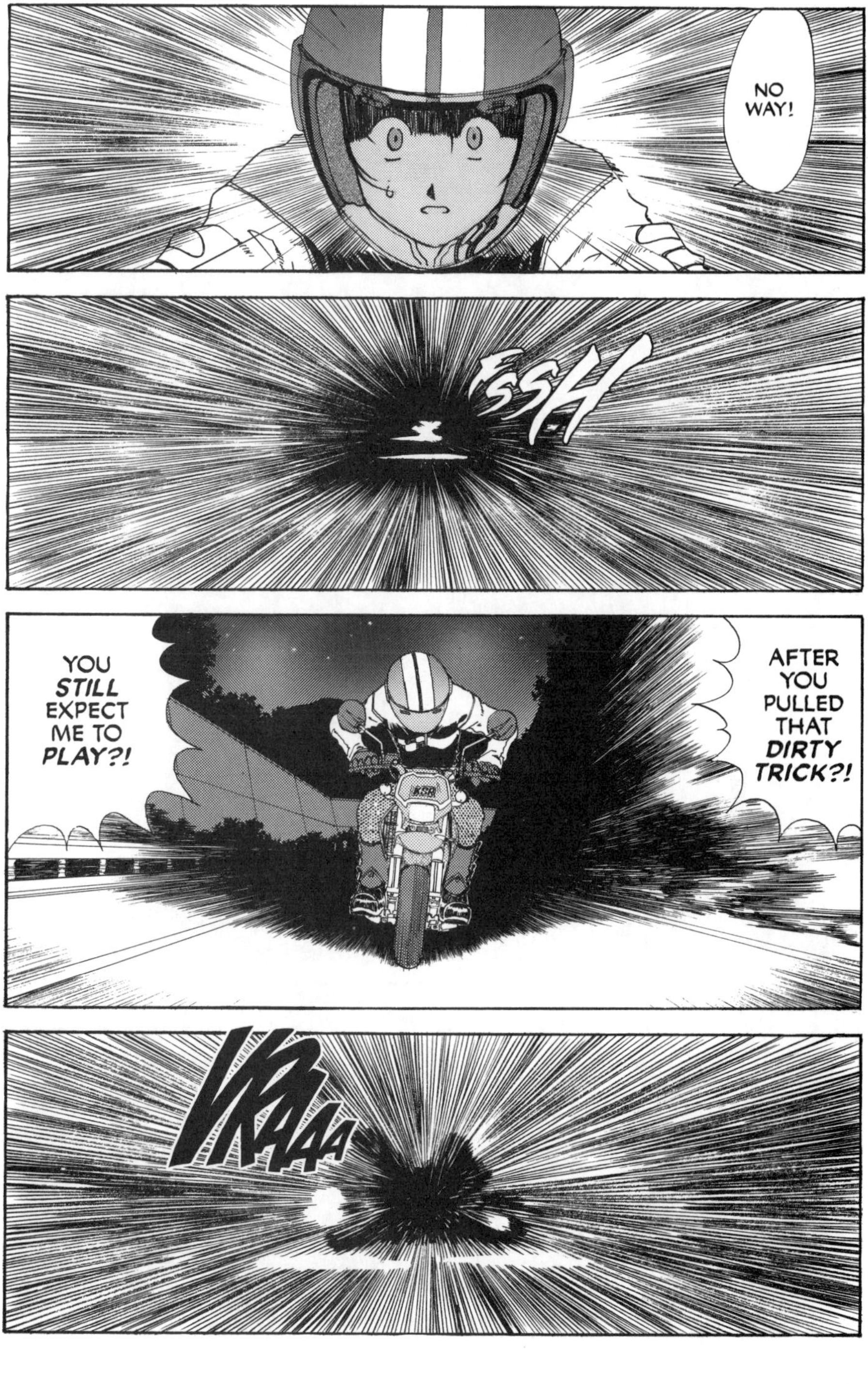
NO WAY!
FSSH
YOU STILL EXPECT ME TO PLAY?!
AFTER YOU PULLED THAT DIRTY TRICK?!
VRAAAA

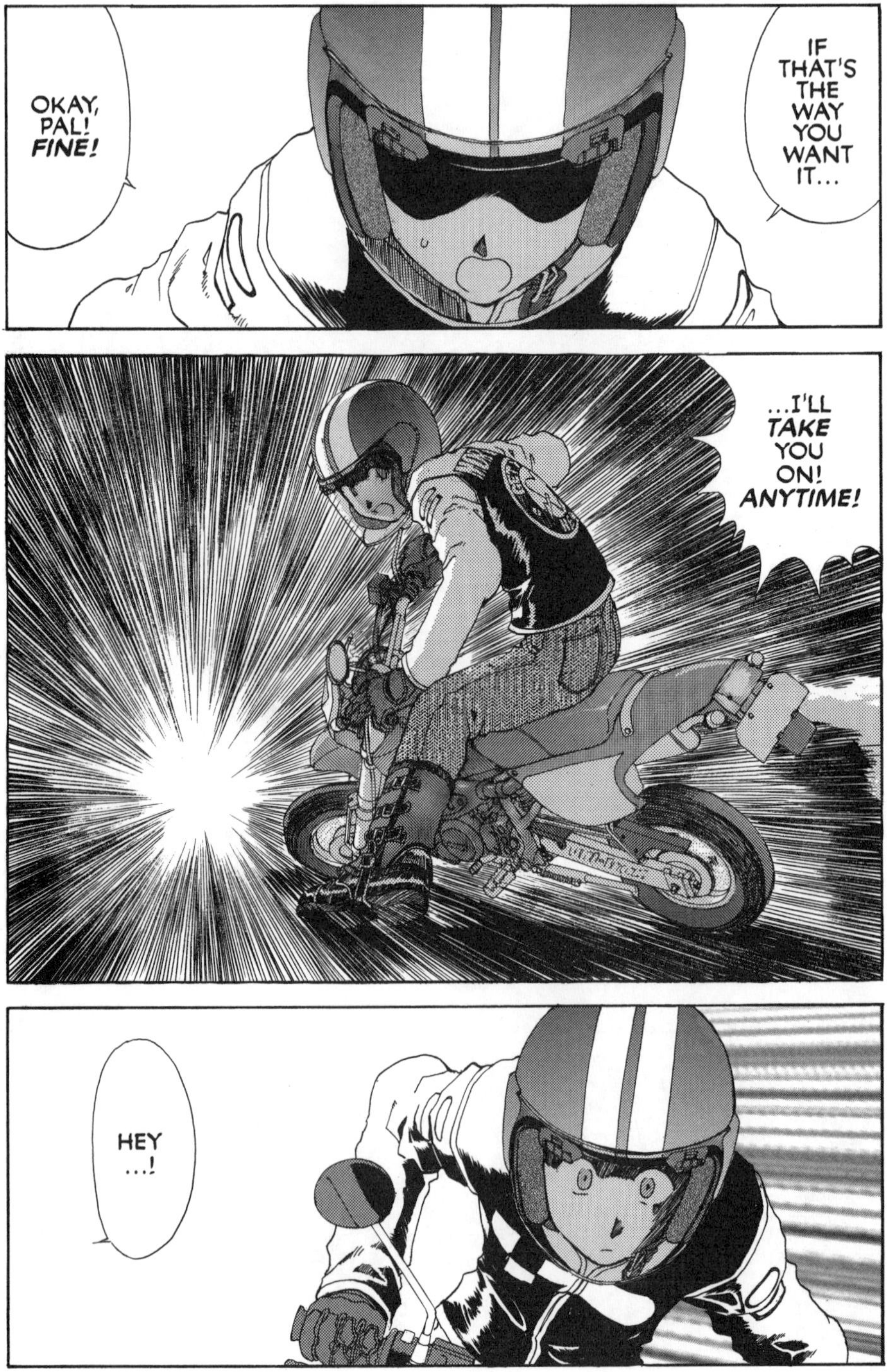
OKAY, PAL! FINE!
IF THAT'S THE WAY YOU WANT IT...
...I'LL TAKE YOU ON! ANYTIME!
HEY ...!

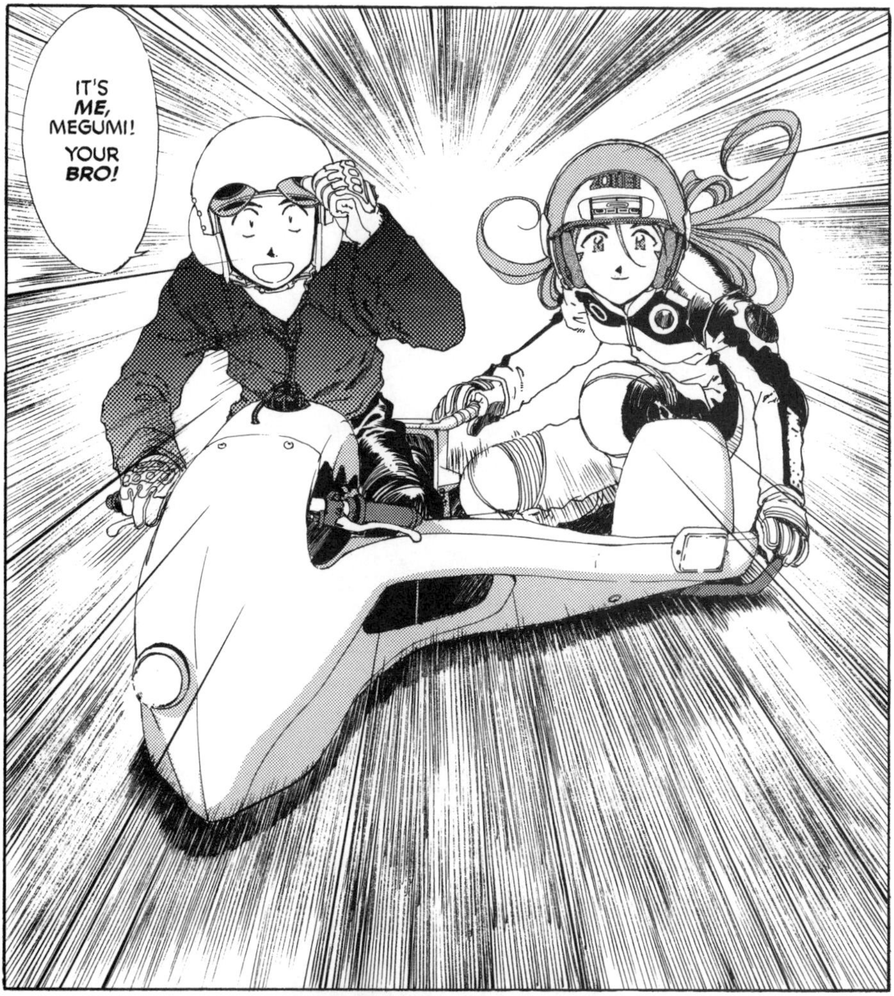
IT'S *ME,* MEGUMI! YOUR *BRO!*
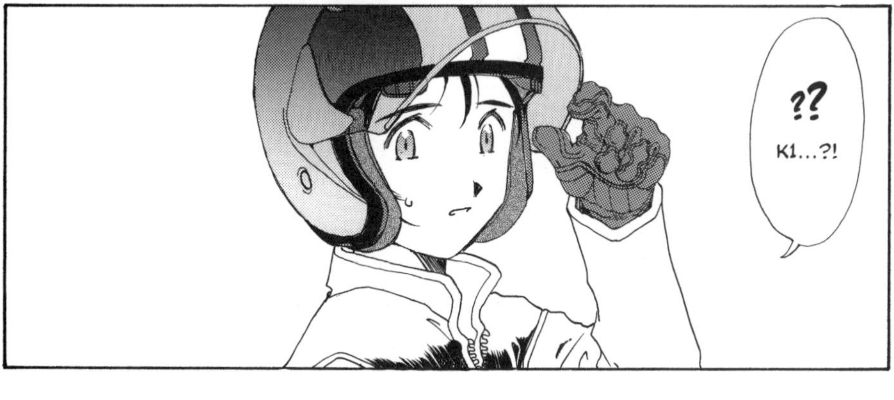
?? K1...?!

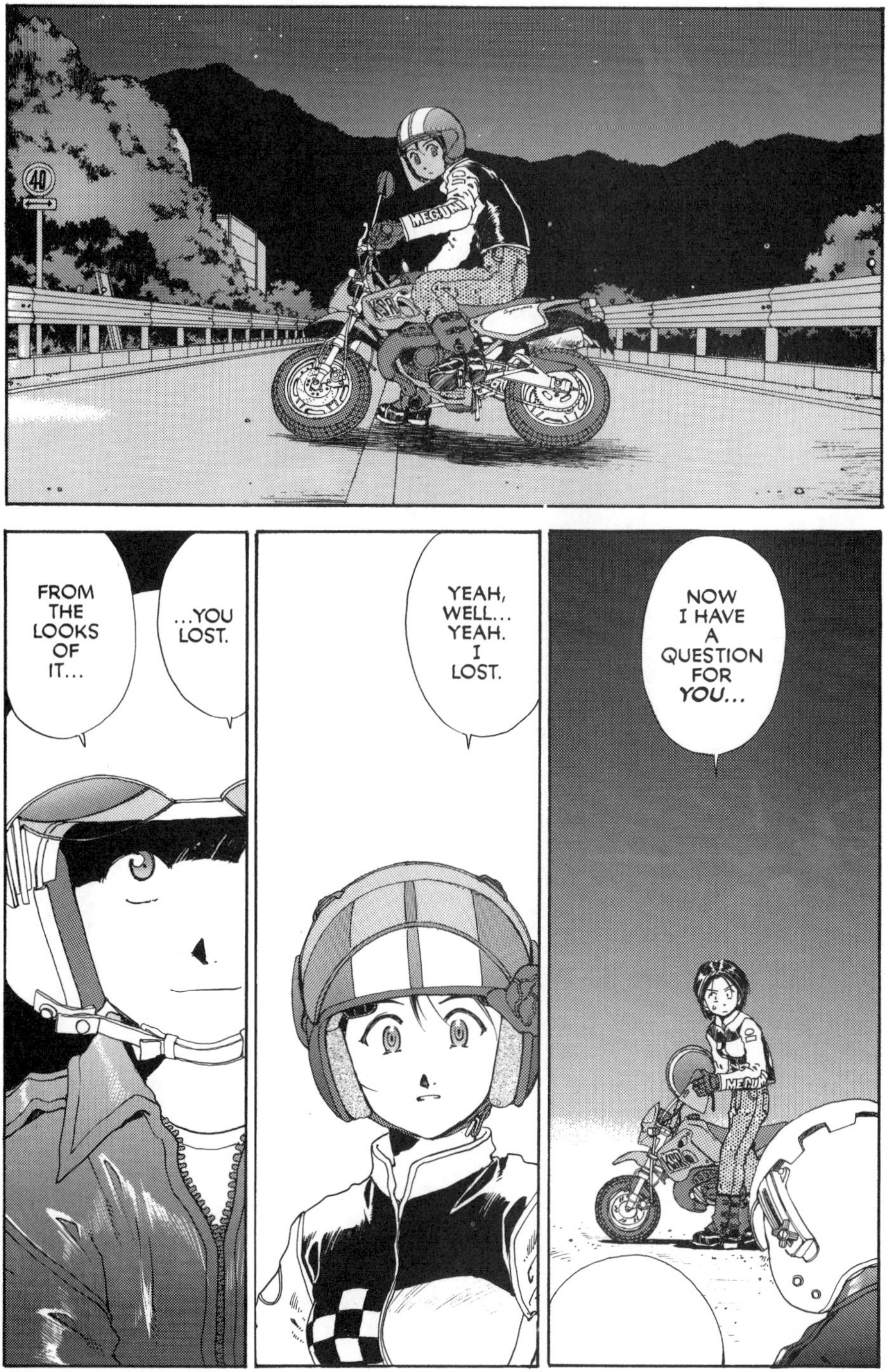
40
MEGUMI
FROM THE LOOKS OF IT...
...YOU LOST.
YEAH, WELL... YEAH. I LOST.
NOW I HAVE A QUESTION FOR *YOU*...
MEGUMI

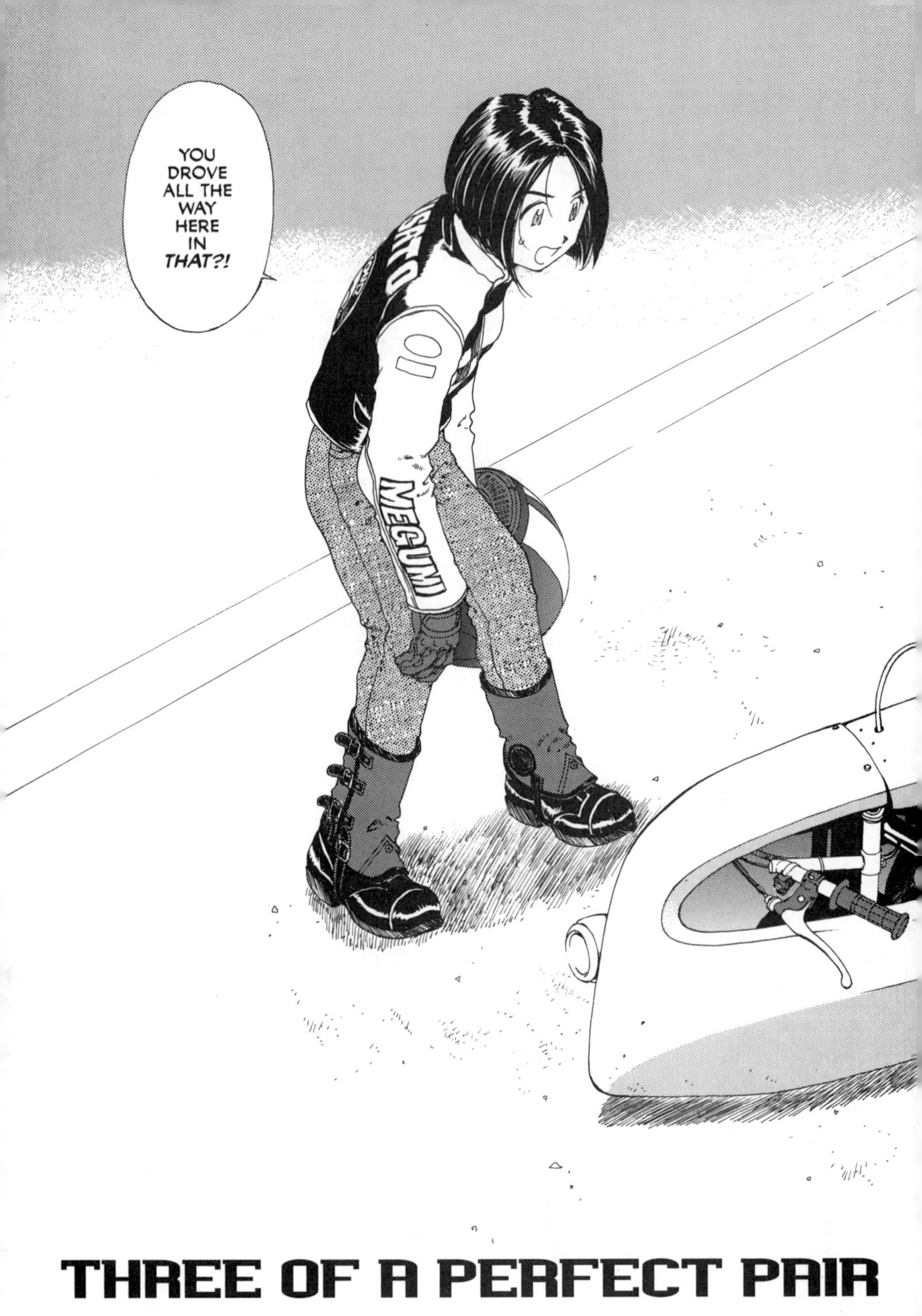
YOU DROVE ALL THE WAY HERE IN *THAT?!*
MEGUMI

THREE OF A PERFECT PAIR

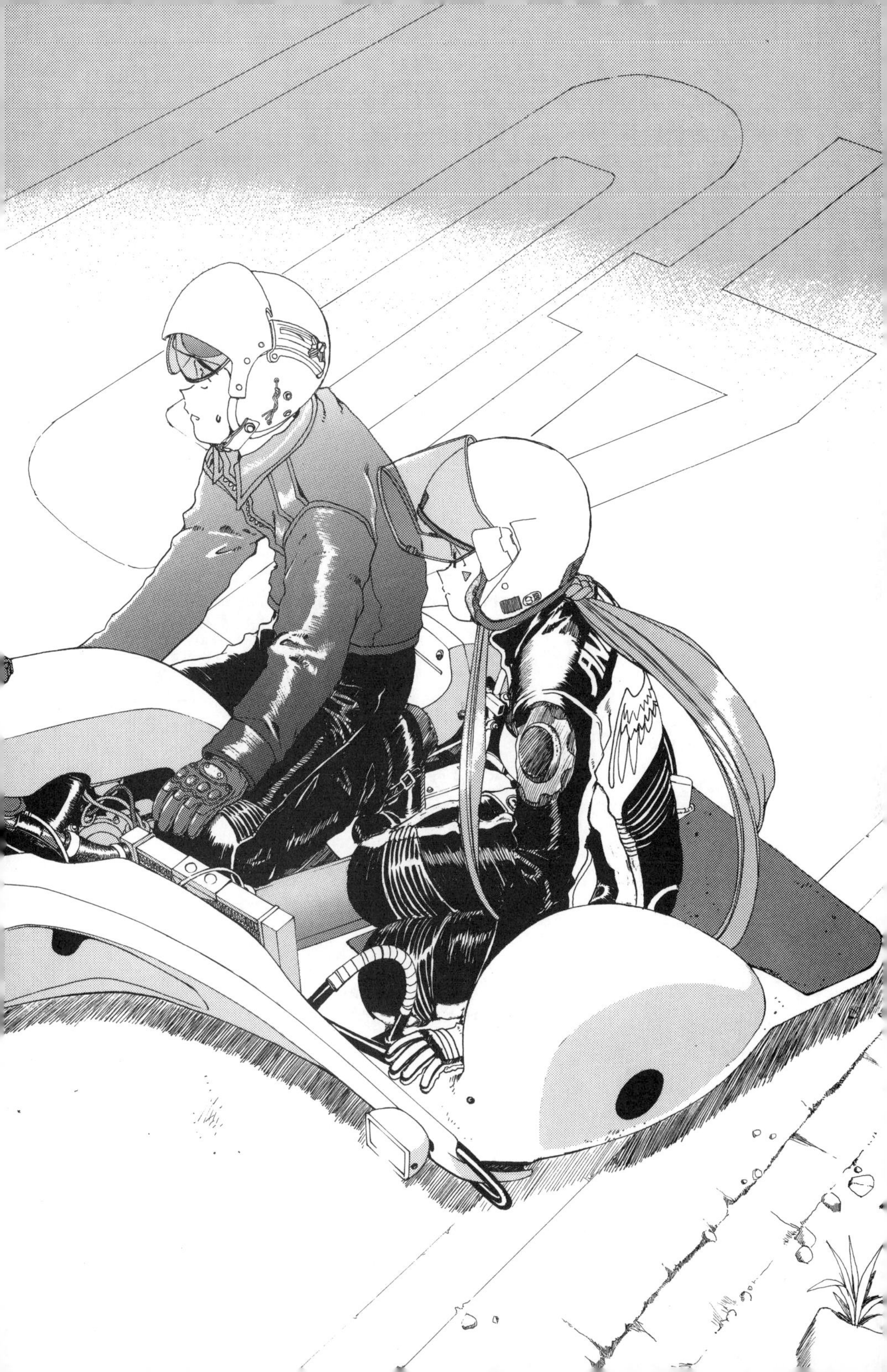

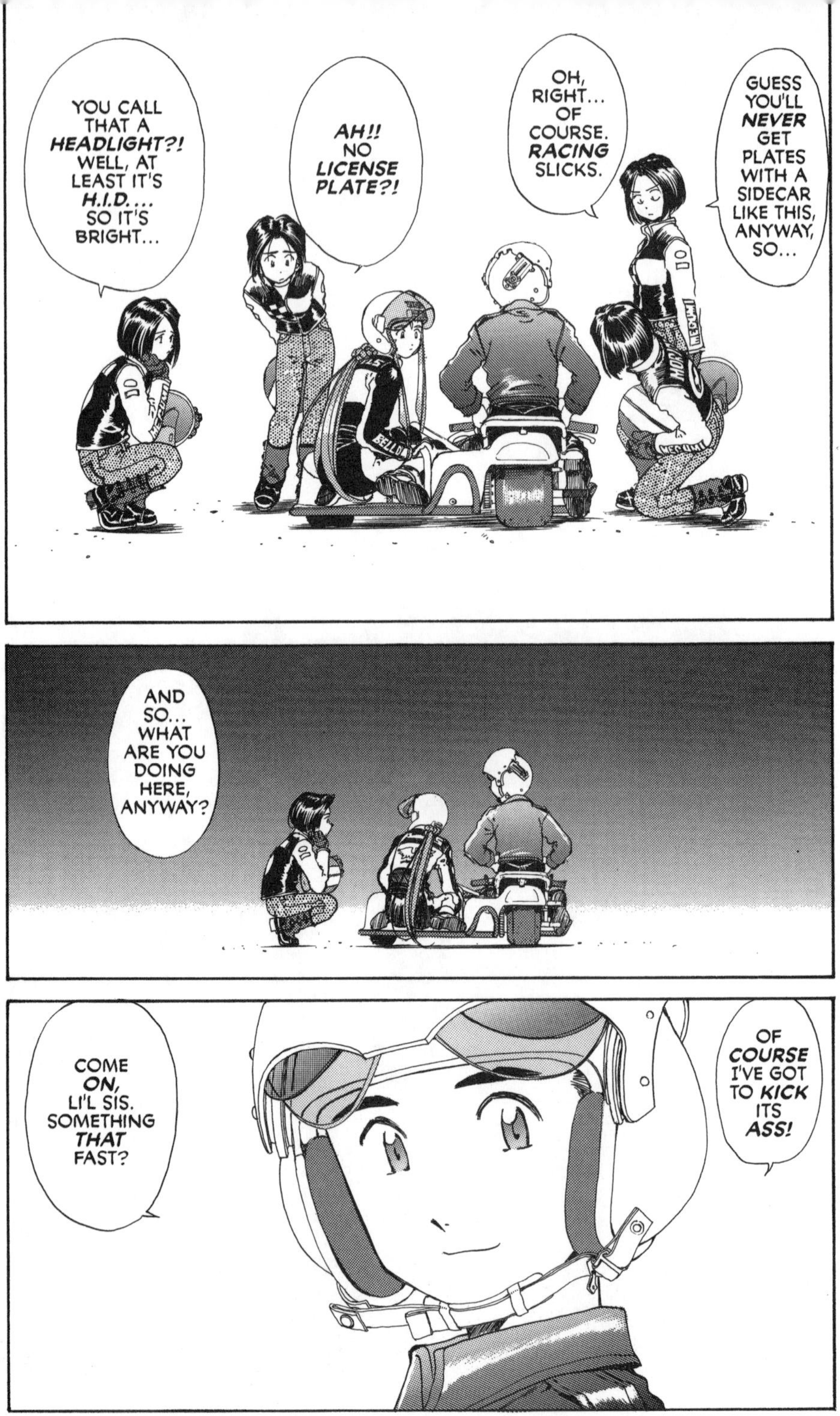
YOU CALL THAT A HEADLIGHT?! WELL, AT LEAST IT'S H.I.D.... SO IT'S BRIGHT...
AH!! NO LICENSE PLATE?!
OH, RIGHT... OF COURSE. RACING SLICKS.
GUESS YOU'LL NEVER GET PLATES WITH A SIDECAR LIKE THIS, ANYWAY, SO...
AND SO... WHAT ARE YOU DOING HERE, ANYWAY?
COME ON, LI'L SIS. SOMETHING THAT FAST?
OF COURSE I'VE GOT TO KICK ITS ASS!

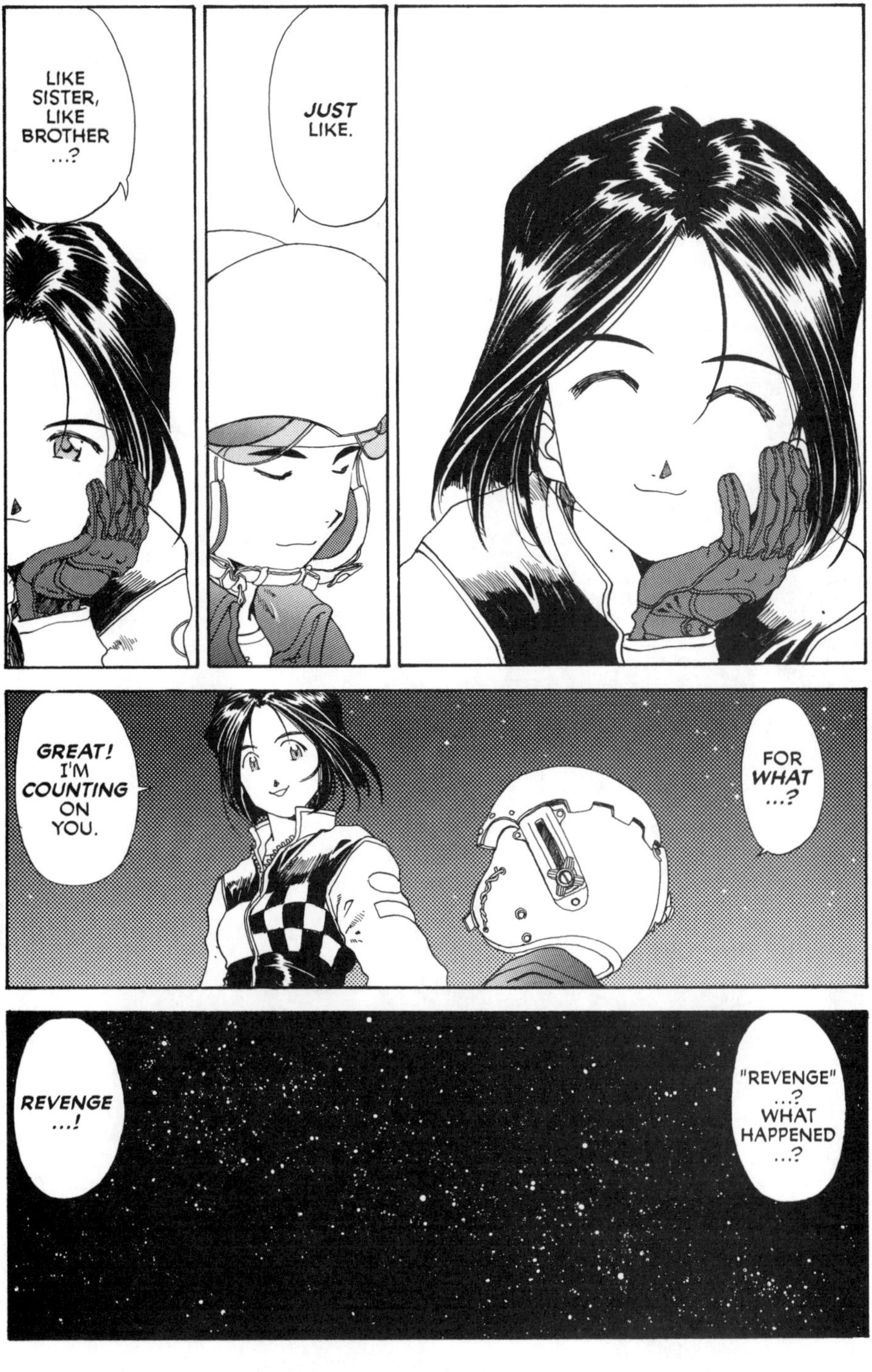
LIKE SISTER, LIKE BROTHER ...?
JUST LIKE.
GREAT! I'M COUNTING ON YOU.
FOR WHAT ...?
REVENGE ...!
"REVENGE" ...? WHAT HAPPENED ...?

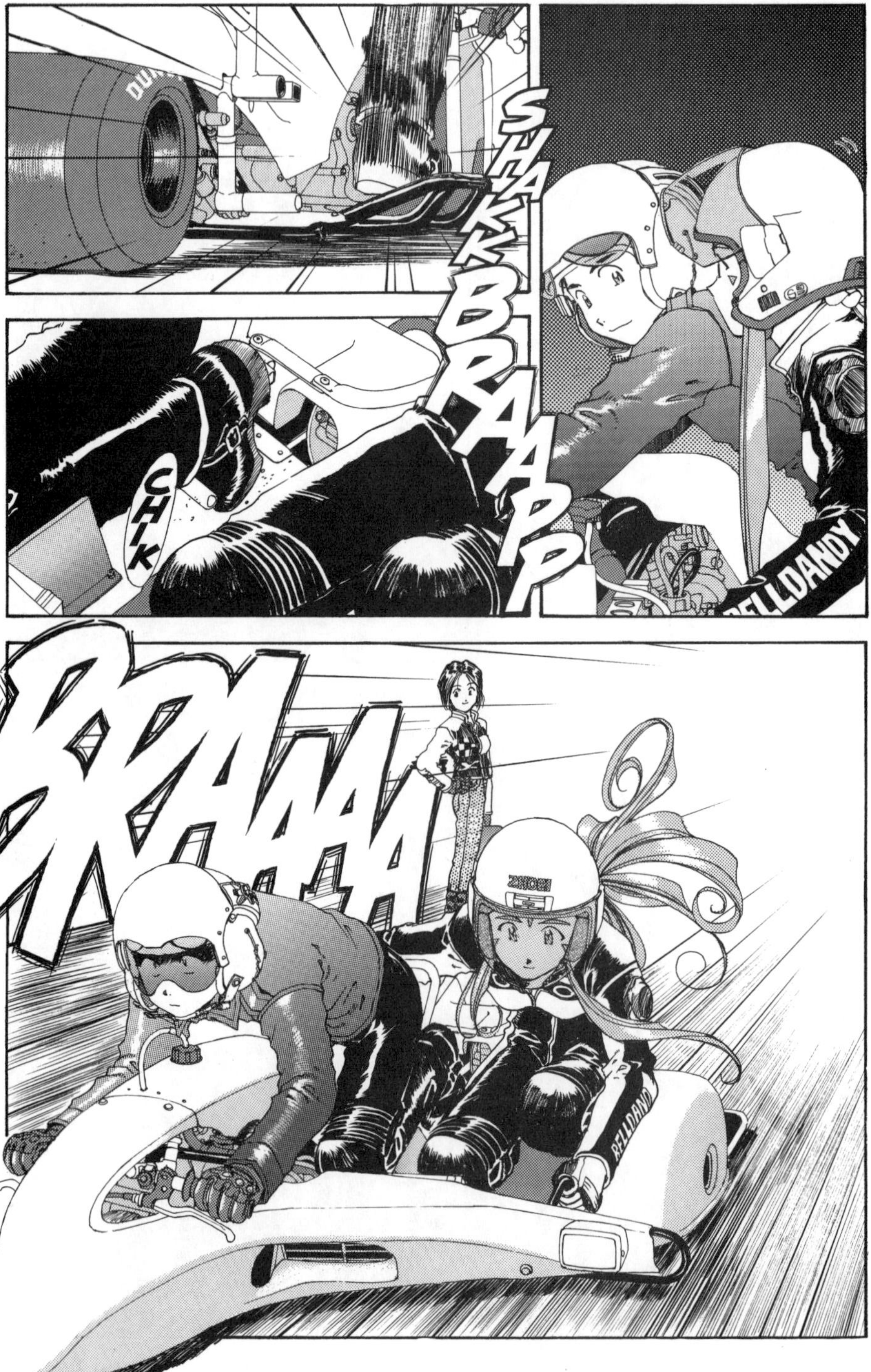
SHAKKBRAAAPP
CHIK
BELLDANDY
BRAAAA
BELLDANDY

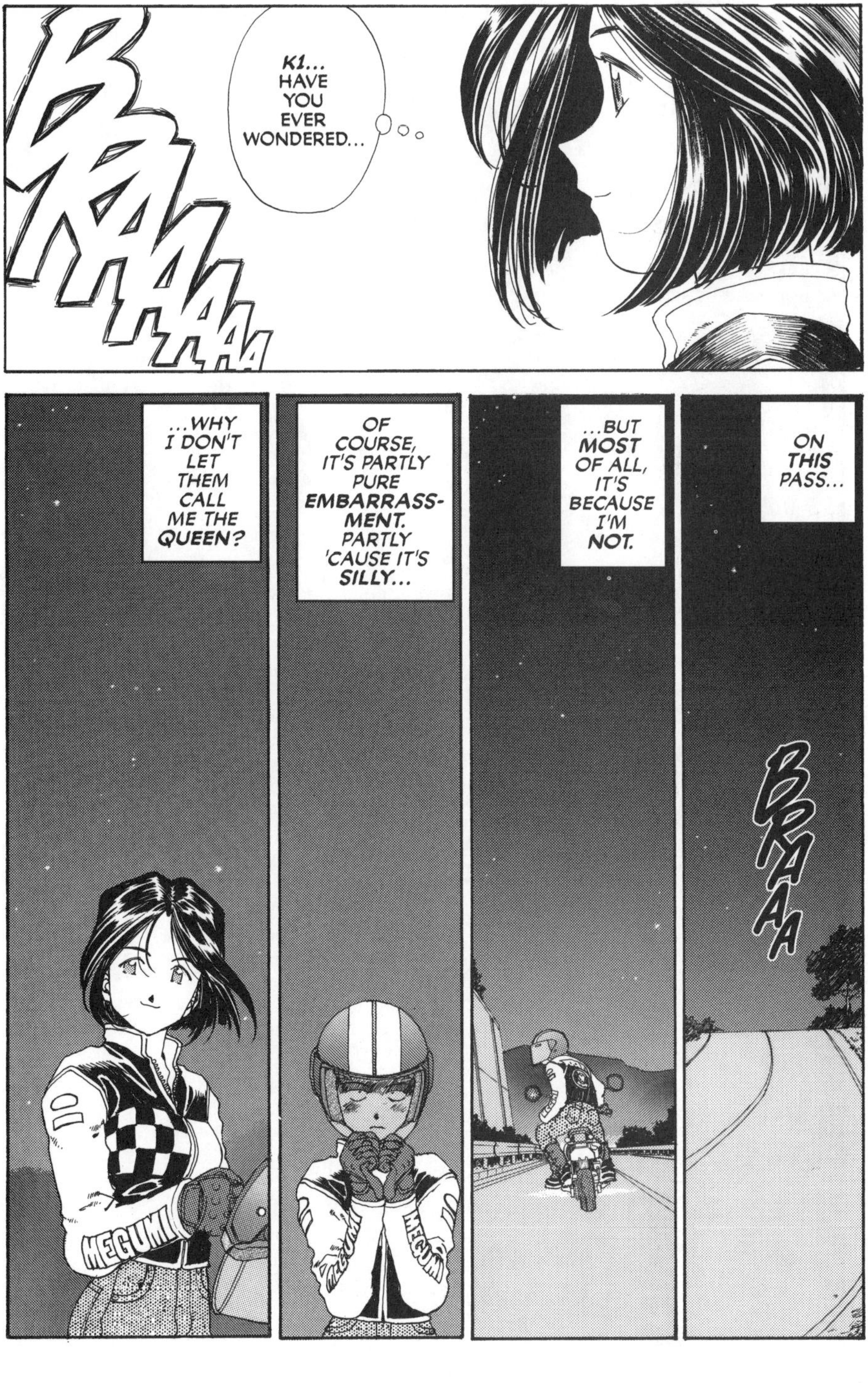
BRAAAAA
K1... HAVE YOU EVER WONDERED...
...WHY I DON'T LET THEM CALL ME THE QUEEN?
OF COURSE, IT'S PARTLY PURE EMBARRASSMENT. PARTLY 'CAUSE IT'S SILLY...
...BUT MOST OF ALL, IT'S BECAUSE I'M NOT.
ON THIS PASS...
BRAAAA
MEGUMI

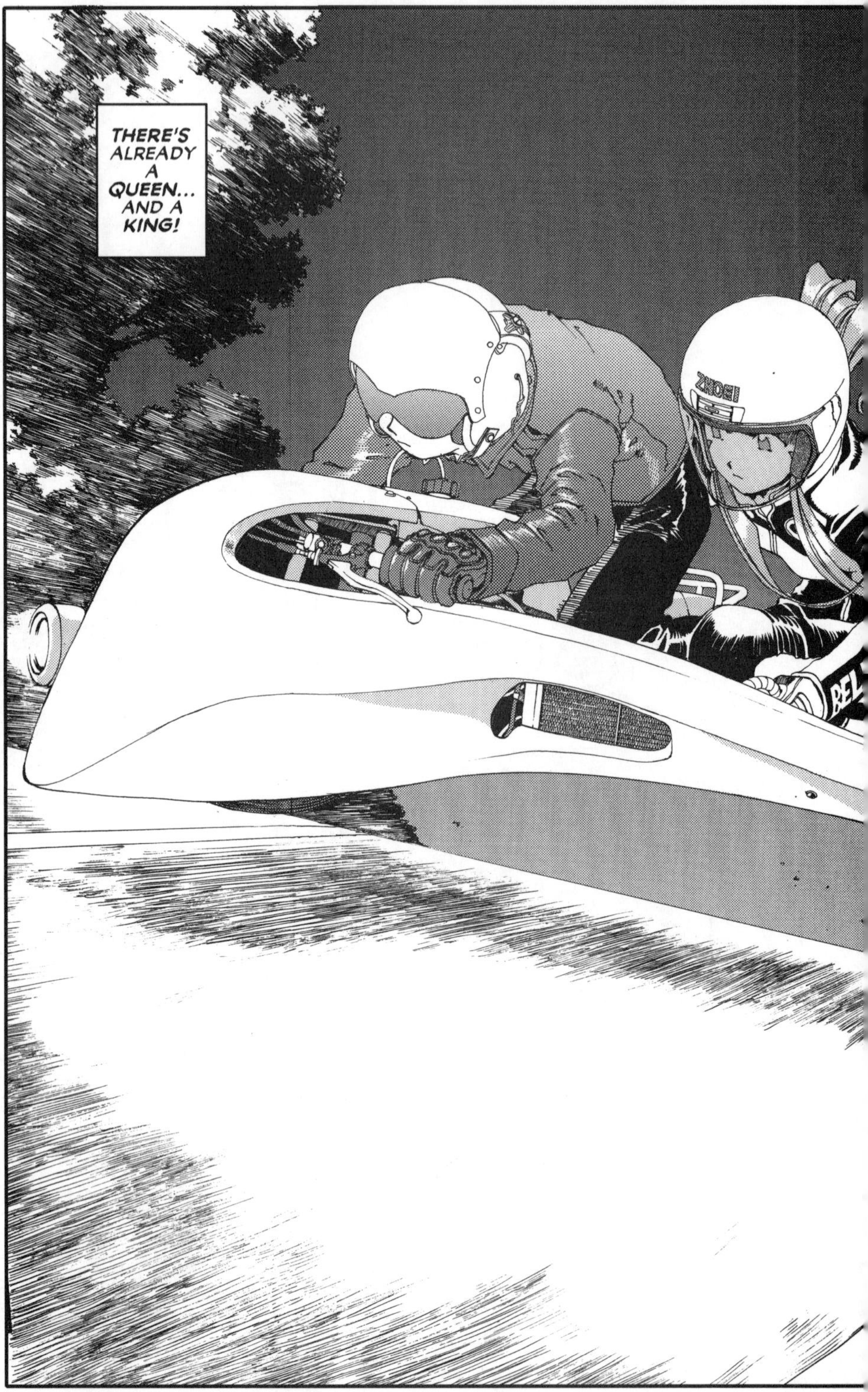
THERE'S ALREADY A QUEEN... AND A KING!

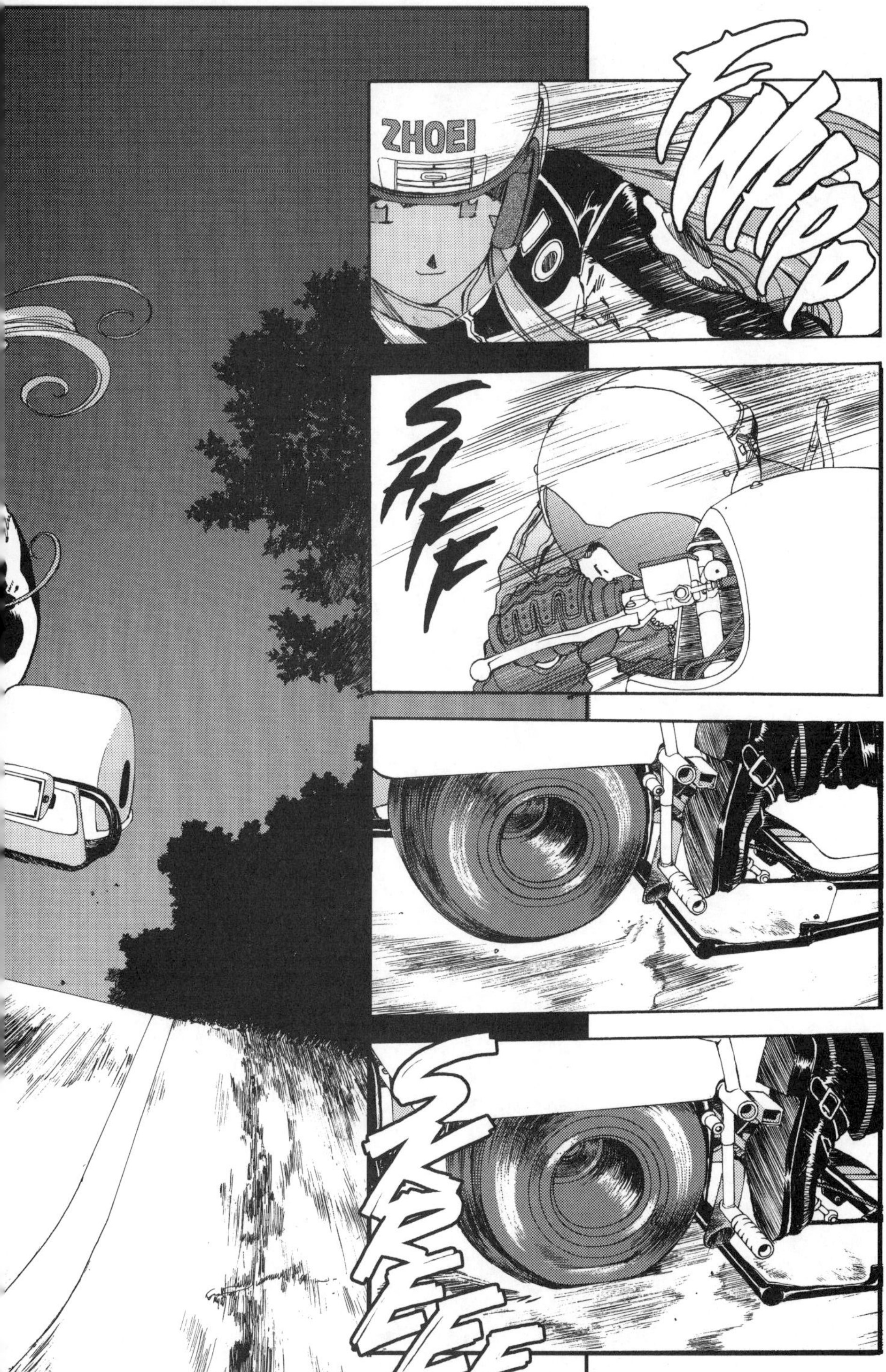
ZHOEI
FWHIP
SHFF
SKREEEE

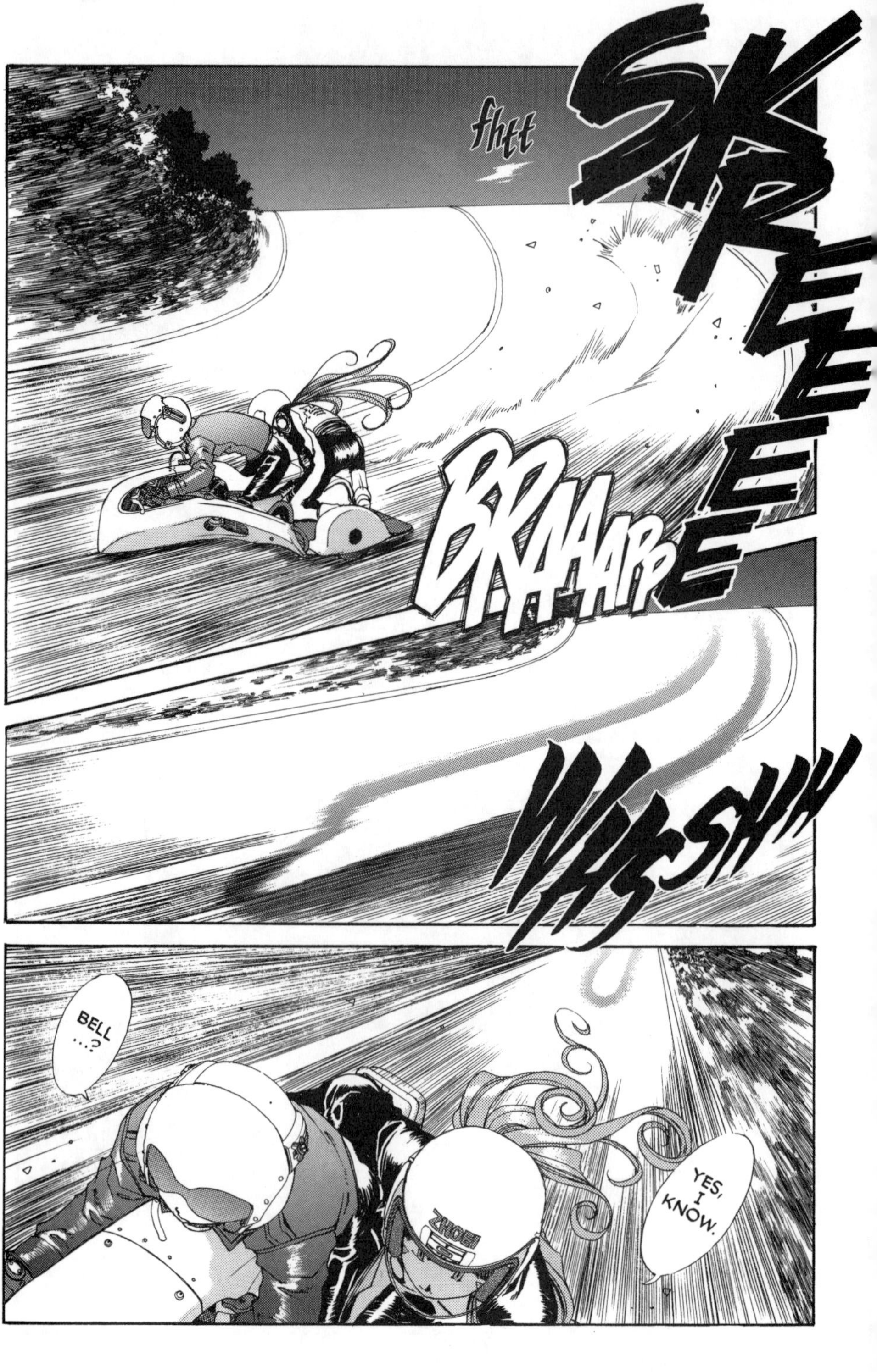
fhtt
SKREEEEE
BRAAAAPP
WHSSHH
BELL ...?
YES, I KNOW.

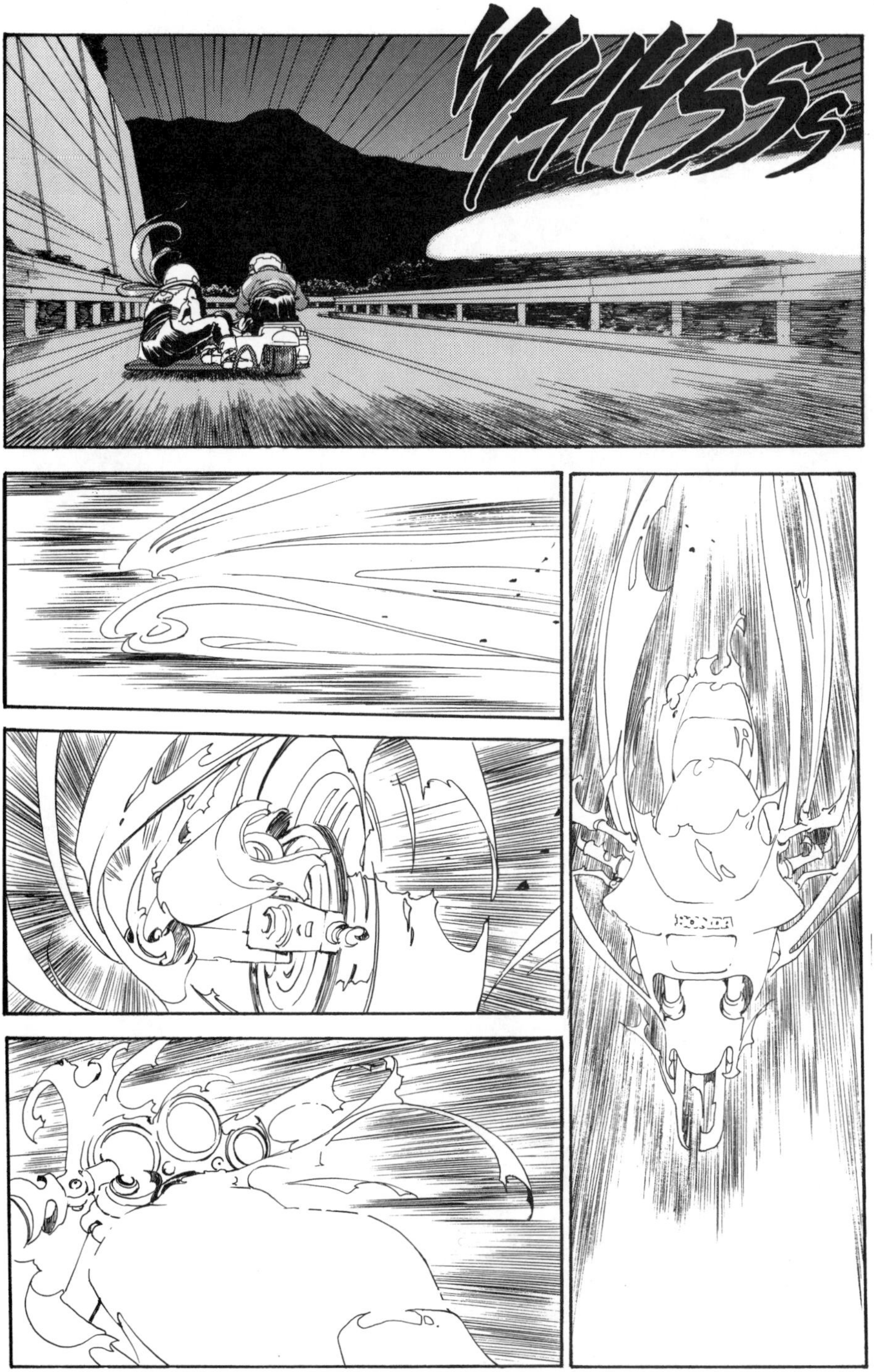
WHHSSs
HONDA

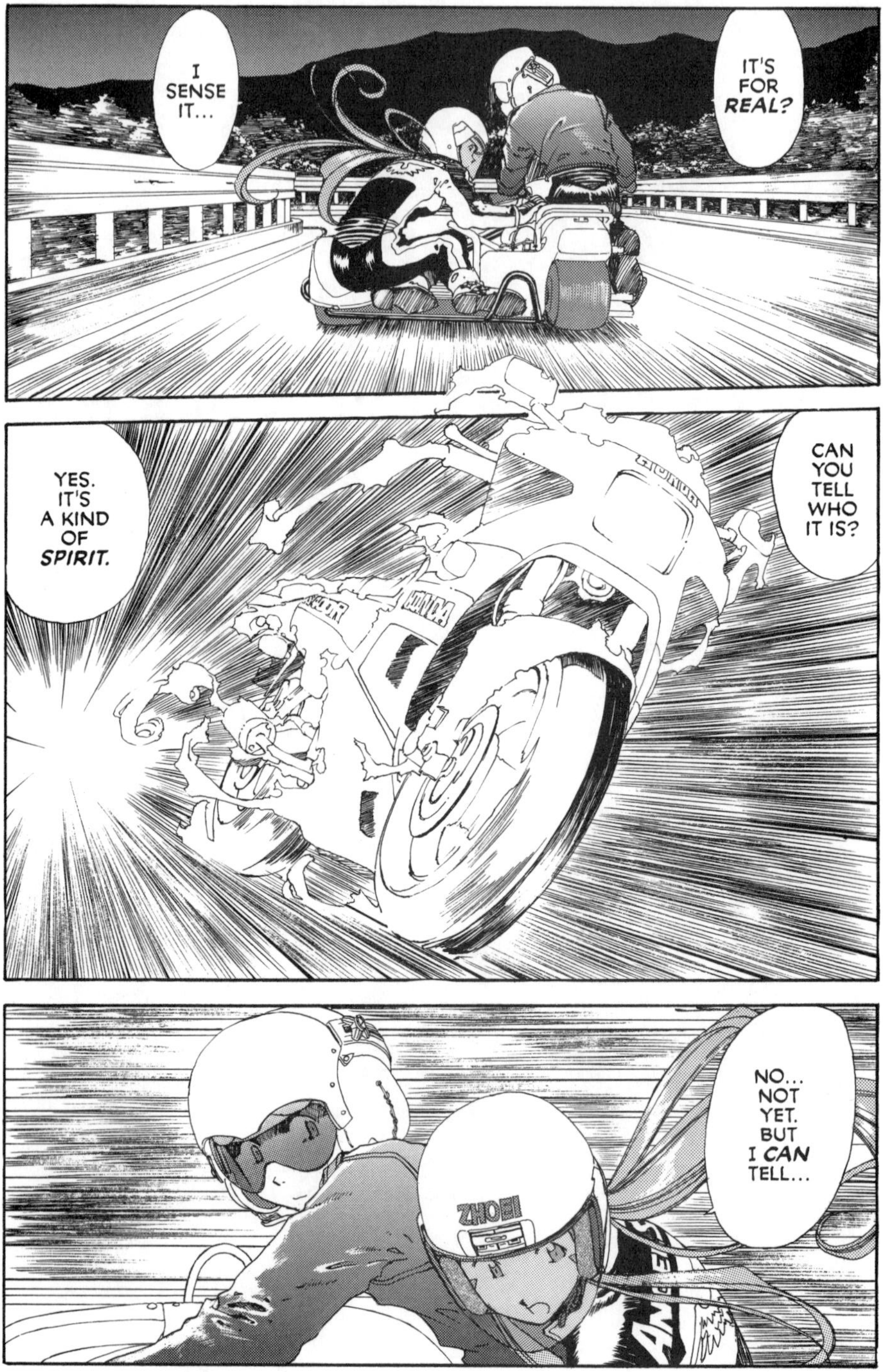
I SENSE IT...
IT'S FOR *REAL?*
YES. IT'S A KIND OF *SPIRIT.*
CAN YOU TELL WHO IT IS?
NO... NOT YET. BUT I *CAN* TELL...

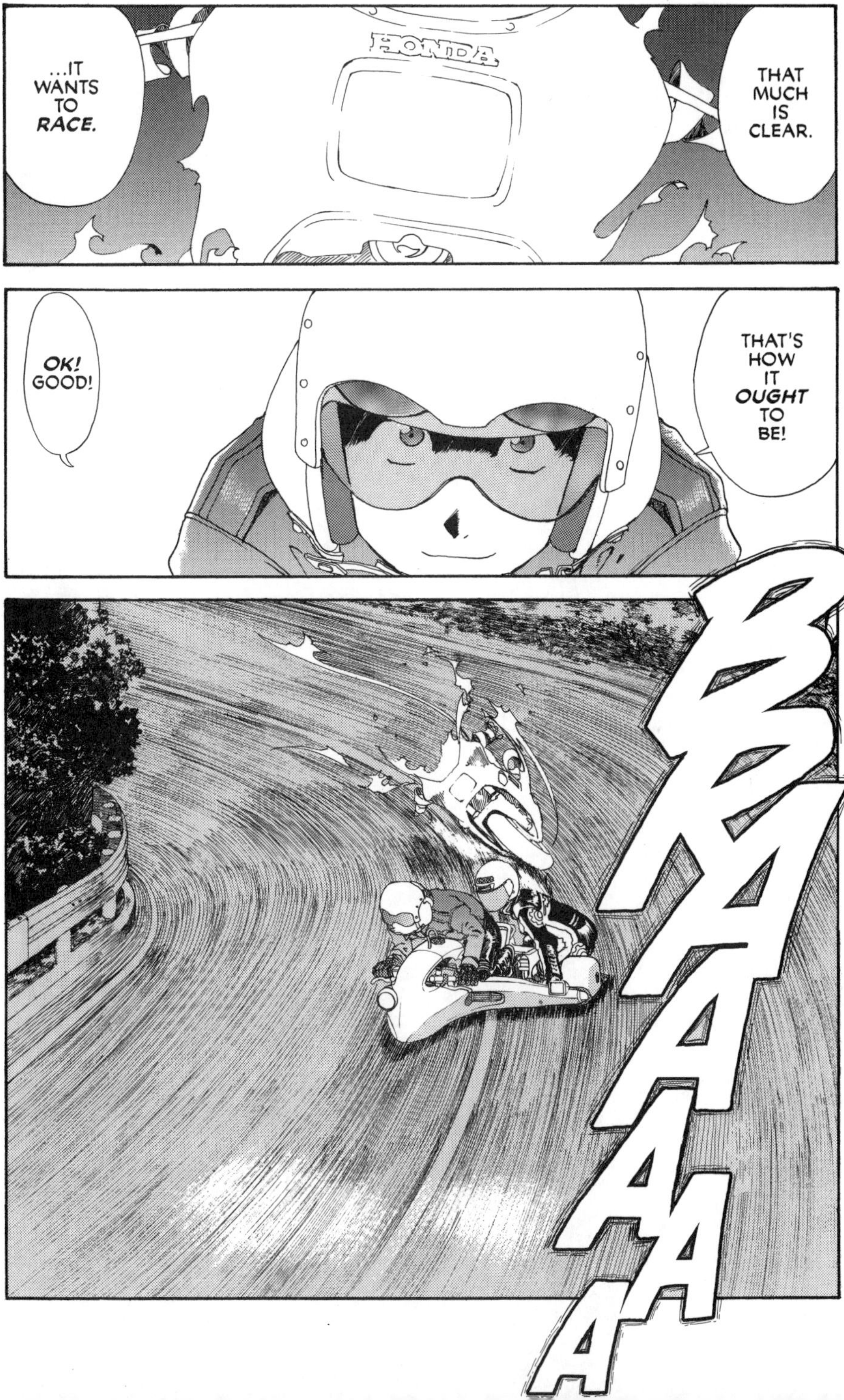

...IT WANTS TO *RACE.*
THAT MUCH IS CLEAR.
OK! GOOD!
THAT'S HOW IT *OUGHT* TO BE!
BRAAAAAAAA

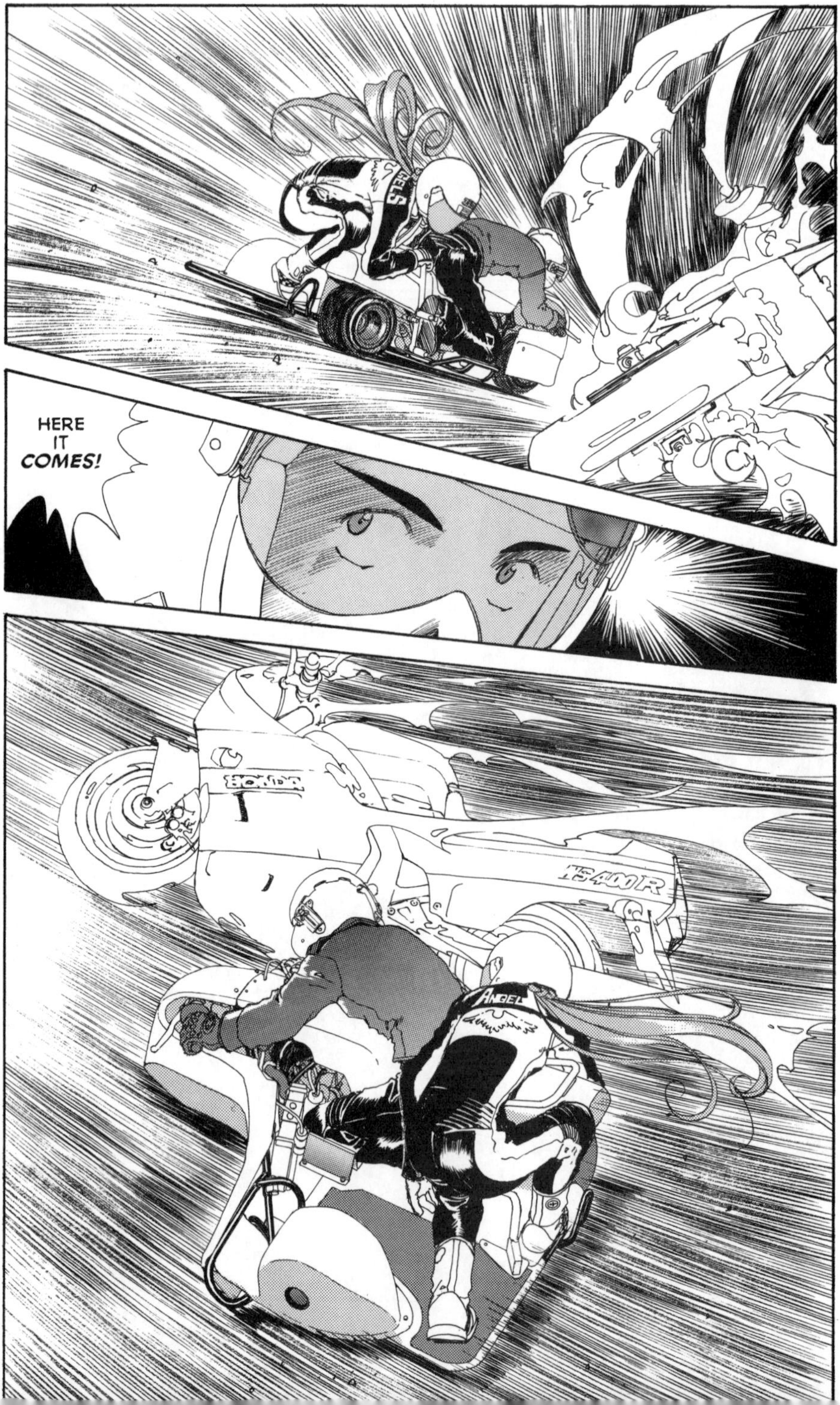
HERE IT COMES!
HONDA
NS400R
ANGEL

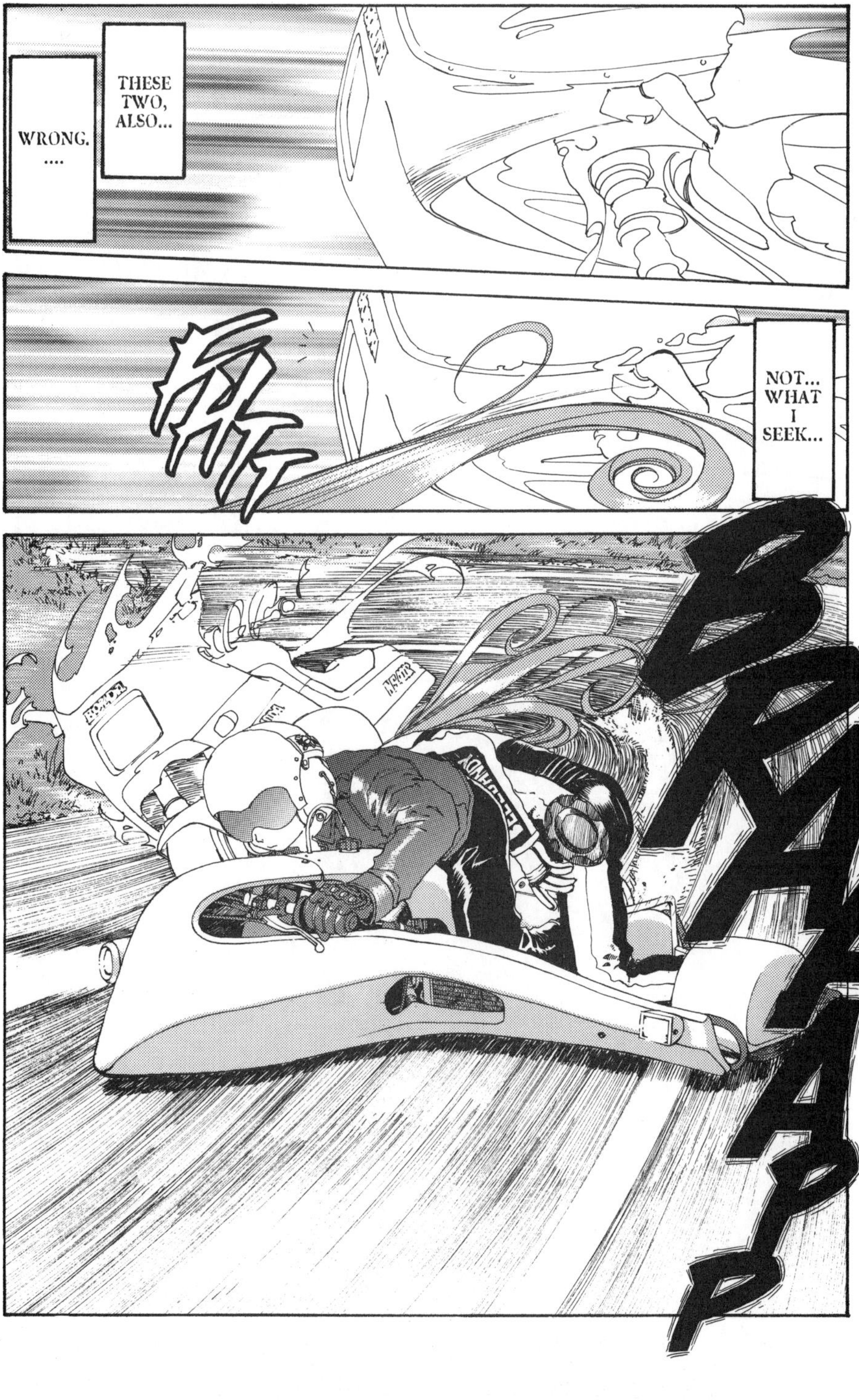
THESE TWO, ALSO...
WRONG. ....
NOT... WHAT I SEEK...
BRAAAAPP

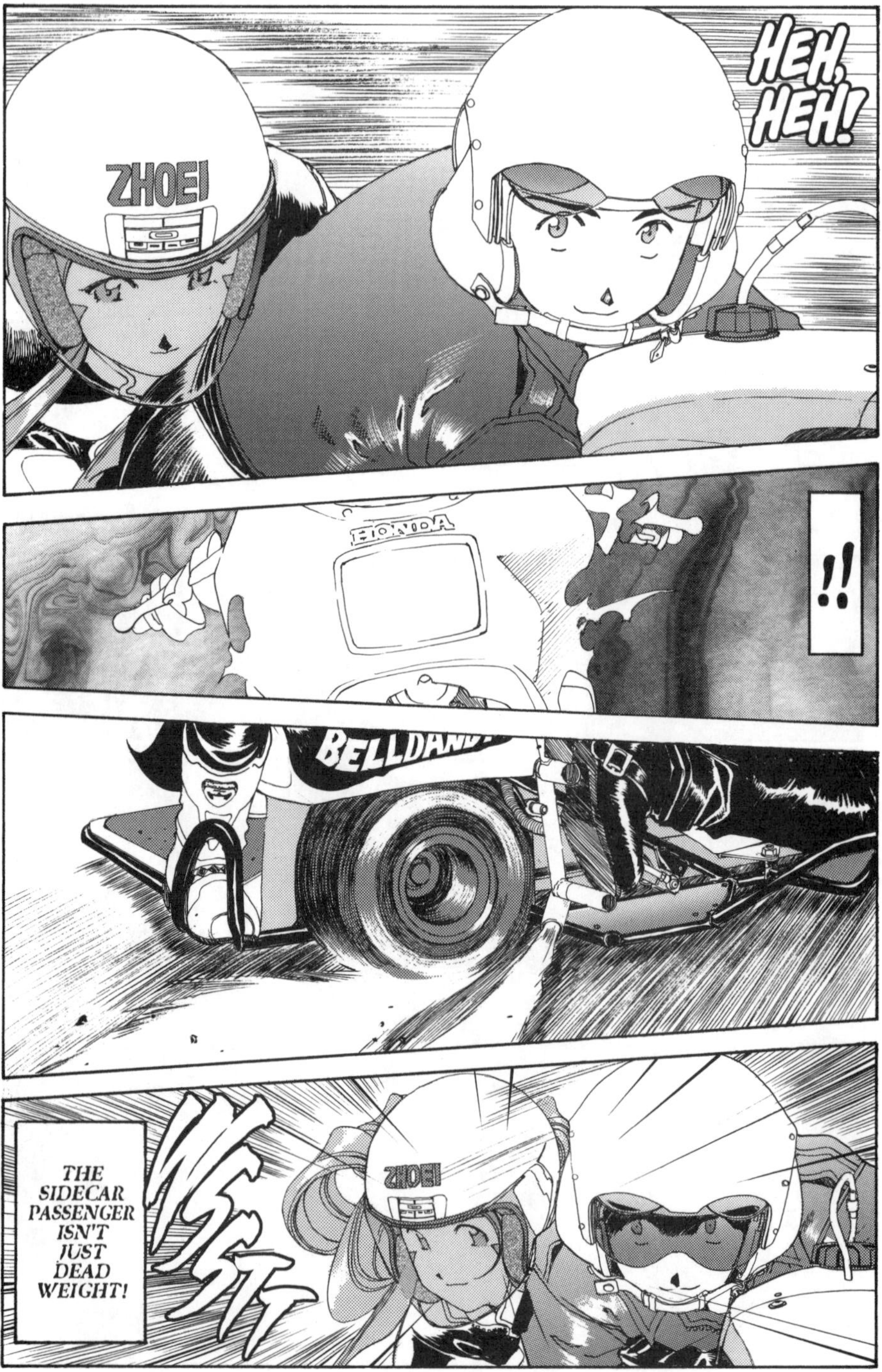
ZHOEI
HEH, HEH!
HONDA
!!
THE SIDECAR PASSENGER ISN'T JUST DEAD WEIGHT!
WSSTT

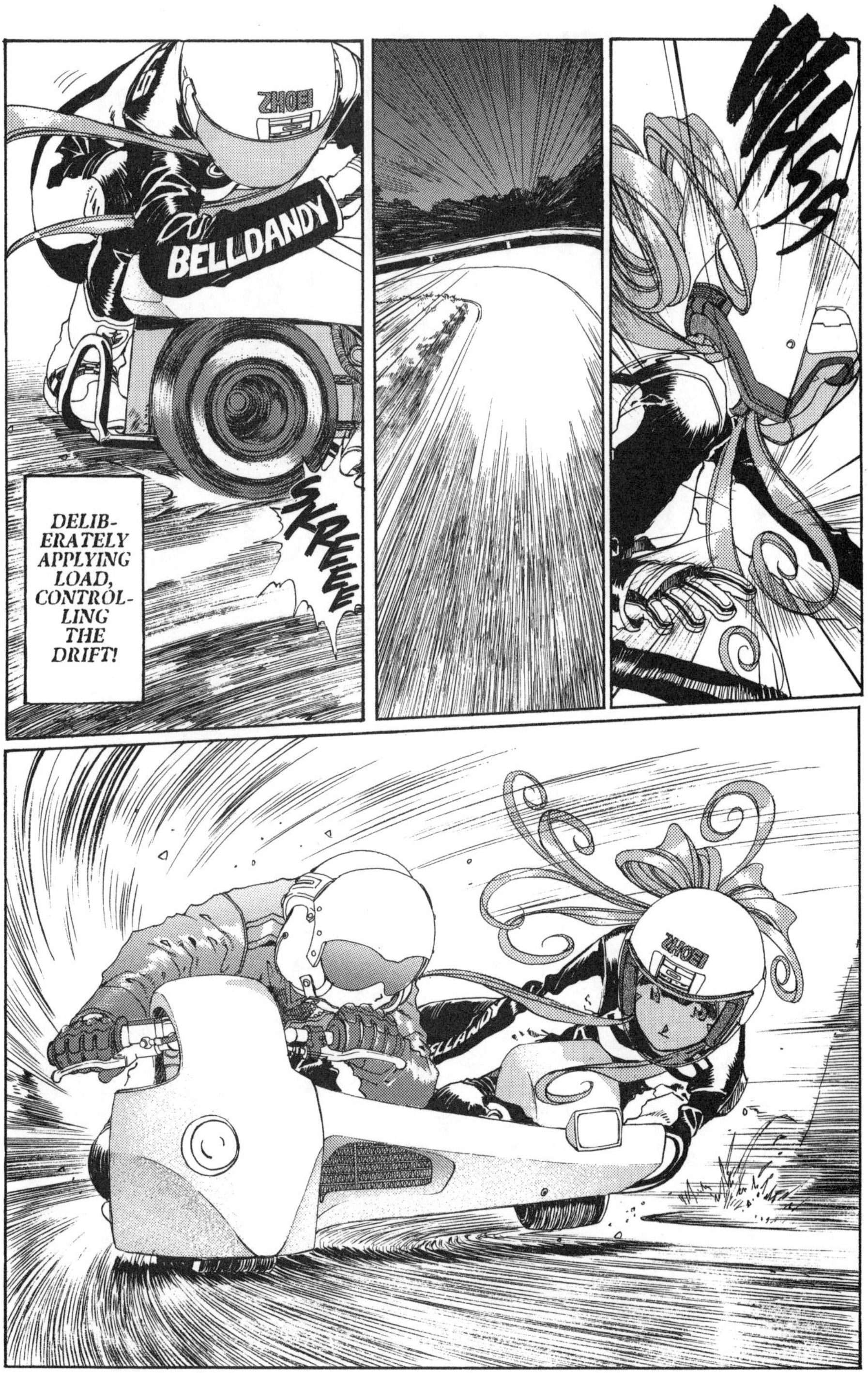
BELLDANDY
DELIB-ERATELY APPLYING LOAD, CONTROL-LING THE DRIFT!
SKREEEE
WHSS

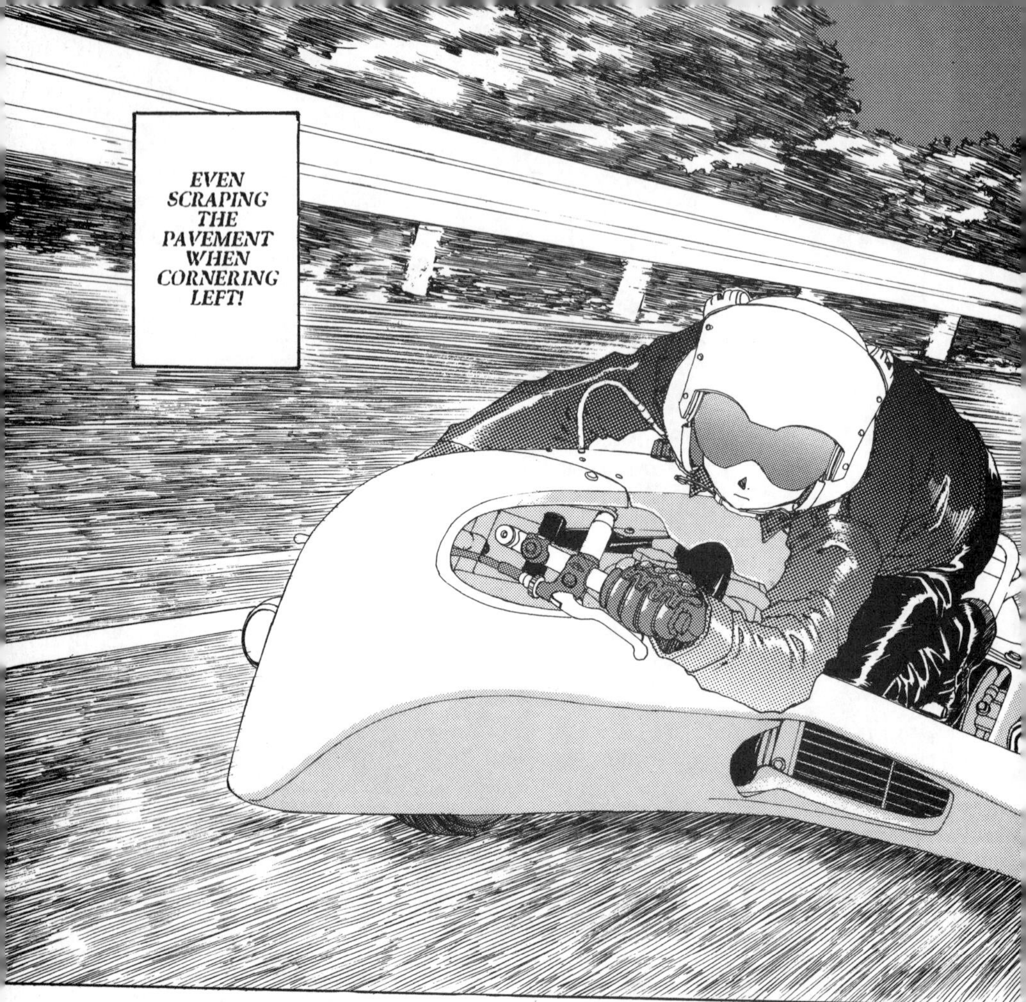
EVEN SCRAPING THE PAVEMENT WHEN CORNERING LEFT!

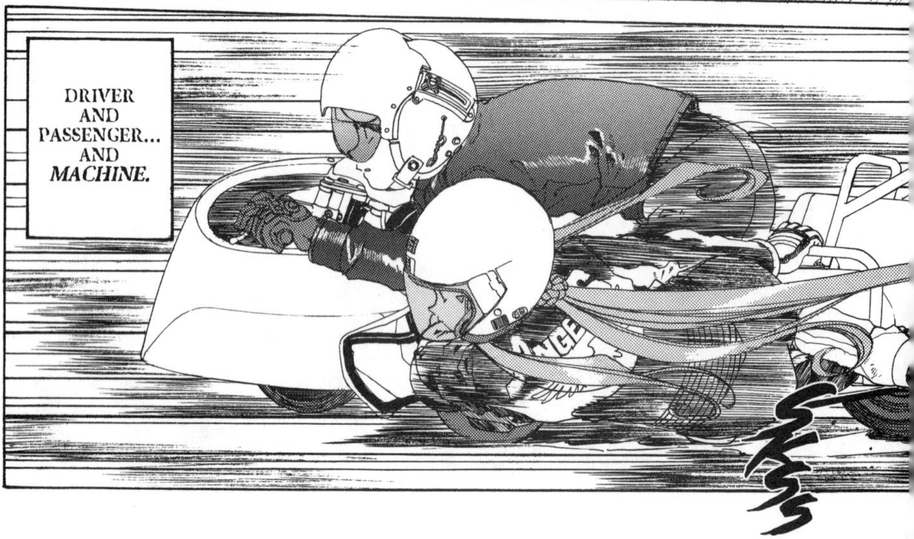
DRIVER AND PASSENGER... AND *MACHINE.*

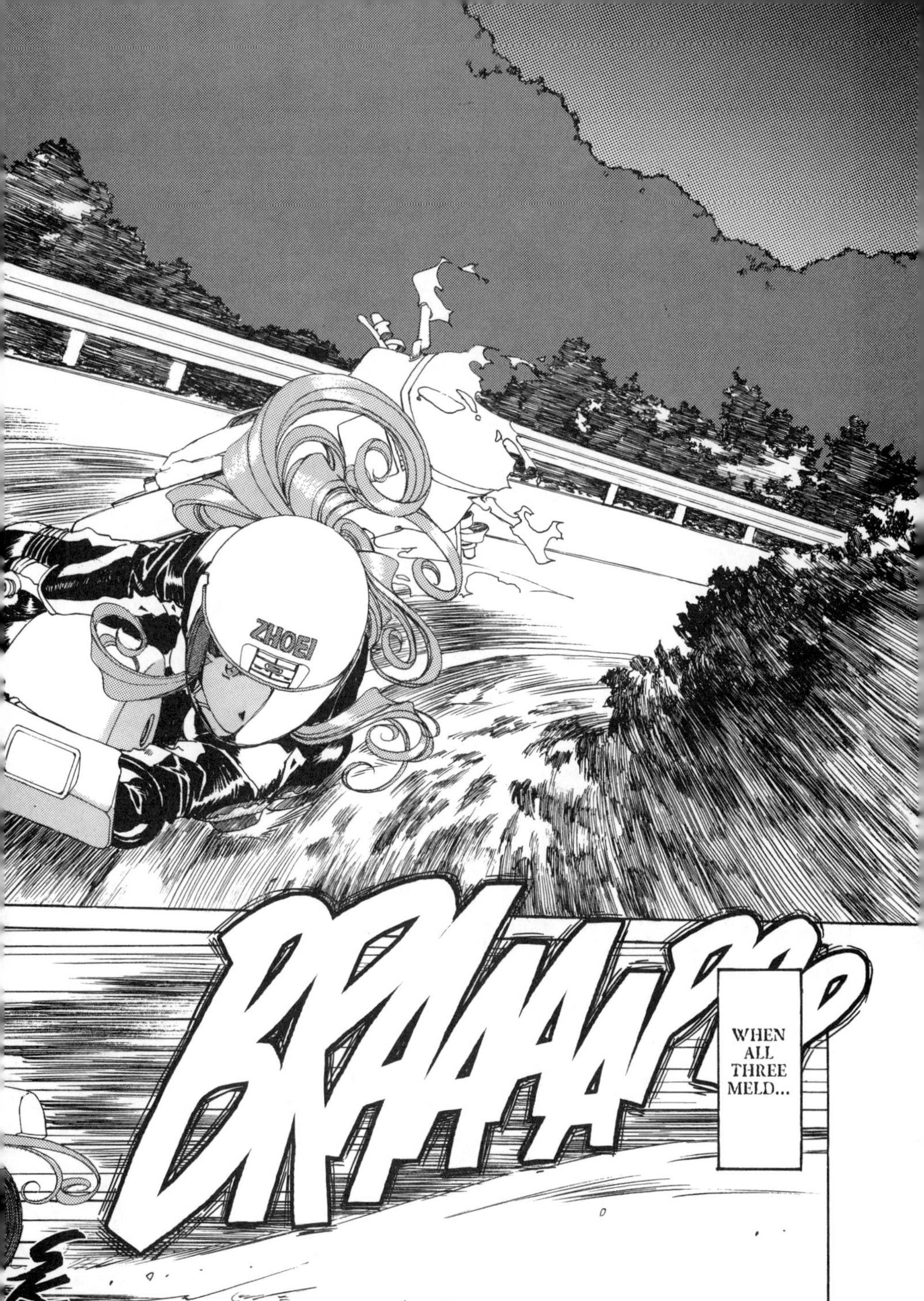
ZHOEI
WHEN ALL THREE MELD...

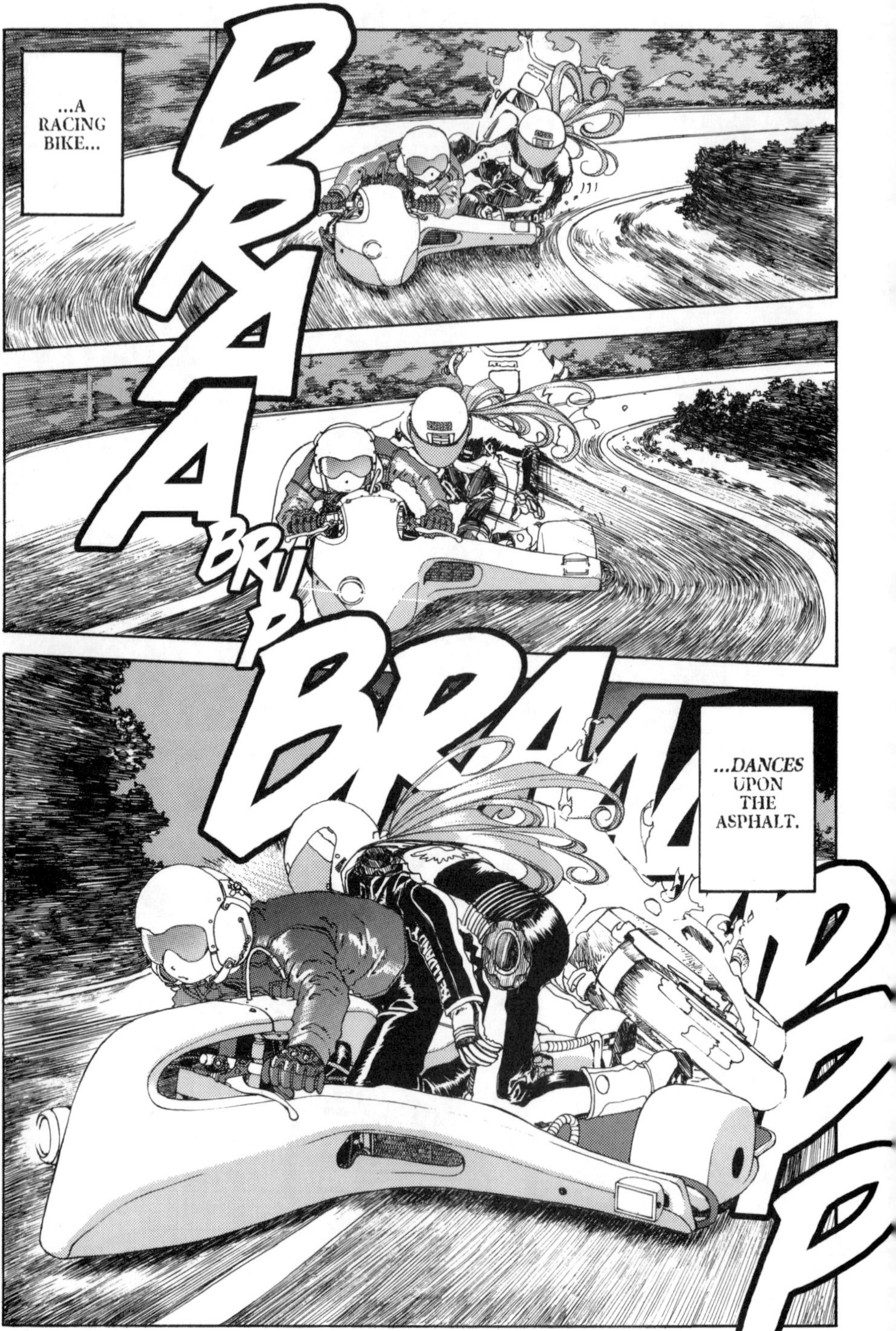
...A RACING BIKE...
BRAAA
BRUP
BRAAAP
...DANCES UPON THE ASPHALT.
PPPP

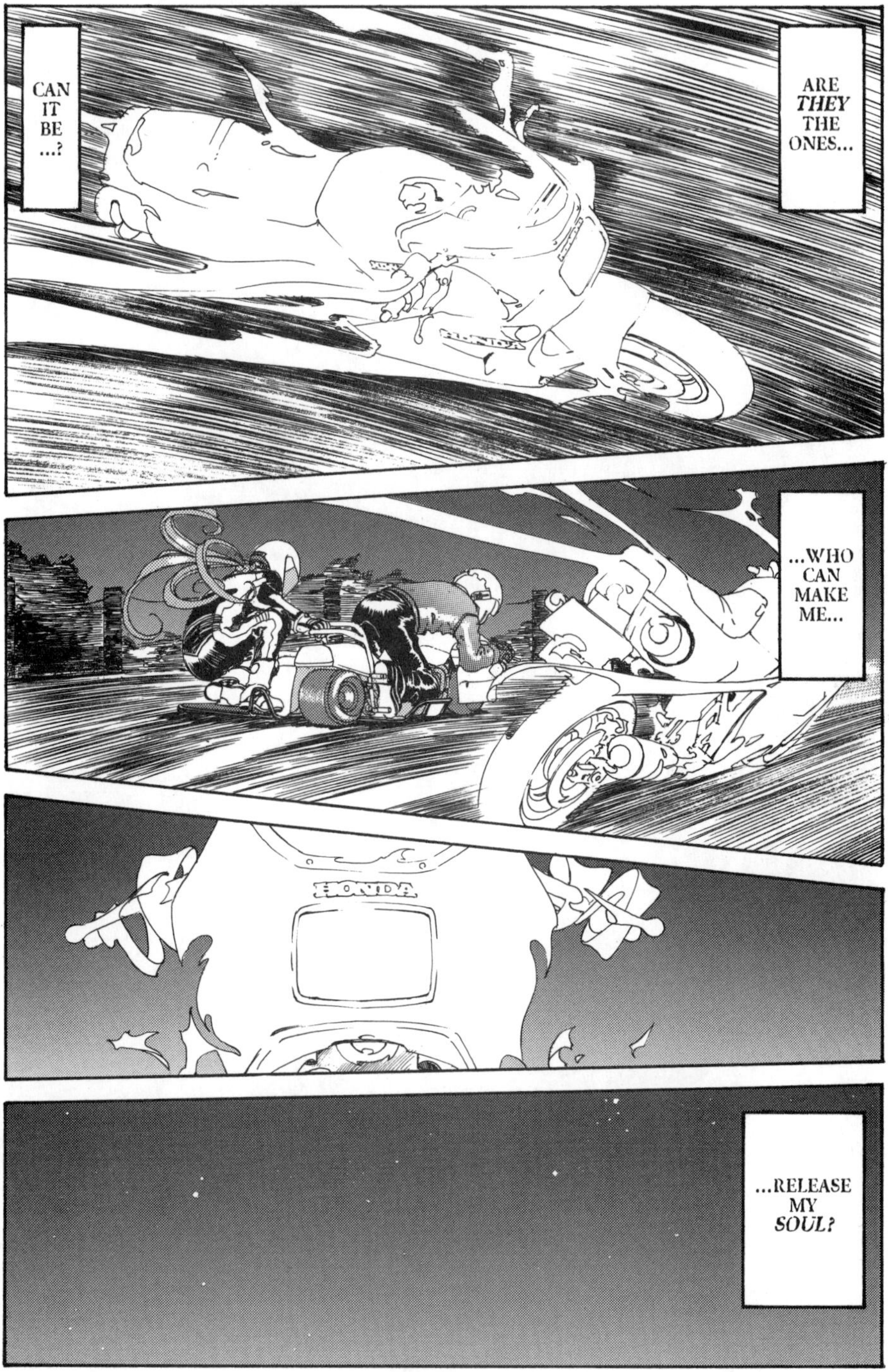
CAN IT BE ...?
ARE *THEY* THE ONES...
...WHO CAN MAKE ME...
HONDA
...RELEASE MY *SOUL?*

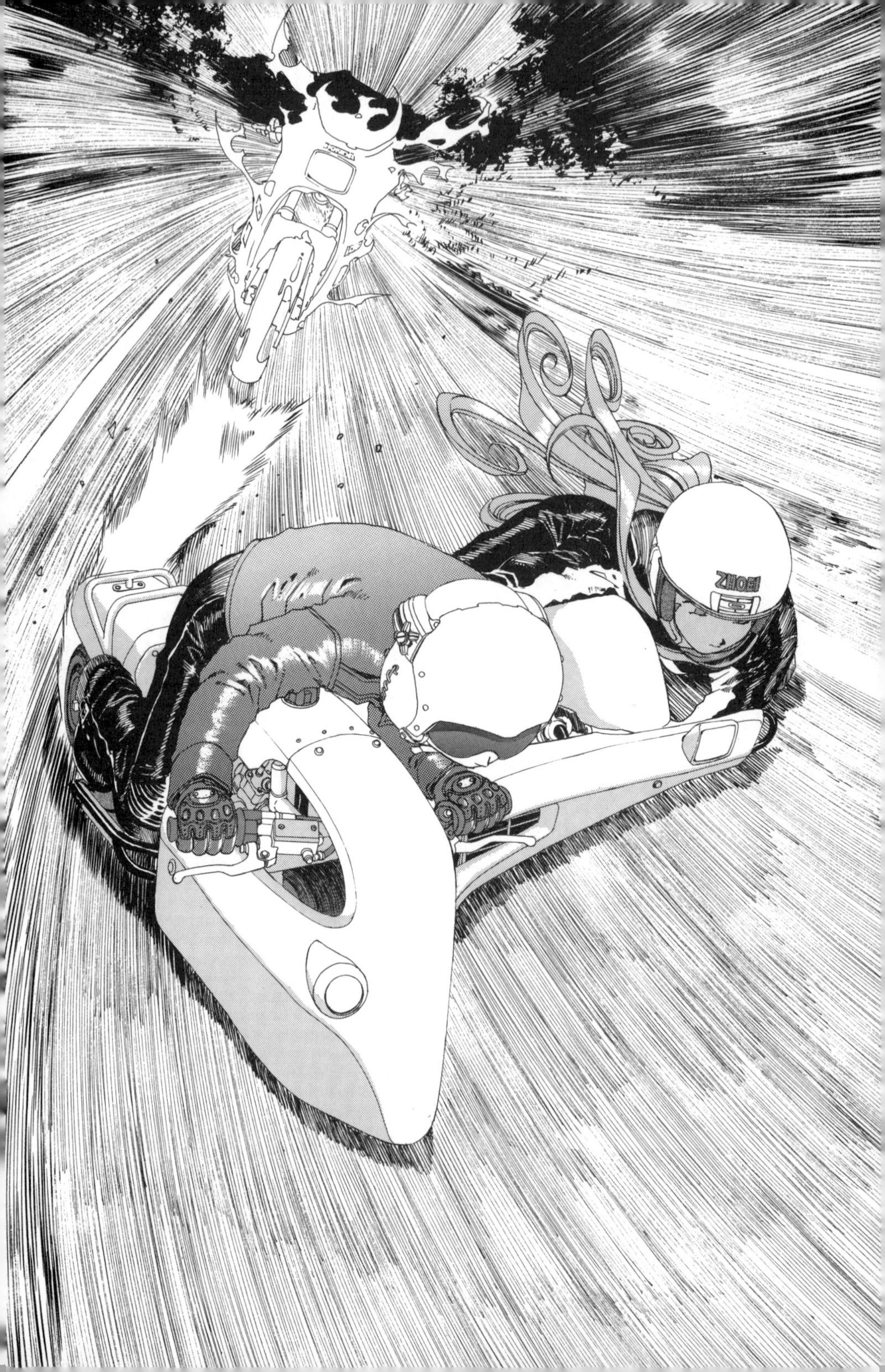

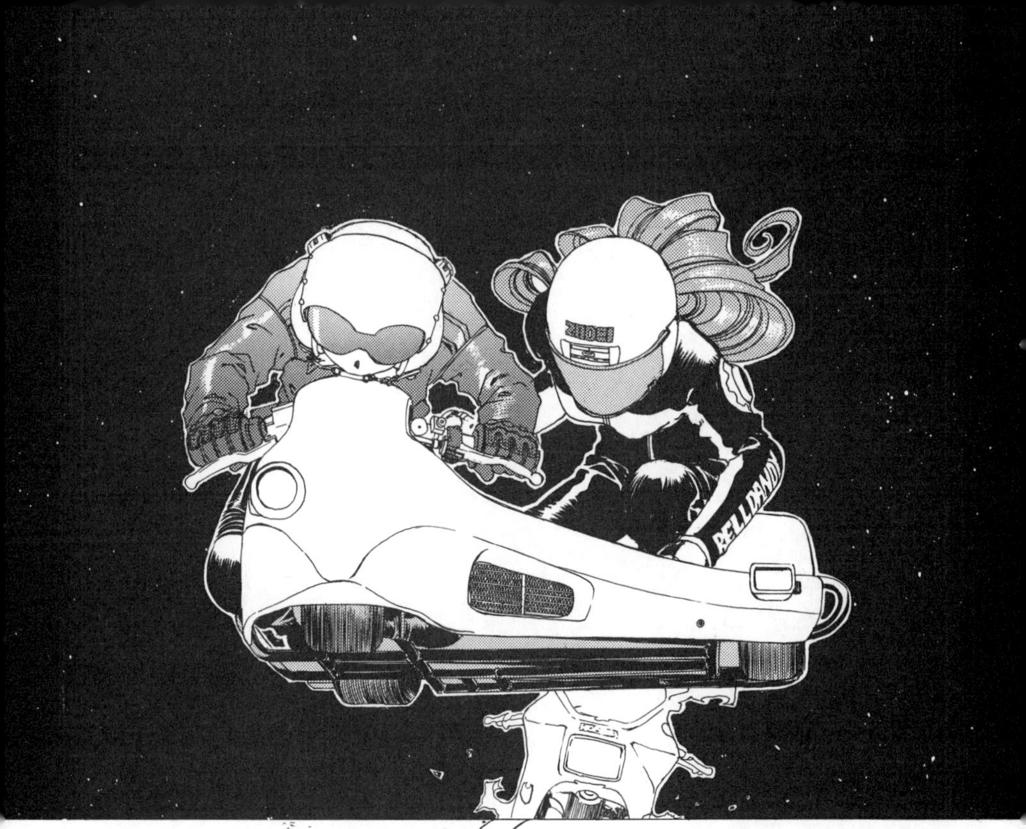
BELLDANDY

WELCOME BACK

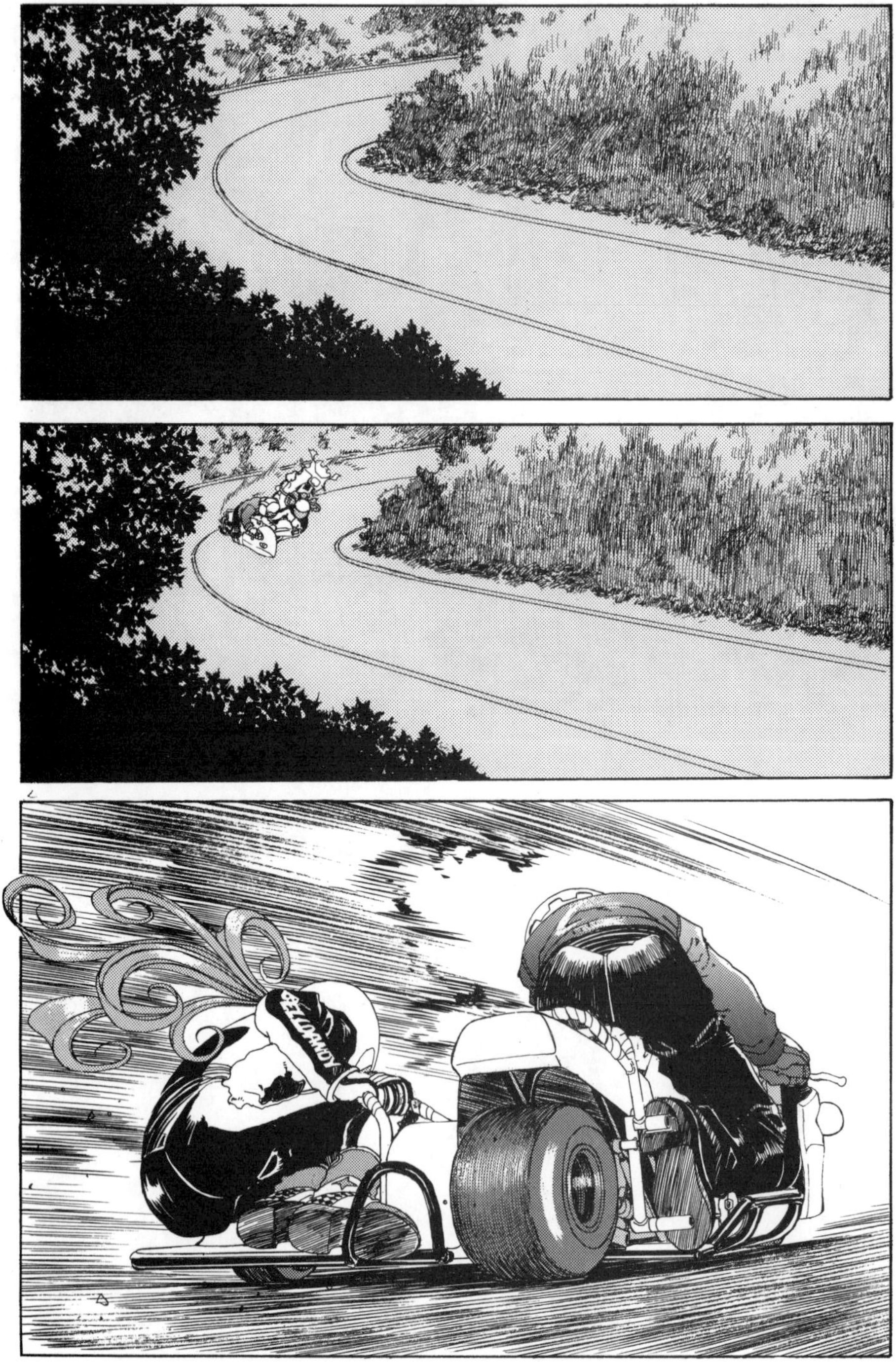

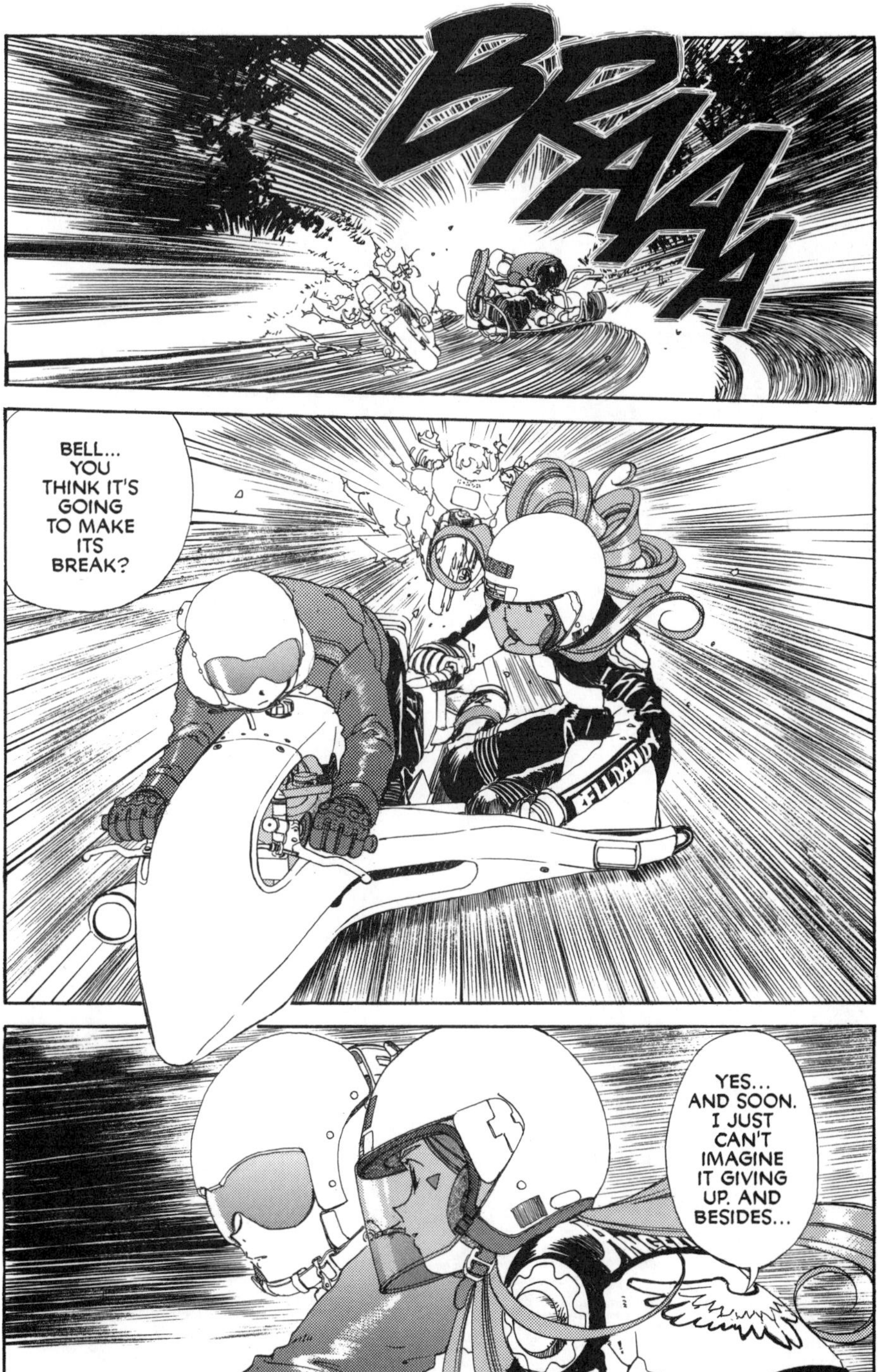
BRAAA
BELL... YOU THINK IT'S GOING TO MAKE ITS BREAK?
BELL DANDY
YES... AND SOON. I JUST CAN'T IMAGINE IT GIVING UP. AND BESIDES...

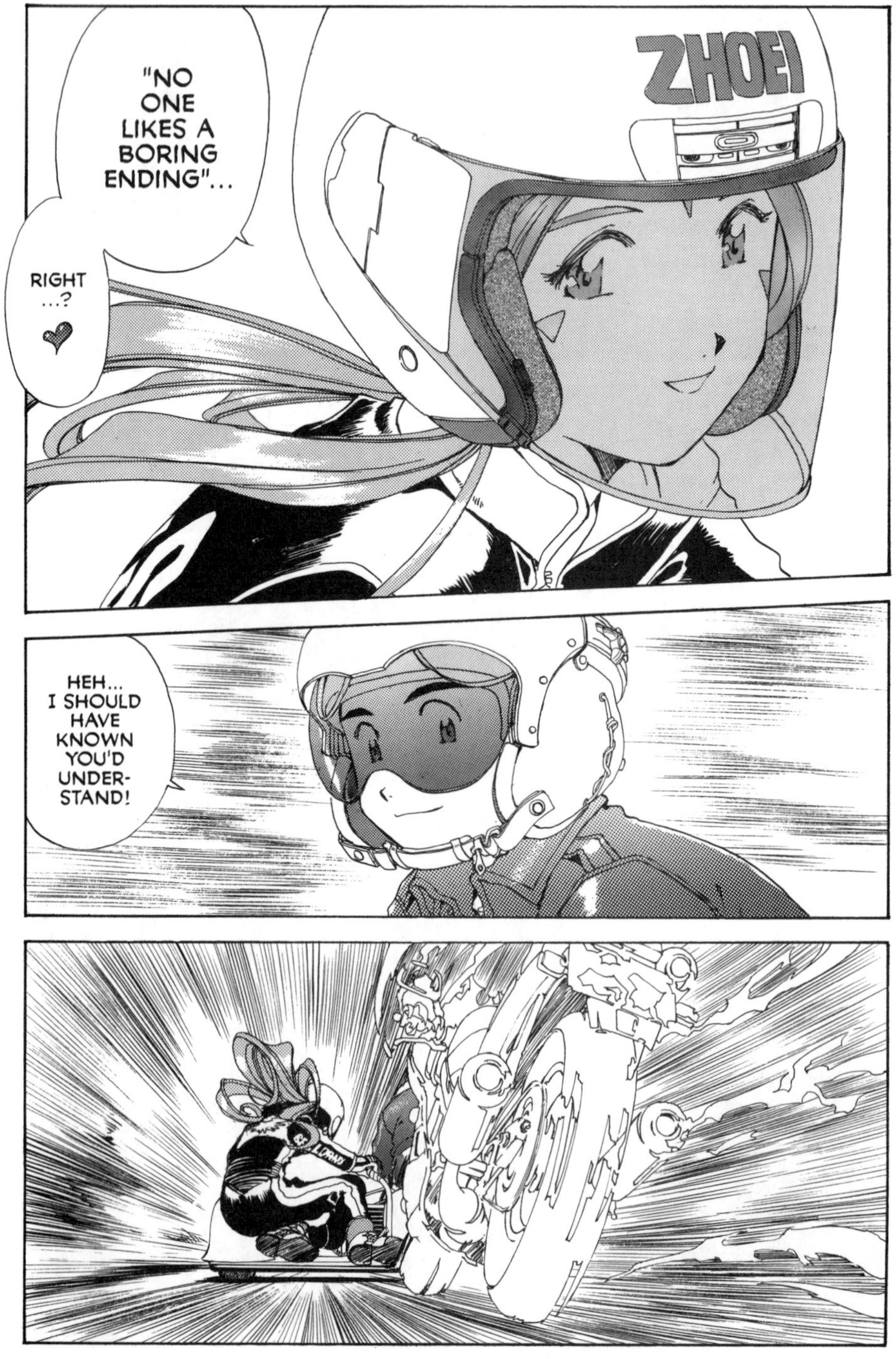
"NO ONE LIKES A BORING ENDING"...
RIGHT ...? ♥
ZHOEI
HEH... I SHOULD HAVE KNOWN YOU'D UNDER-STAND!

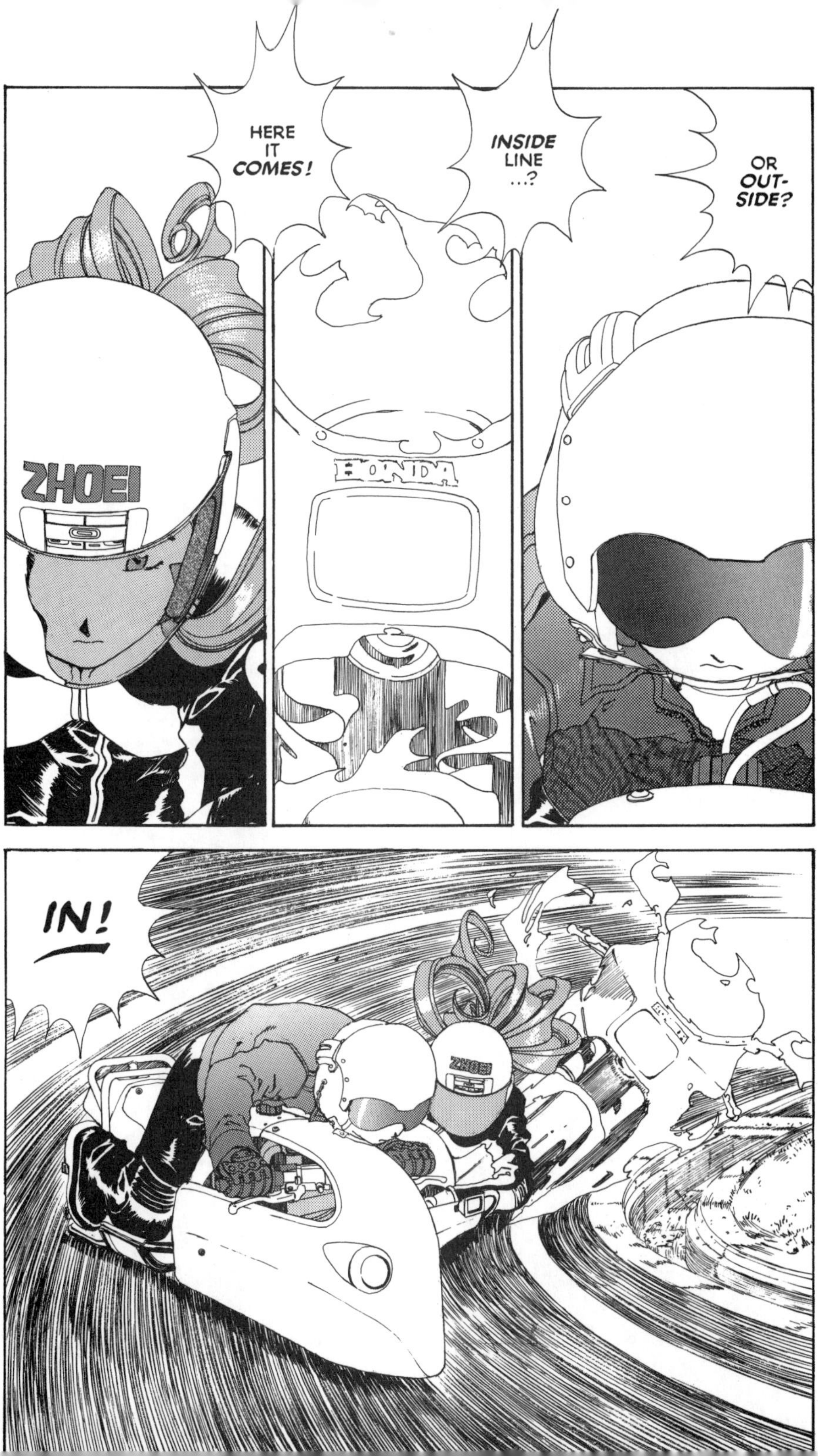
HERE IT COMES!
INSIDE LINE ...?
OR OUT-SIDE?
IN!

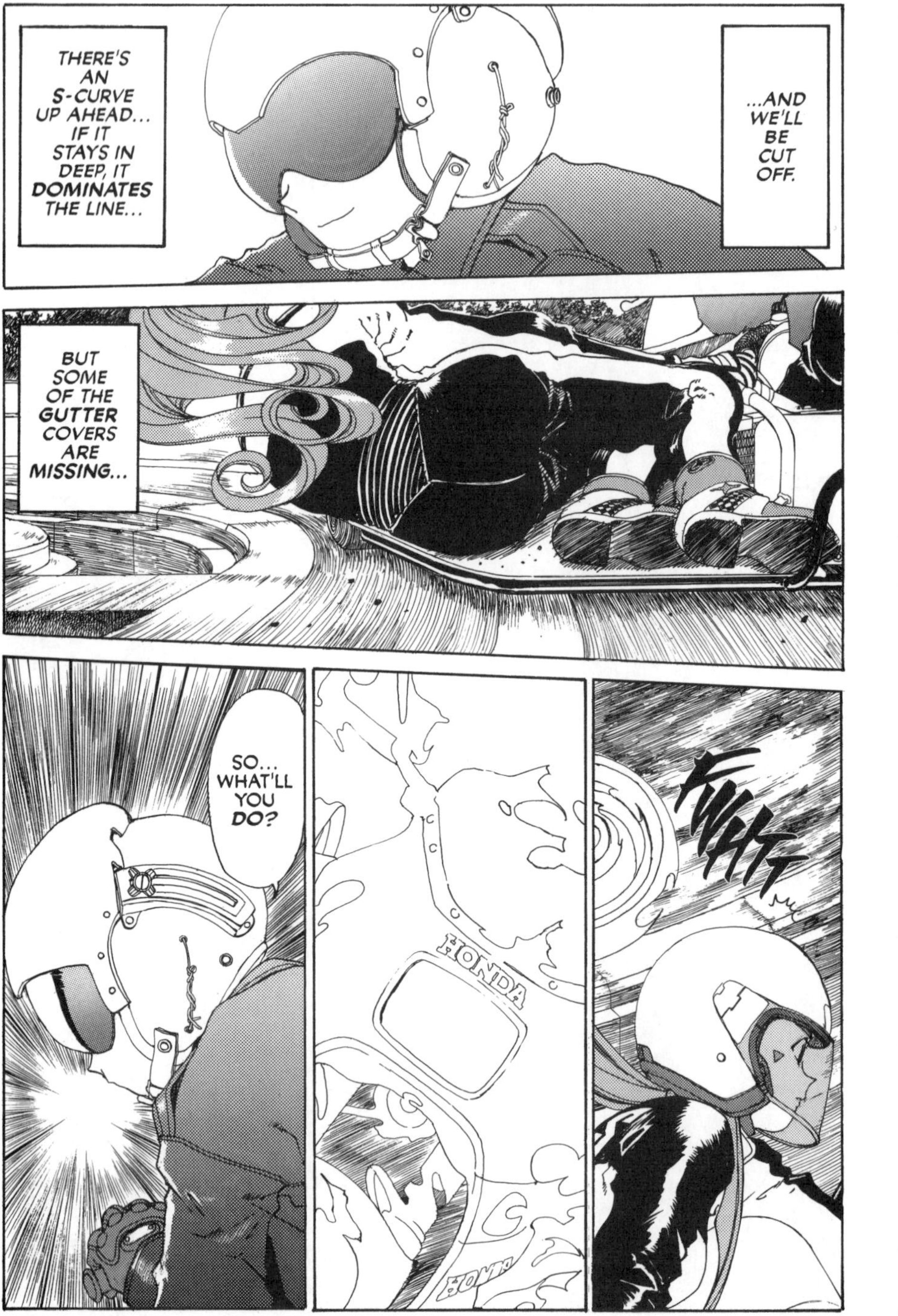
THERE'S AN S-CURVE UP AHEAD... IF IT STAYS IN DEEP, IT DOMINATES THE LINE...
...AND WE'LL BE CUT OFF.
BUT SOME OF THE GUTTER COVERS ARE MISSING...
SO... WHAT'LL YOU DO?
HONDA
FWHTT
HONDA

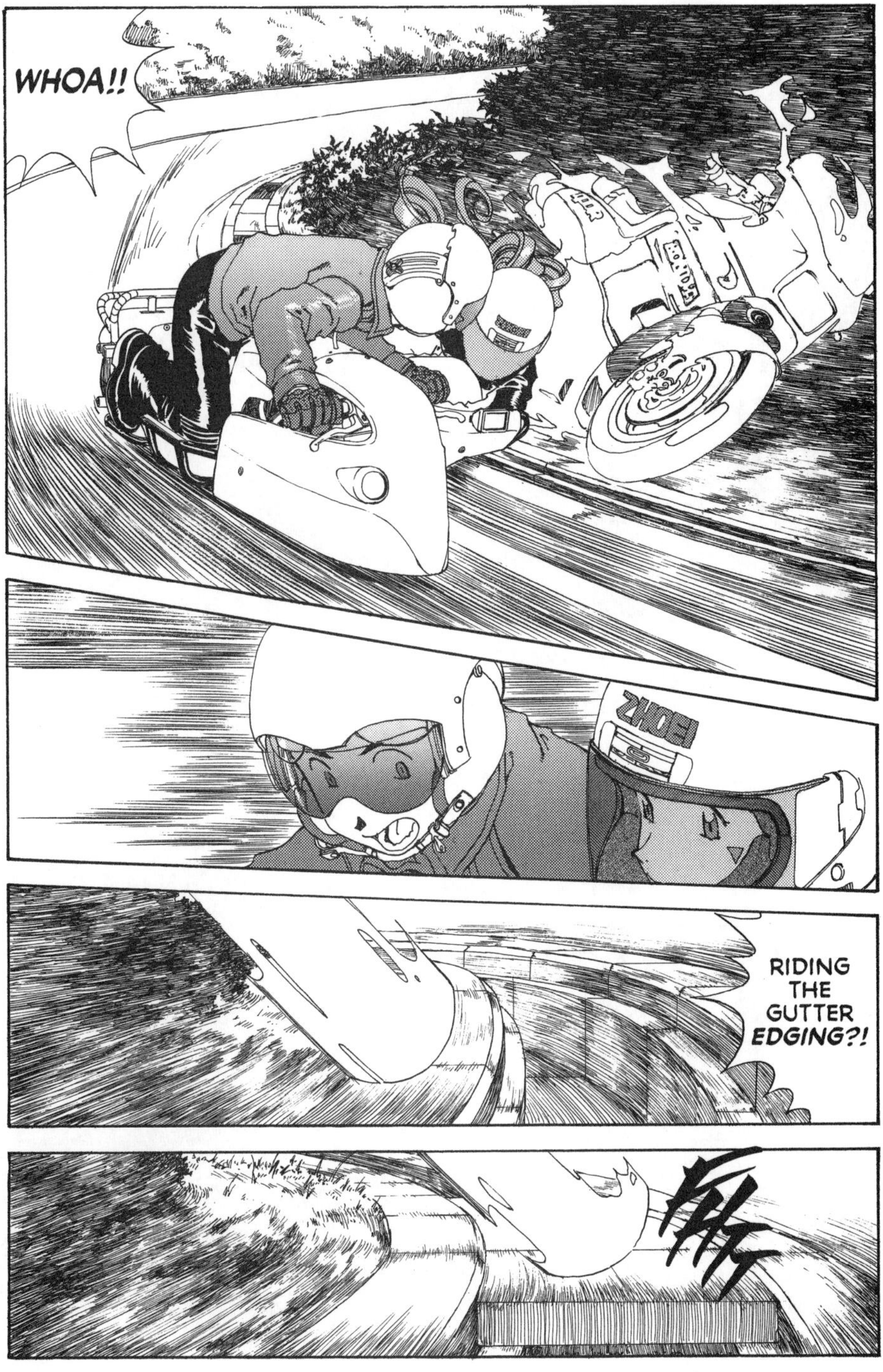
WHOA!!
RIDING THE GUTTER *EDGING?!*

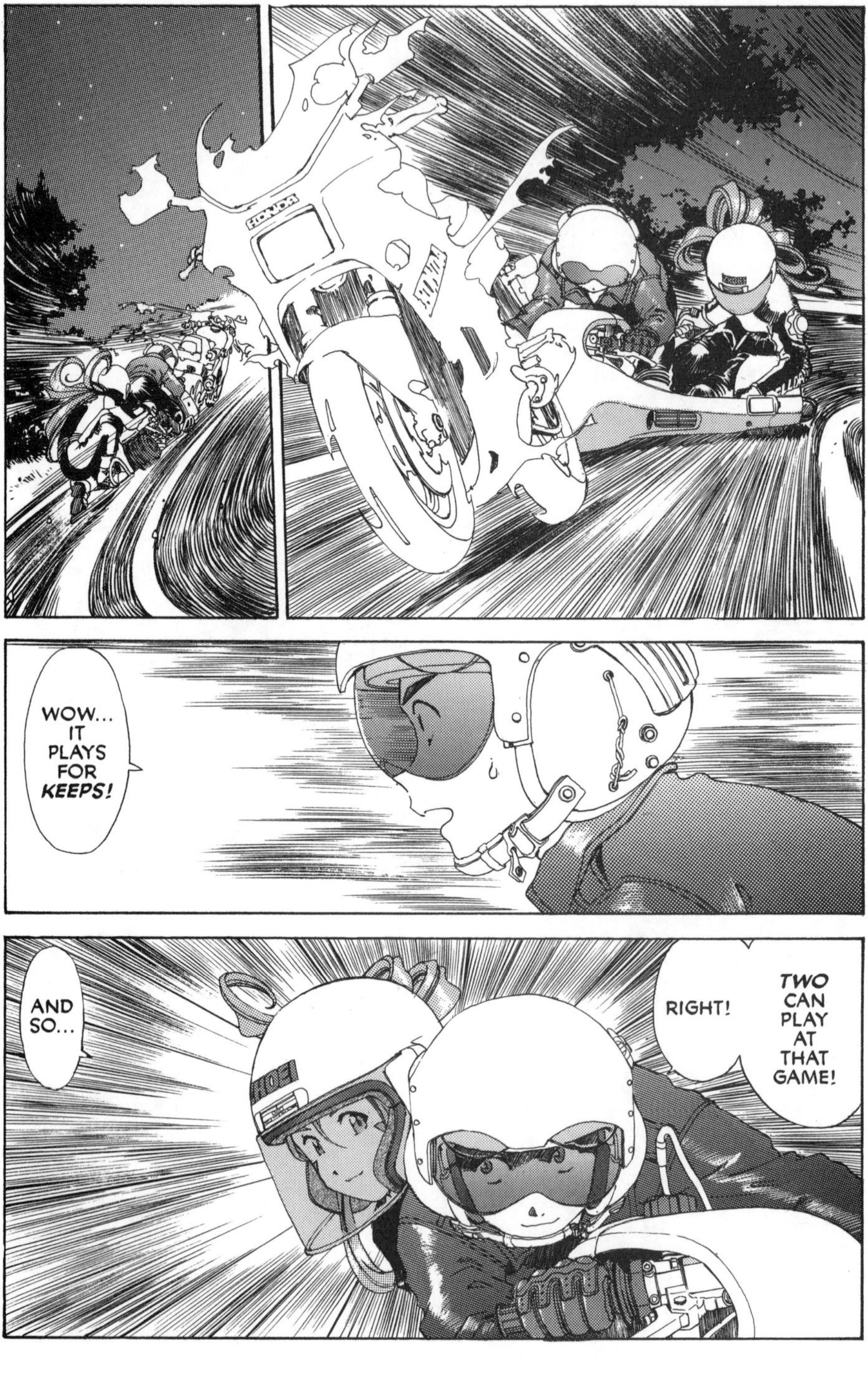
WOW... IT PLAYS FOR *KEEPS!*
AND SO...
RIGHT!
TWO CAN PLAY AT THAT GAME!

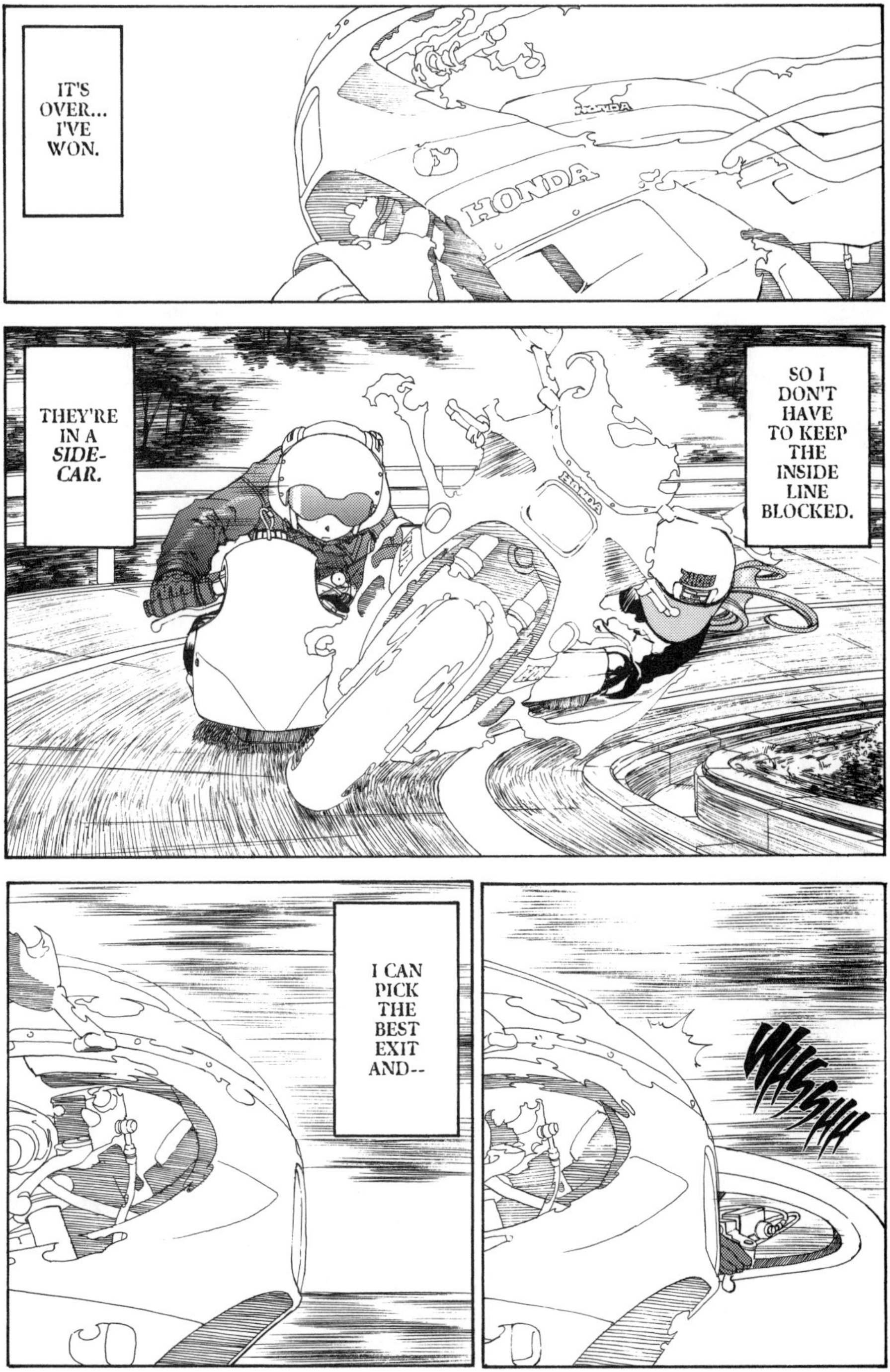
IT'S OVER... I'VE WON.
HONDA
THEY'RE IN A *SIDE-CAR.*
SO I DON'T HAVE TO KEEP THE INSIDE LINE BLOCKED.
I CAN PICK THE BEST EXIT AND--
WHSSHH

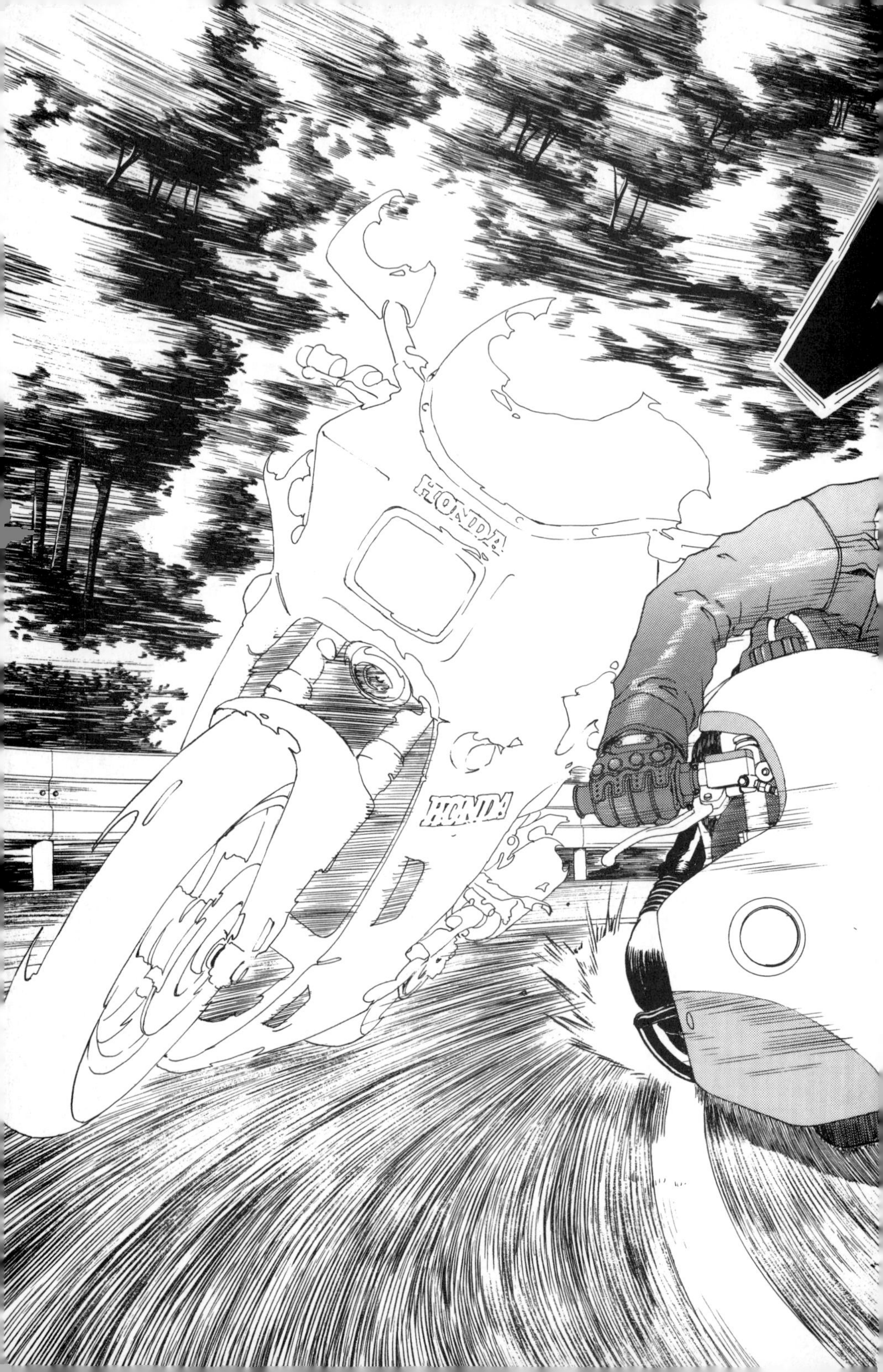
HONDA
HONDA

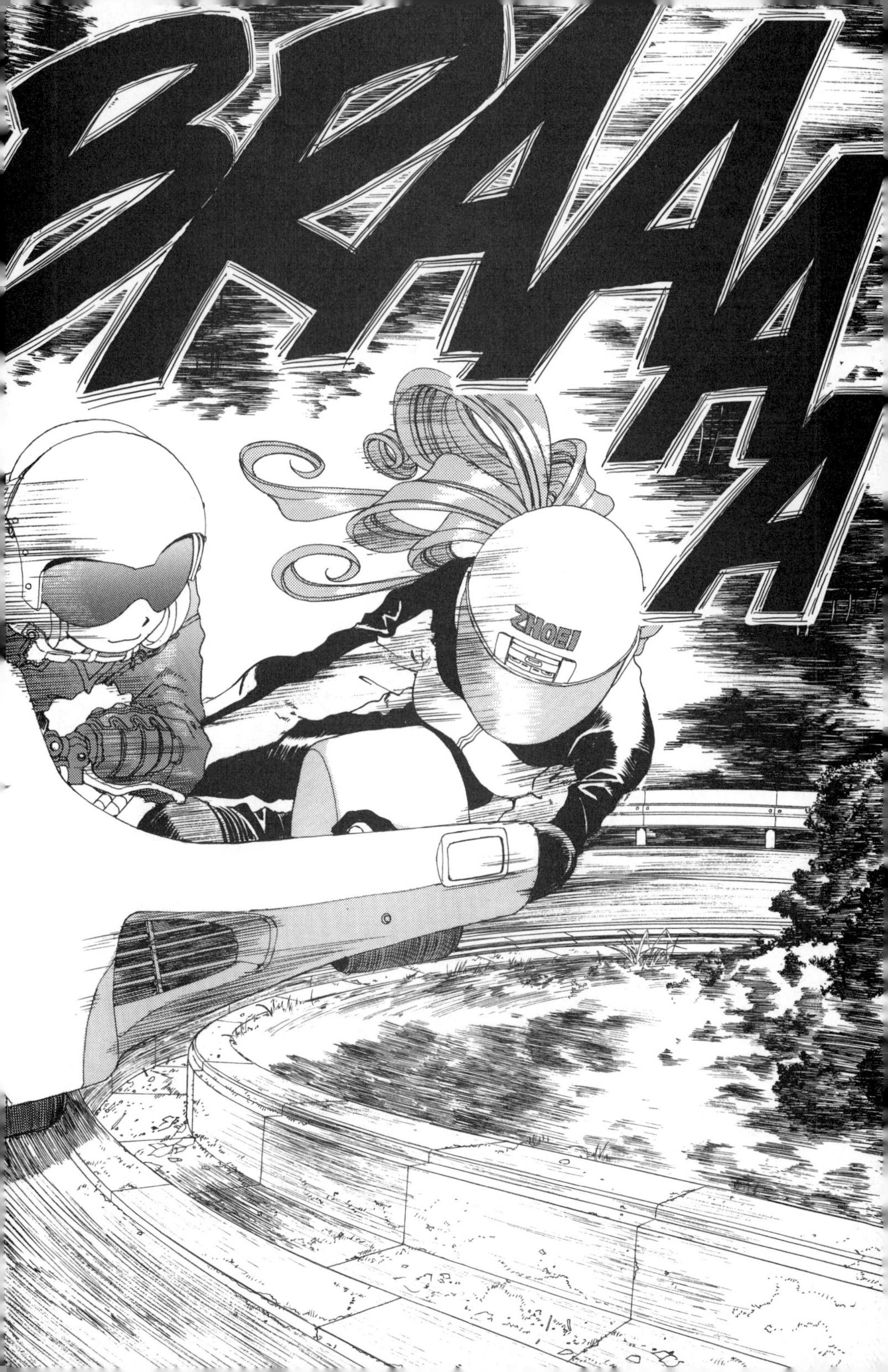

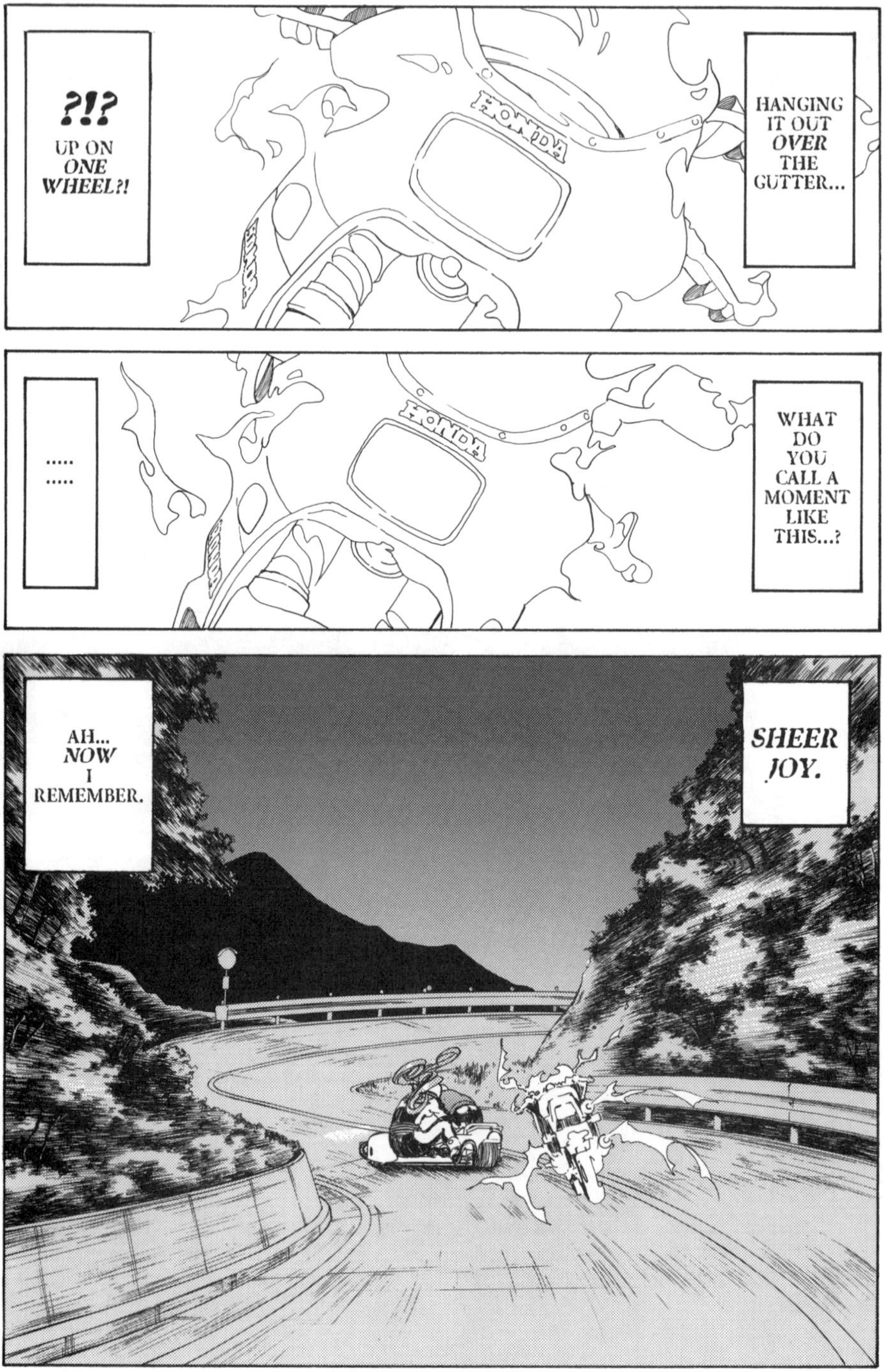
?!? UP ON *ONE* *WHEEL?!*
HANGING IT OUT *OVER* THE GUTTER...
.....
.....
WHAT DO YOU CALL A MOMENT LIKE THIS...?
AH... *NOW* I REMEMBER.
SHEER JOY.

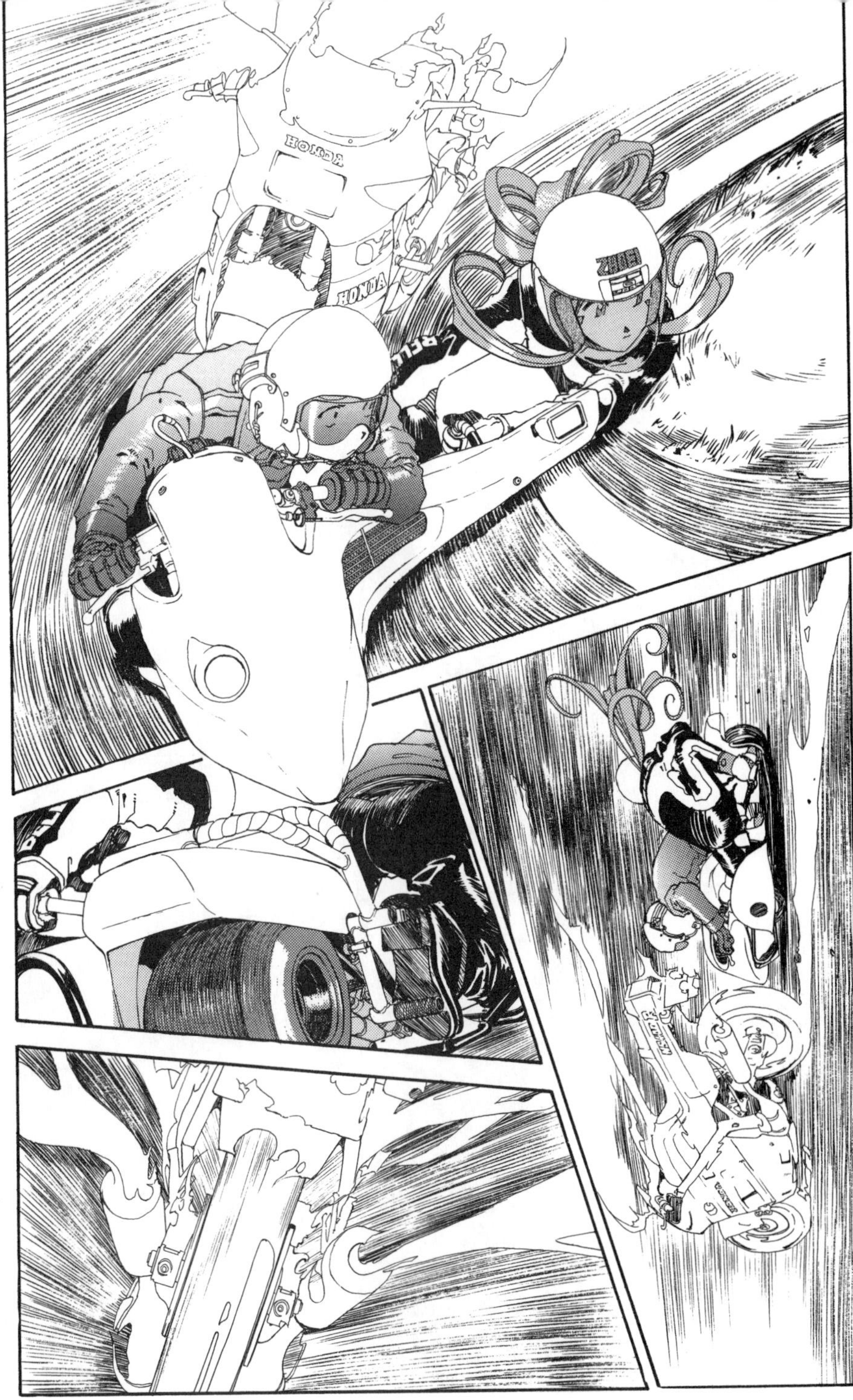
HONDA

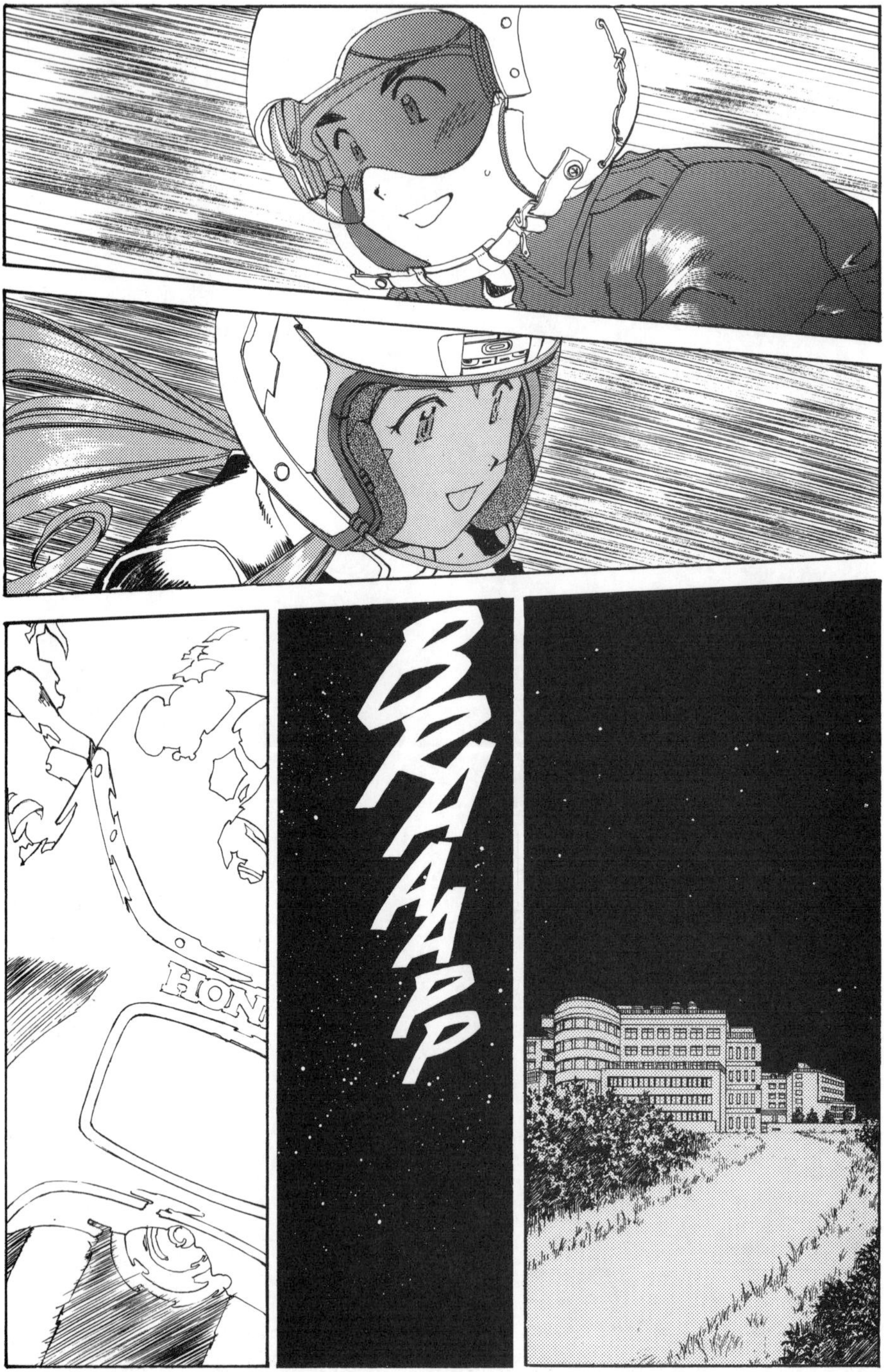
BRAAAPP

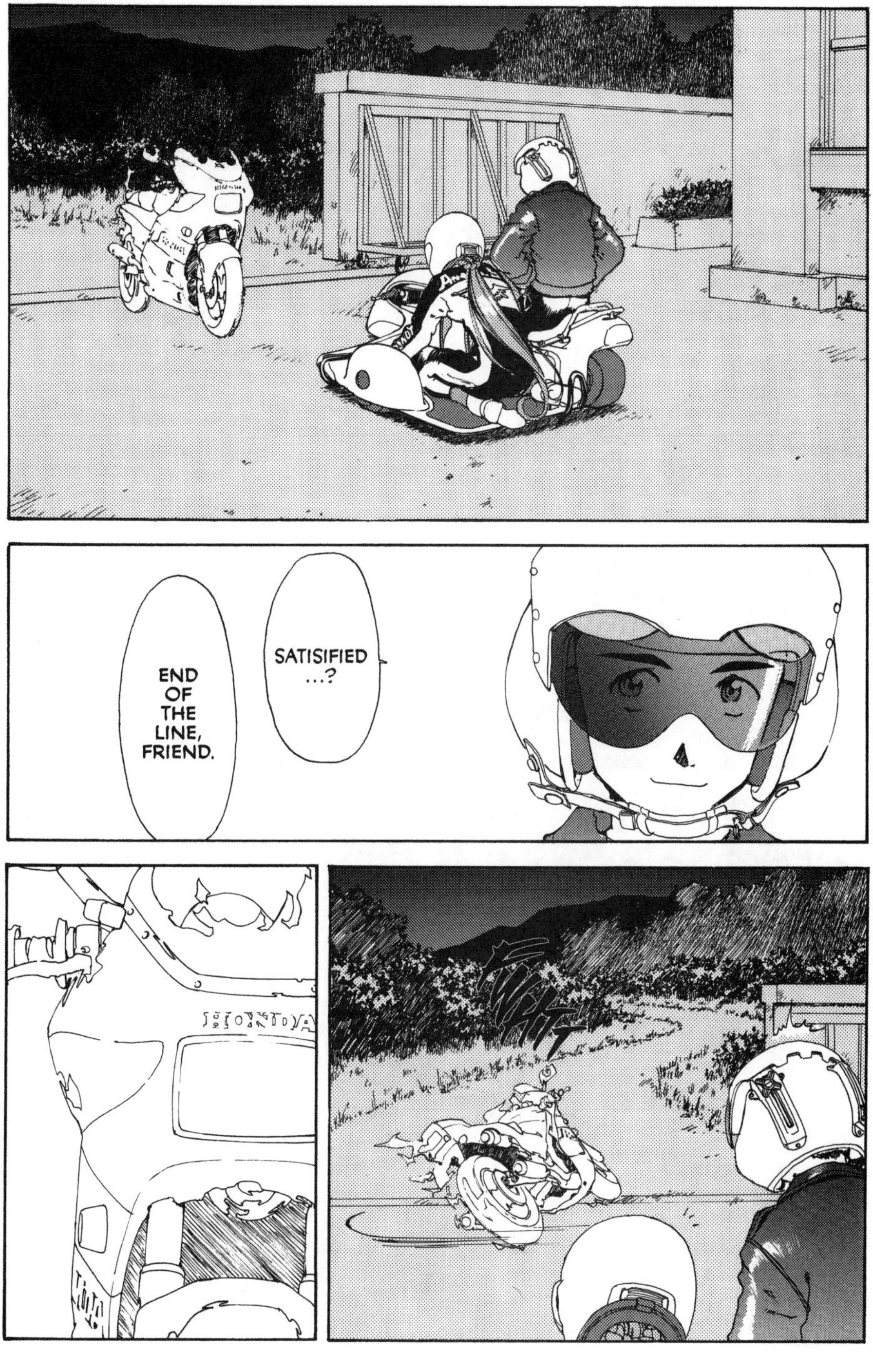
SATISIFIED …?
END OF THE LINE, FRIEND.
HONDA

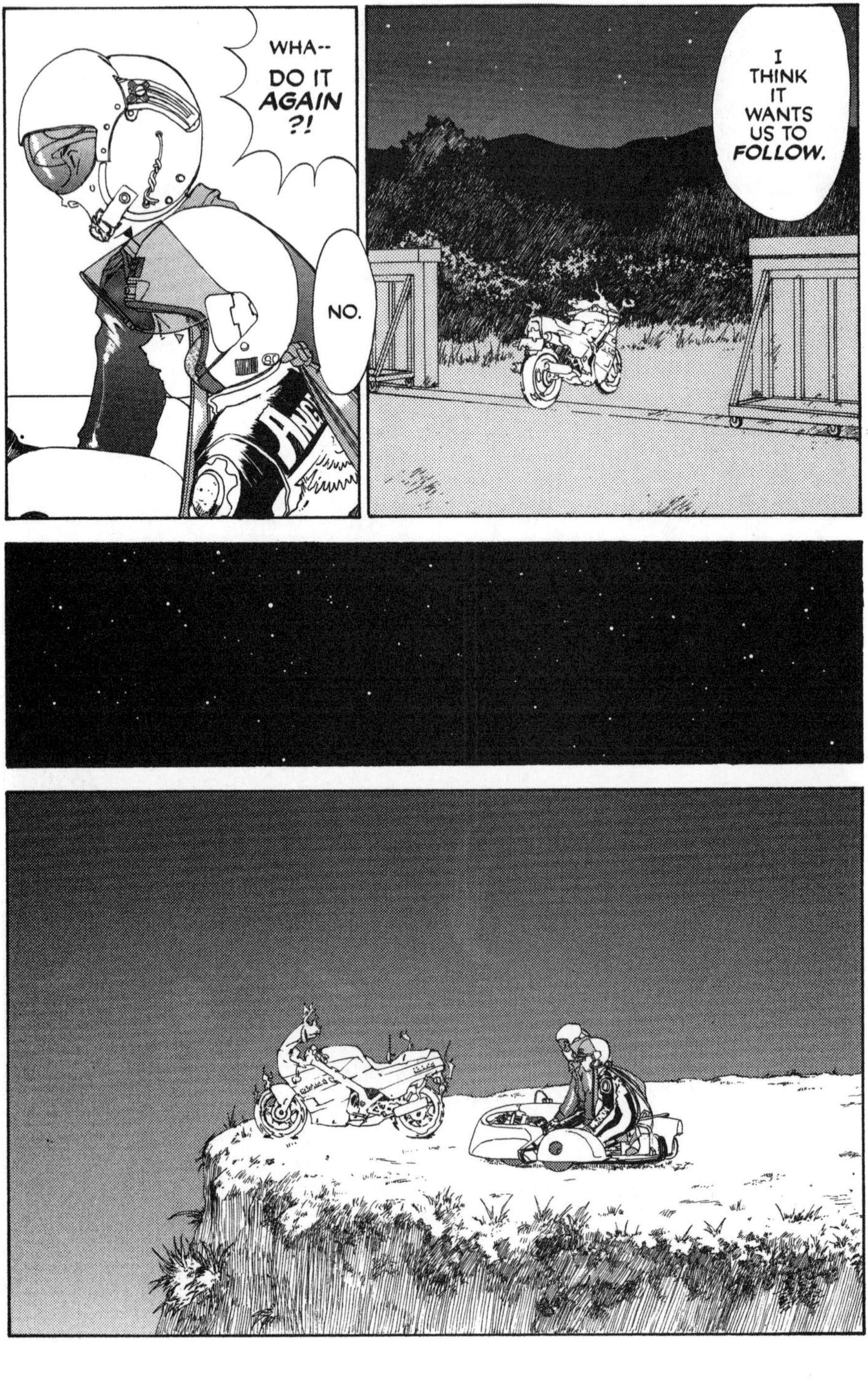
WHA-- DO IT AGAIN?!
NO.
I THINK IT WANTS US TO FOLLOW.

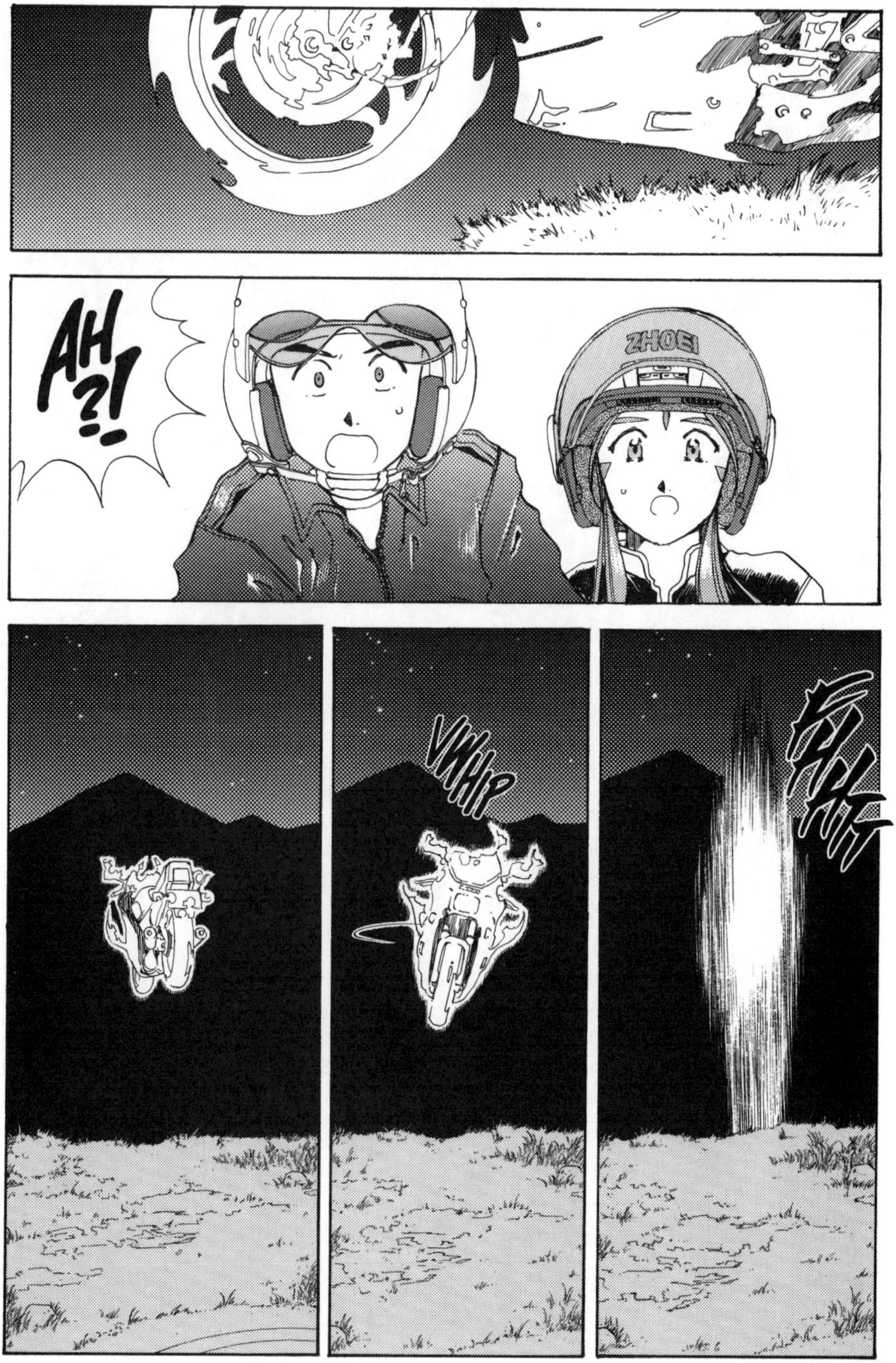
AH?!
VWHIP

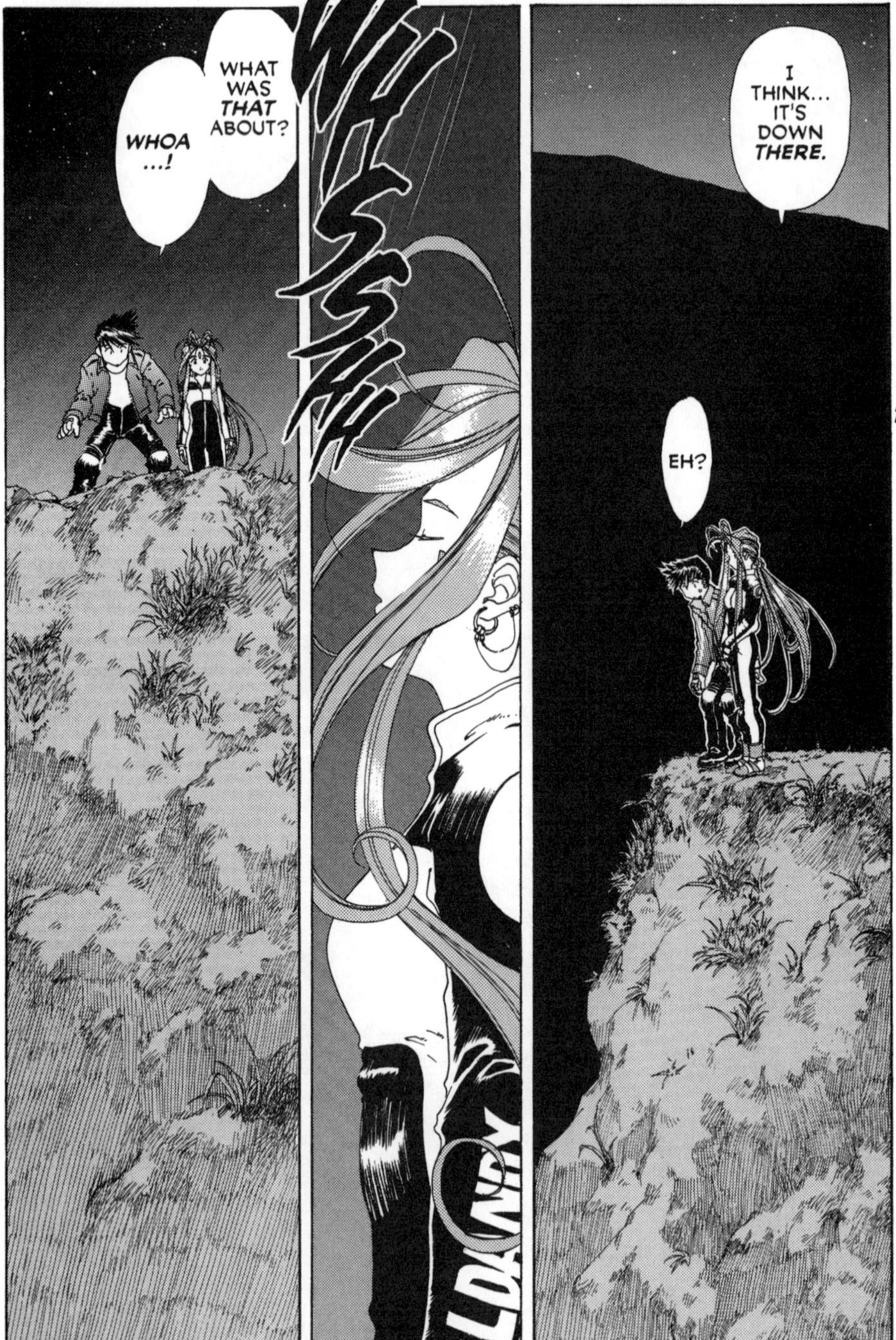
WHOA ...!
WHAT WAS THAT ABOUT?
WHSSHH
I THINK... IT'S DOWN THERE.
EH?

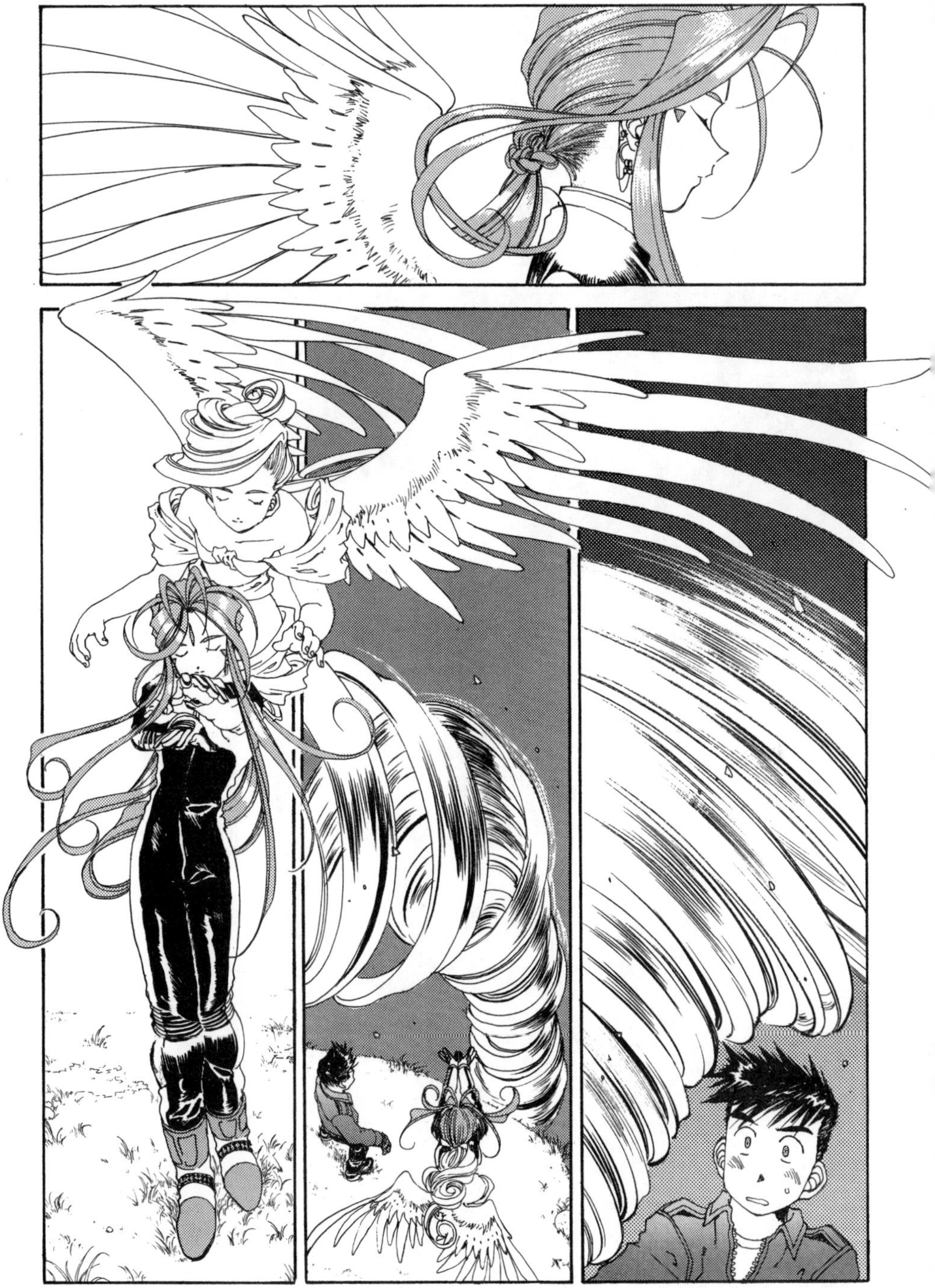

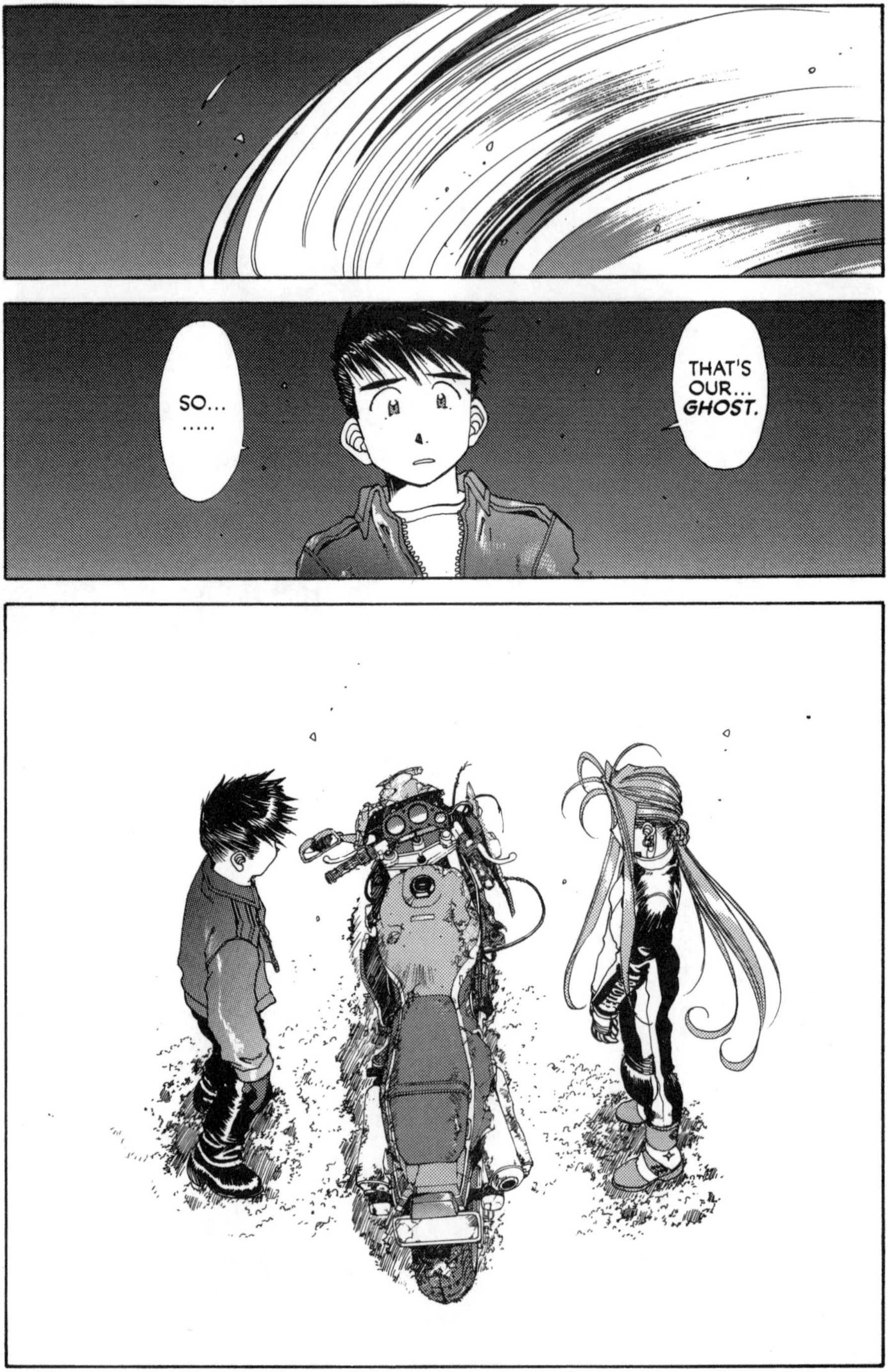
SO...
.....
THAT'S OUR... *GHOST.*

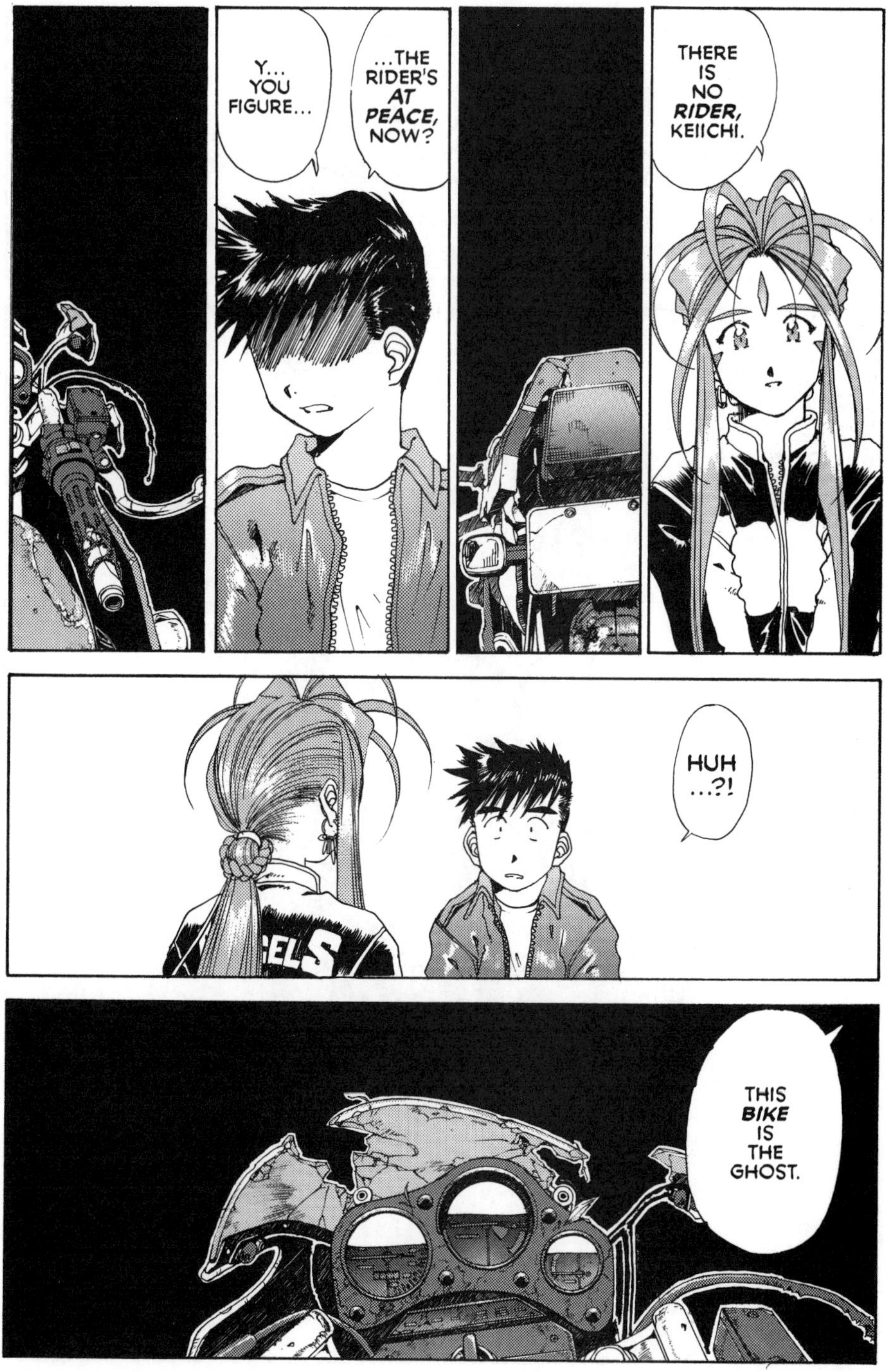
Y... YOU FIGURE...
...THE RIDER'S AT PEACE, NOW?
THERE IS NO RIDER, KEIICHI.
HUH ...?!
THIS BIKE IS THE GHOST.

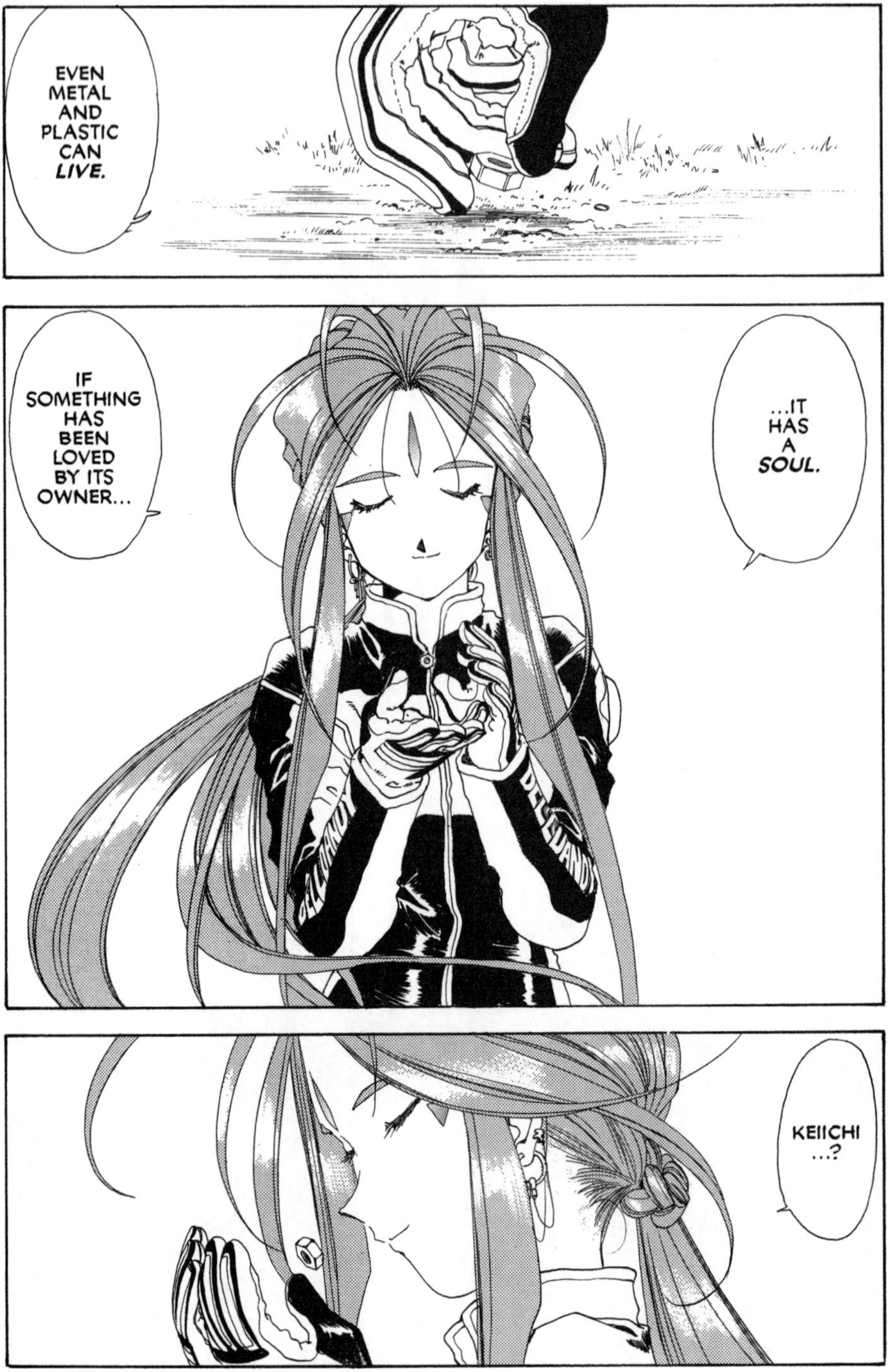
EVEN METAL AND PLASTIC CAN *LIVE.*
IF SOMETHING HAS BEEN LOVED BY ITS OWNER...
...IT HAS A *SOUL.*
KEIICHI ...?

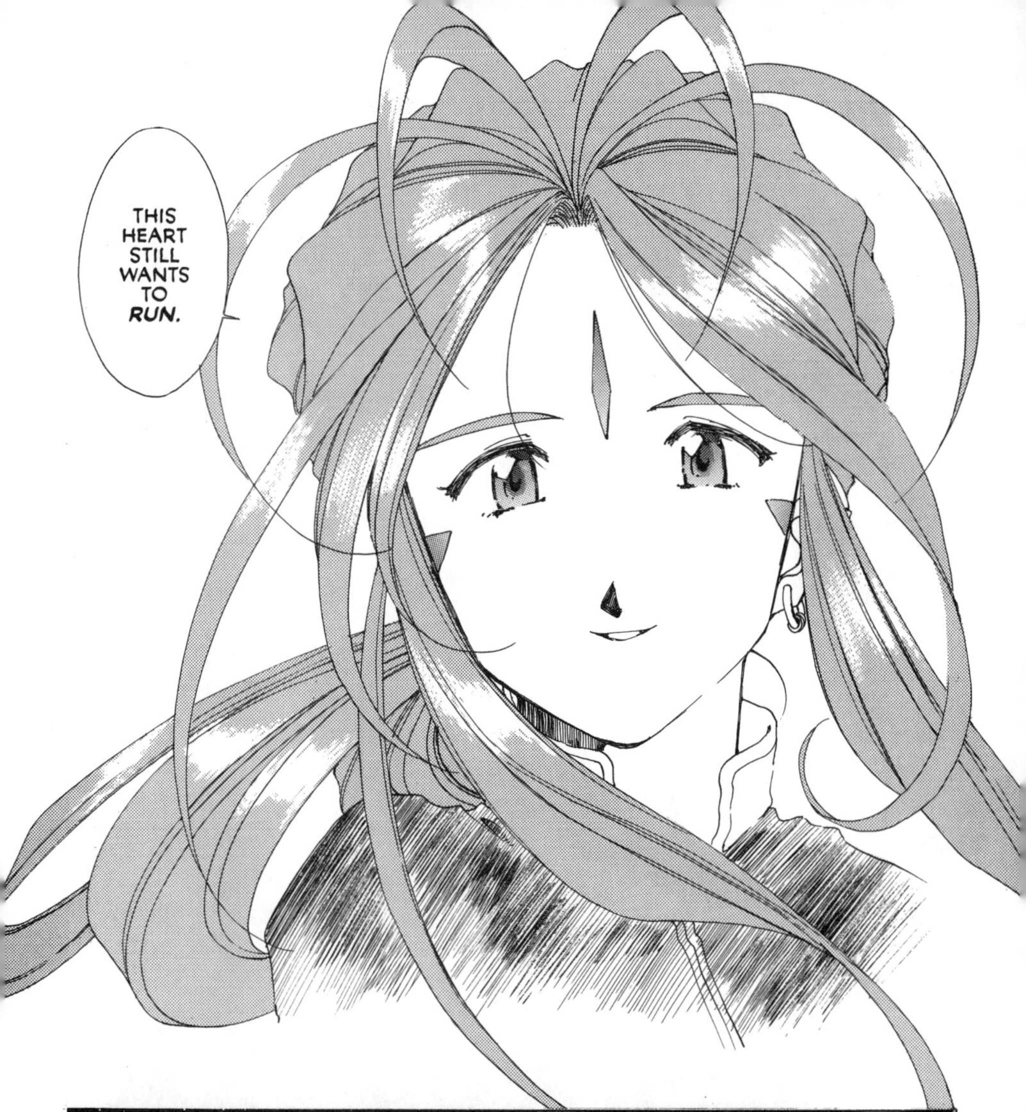
THIS HEART STILL WANTS TO *RUN.*

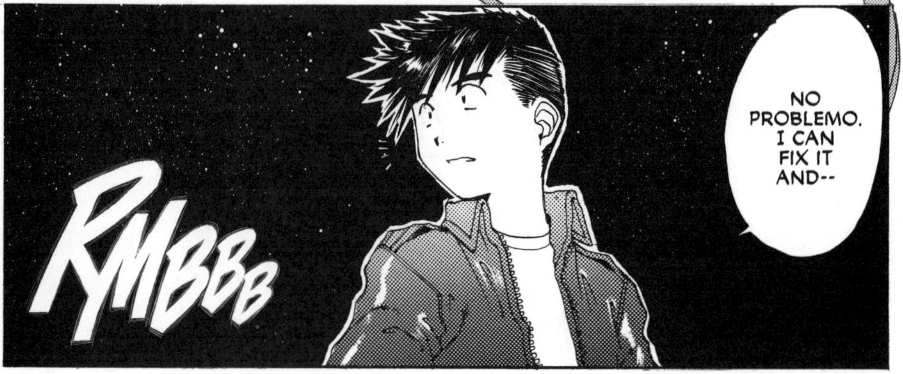
RMBBB
NO PROBLEMO. I CAN FIX IT AND--

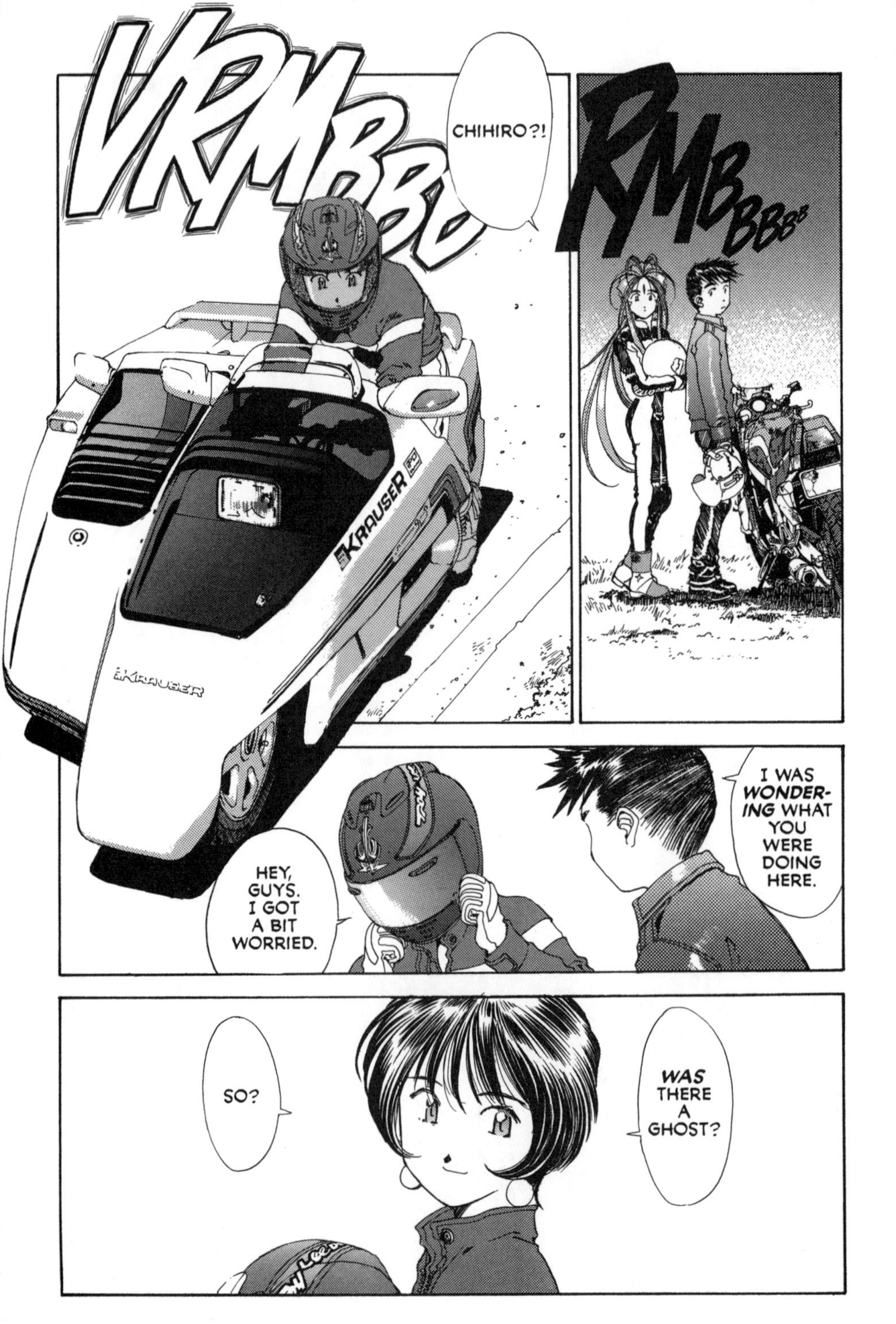
CHIHIRO?!
HEY, GUYS. I GOT A BIT WORRIED.
I WAS *WONDERING* WHAT YOU WERE DOING HERE.
SO?
WAS THERE A GHOST?

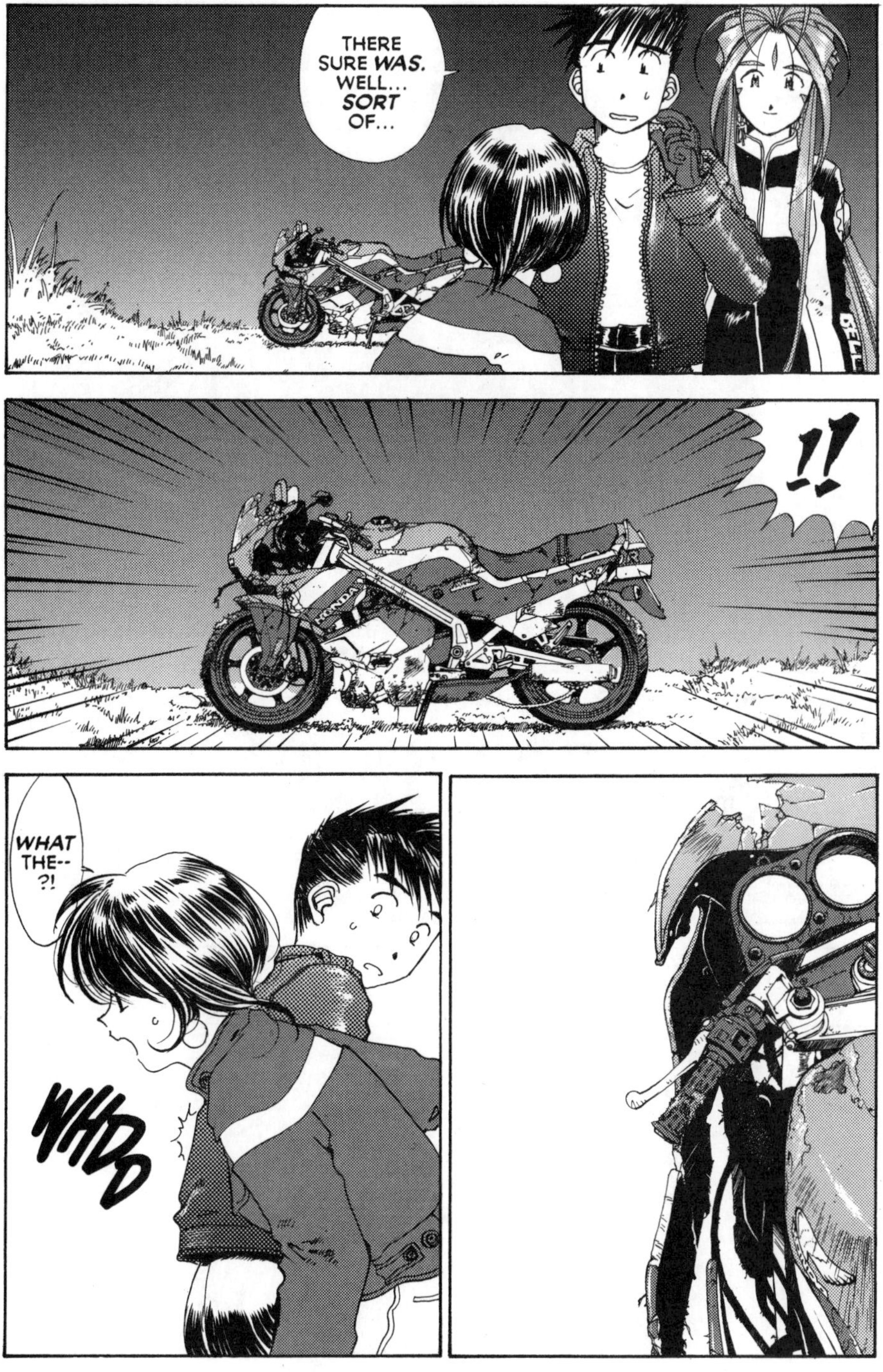
THERE SURE WAS. WELL... SORT OF...
!!
WHAT THE-- ?!
WHUD

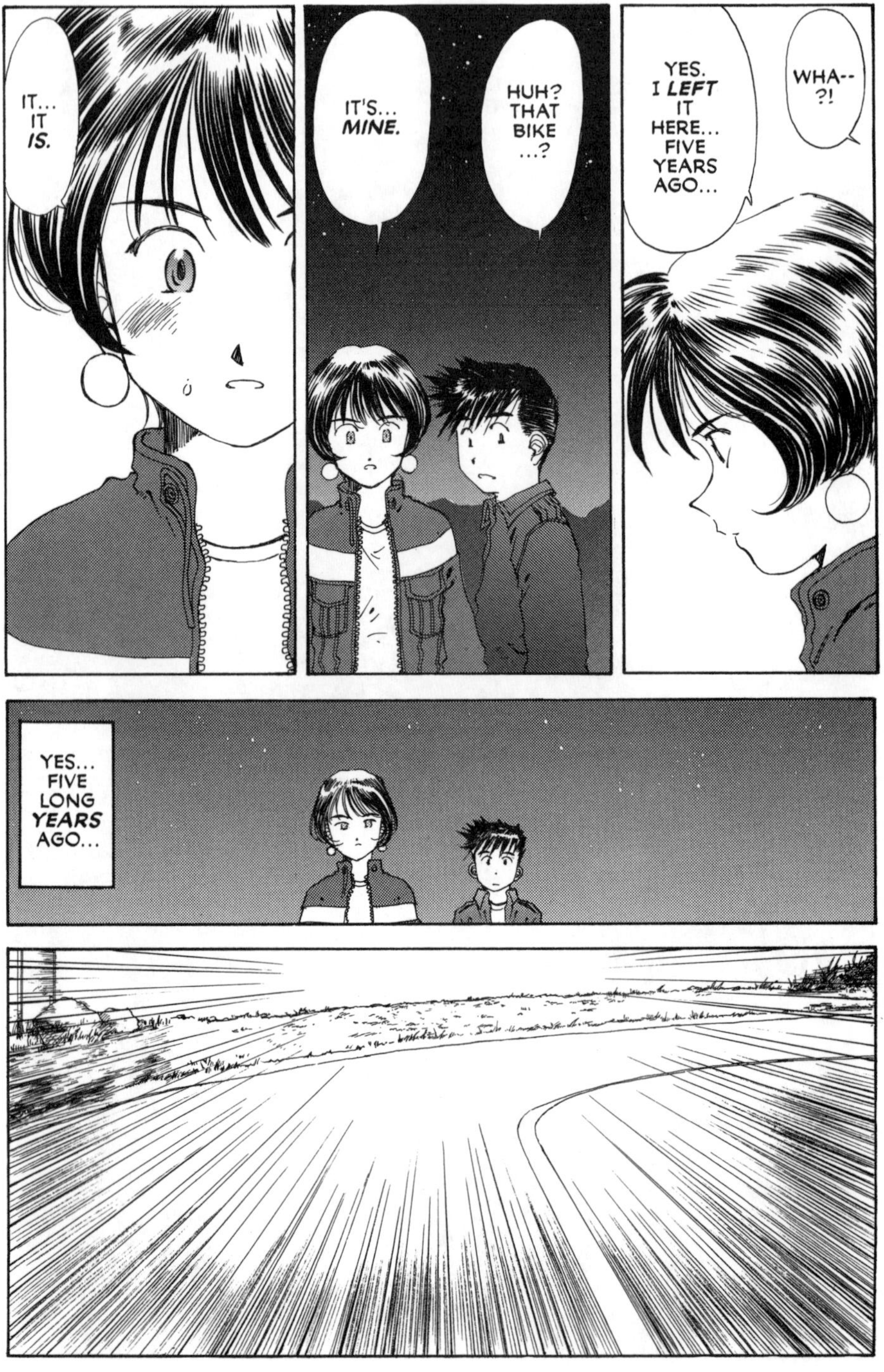
IT... IT *IS.*
IT'S... ***MINE.***
HUH? THAT BIKE ...?
YES. I ***LEFT*** IT HERE... FIVE YEARS AGO...
WHA-- ?!
YES... FIVE LONG ***YEARS*** AGO...

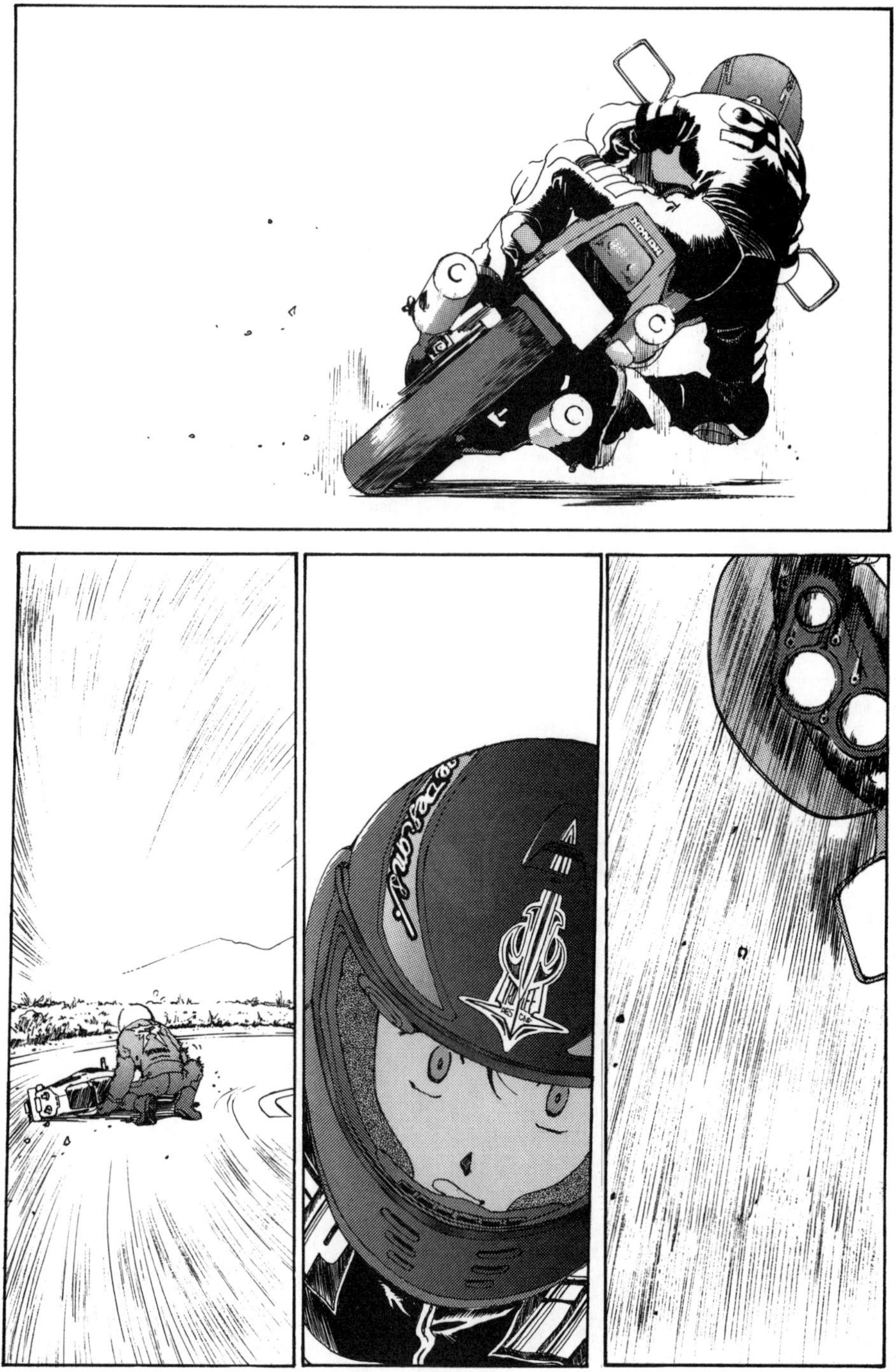

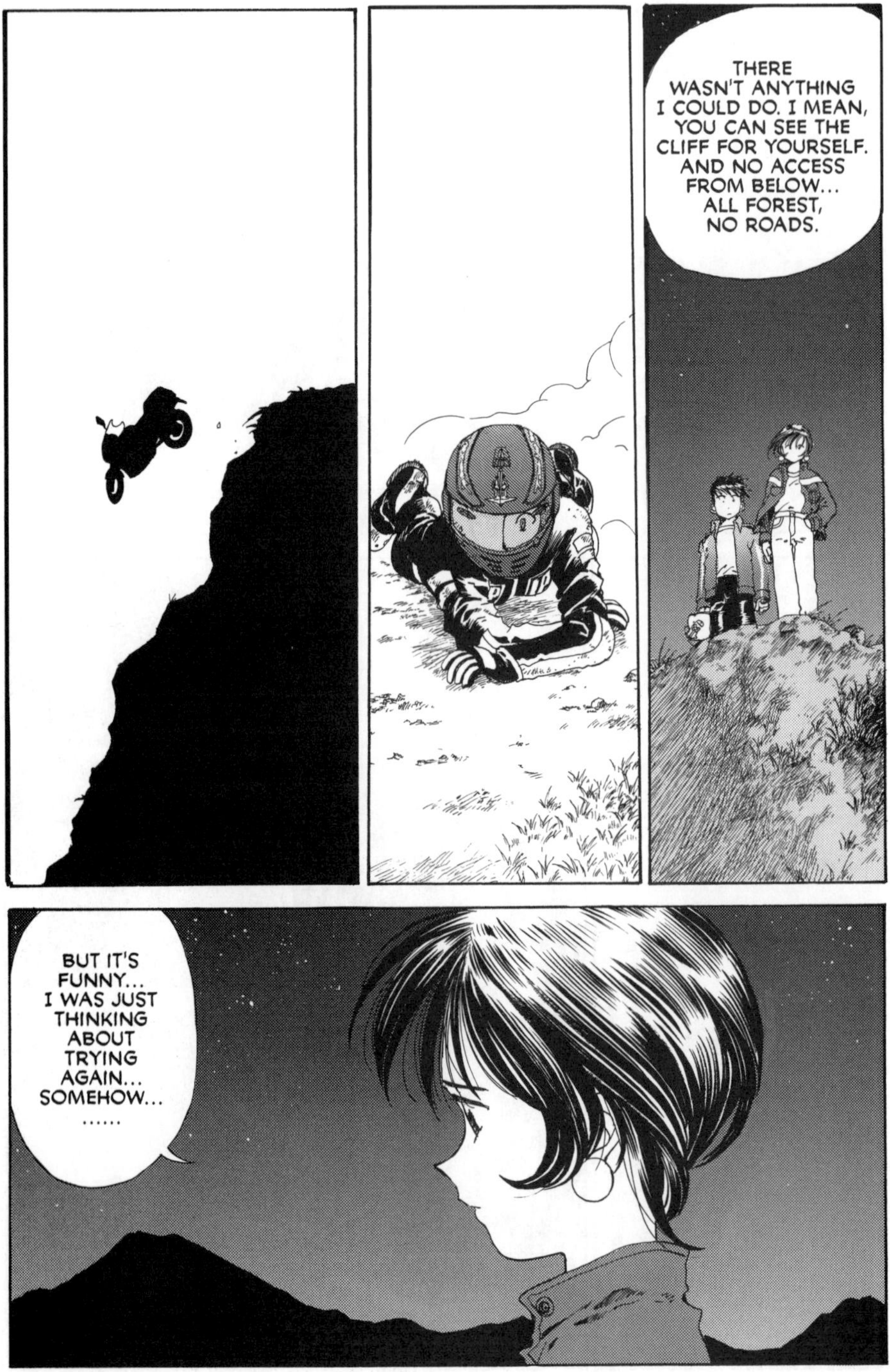
THERE WASN'T ANYTHING I COULD DO. I MEAN, YOU CAN SEE THE CLIFF FOR YOURSELF. AND NO ACCESS FROM BELOW... ALL FOREST, NO ROADS.
BUT IT'S FUNNY... I WAS JUST THINKING ABOUT TRYING AGAIN... SOMEHOW... ......

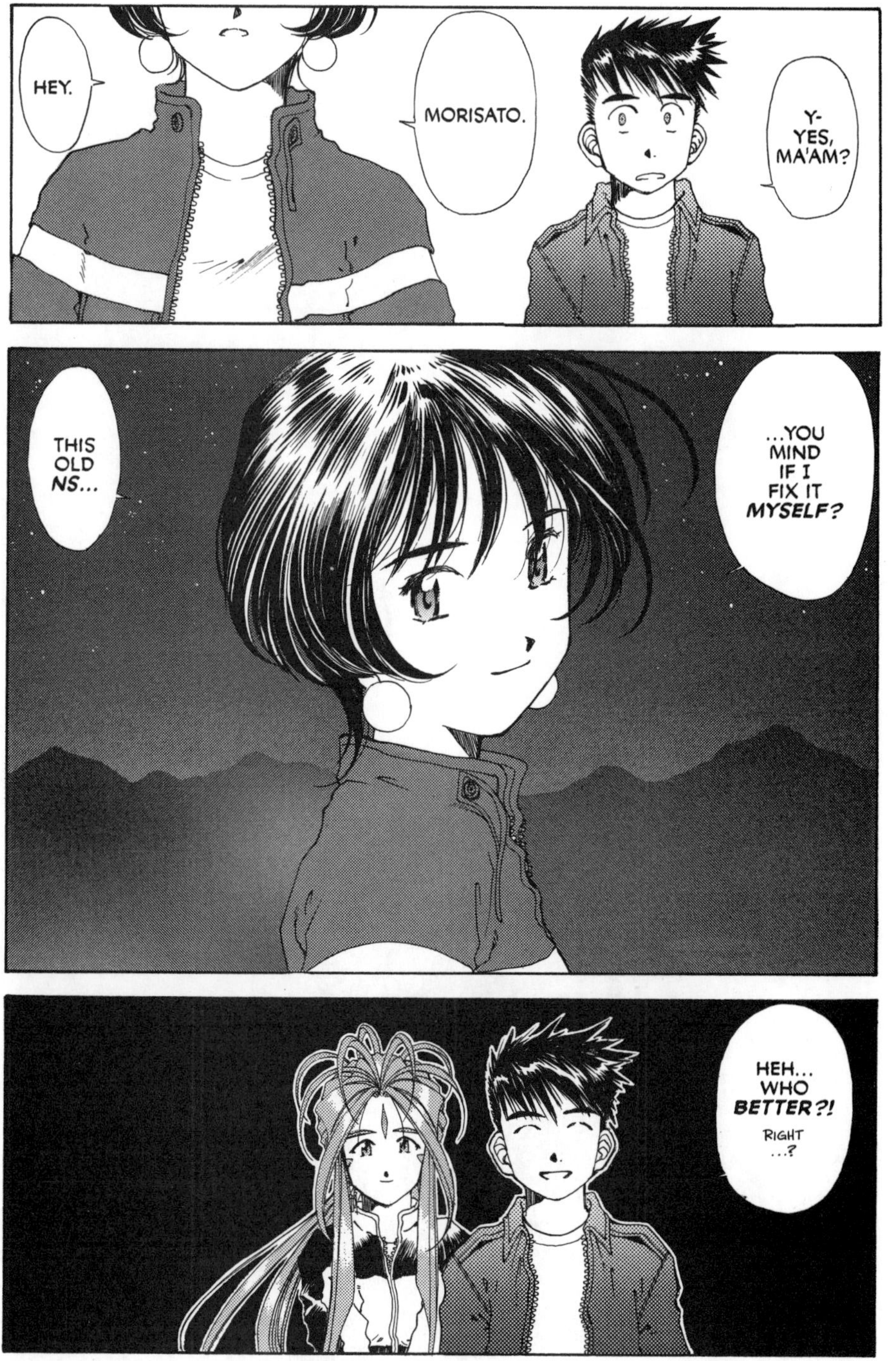
HEY.
MORISATO.
Y-YES, MA'AM?
THIS OLD *NS*...
...YOU MIND IF I FIX IT *MYSELF?*
HEH... WHO *BETTER?!*
RIGHT ...?

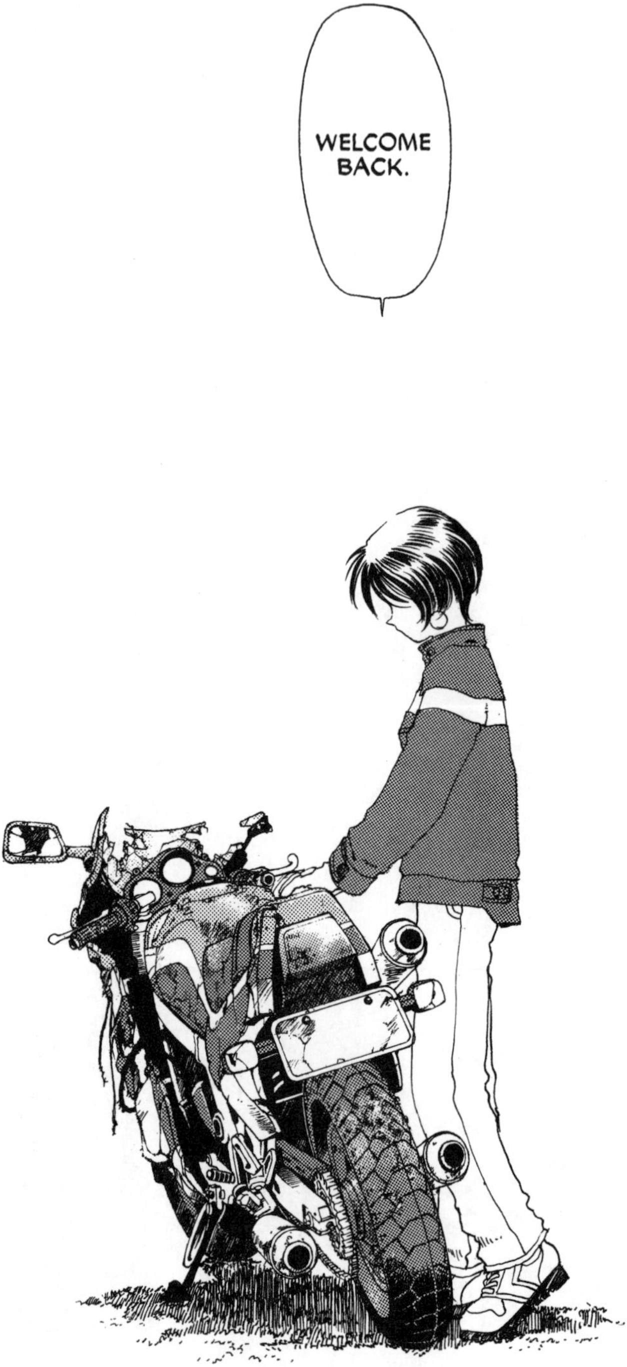
WELCOME BACK.

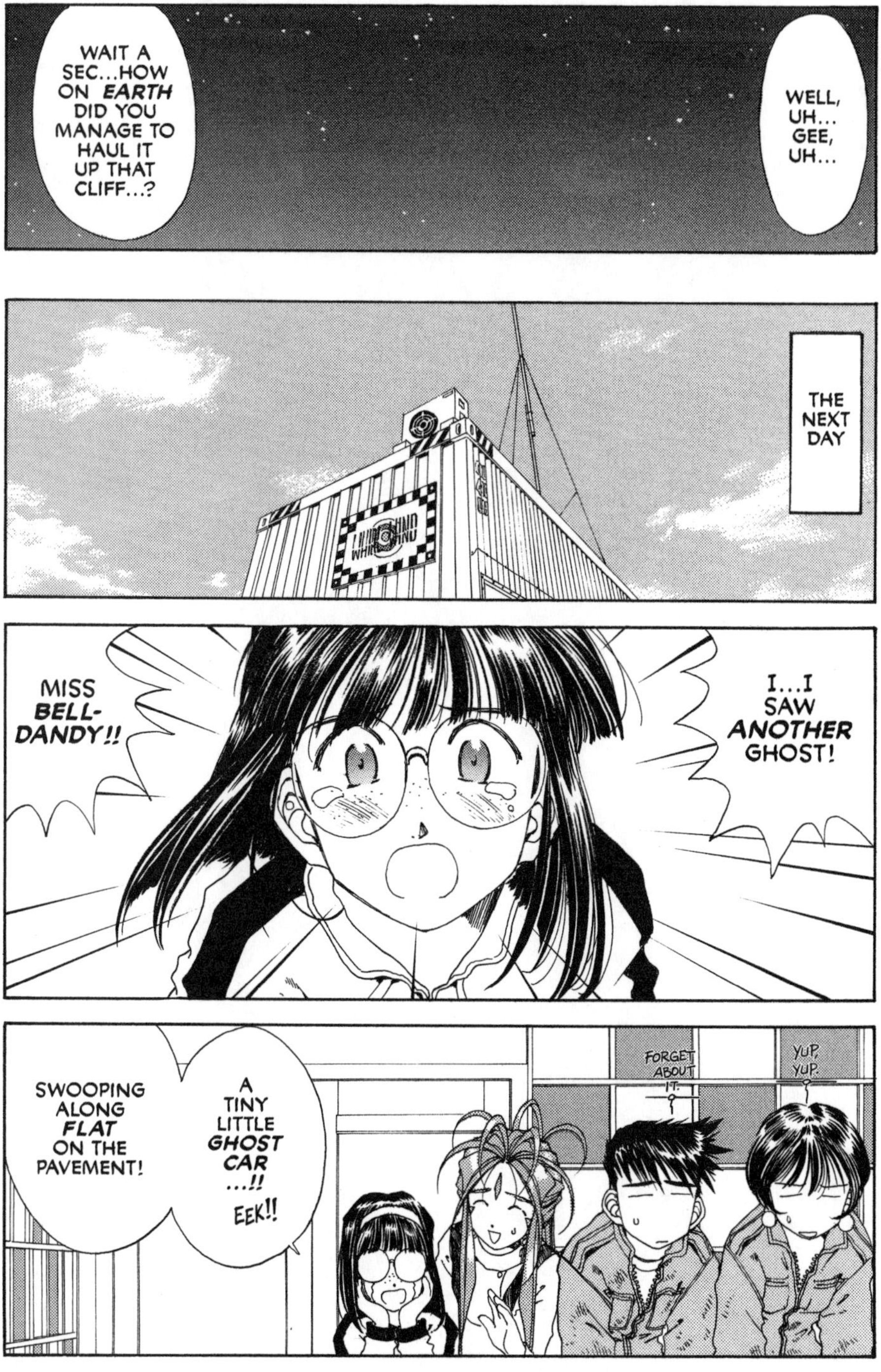
WAIT A SEC...HOW ON EARTH DID YOU MANAGE TO HAUL IT UP THAT CLIFF...?
WELL, UH... GEE, UH...
THE NEXT DAY
MISS BELL-DANDY!!
I...I SAW ANOTHER GHOST!
SWOOPING ALONG FLAT ON THE PAVEMENT!
A TINY LITTLE GHOST CAR ...!!
EEK!!
FORGET ABOUT IT.
YUP, YUP.

MEET DOCTOR MOREAU

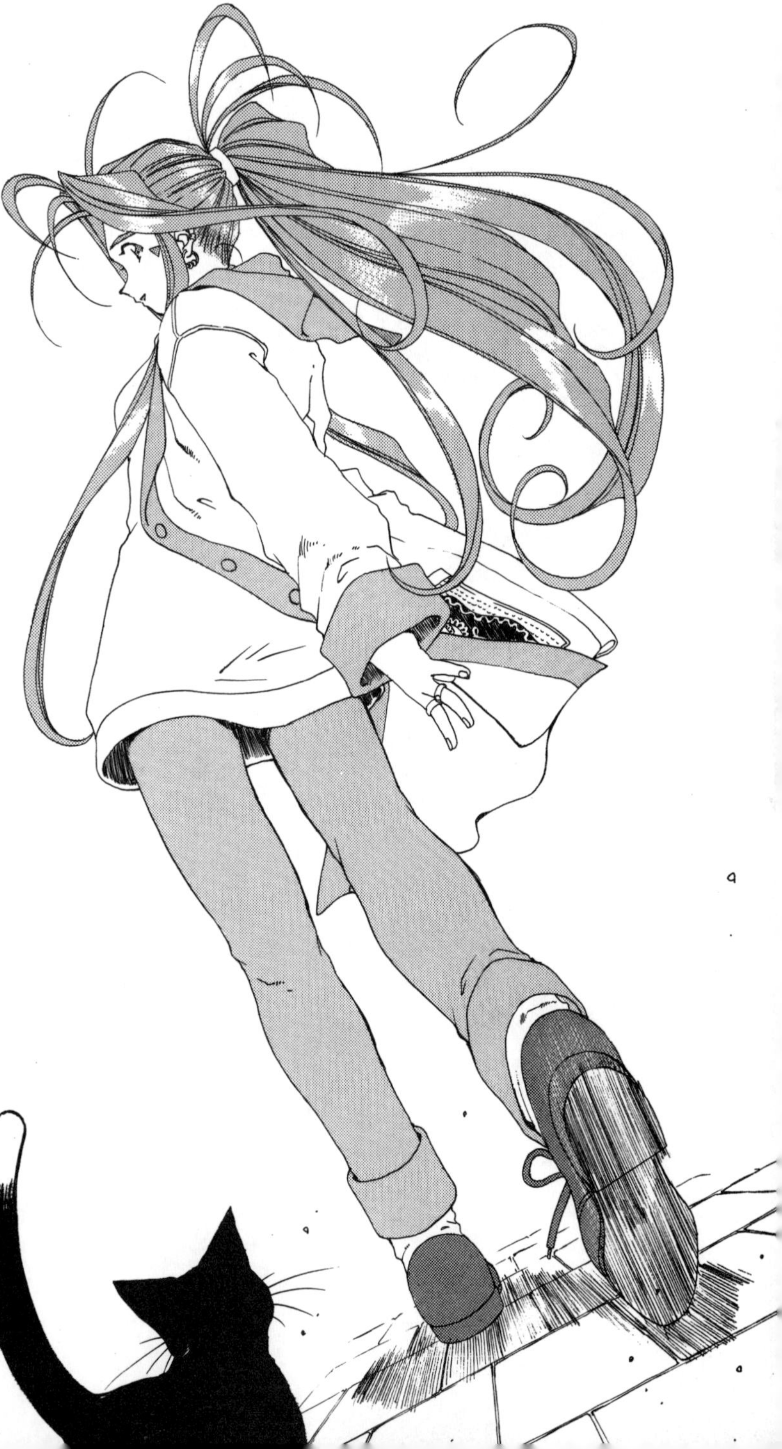

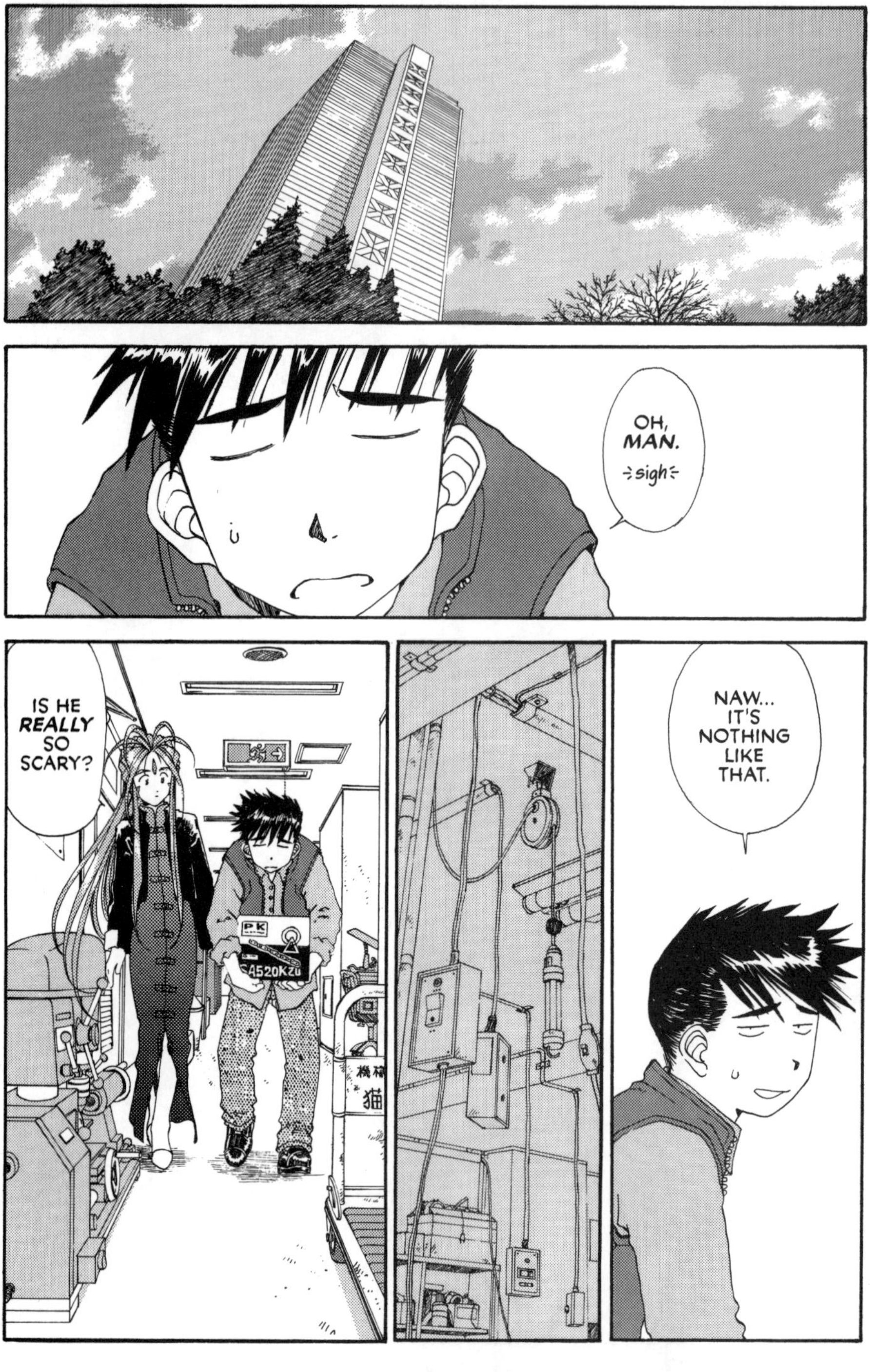
OH, MAN.
sigh
IS HE REALLY SO SCARY?
NAW... IT'S NOTHING LIKE THAT.

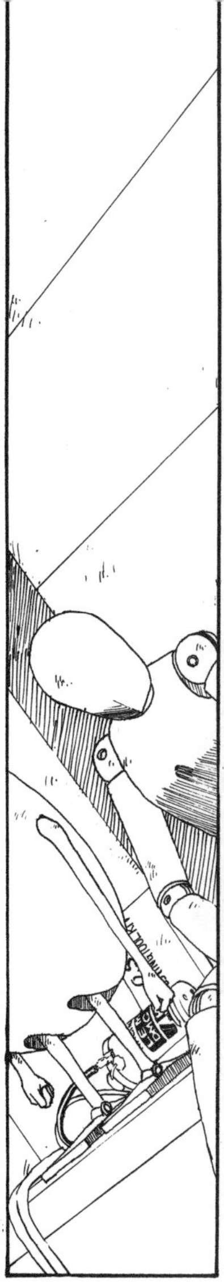
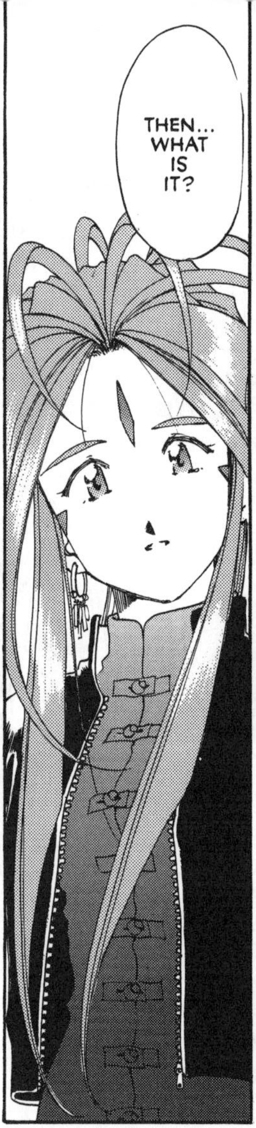
THEN... WHAT IS IT?
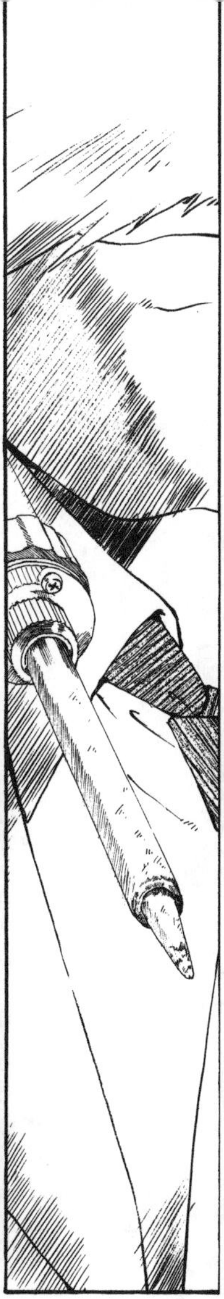
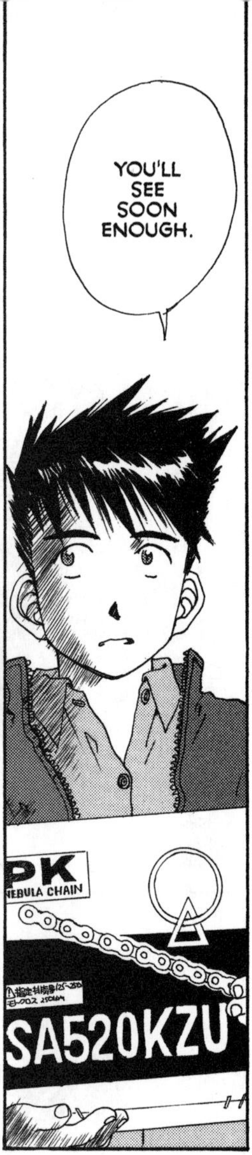
YOU'LL SEE SOON ENOUGH.
PK
NEBULA CHAIN
SA520KZU
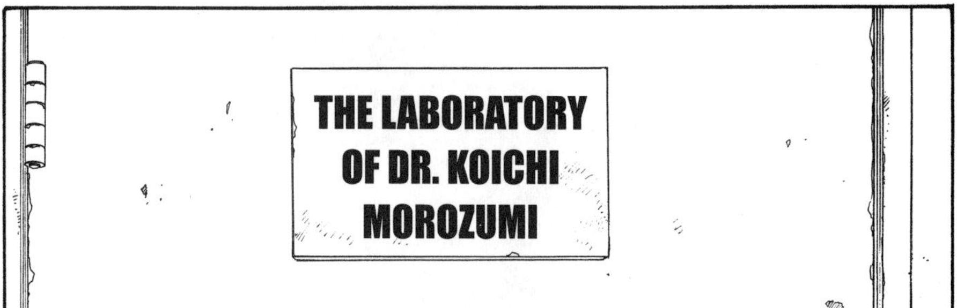
THE LABORATORY OF DR. KOICHI MOROZUMI

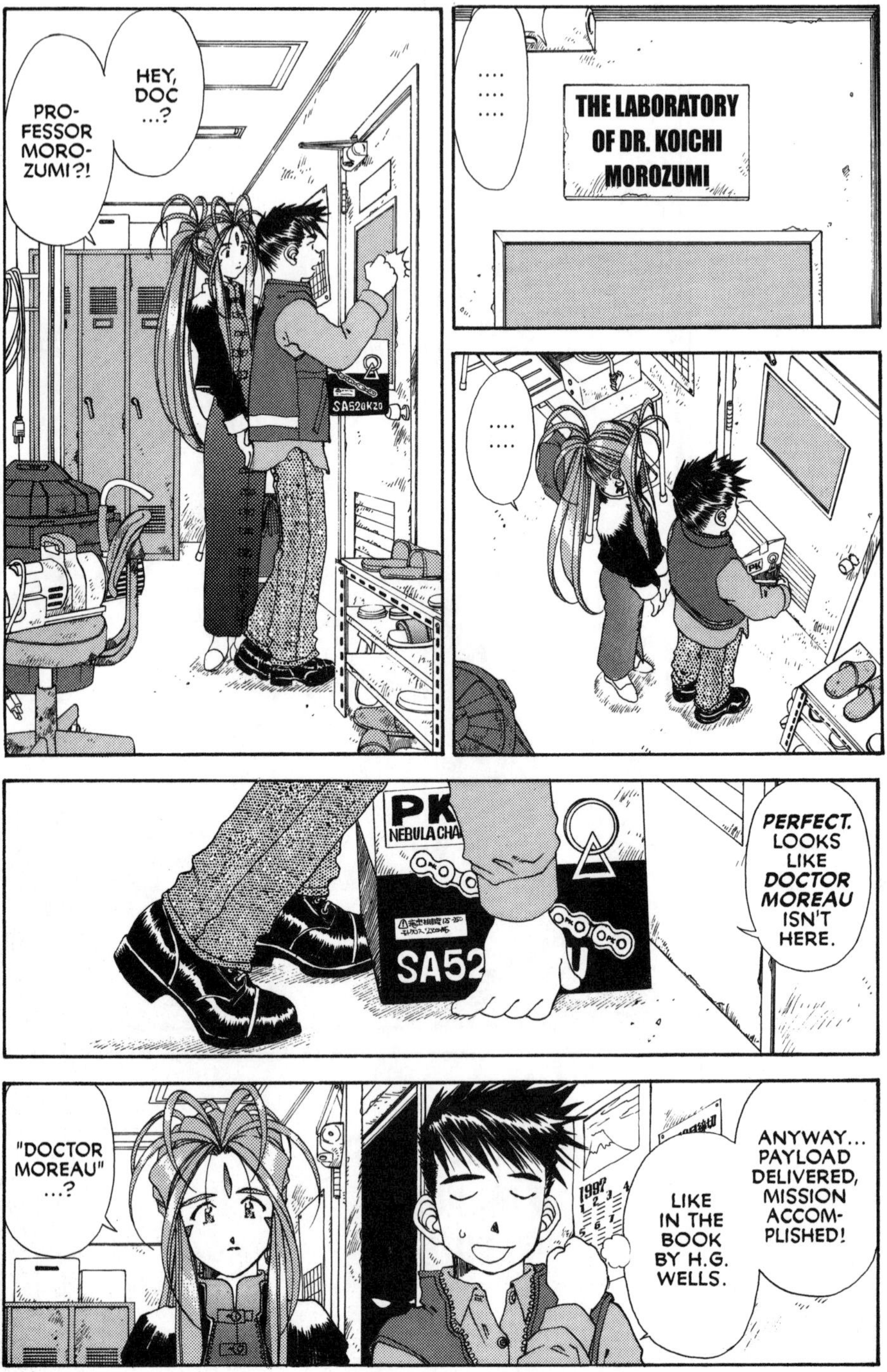
HEY, DOC ...?
PRO-FESSOR MORO-ZUMI?!
....
....
....
THE LABORATORY OF DR. KOICHI MOROZUMI
....
....
PERFECT. LOOKS LIKE DOCTOR MOREAU ISN'T HERE.
"DOCTOR MOREAU" ...?
ANYWAY... PAYLOAD DELIVERED, MISSION ACCOM-PLISHED!
LIKE IN THE BOOK BY H.G. WELLS.

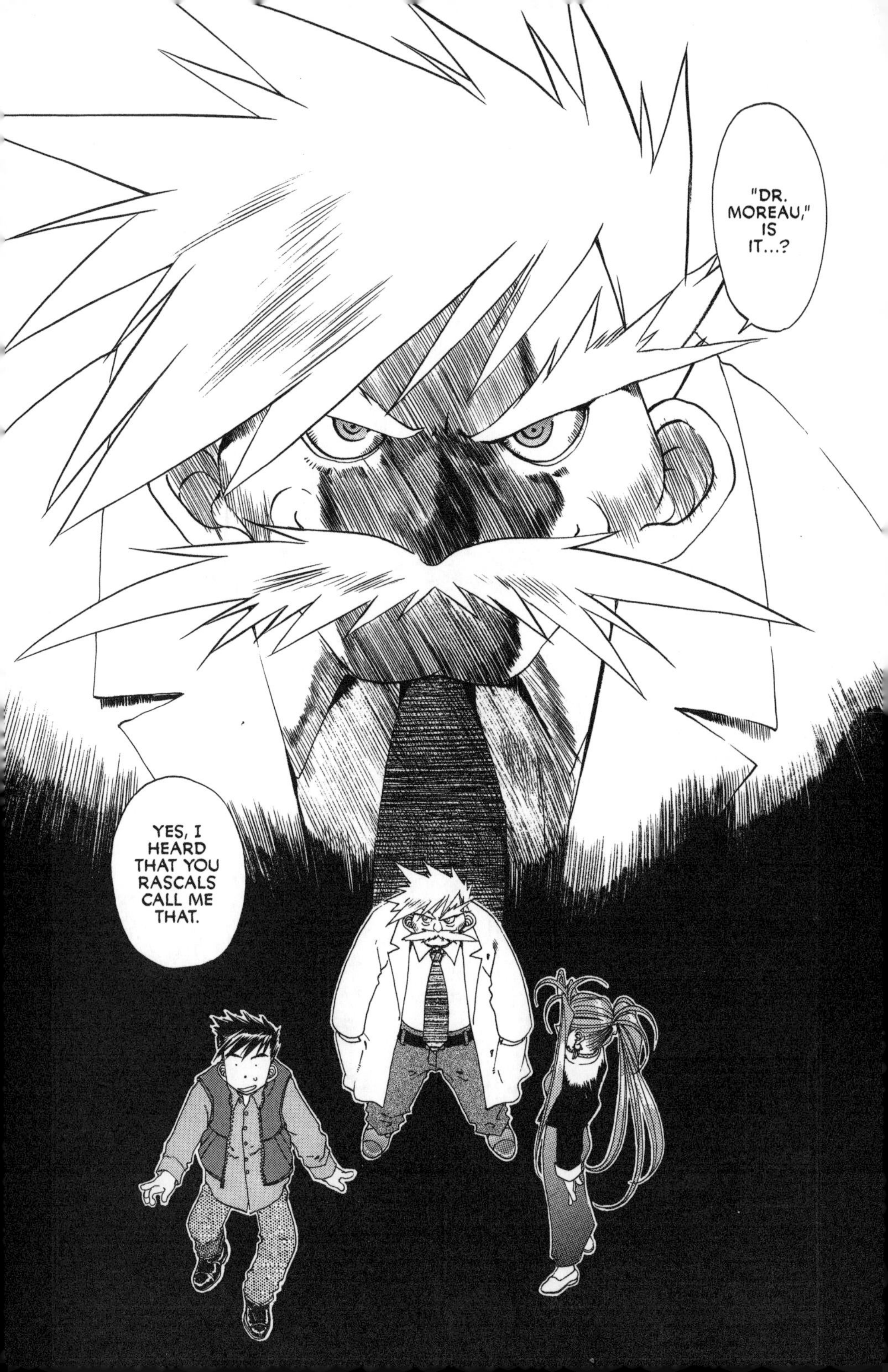
"DR. MOREAU," IS IT...?
YES, I HEARD THAT YOU RASCALS CALL ME THAT.

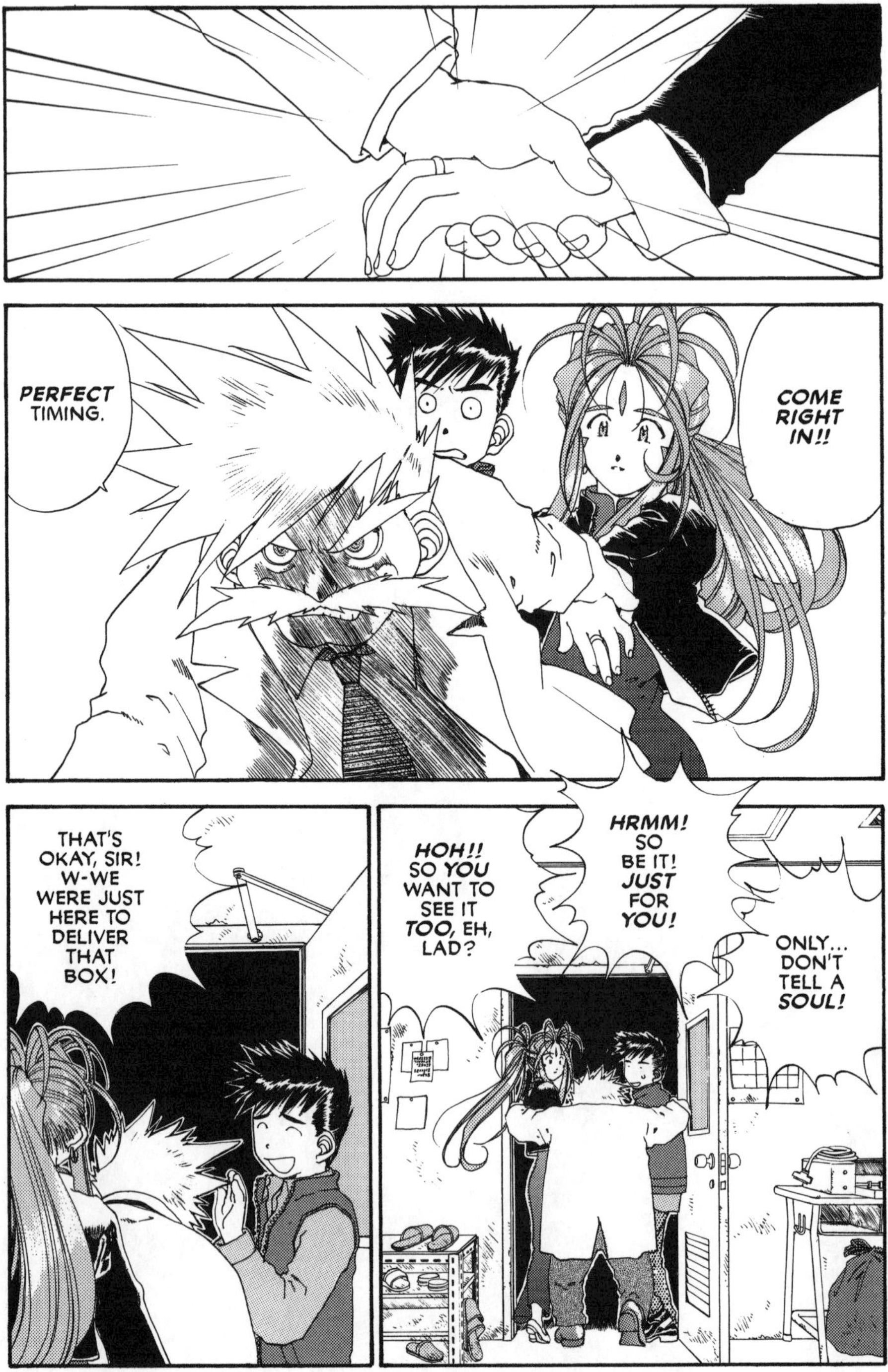
PERFECT TIMING.
COME RIGHT IN!!
THAT'S OKAY, SIR! W-WE WERE JUST HERE TO DELIVER THAT BOX!
HOH!! SO *YOU* WANT TO SEE IT *TOO*, EH, LAD?
HRMM! SO BE IT! *JUST* FOR *YOU!*
ONLY... DON'T TELL A *SOUL!*

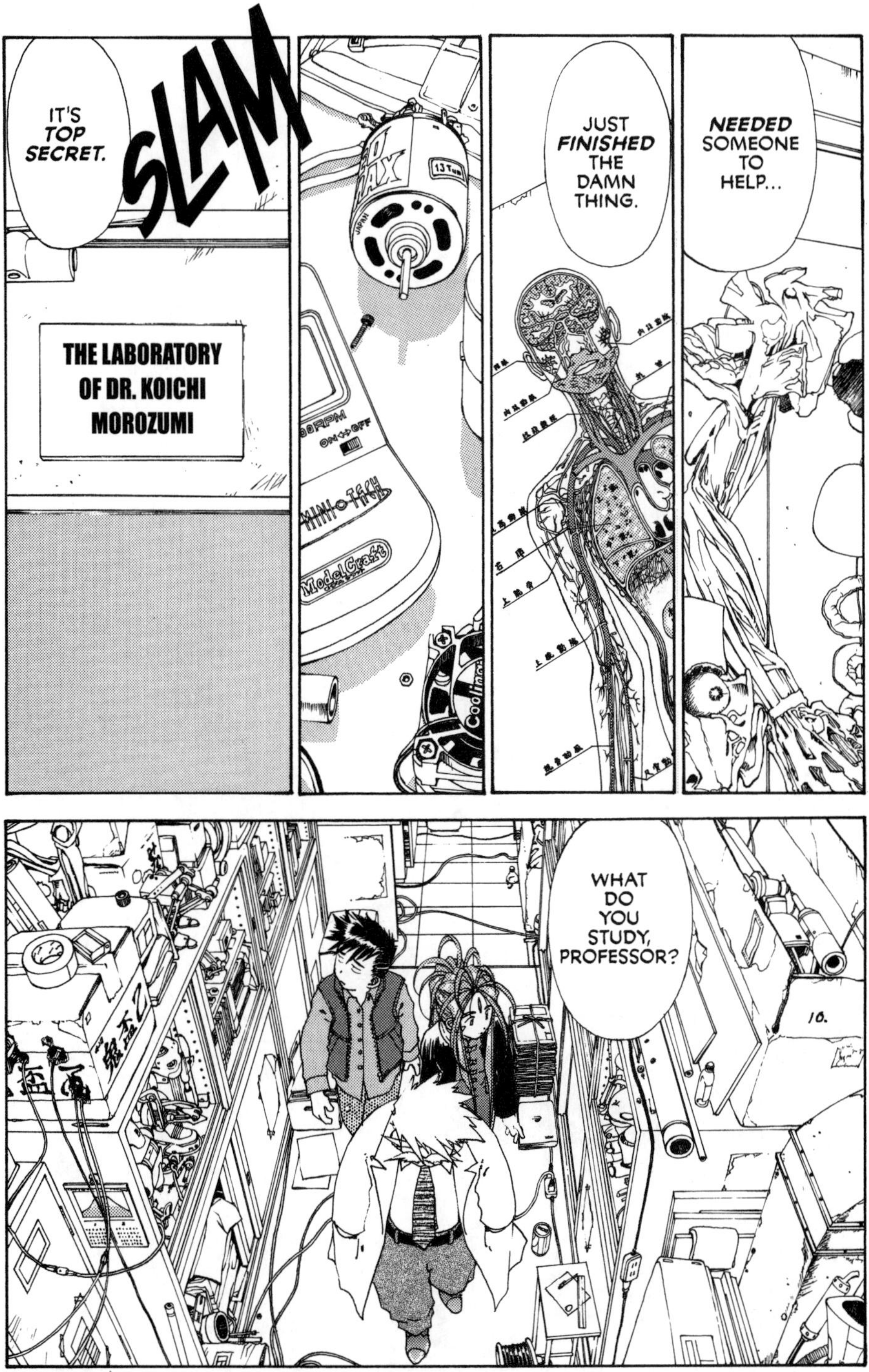
IT'S *TOP* SECRET.
SLAM
THE LABORATORY OF DR. KOICHI MOROZUMI
JUST *FINISHED* THE DAMN THING.
NEEDED SOMEONE TO HELP...
WHAT DO YOU STUDY, PROFESSOR?

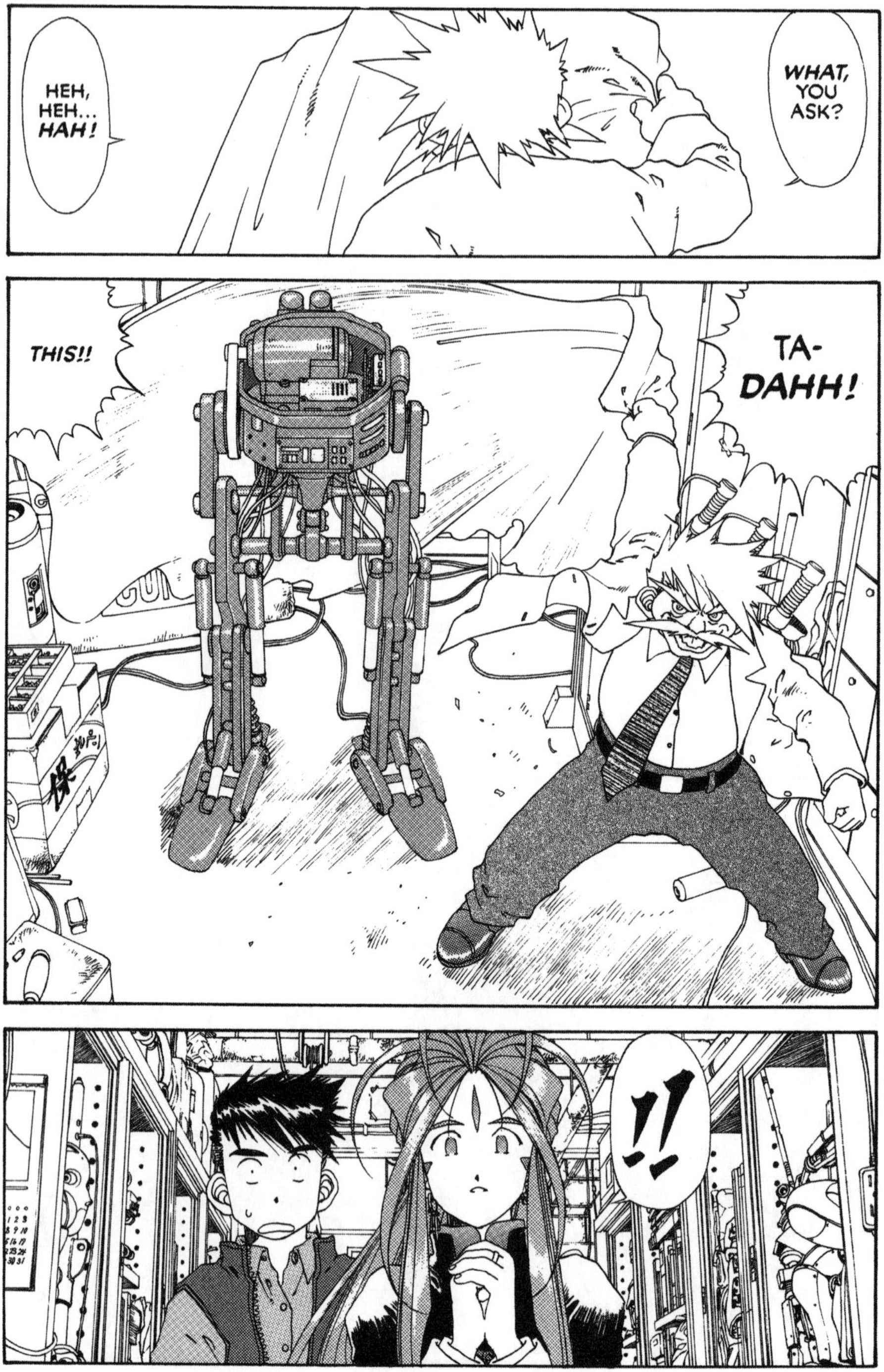
HEH, HEH... HAH!
WHAT, YOU ASK?
THIS!!
TA-DAHH!
!!

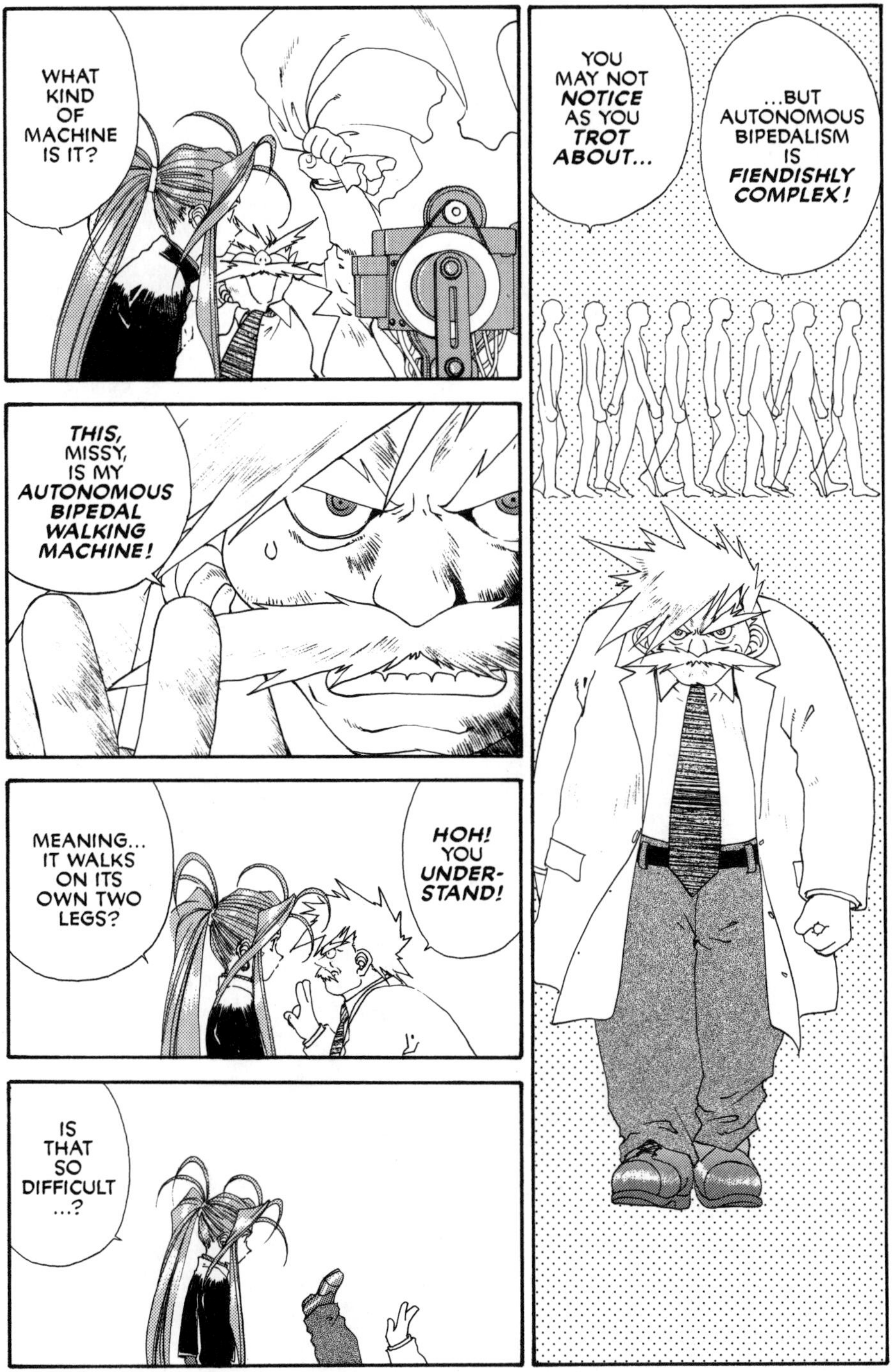
WHAT KIND OF MACHINE IS IT?
THIS, MISSY, IS MY AUTONOMOUS BIPEDAL WALKING MACHINE!
MEANING... IT WALKS ON ITS OWN TWO LEGS?
HOH! YOU UNDER-STAND!
IS THAT SO DIFFICULT ...?
YOU MAY NOT NOTICE AS YOU TROT ABOUT...
...BUT AUTONOMOUS BIPEDALISM IS FIENDISHLY COMPLEX!

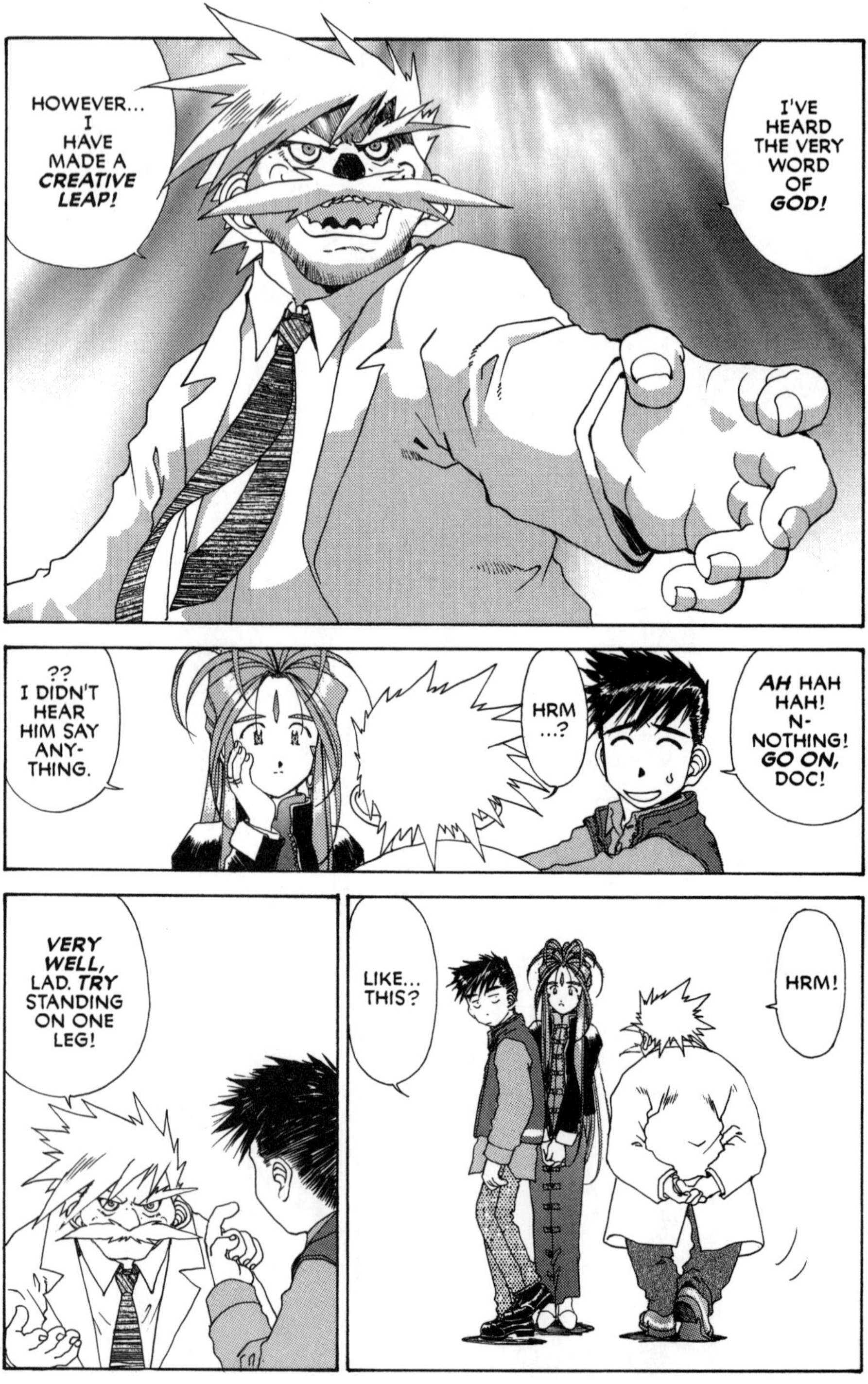
HOWEVER... I HAVE MADE A CREATIVE LEAP!
I'VE HEARD THE VERY WORD OF GOD!
?? I DIDN'T HEAR HIM SAY ANY-THING.
HRM ...?
AH HAH HAH! N-NOTHING! GO ON, DOC!
VERY WELL, LAD. TRY STANDING ON ONE LEG!
LIKE... THIS?
HRM!

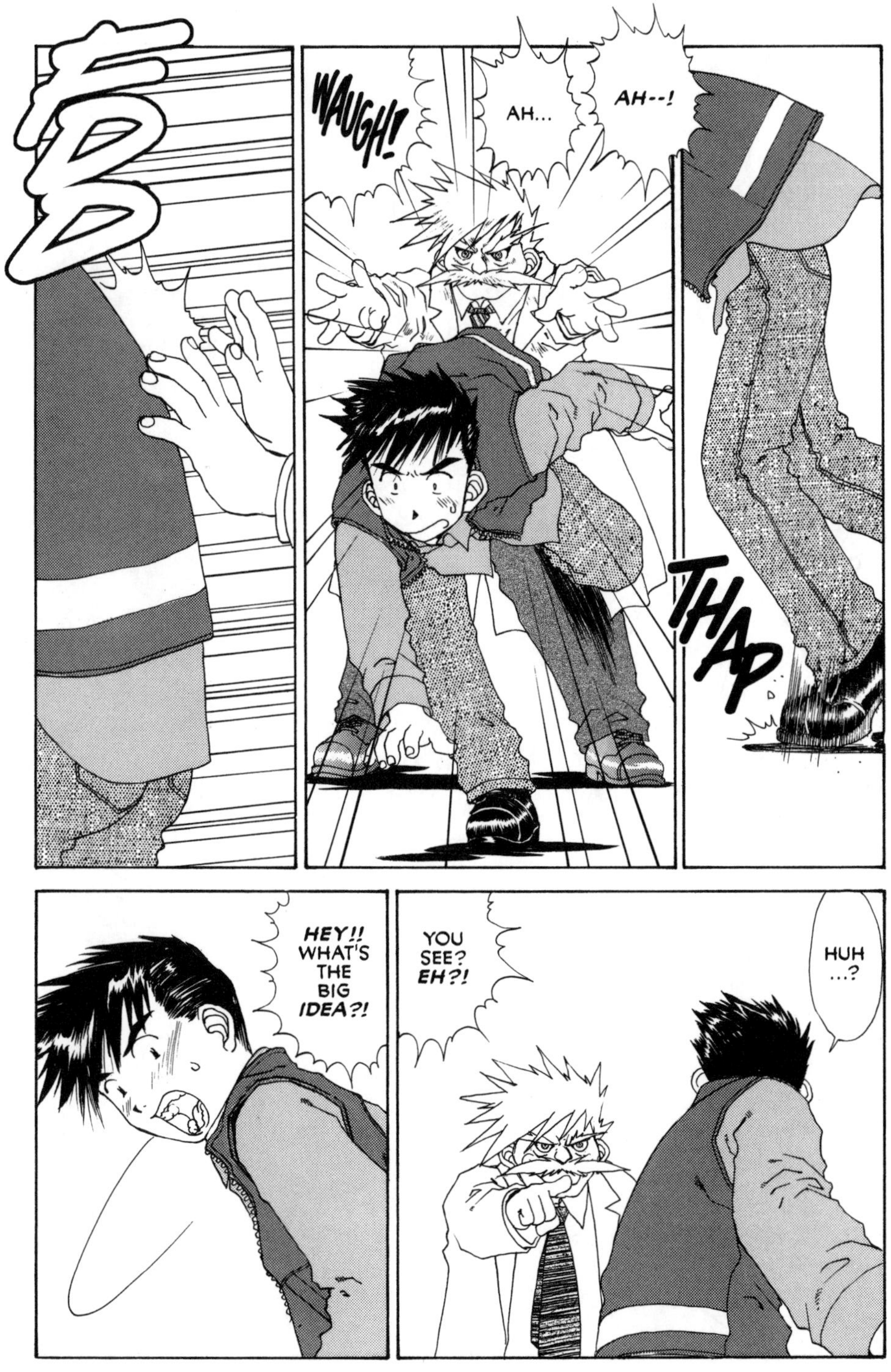
WAUGH!
AH...
AH--!
THAP
HEY!! WHAT'S THE BIG IDEA?!
YOU SEE? EH?!
HUH ...?

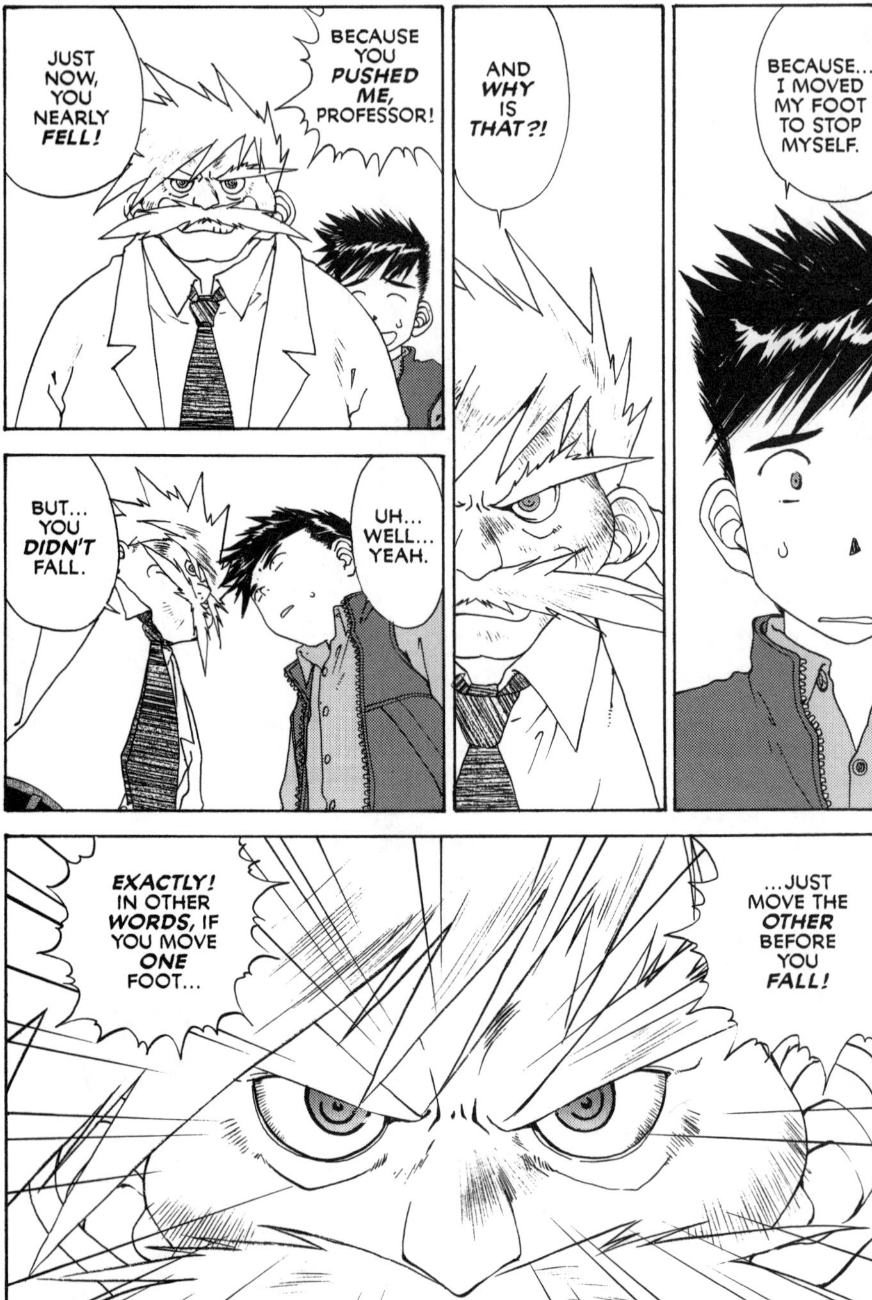
JUST NOW, YOU NEARLY **FELL!**
BECAUSE YOU ***PUSHED ME,*** PROFESSOR!
BUT... YOU ***DIDN'T*** FALL.
UH... WELL... YEAH.
AND ***WHY*** IS ***THAT?!***
BECAUSE... I MOVED MY FOOT TO STOP MYSELF.
EXACTLY! IN OTHER ***WORDS,*** IF YOU MOVE ***ONE*** FOOT...
...JUST MOVE THE ***OTHER*** BEFORE YOU ***FALL!***

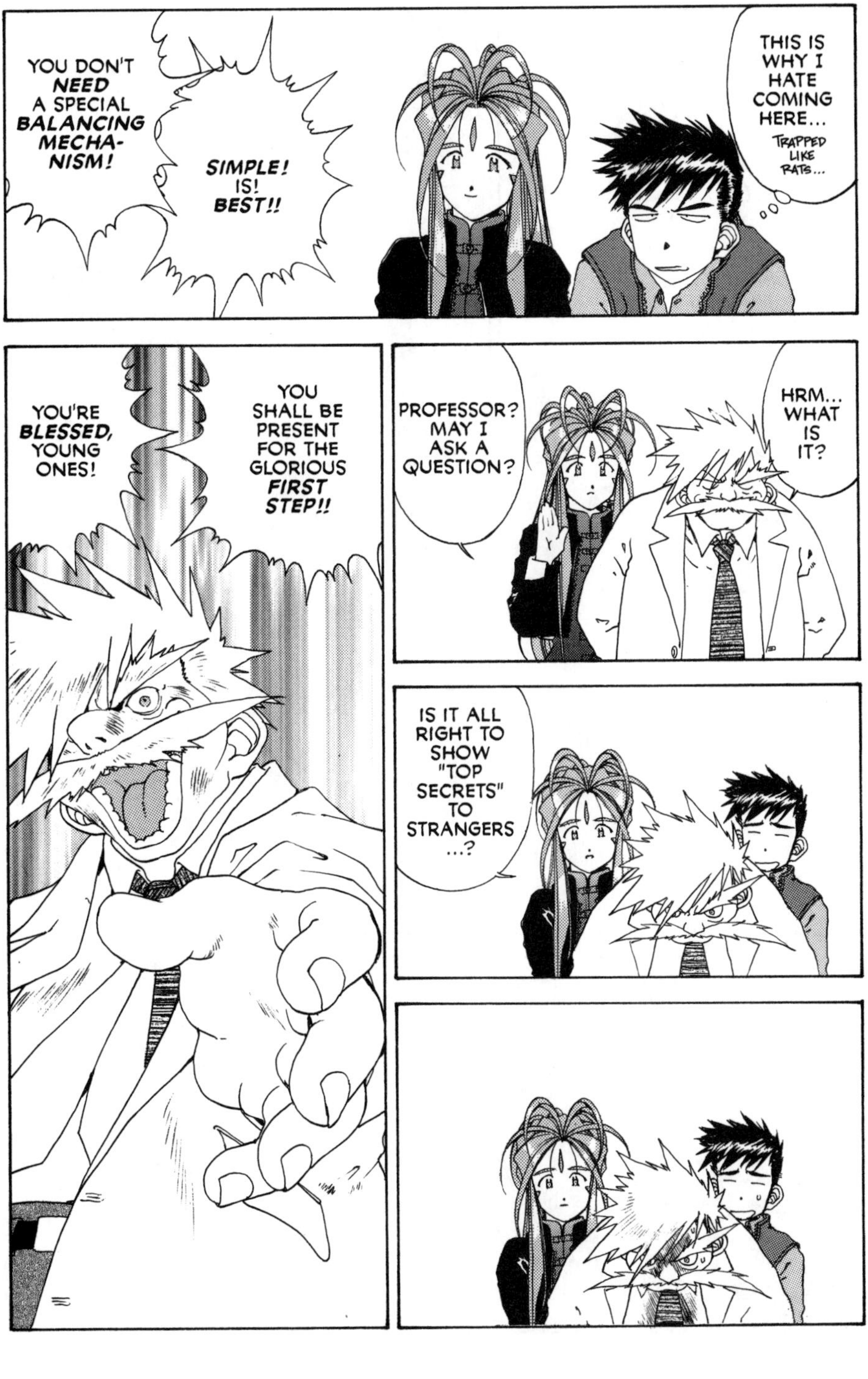

YOU DON'T NEED A SPECIAL BALANCING MECHA-NISM!
SIMPLE! IS! BEST!!
THIS IS WHY I HATE COMING HERE...
TRAPPED LIKE RATS...
YOU'RE BLESSED, YOUNG ONES!
YOU SHALL BE PRESENT FOR THE GLORIOUS FIRST STEP!!
PROFESSOR? MAY I ASK A QUESTION?
HRM... WHAT IS IT?
IS IT ALL RIGHT TO SHOW "TOP SECRETS" TO STRANGERS ...?

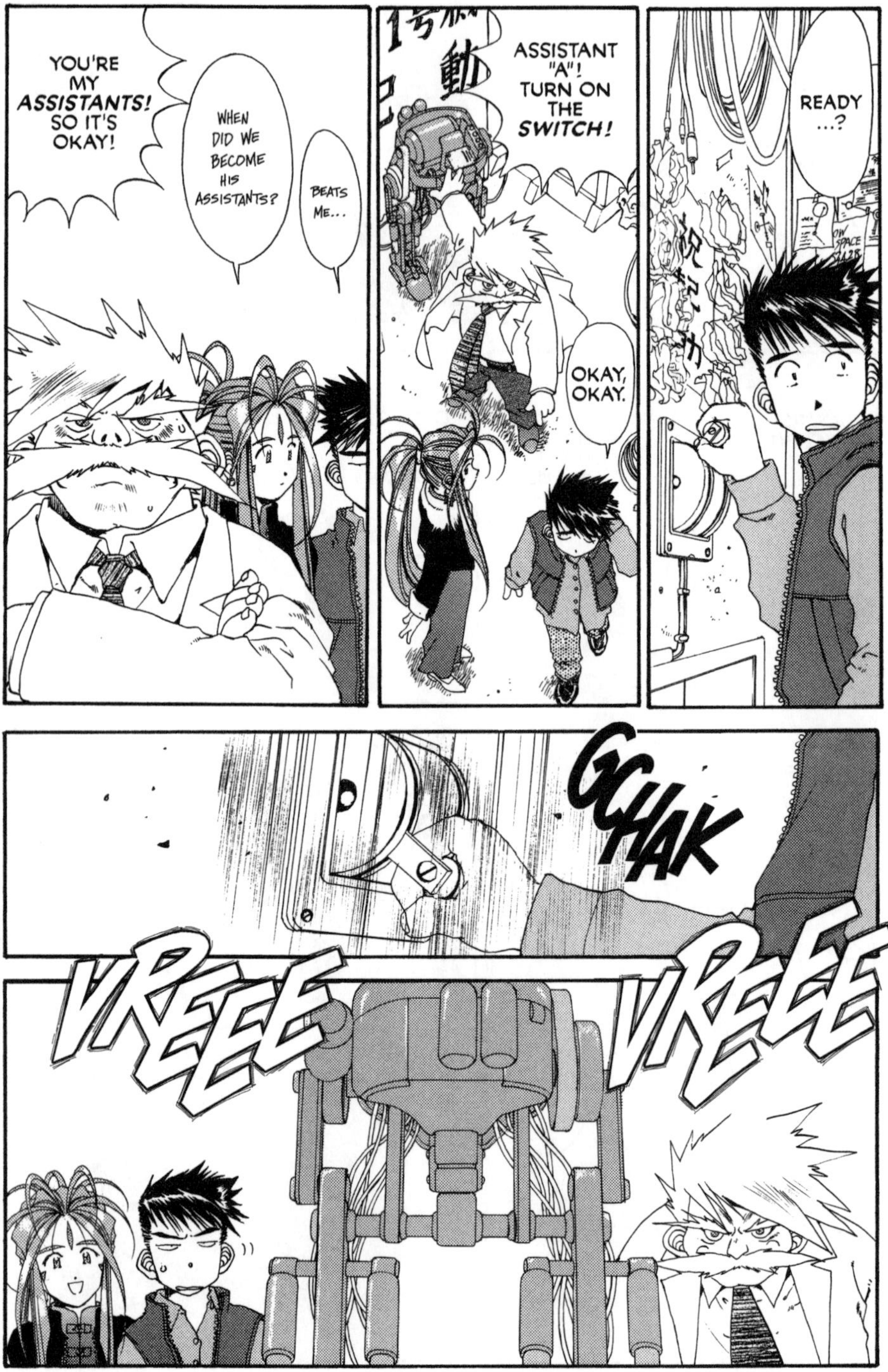
YOU'RE MY ASSISTANTS! SO IT'S OKAY!
WHEN DID WE BECOME HIS ASSISTANTS?
BEATS ME...
ASSISTANT "A"! TURN ON THE SWITCH!
OKAY, OKAY.
READY ...?
GCHAK
VREEE
VREEE

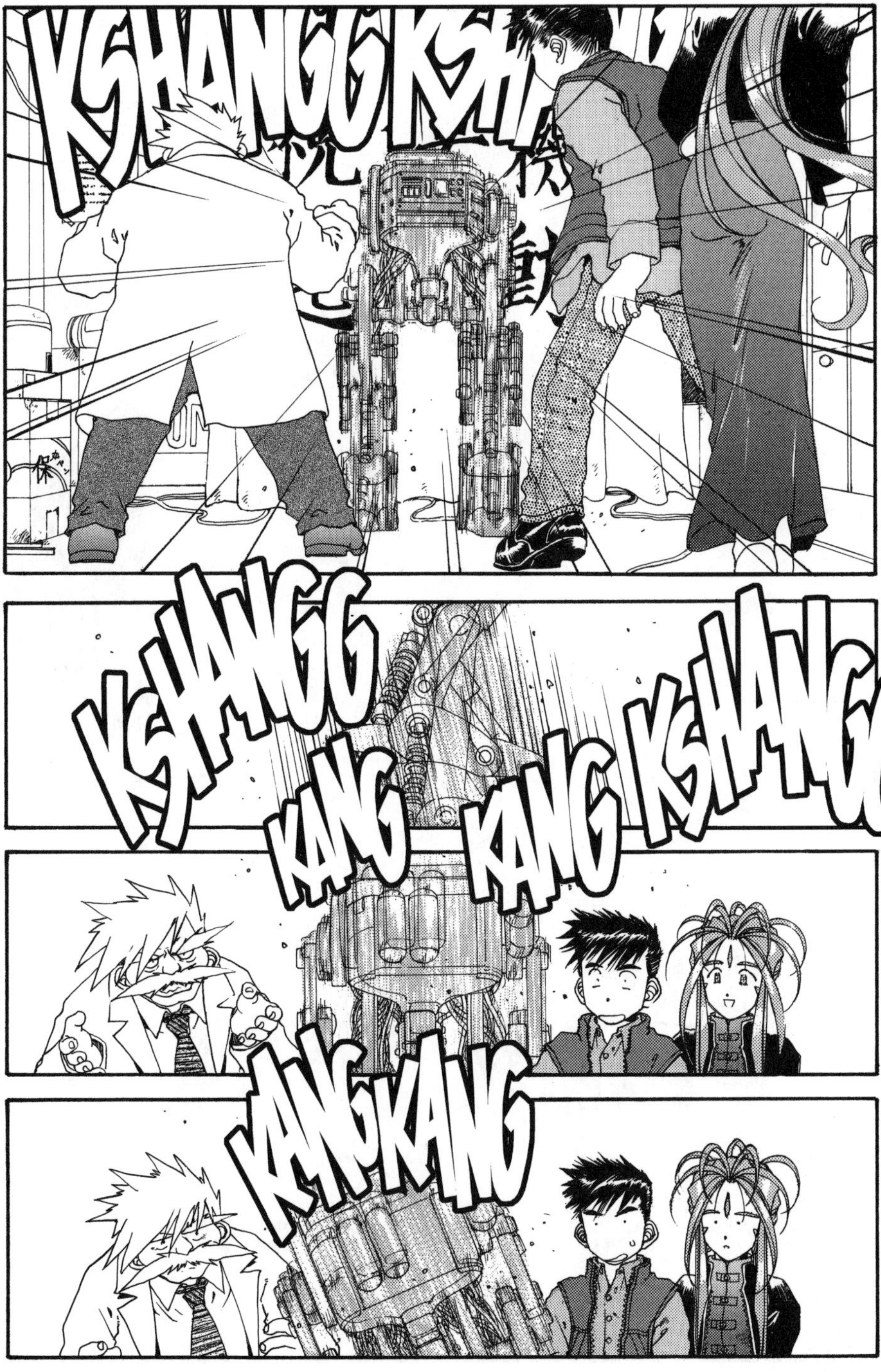
KSHANGG
KSHA
KSHANGG
KANG
KANG
KSHANGG
KANG KANG

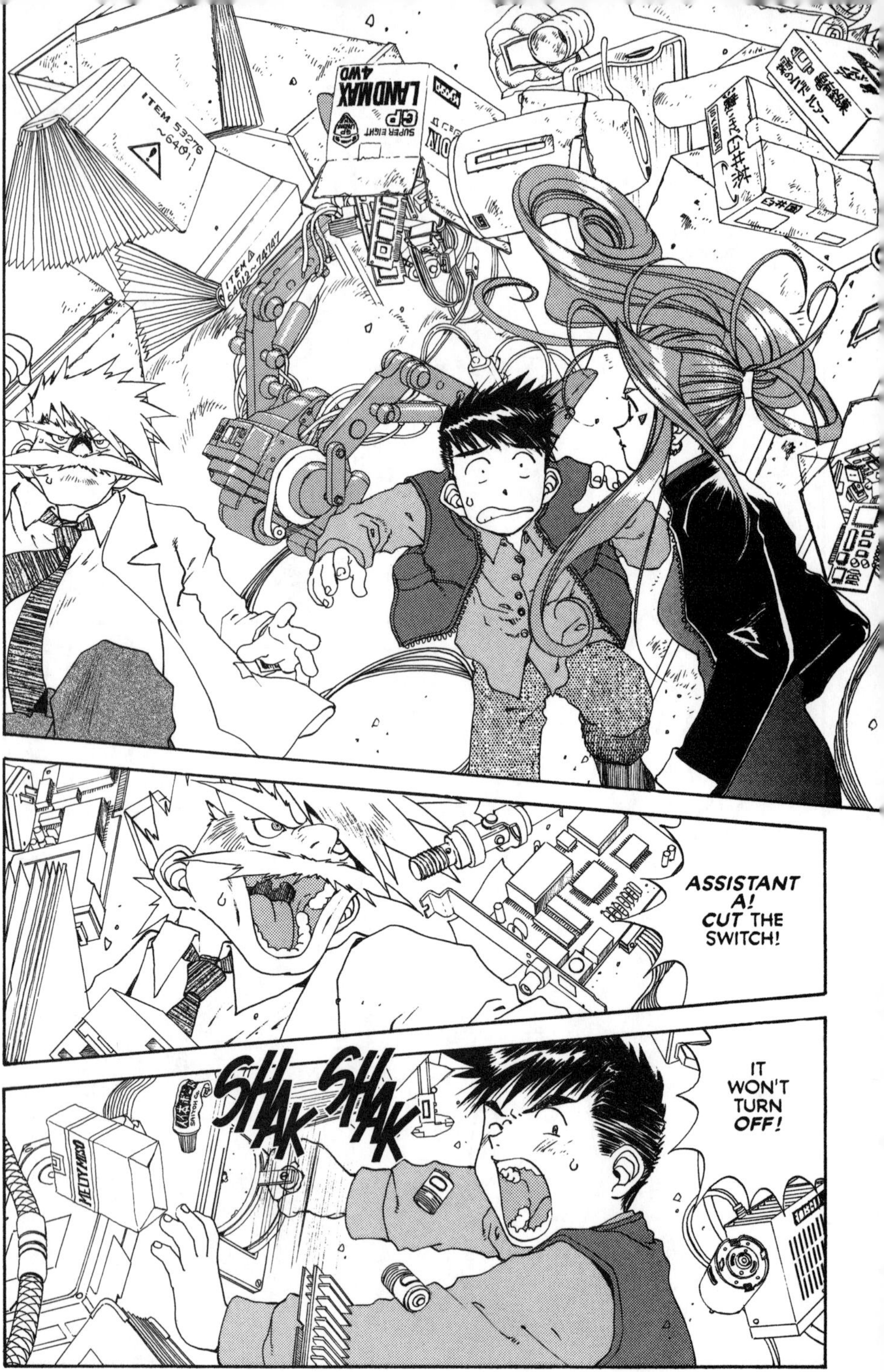
ASSISTANT A! CUT THE SWITCH!
SHAK SHAK
IT WON'T TURN OFF!

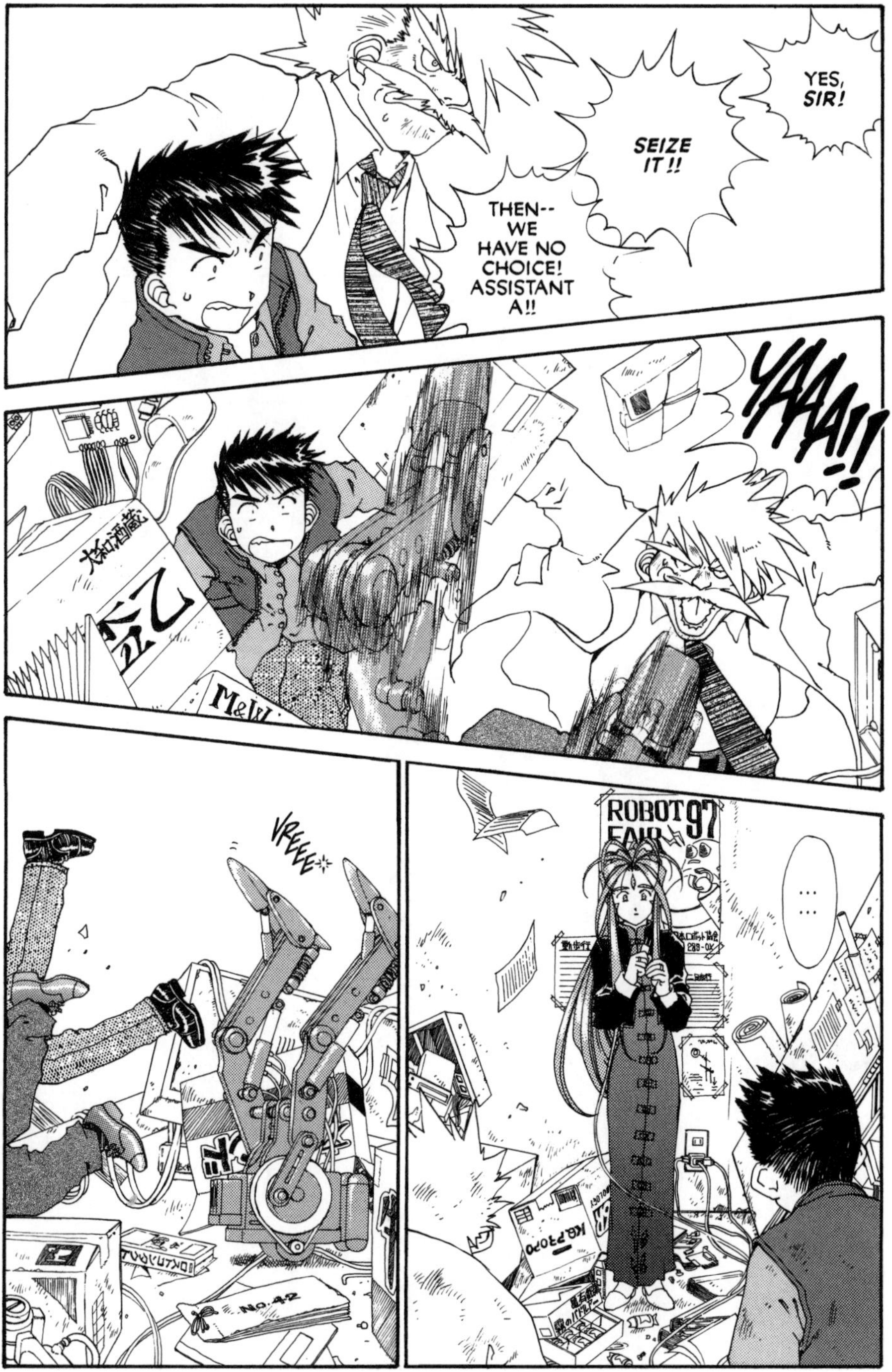
THEN-- WE HAVE NO CHOICE! ASSISTANT A!!
SEIZE IT!!
YES, SIR!
YAAA!!
大和酒蔵
M&W
VREEE
No. 42
ROBOT FAIR 97
... ...

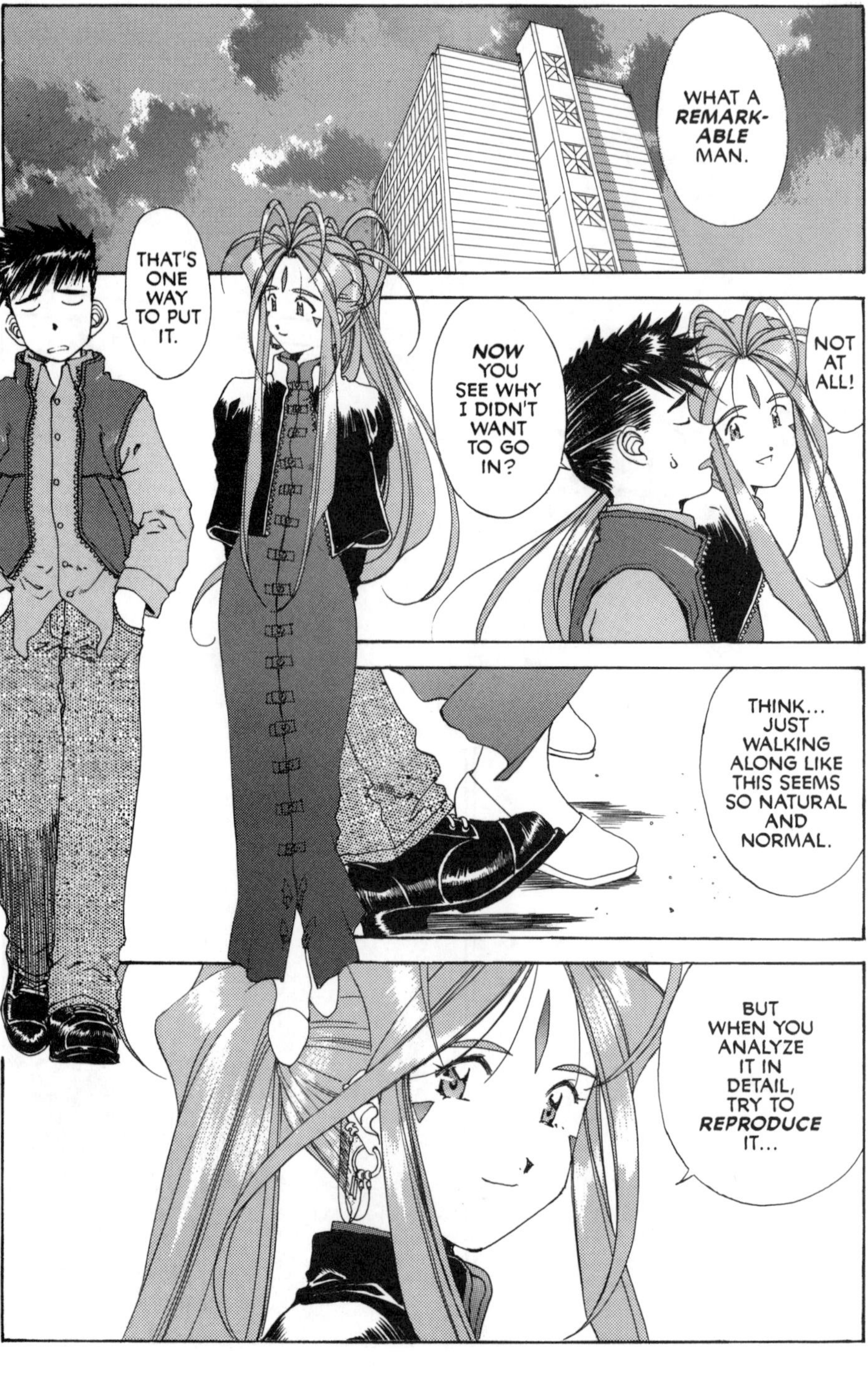
WHAT A *REMARKABLE* MAN.
THAT'S ONE WAY TO PUT IT.
NOW YOU SEE WHY I DIDN'T WANT TO GO IN?
NOT AT ALL!
THINK... JUST WALKING ALONG LIKE THIS SEEMS SO NATURAL AND NORMAL.
BUT WHEN YOU ANALYZE IT IN DETAIL, TRY TO *REPRODUCE* IT...

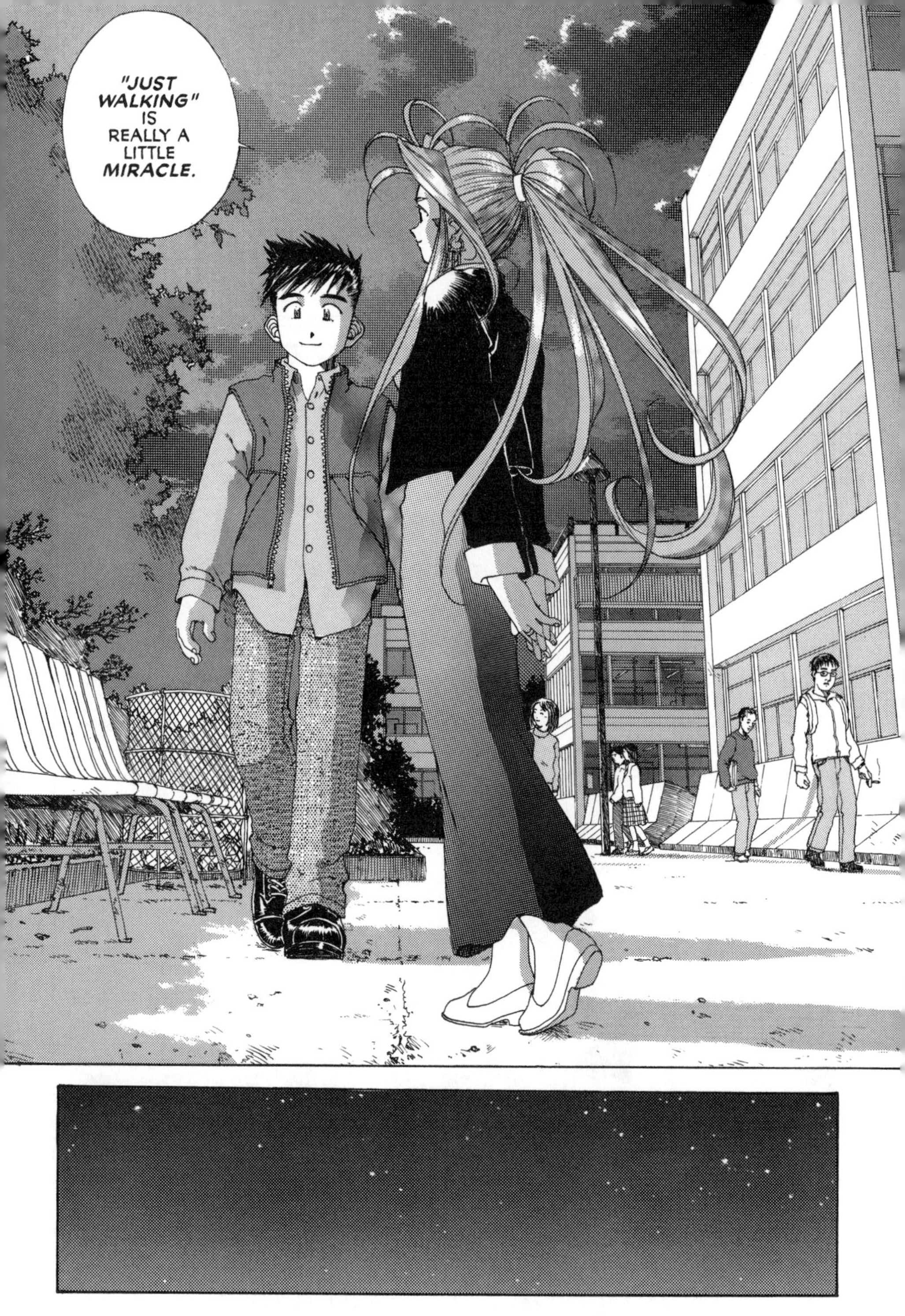
"JUST WALKING" IS REALLY A LITTLE MIRACLE.

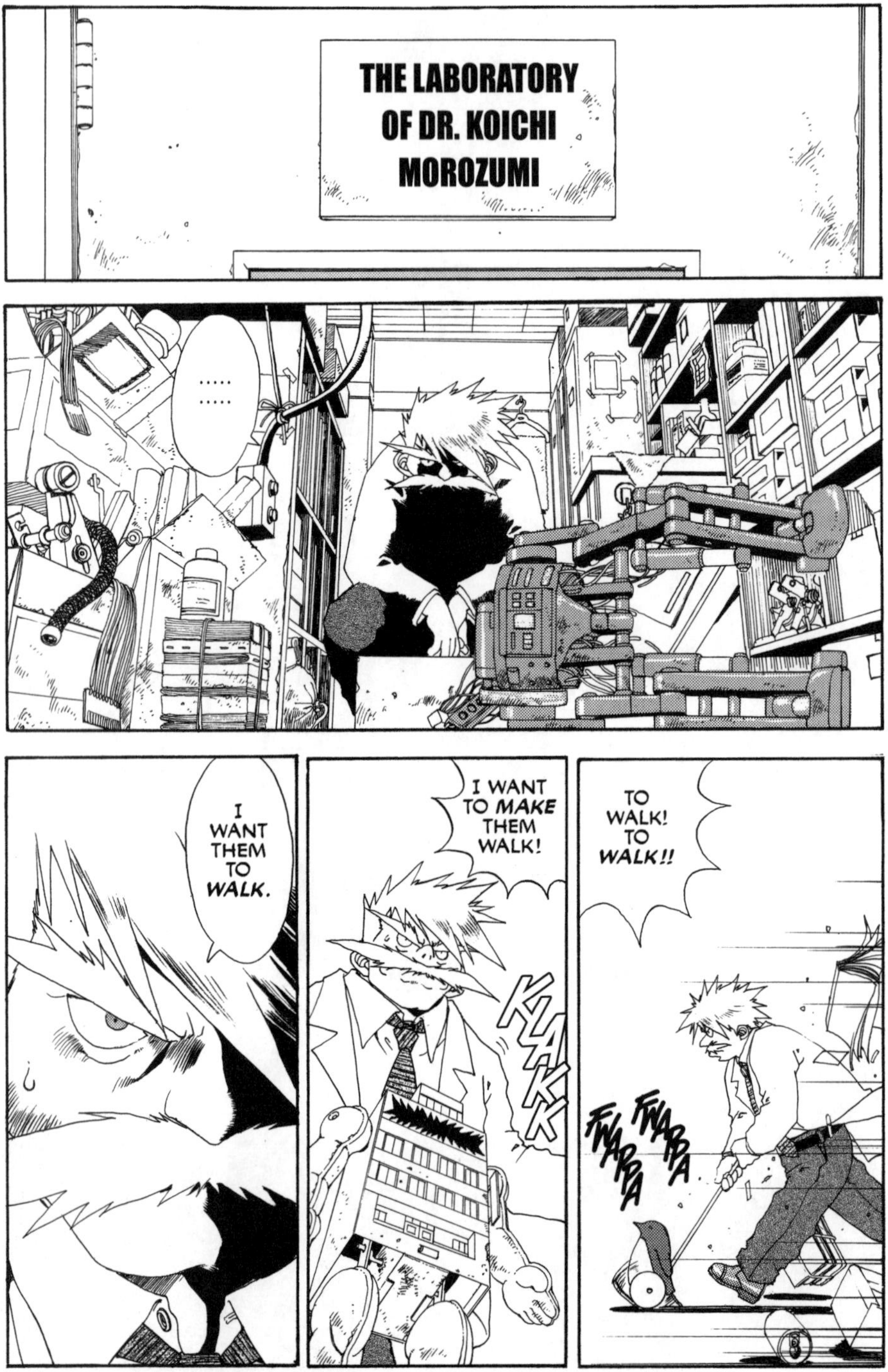
THE LABORATORY OF DR. KOICHI MOROZUMI
......
......
I WANT THEM TO *WALK.*
I WANT TO *MAKE* THEM WALK!
KLAKK
TO WALK! TO *WALK!!*
FWABA
FWABA

ACTUALLY, HONDA HAS NOW SUCCEEDED IN CREATING A FULLY AUTONOMOUS BIPEDAL ROBOT ("ASIMO"). BUT IN THIS STORY, THAT STILL HASN'T HAPPENED.

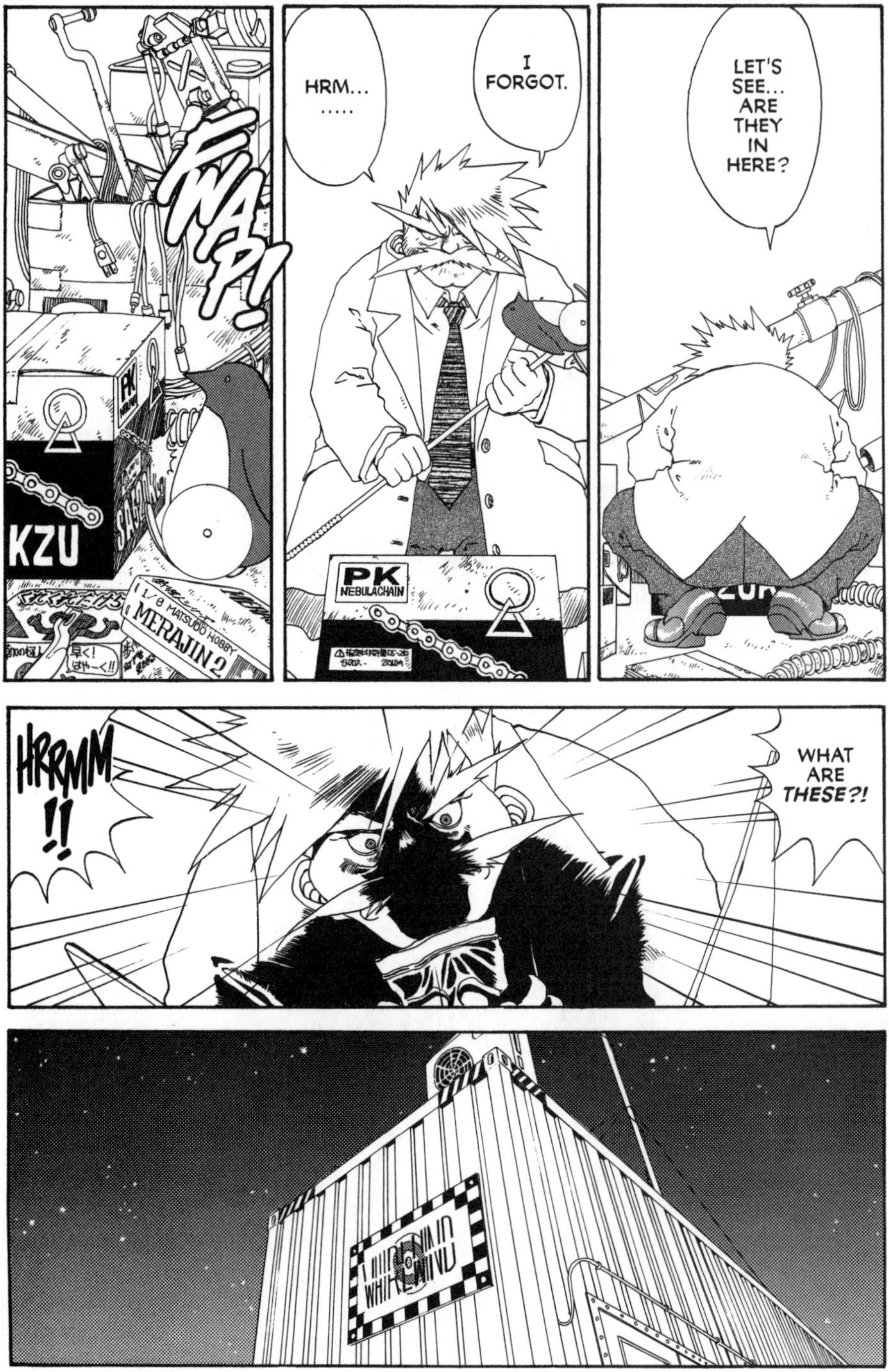
FWAP!
KZU
1/8 MATSUDO HOBBY
MERAJIN 2
早く! はやーく!!
HRM... .....
I FORGOT.
PK
NEBULACHAIN
LET'S SEE... ARE THEY IN HERE?
HRRMM!!
WHAT ARE *THESE?!*

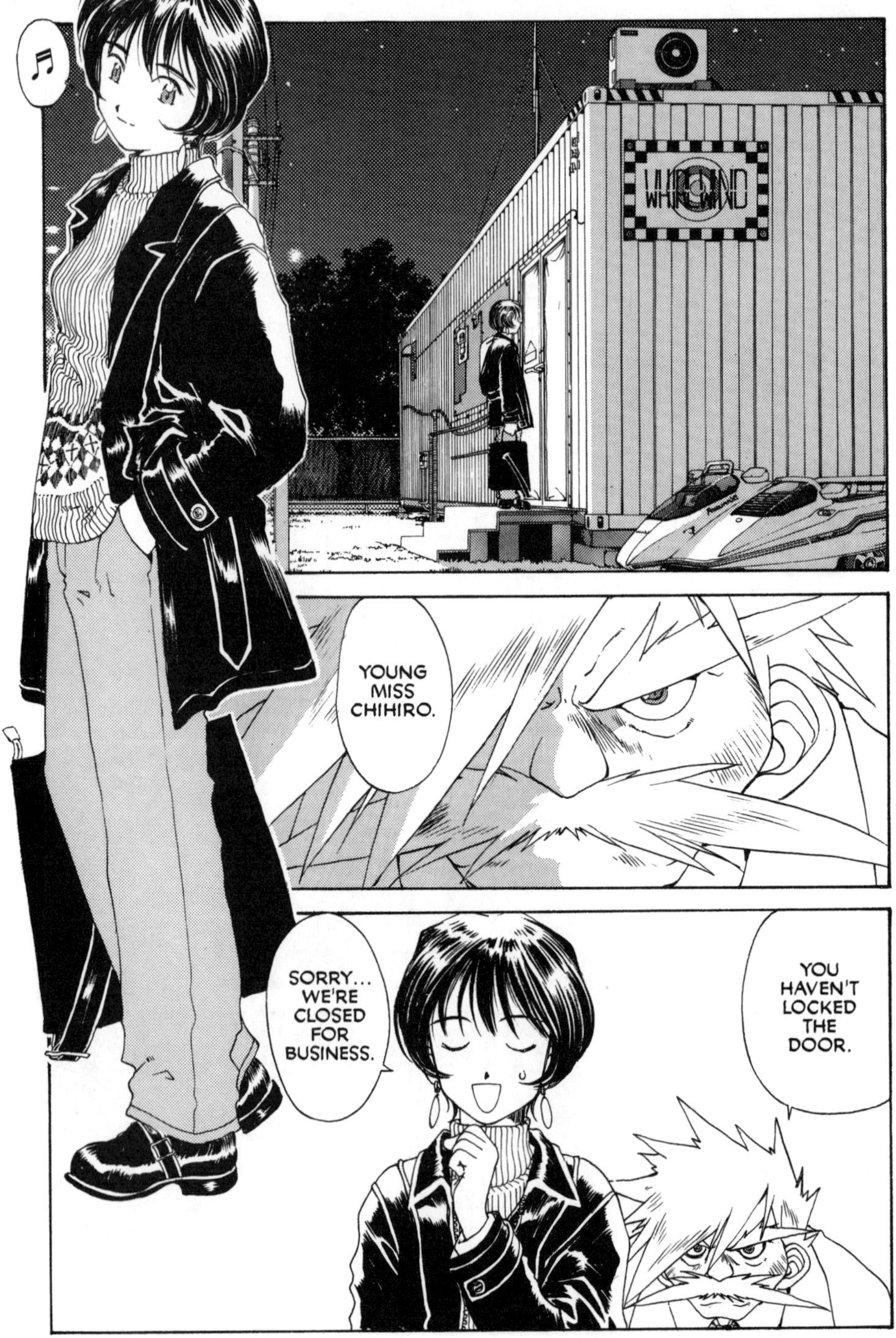
♪
YOUNG MISS CHIHIRO.
SORRY... WE'RE CLOSED FOR BUSINESS.
YOU HAVEN'T LOCKED THE DOOR.

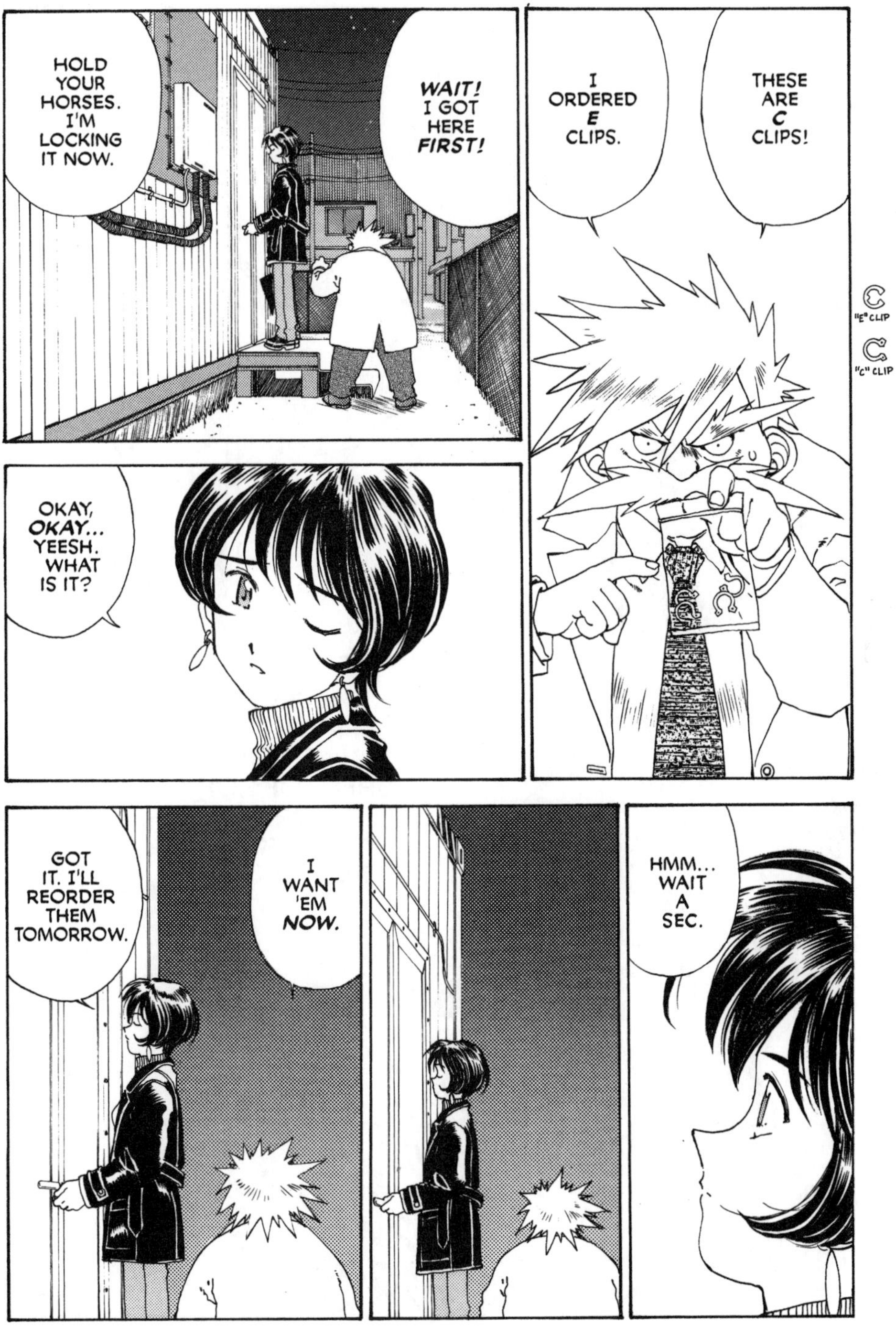
HOLD YOUR HORSES. I'M LOCKING IT NOW.
WAIT! I GOT HERE FIRST!
OKAY, OKAY... YEESH. WHAT IS IT?
I ORDERED E CLIPS.
THESE ARE C CLIPS!
"E" CLIP
"C" CLIP
GOT IT. I'LL REORDER THEM TOMORROW.
I WANT 'EM NOW.
HMM... WAIT A SEC.

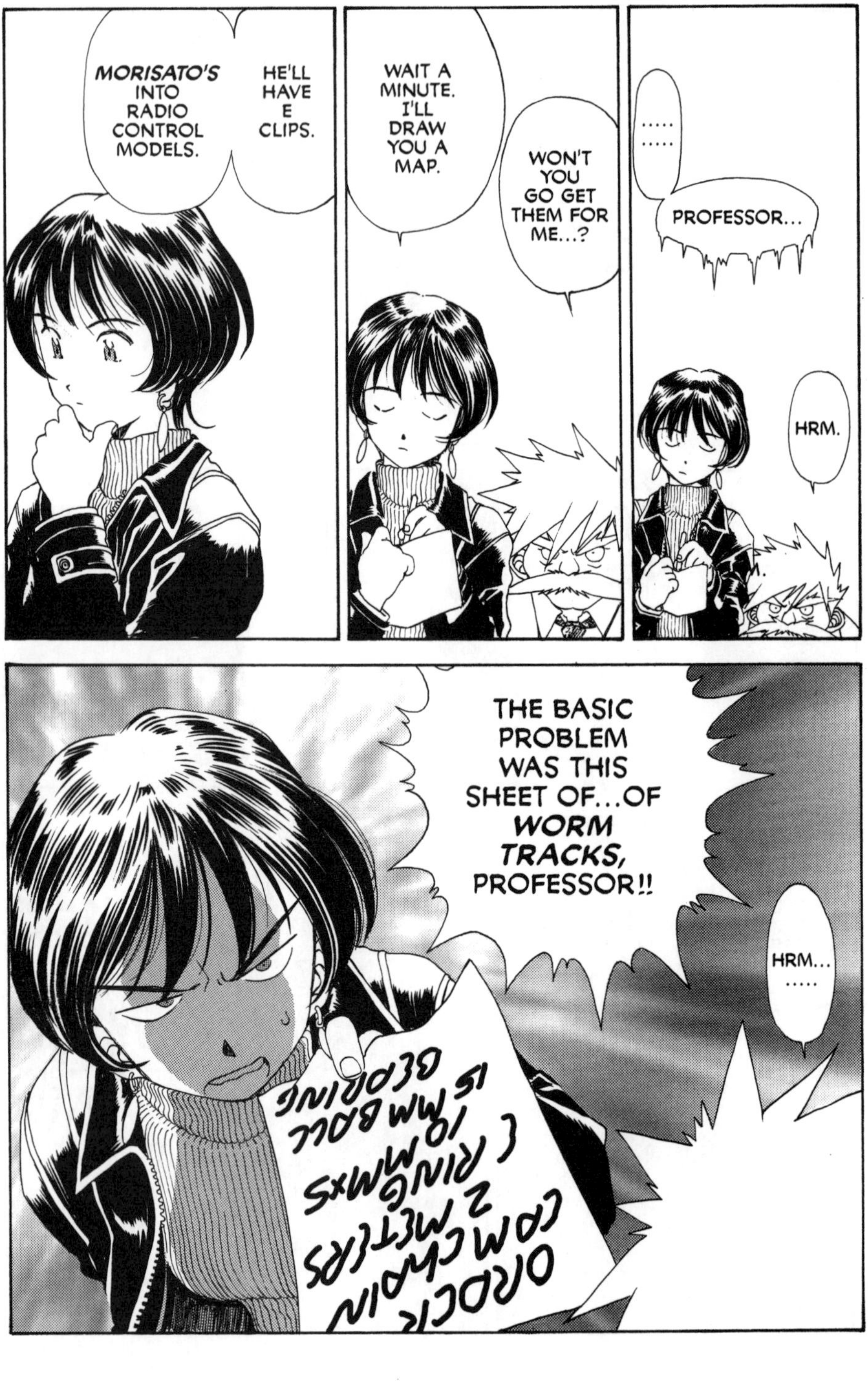
MORISATO'S INTO RADIO CONTROL MODELS.
HE'LL HAVE E CLIPS.
WAIT A MINUTE. I'LL DRAW YOU A MAP.
WON'T YOU GO GET THEM FOR ME...?
....
PROFESSOR...
HRM.
THE BASIC PROBLEM WAS THIS SHEET OF...OF WORM TRACKS, PROFESSOR!!
HRM... .....

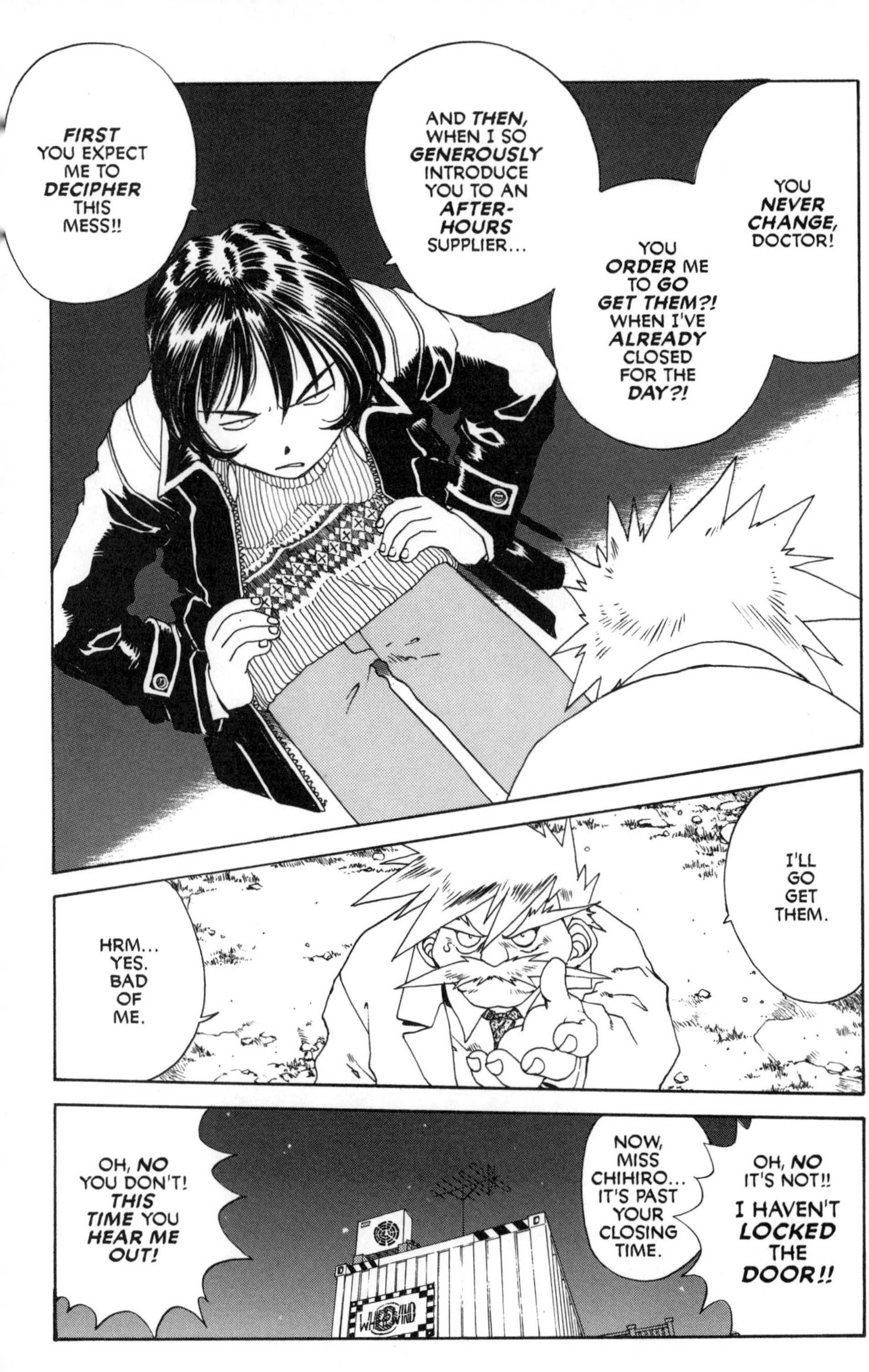
FIRST YOU EXPECT ME TO DECIPHER THIS MESS!!
AND THEN, WHEN I SO GENEROUSLY INTRODUCE YOU TO AN AFTER-HOURS SUPPLIER...
YOU ORDER ME TO GO GET THEM?! WHEN I'VE ALREADY CLOSED FOR THE DAY?!
YOU NEVER CHANGE, DOCTOR!
HRM... YES. BAD OF ME.
I'LL GO GET THEM.
OH, NO YOU DON'T! THIS TIME YOU HEAR ME OUT!
NOW, MISS CHIHIRO... IT'S PAST YOUR CLOSING TIME.
OH, NO IT'S NOT!!
I HAVEN'T LOCKED THE DOOR!!

ANDROID DREAMS

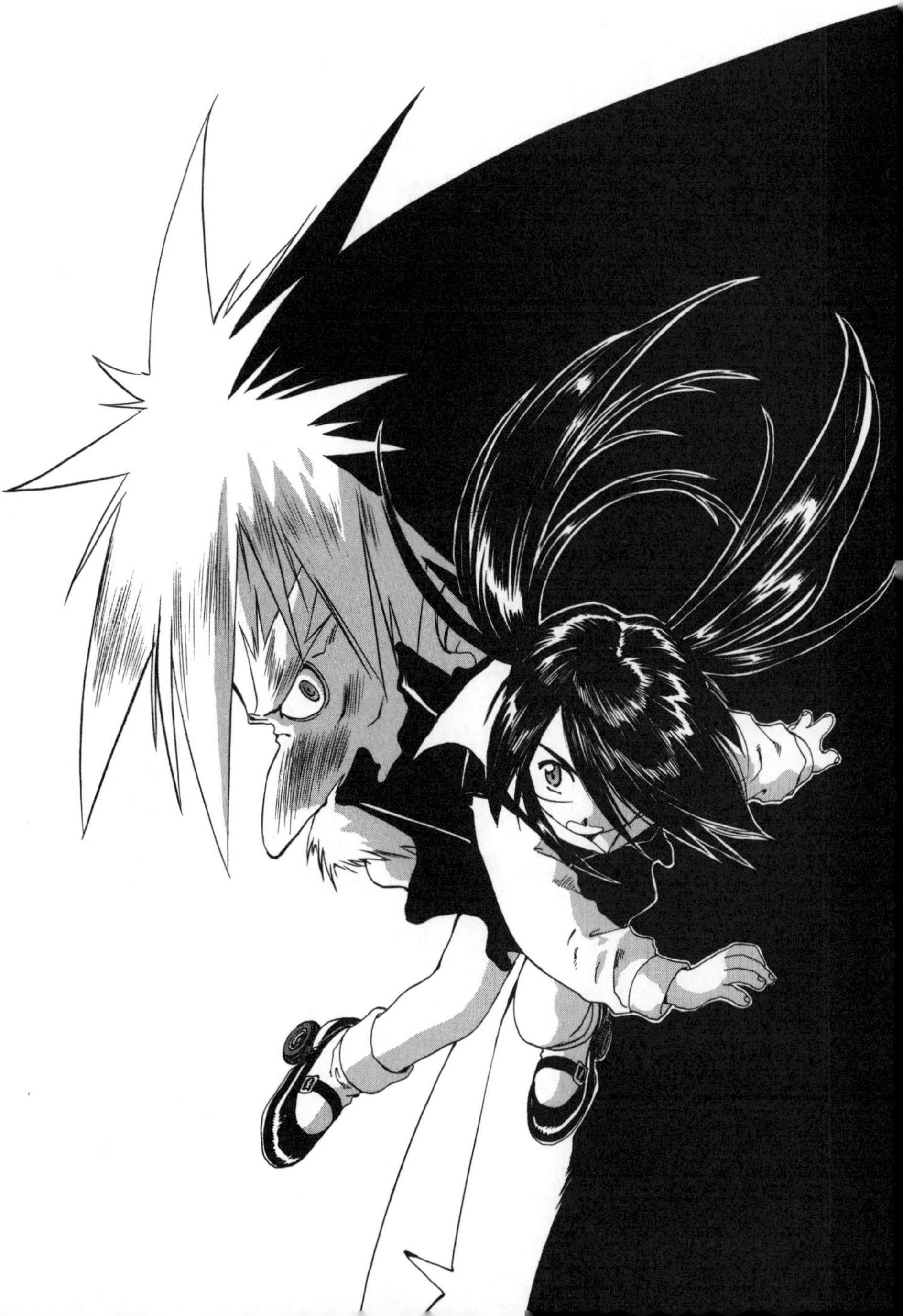

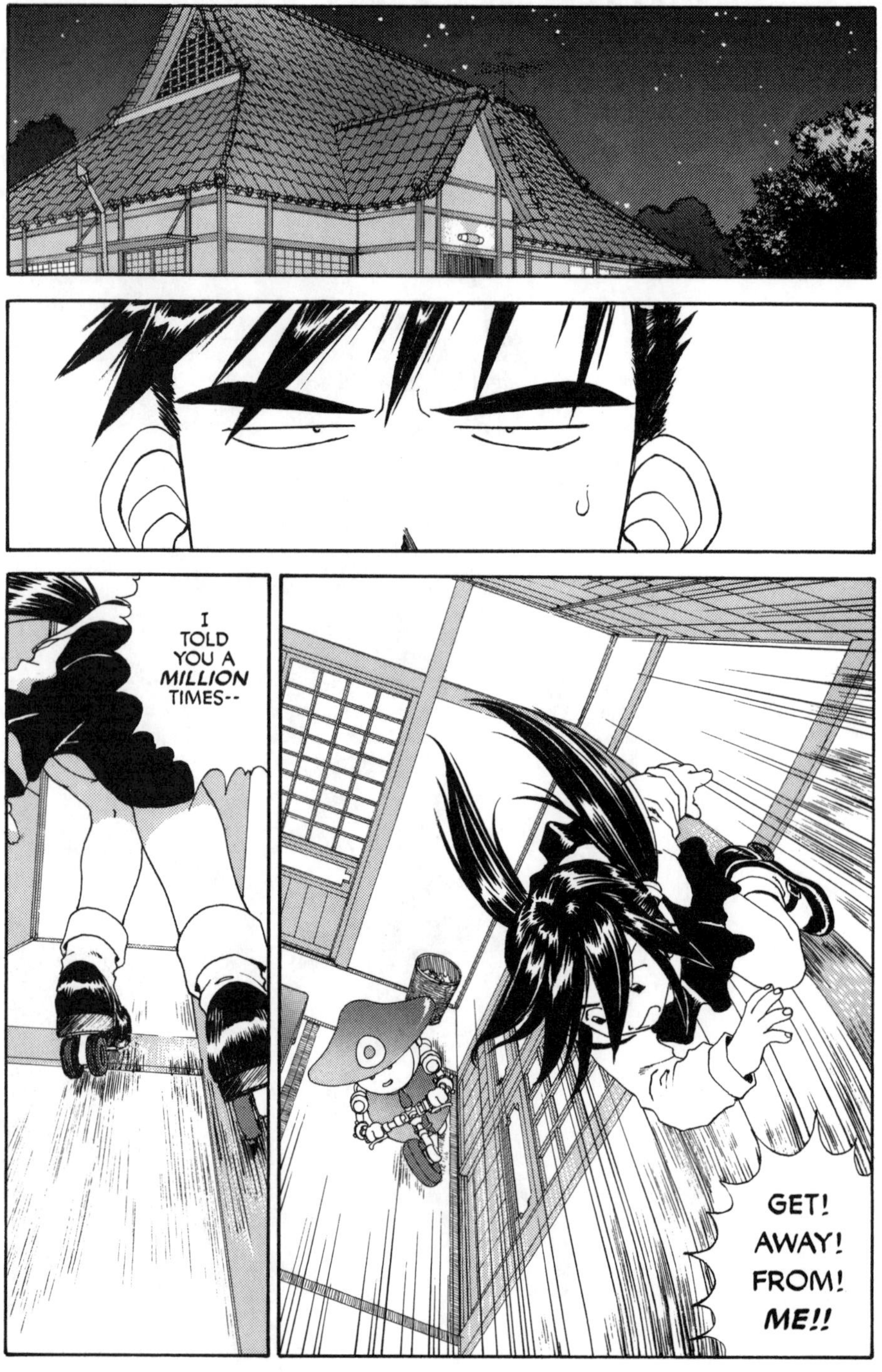
I TOLD YOU A *MILLION* TIMES--
GET! AWAY! FROM! *ME!!*

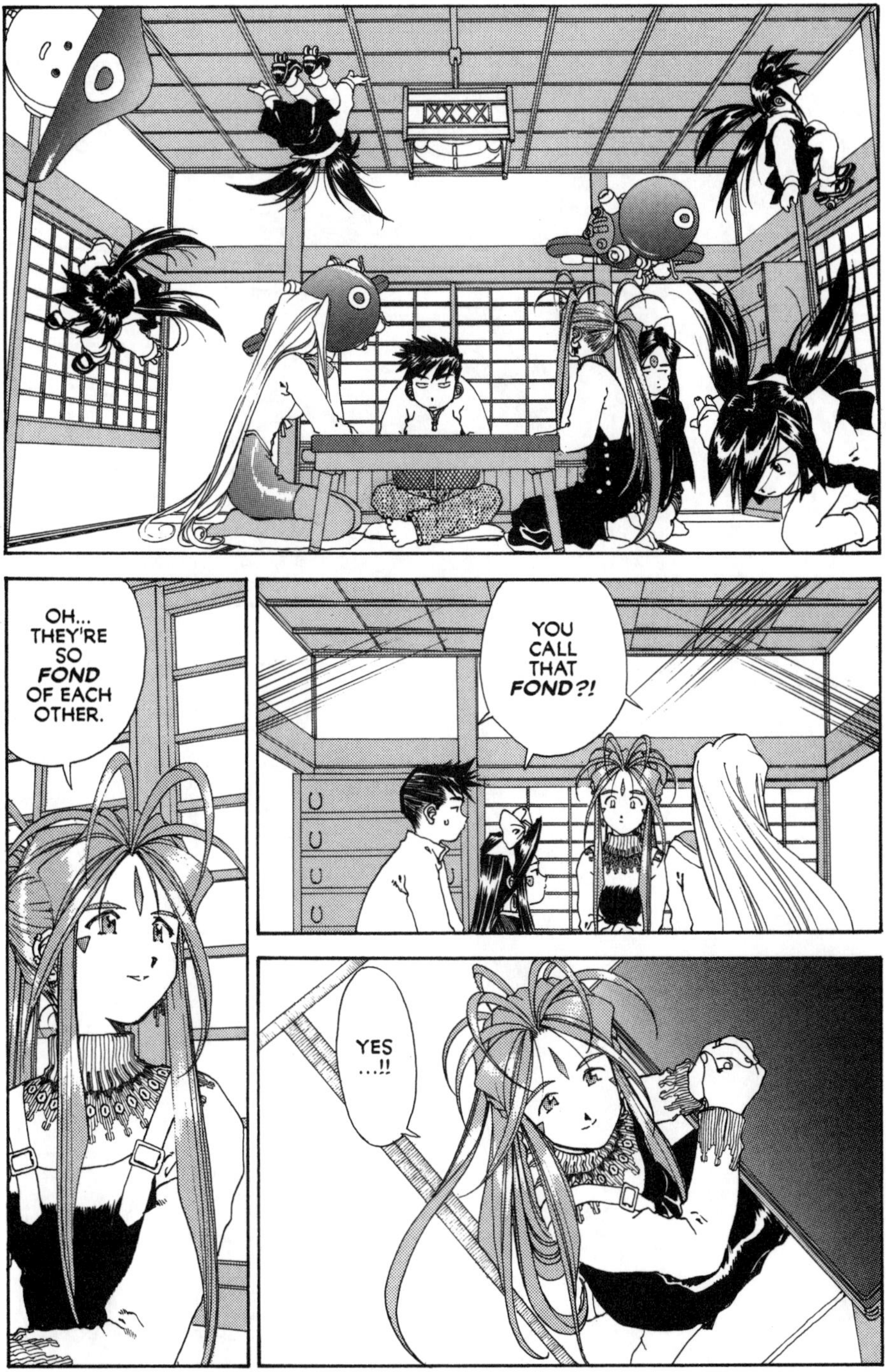
OH... THEY'RE SO *FOND* OF EACH OTHER.
YOU CALL THAT *FOND?!*
YES ...!!

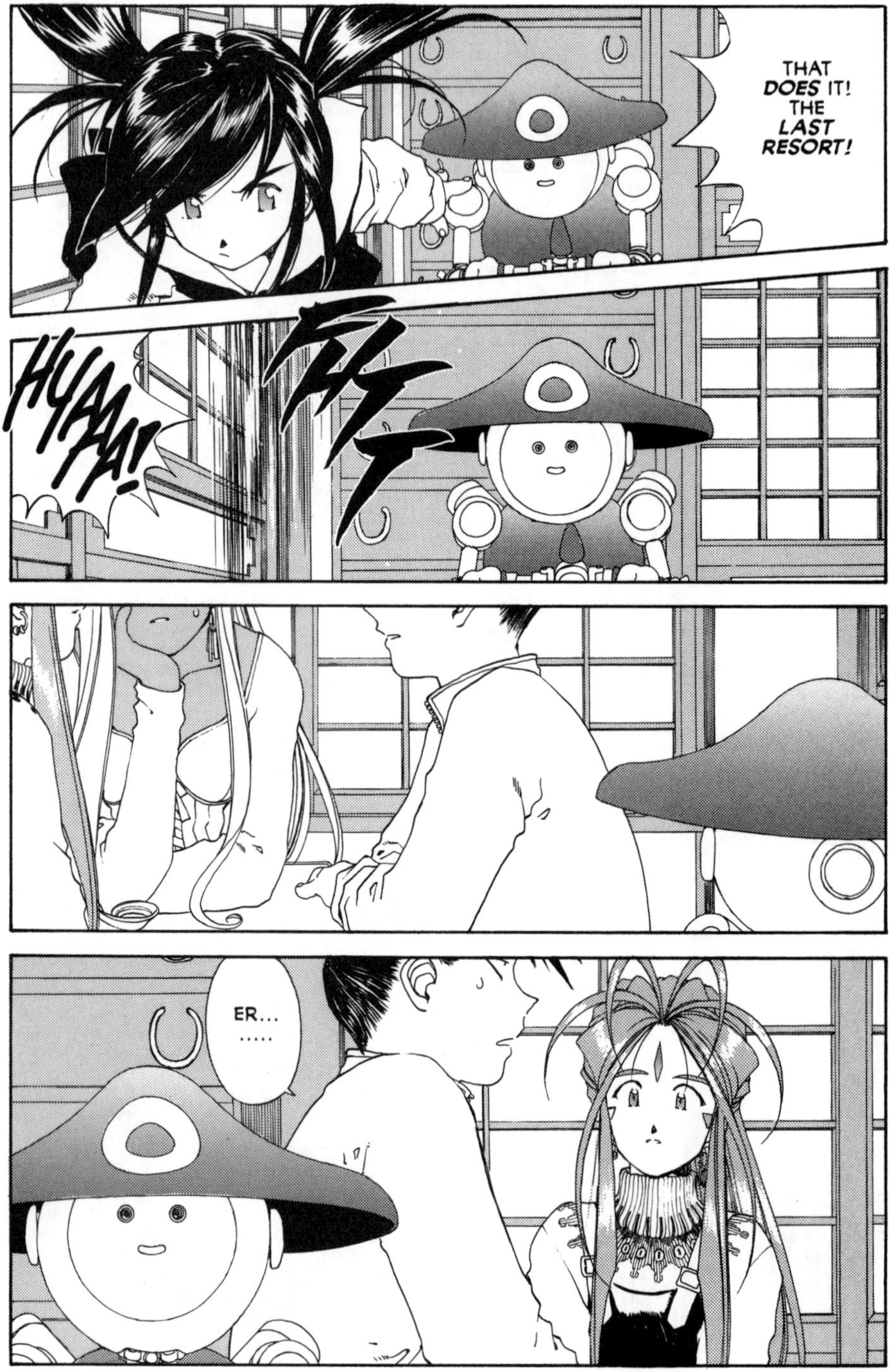
THAT DOES IT! THE LAST RESORT!
HYAAAA!
FWT
ER... ......

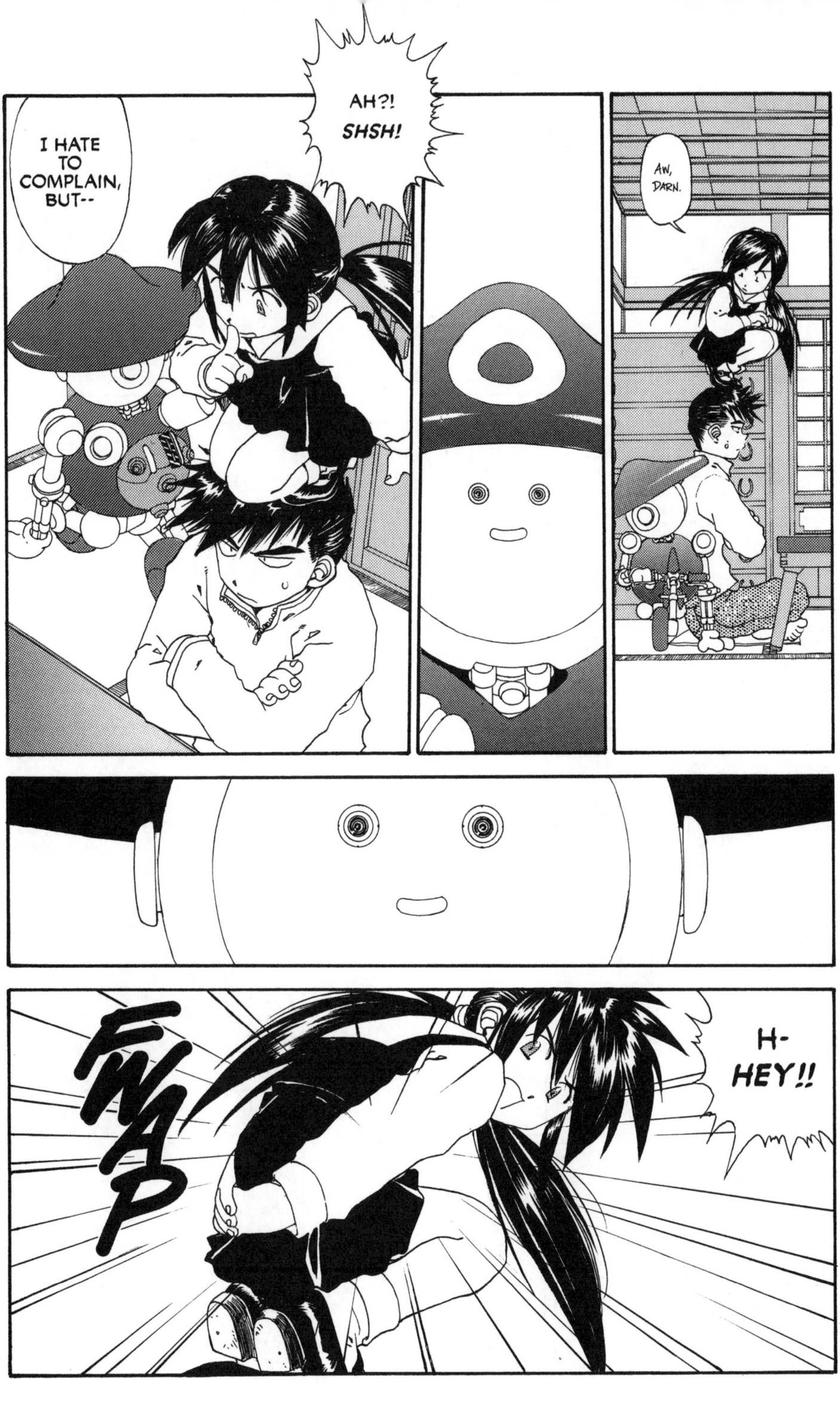
I HATE TO COMPLAIN, BUT--
AH?! SHSH!
AW, DARN.
FWAP
H- HEY!!

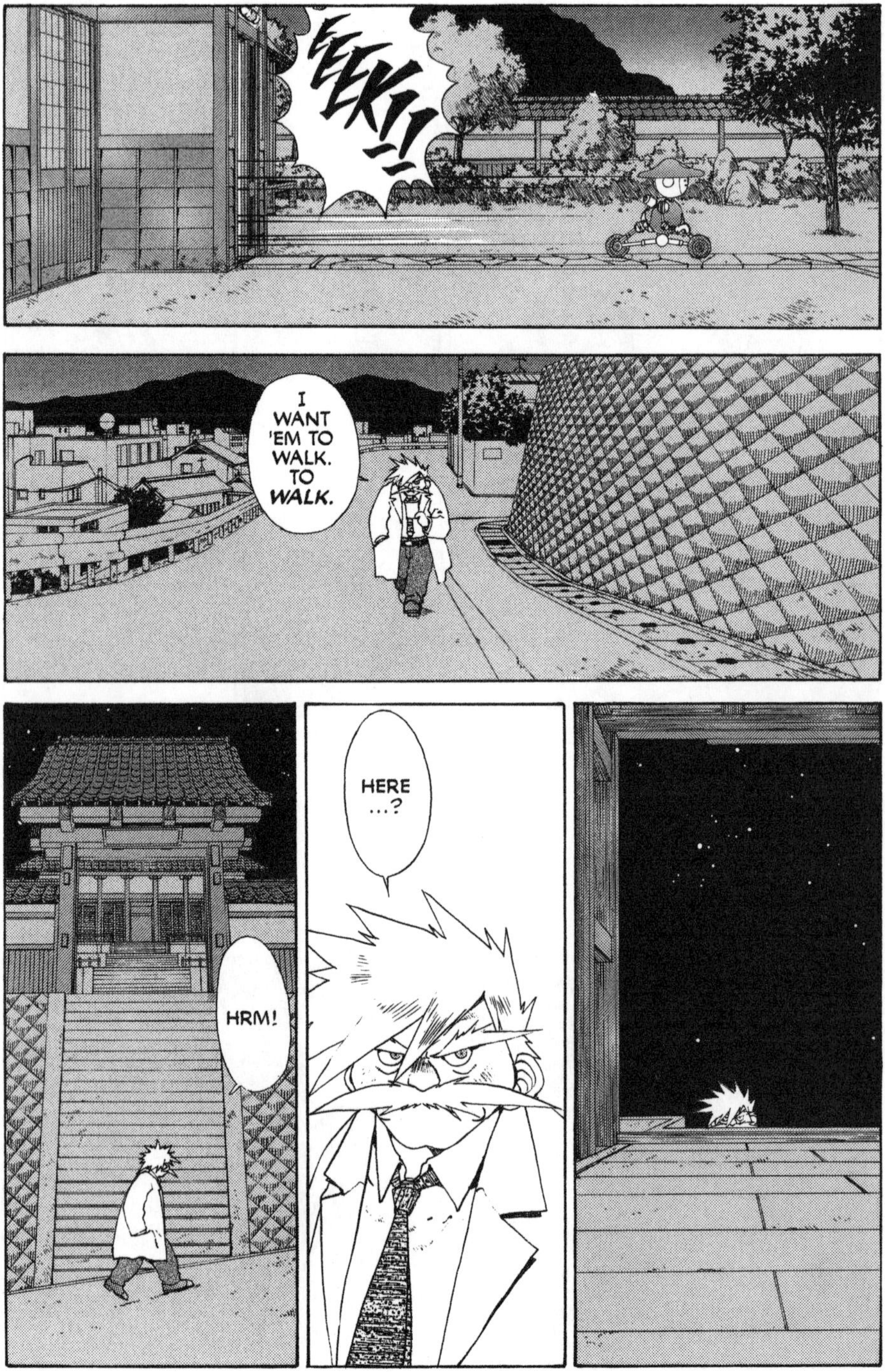
EEEKK!!!
I WANT 'EM TO WALK. TO *WALK*.
HRM!
HERE ...?

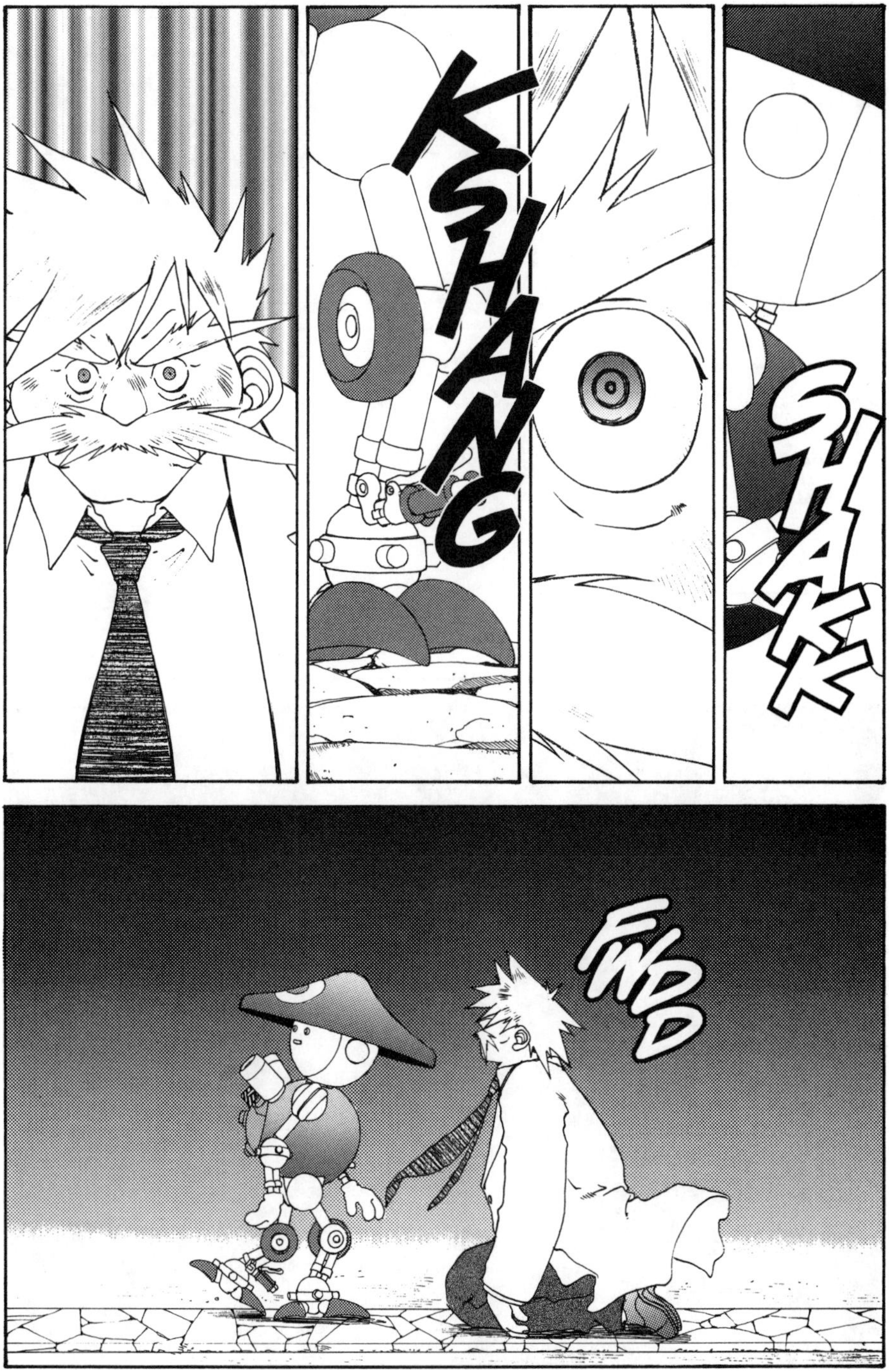
KSHANG
SHAKK
FWD

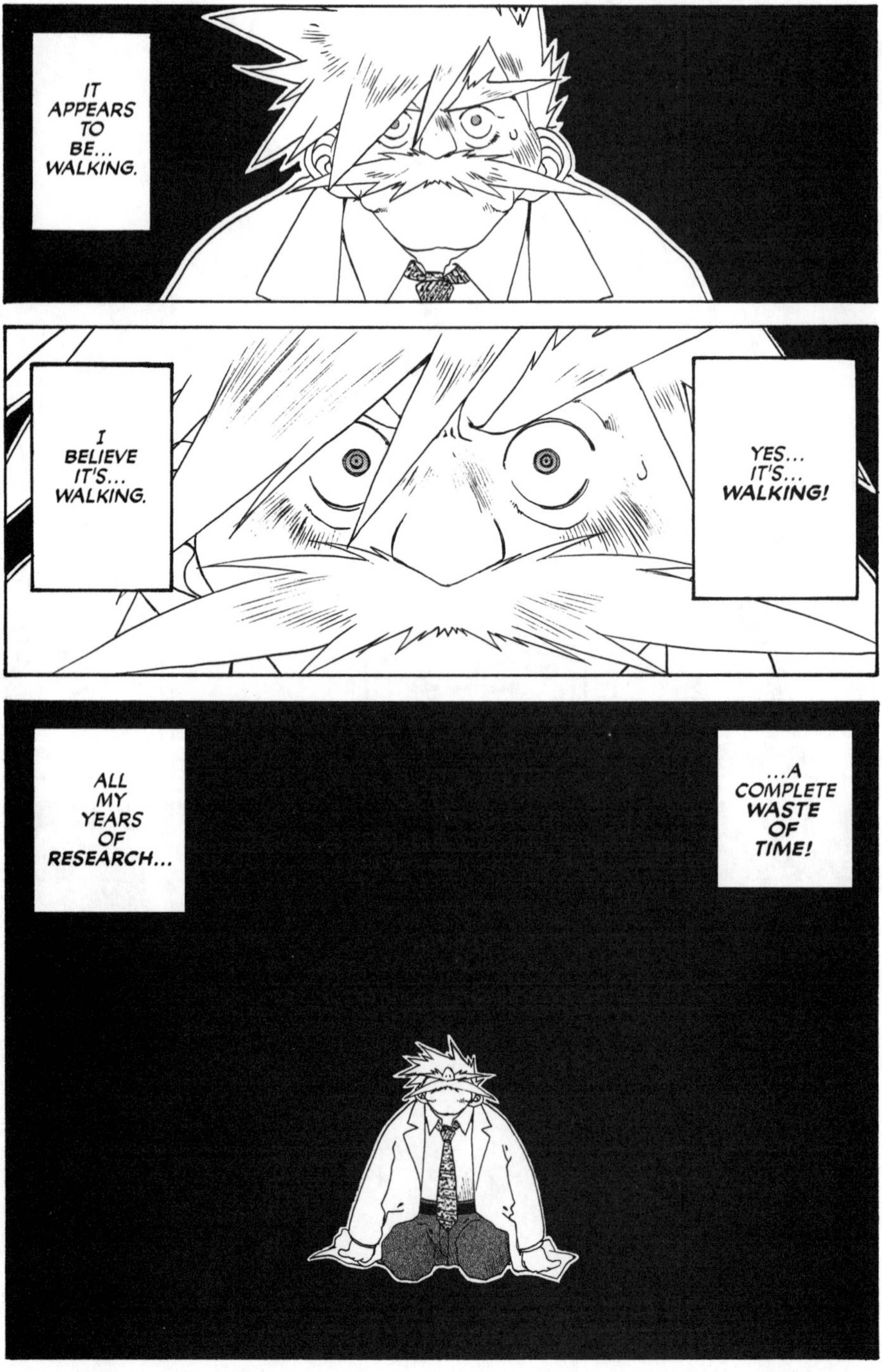
IT APPEARS TO BE... WALKING.
I BELIEVE IT'S... WALKING.
YES... IT'S... WALKING!
ALL MY YEARS OF RESEARCH...
...A COMPLETE WASTE OF TIME!

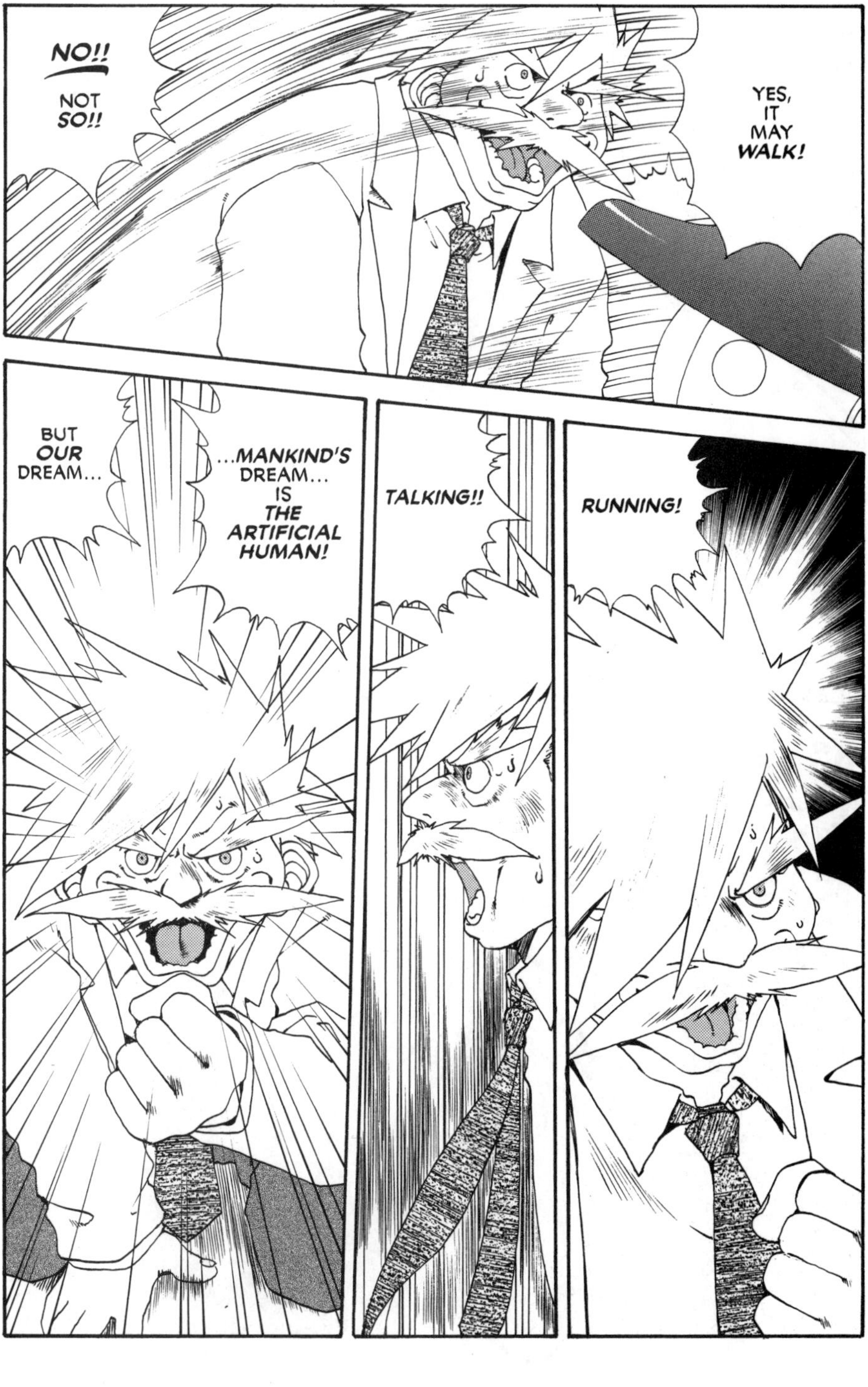
NO!!
NOT SO!!
YES, IT MAY WALK!
BUT OUR DREAM...
...MANKIND'S DREAM... IS THE ARTIFICIAL HUMAN!
TALKING!!
RUNNING!

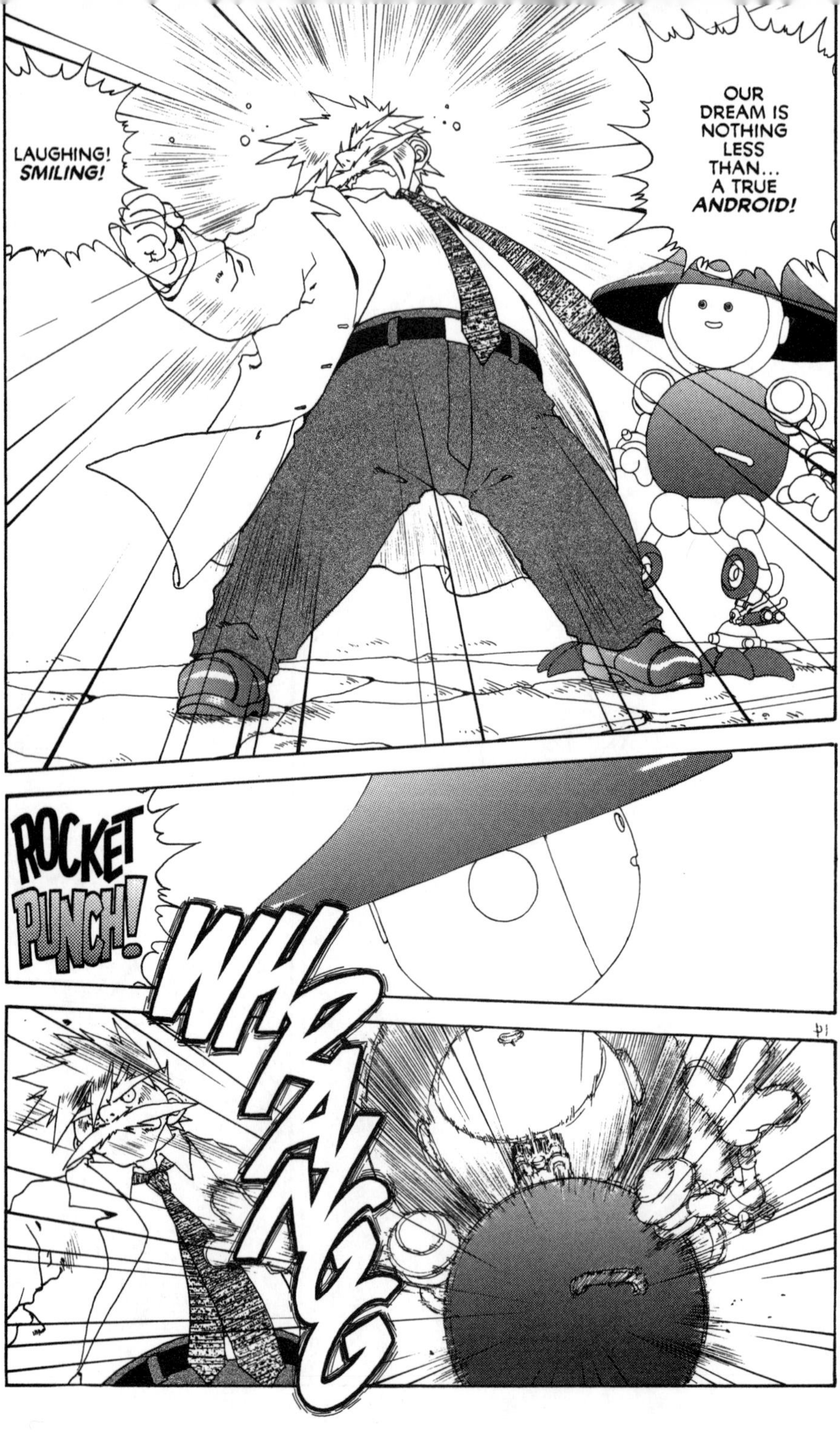
LAUGHING! *SMILING!*
OUR DREAM IS NOTHING LESS THAN... A TRUE *ANDROID!*
ROCKET PUNCH!
WHRANGG

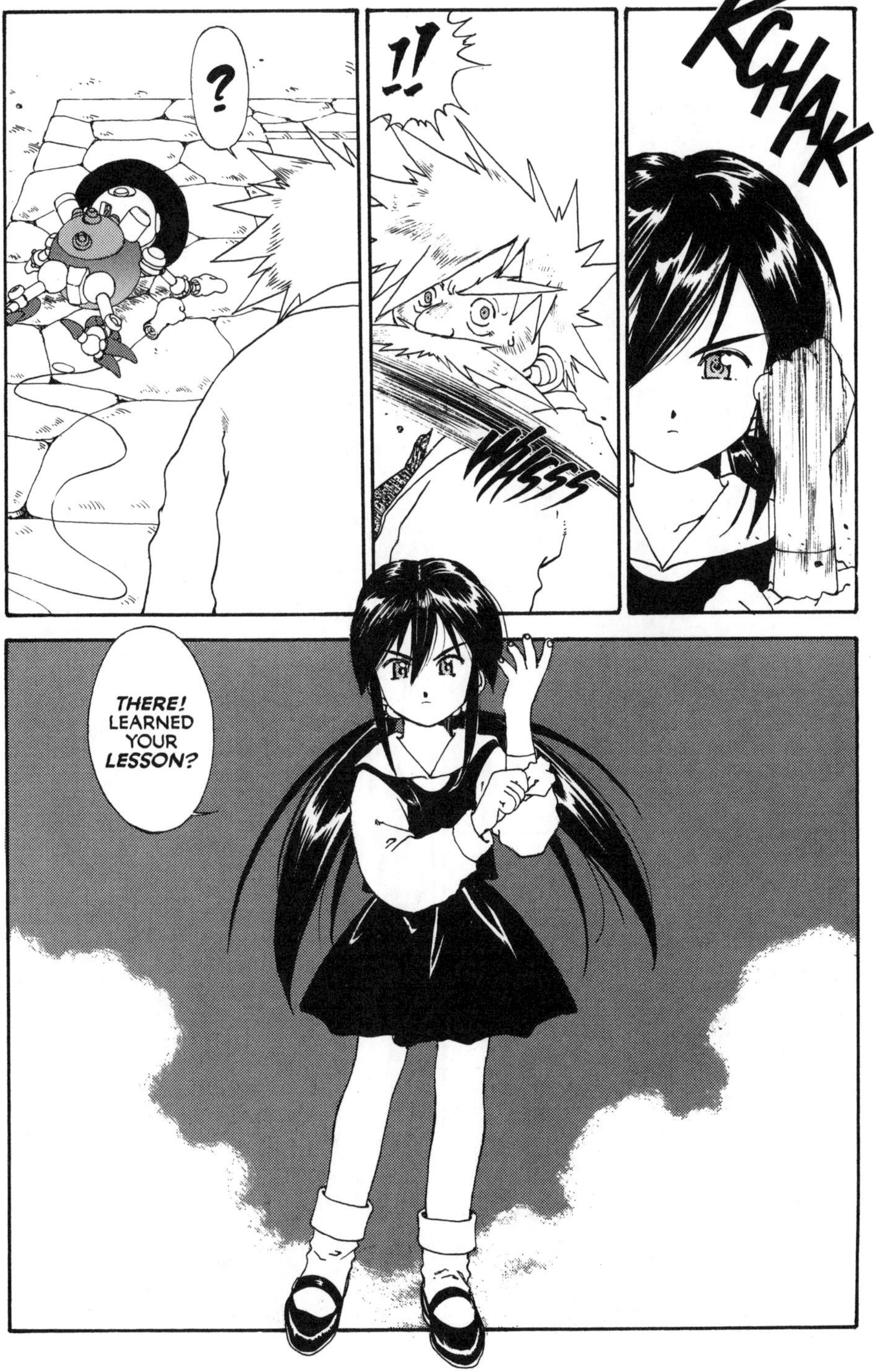
?
!!
WHSSS
KCHAK
THERE! LEARNED YOUR LESSON?

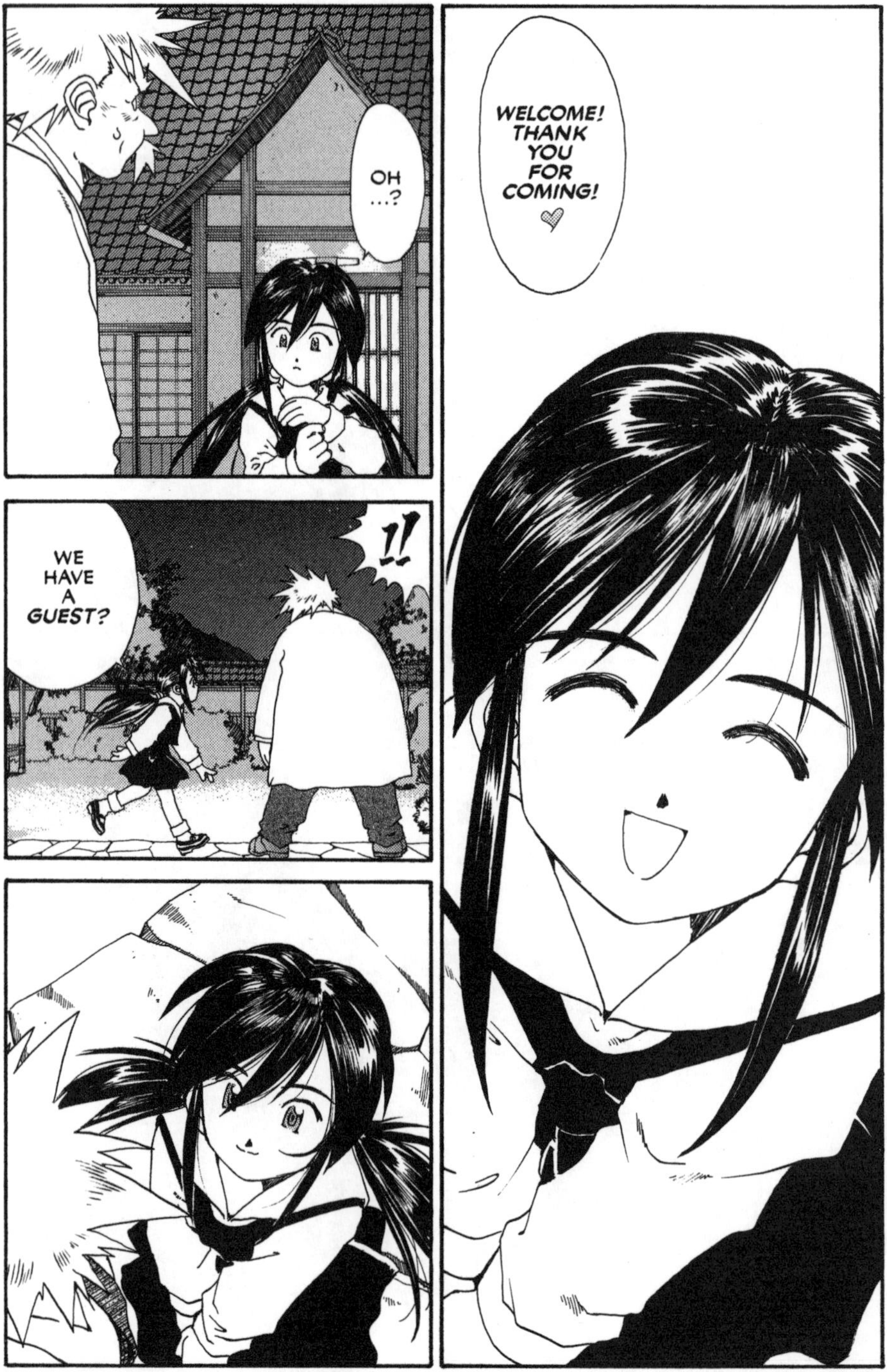
OH ...?
WE HAVE A GUEST?
!!
WELCOME! THANK YOU FOR COMING! ♥

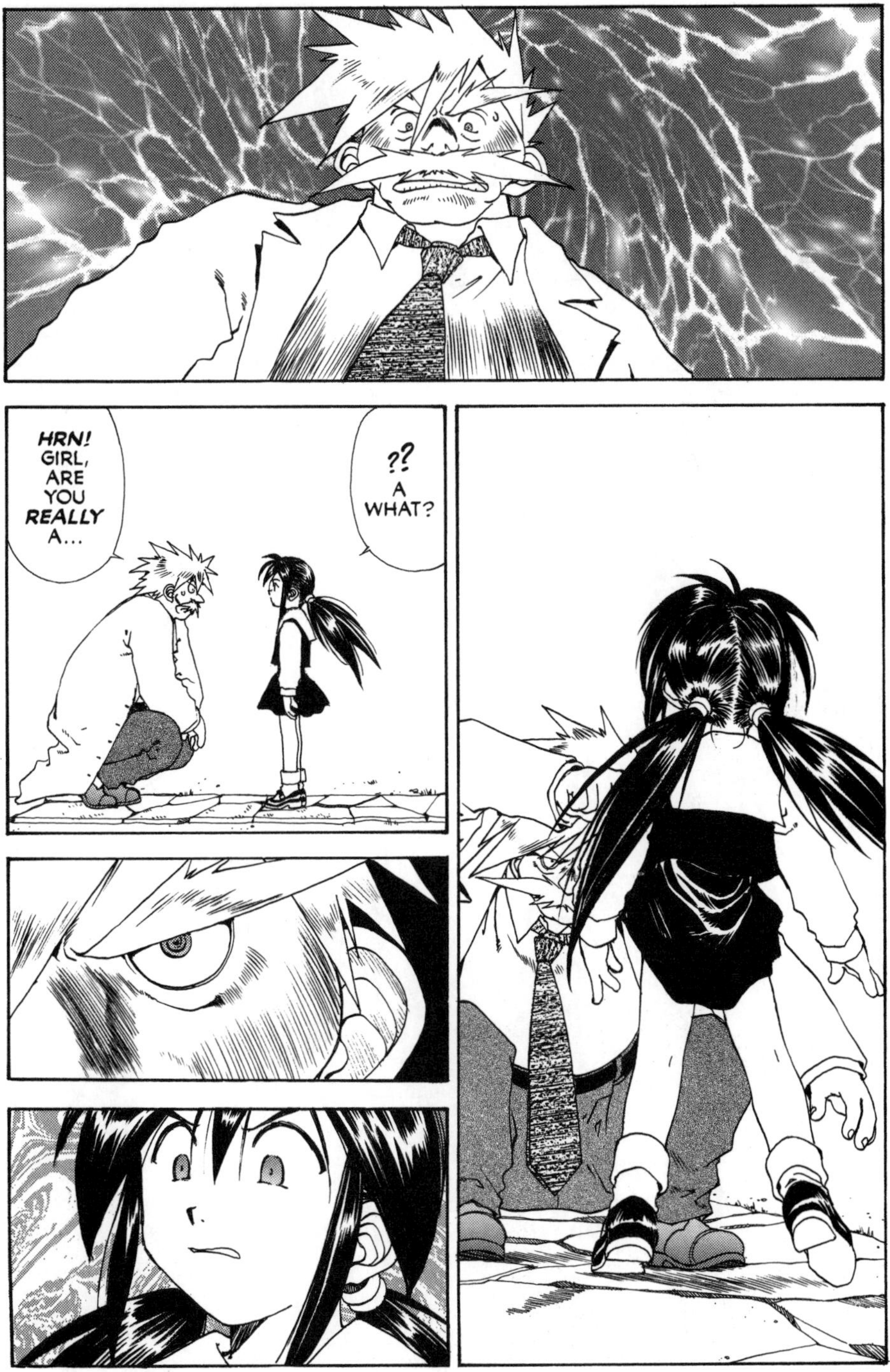
HRN! GIRL, ARE YOU **REALLY** A...
?? A WHAT?

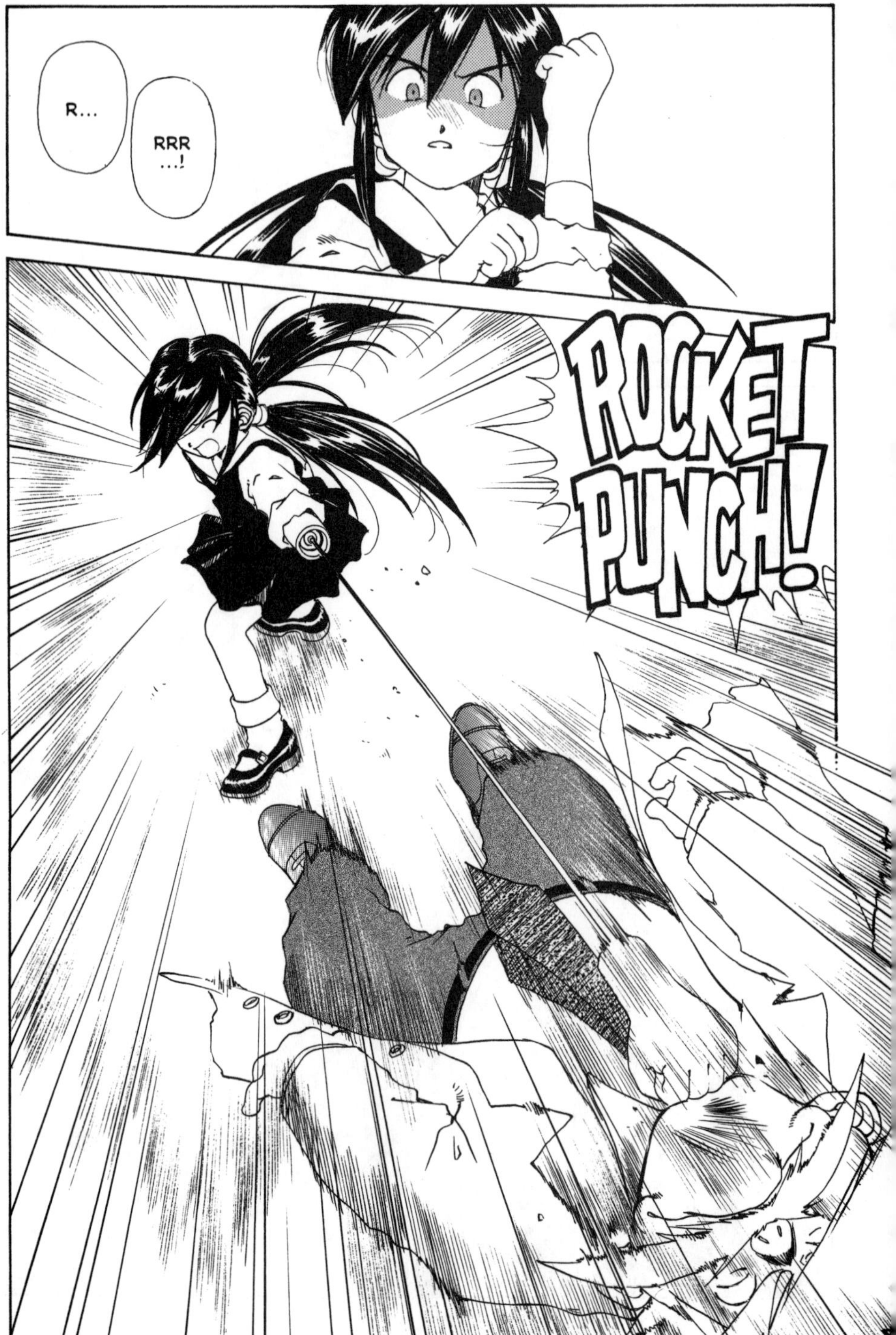
R...
RRR ...!
ROCKET PUNCH!

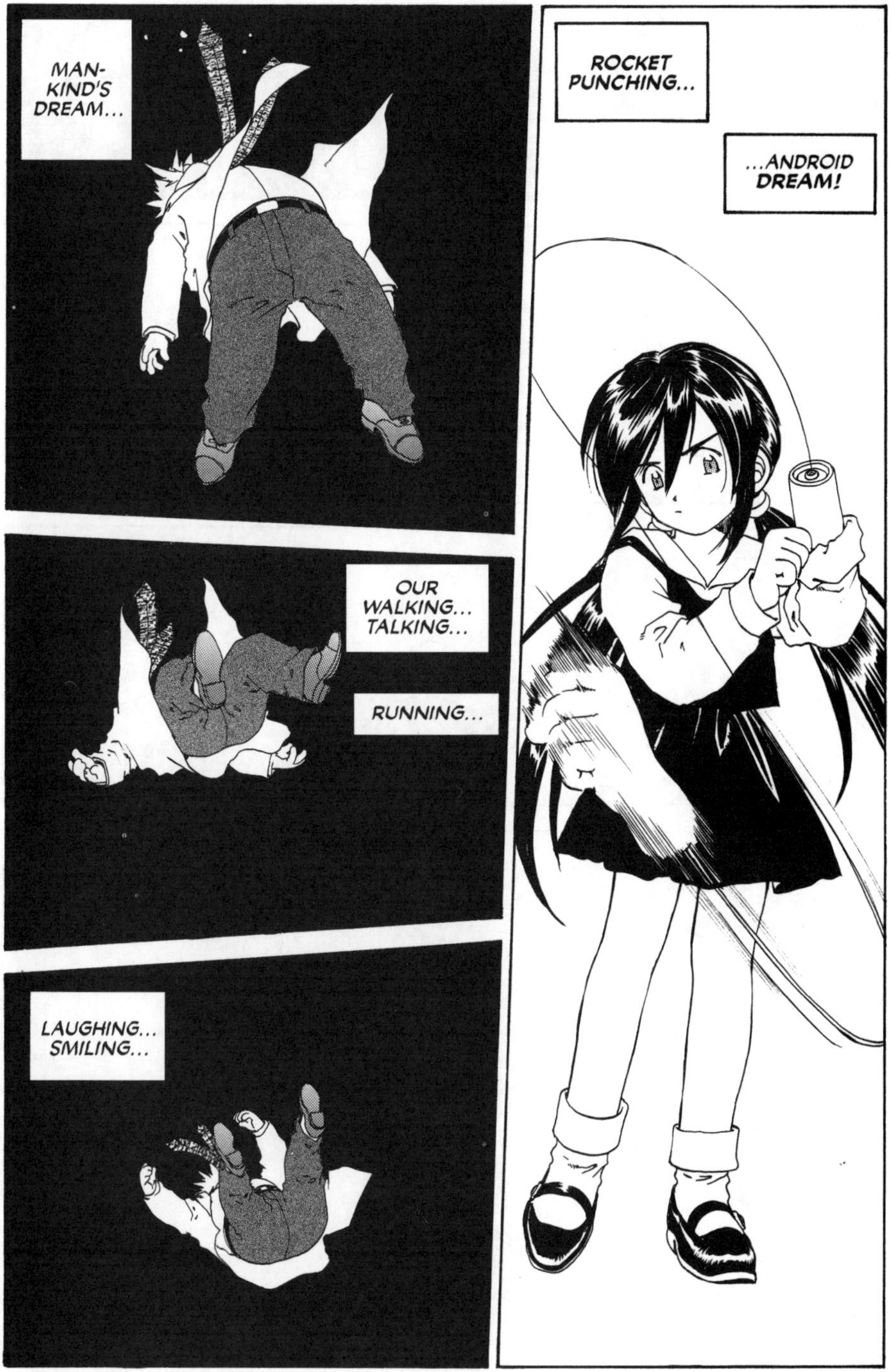
MAN-KIND'S DREAM...
OUR WALKING... TALKING...
RUNNING...
LAUGHING... SMILING...
ROCKET PUNCHING...
...ANDROID DREAM!

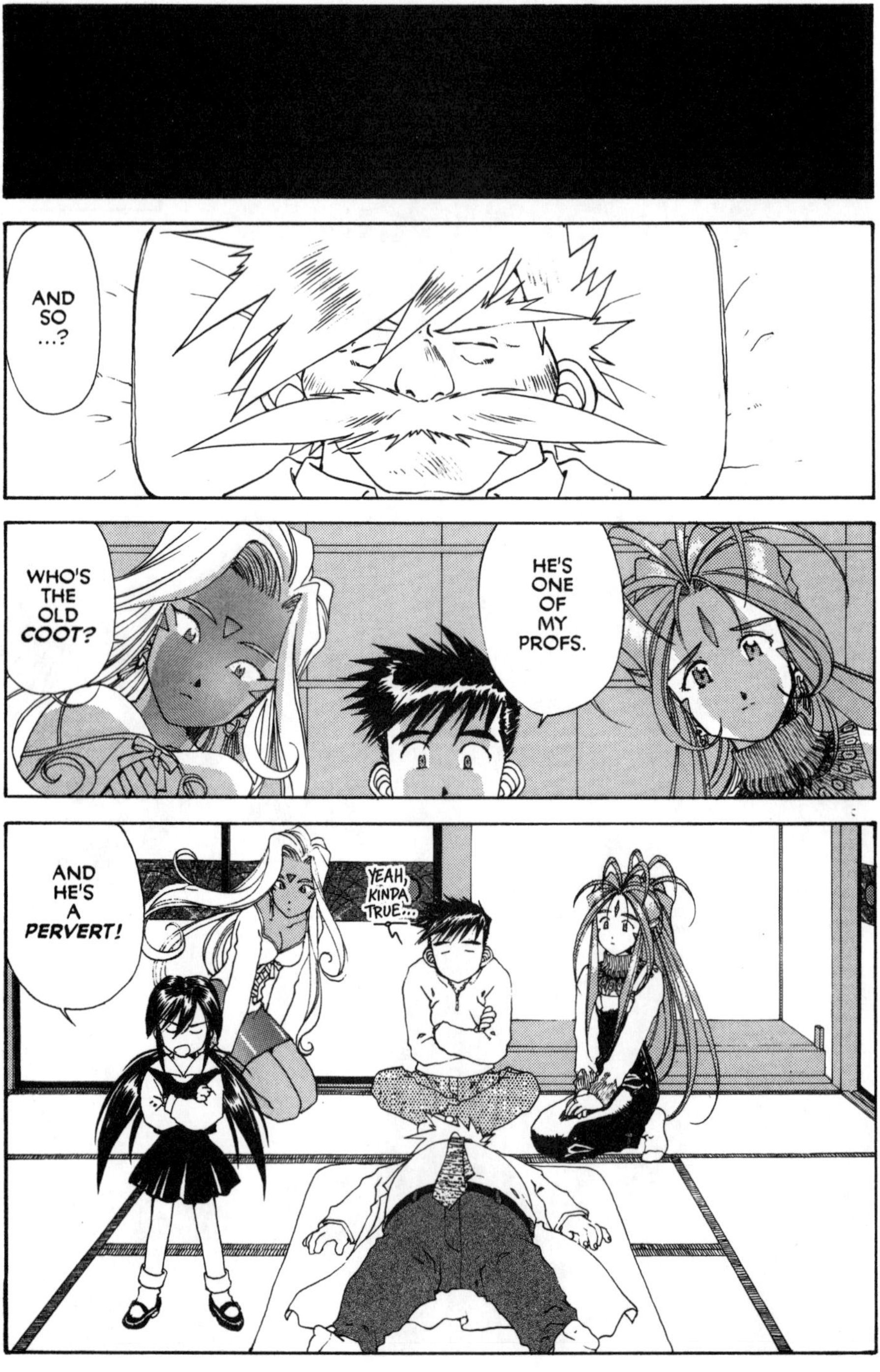
AND SO ...?
WHO'S THE OLD COOT?
HE'S ONE OF MY PROFS.
AND HE'S A PERVERT!
YEAH, KINDA TRUE...

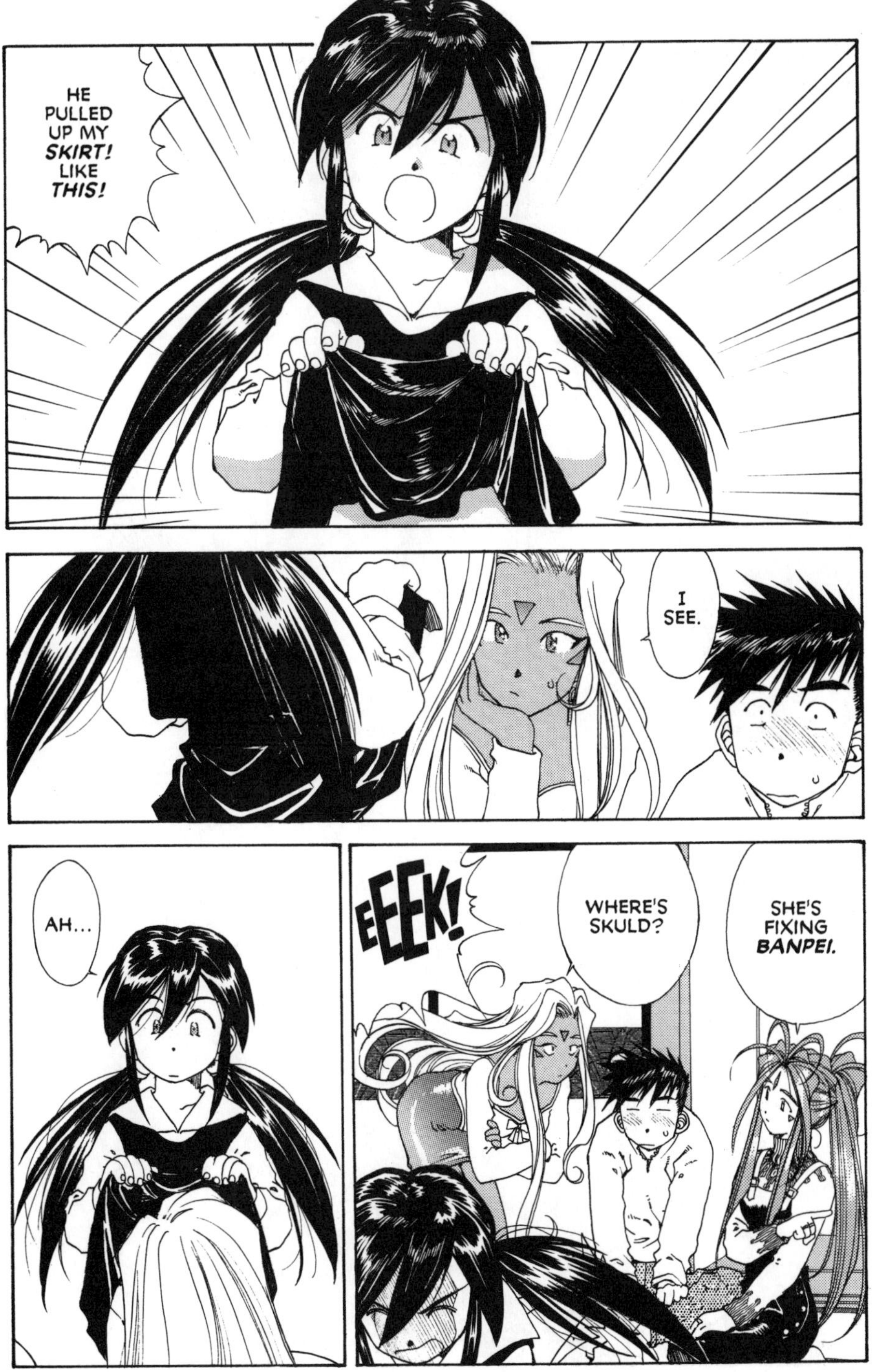
HE PULLED UP MY *SKIRT!* LIKE *THIS!*
I SEE.
AH...
EEEK!
WHERE'S SKULD?
SHE'S FIXING *BANPEI.*

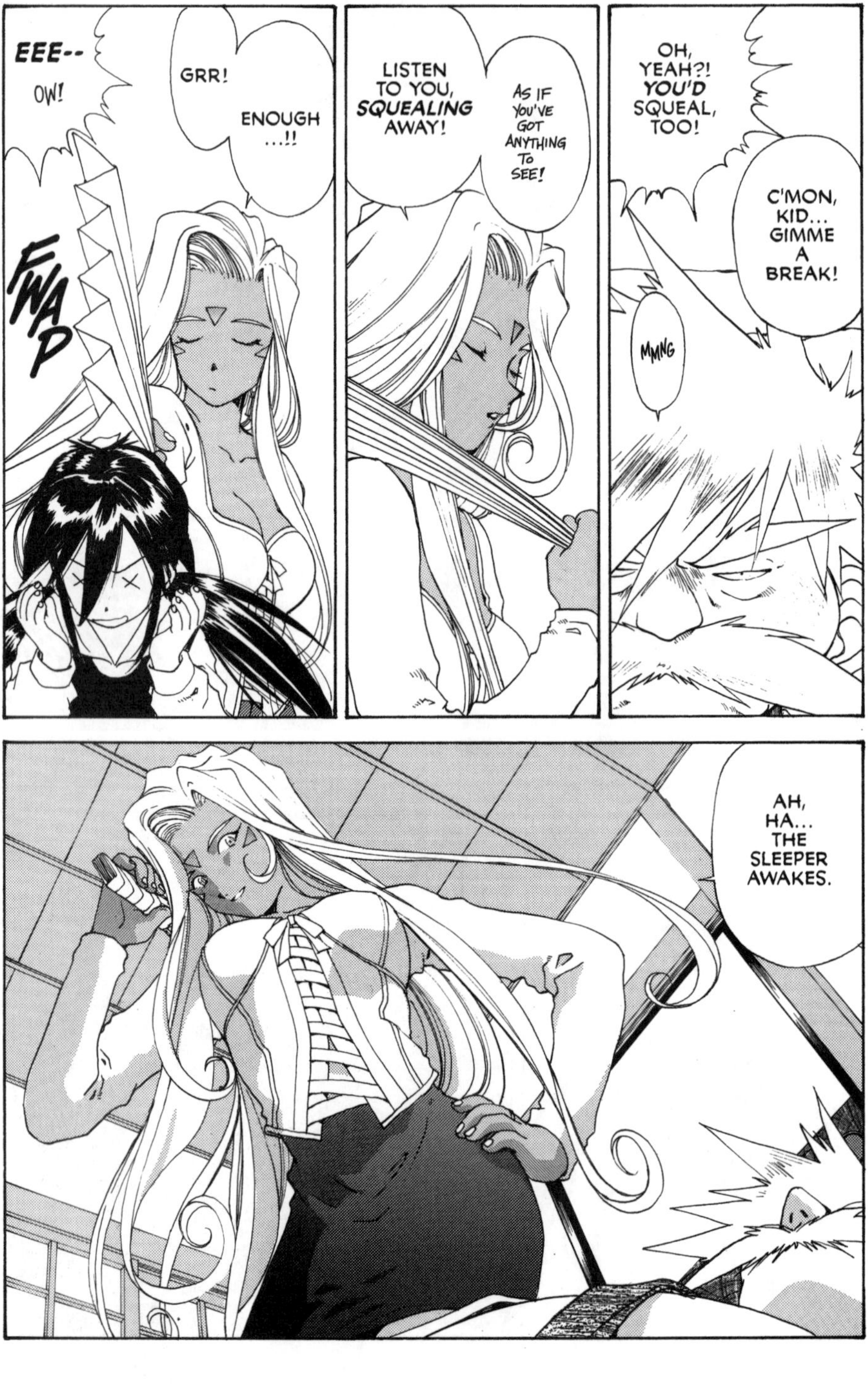
EEE--
OW!
GRR!
ENOUGH ...!!
FWAP
LISTEN TO YOU, SQUEALING AWAY!
AS IF YOU'VE GOT ANYTHING TO SEE!
OH, YEAH?! YOU'D SQUEAL, TOO!
C'MON, KID... GIMME A BREAK!
MMNG
AH, HA... THE SLEEPER AWAKES.

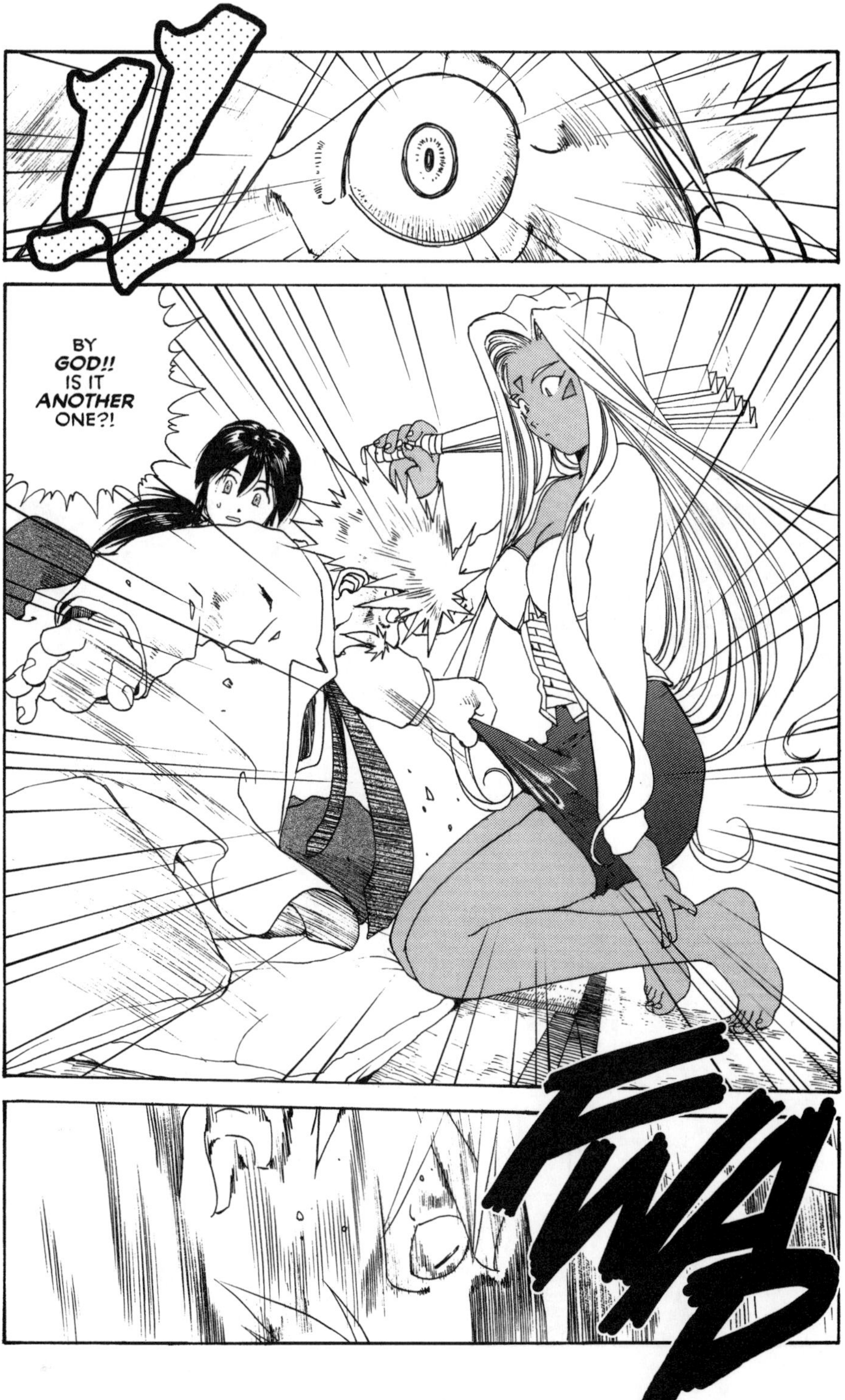
!!
BY *GOD!!* IS IT *ANOTHER* ONE?!
FWAP

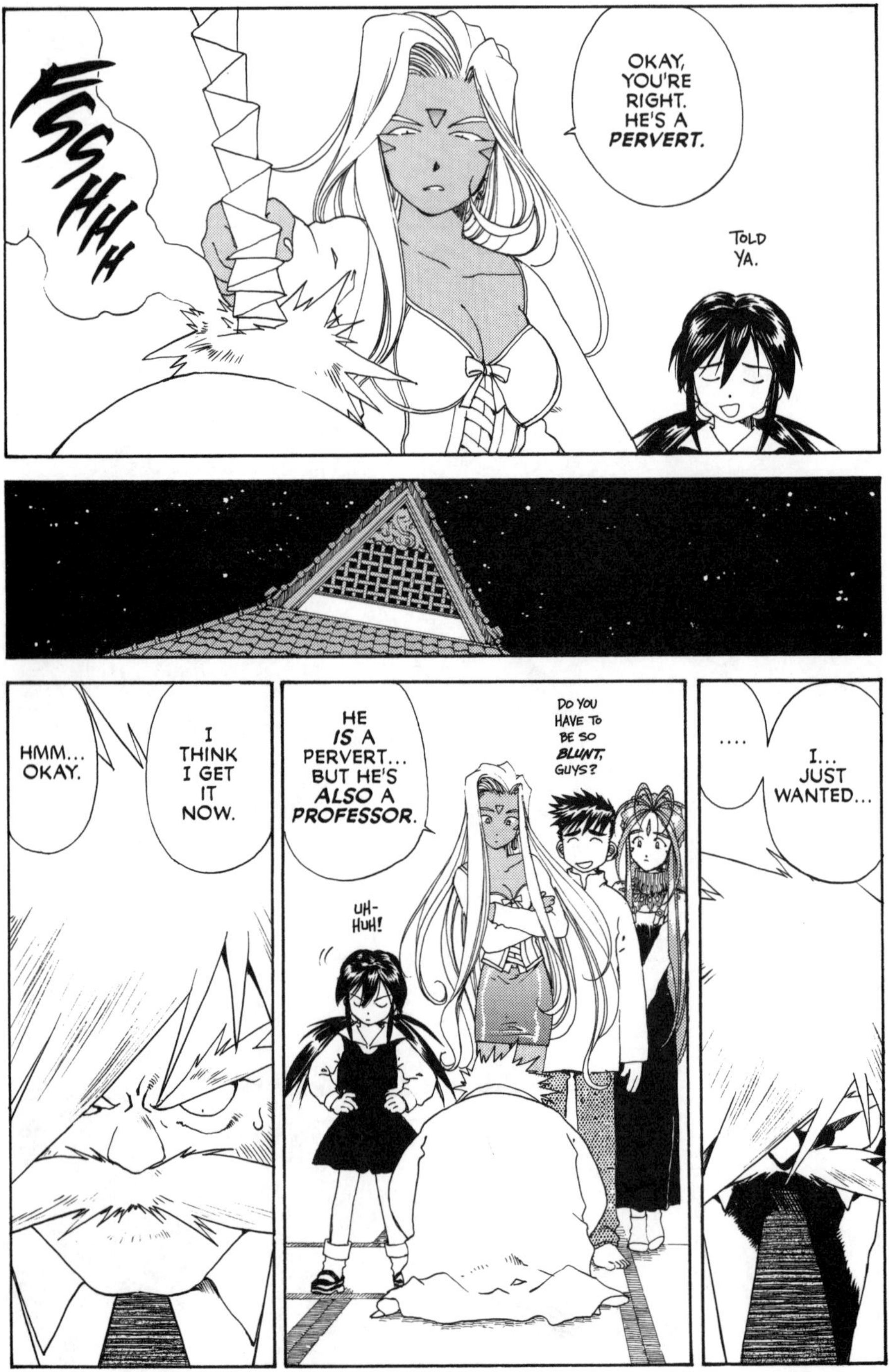
FSSHHHH
OKAY, YOU'RE RIGHT. HE'S A PERVERT.
TOLD YA.
HMM... OKAY.
I THINK I GET IT NOW.
HE IS A PERVERT... BUT HE'S ALSO A PROFESSOR.
DO YOU HAVE TO BE SO BLUNT, GUYS?
UH-HUH!
....
I... JUST WANTED...

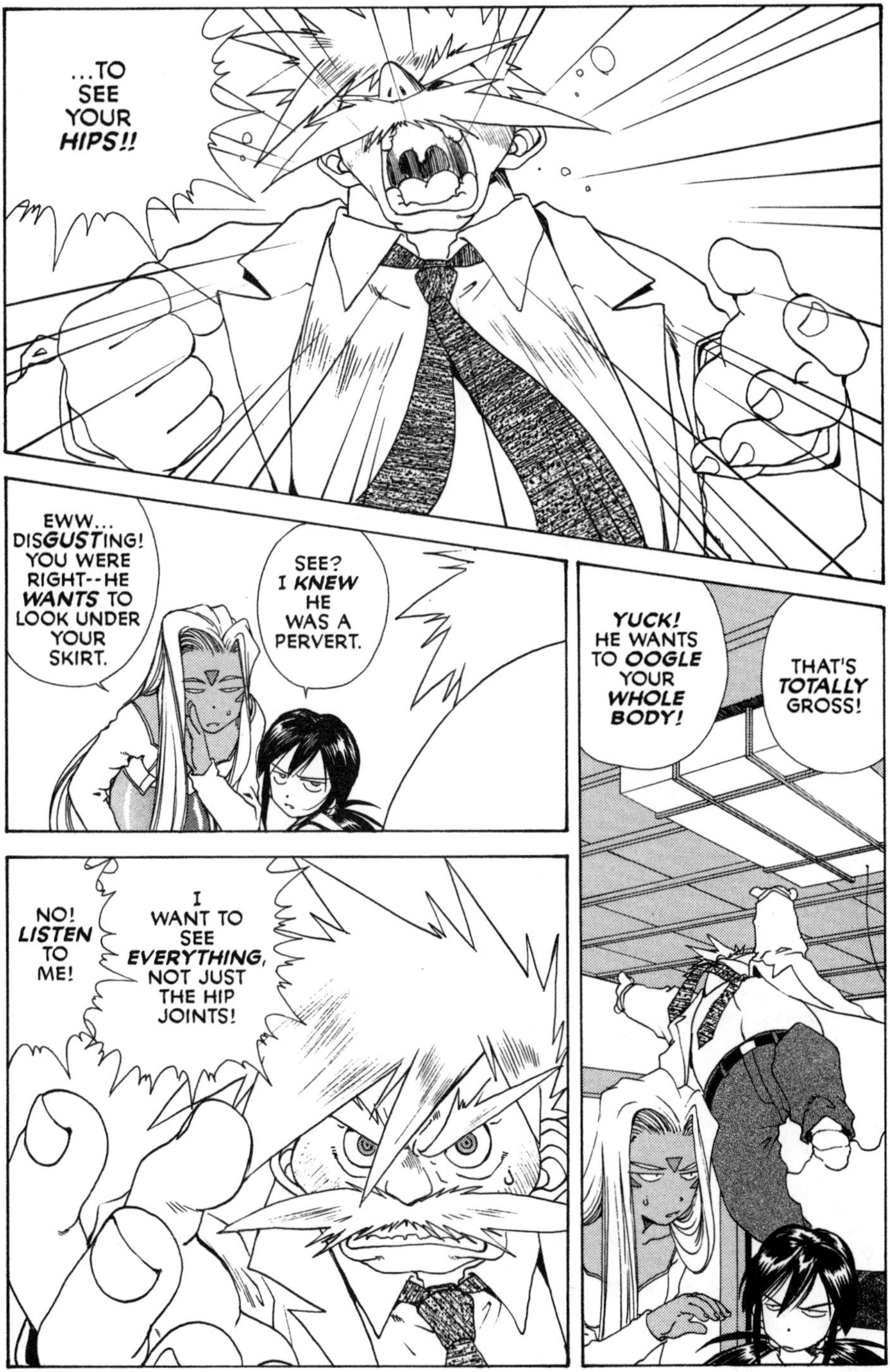
...TO SEE YOUR HIPS!!
EWW... DISGUSTING! YOU WERE RIGHT--HE WANTS TO LOOK UNDER YOUR SKIRT.
SEE? I KNEW HE WAS A PERVERT.
NO! LISTEN TO ME!
I WANT TO SEE EVERYTHING, NOT JUST THE HIP JOINTS!
YUCK! HE WANTS TO OOGLE YOUR WHOLE BODY!
THAT'S TOTALLY GROSS!

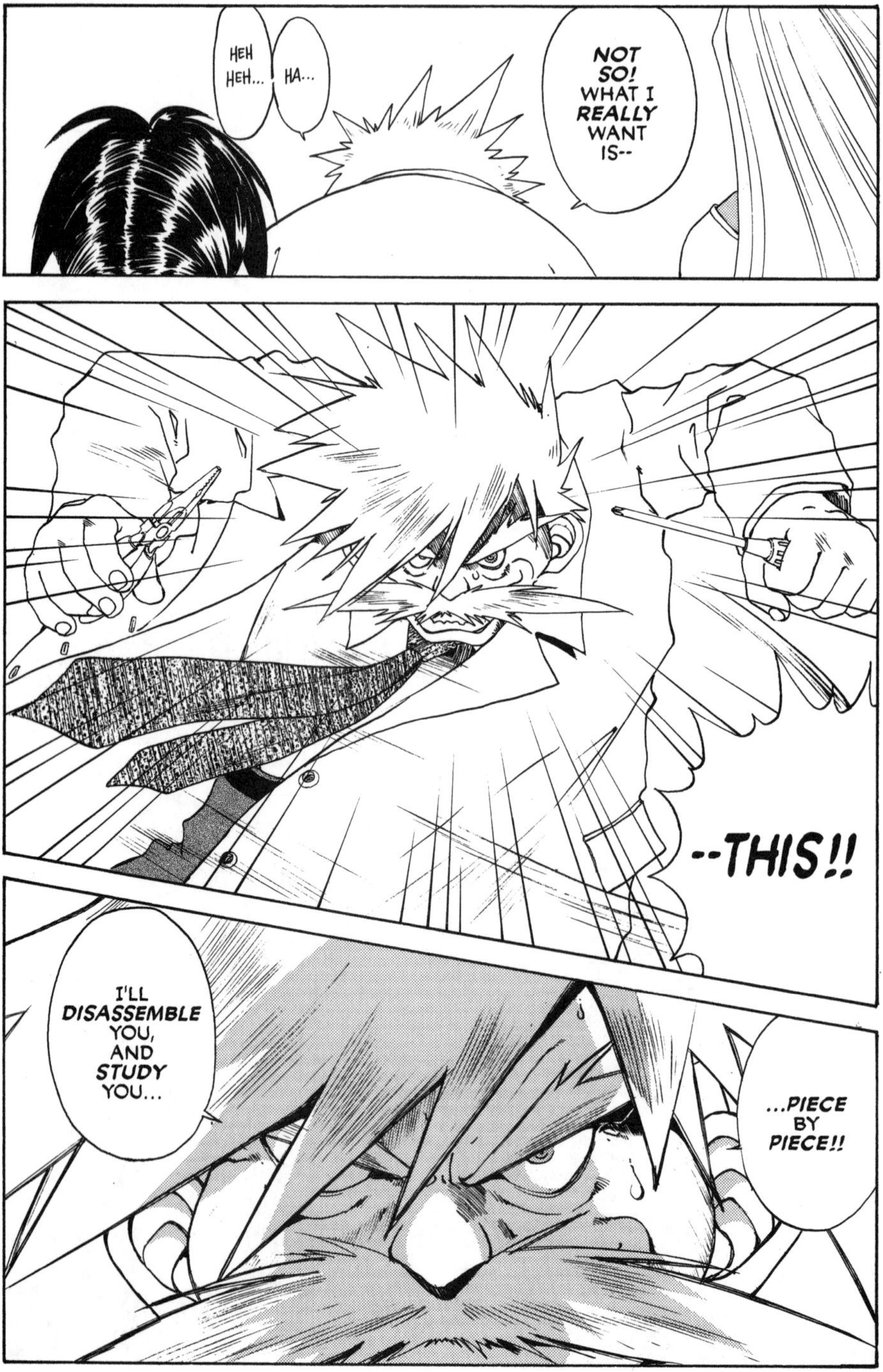
HEH HEH...
HA...
NOT SO! WHAT I *REALLY* WANT IS--
--THIS!!
I'LL *DISASSEMBLE* YOU, AND *STUDY* YOU...
...PIECE BY PIECE!!

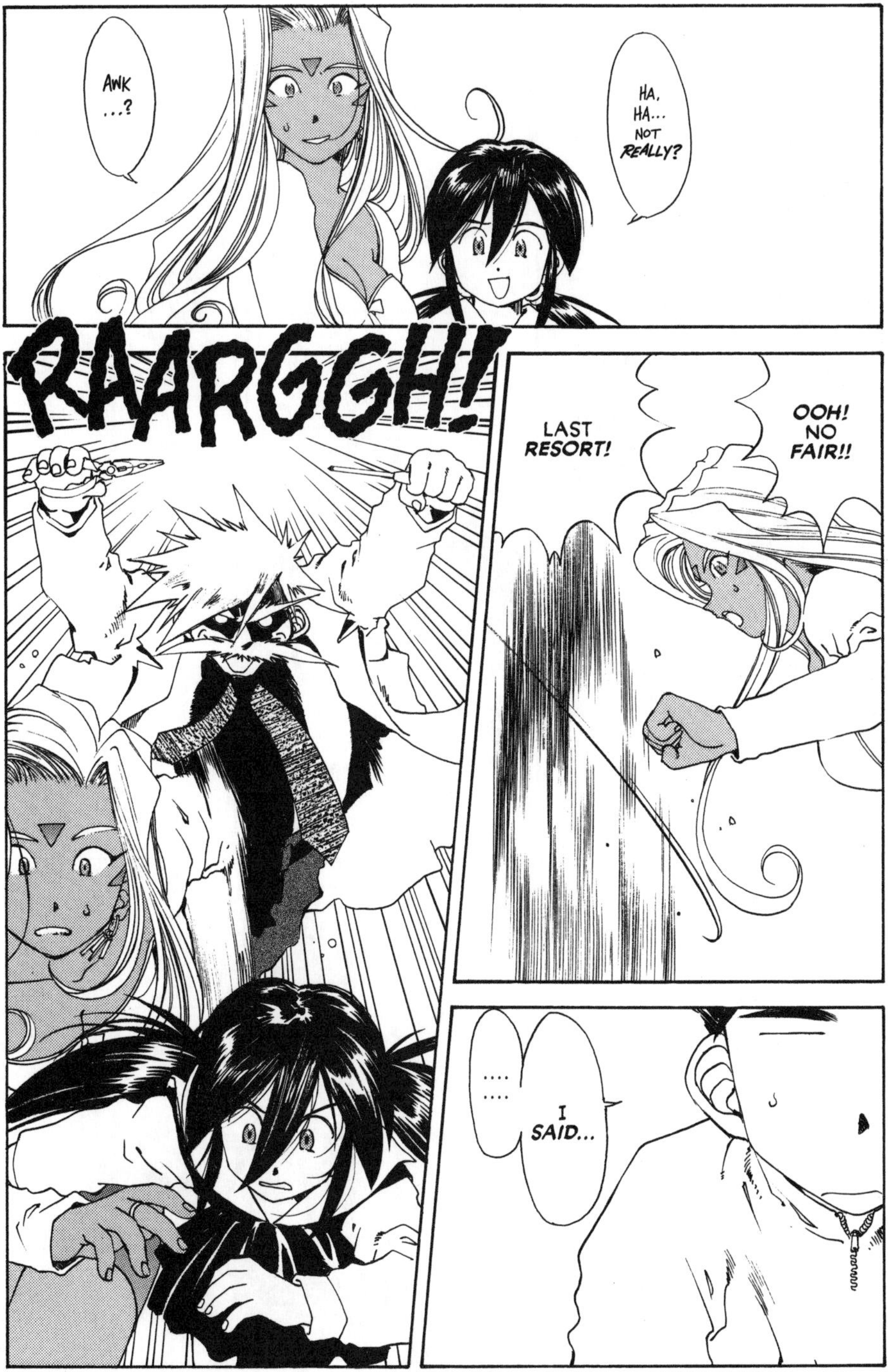
AWK ...?
HA, HA... NOT REALLY?
RAARGGH!
LAST RESORT!
OOH! NO FAIR!!
....
....
I SAID...

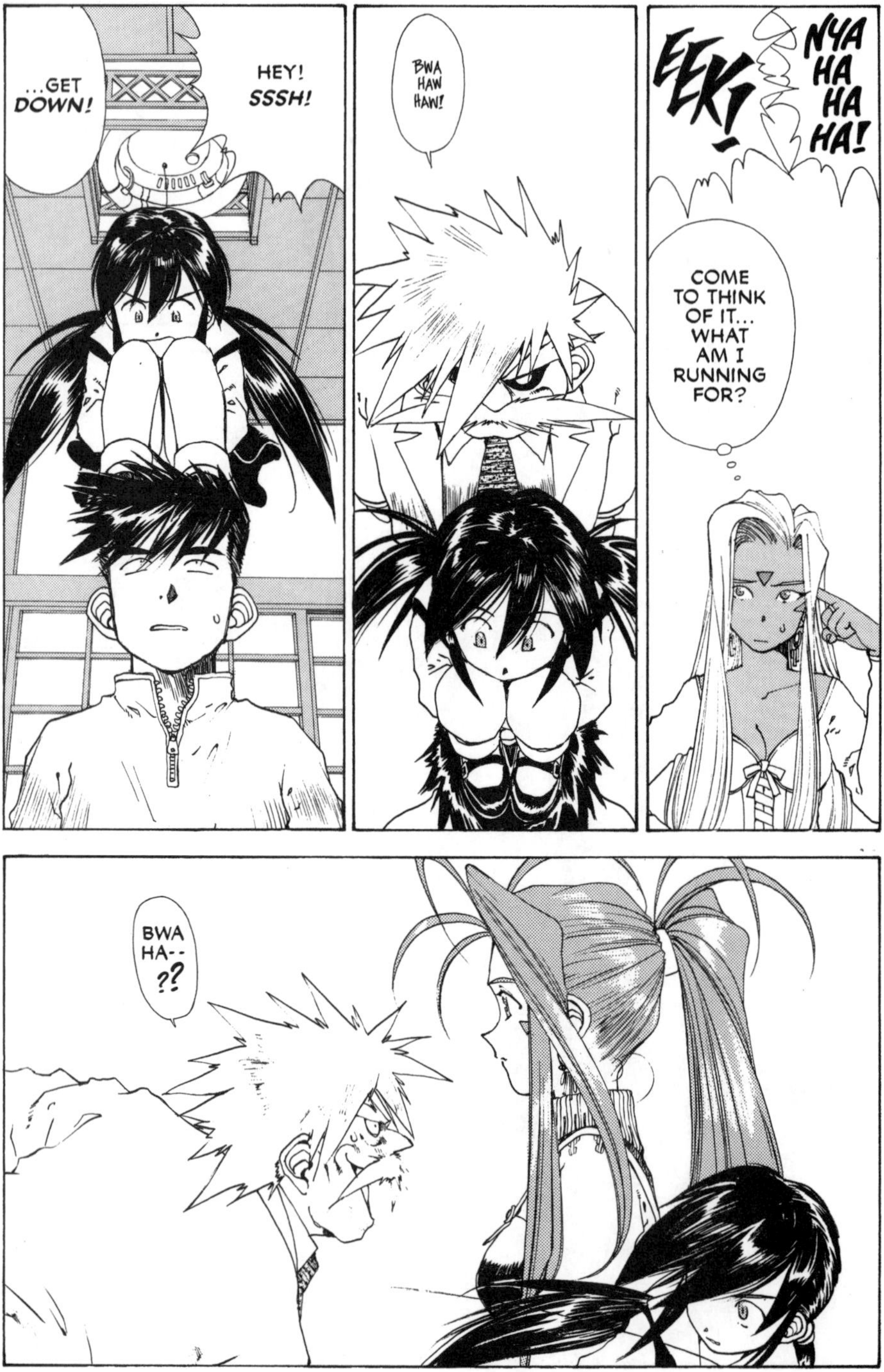
...GET DOWN!
HEY! SSSH!
BWA HAW HAW!
EEK!
NYA HA HA HA!
COME TO THINK OF IT... WHAT AM I RUNNING FOR?
BWA HA-- ??

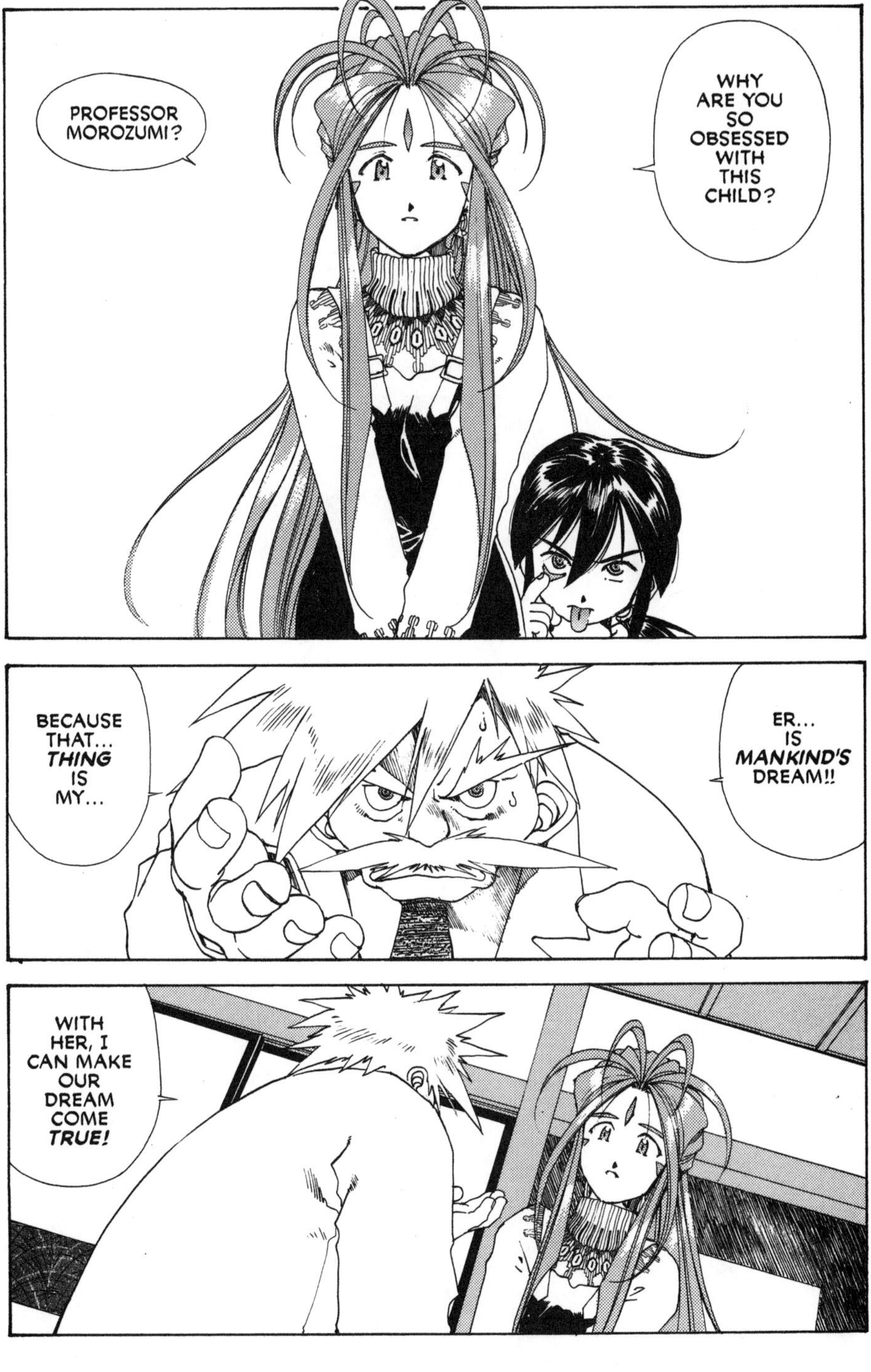
PROFESSOR MOROZUMI?
WHY ARE YOU SO OBSESSED WITH THIS CHILD?
BECAUSE THAT... *THING* IS MY...
ER... IS *MANKIND'S* DREAM!!
WITH HER, I CAN MAKE OUR DREAM COME *TRUE!*

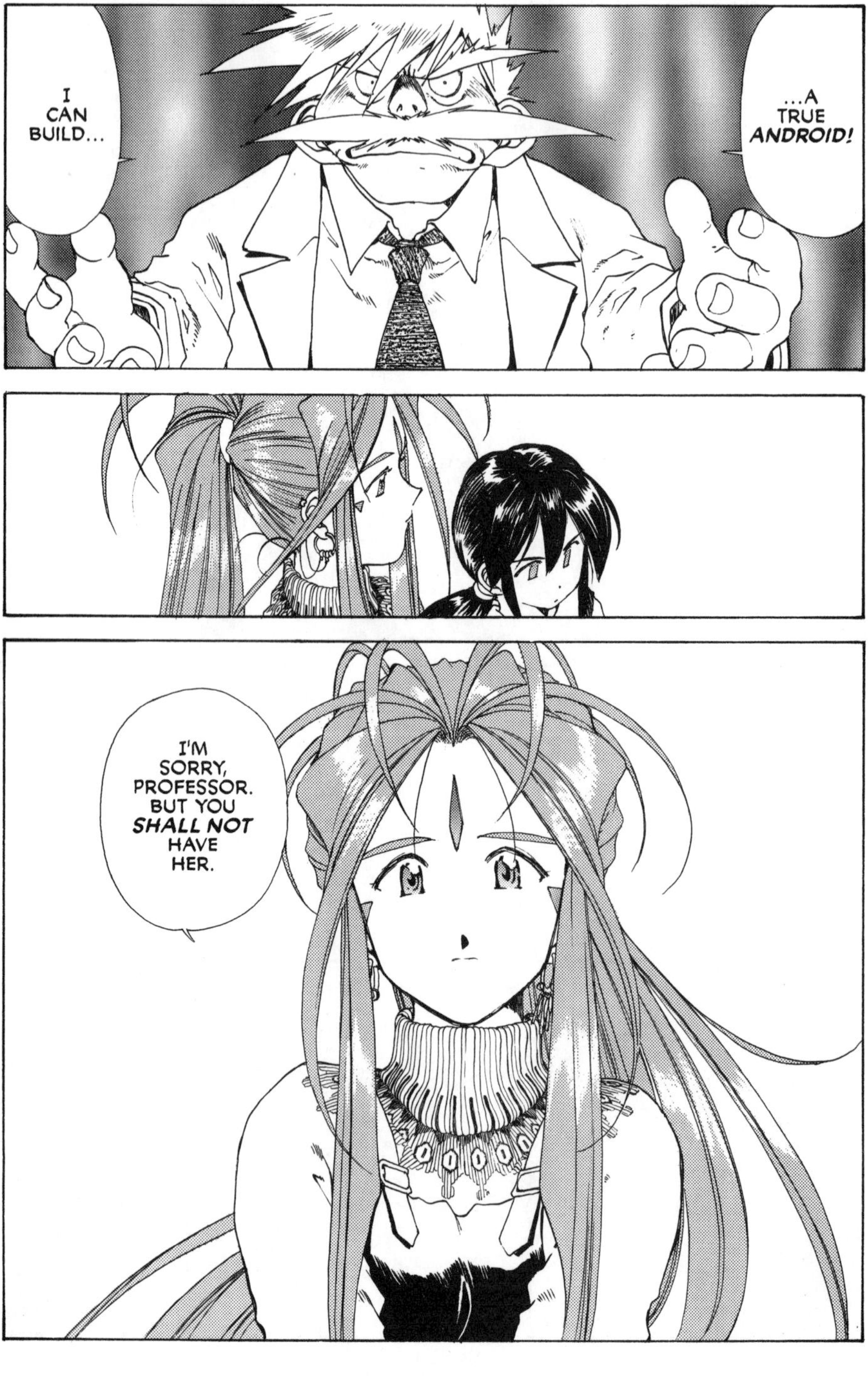
I CAN BUILD...
...A TRUE ANDROID!
I'M SORRY, PROFESSOR. BUT YOU SHALL NOT HAVE HER.

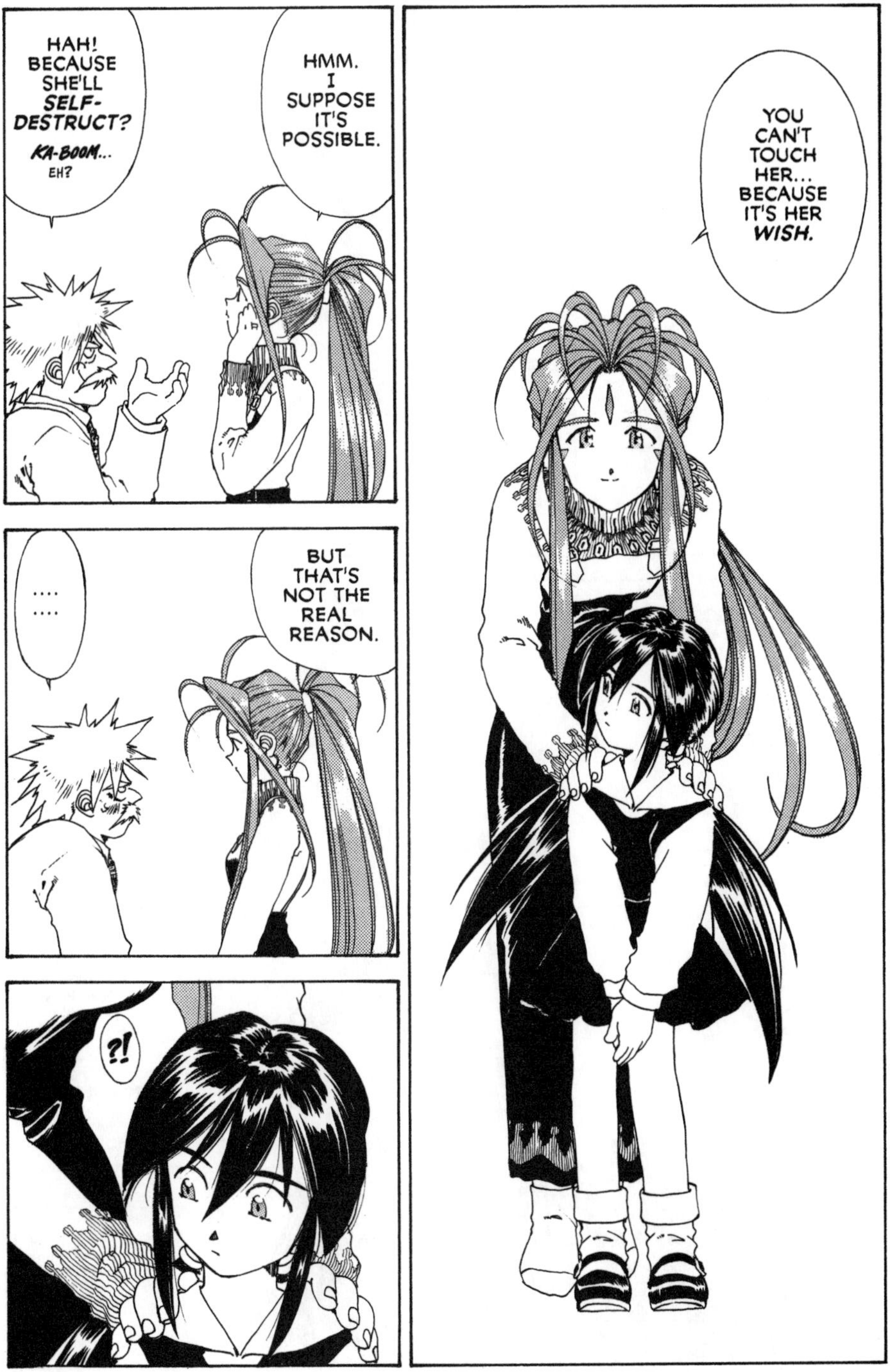

HAH! BECAUSE SHE'LL *SELF-DESTRUCT?*
KA-BOOM...
EH?
HMM. I SUPPOSE IT'S POSSIBLE.
....
BUT THAT'S NOT THE REAL REASON.
?!
YOU CAN'T TOUCH HER... BECAUSE IT'S HER *WISH.*

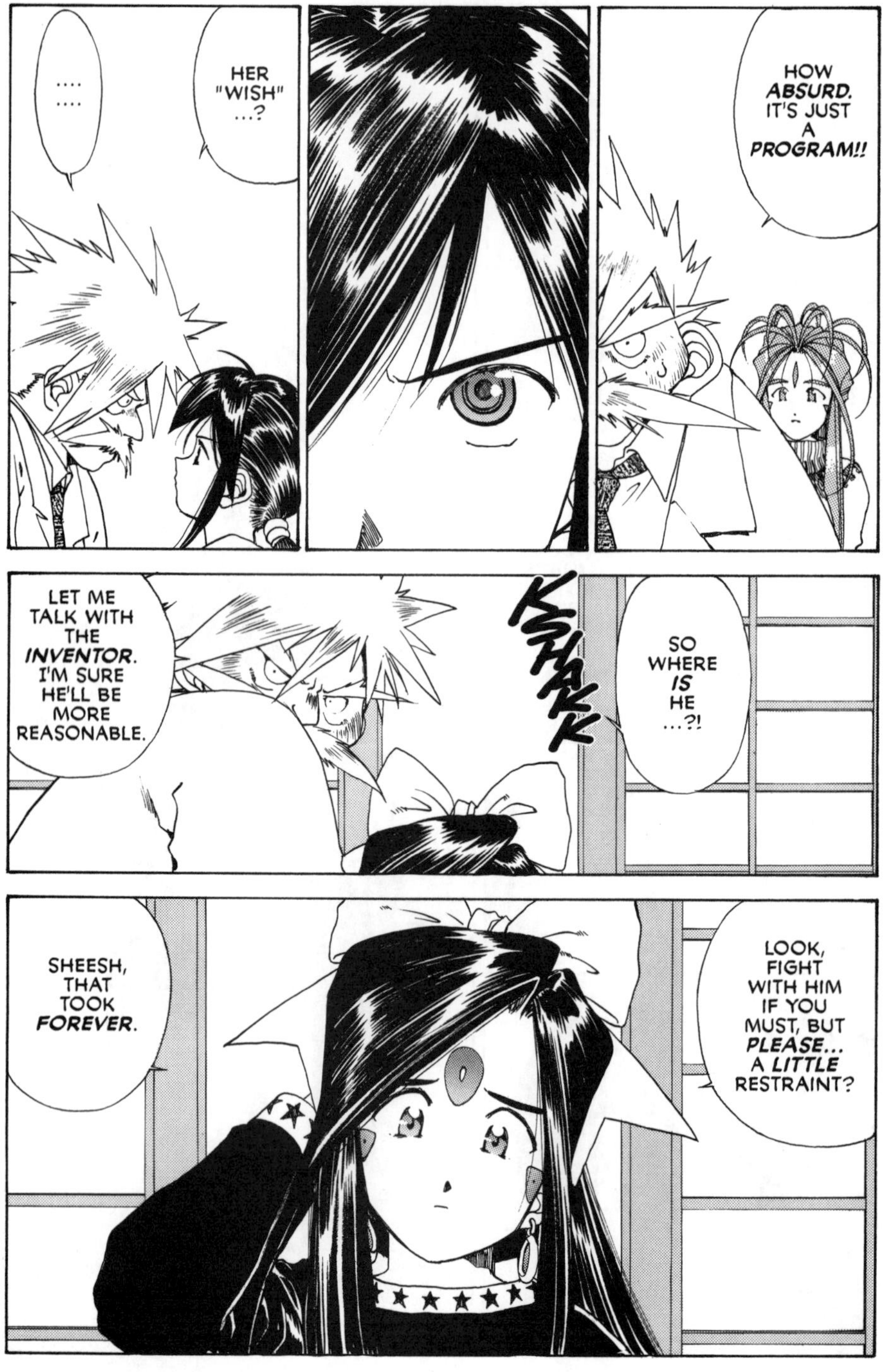
....
....
HER "WISH" ...?
HOW ABSURD. IT'S JUST A PROGRAM!!
LET ME TALK WITH THE INVENTOR. I'M SURE HE'LL BE MORE REASONABLE.
KSHAKK
SO WHERE IS HE ...?!
SHEESH, THAT TOOK FOREVER.
LOOK, FIGHT WITH HIM IF YOU MUST, BUT PLEASE... A LITTLE RESTRAINT?

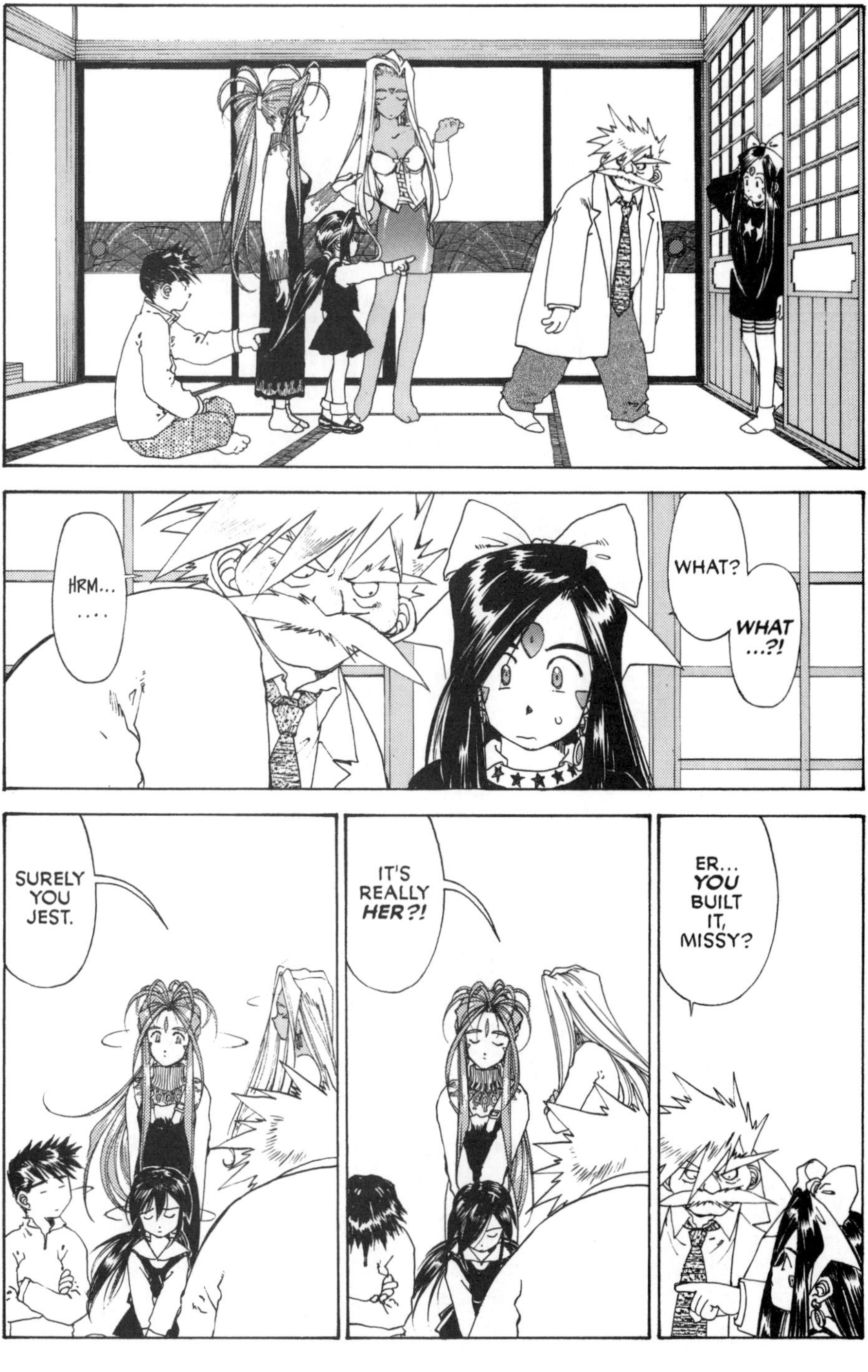
HRM... ....
WHAT?
WHAT ...?!
SURELY YOU JEST.
IT'S REALLY HER?!
ER... YOU BUILT IT, MISSY?

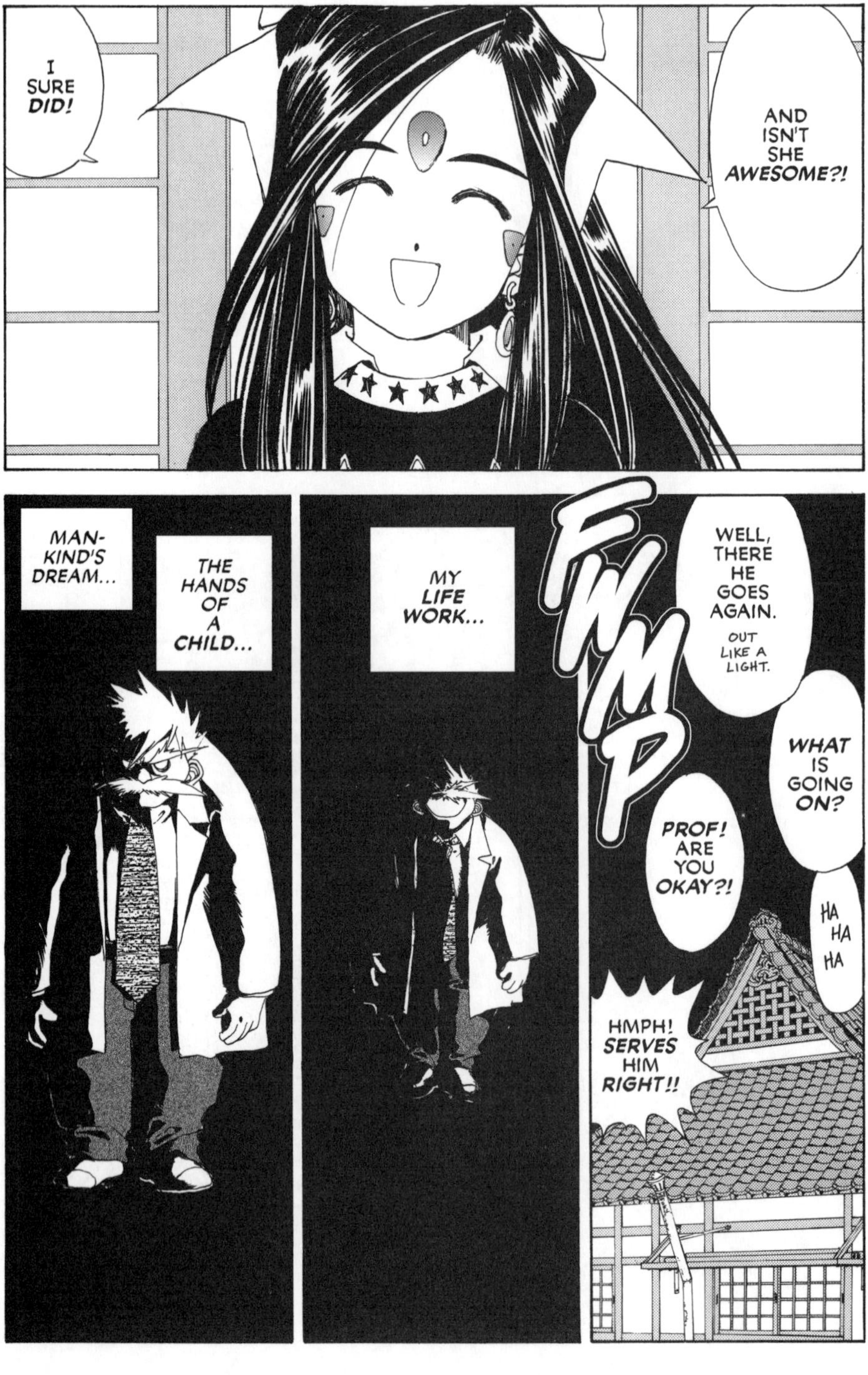
I SURE DID!
AND ISN'T SHE AWESOME?!
MAN-KIND'S DREAM...
THE HANDS OF A CHILD...
MY LIFE WORK...
FWMP
WELL, THERE HE GOES AGAIN.
OUT LIKE A LIGHT.
WHAT IS GOING ON?
PROF! ARE YOU OKAY?!
HA HA HA
HMPH! SERVES HIM RIGHT!!

THE TRAP OF DOCTOR MOREAU!

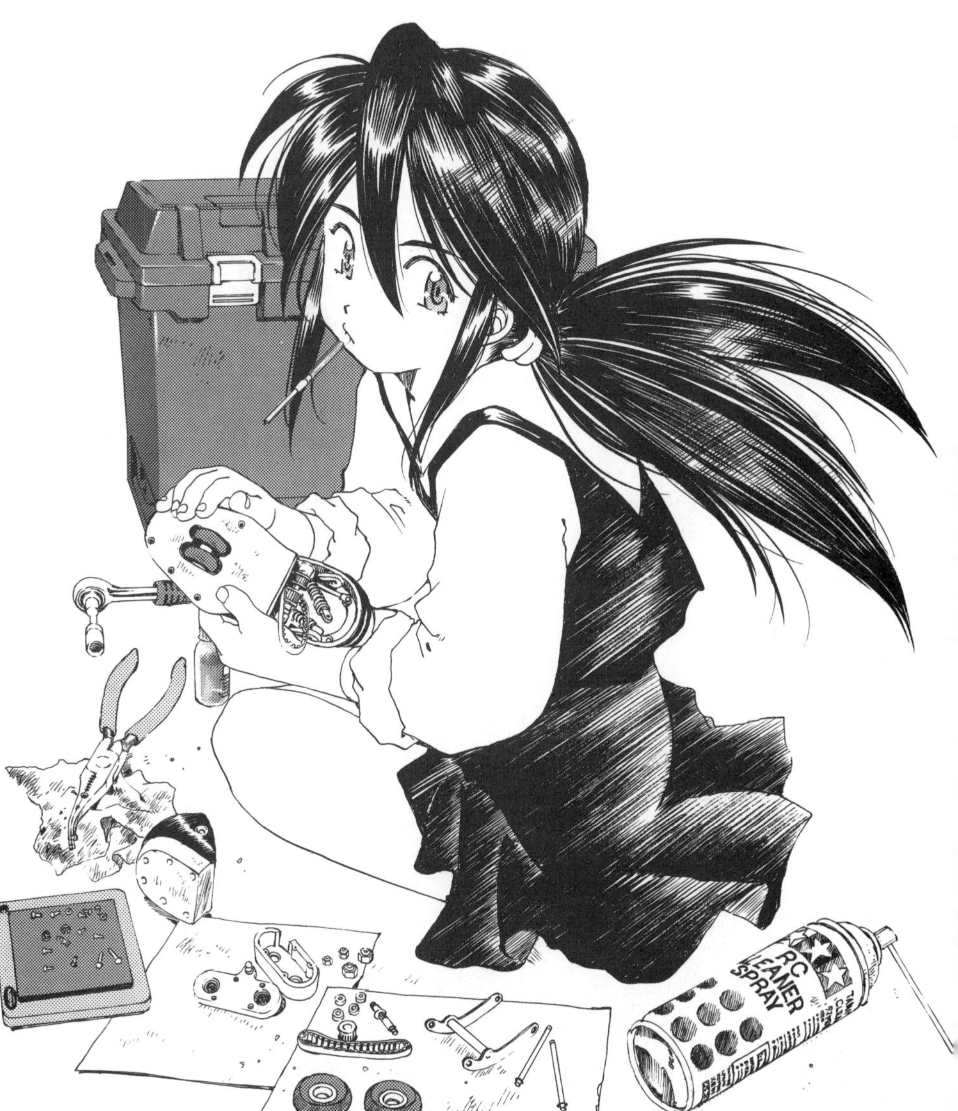
RC
SPRAY

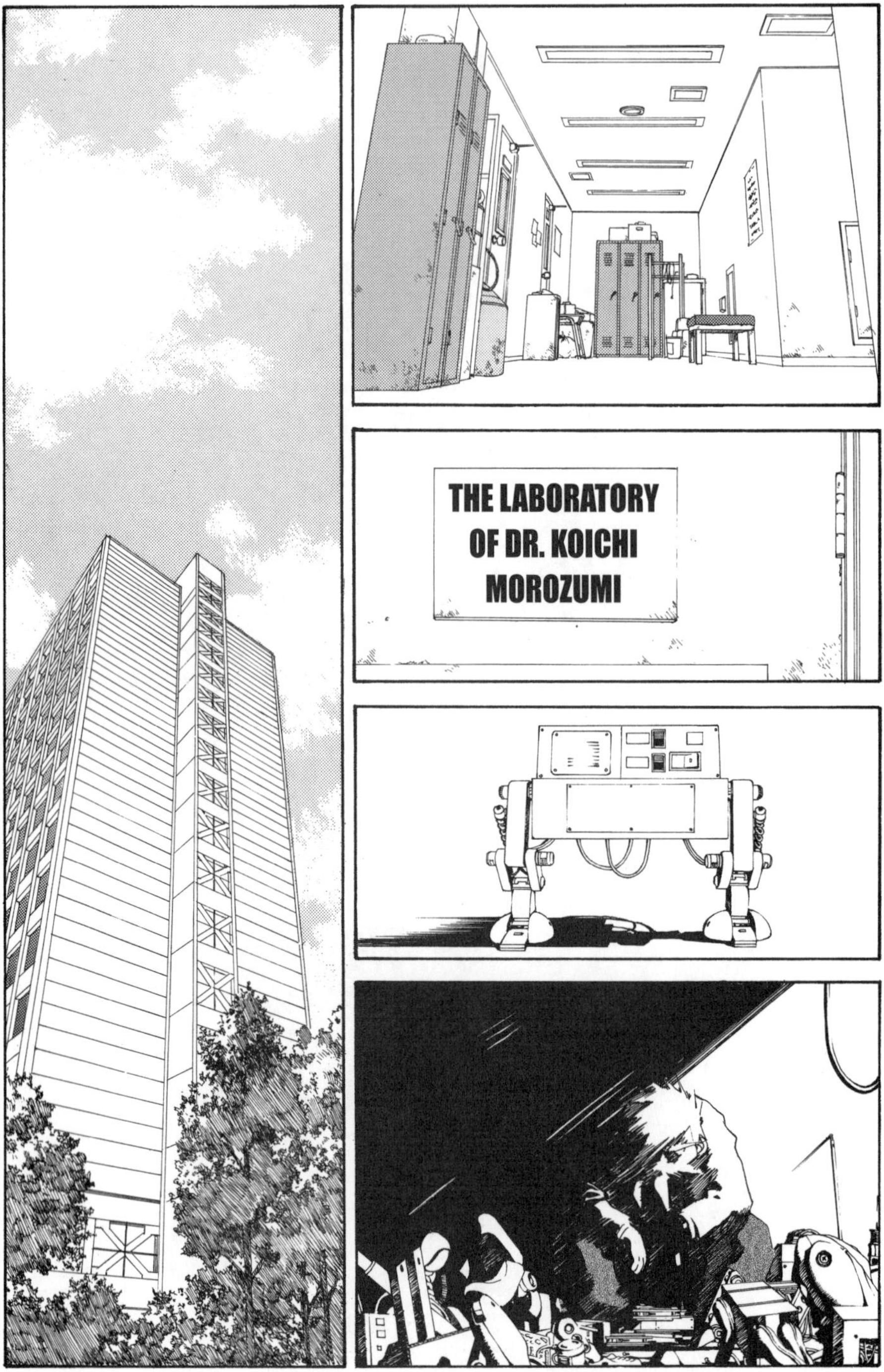
THE LABORATORY
OF DR. KOICHI
MOROZUMI

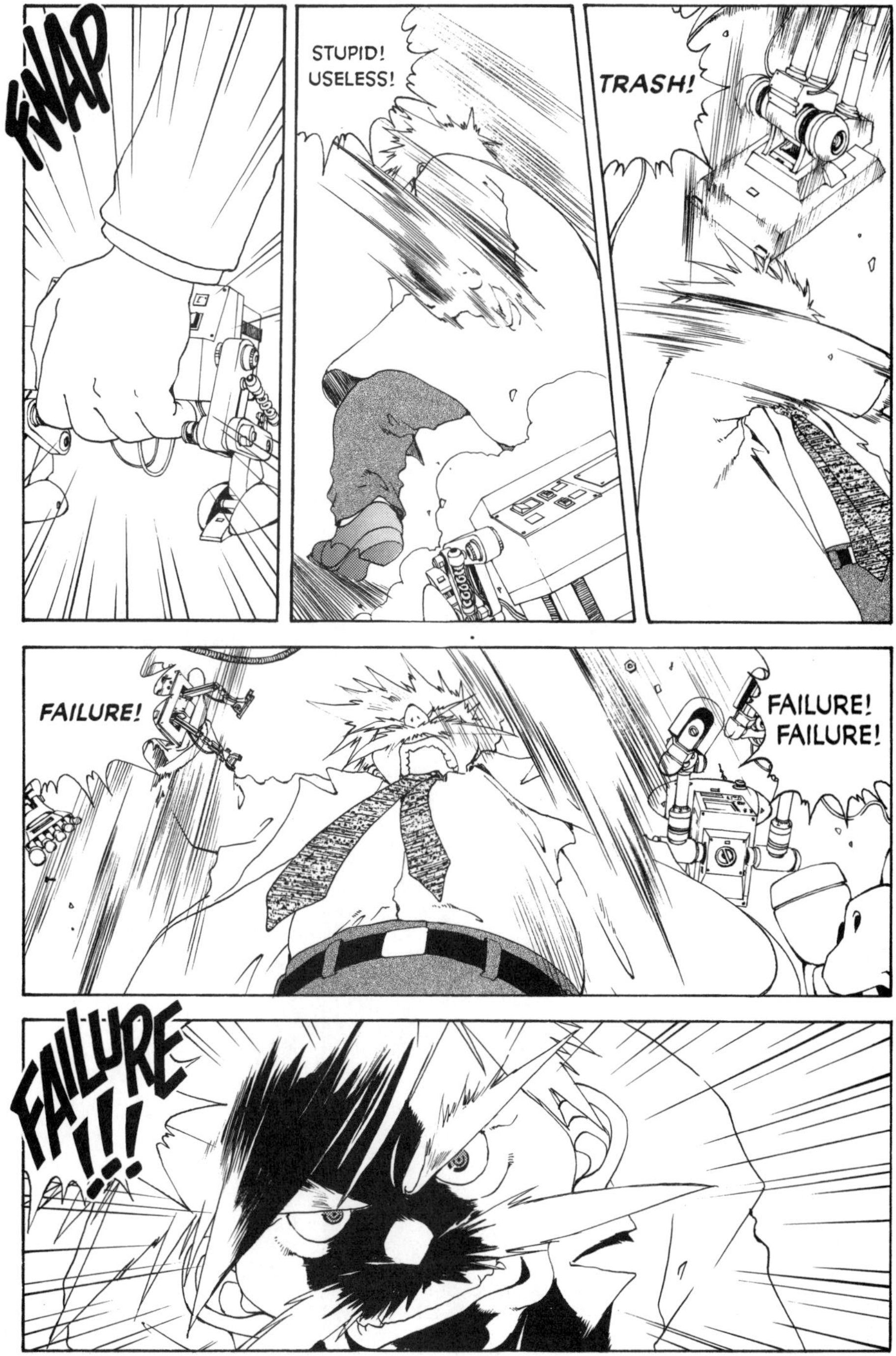
FWAP
STUPID!
USELESS!
TRASH!
FAILURE!
FAILURE!
FAILURE!
FAILURE!!!

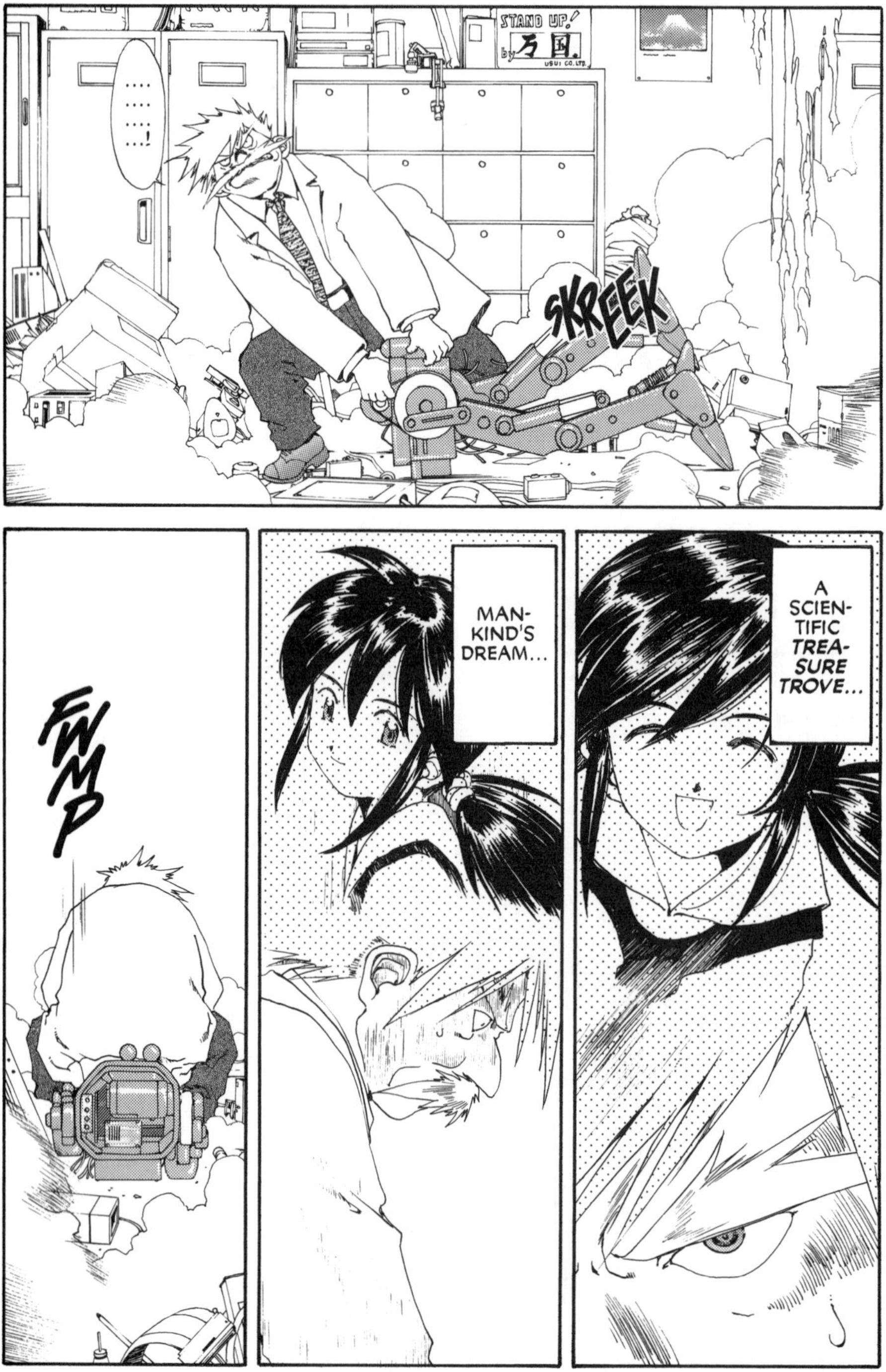
STAND UP! by 万国.
USUI CO. LTD.
.........!
SKREEK
FWMP
MAN-KIND'S DREAM...
A SCIENTIFIC TREASURE TROVE...

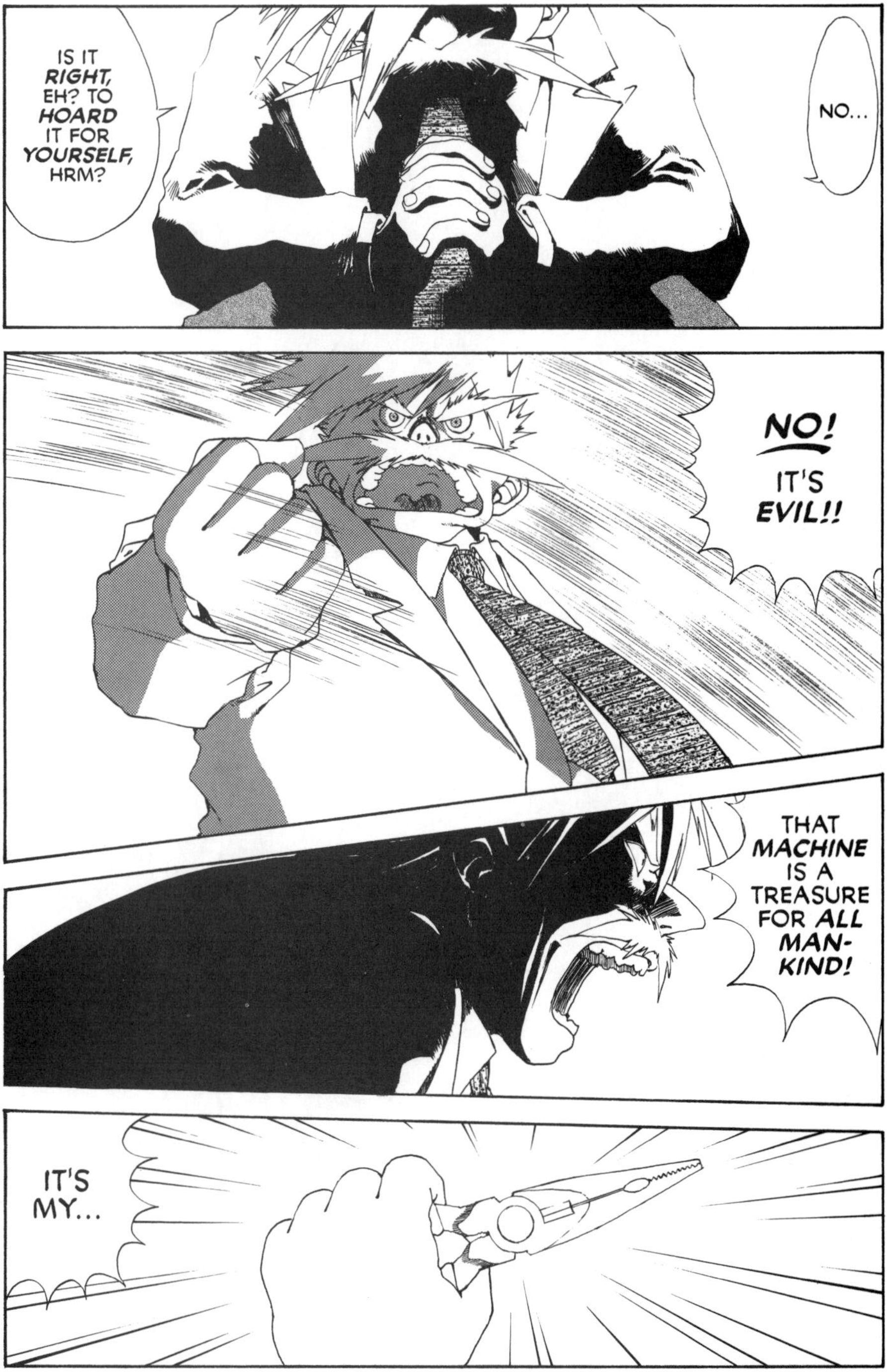
IS IT *RIGHT,* EH? TO *HOARD* IT FOR *YOURSELF,* HRM?
NO...
NO! IT'S *EVIL!!*
THAT *MACHINE* IS A TREASURE FOR *ALL MAN-KIND!*
IT'S MY...

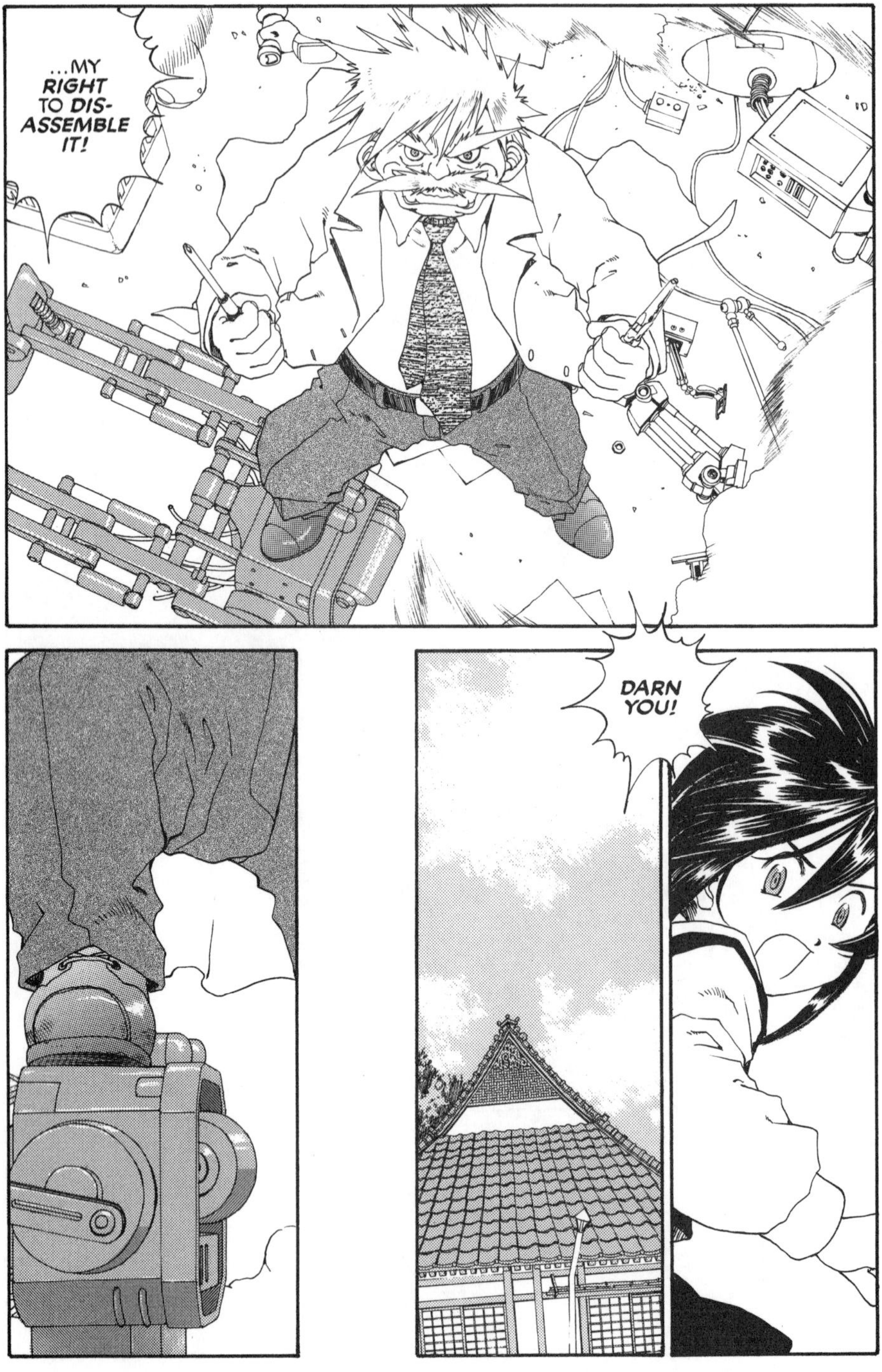
...MY RIGHT TO DIS-ASSEMBLE IT!
DARN YOU!

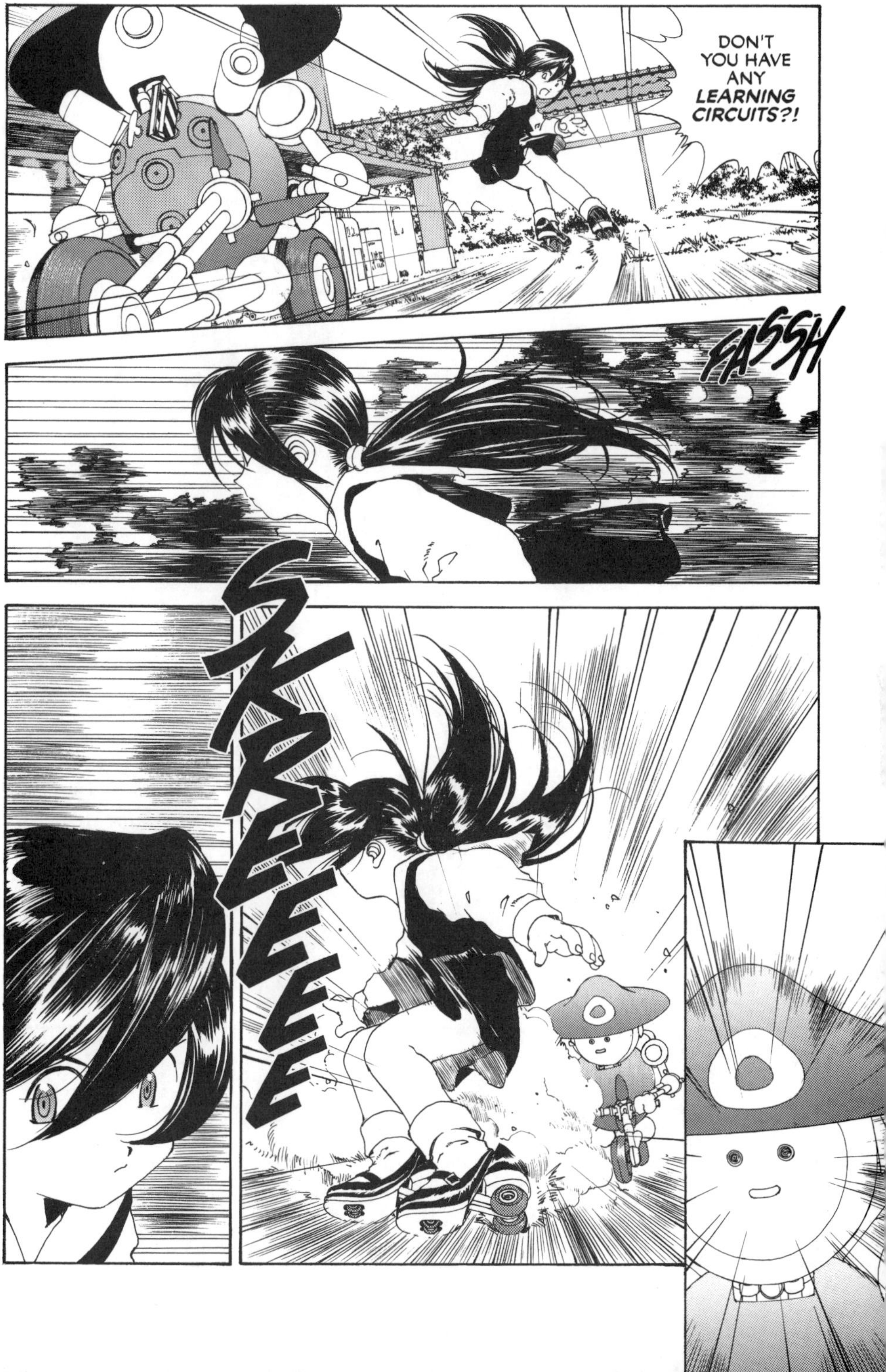
DON'T YOU HAVE ANY *LEARNING CIRCUITS?!*
FASSH
SKREEEEEEE

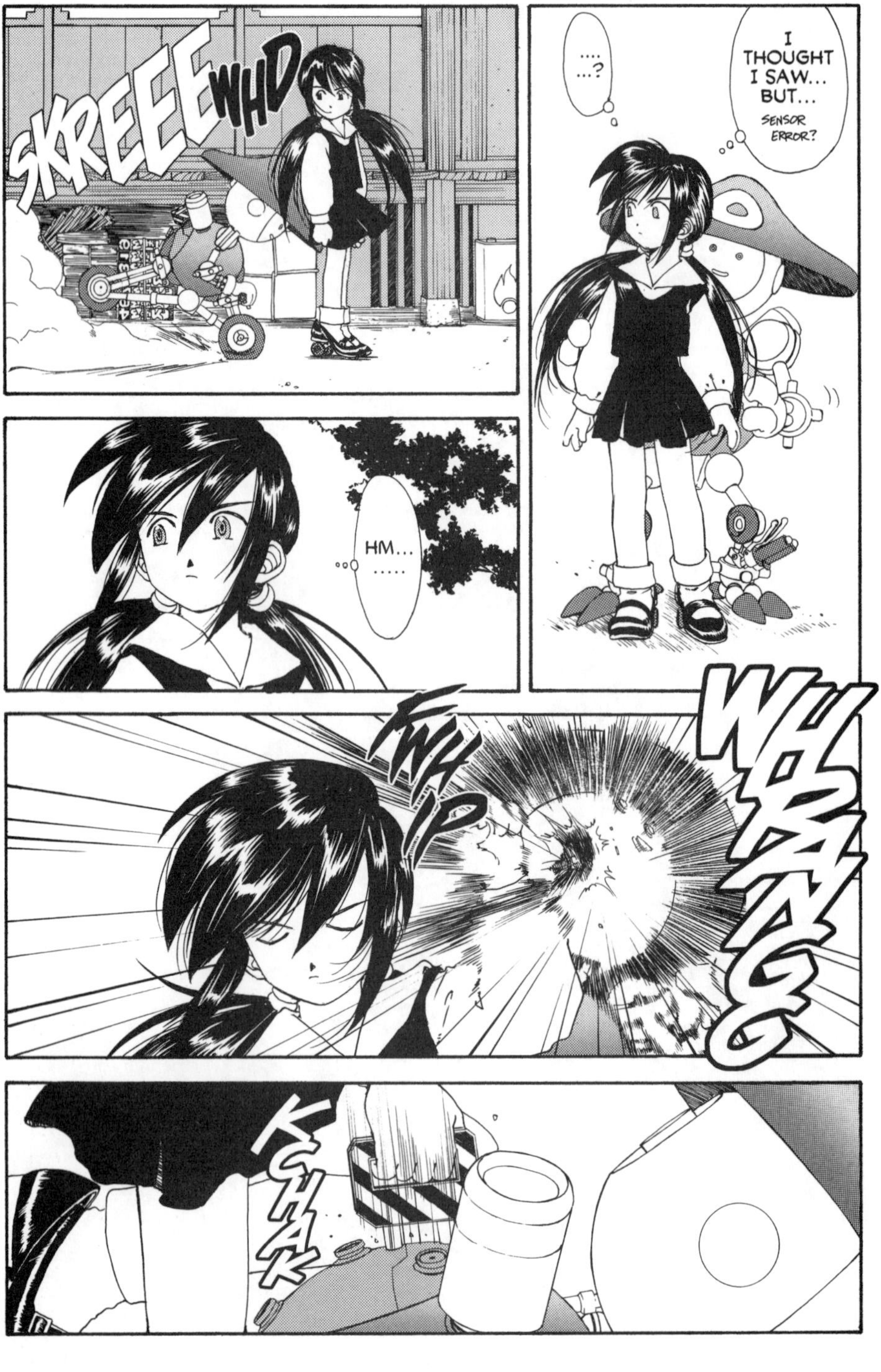
SKREEEWHD
HM...
.....
....
...?
I THOUGHT I SAW... BUT...
SENSOR ERROR?
FWHIP
WHANGG
KCHAK

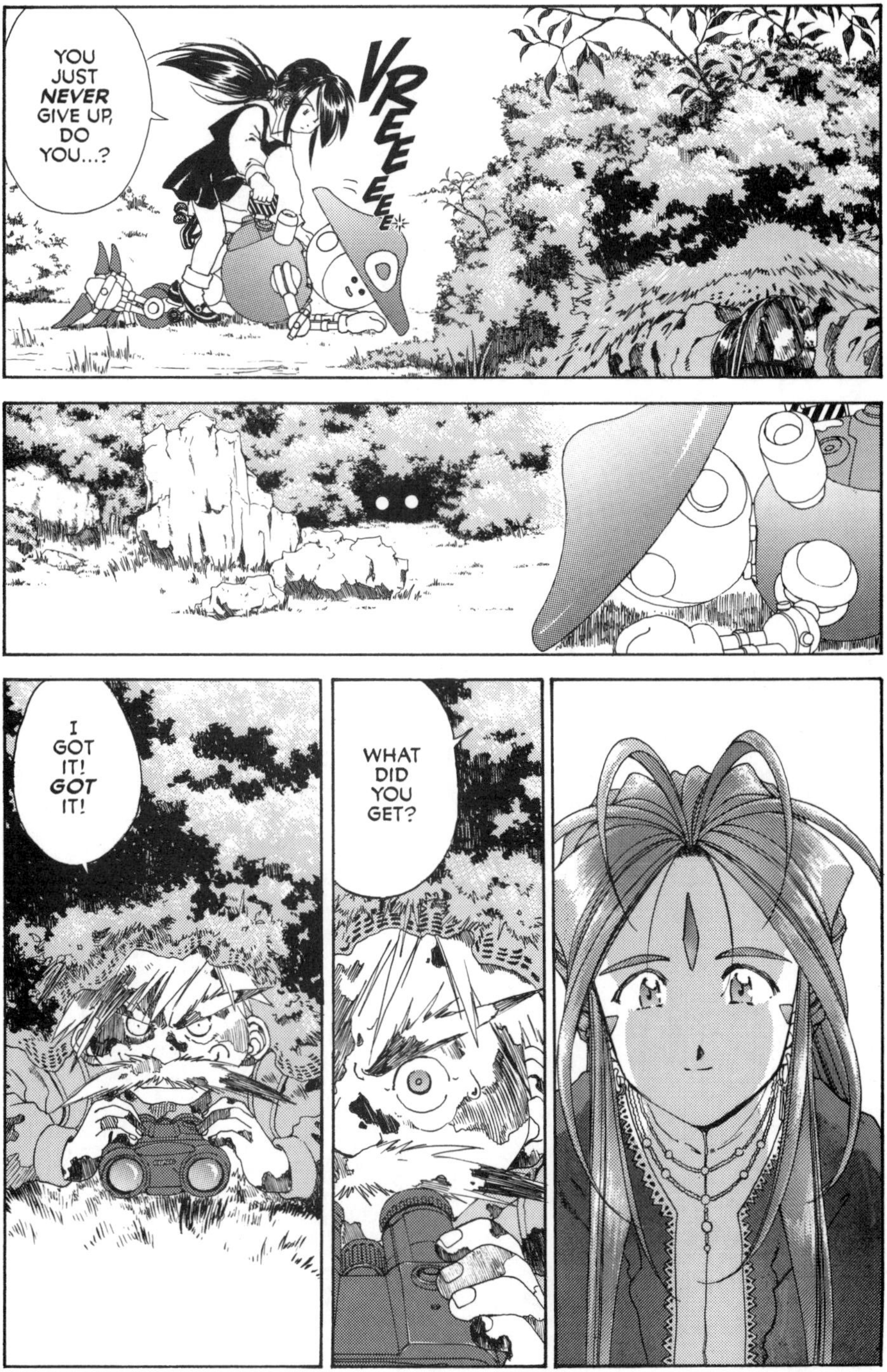
YOU JUST **NEVER** GIVE UP, DO YOU...?
VREEEEEE
I GOT IT! **GOT** IT!
WHAT DID YOU GET?

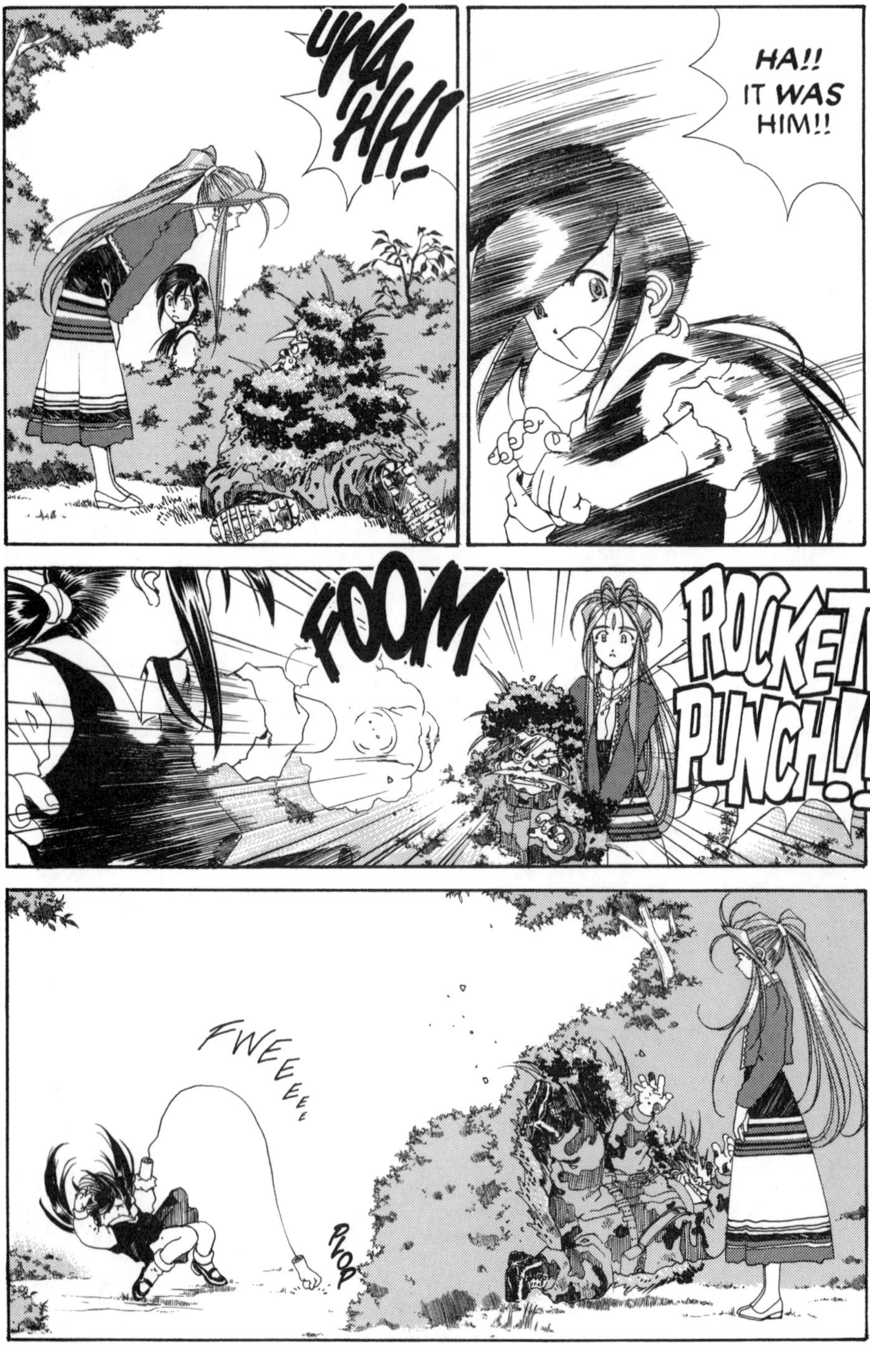
UWAHH!
HA!! IT WAS HIM!!
FOOM
ROCKET PUNCH!!!
FWEEEEE
PLOP

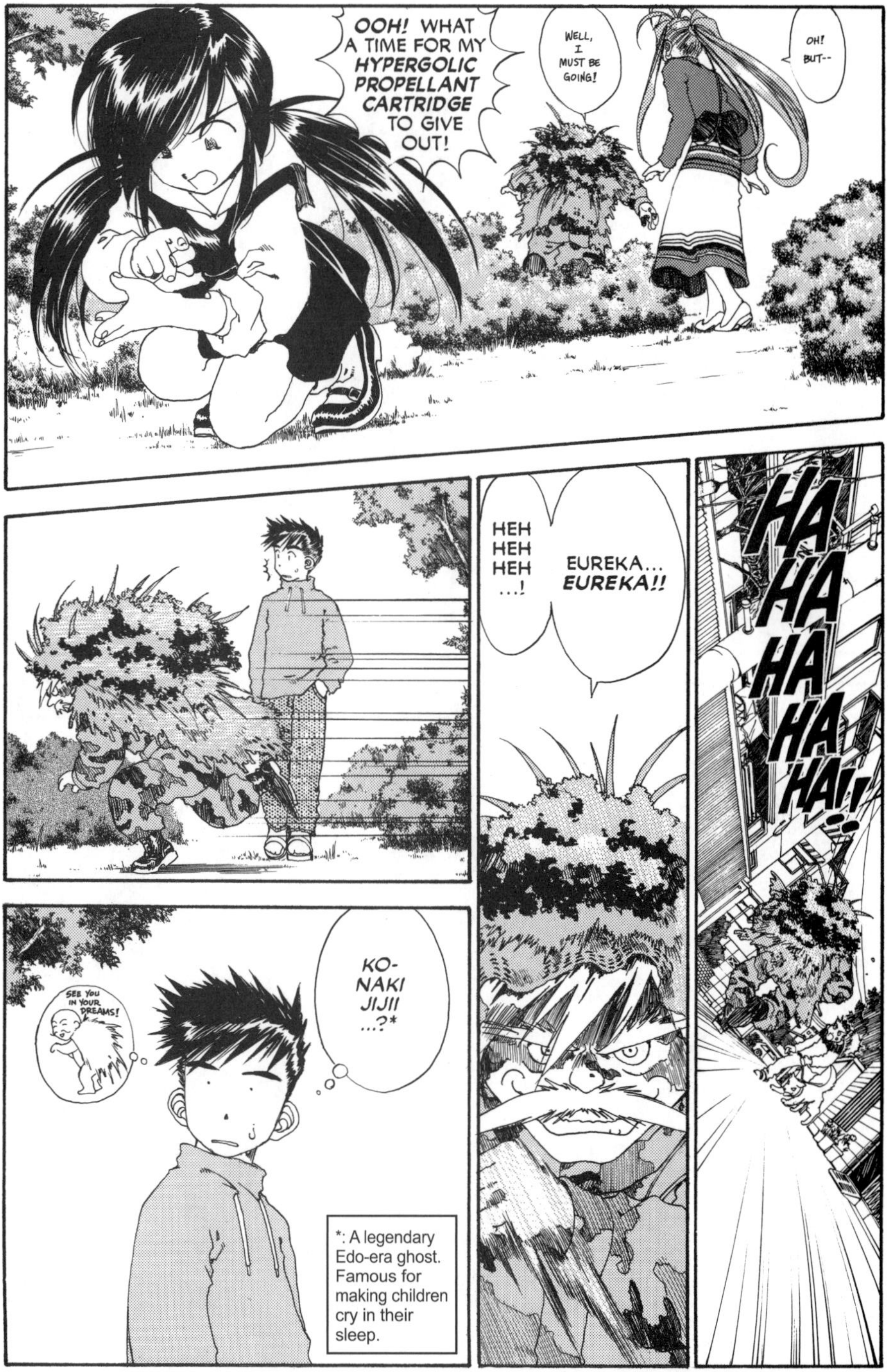
OOH! WHAT A TIME FOR MY HYPERGOLIC PROPELLANT CARTRIDGE TO GIVE OUT!
WELL, I MUST BE GOING!
OH! BUT--
SEE YOU IN YOUR DREAMS!
KO-NAKI JIJII ...?*
*: A legendary Edo-era ghost. Famous for making children cry in their sleep.
HEH HEH HEH ...!
EUREKA... EUREKA!!
HA HA HA HA HA HA!!

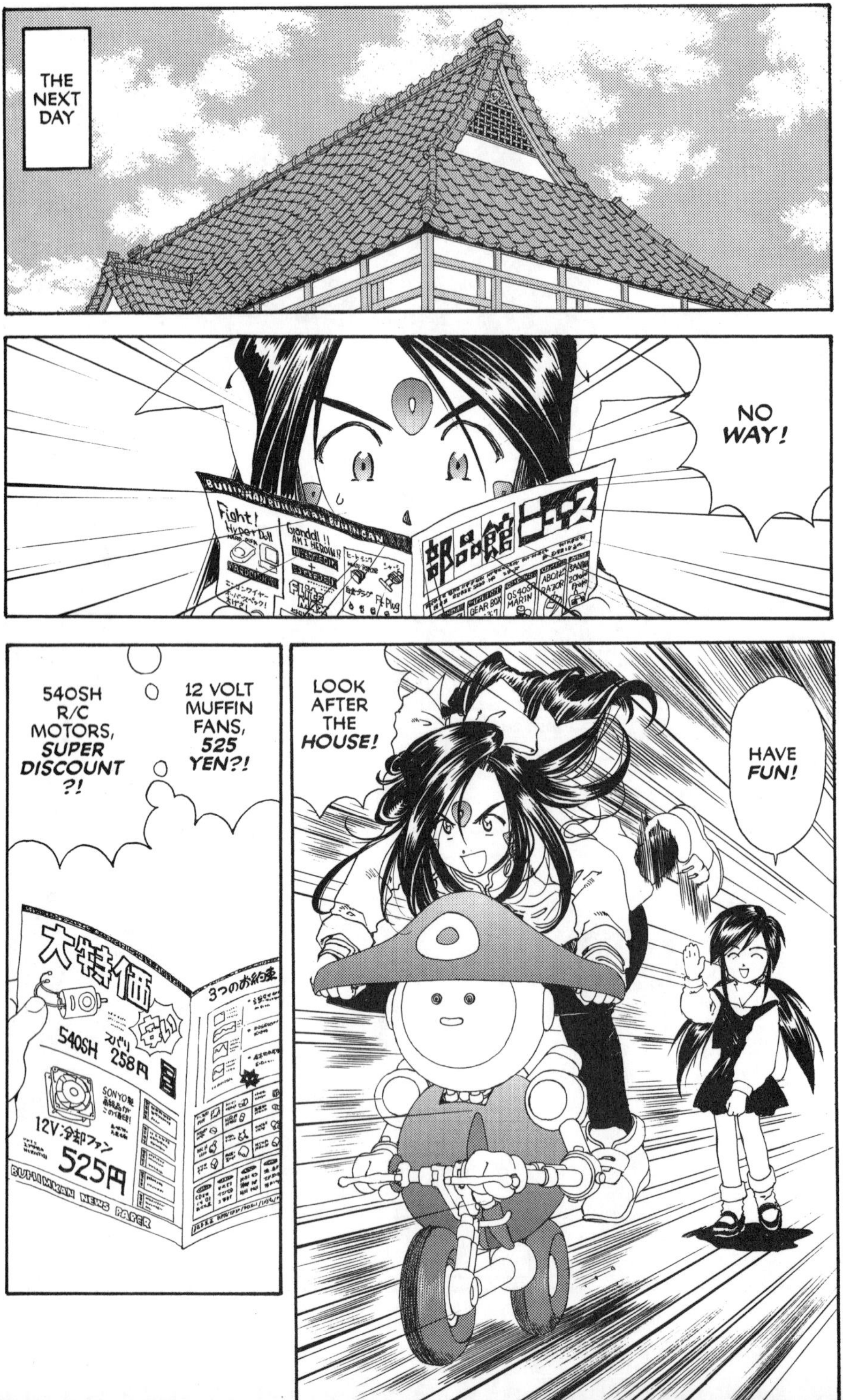
THE NEXT DAY
NO WAY!
部品館ニュース
Fight! Hyper Doll
540SH R/C MOTORS, SUPER DISCOUNT?!
12 VOLT MUFFIN FANS, 525 YEN?!
大特価
3つのお約束
540SH
258円
12V冷却ファン
525円
BUHIMKAN NEWS PAPER
LOOK AFTER THE HOUSE!
HAVE FUN!

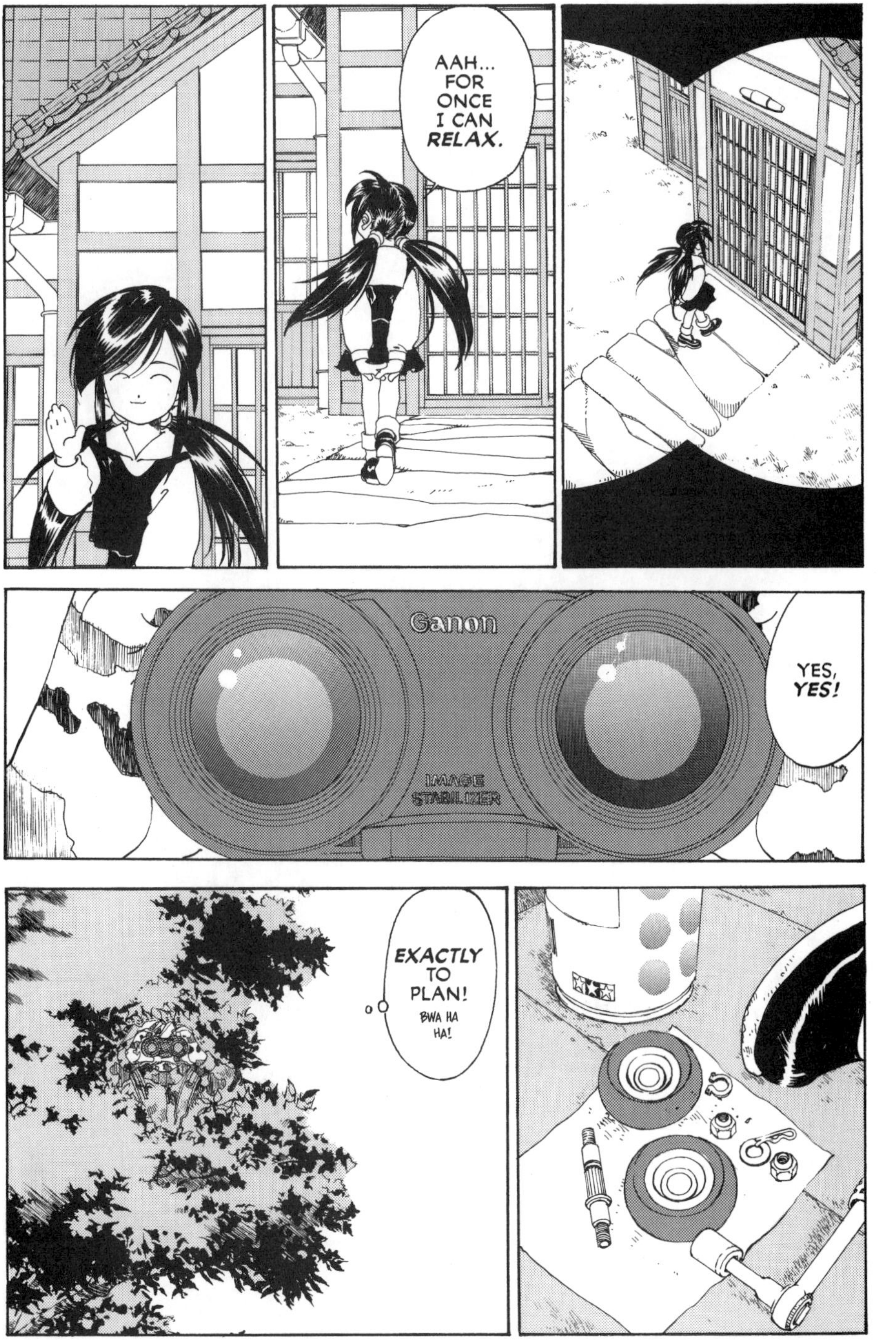
AAH... FOR ONCE I CAN *RELAX*.
Ganon
IMAGE STABILIZER
YES, *YES!*
EXACTLY TO PLAN!
BWA HA HA!

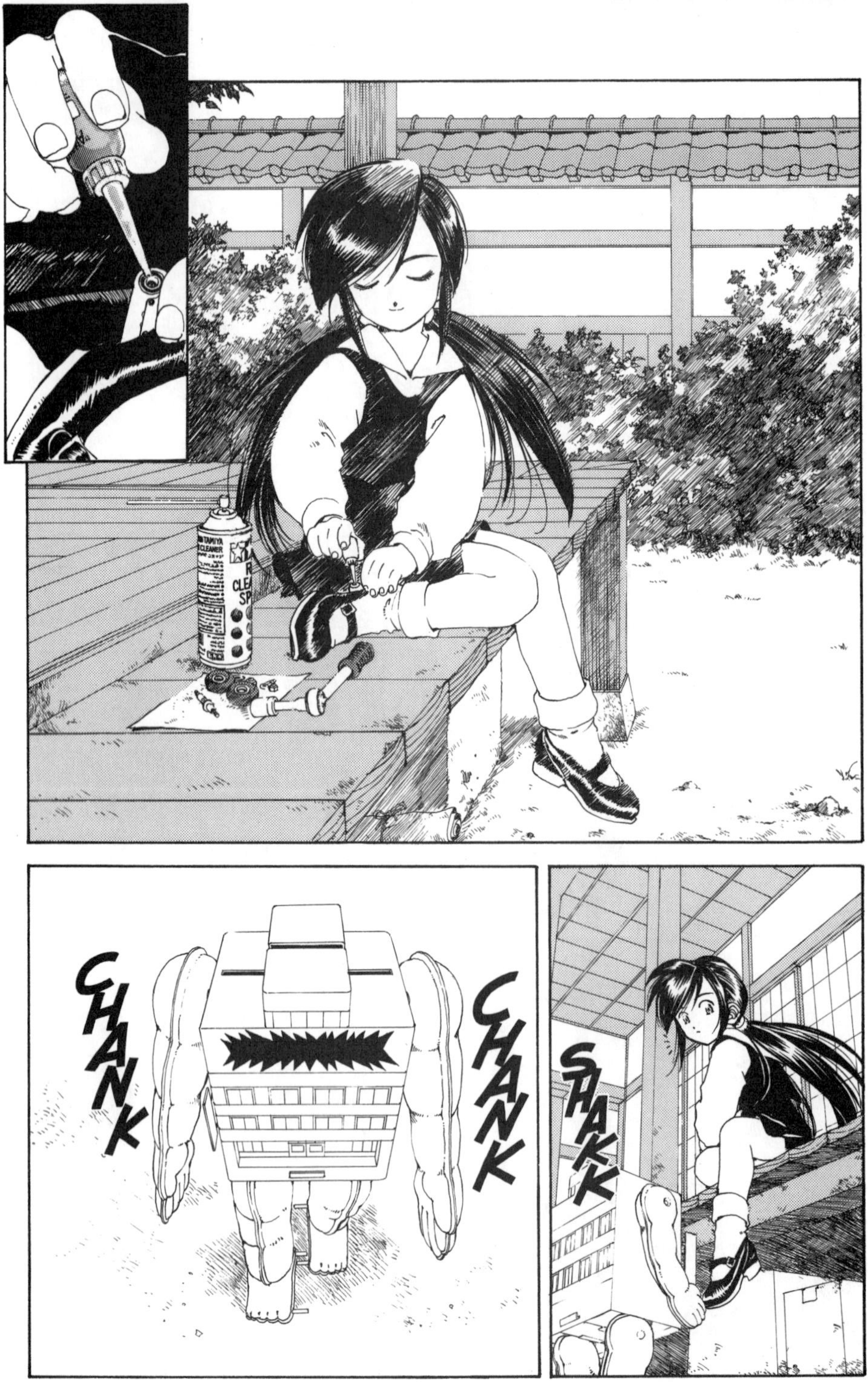
CHANK
CHANK
SHAKK

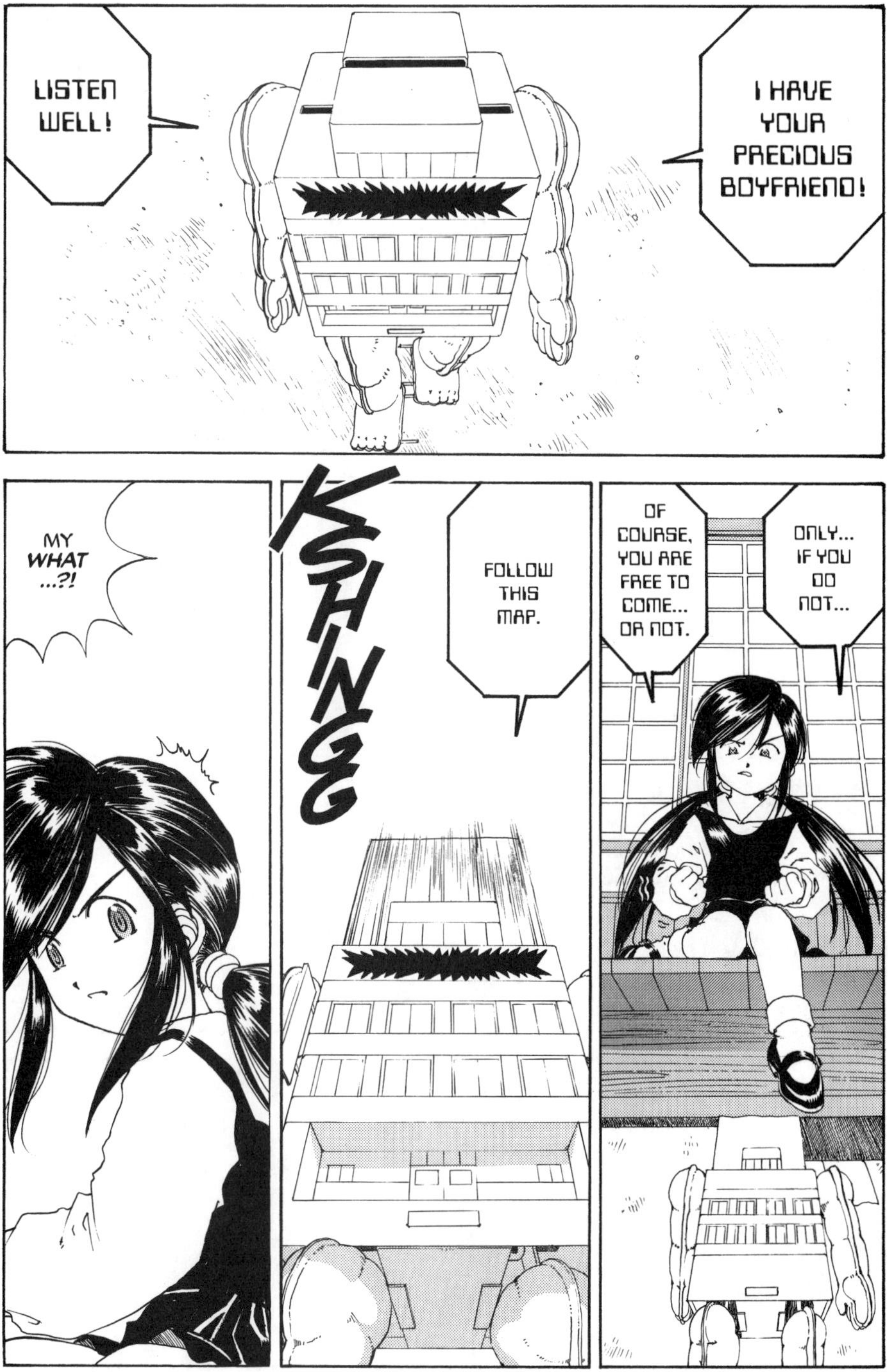
LISTEN WELL!
I HAVE YOUR PRECIOUS BOYFRIEND!
MY WHAT ...?!
KSHINGG
FOLLOW THIS MAP.
OF COURSE, YOU ARE FREE TO COME... OR NOT.
ONLY... IF YOU DO NOT...

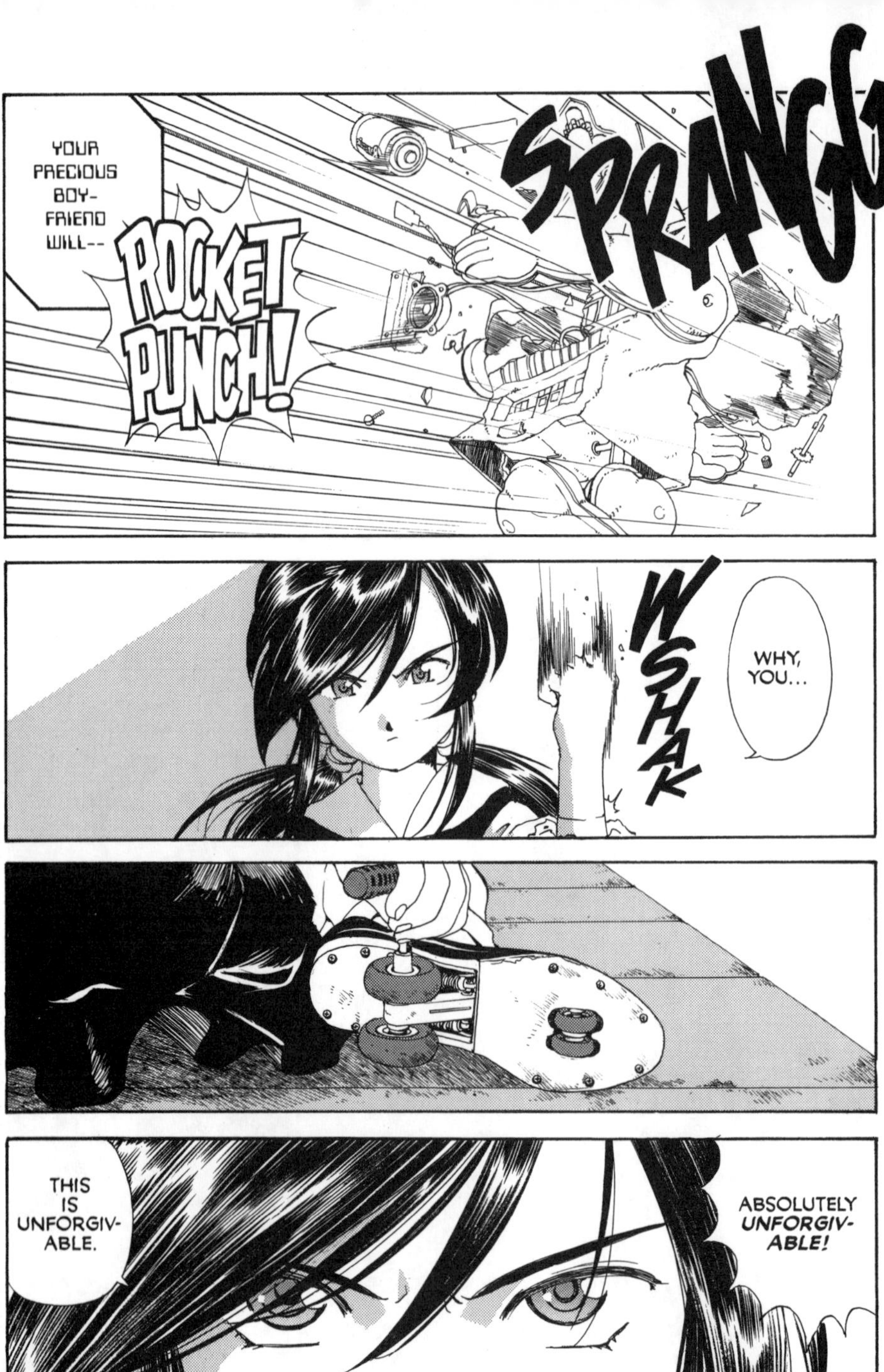
YOUR PRECIOUS BOY-FRIEND WILL--
ROCKET PUNCH!
SPRANGG
WSHAK
WHY, YOU...
THIS IS UNFORGIV-ABLE.
ABSOLUTELY *UNFORGIV-ABLE!*

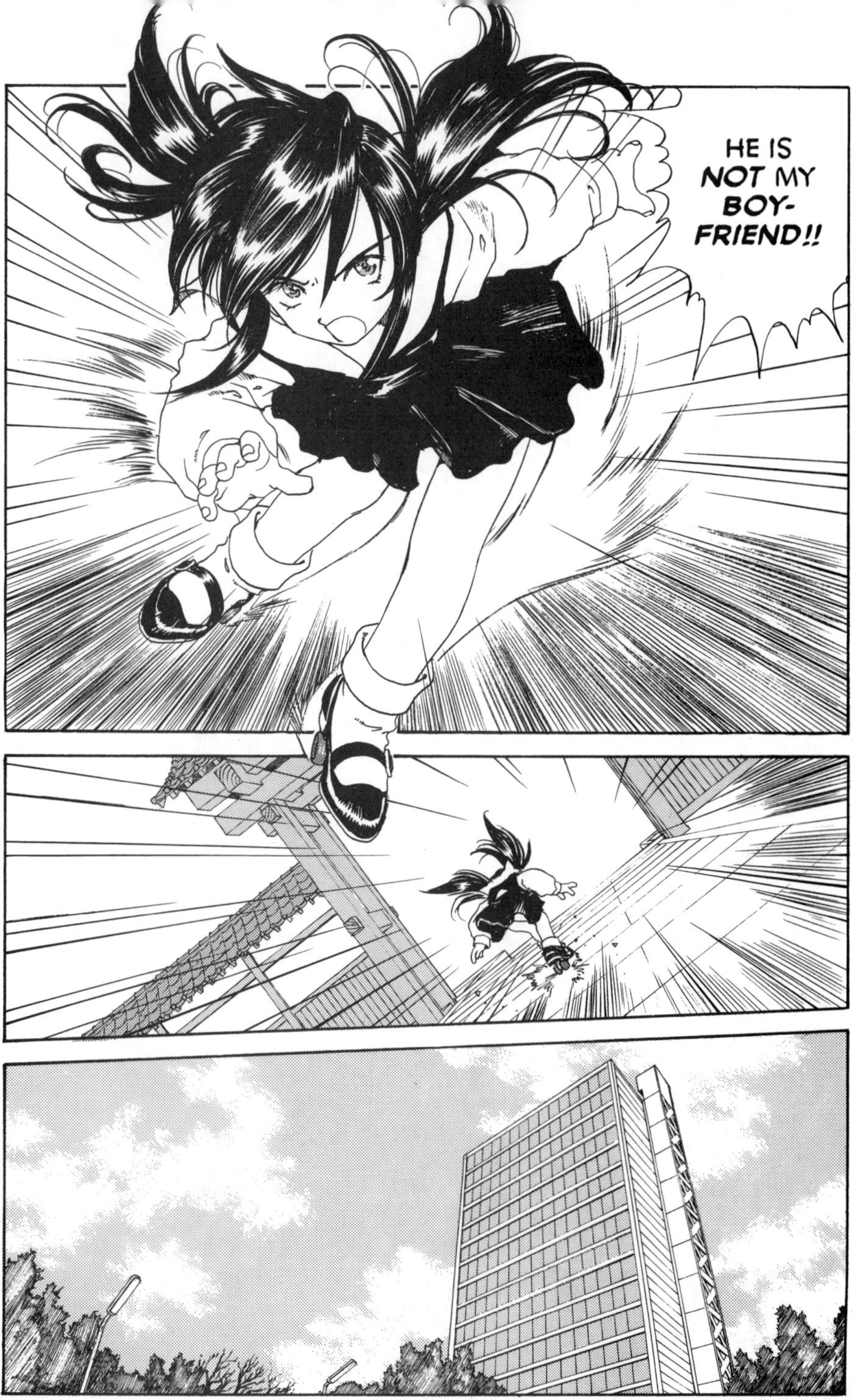
HE IS NOT MY BOY-FRIEND!!

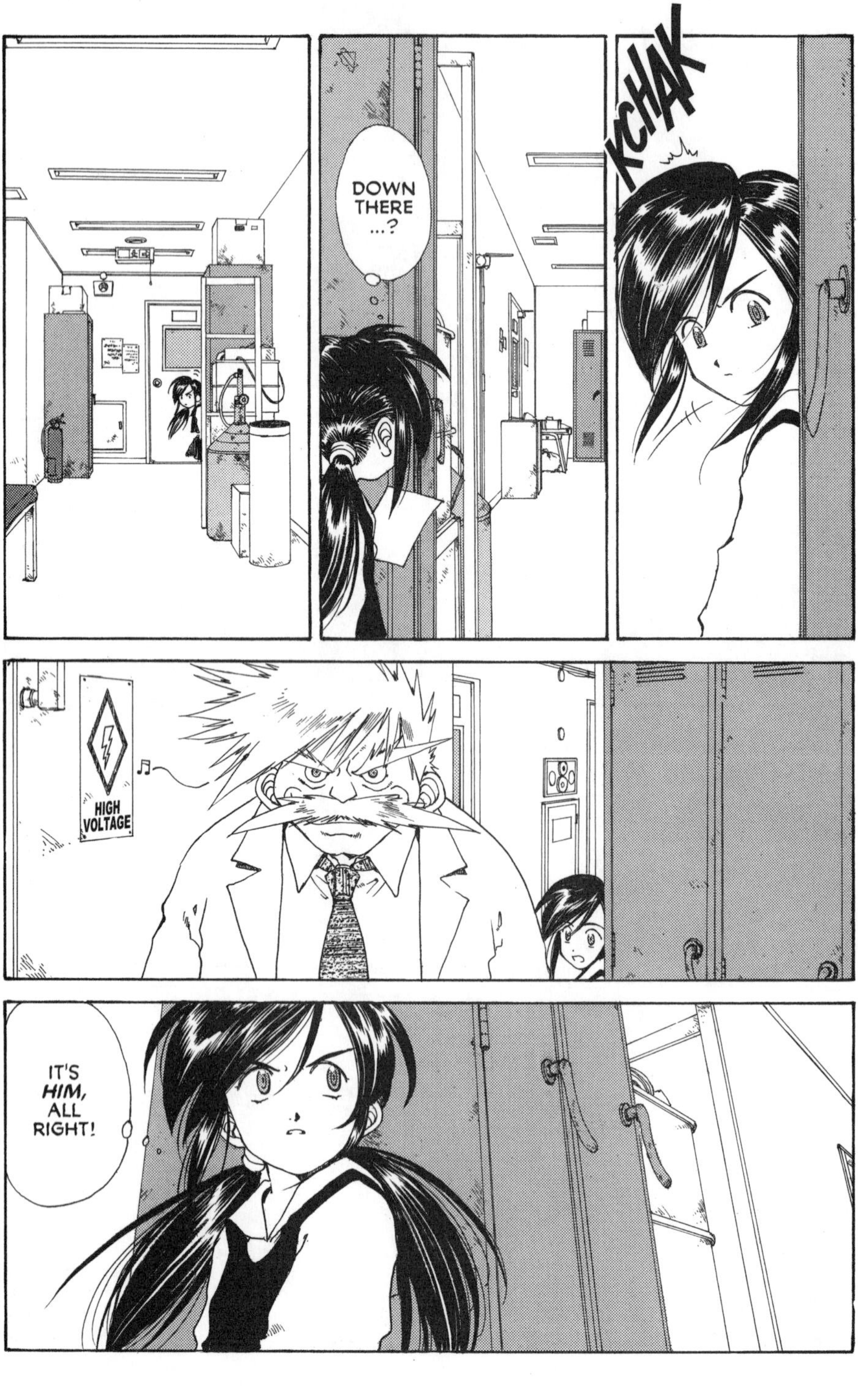
DOWN THERE ...?
KCHAK
HIGH VOLTAGE
♫
IT'S *HIM*, ALL RIGHT!

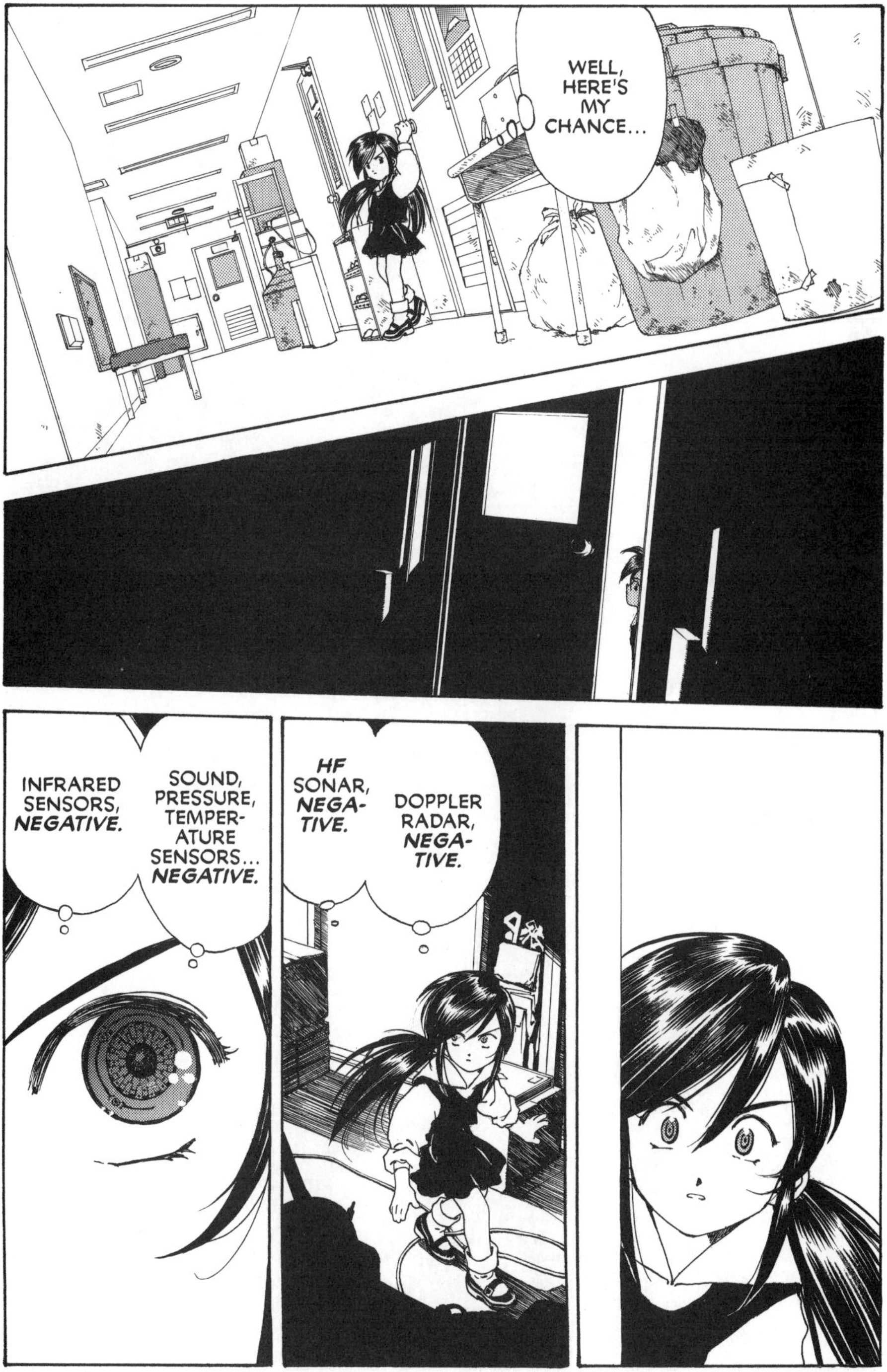
WELL, HERE'S MY CHANCE...
INFRARED SENSORS, *NEGATIVE.*
SOUND, PRESSURE, TEMPER-ATURE SENSORS... *NEGATIVE.*
HF SONAR, *NEGA-TIVE.*
DOPPLER RADAR, *NEGA-TIVE.*

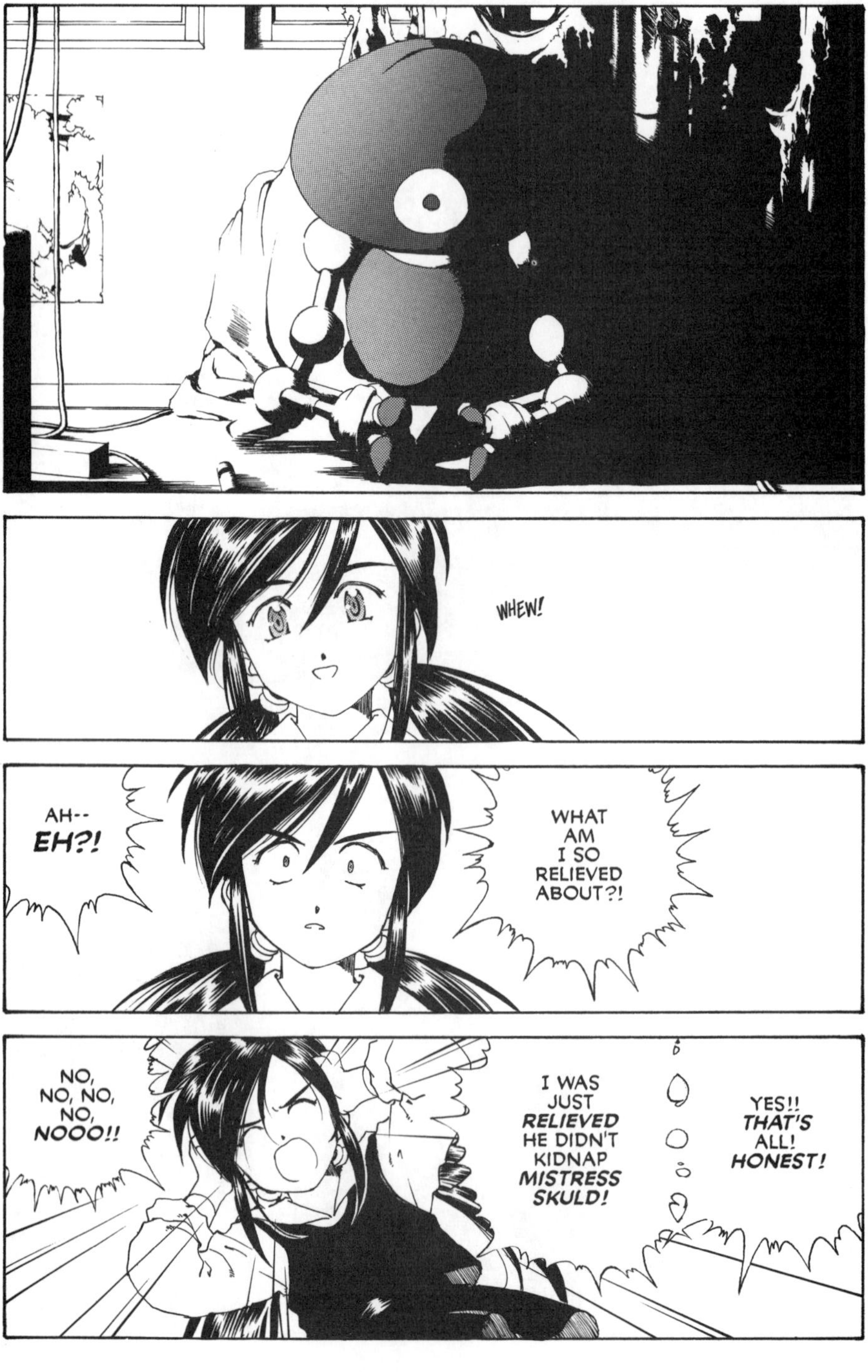
WHEW!
AH--
EH?!
WHAT AM I SO RELIEVED ABOUT?!
NO, NO, NO, NO, *NOOO!!*
I WAS JUST *RELIEVED* HE DIDN'T KIDNAP *MISTRESS SKULD!*
YES!! *THAT'S ALL! HONEST!*

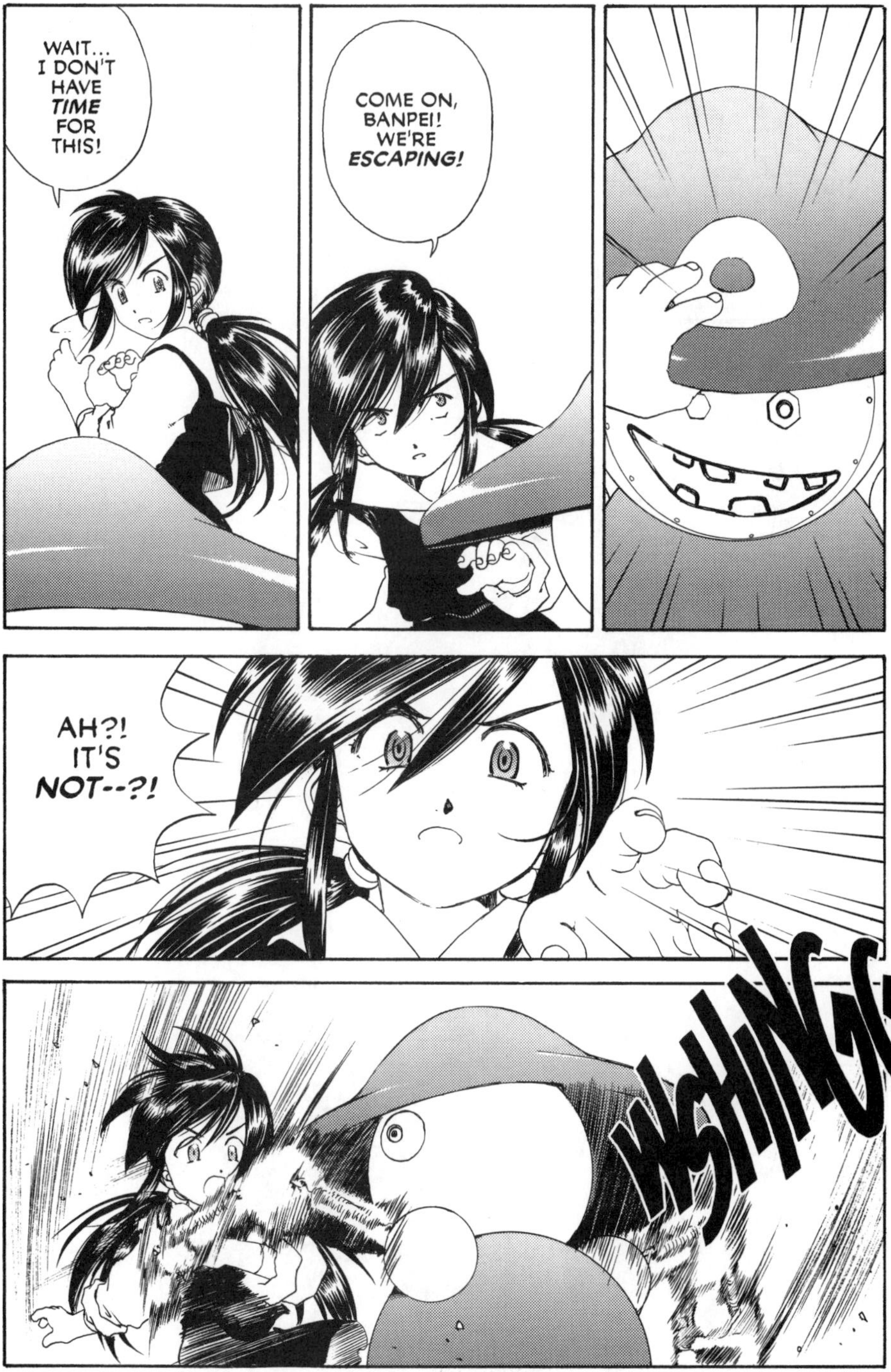
WAIT... I DON'T HAVE *TIME* FOR THIS!
COME ON, BANPEI! WE'RE *ESCAPING!*
AH?! IT'S *NOT--?!*
WSHINGG

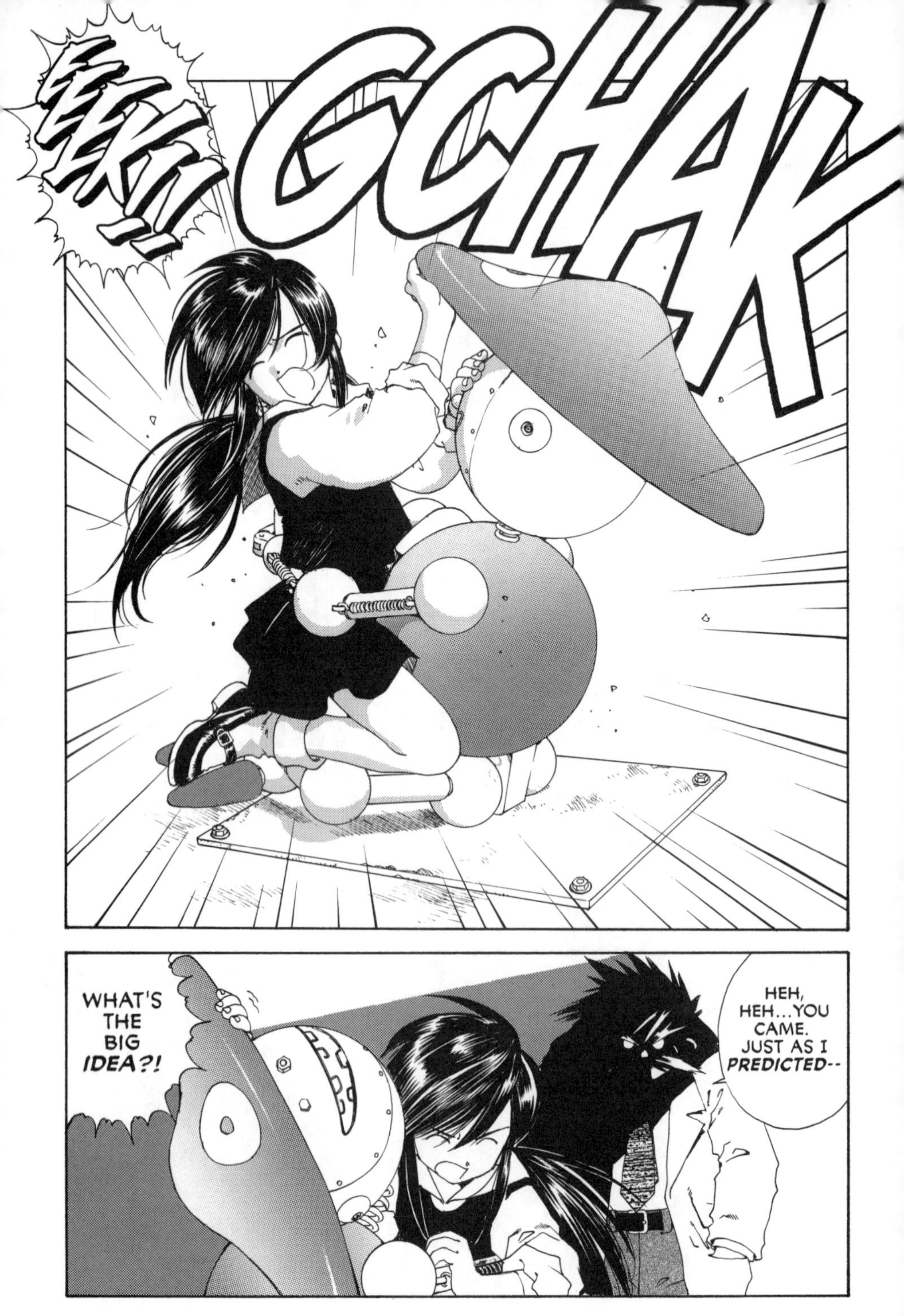
EEEK!!
GCHAK
WHAT'S THE BIG IDEA?!
HEH, HEH...YOU CAME. JUST AS I PREDICTED--

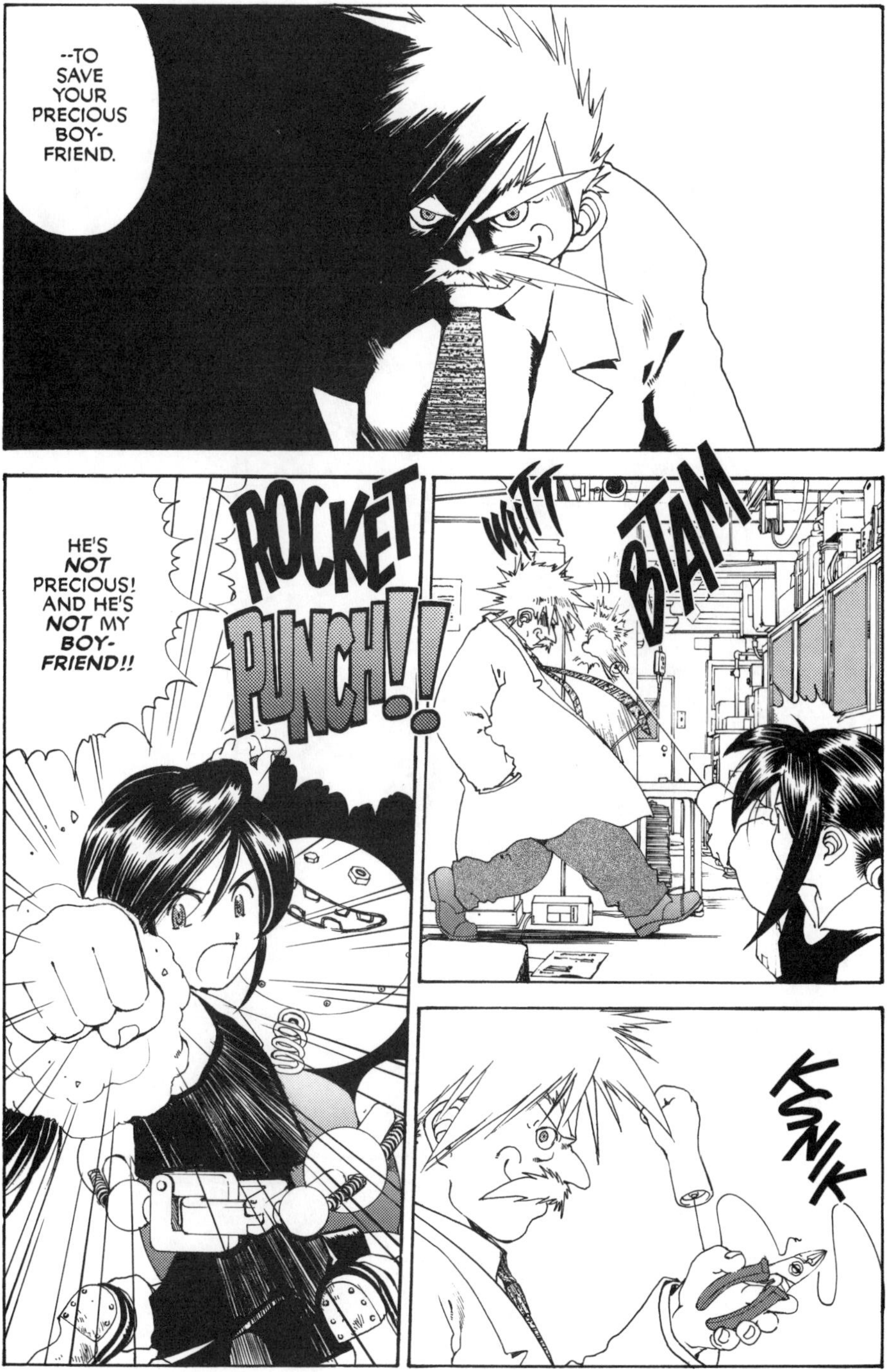
--TO SAVE YOUR PRECIOUS BOY-FRIEND.
HE'S *NOT* PRECIOUS! AND HE'S *NOT* MY *BOY-FRIEND!!*
ROCKET PUNCH!!!
WHTT
BTAM
KSNIK

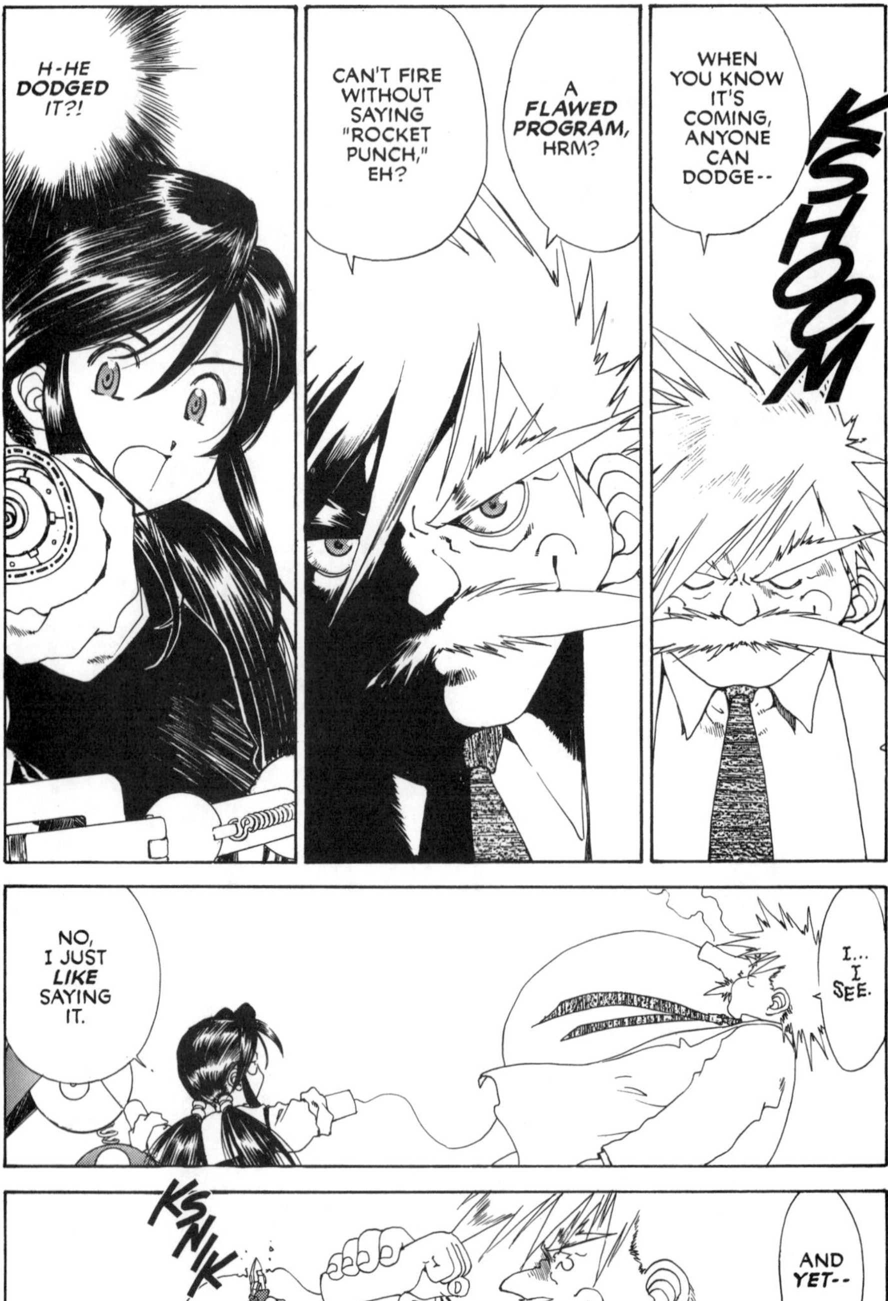
H-HE **DODGED** IT?!
CAN'T FIRE WITHOUT SAYING "ROCKET PUNCH," EH?
A ***FLAWED PROGRAM,*** HRM?
WHEN YOU KNOW IT'S COMING, ANYONE CAN DODGE--
KSHOOOM
NO, I JUST ***LIKE*** SAYING IT.
I... I SEE.
KSNIK
AND ***YET***--

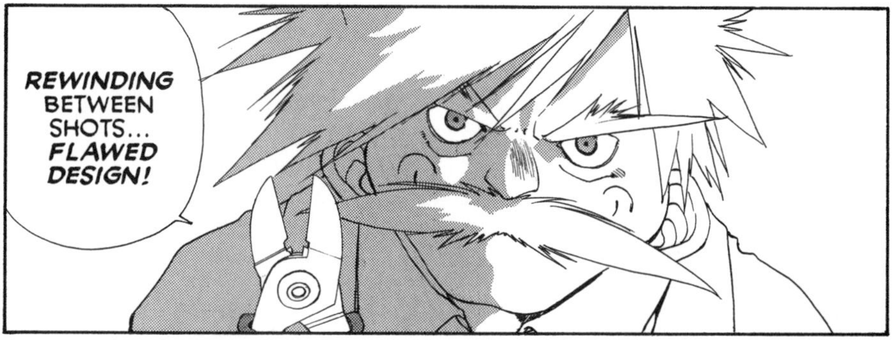
REWINDING BETWEEN SHOTS... FLAWED DESIGN!

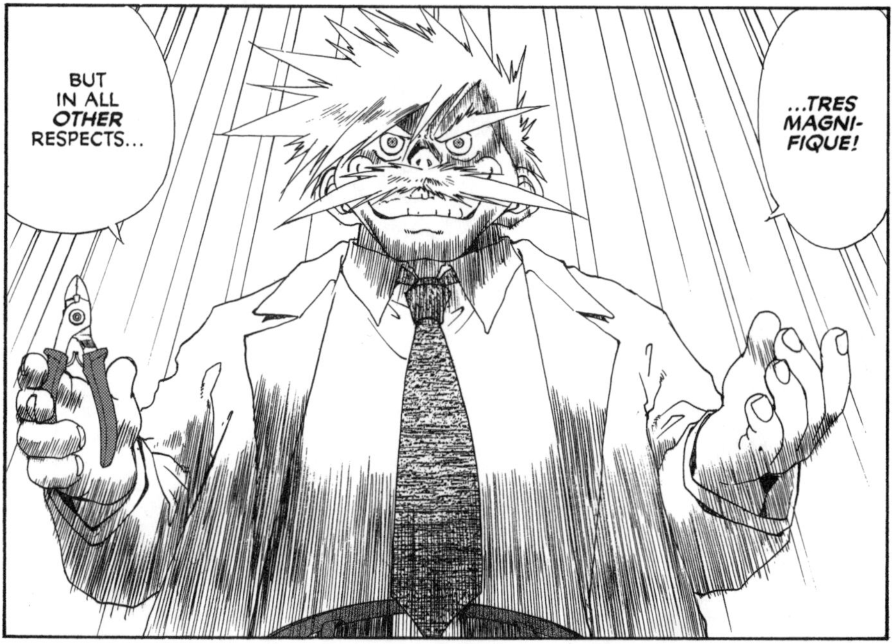
BUT IN ALL OTHER RESPECTS...
...TRES MAGNI-FIQUE!

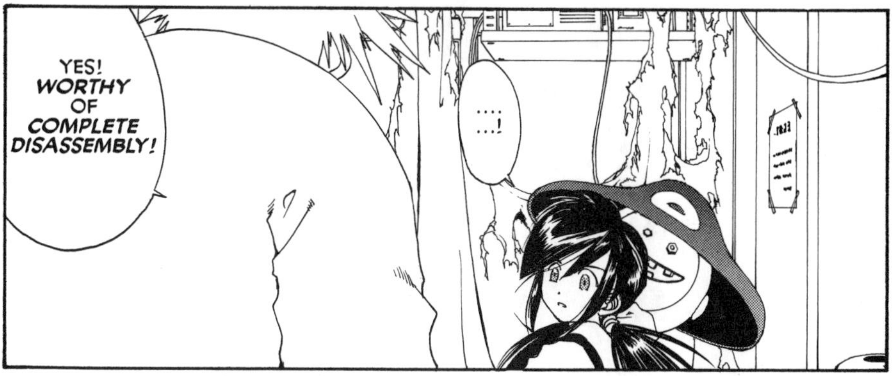
YES! WORTHY OF COMPLETE DISASSEMBLY!
....
...!

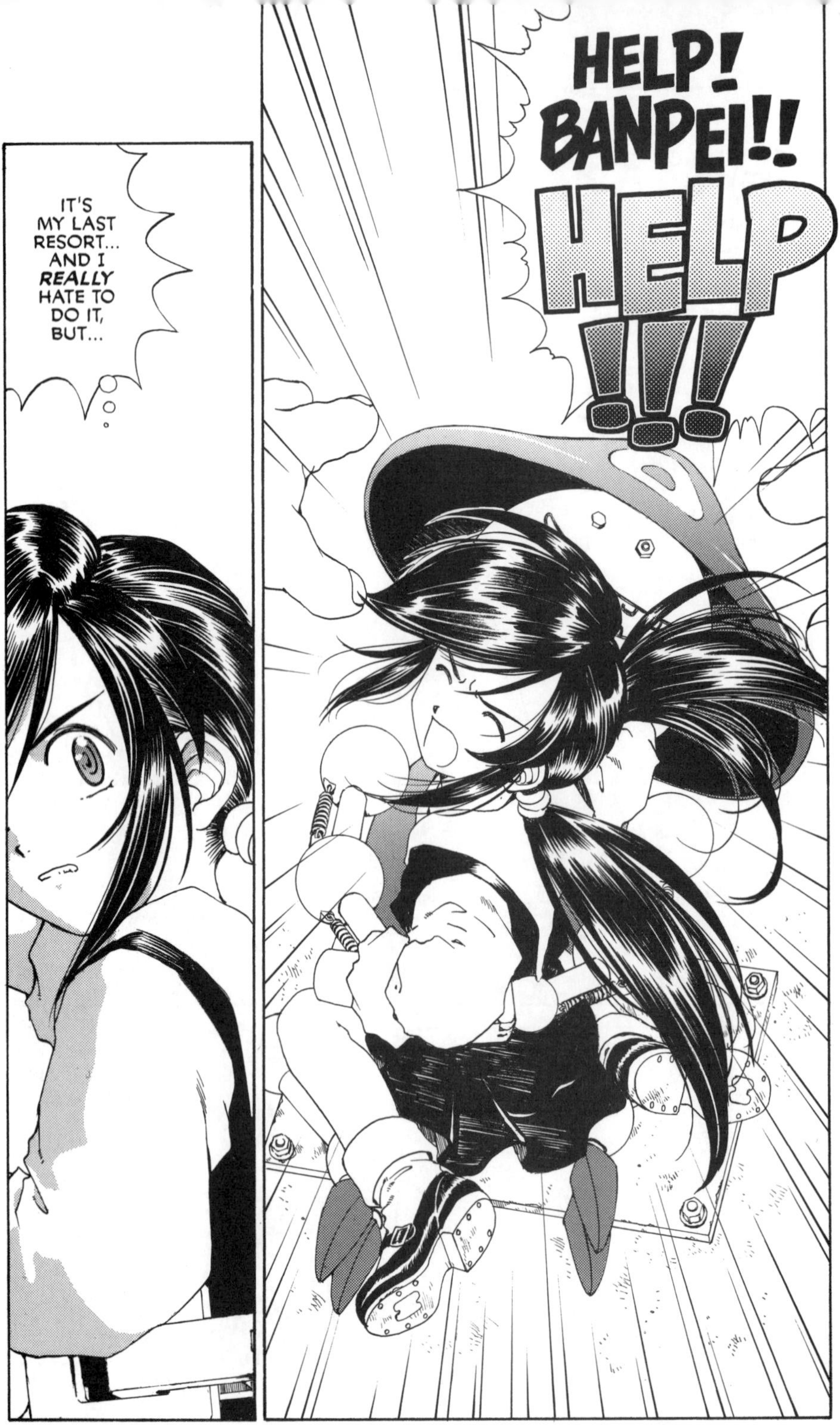
IT'S MY LAST RESORT... AND I *REALLY* HATE TO DO IT, BUT...
HELP! BANPEI!! HELP!!!

MAN? MACHINE?

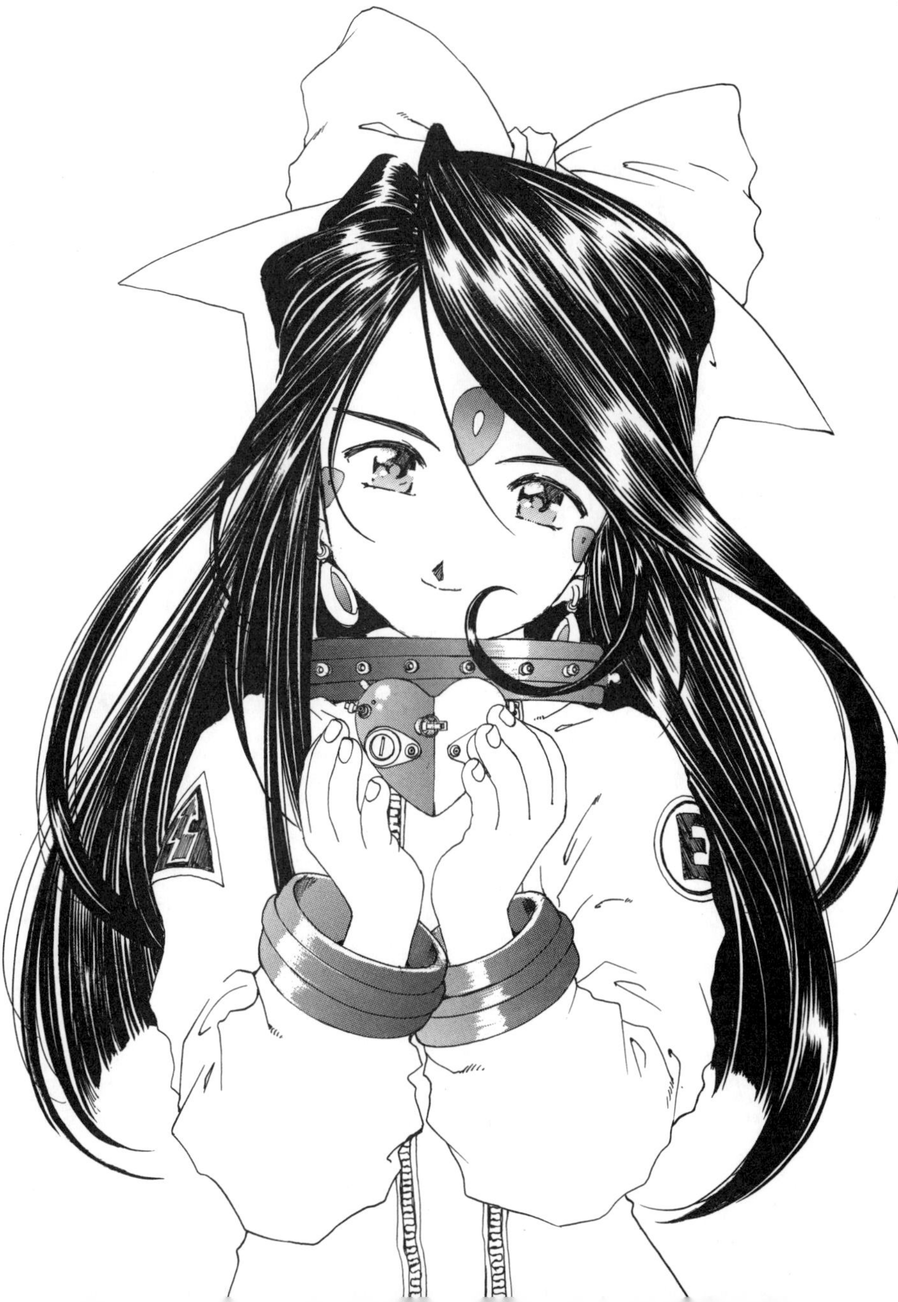

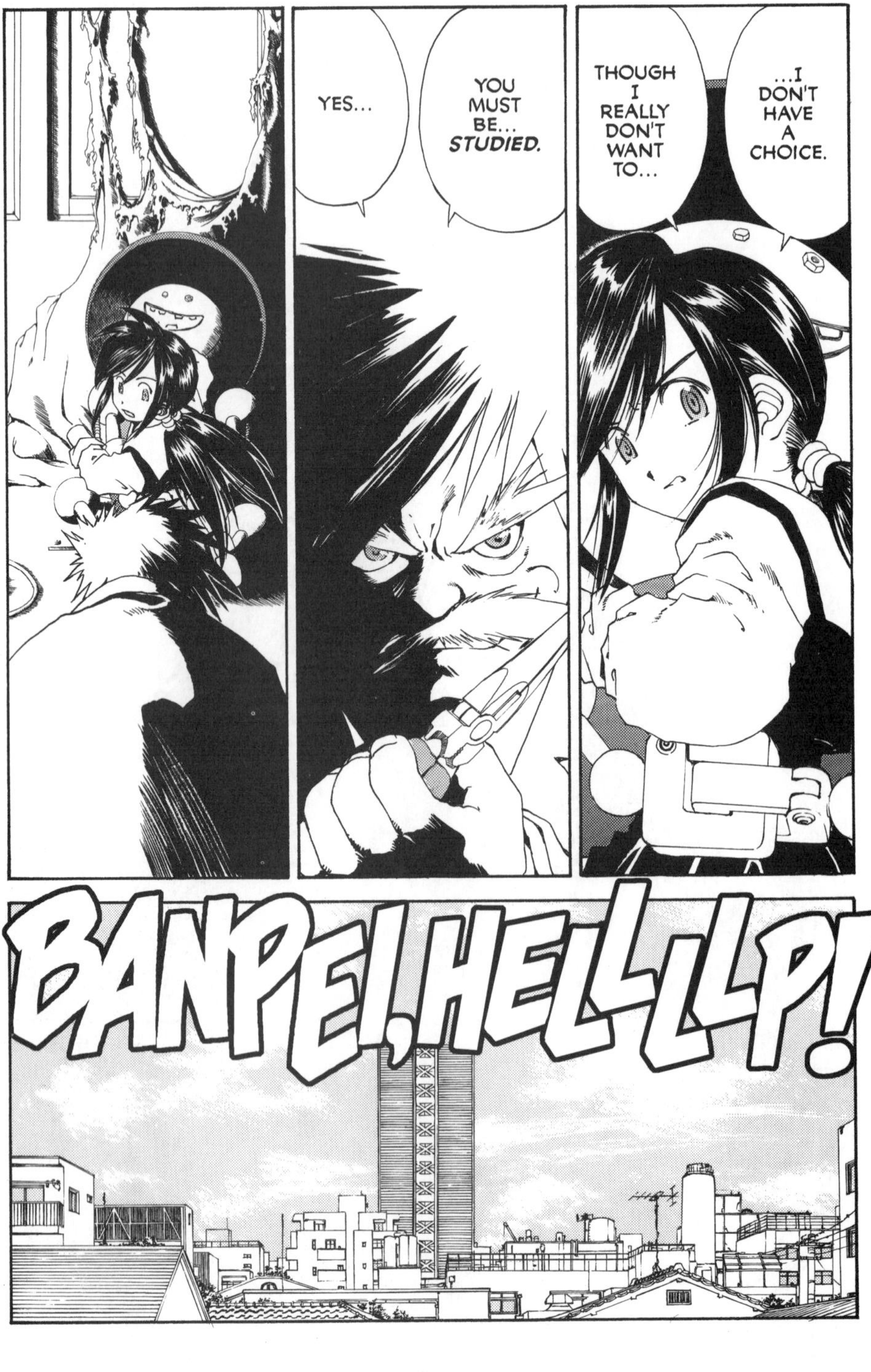

YES...
YOU MUST BE... *STUDIED.*
THOUGH I REALLY DON'T WANT TO...
...I DON'T HAVE A CHOICE.
BANPEI, HELLLP!

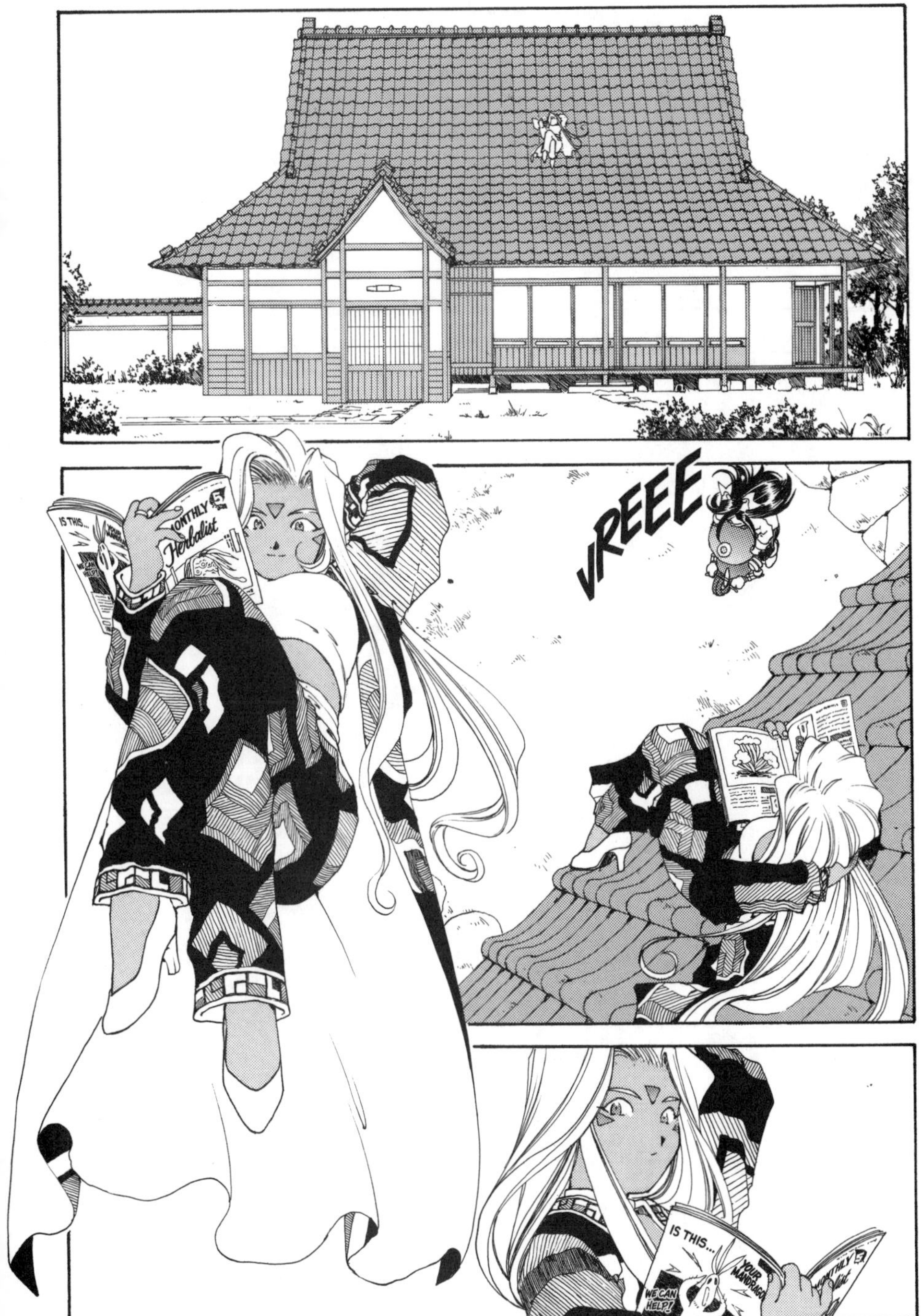
IS THIS...
WE CAN HELP!
MONTHLY Herbalist
VREEE
IS THIS...
YOUR MANDRAGO
WE CAN HELP!

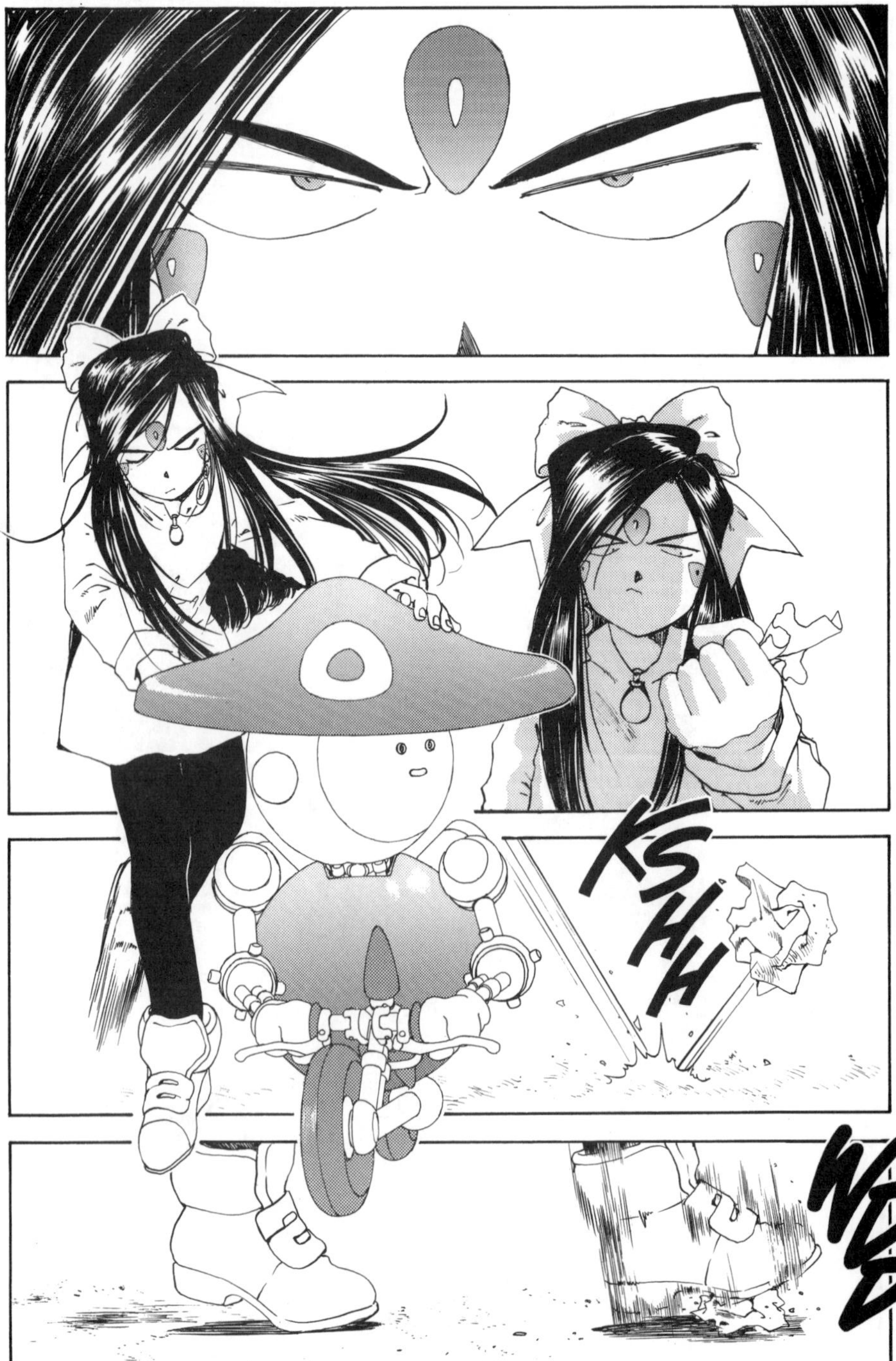
KSHHH
WD

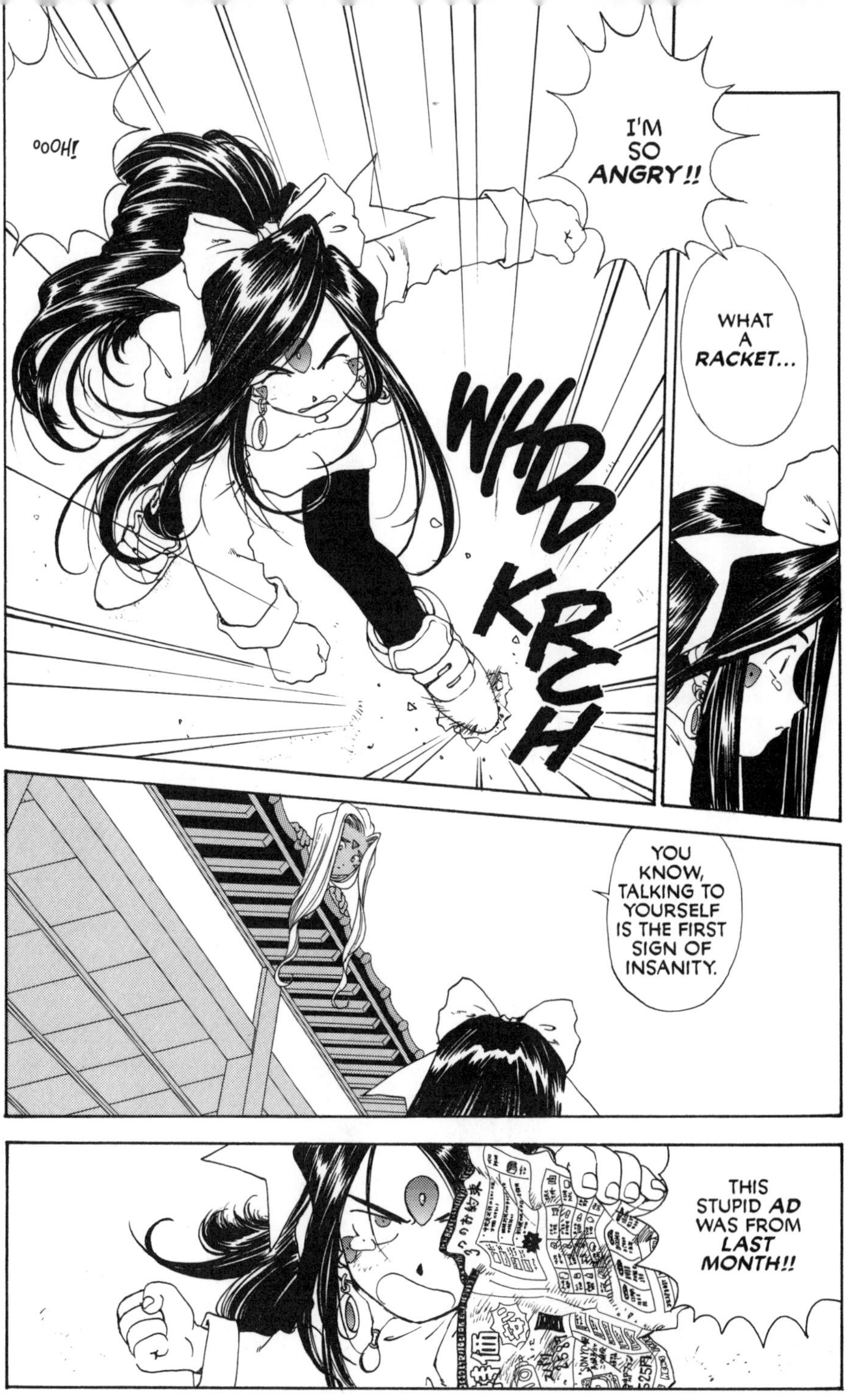
OOOH!
I'M SO ANGRY!!
WHDD KRCH
WHAT A RACKET...
YOU KNOW, TALKING TO YOURSELF IS THE FIRST SIGN OF INSANITY.
THIS STUPID AD WAS FROM LAST MONTH!!

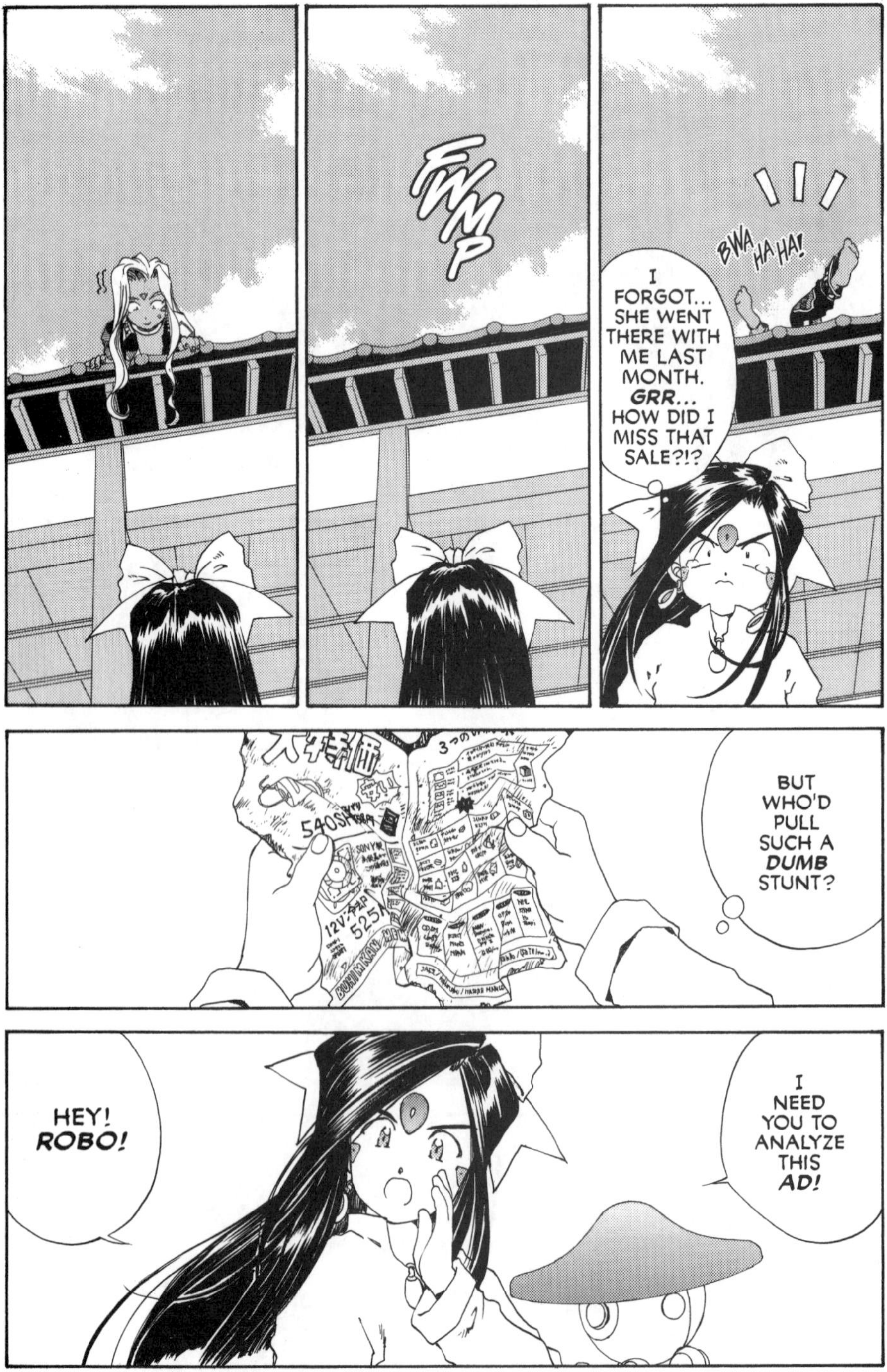
FWMP
I FORGOT... SHE WENT THERE WITH ME LAST MONTH. GRR... HOW DID I MISS THAT SALE?!?
BWA HA HA!
BUT WHO'D PULL SUCH A DUMB STUNT?
HEY! ROBO!
I NEED YOU TO ANALYZE THIS AD!

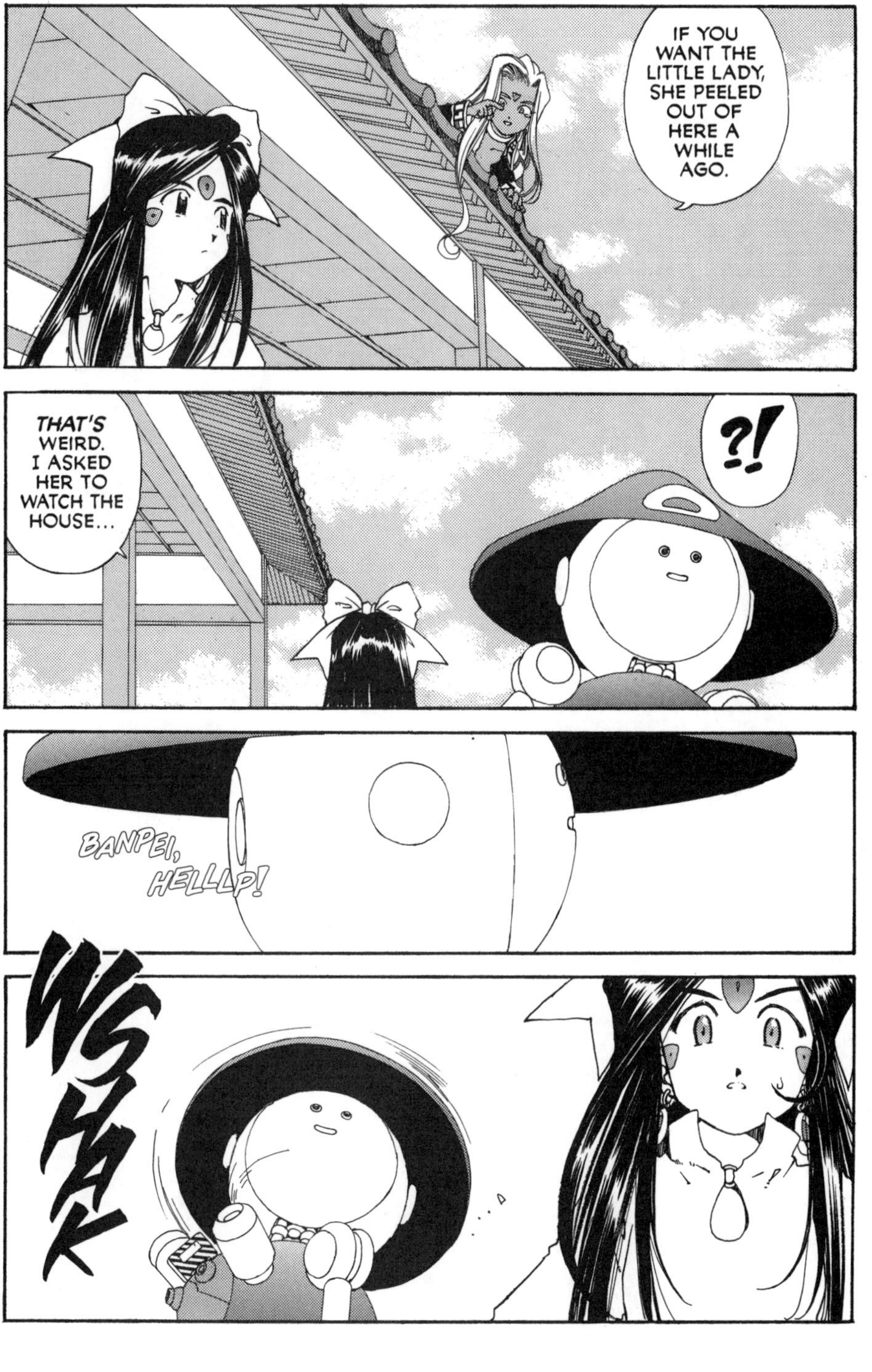
IF YOU WANT THE LITTLE LADY, SHE PEELED OUT OF HERE A WHILE AGO.
THAT'S WEIRD. I ASKED HER TO WATCH THE HOUSE...
?!
BANPEI, HELLLP!
WSHAK
...

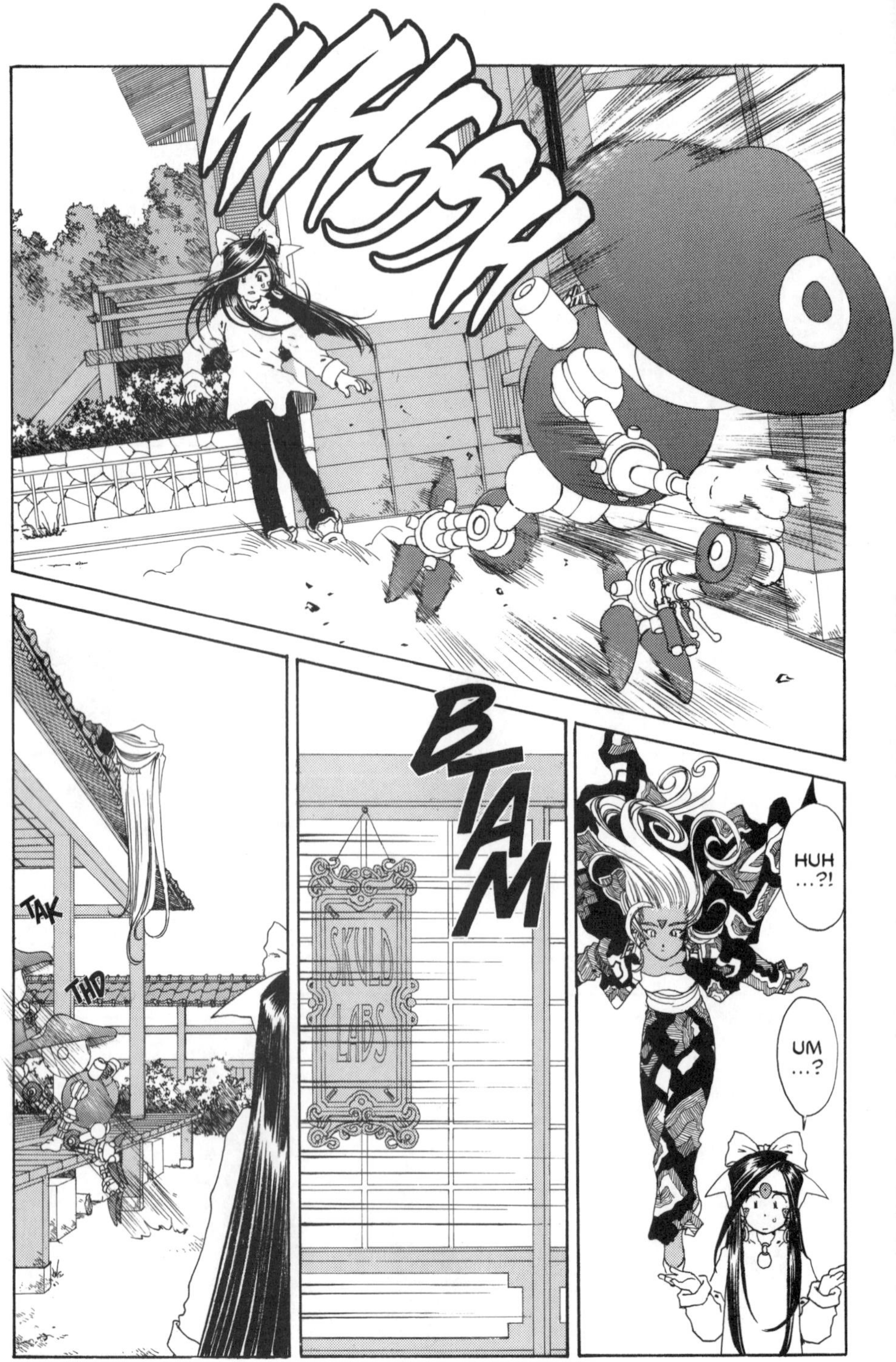
WHSSH
TAK
THD
BTAM
HUH ...?!
UM ...?

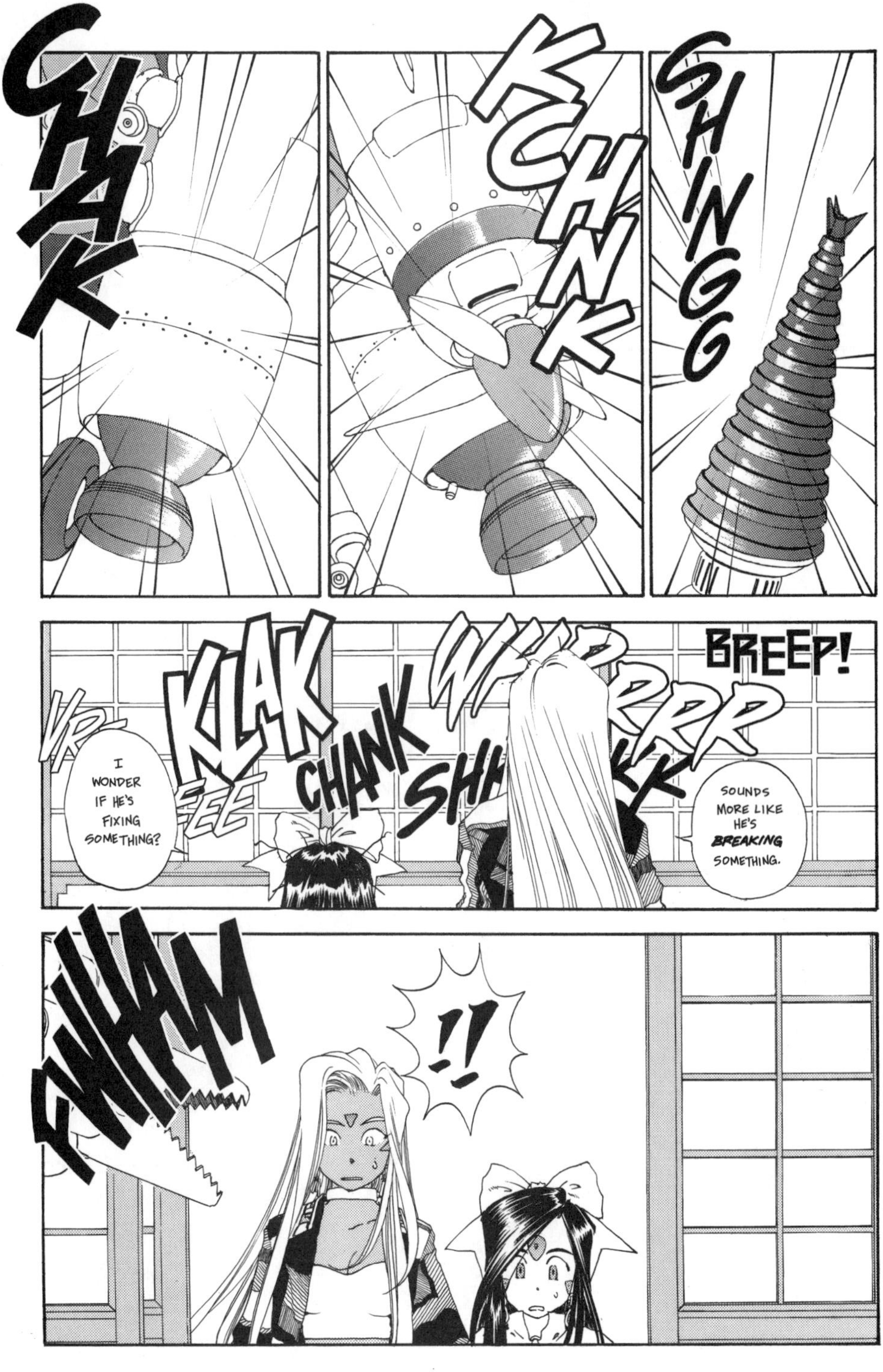
CHAK
KCHNK
SHINGG
KLAK
CHANK
BREEP!
I WONDER IF HE'S FIXING SOMETHING?
SOUNDS MORE LIKE HE'S **BREAKING** SOMETHING.
FWHAM
!!

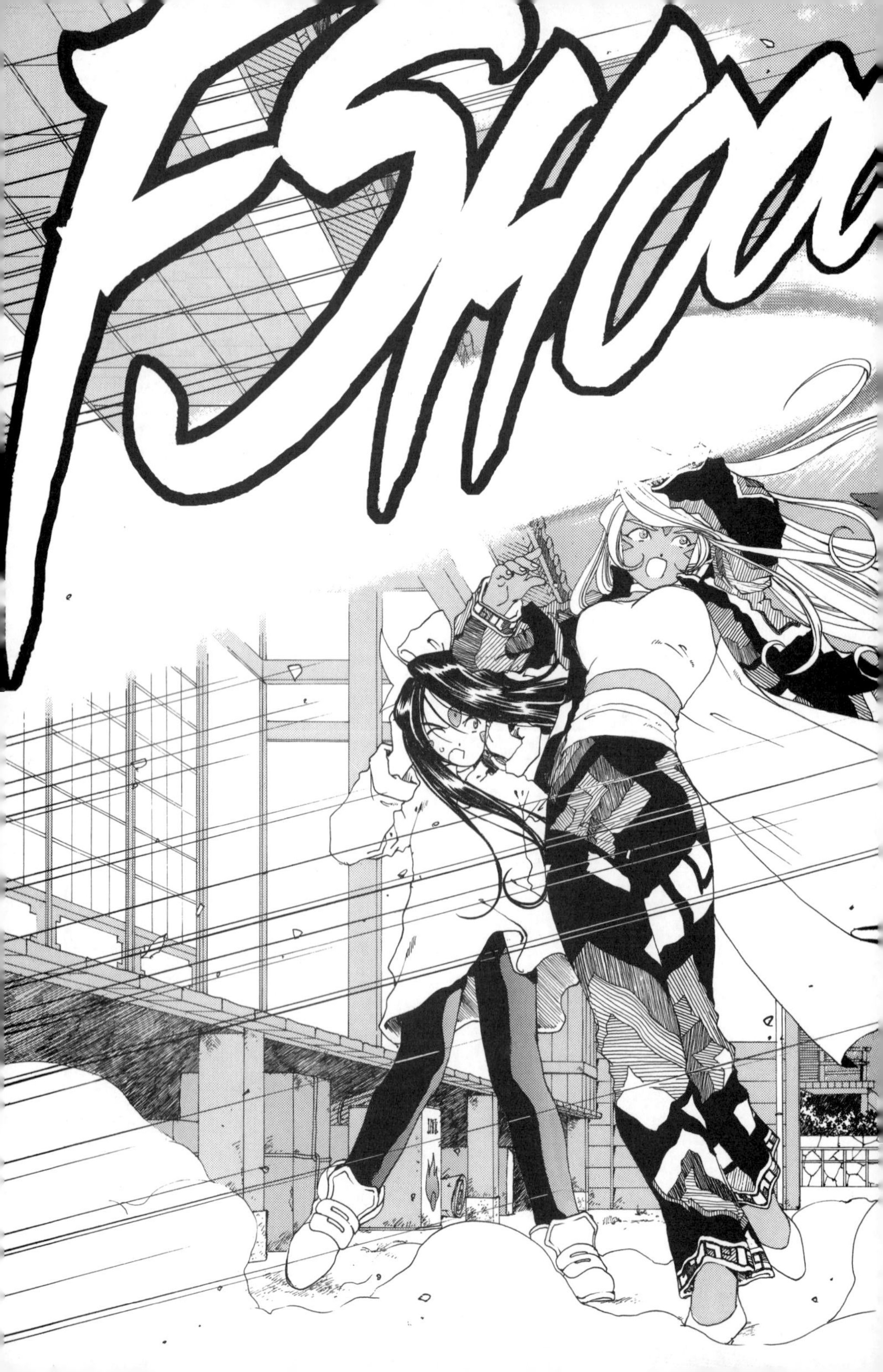
FSHAA

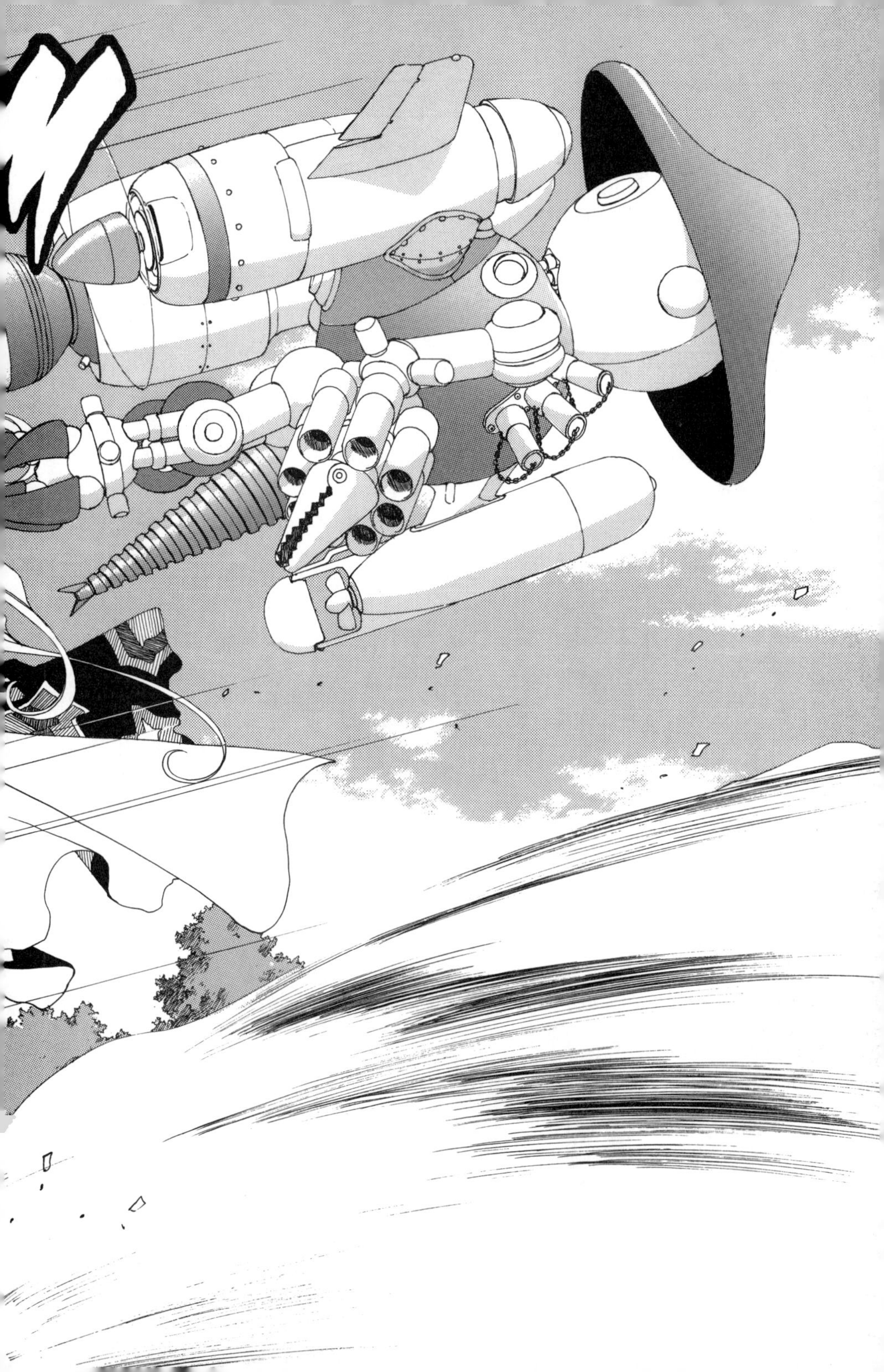

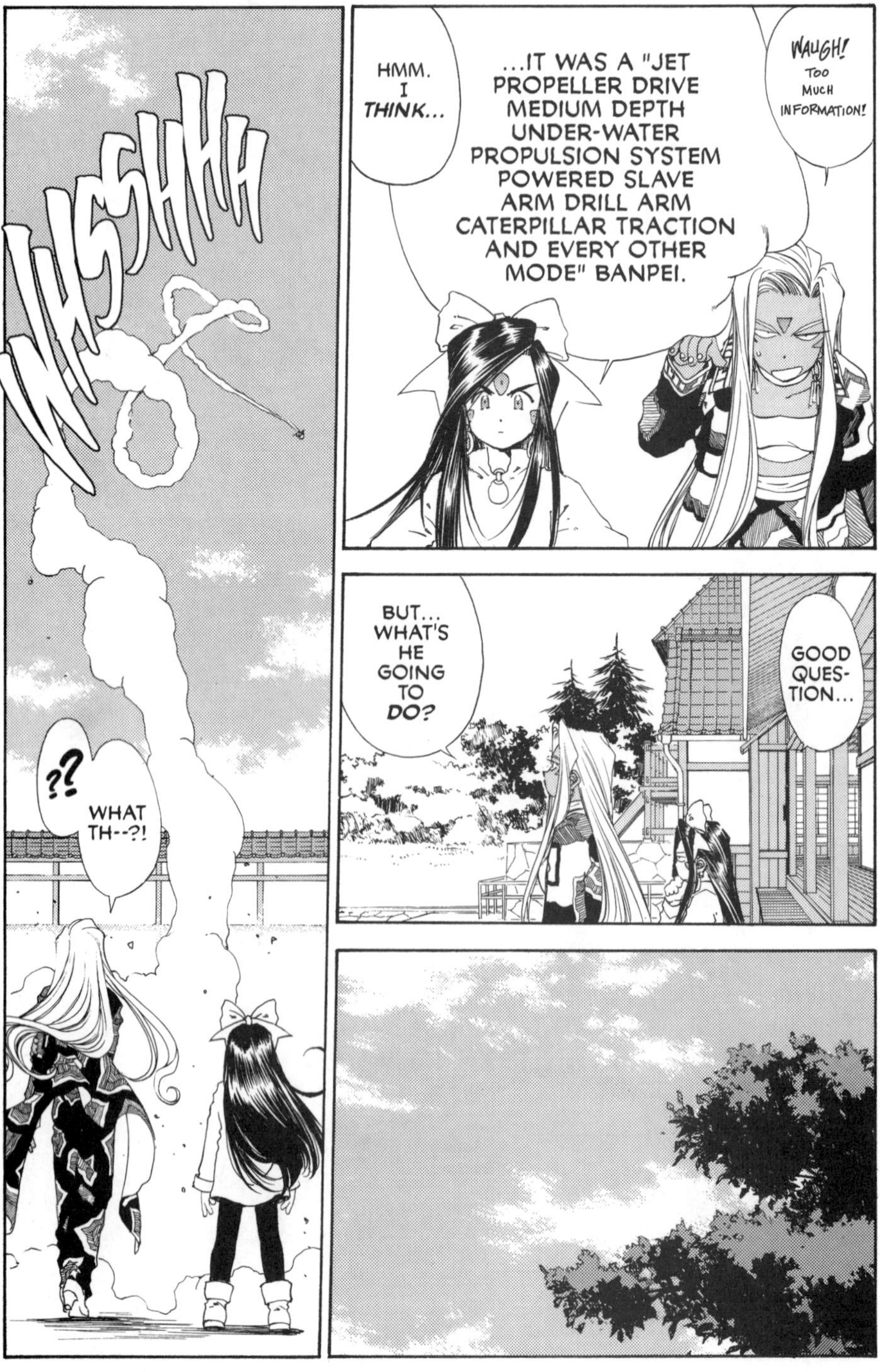
WHSHHH
??
WHAT TH--?!
HMM. I *THINK*...
...IT WAS A "JET PROPELLER DRIVE MEDIUM DEPTH UNDER-WATER PROPULSION SYSTEM POWERED SLAVE ARM DRILL ARM CATERPILLAR TRACTION AND EVERY OTHER MODE" BANPEI.
WAUGH! TOO MUCH INFORMATION!
BUT... WHAT'S HE GOING TO *DO?*
GOOD QUES-TION...

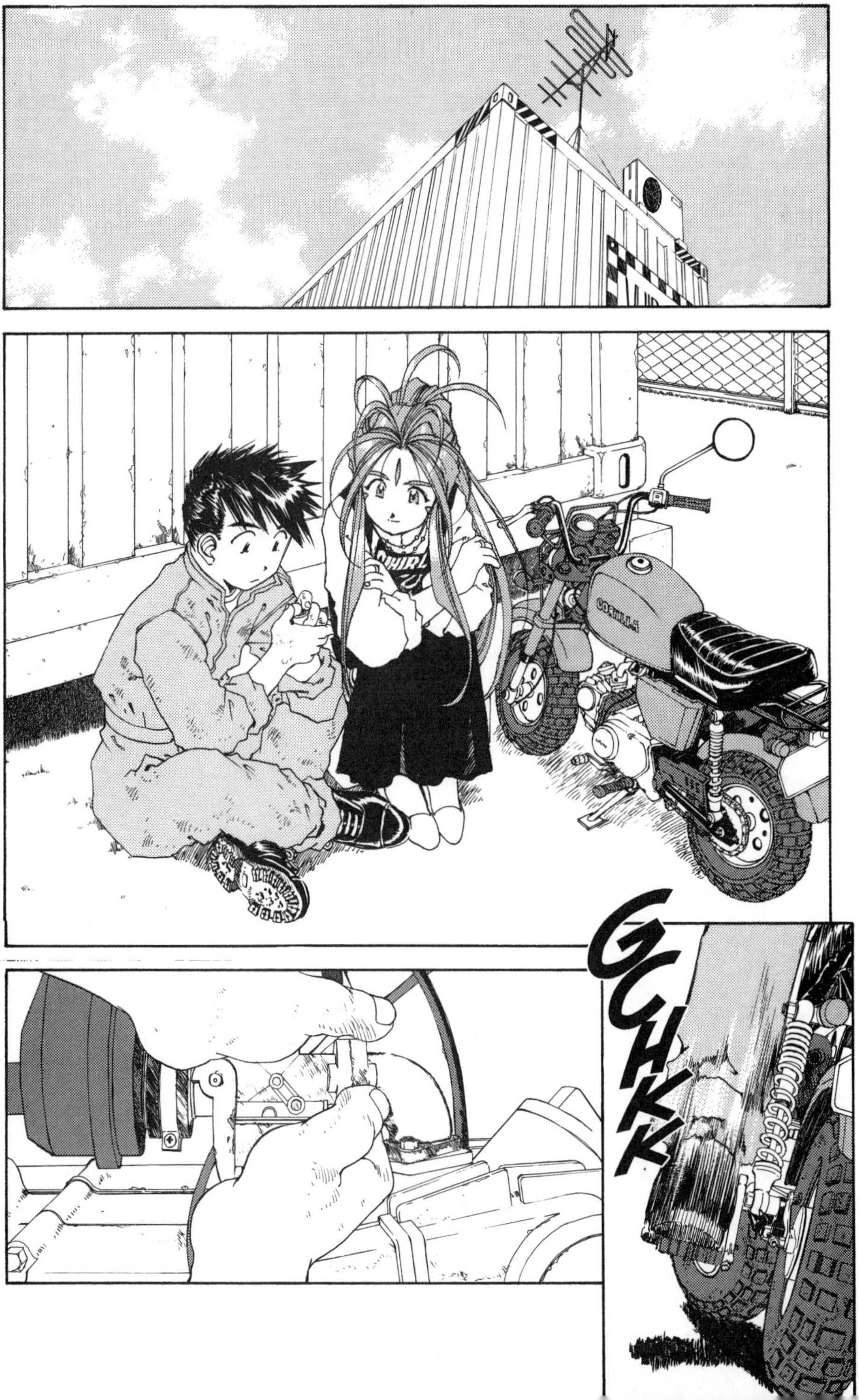
GORILLA
GCHKK

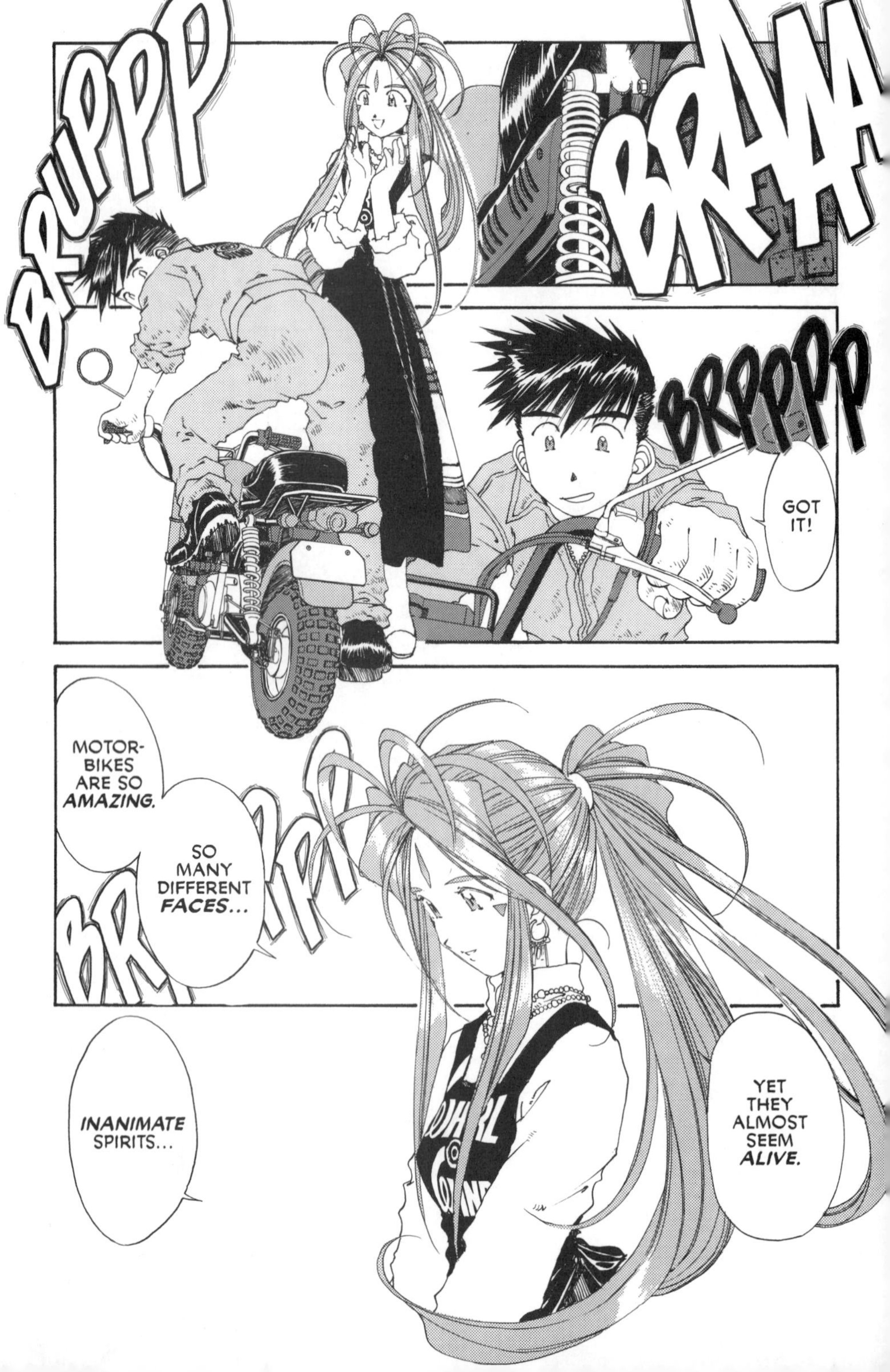
BRUPPP
BRAAA
BRPPPP
GOT IT!
MOTOR-BIKES ARE SO AMAZING.
SO MANY DIFFERENT FACES...
BRPPP
INANIMATE SPIRITS...
YET THEY ALMOST SEEM ALIVE.

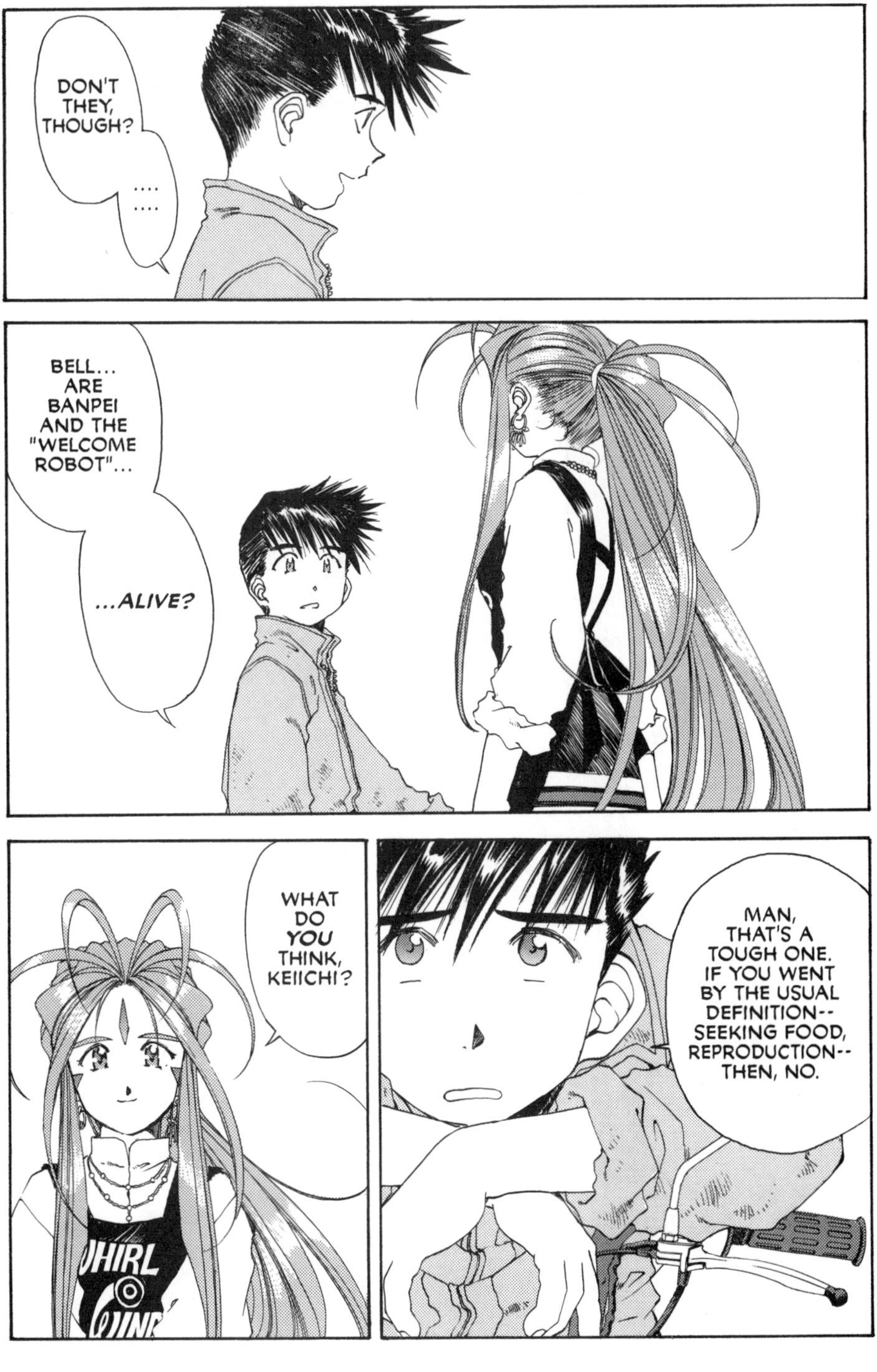
DON'T THEY, THOUGH?
....
....
BELL... ARE BANPEI AND THE "WELCOME ROBOT"...
...ALIVE?
WHAT DO YOU THINK, KEIICHI?
MAN, THAT'S A TOUGH ONE. IF YOU WENT BY THE USUAL DEFINITION-- SEEKING FOOD, REPRODUCTION-- THEN, NO.

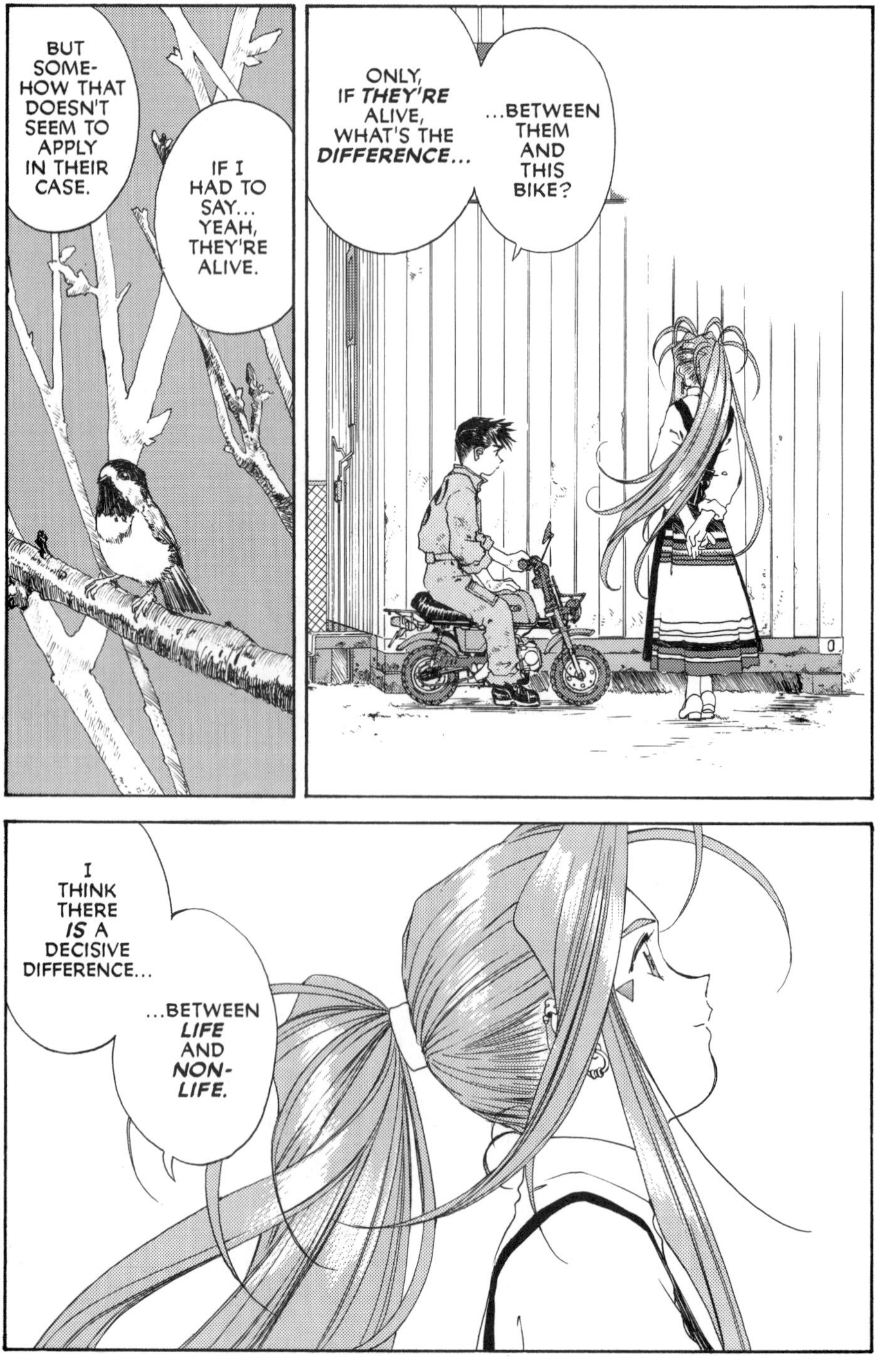
BUT SOME-HOW THAT DOESN'T SEEM TO APPLY IN THEIR CASE.
IF I HAD TO SAY... YEAH, THEY'RE ALIVE.
ONLY, IF *THEY'RE* ALIVE, WHAT'S THE *DIFFERENCE*...
...BETWEEN THEM AND THIS BIKE?
I THINK THERE *IS* A DECISIVE DIFFERENCE...
...BETWEEN *LIFE* AND *NON-LIFE.*

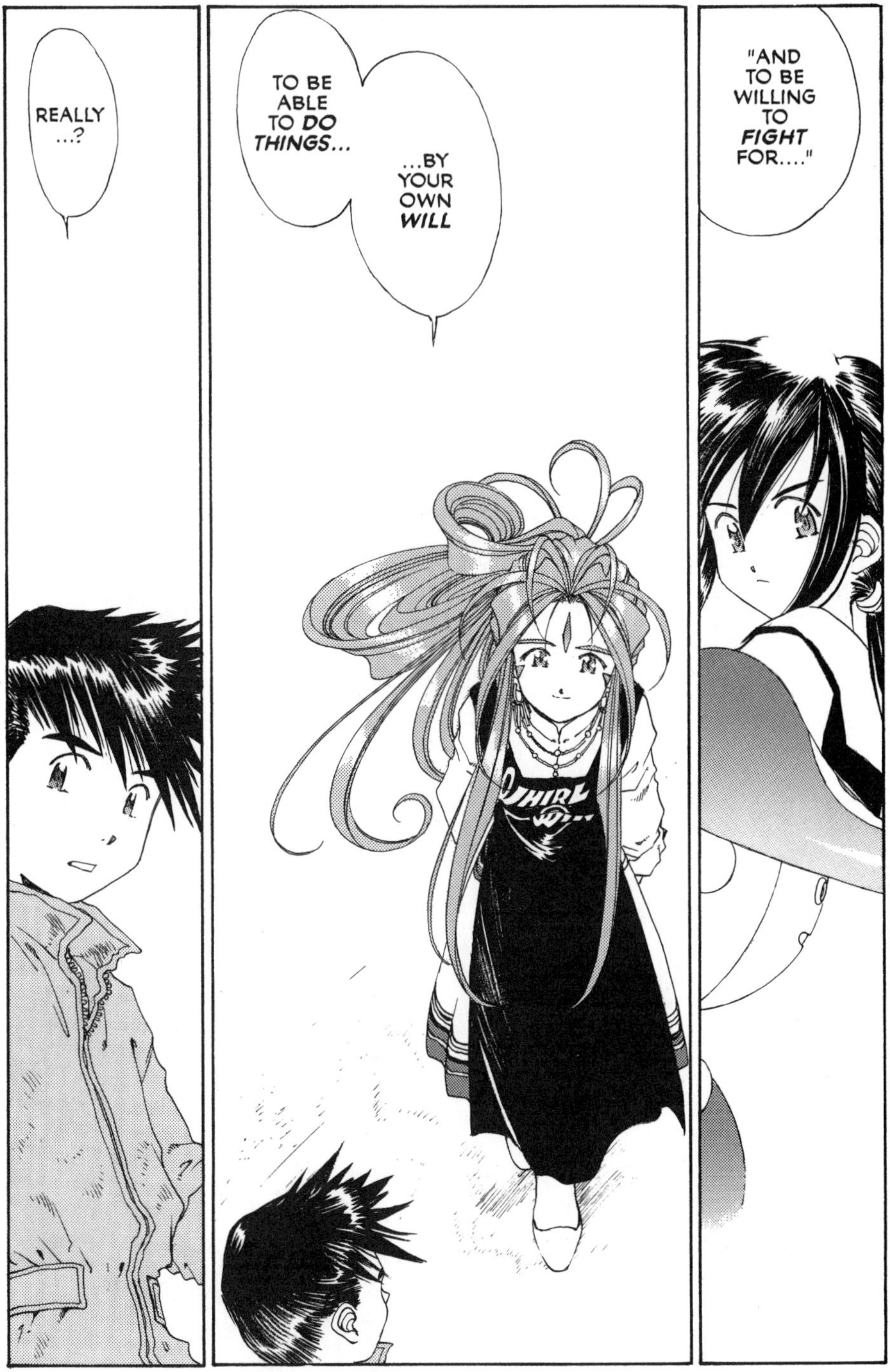
REALLY ...?
TO BE ABLE TO ***DO THINGS...***
...BY YOUR OWN ***WILL***
"AND TO BE WILLING TO ***FIGHT*** FOR...."

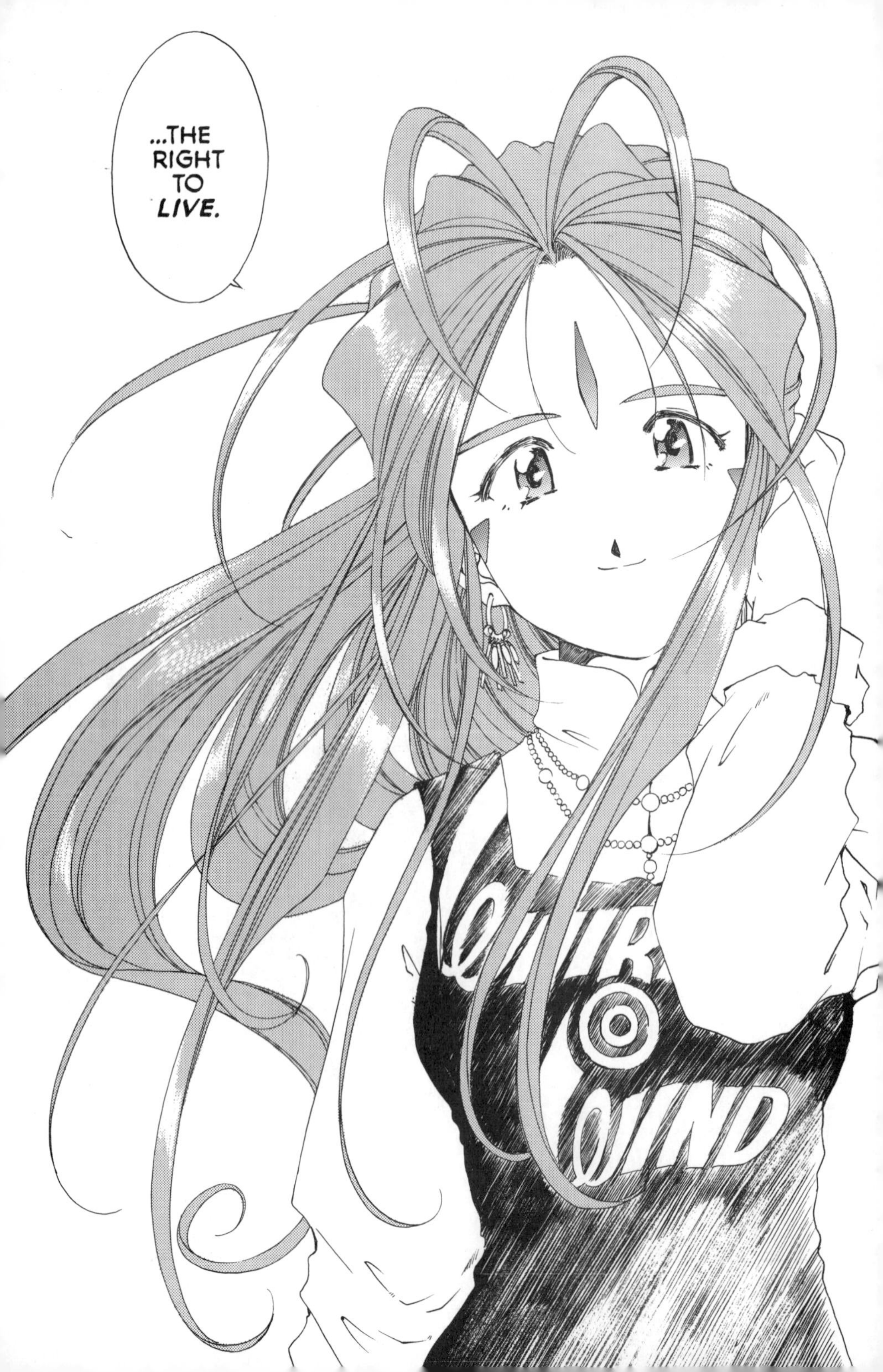
...THE RIGHT TO *LIVE.*

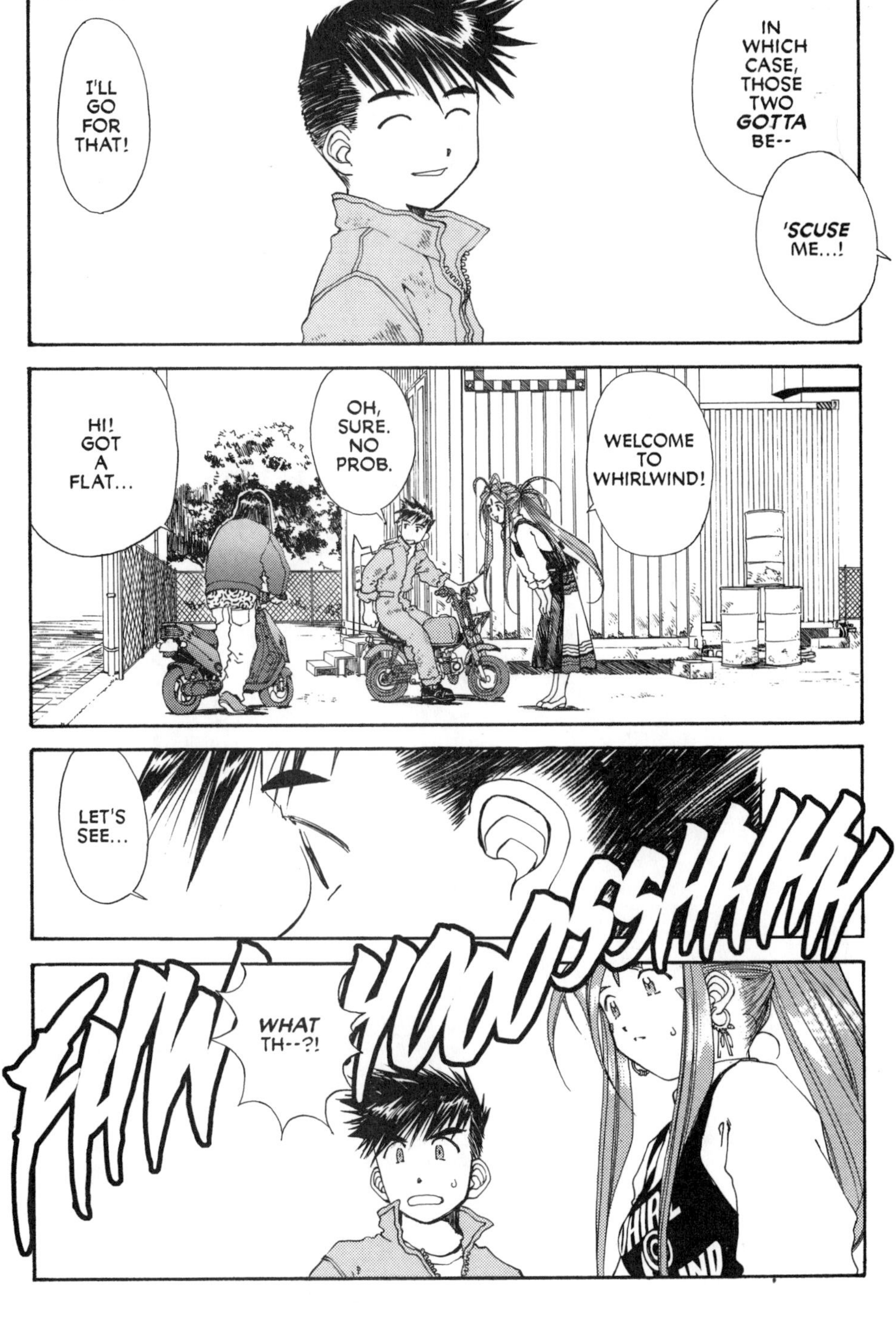
I'LL GO FOR THAT!
IN WHICH CASE, THOSE TWO *GOTTA* BE--
'SCUSE ME...!
HI! GOT A FLAT...
OH, SURE. NO PROB.
WELCOME TO WHIRLWIND!
LET'S SEE...
FWW
WHAT TH--?!
YOOOSSHHHH

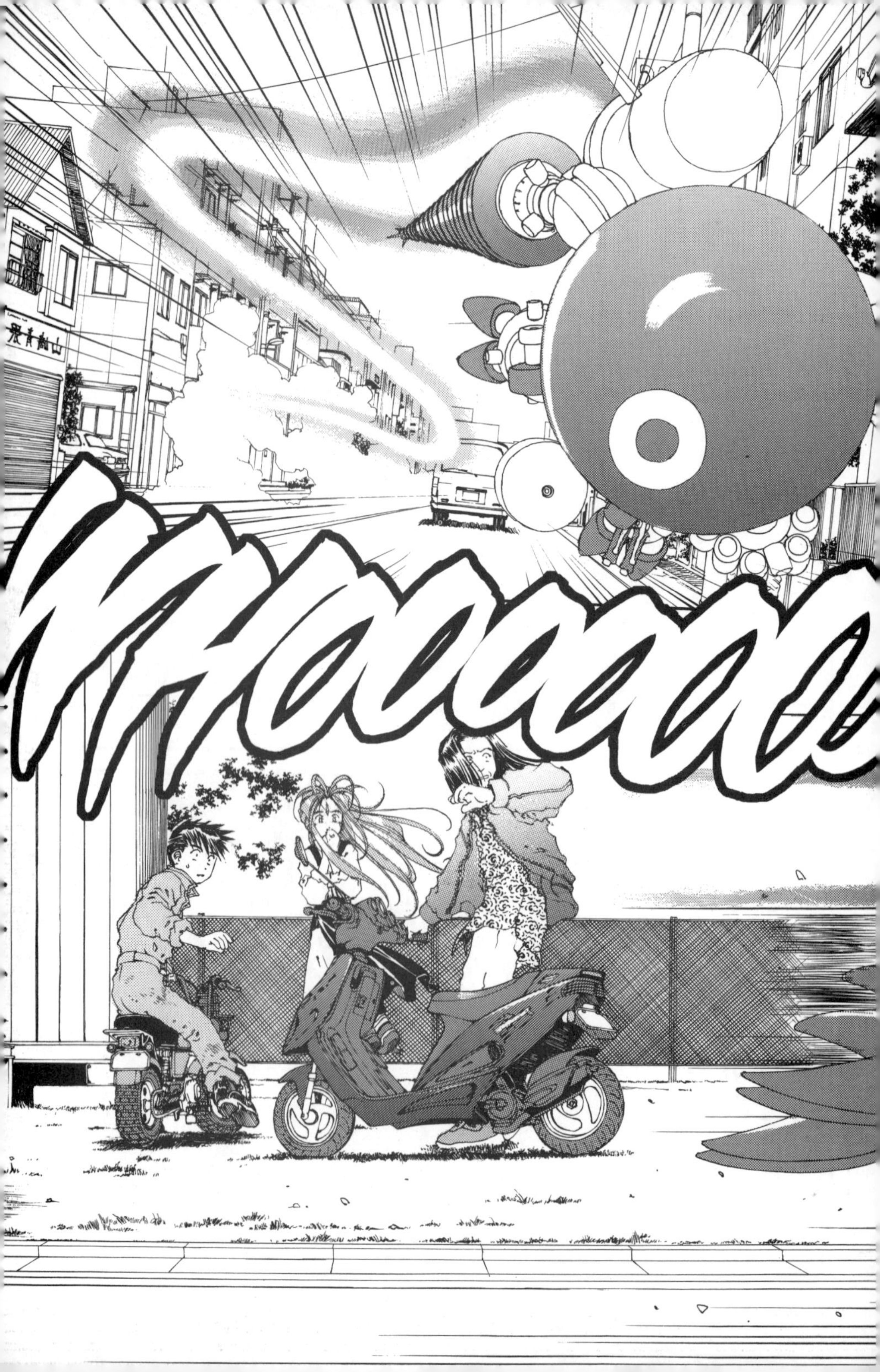

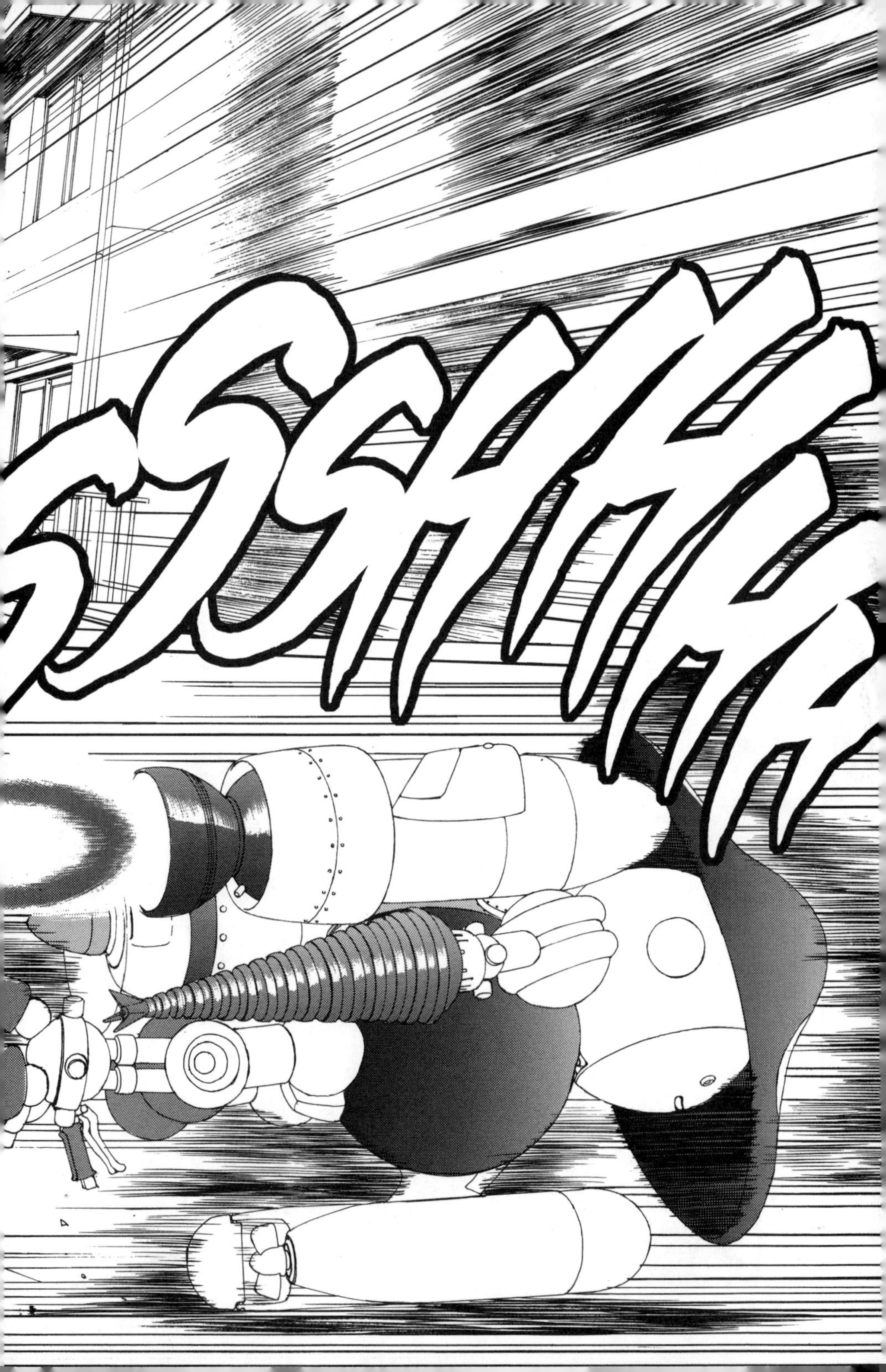
SSHHHH

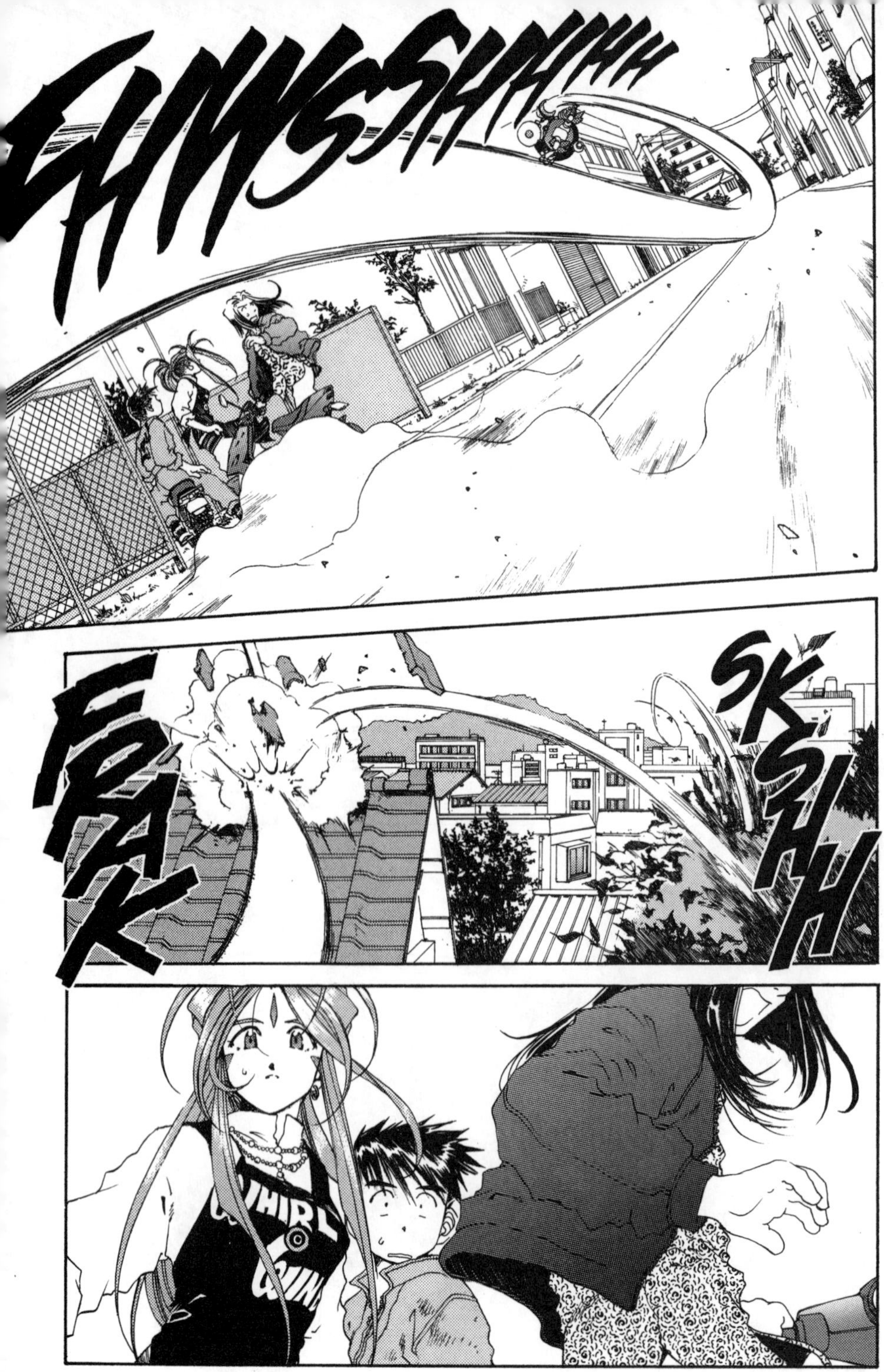
ZWWSHHHHH
FRAK
SKSHH

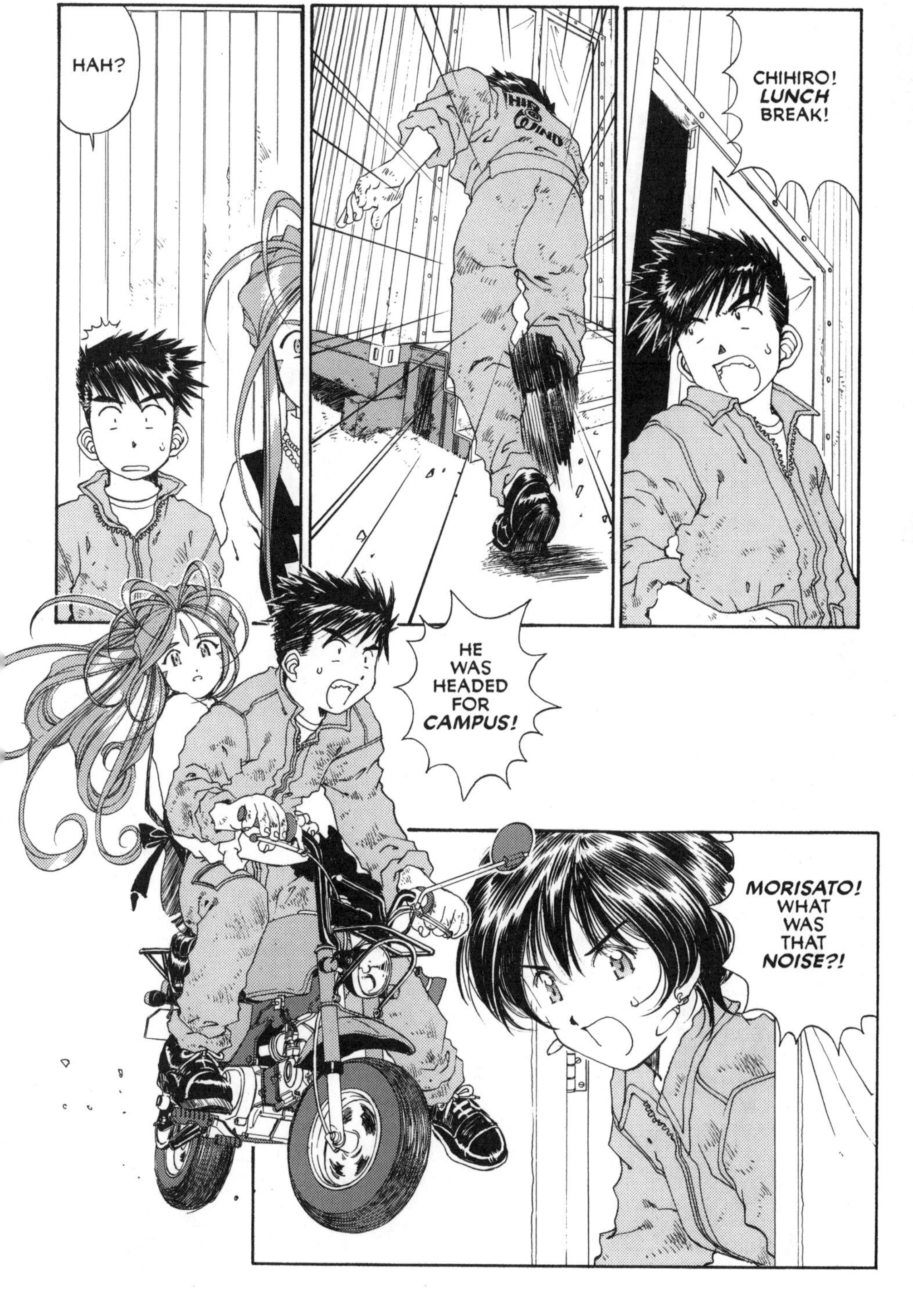
HAH?
CHIHIRO! *LUNCH* BREAK!
HE WAS HEADED FOR *CAMPUS!*
MORISATO! WHAT WAS THAT *NOISE?!*

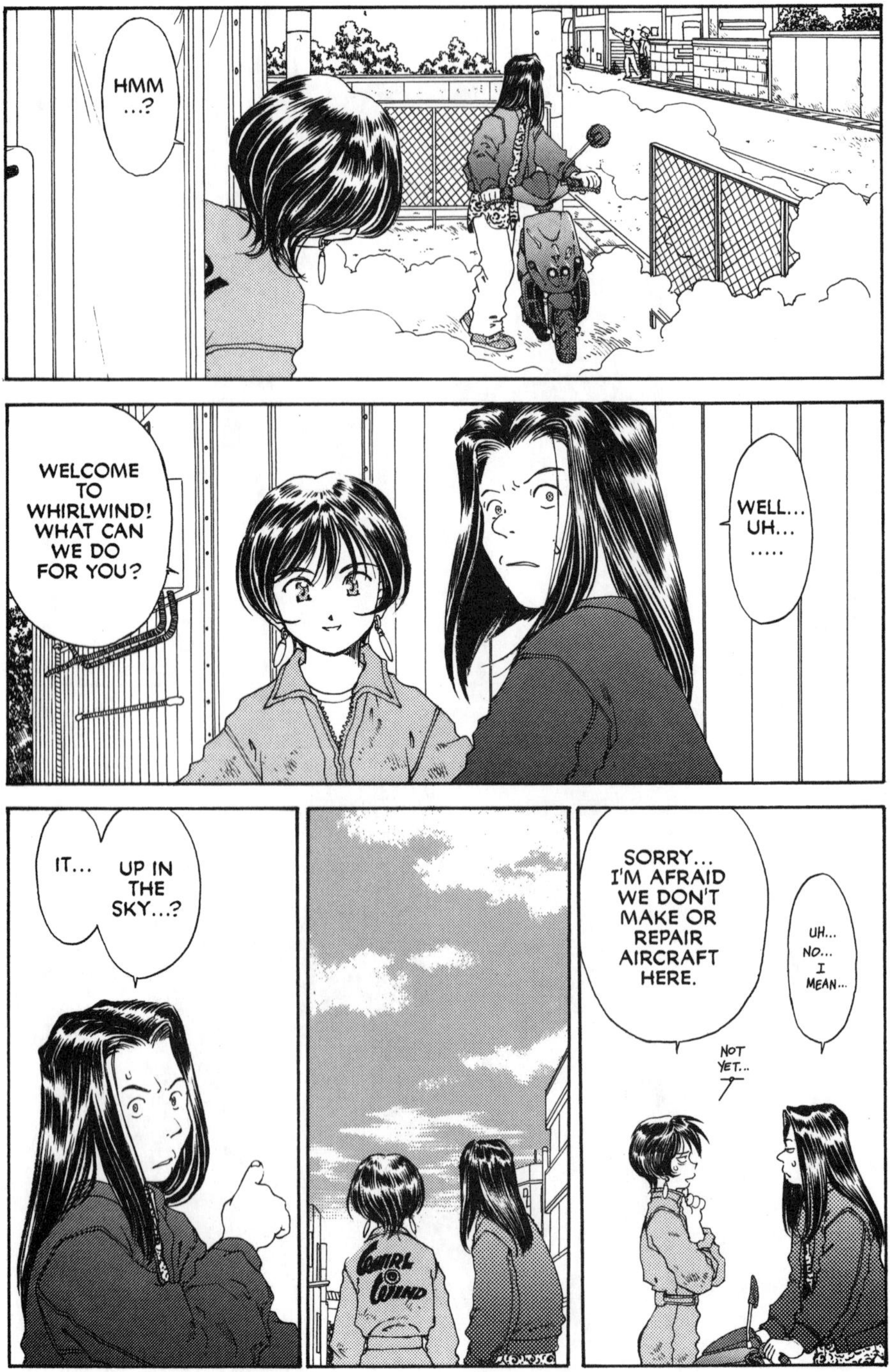
HMM ...?
WELCOME TO WHIRLWIND! WHAT CAN WE DO FOR YOU?
WELL... UH... .....
IT...
UP IN THE SKY...?
SORRY... I'M AFRAID WE DON'T MAKE OR REPAIR AIRCRAFT HERE.
NOT YET...
UH... NO... I MEAN...

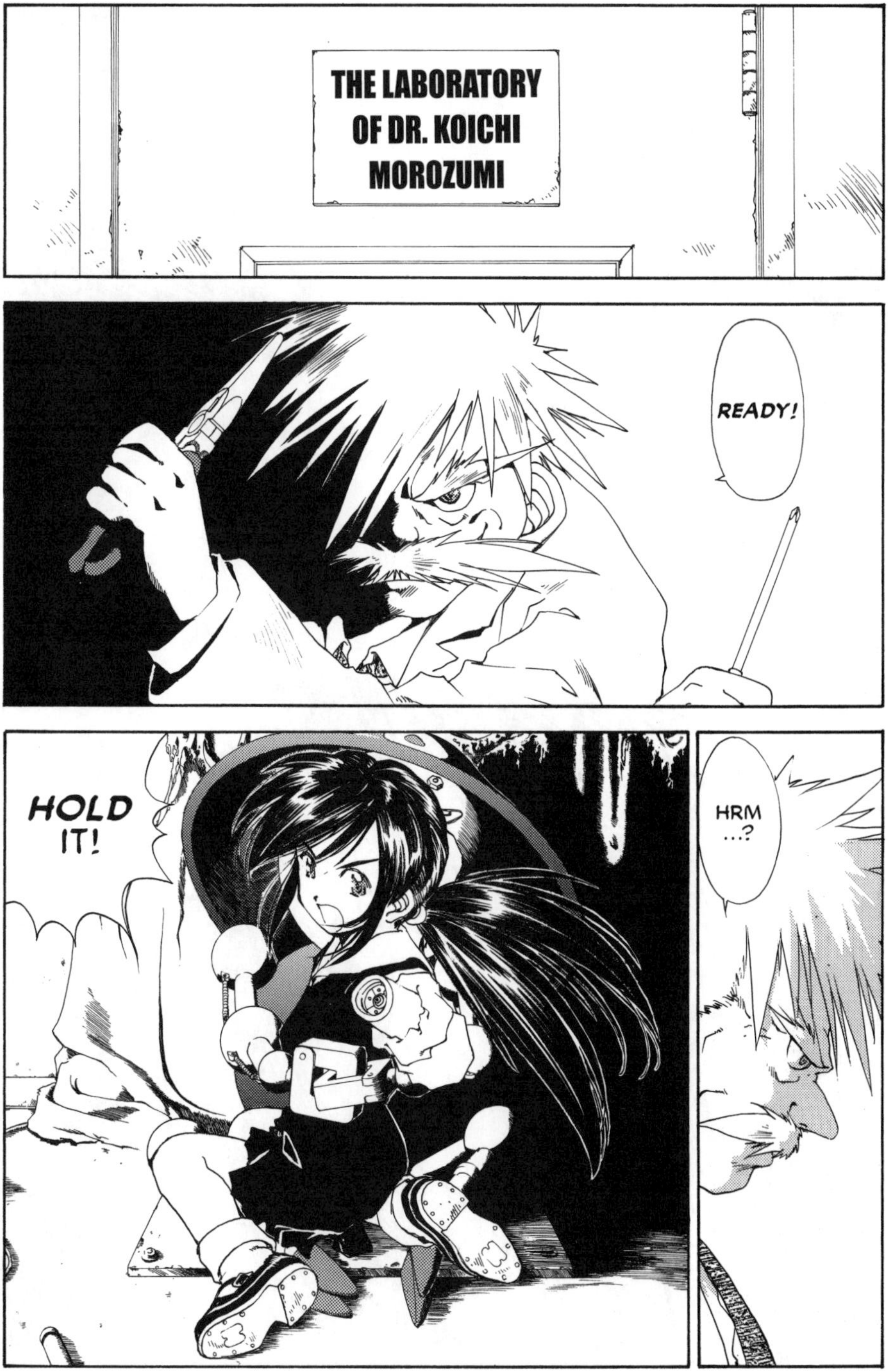
THE LABORATORY OF DR. KOICHI MOROZUMI
READY!
HOLD IT!
HRM ...?

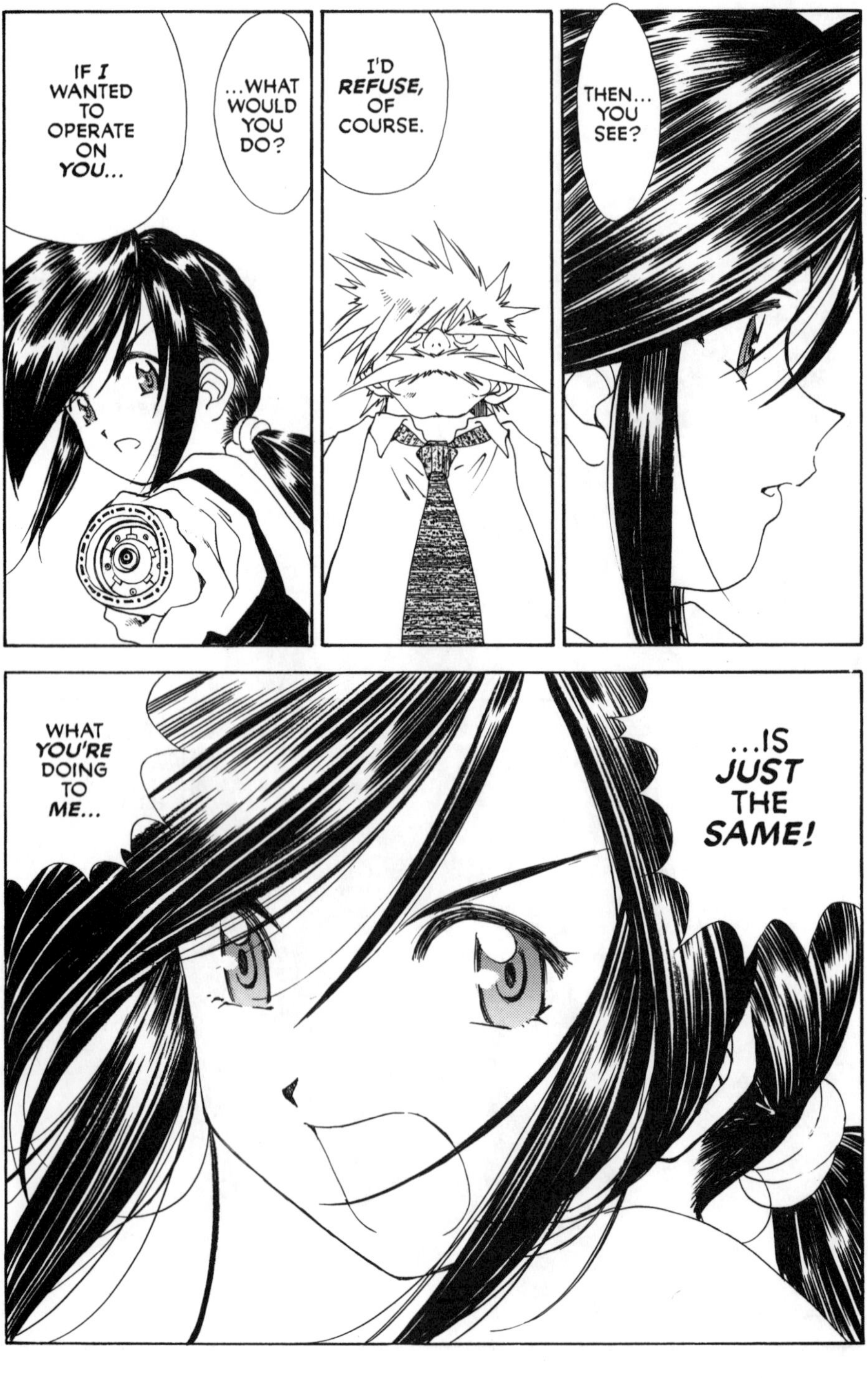
IF *I* WANTED TO OPERATE ON *YOU*...
...WHAT WOULD YOU DO?
I'D *REFUSE,* OF COURSE.
THEN... YOU SEE?
WHAT *YOU'RE* DOING TO *ME*...
...IS *JUST* THE *SAME!*

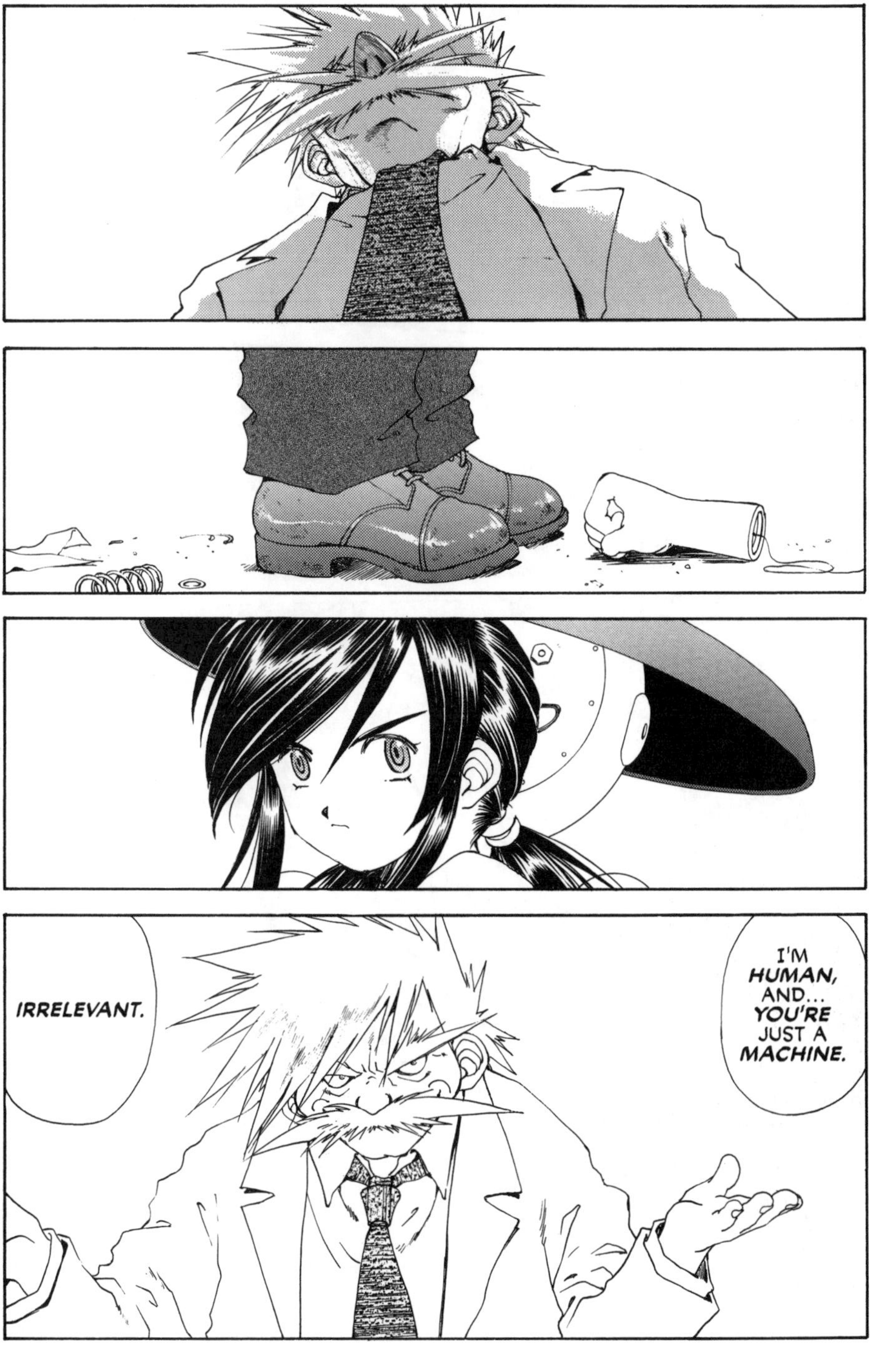
IRRELEVANT.
I'M HUMAN, AND... YOU'RE JUST A MACHINE.

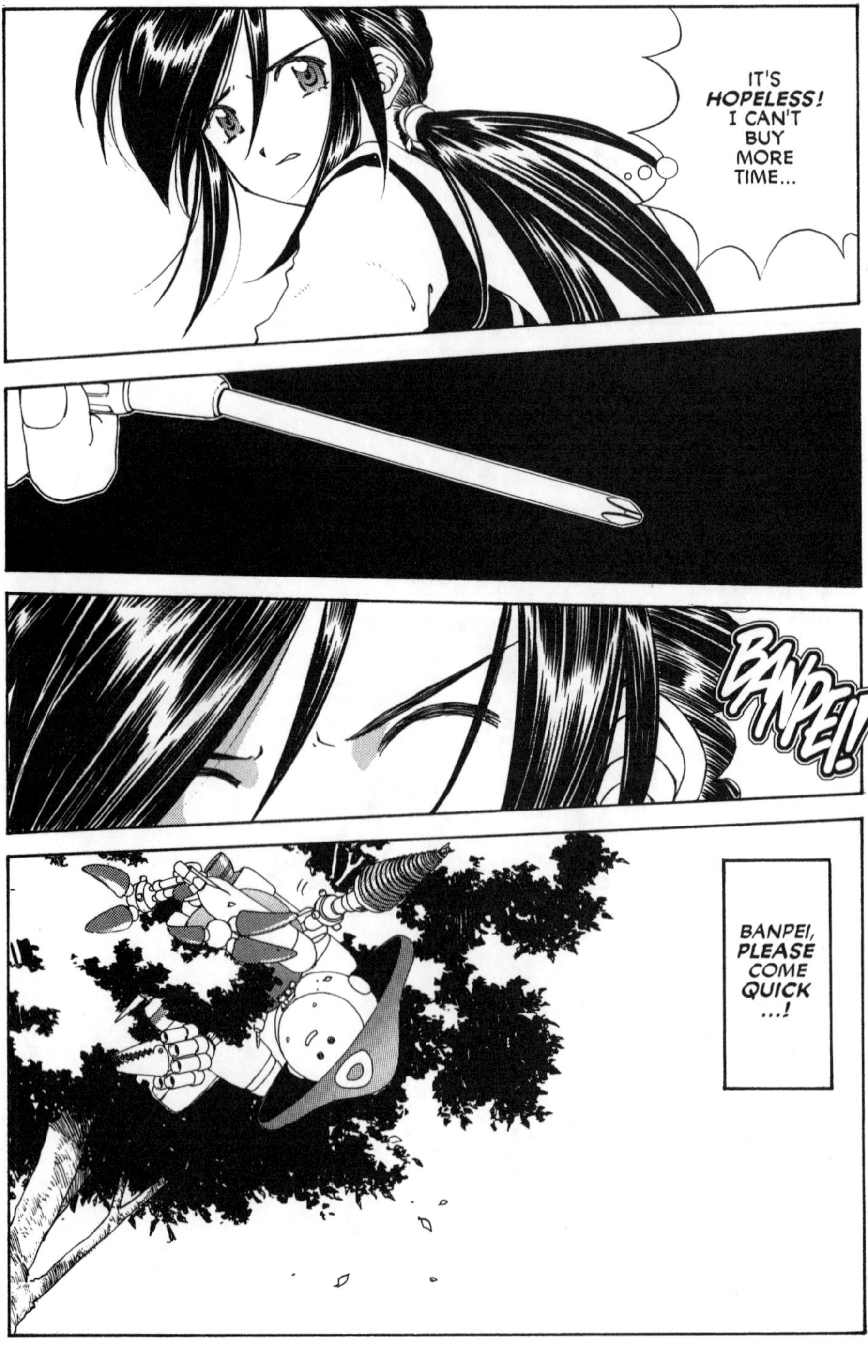
IT'S HOPELESS! I CAN'T BUY MORE TIME...
BANPEI!!
BANPEI, PLEASE COME QUICK ...!

THE SIGN OF LIFE

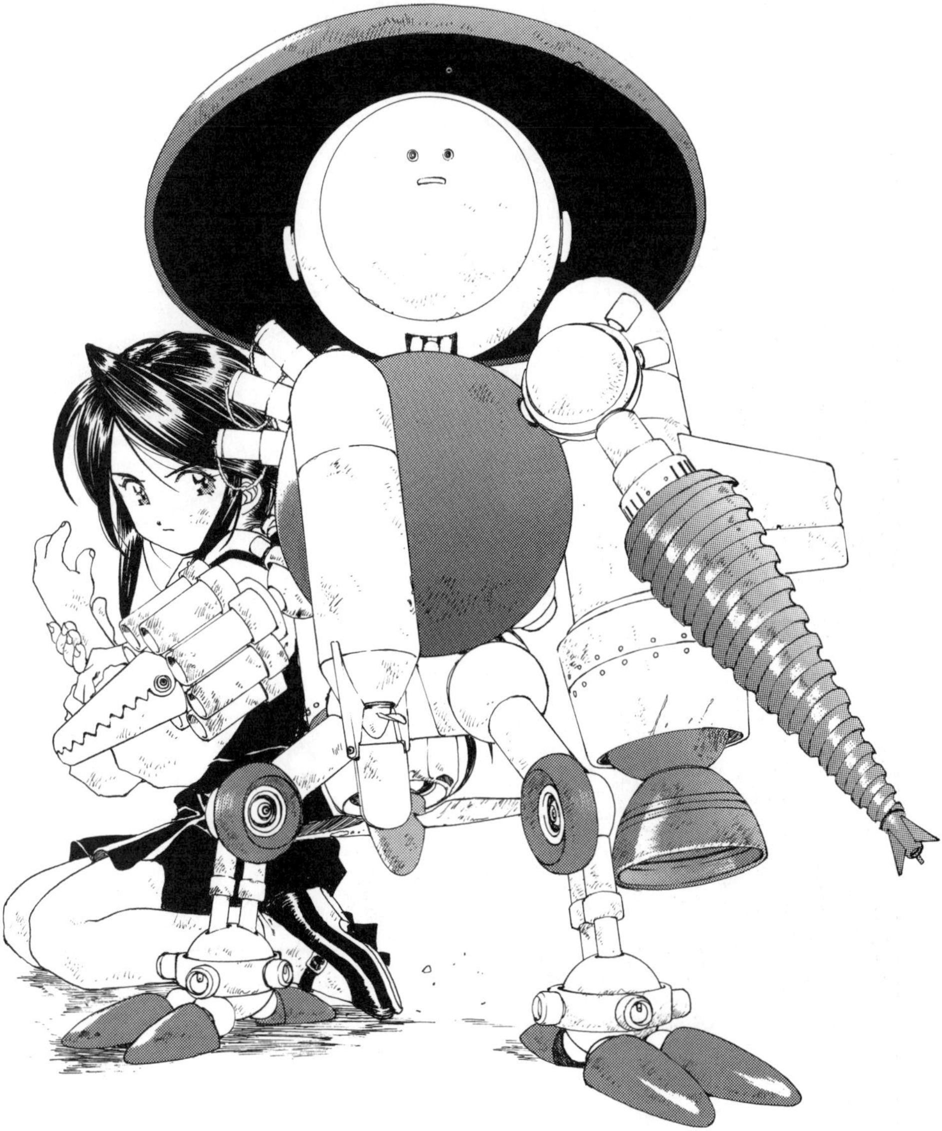

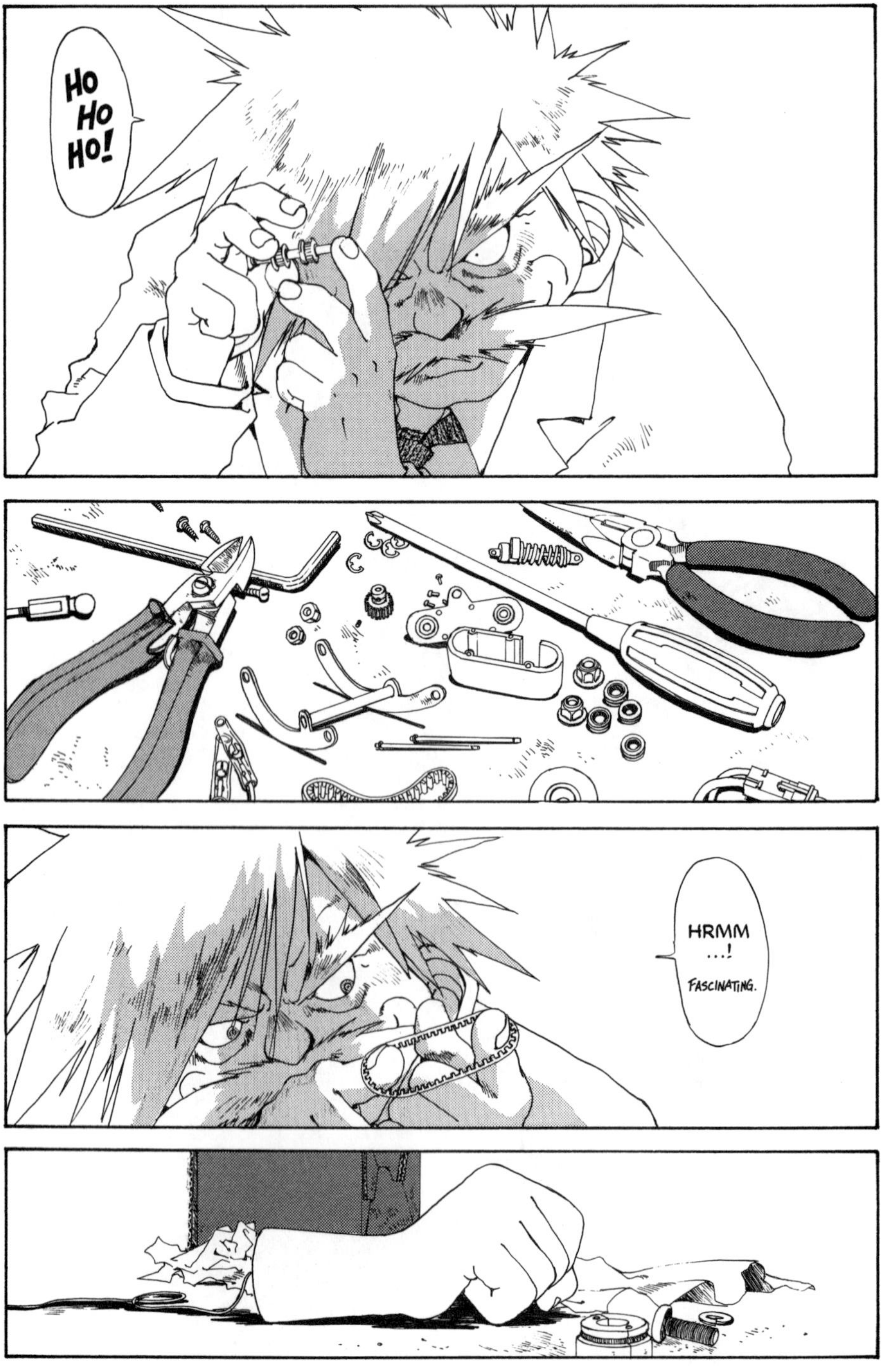
HO HO HO!
HRMM ...! FASCINATING.

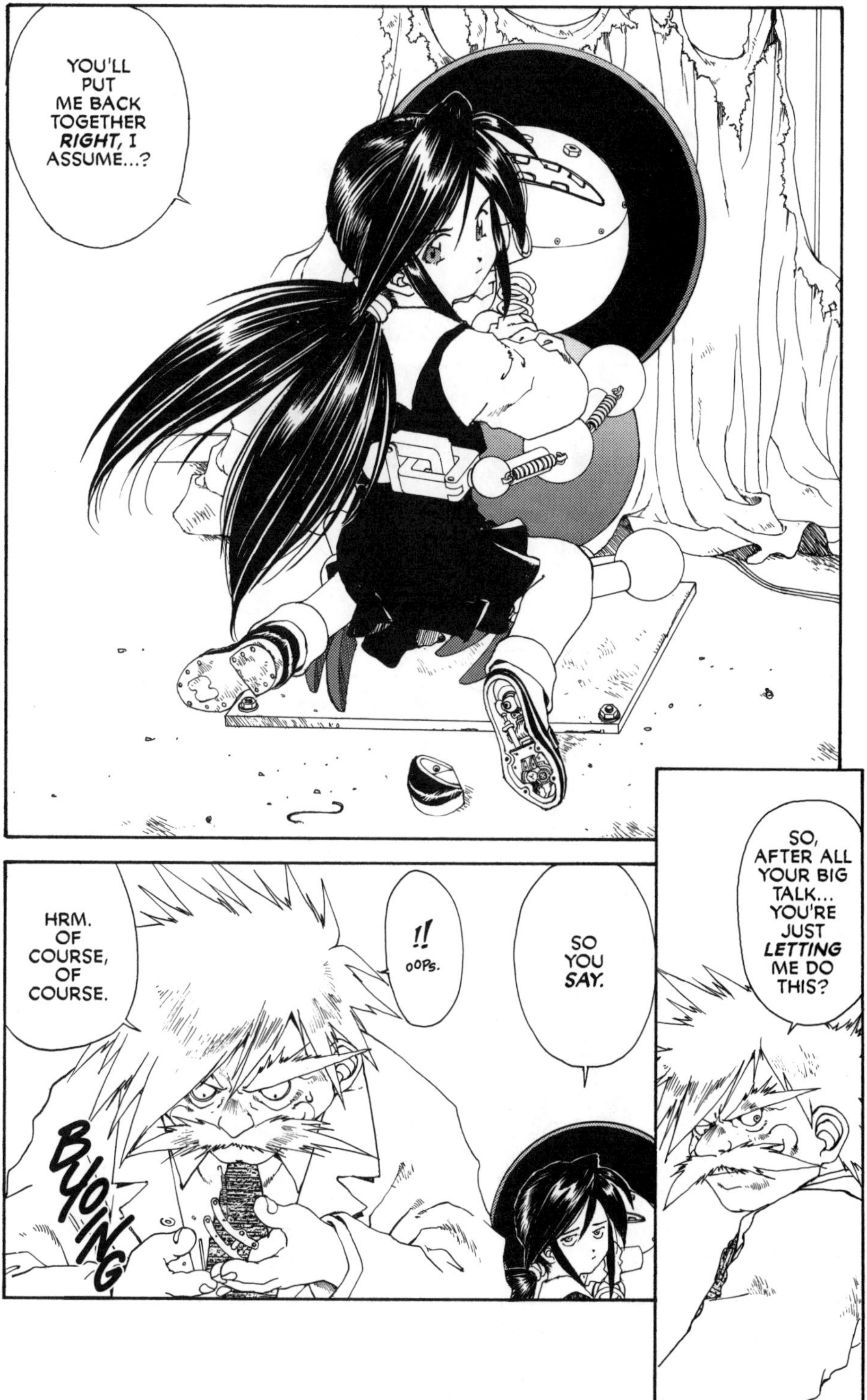
YOU'LL PUT ME BACK TOGETHER *RIGHT,* I ASSUME...?
HRM. OF COURSE, OF COURSE.
BUYOING
!! OOPS.
SO YOU *SAY.*
SO, AFTER ALL YOUR BIG TALK... YOU'RE JUST *LETTING* ME DO THIS?

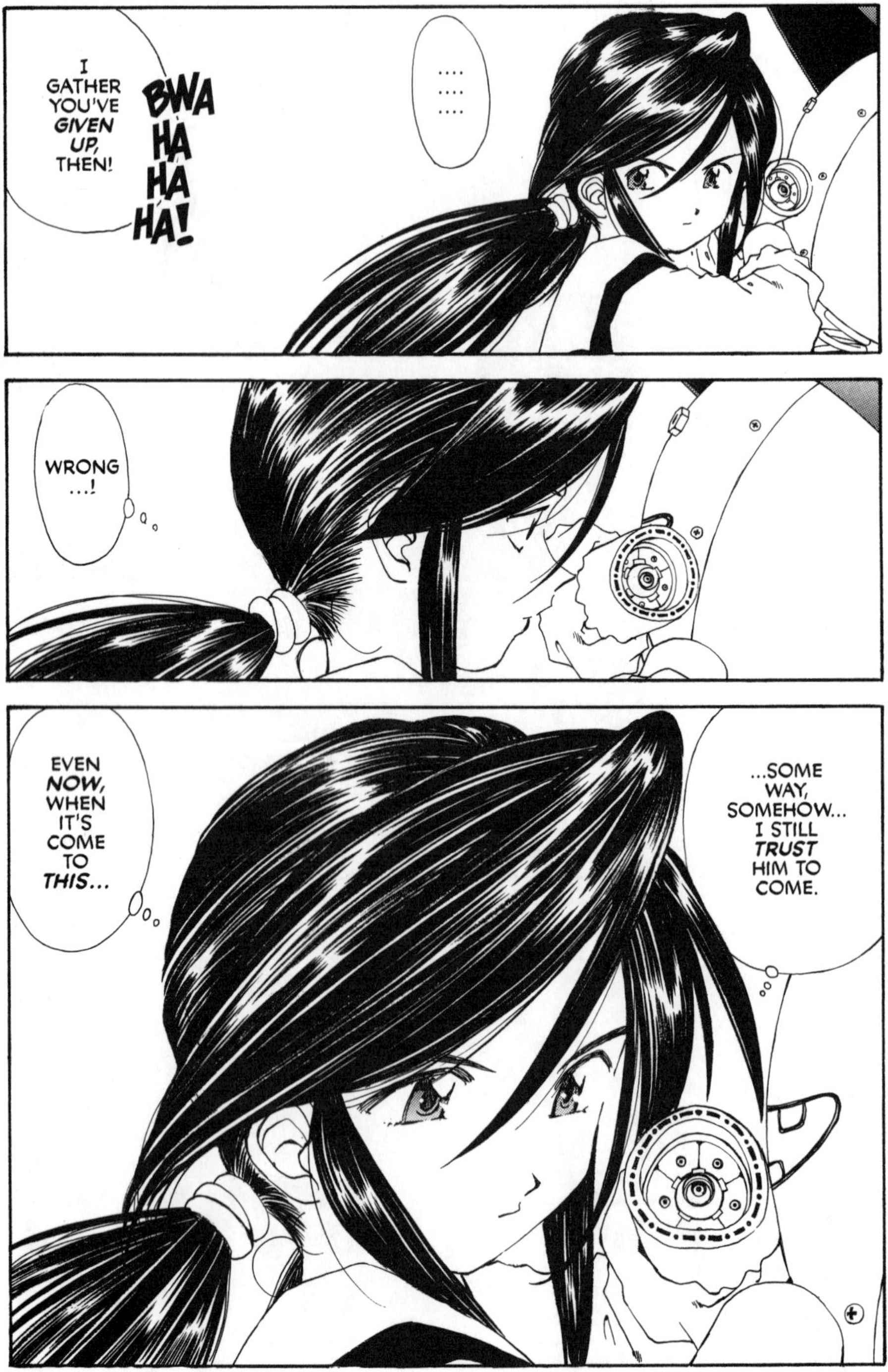
I GATHER YOU'VE *GIVEN UP,* THEN!
BWA HA HA HA!
....
....
....
WRONG ...!
EVEN *NOW,* WHEN IT'S COME TO *THIS...*
...SOME WAY, SOMEHOW... I STILL *TRUST* HIM TO COME.

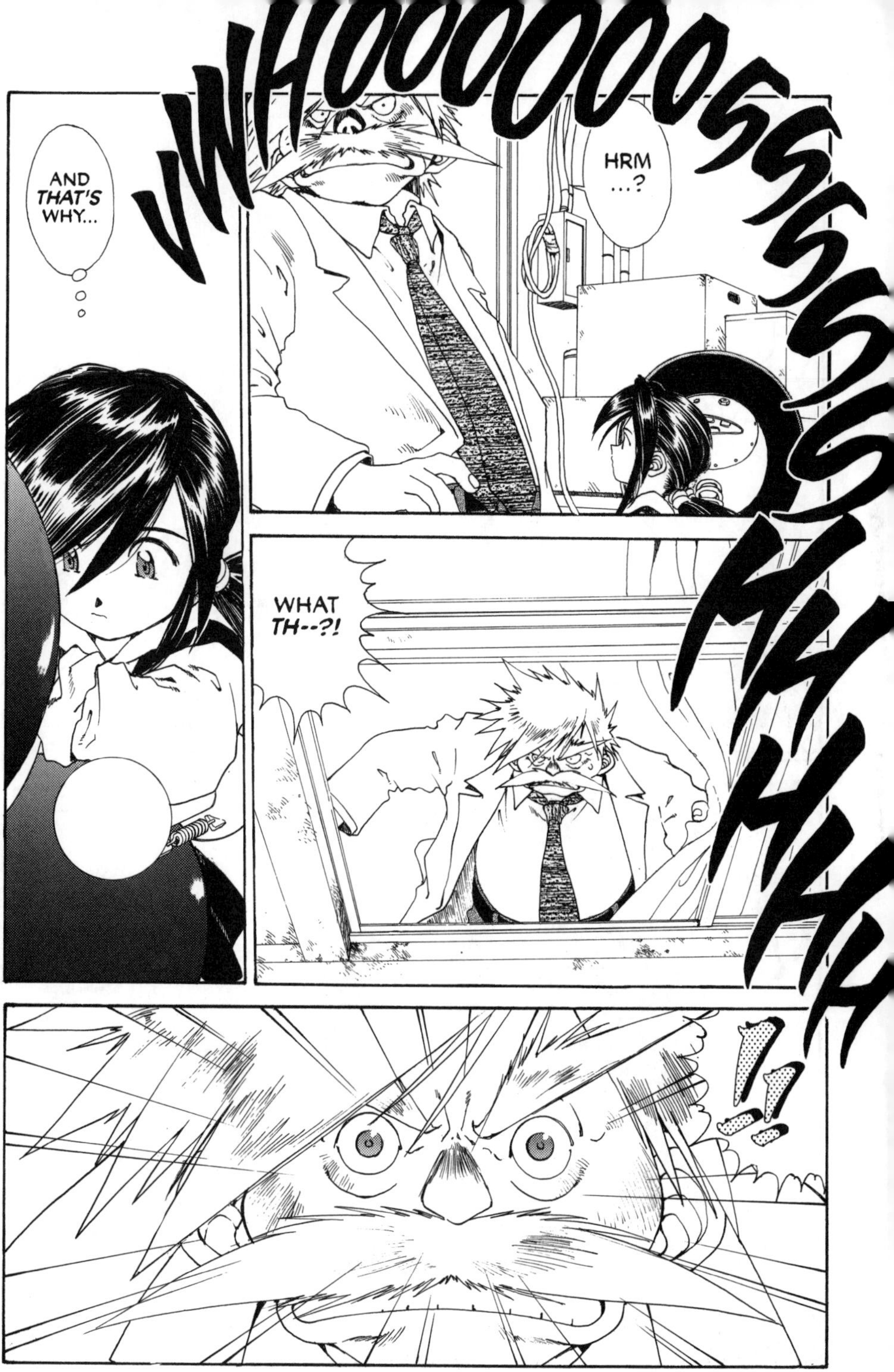
AND THAT'S WHY...
VWHOOOOOOSSSSSSHHHHHH
HRM ...?
WHAT TH--?!
!!

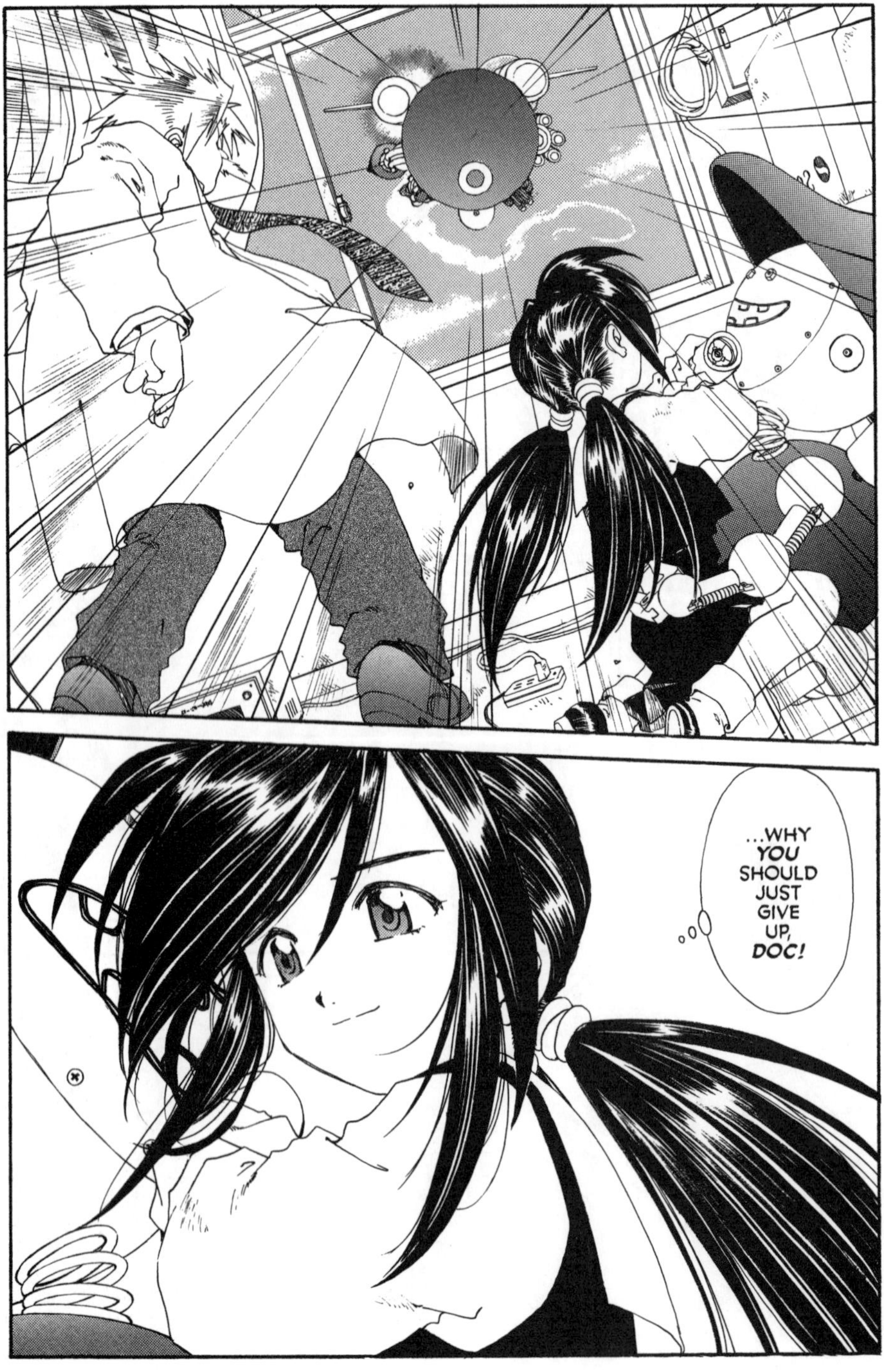
...WHY *YOU* SHOULD JUST GIVE UP, *DOC!*

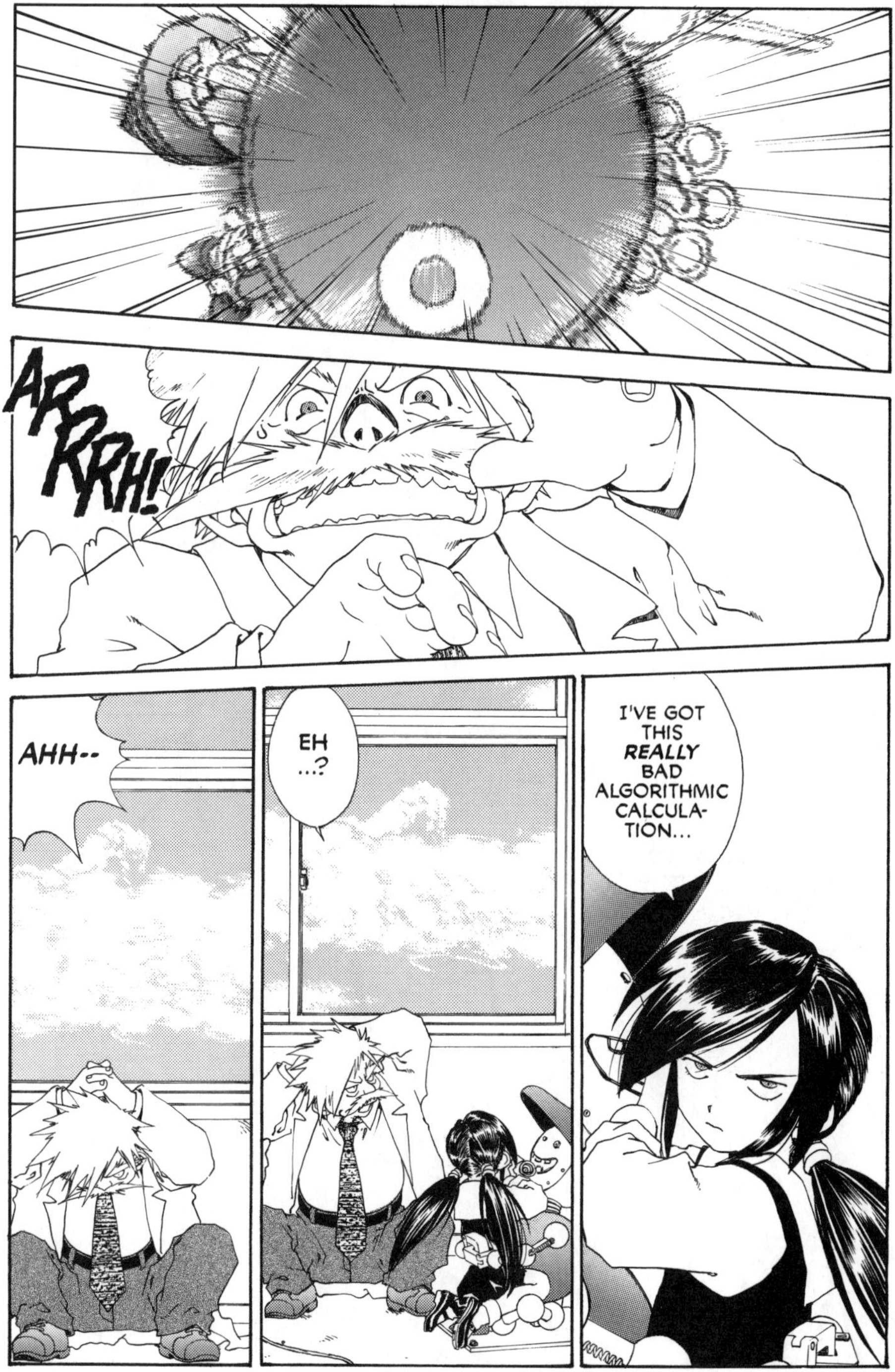
ARRRH!
AHH--
EH ...?
I'VE GOT THIS *REALLY* BAD ALGORITHMIC CALCULA-TION...

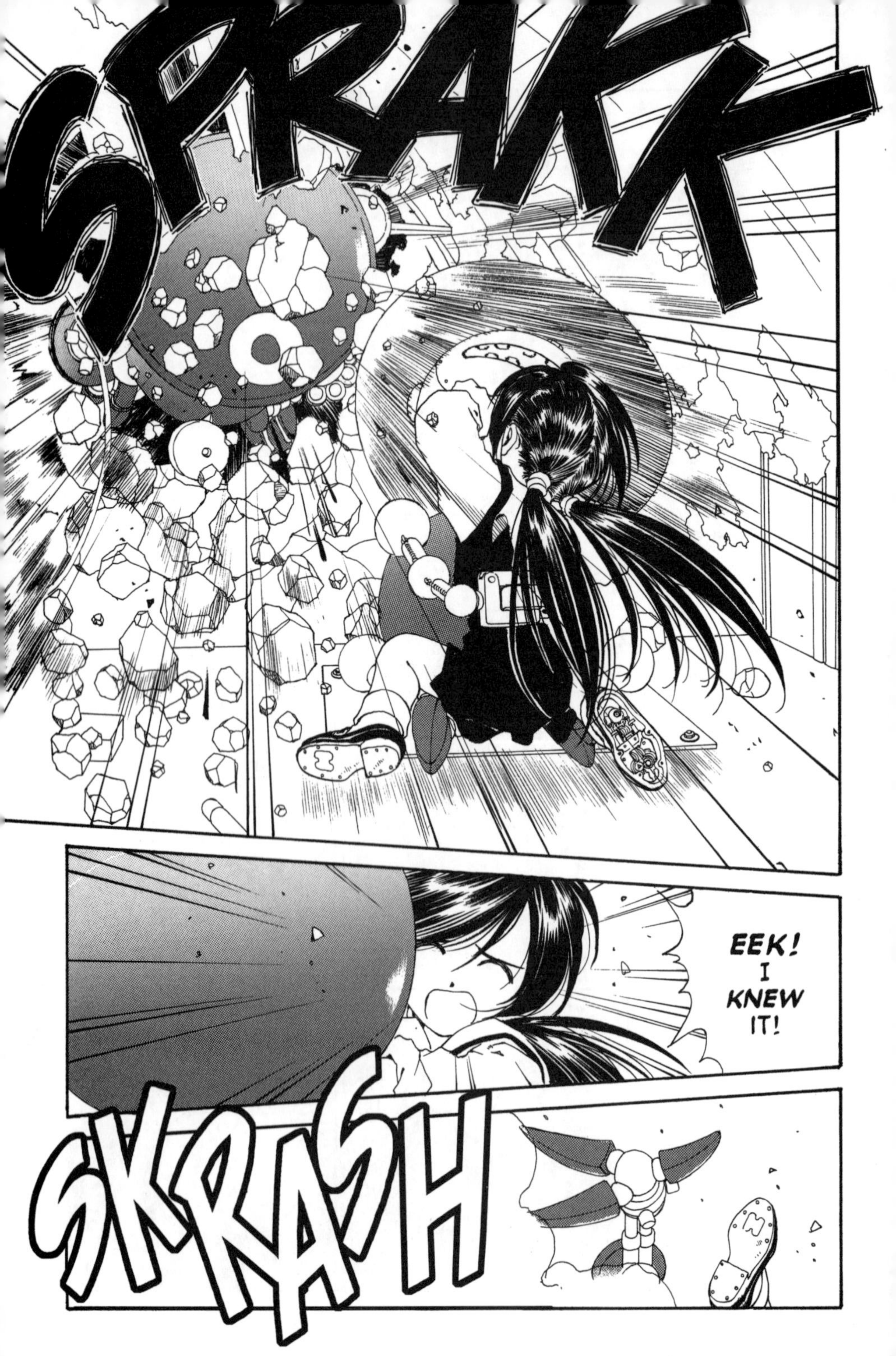
SPAKK
EEK! I KNEW IT!
SKRASH

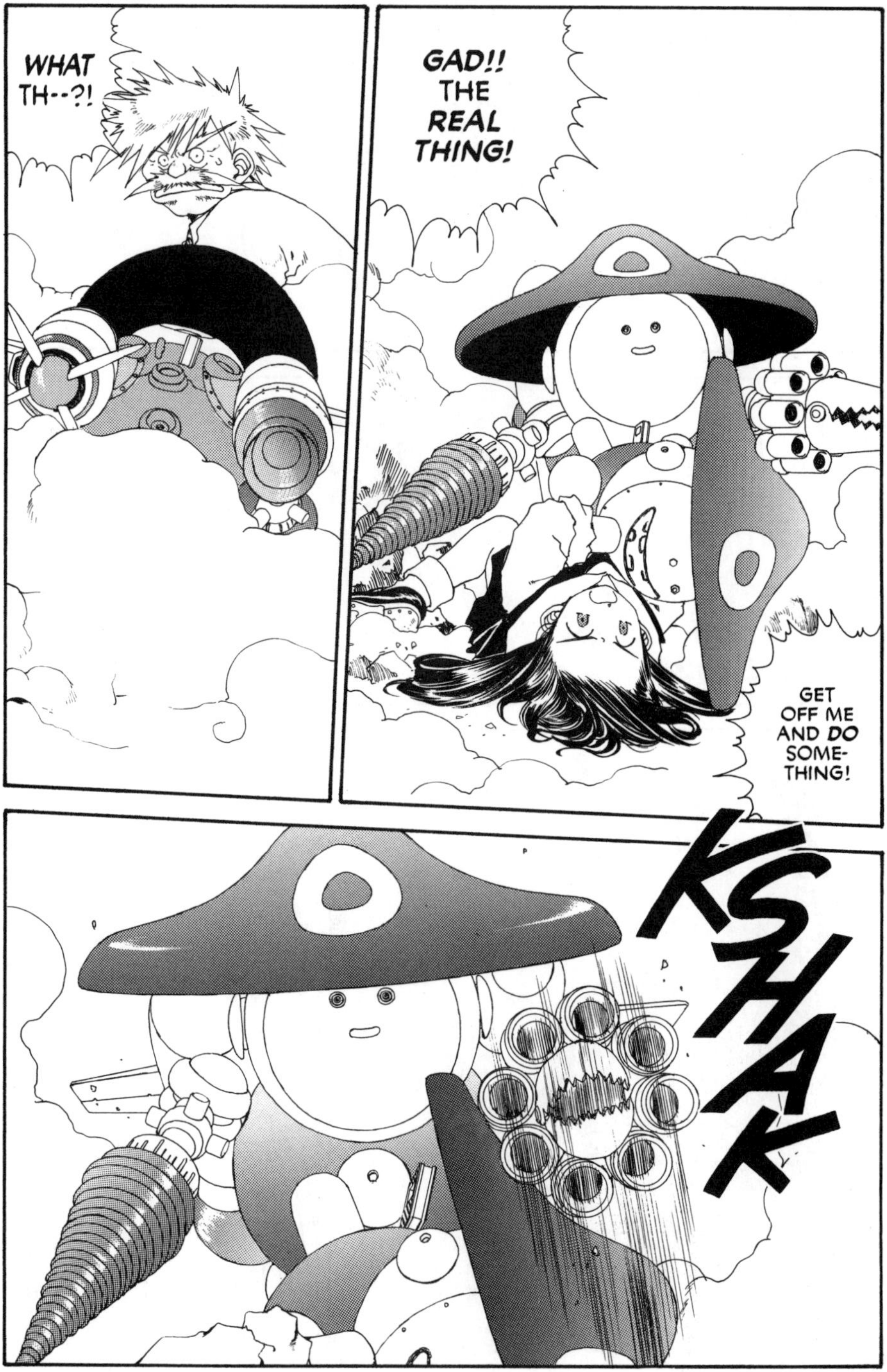
WHAT TH--?!
GAD!! THE REAL THING!
GET OFF ME AND DO SOME-THING!
KSHAK

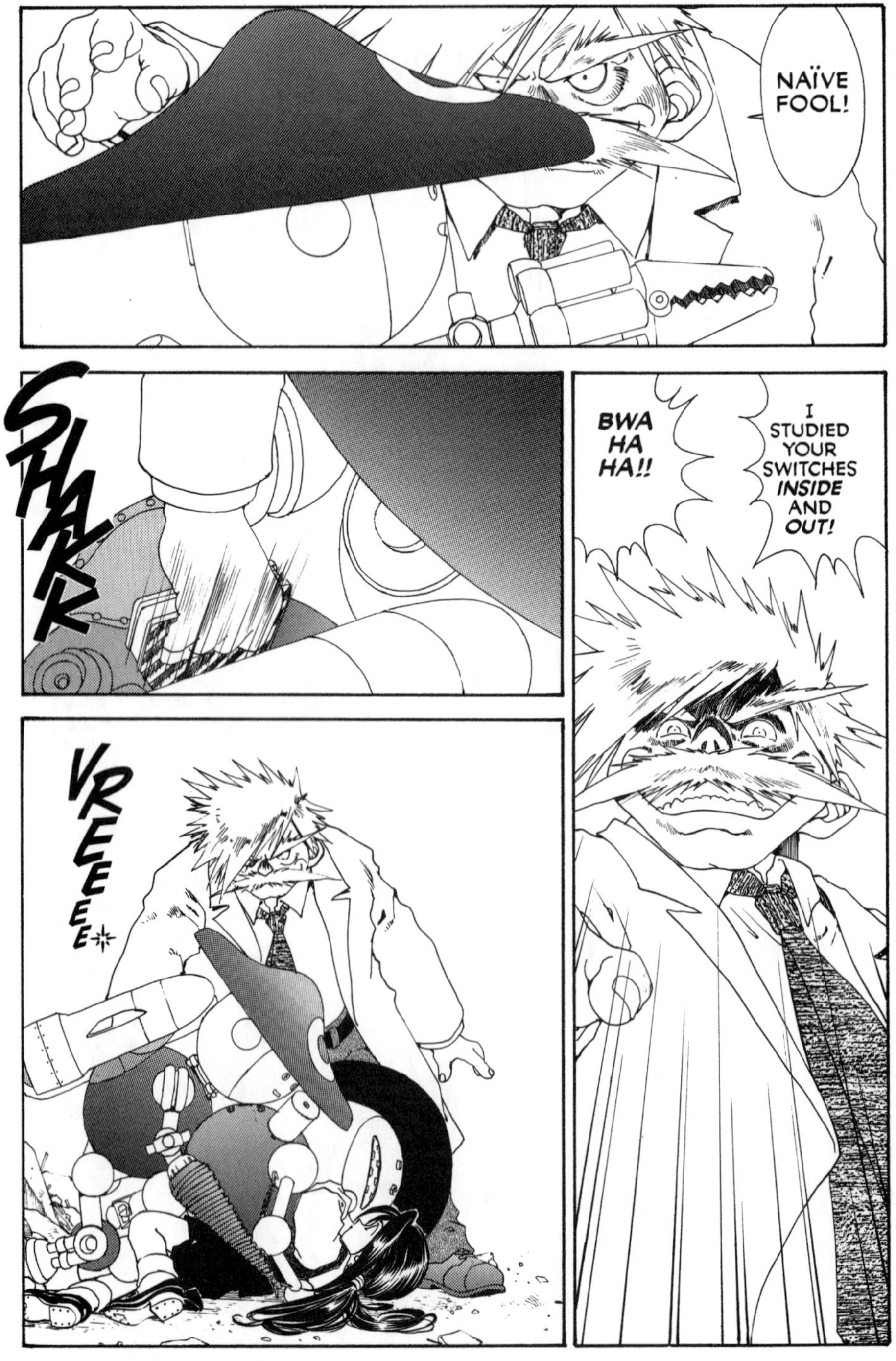
NAÏVE FOOL!
SHAKK
VREEEEE
BWA HA HA!!
I STUDIED YOUR SWITCHES *INSIDE* AND *OUT!*

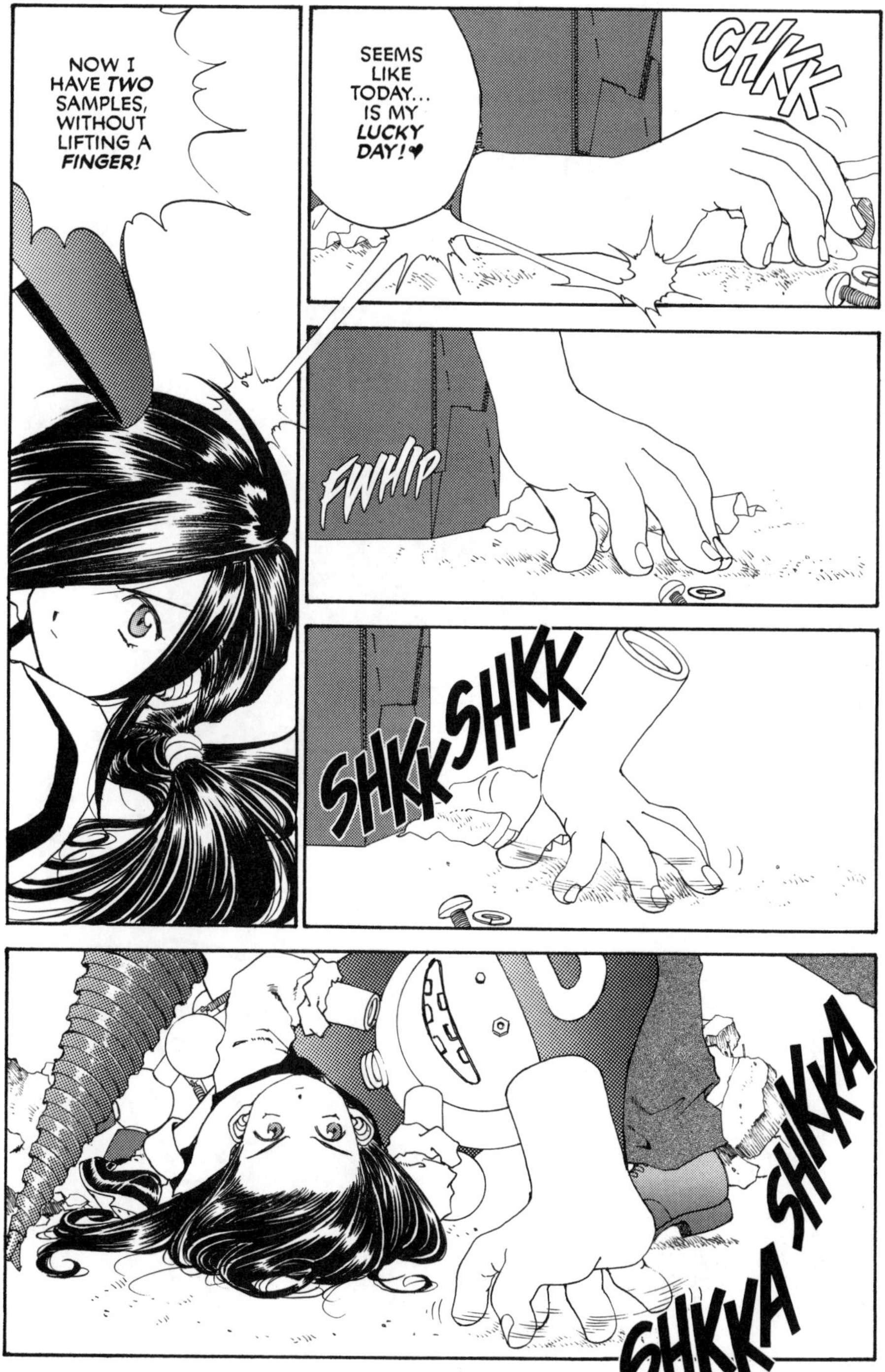
NOW I HAVE **TWO** SAMPLES, WITHOUT LIFTING A **FINGER!**
SEEMS LIKE TODAY... IS MY **LUCKY DAY!**♥
CHKK
FWHIP
SHKK SHKK
SHKKA SHKKA SHKKA

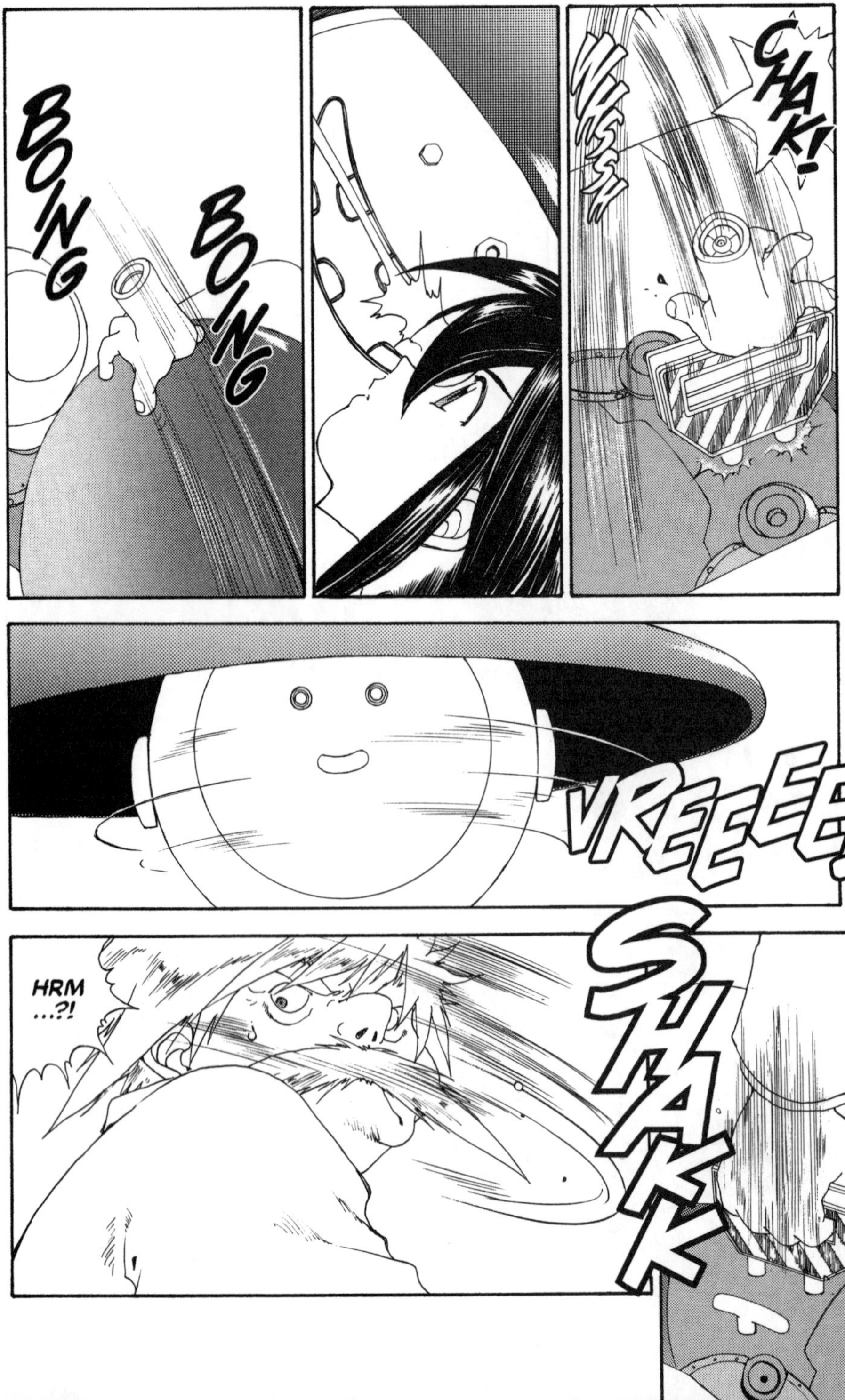
BOING
BOING
WHSSH
CHAK!
VREEEEE!
HRM ...?!
SHAKK

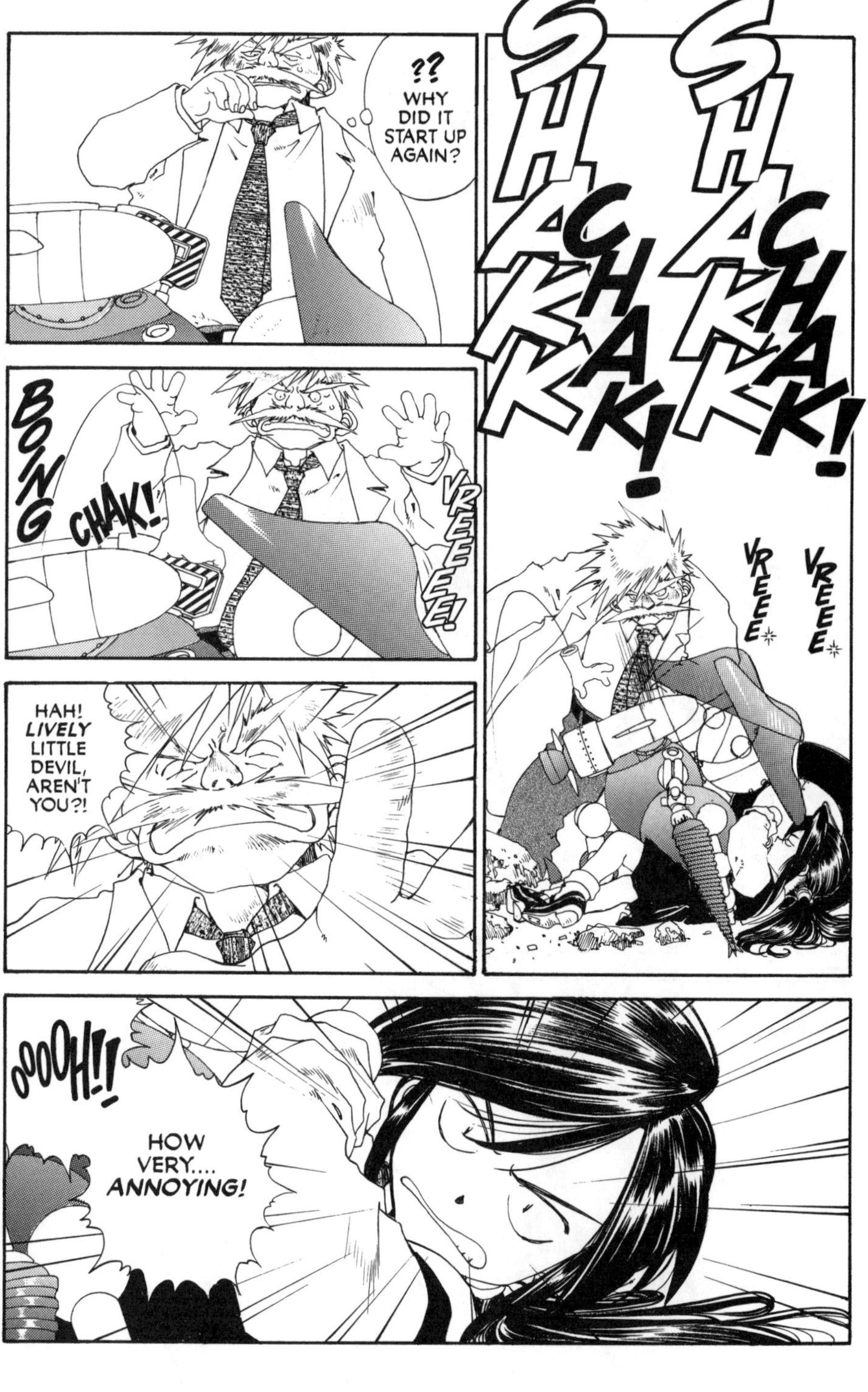
??
WHY DID IT START UP AGAIN?
BOING
CHAK!
VREEEE!
HAH! *LIVELY* LITTLE DEVIL, AREN'T YOU?!
SHACHAKK!
SHACHAKK!
VREEE
VREEE
OOOOH!!!
HOW VERY.... ***ANNOYING!***

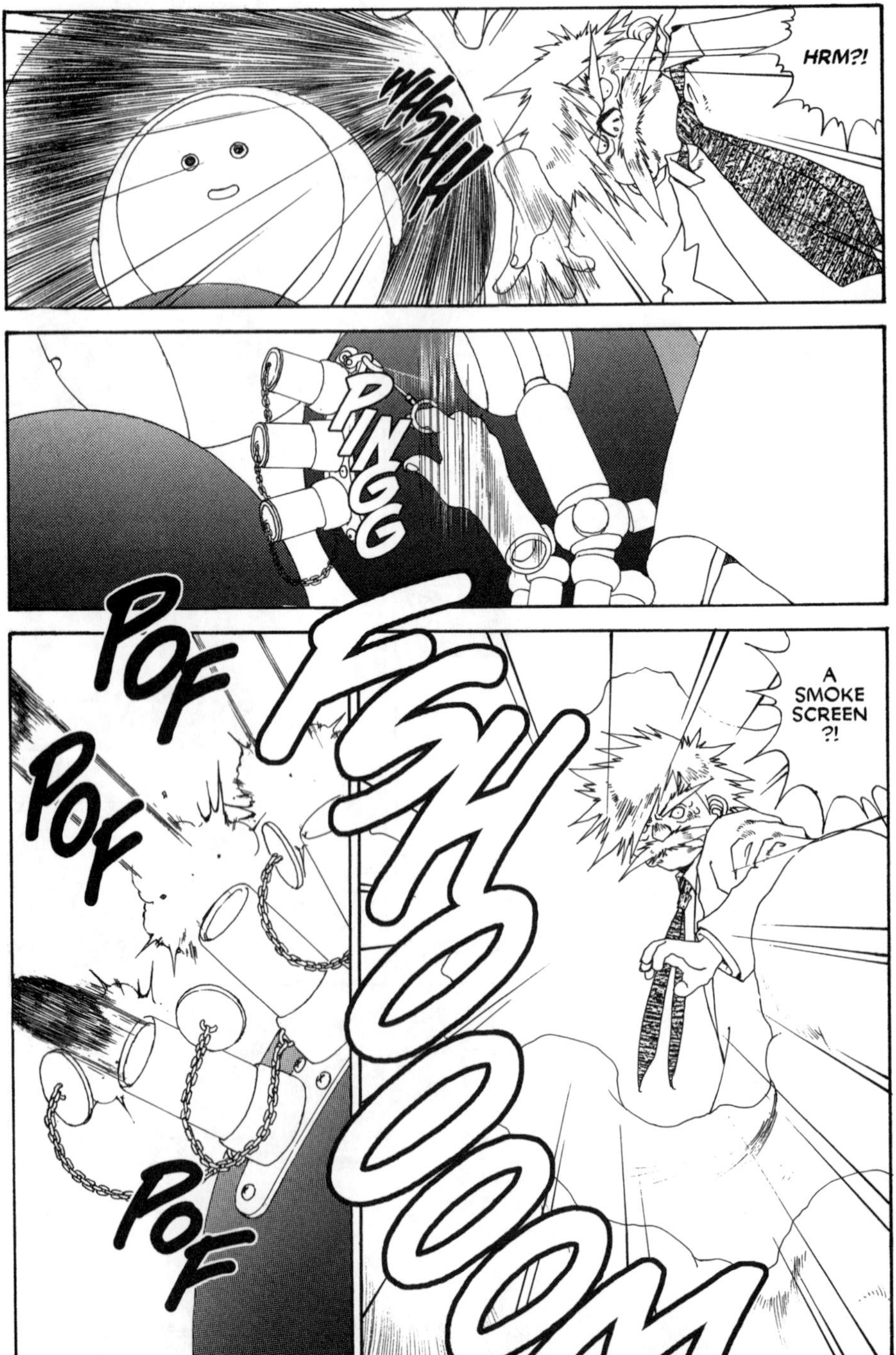
WHSHHH
HRM?!
PINGG
POF
POF
POF
FSHOOOOOM
A SMOKE SCREEN ?!

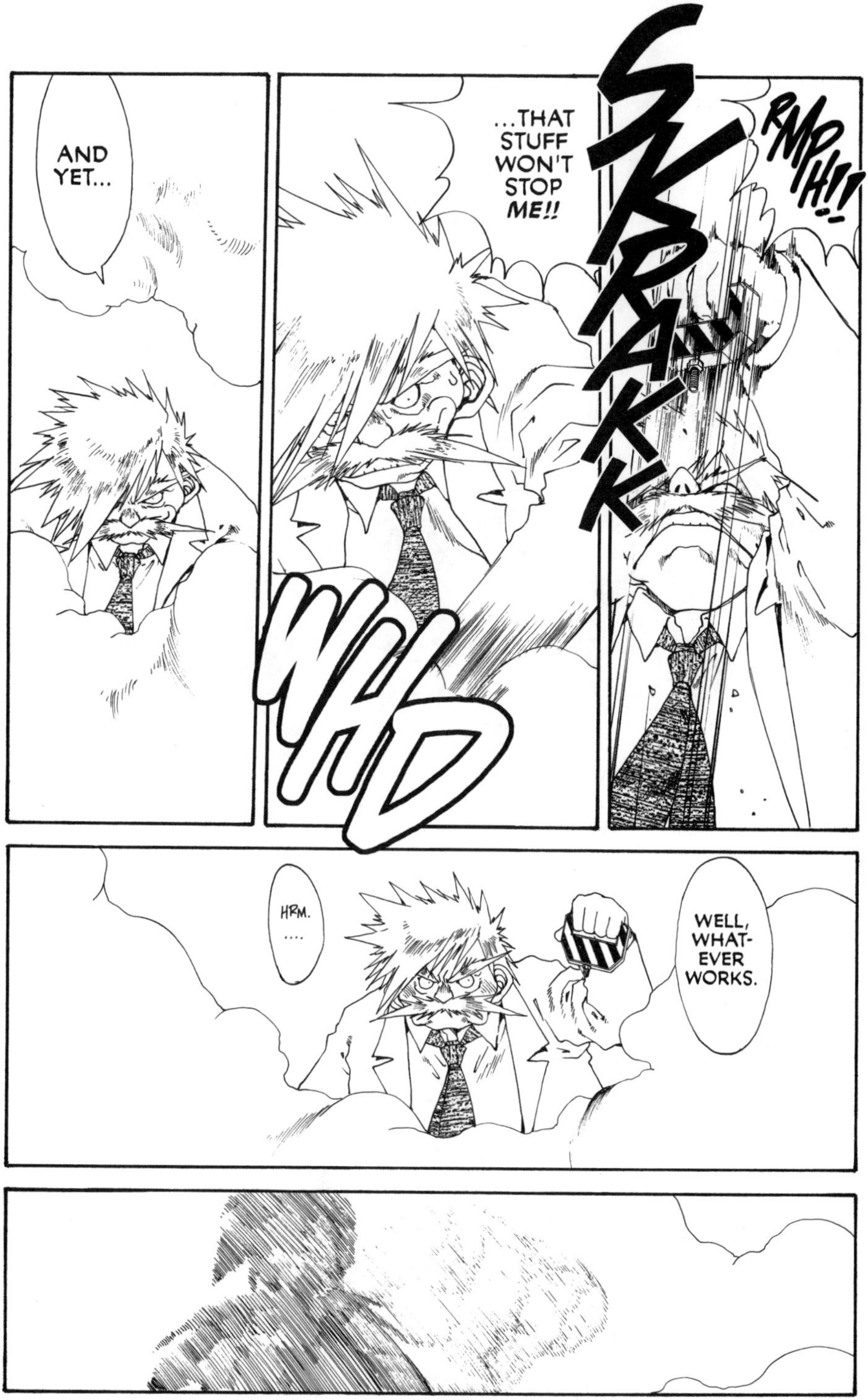
AND YET...
...THAT STUFF WON'T STOP ME!!
WHD
SKRAKK
RMPH!!
HRM. ....
WELL, WHAT-EVER WORKS.

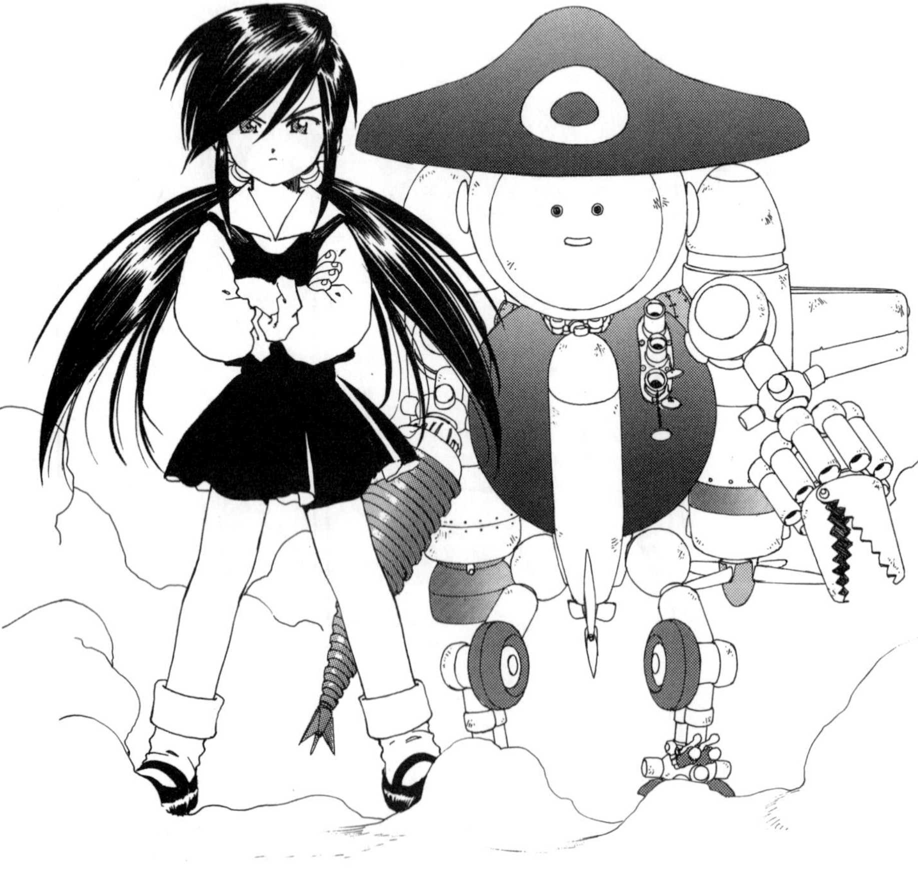

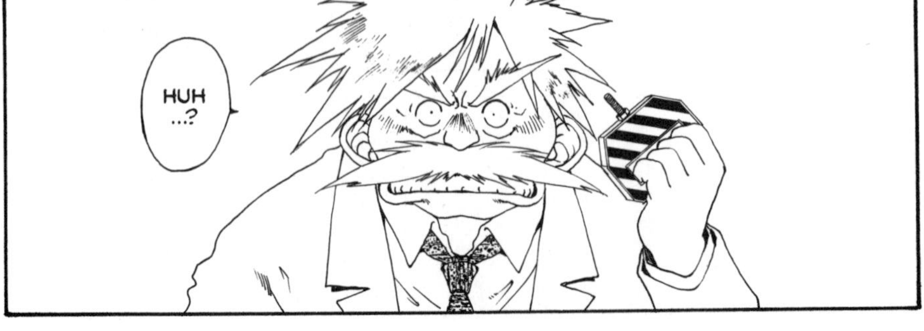
HUH
...?

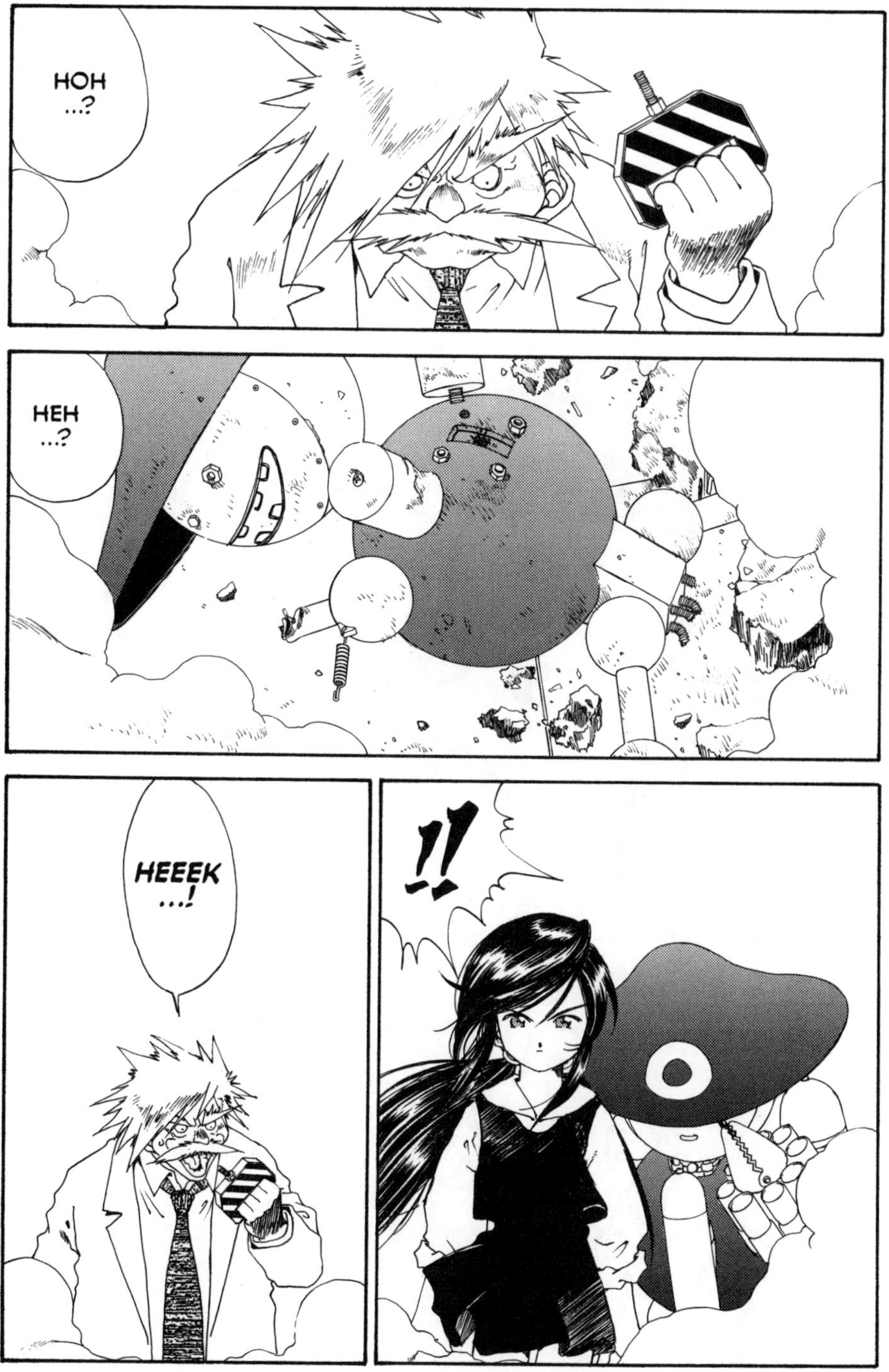
HOH ...?
HEH ...?
HEEEK ...!
!!

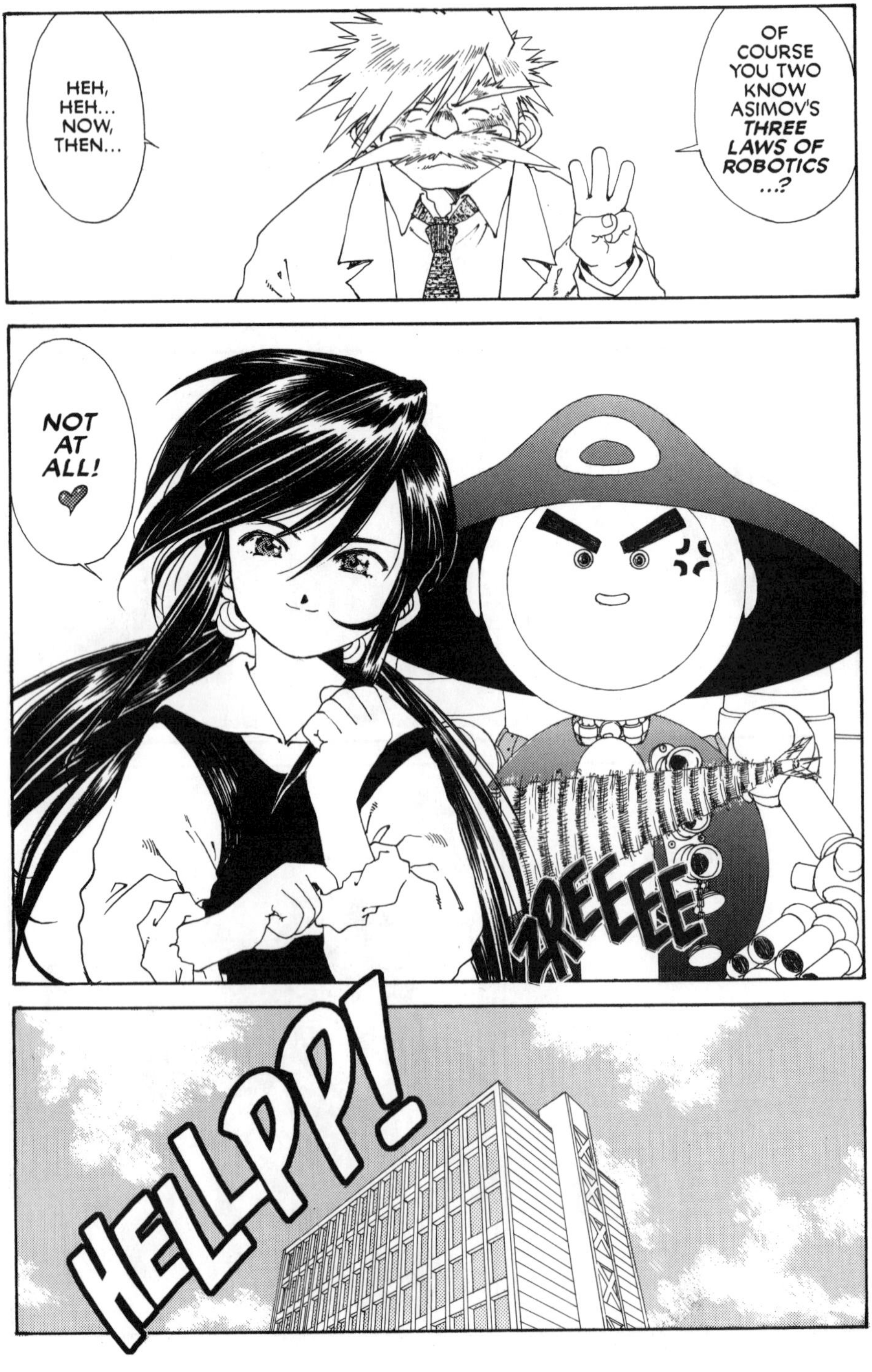
HEH, HEH... NOW, THEN...
OF COURSE YOU TWO KNOW ASIMOV'S *THREE LAWS OF ROBOTICS* ...?
NOT AT ALL! ♥
ZREEEEE
HELLPP!

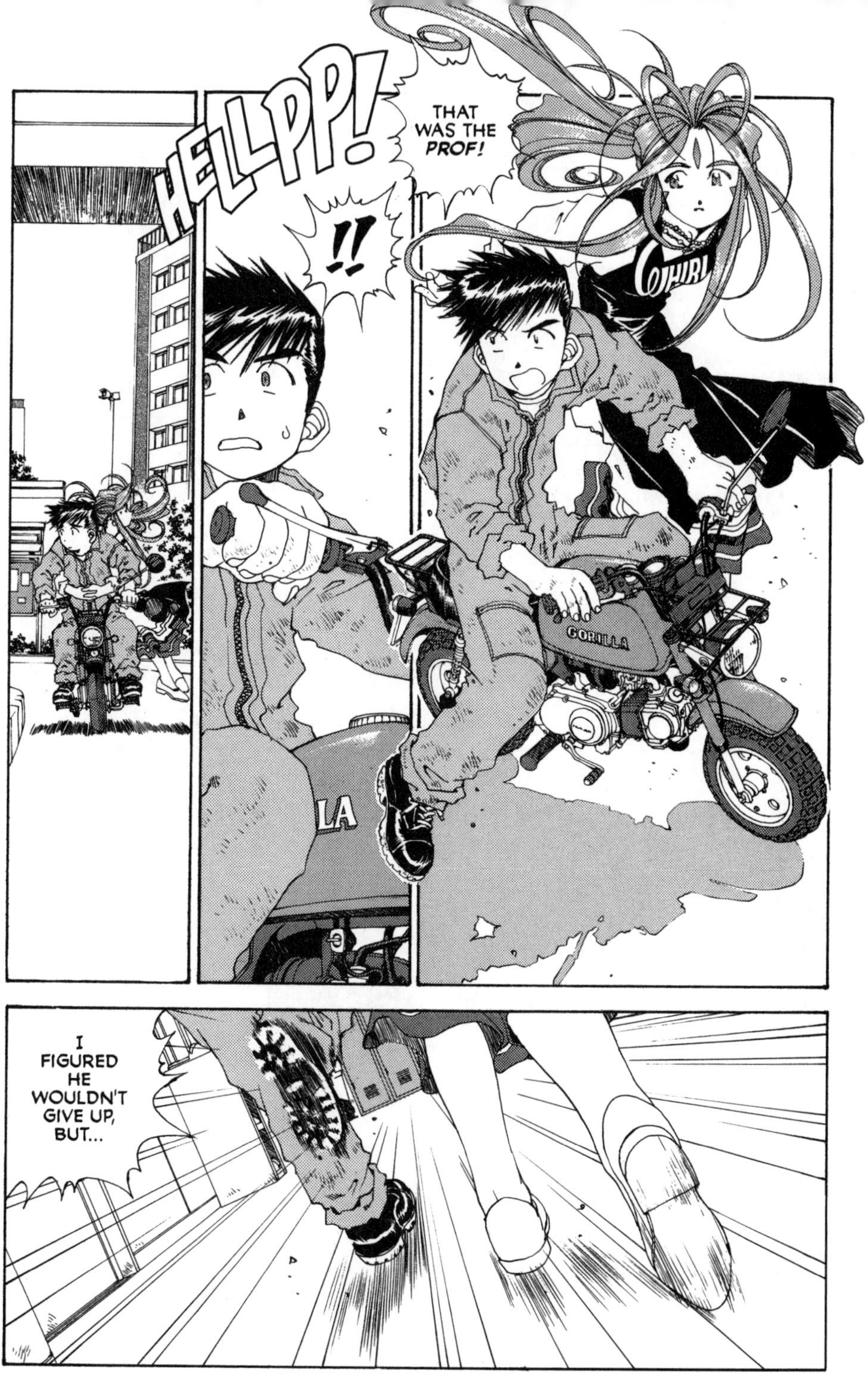
HELLPP!
!!
THAT WAS THE PROF!
GORILLA
I FIGURED HE WOULDN'T GIVE UP, BUT...

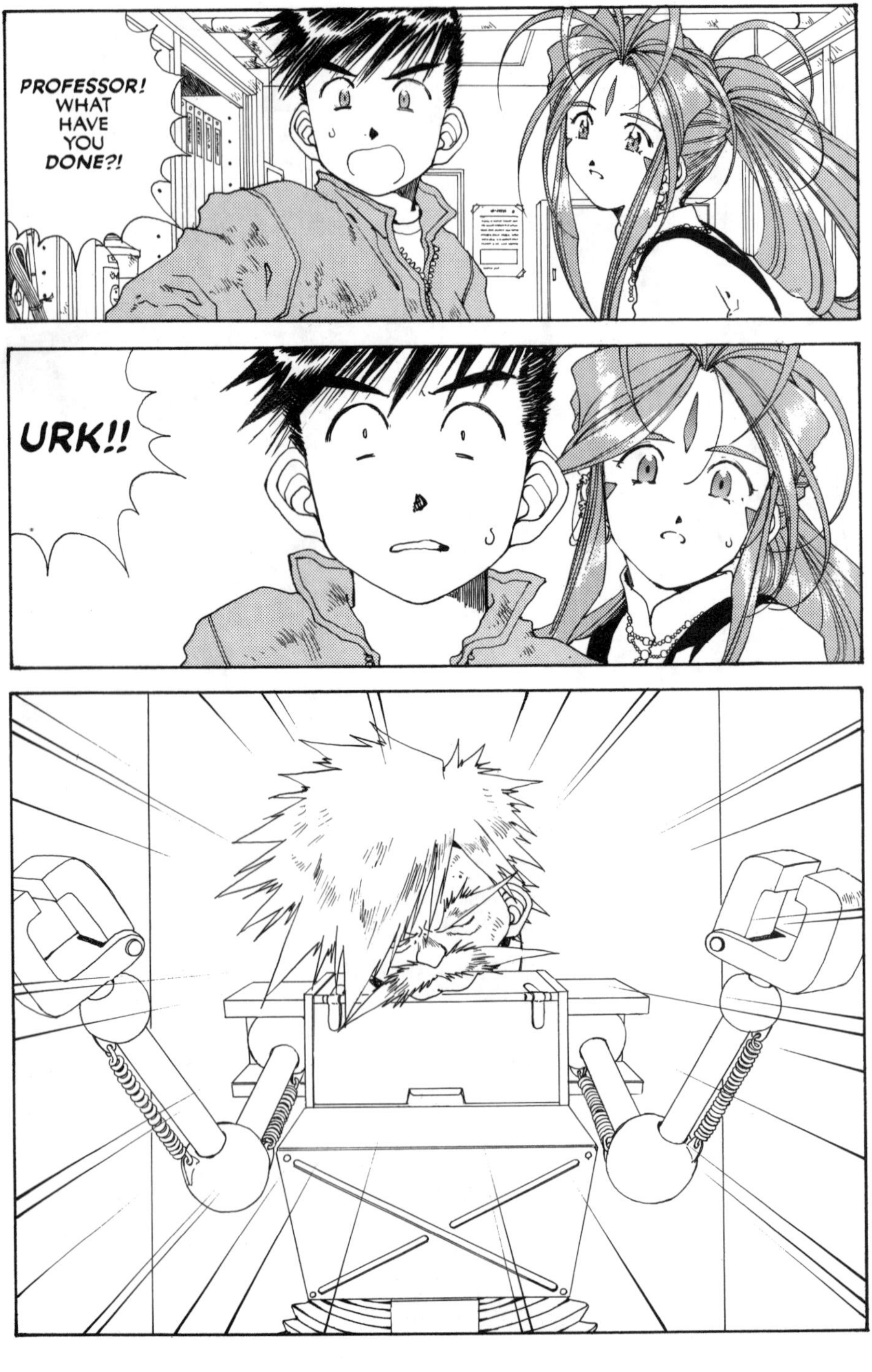
PROFESSOR! WHAT HAVE YOU DONE?!
URK!!

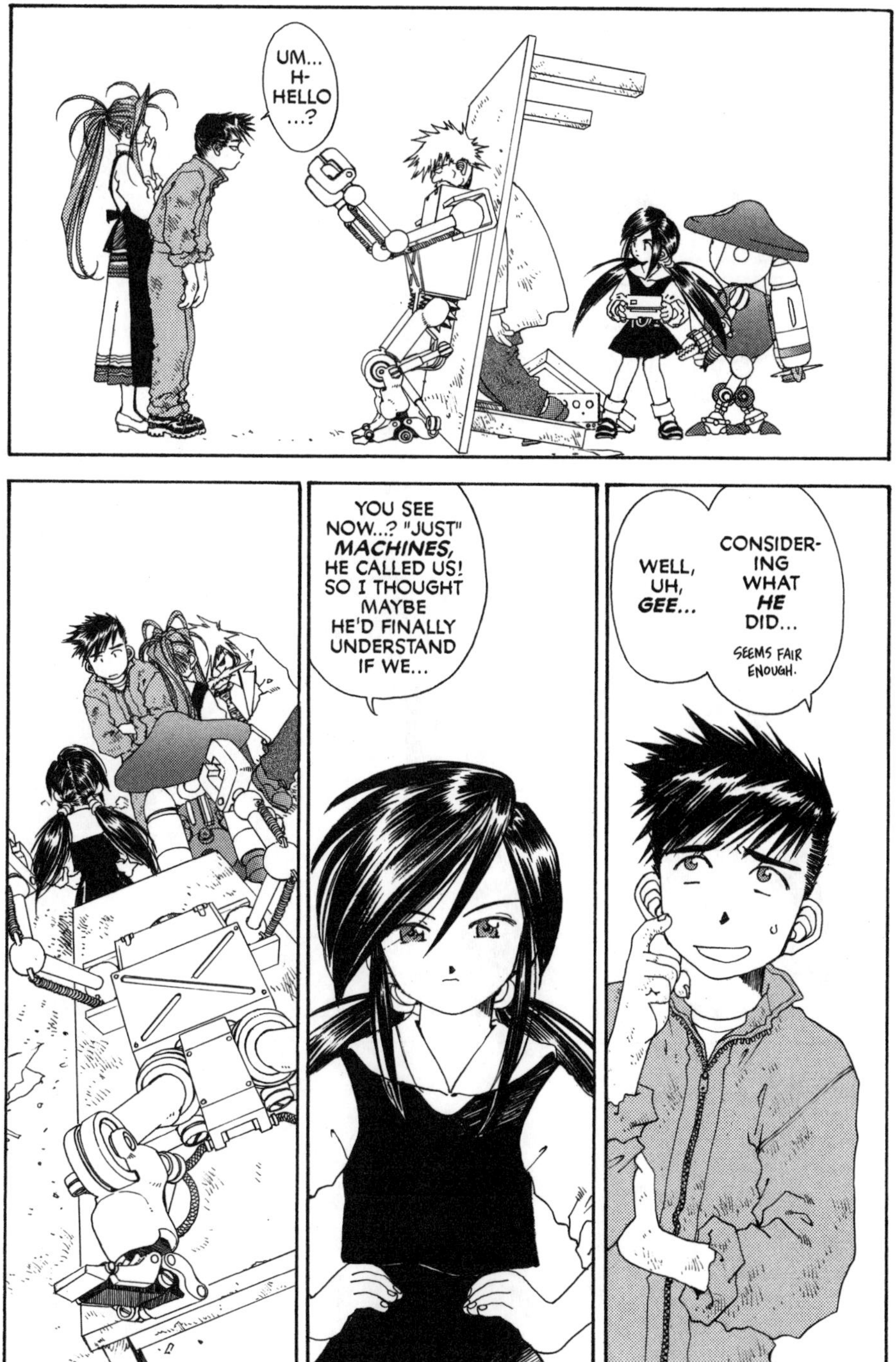
UM... H-HELLO ...?
YOU SEE NOW...? "JUST" MACHINES, HE CALLED US! SO I THOUGHT MAYBE HE'D FINALLY UNDERSTAND IF WE...
WELL, UH, GEE...
CONSIDER-ING WHAT HE DID...
SEEMS FAIR ENOUGH.

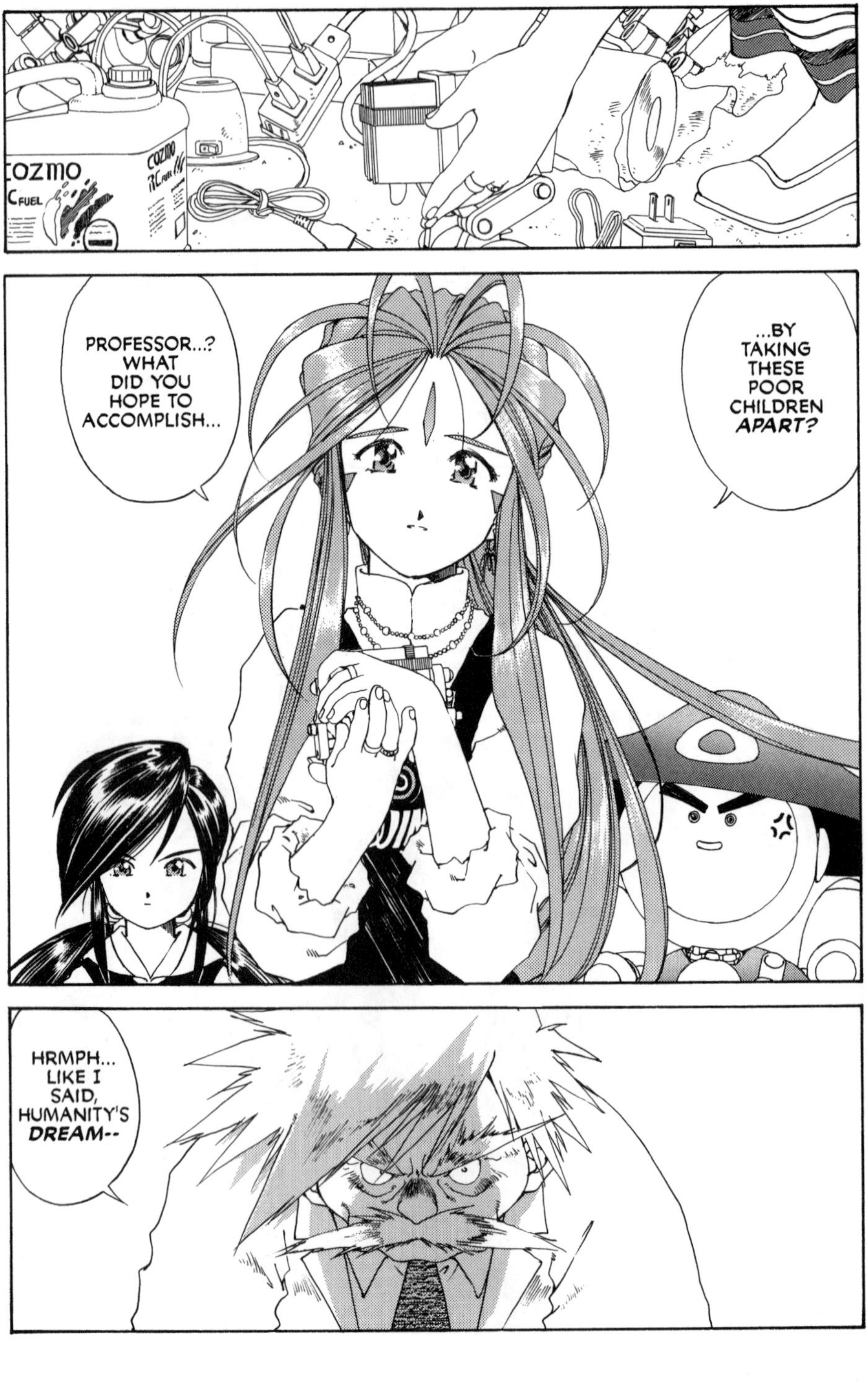
COZMO RC FUEL
PROFESSOR...? WHAT DID YOU HOPE TO ACCOMPLISH...
...BY TAKING THESE POOR CHILDREN *APART?*
HRMPH... LIKE I SAID, HUMANITY'S ***DREAM--***

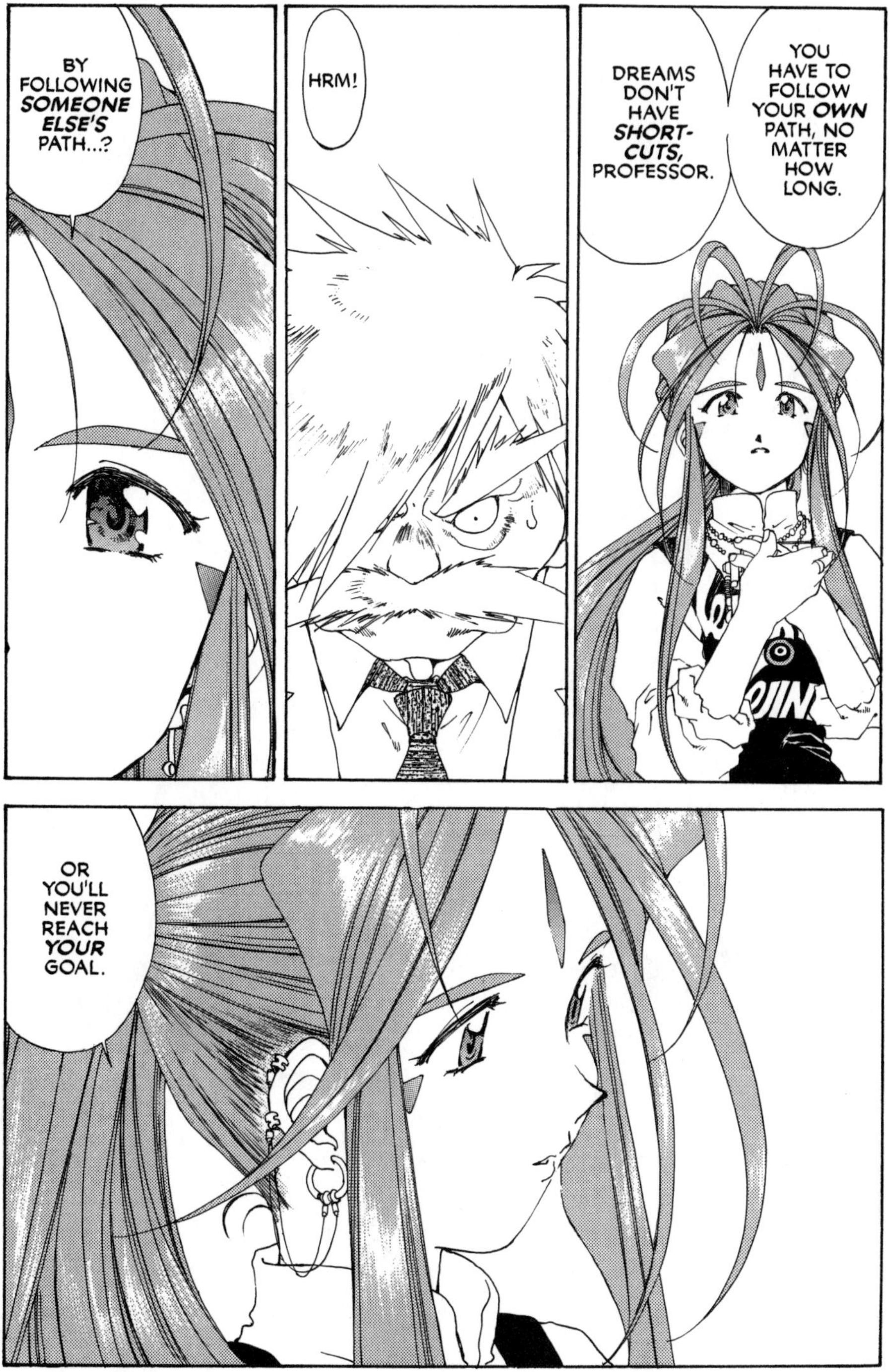
BY FOLLOWING SOMEONE ELSE'S PATH...?
HRM!
DREAMS DON'T HAVE SHORT-CUTS, PROFESSOR.
YOU HAVE TO FOLLOW YOUR OWN PATH, NO MATTER HOW LONG.
OR YOU'LL NEVER REACH YOUR GOAL.

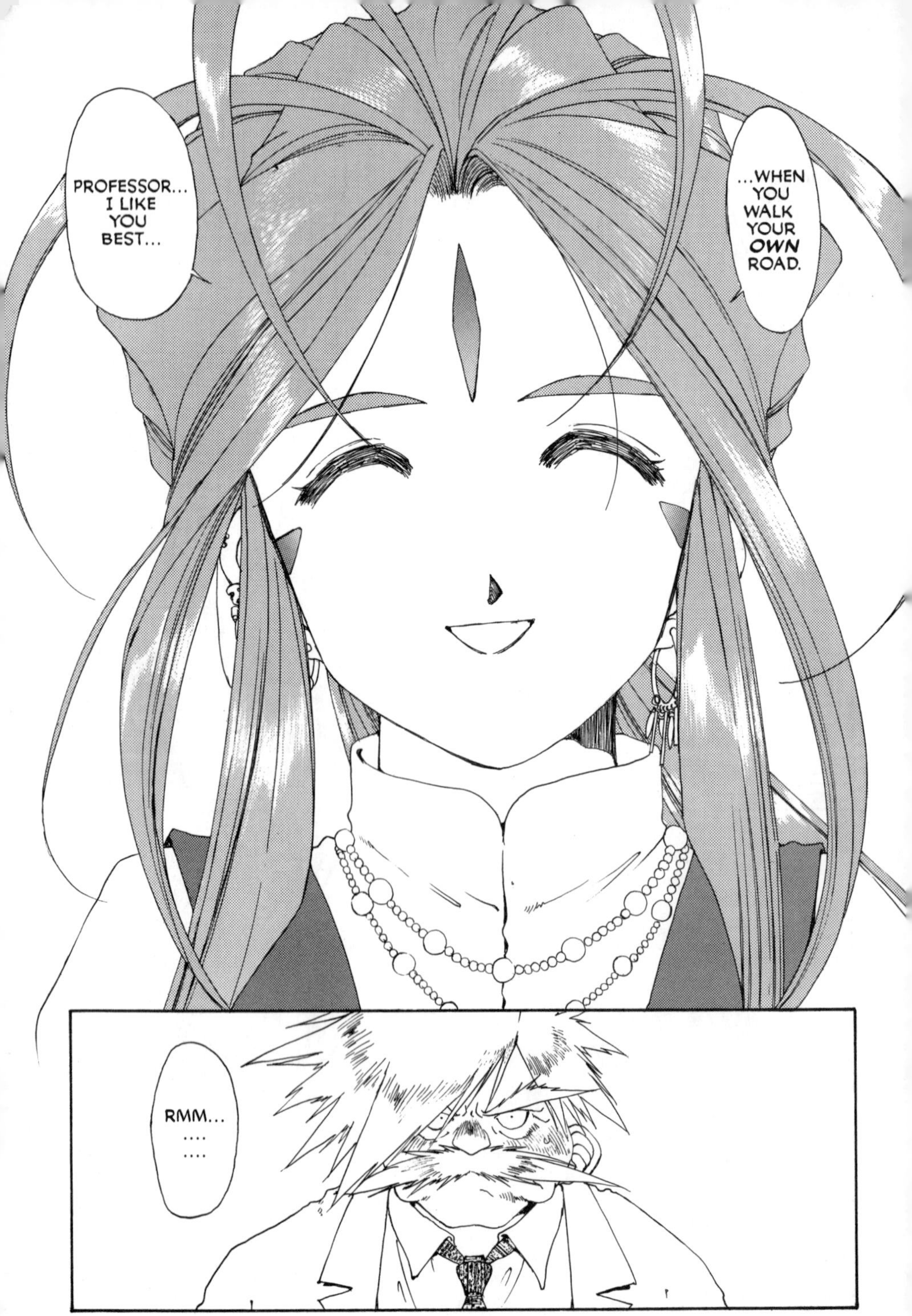
PROFESSOR... I LIKE YOU BEST...
...WHEN YOU WALK YOUR *OWN* ROAD.
RMM... ....

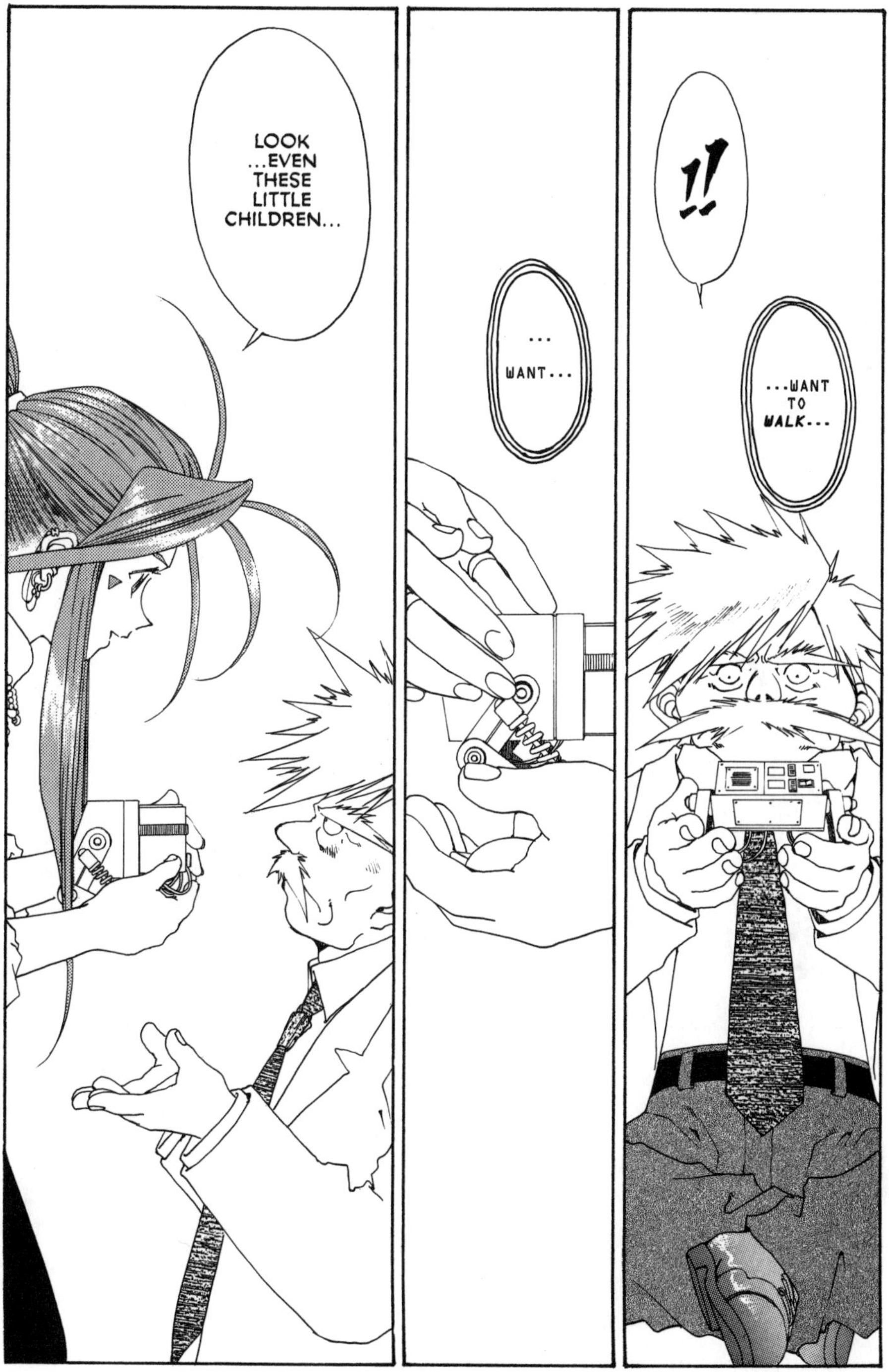
LOOK ...EVEN THESE LITTLE CHILDREN...
... WANT...
!!
...WANT TO WALK...

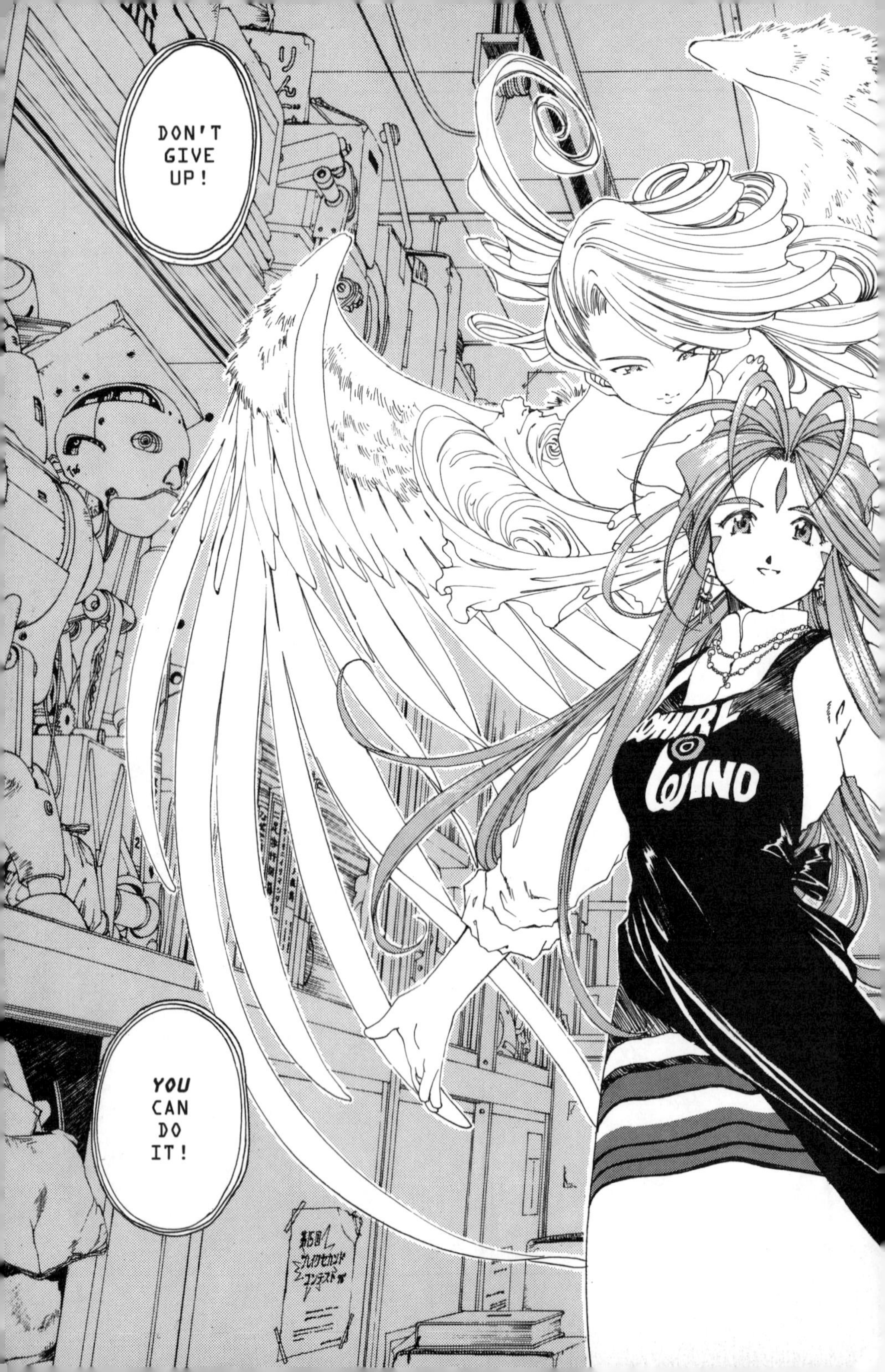
DON'T GIVE UP!
YOU CAN DO IT!

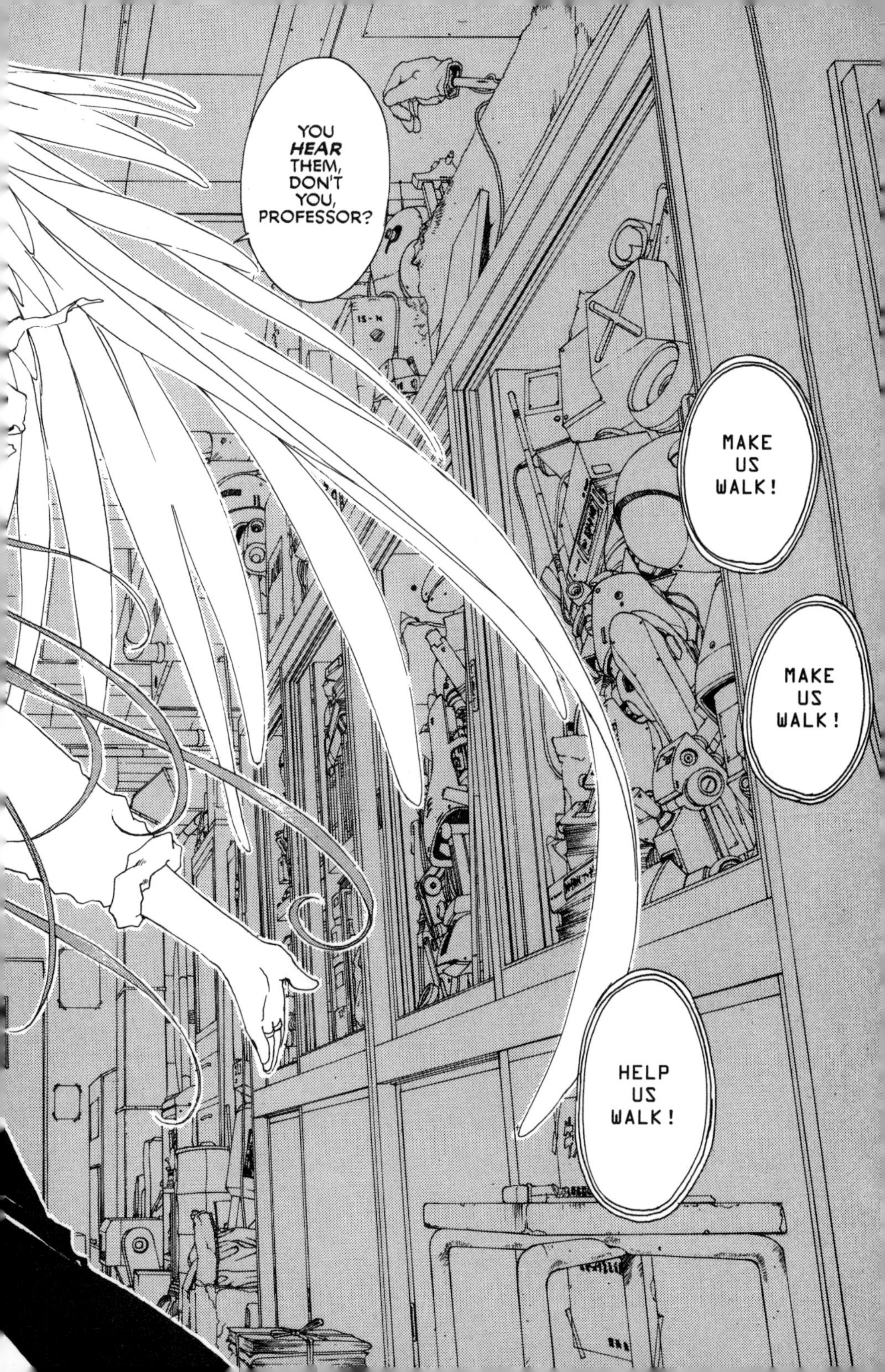
YOU *HEAR* THEM, DON'T YOU, PROFESSOR?
MAKE US WALK!
MAKE US WALK!
HELP US WALK!

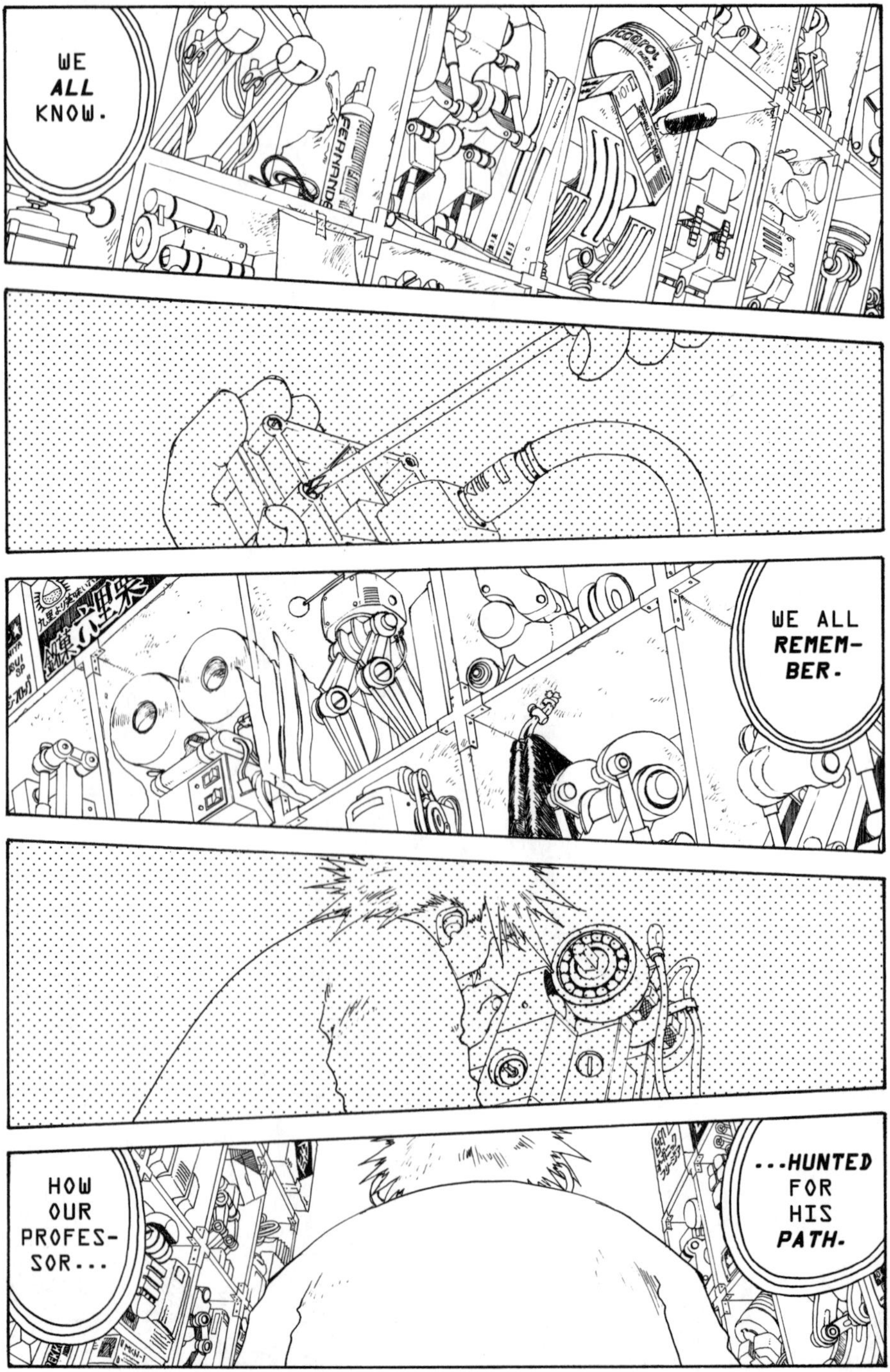
WE ALL KNOW.
WE ALL REMEMBER.
HOW OUR PROFESSOR...
...HUNTED FOR HIS PATH.

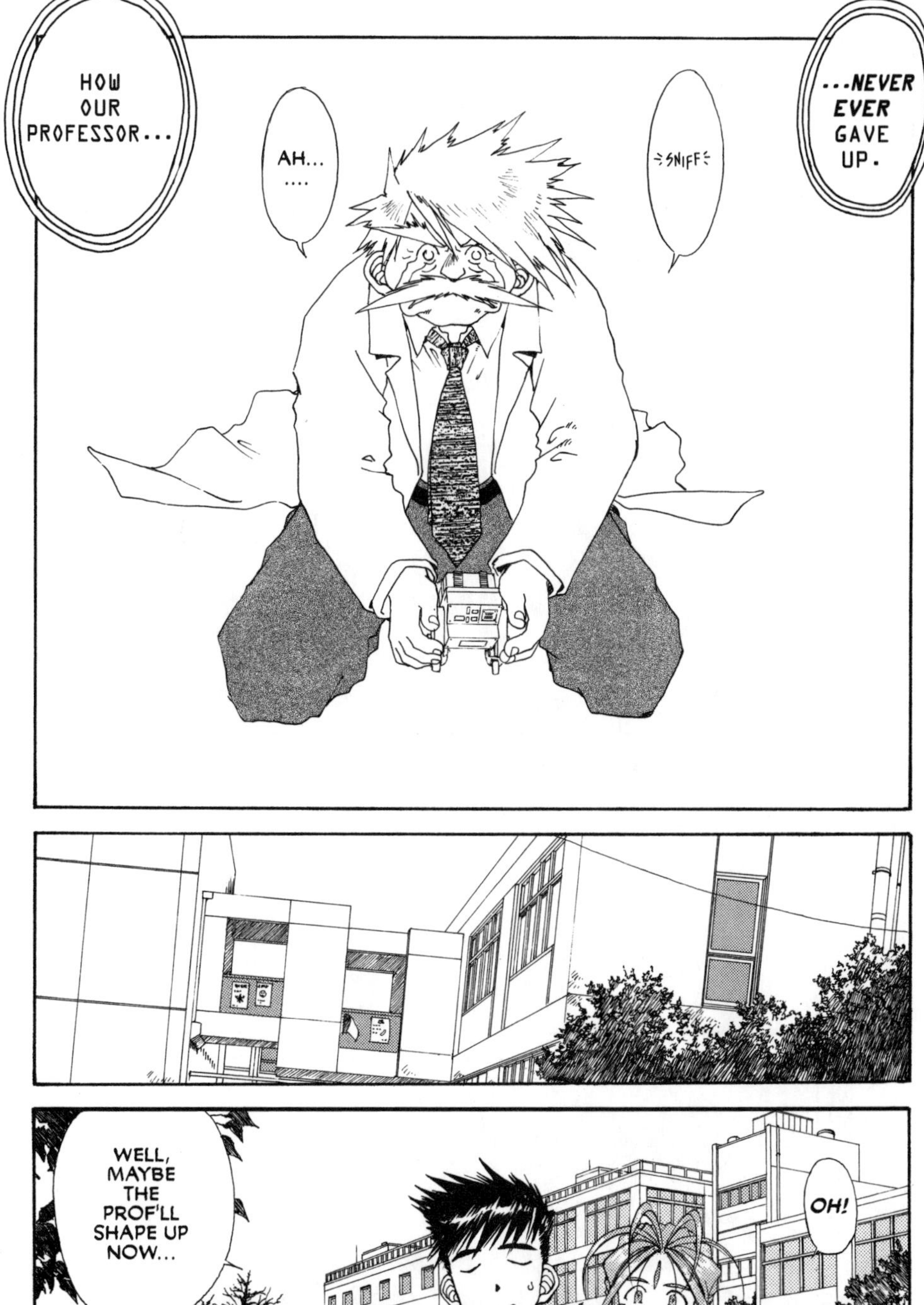
HOW OUR PROFESSOR...
AH... ....
SNIFF
...NEVER EVER GAVE UP.
WELL, MAYBE THE PROF'LL SHAPE UP NOW...
OH!

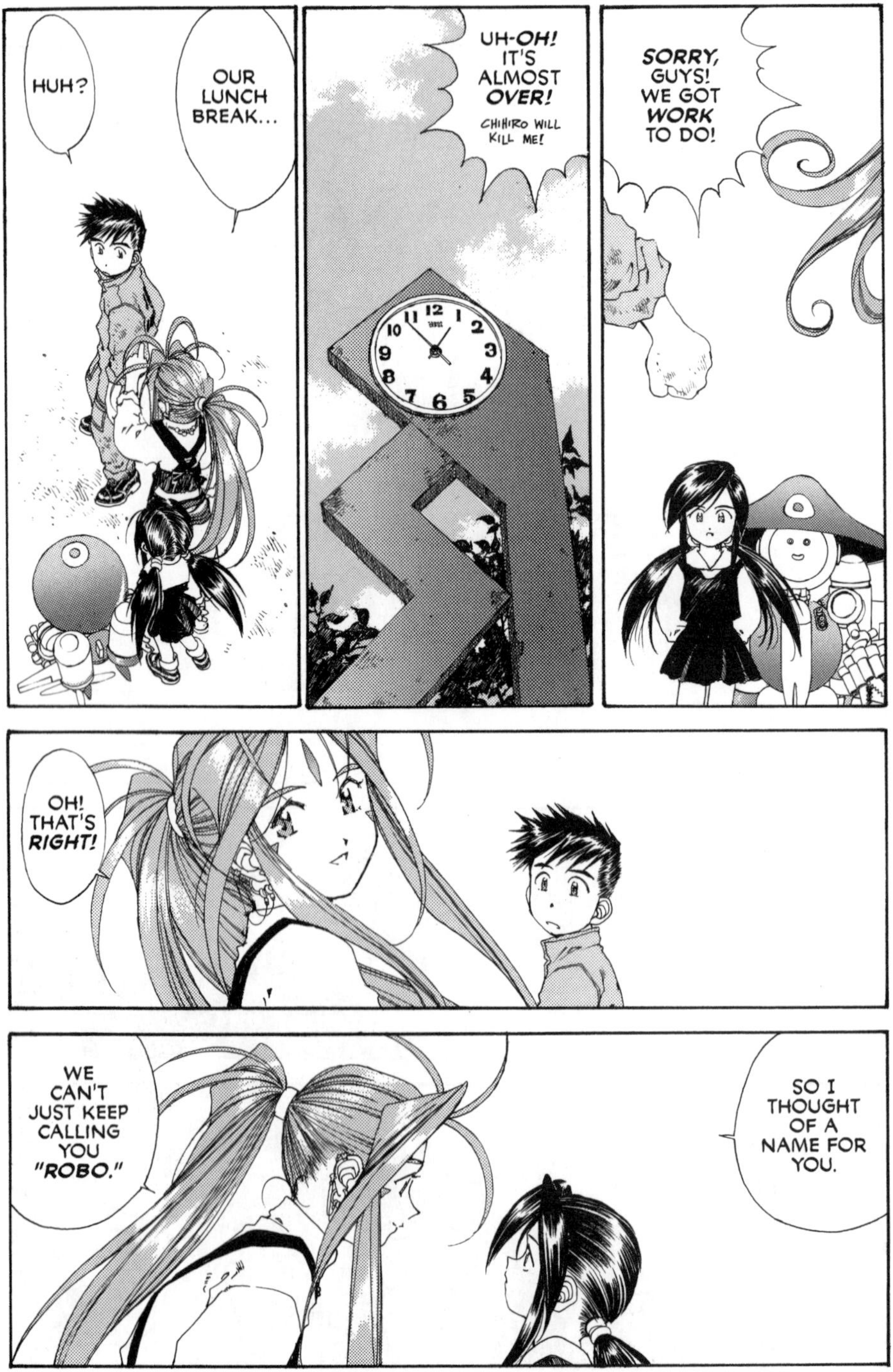
HUH?
OUR LUNCH BREAK...
UH-OH! IT'S ALMOST OVER!
CHIHIRO WILL KILL ME!
SORRY, GUYS! WE GOT WORK TO DO!
OH! THAT'S RIGHT!
WE CAN'T JUST KEEP CALLING YOU "ROBO."
SO I THOUGHT OF A NAME FOR YOU.

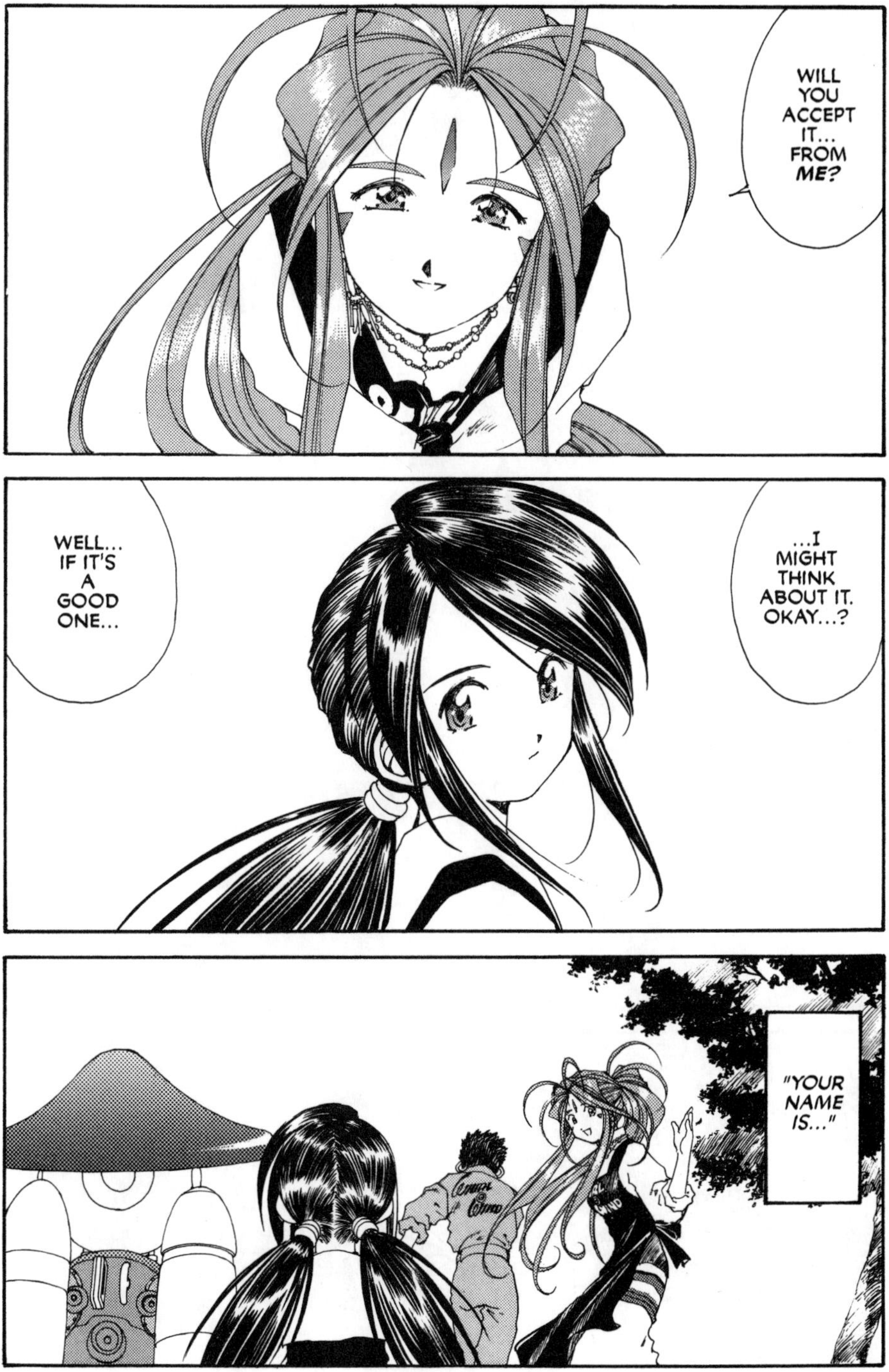
WILL YOU ACCEPT IT... FROM *ME?*
WELL... IF IT'S A GOOD ONE...
...I MIGHT THINK ABOUT IT. OKAY...?
"YOUR NAME IS..."

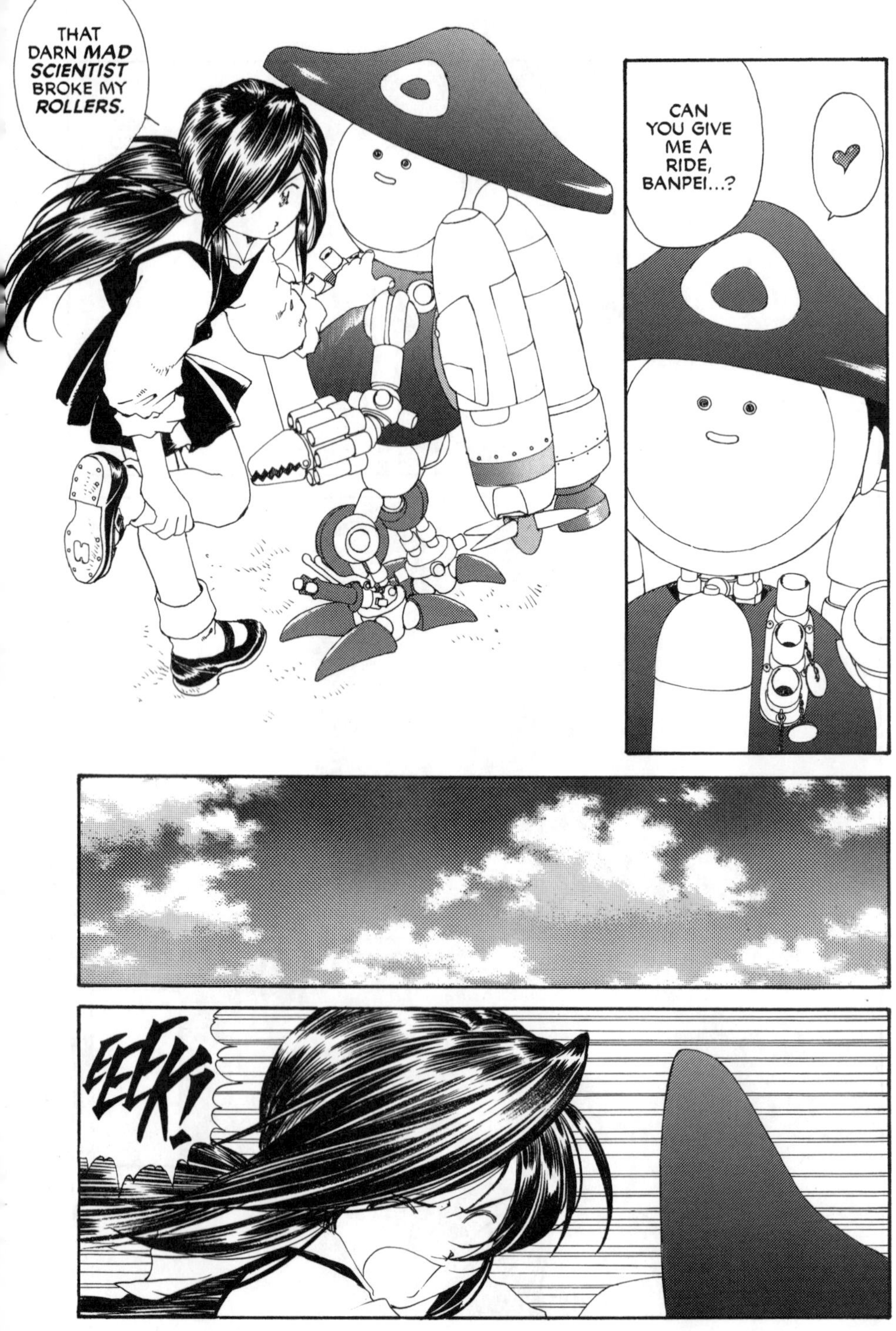
THAT DARN *MAD SCIENTIST* BROKE MY *ROLLERS.*
CAN YOU GIVE ME A RIDE, BANPEI...?
EEEK!

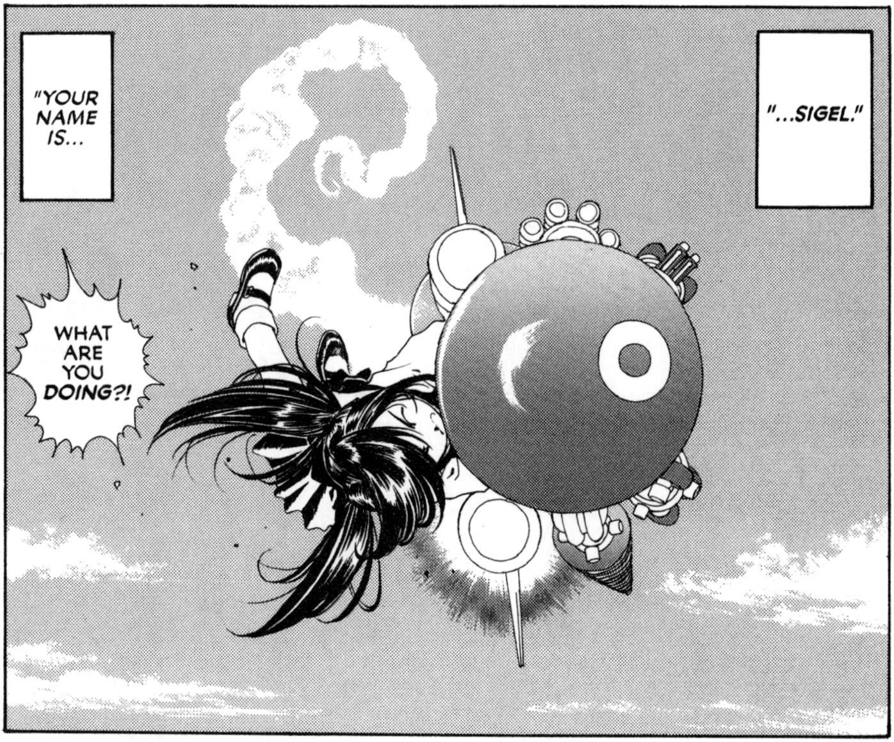
"YOUR NAME IS...
WHAT ARE YOU DOING?!
"...SIGEL."

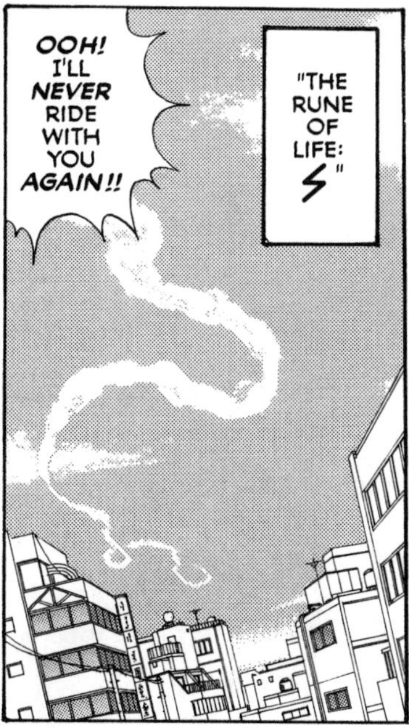
OOH! I'LL NEVER RIDE WITH YOU AGAIN!!
"THE RUNE OF LIFE: ᛋ"

AND AS FOR DOCTOR MOREAU?

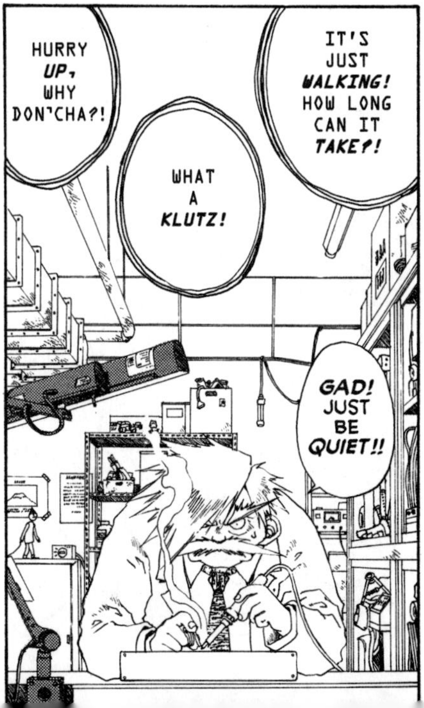
HURRY UP, WHY DON'CHA?!
WHAT A KLUTZ!
IT'S JUST WALKING! HOW LONG CAN IT TAKE?!
GAD! JUST BE QUIET!!

DOCTOR MOREAU'S
Secrets of Creativity!

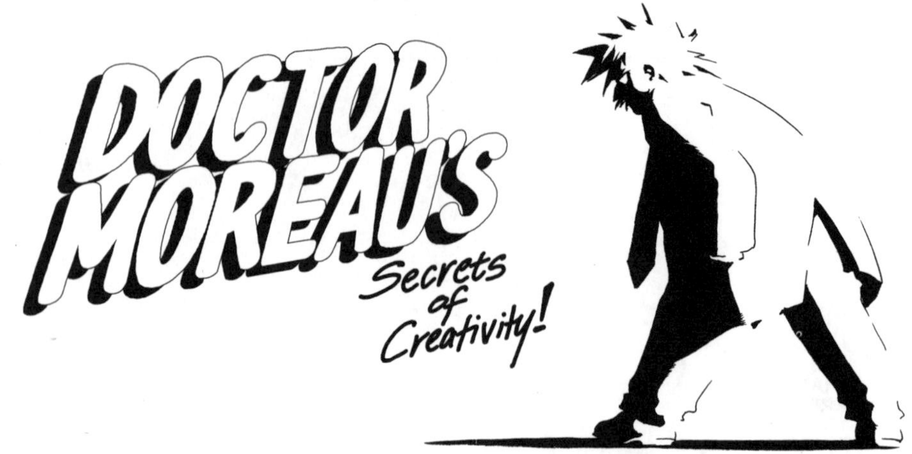

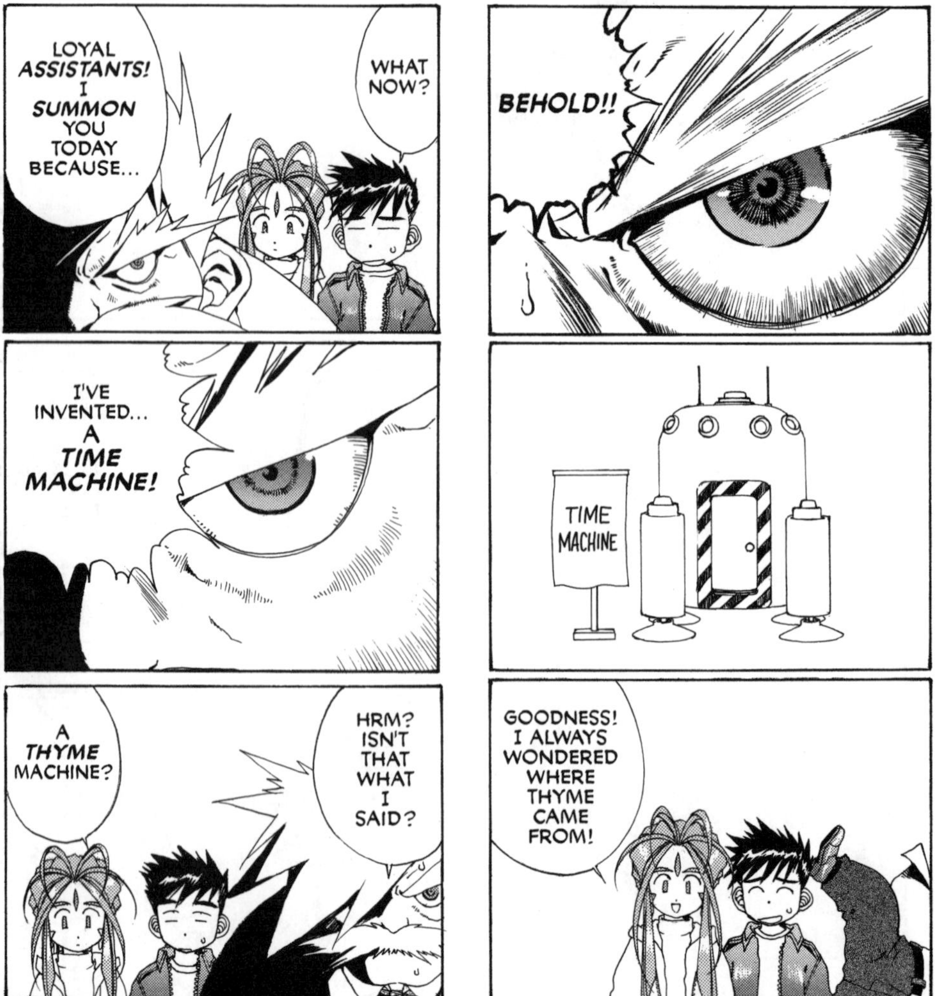

LOYAL ASSISTANTS! I SUMMON YOU TODAY BECAUSE...
WHAT NOW?
BEHOLD!!
I'VE INVENTED... A TIME MACHINE!
TIME MACHINE
A THYME MACHINE?
HRM? ISN'T THAT WHAT I SAID?
GOODNESS! I ALWAYS WONDERED WHERE THYME CAME FROM!

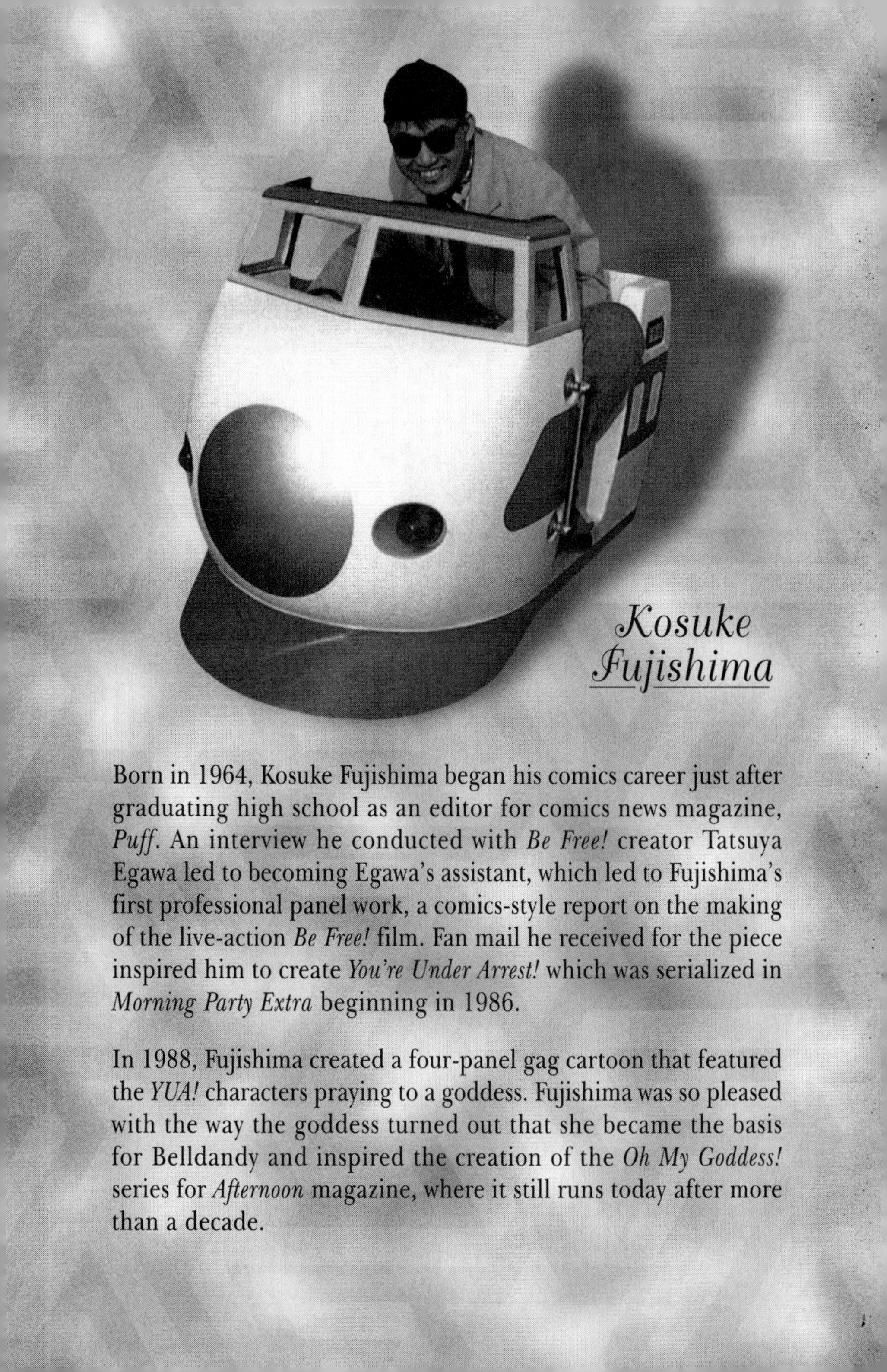

Kosuke Fujishima

Born in 1964, Kosuke Fujishima began his comics career just after graduating high school as an editor for comics news magazine, *Puff*. An interview he conducted with *Be Free!* creator Tatsuya Egawa led to becoming Egawa's assistant, which led to Fujishima's first professional panel work, a comics-style report on the making of the live-action *Be Free!* film. Fan mail he received for the piece inspired him to create *You're Under Arrest!* which was serialized in *Morning Party Extra* beginning in 1986.

In 1988, Fujishima created a four-panel gag cartoon that featured the *YUA!* characters praying to a goddess. Fujishima was so pleased with the way the goddess turned out that she became the basis for Belldandy and inspired the creation of the *Oh My Goddess!* series for *Afternoon* magazine, where it still runs today after more than a decade.

KOSUKE FUJISHIMA'S

Oh My Goddess!

The stories following the misadventures of Keiichi Morisato and the trio of lovely goddesses who live with him explode into a fantastic romantic comedy!

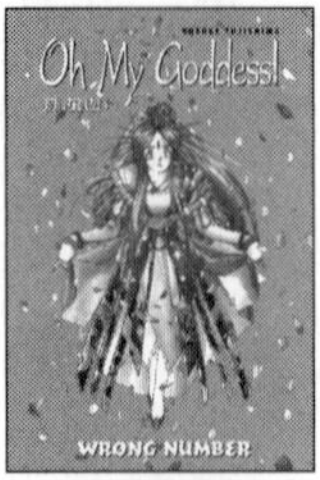
Oh My Goddess!
WRONG NUMBER

Volume 1
WRONG NUMBER
160-page B&W paperback
ISBN: 1-56971-669-2 $13.95

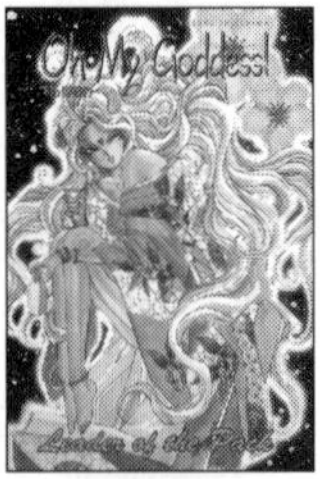
Oh My Goddess!

Volume 2
LEADER OF THE PACK
152-page B&W paperback
ISBN: 1-56971-764-8 $13.95

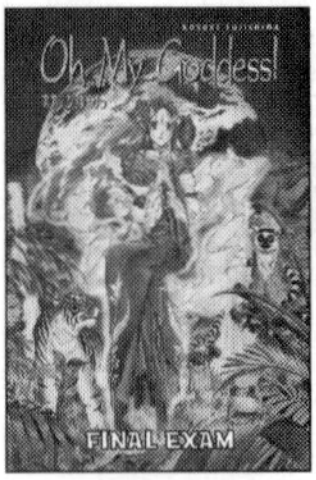
Oh My Goddess!
FINAL EXAM

Volume 3
FINAL EXAM
152-page B&W paperback
ISBN: 1-56971-765-6 $13.95

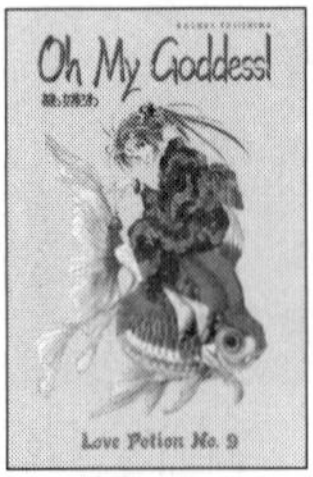
Oh My Goddess!
Love Potion No. 9

Volume 4
LOVE POTION NO. 9
192-page B&W paperback
ISBN: 1-56971-252-2 $14.95

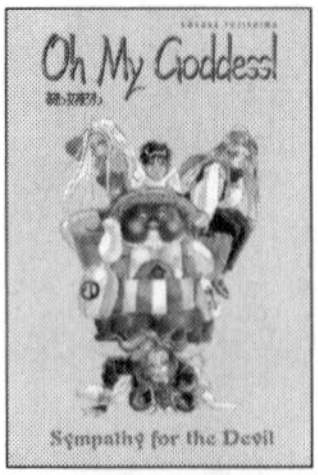
Oh My Goddess!
Sympathy for the Devil

Volume 5
SYMPATHY FOR THE DEVIL
160-page B&W paperback
ISBN: 1-56971-329-4 $12.95

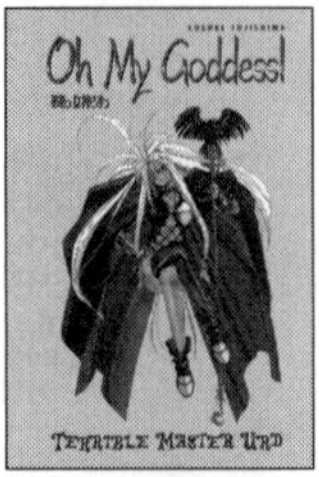
Oh My Goddess!
TERRIBLE MASTER URD

Volume 6
TERRIBLE MASTER URD
176-page B&W paperback
ISBN: 1-56971-369-3 $12.95

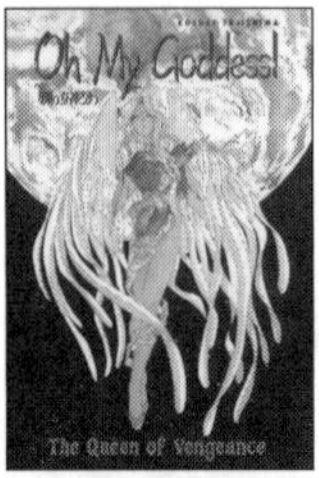
Oh My Goddess!
The Queen of Vengeance

Volume 7
THE QUEEN OF VENGEANCE
152-page B&W paperback
ISBN: 1-56971-431-2 $13.95

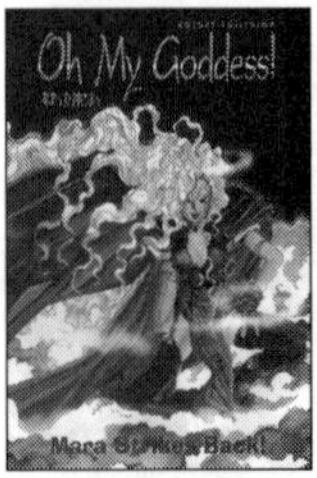
Oh My Goddess!

Volume 8
MARA STRIKES BACK
176-page B&W paperback
ISBN: 1-56971-449-5 $14.95

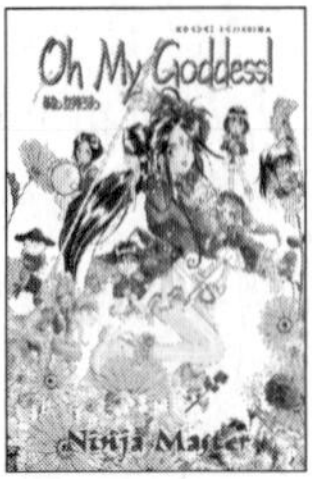
Oh My Goddess!

Volume 9
NINJA MASTER
152-page B&W paperback
ISBN: 1-56971-474-6 $13.95

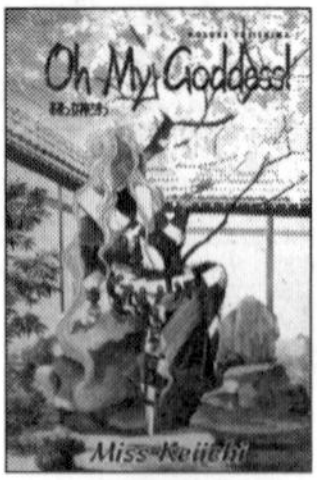
Oh My Goddess!

Volume 10
MISS KEIICHI
232-page B&W paperback
ISBN: 1-56971-522-X $16.95

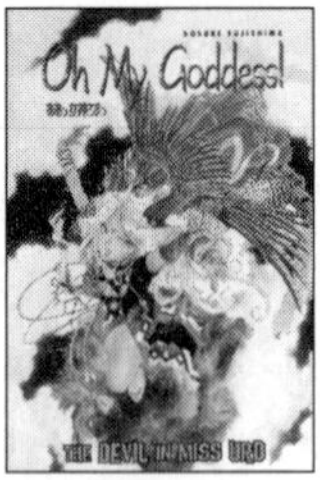
Oh My Goddess!
THE DEVIL IN MISS URD

Volume 11
THE DEVIL IN MISS URD
176-page B&W paperback
ISBN: 1-56971-540-8 $14.95

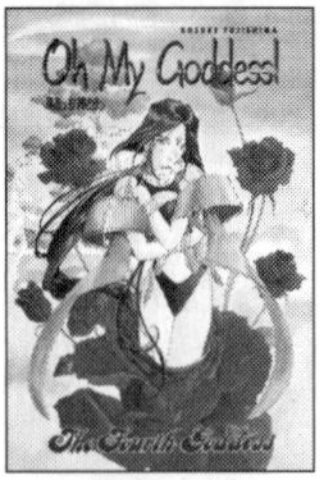
Oh My Goddess!

Volume 12
THE FOURTH GODDESS
280-page B&W paperback
ISBN: 1-56971-551-3 $18.95

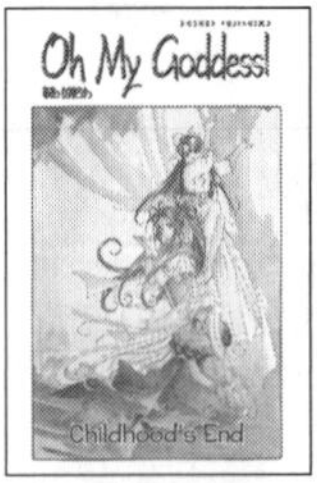
Oh My Goddess!
Childhood's End

Volume 13
CHILDHOOD'S END
216-page B&W paperback
ISBN: 1-56971-685-4 $15.95

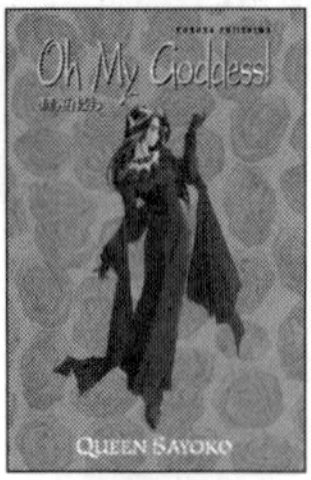
Oh My Goddess!
QUEEN SAYOKO

Volume 14
QUEEN SAYOKO
240-page B&W paperback
ISBN: 1-56971-766-4 $16.95

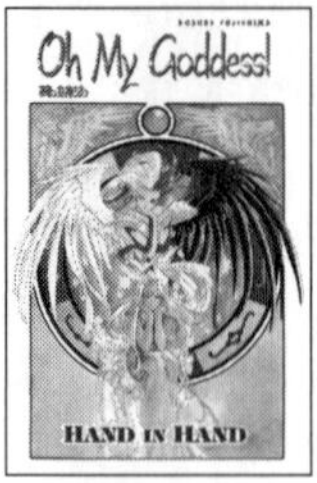
Oh My Goddess!
HAND IN HAND

Volume 15
HAND IN HAND
256-page B&W paperback
ISBN: 1-56971-921-7 $17.95

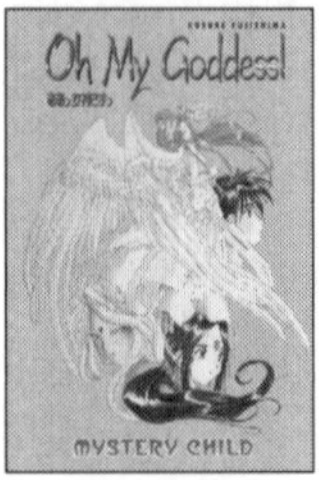
Oh My Goddess!
MYSTERY CHILD

Volume 16
MYSTERY CHILD
272-page B&W paperback
ISBN: 1-56971-950-0 $17.95

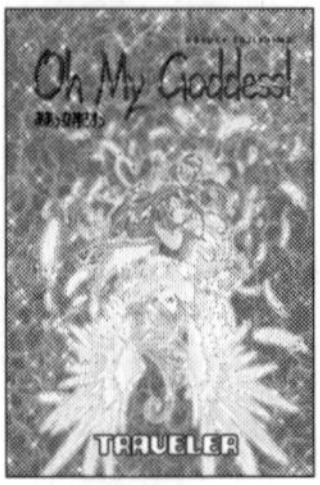
Oh My Goddess!
TRAVELER

Volume 17
TRAVELER
256-page B&W paperback
ISBN: 1-56971-986-1 $17.95

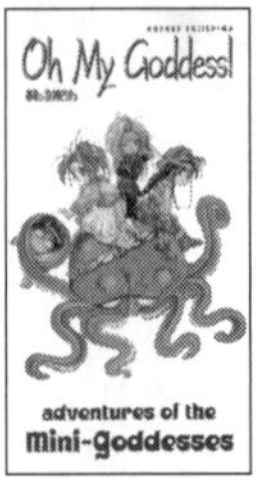
Oh My Goddess!
adventures of the
Mini-goddesses

ADVENTURES OF THE MINI-GODDESSES
88-page B&W paperback
ISBN: 1-56971-421-5 $9.95

STUDIO PROTEUS

AVAILABLE AT YOUR LOCAL COMICS SHOP OR BOOKSTORE

To find a comics shop in your area, call 1-888-266-4226

For more information or to order direct: • On the web: www.darkhorse.com • E-mail: mailorder@darkhorse.com • Phone: 1-800-862-0052 or (503) 652-9701 Mon.-Sat. 9 A.M. to 5 P.M. Pacific Time

DARK HORSE MANGA

THE LEGEND OF MOTHER SARAH
Katsuhiro Otomo
Tunnel Town
B&W / 1-56971-145-3 / $18.95

LONE WOLF AND CUB
Kazuo Koike and Goseki Kojima
Volume 1: The Assassin's Road
296-page B&W / 1-56971-502-5 / $9.95

Volume 2: The Gateless Barrier
296-page B&W / 1-56971-503-3 / $9.95

Volume 3: The Flute of the Fallen Tiger
304-page B&W / 1-56971-504-1 / $9.95

Volume 4: The Bell Warden
304-page B&W / 1-56971-505-X / $9.95

Volume 5: Black Wind
288-page B&W / 1-56971-506-8 / $9.95

Volume 6: Lanterns for the Dead
288-page B&W / 1-56971-507-6 / $9.95

Volume 7: Cloud Dragon, Wind Tiger
320-page B&W / 1-56971-508-4 / $9.95

Volume 8: Chains of Death
304-page B&W / 1-56971-509-2 / $9.95

Volume 9: Echo of the Assassin
288-page B&W / 1-56971-510-6 / $9.95

Volume 10: Hostage Child
320-page B&W / 1-56971-511-4 / $9.95

Volume 11: Talisman of Hades
320-page B&W / 1-56971-512-2 / $9.95

Volume 12: Shattered Stones
304-page B&W / 1-56971-513-0 / $9.95

Volume 13: The Moon in the East,
The Sun in the West
320-page B&W / 1-56971-585-8 / $9.95

Volume 14: The Day of the Demons
320-page B&W / 1-56971-586-6 / $9.95

Volume 15: Brothers of the Grass
352-page B&W / 1-56971-587-4 / $9.95

Volume 16: The Gateway into Winter
320-page B&W / 1-56971-588-2 / $9.95

Volume 17: Will of the Fang
320-page B&W / 1-56971-589-0 / $9.95

Volume 18: Twilight of the Kurokuwa
320-page B&W / 1-56971-590-4 / $9.95

Volume 19: The Moon in Our Hearts
320-page B&W / 1-56971-591-2 / $9.95

Volume 20: A Taste of Poison
320-page B&W / 1-56971-592-0 / $9.95

Volume 21: Fragrance of Death
320-page B&W / 1-56971-593-9 / $9.95

Volume 22: Heaven and Earth
288-page B&W / 1-56971-594-7 / $9.95

Volume 23: Tears of Ice
320-page B&W / 1-56971-595-5 / $9.95

Volume 24: In These Small Hands
320-page B&W / 1-56971-596-3 / $9.95

Volume 25: Perhaps in Death
320-page B&W / 1-56971-597-1 / $9.95

Volume 26: Struggle in the Dark
312-page B&W / 1-56971-598-X / $9.95

Volume 27: Battle's Eve
300-page B&W / 1-56971-599-8 / $9.95

Volume 28: The Lotus Throne
320-page B&W / 1-56971-600-5 / $9.95

LOST WORLD
Osamu Tezuka
248-page B&W / 1-56971-865-2 / $14.95

METROPOLIS
Osamu Tezuka
168-page B&W / 1-56971-864-4 / $13.95

NEXTWORLD
Osamu Tezuka
Volume 1
160-page B&W / 1-56971-866-0 / $13.95

Volume 2
168-page B&W / 1-56971-867-9 / $13.95

ORION
Masamune Shirow
272-page B&W / 1-56971-572-6 / $19.95

OUTLANDERS
Johji Manabe
Volume 2
192-page B&W / 1-56971-162-3 / $13.95

Volume 3
160-page B&W / 1-56971-163-1 / $13.95

Volume 4
168-page B&W / 1-56971-069-4 / $12.95

Volume 5
216-page B&W / 1-56971-275-1 / $14.95

Volume 6
200-page B&W / 1-56971-423-1 / $14.95

Volume 7
184-page B&W / 1-56971-424-X / $14.95

Volume 8
176-page B&W / 1-56971-425-8 / $14.95

SERAPHIC FEATHER
Hiroyuki Utatane, Toshiya Takeda,
Yo Morimoto
Volume 1: Crimson Angel
232-page B&W / 1-56971-555-6 / $17.95

Volume 2: Seeds of Chaos
240-page B&W / 1-56971-739-7 / $17.95

Volume 3: Target Zone
240-page B&W / 1-56971-912-8 / $17.95

Volume 4: Dark Angel
240-page B&W / 1-56971-913-6 / $17.95

SHADOW LADY
Masakazu Katsura
Volume 1: Dangerous Love
200-page B&W / 1-56971-408-8 / $17.95

Volume 2: The Awakening
184-page B&W / 1-56971-446-0 / $15.95

Volume 3: Sudden Death
176-page B&W / 1-56971-477-0 / $14.95

SHADOW STAR
Mohiro Kitoh
Volume 1: Shadow Star
192-page B&W / 1-56971-548-3 / $15.95

Volume 2: Darkness Visible
182-page B&W / 1-56971-740-0 / $14.95

Volume 3: Shadows of the Past
144-page B&W / 1-56971-743-5 / $13.95

Volume 4: Nothing but the Truth
160-page B&W / 1-56971-920-9 / $14.95

Volume 5: A Flower's Fragrance
208-page B&W / 1-56971-990-X / $15.95

3X3 EYES
Yuzo Takada
Volume 1: House of Demons
160-page B&W / 1-56971-930-6 / $14.95

Volume 2: Curse of the Gesu
152-page B&W / 1-56971-931-4 / $14.95

Volume 3: Flight of the Demon
208-page B&W / 1-56971-553-X / $15.95

Volume 4: Blood of the Sacred Demon
144-page B&W / 1-56971-735-4 / $15.95

Volume 5: Summoning of the Beast
152-page B&W / 1-56971-747-8 / $14.95

Volume 6: Key to the Sacred Land
136-page B&W / 1-56971-881-4 / $13.95

Volume 7: The Shadow of the Kunlun
224-page B&W / 1-56971-981-0 / $17.95

AVAILABLE AT YOUR LOCAL COMICS SHOP OR BOOKSTORE
To find a comics shop in your area, call **1-888-266-4226**
For more information or to order direct: • On the web: www.darkhorse.com • E-mail: mailorder@darkhorse.com
• Phone: 1-800-862-0052 or (503) 652-9701 Mon.-Sat. 9 A.M. to 5 P.M. Pacific Time